Praise for David P. Moessner's, *Luke the Historian of Israel's Legacy, Theologian of Israel's 'Christ.' A New Reading of the 'Gospel Acts' of Luke*

"David Moessner's collection of learned essays impressively synthesizes his sustained scholarly exploration of Luke-Acts as a coherent narrative. Moessner portrays Luke as simultaneously a Hellenistic historian embodying Greco-Roman literary theory and practice and a biblical theologian deeply engaged with interpretation of Israel's Scripture. No other scholar has so carefully delineated the implications of reading Luke's work as a fusion of these streams of tradition. This book is essential reading for interpreters of Luke's Gospel and the Acts of the Apostles."
  RICHARD B. HAYS, *George Washington Ivey Professor of New Testament*, The Divinity School, Duke University

"This volume brings together previously published essays by David Moessner, a leading and distinctive voice in Lukan studies for over three decades. But this is more than a collection of disparate and occasional essays; by providing contextualizing introductions to each of the five parts and re-configuring each of the essays, Moessner offers an internally coherent and brilliantly compelling thesis: Luke the Hellenistic historian and biblical theologian has deployed various rhetorical conventions and a configuring and re-configuring of Israel's scriptures and "things that have come to full flowering among us" to present the "plan of God" who intends to act salvifically through Israel's suffering Christ for Israel and the world. This volume demands and deserves a hearing with every serious student of Luke and Acts."
  MIKEAL C. PARSONS, *Professor and Macon Chair in Religion*, Baylor University

"Moessner's essays, spanning over 30 years of study of the Lukan writings, profoundly affect ourunderstanding of Luke's literary and theological achievements. The insistence on seeing Luke and Acts as a single whole ('Gospel Acts'), the comparisons drawn between Luke and other historians of the time, especially those writing large-scale histories, and the analysis of the fundamental importance of Jewish scripture for Luke, are timely and compelling. The resulting picture of Luke as a 'biblical theologian', precisely as a 'historian', is hugely impressive in its scope and detail. Moessner's work will be essential reading for all engaged in Lukan studies for many yearsto come."
  CHRISTOPHER TUCKETT, *Emeritus Professor of New Testament Studies*, University of Oxford

"Professor Moessner has for many years made significant contributions to our understanding of Luke-Acts, contributions based in part on his deep learning in ancient literary theory, in part on his close exegesis of Luke's language, and in part on his firm grasp of the theological framework within which Luke works. The present volume of studies enables scholars – who may have been aware only of scattered essays – to appreciate the full range and depth of his scholarship."
  LUKE TIMOTHY JOHNSON, *Robert W. Woodruff Professor of New Testament and Christian Origins*, Emory University

"David Moessner has devoted decades to puzzling out the narrative poetics and biblical theology of the double-work, Luke-Acts. These rich and insightful essays are filled with the important results of his research, both in Hellenistic historiography and in patient reading of the Lukan work itself, in conversation with scholarship on ancient historiography, rhetoric, and narrative poetics, contemporary narrative theory, and biblical theology. The present volume offers a fresh and comprehensive picture of the compositional praxis and results of the work of 'the first biblical theologian' with which all New Testament scholars will want to contend."
  MARGARET M. MITCHELL, *Shailer Mathews Professor of New Testament and Early Christian Literature*, The University of Chicago

"We have here, in this important collection, the fruits of a life-time of informed reflection on Luke and Acts in their original literary setting. The exegetical proposals are argued with exceptional care, the comparisons with Hellenistic literature are uniformly insightful, and the attempt to read Luke-Acts through Greco-Roman historiography is convincing."
  DALE C. ALLISON, Jr., Princeton Theological Seminary

"David Moessner setzt bei den Aporien des Zueinanders von Lukasevangelium und Apostelgeschichte an. Da er die Einheit der beiden als antiken Vorgaben folgende Erzählung ernst nimmt, gelingt es ihm, viele Aporien bisheriger Forschung einer Lösung zuzuführen. Moessner beschreibt Lukas konsequent als rhetorisch begabten Theologen, dessen Werk nicht als antike Biographie, sondern als *historia* zu deuten ist: Das lukanische Doppelwerk versteht Moessner als Erzählung über das Ziel der Schriften Israels, welches durch den Gesalbten Israels, Jesus von Nazaret, in Szene gesetzt wird. Der Text ist Schrift über den ‚Plan Gottes' mit Israel und derWelt. Moessner hat hier weit mehr als eine Sammlung von Aufsätzen vorgelegt, nämlich das gewichtige, hoch spannend zu lesende Resultat der Forschung vieler Jahre. Wer sich mit dem lukanischen Doppelwerk beschäftigt, sollte an diesem Buch nicht vorüber gehen."
  TOBIAS NICKLAS, Universität Regensburg

David Paul Moessner
Luke the Historian of Israel's Legacy, Theologian of Israel's 'Christ'

Beihefte zur Zeitschrift
für die neutestamentliche
Wissenschaft

Edited by
James D. G. Dunn, Carl R. Holladay,
Hermann Lichtenberger, Jens Schröter,
Gregory E. Sterling and Michael Wolter

Volume 182

David Paul Moessner

Luke the Historian of Israel's Legacy, Theologian of Israel's 'Christ'

A New Reading of the 'Gospel Acts' of Luke

DE GRUYTER

ISBN 978-3-11-061043-7
e-ISBN (PDF) 978-3-11-025540-9
e-ISBN (EPUB) 978-3-11-039196-1
ISSN 0171-6441

Library of Congress Cataloging-in-Publication Data
A CIP catalog record for this book has been applied for at the Library of Congress.

Bibliografische Information der Deutschen Nationalbibliothek
Die Deutsche Nationalbibliothek verzeichnet diese Publikation in der Deutschen Nationalbibliografie; detaillierte bibliografische Daten sind im Internet über http://dnb.dnb.de abrufbar.

© 2018 Walter de Gruyter GmbH, Berlin/Boston
This volume is text- and page-identical with the hardback published in 2016.
Printing and binding: CPI books GmbH, Leck
Typesetting: Dörlemann Satz, Lemförde

♾ Printed on acid-free paper
Printed in Germany

www.degruyter.com

Dedicated to a 'Beloved Son'
Whose Lord was 'at his right hand continually'
David Stevenson Moessner (1988–2015)

Table of contents

Introduction:
Enigma in Two volumes —— 1
The 'Gospel Acts' of Luke: Hellenistic History as 'Biblical' Theology —— 1
  The Luke-Acts Conundrum —— 1
  Events, Fiction, and the Hermeneutics of Luke's Narrative
    Persuasion —— 3
  Biblical Texts and Intertexts as Narrative 'Arranging' and Intratextual
    'Sequencing' for Luke the Hellenistic Historian and 'Biblical'
    Theologian —— 7

Part I: Luke's 'Gospel Acts' and the Genre of the Gospels —— 11
Chapter One: How Luke Writes —— 13
Chapter Two: Re-Reading Talbert's Luke: The *Bios* of "Balance" or the "Bias" of
  History? —— 39
[SHORT EXCURSUS: **Richard Burridge's** *What are the Gospels?*
  A Comparison with Graeco-Roman Biography, Cambridge University
  Press, 1992] —— 64

Part II: Luke's Prologues and Hellenistic Narrative Hermeneutics —— 67
Chapter Three: The Author 'Luke': "As One Who Has a Thoroughly Informed
  Familiarity with All the Events from the Top" (παρηκολουθηκότι ἄνωθεν
  πᾶσιν ἀκριβῶς, Luke 1:3a) —— 68
Chapter Four: The Meaning of ΚΑΘΕΞΗΣ in Luke's Two-Volume Narrative —— 108

Part III: Luke among Hellenistic Historians —— 125
Chapter Five: 'Listening Posts' Along the Way: 'Synchronisms' as Metaleptic
  Prompts to the 'Continuity of the Narrative' in **Polybius's** *Histories* and in
  Luke's 'Gospel Acts' —— 127
Chapter Six: 'Managing' the Audience: **Diodorus Siculus** and Luke the Evangelist
  on Designing Authorial Intent —— 154
Chapter Seven: *A New Reading of Luke's 'Gospel Acts'*: Acts as the
  'Metaleptic' Collapse of Luke and **Dionysius of Halicarnassus's** Narrative
  'Arrangement' (οἰκονομία) as the Hermeneutical Keys to Luke's
  Re-Visioning of the "Many" —— 172

Part IV: Luke's *Theologia Crucis*. The Suffering Servant(s) of the Lord: Moses, David, the Suffering Righteous, and Jesus and "All The Prophets" —— 201

Chapter Eight: Luke 9:1–50: Luke's Preview of the Journey of the Prophet like Moses of Deuteronomy —— 205

Chapter Nine: "The Christ Must Suffer": New Light On The Jesus – Peter, Stephen, Paul Parallels in Luke's 'Gospel Acts' —— 238

Chapter Ten: Luke's "Plan of God" from the Greek Psalter: The Rhetorical Thrust of 'The Prophets and the Psalms' in Peter's Speech at Pentecost —— 272

Part V: Luke, the Church, and Israel's Legacy —— 289

Chapter Eleven: Paul in Acts: Preacher of Eschatological Repentance to Israel —— 292

Chapter Twelve: Das Doppelwerk des Lukas und *Heil als Geschichte*. Oscar Cullmanns auffälliges Schweigen bezüglich des stärksten Befürworters seiner Konzeption der Heilsgeschichte im Neuen Testament —— 302

Conclusion
Luke the Hellenistic Historian of Israel's Legacy, Theologian of Israel's 'Christ' —— 315

I. Luke is a Configurer (ποιητής) of oral and written traditions concerning events and matters purporting to have taken place in the real world of the author. By 'arranging' a new narrative sequence different from a number of predecessors, Luke imparts a new cognitive and affective understanding of these happenings. —— 315

  1. Patterns of Recurrence from Authoritative Written and Oral Traditions —— 317
  2. Patterns of Recurrence of 'First Person' Participation within the Described Events —— 328
  3. Patterns of Recurrence Attributed to an Overarching Divine Will, Fate, or Necessity —— 330

II. Luke is a Manager (οἰκονόμος) of the Narrative 'Economy' (οἰκονομία). As rhetorical elaborator, Luke turns to various tropes of conventional poetics to effect the understanding of the events that he wishes his audience to attain. —— 332

  1. Luke's 'beginning' (ἡ ἀρχή) for his two-volume work forecasts the plot and sets the tone for the whole: Israel's "Christ" of the scriptures "must suffer and rise up" and Jesus of Nazareth is that "Christ." —— 334

2. The ***metaleptic*** collapse within Luke's secondary ***prooimion*** pulls Paul into the 'continuity of the narrative' as central to the two-volume narrative 'arrangement' so that Paul emerges as *chief* "witness" of the Christ's "anointed" sending to Israel and the nations–"to the end of the earth." —— 336

Finale:
Luke the Historian, Biblical Theologian of Israel's "Christ" —— **339**

Bibliography —— 340

Index —— 358

Abbreviations

AB	Anchor Bible
ACCS	Ancient Christian Commentary on Scripture
AGAJU	Arbeiten zur Geschichte des antiken Judentums und des Urchristentums
AJP	*American Journal of Philology*
AnBib	Analecta Biblica
ANQ	*Andover Newton Quarterly*
ATANT	Abhandlungen zur Theologie des Alten und Neuen Testaments
BDAG	Bauer Greek lexicon
BDF	Blass, Friedrich, Albert Debrunner, and Robert W. Funk. *A Greek Grammar of the New Testament and Other Early Christian Literature.* Chicago: University of Chicago Press, 1961.
BECNT	Baker Exegetical Commentary on the New Testament
BETL	Bibliotheca Ephemeridum Theologicarum Lovaniensium
BEvT	Beiträge zur evangelischen Theologie
BGBE	Beiträge zur Geschichte der biblischen Exegese
BHT	Beiträge zur historischen Theologie
Bib	*Biblica*
BWANT	Beiträge zur Wissenschaft vom Alten und Neuen Testament
BZ	*Biblische Zeitschrift*
BZAW	Beihefte zur Zeitschrift für die alttestamentliche Wissenschaft
BZNW	Beihefte zur Zeitschrift für die neutestamentliche Wissenschaft
CBQ	*Catholic Biblical Quarterly*
EHAT	Exegetisches Handbuch zum Alten Testament
EHST	Europäische Hochschulschriften: Theologie
EvT	*Evangelische Theologie*
FBBS	Facet Books, Biblical Series
FC	Fathers of the Church
FRLANT	Forschungen zur Religion und Literatur des Alten und Neuen Testaments
HNT	Handbuch zum Neuen Testament
HTR	*Harvard Theological Review*
IB	*Interpreter's Bible*
ICC	International Critical Commentary
Int	*Interpretation*
JBL	*Journal of Biblical Literature*
JETS	*Journal of the Evangelical Theological Society*
JRS	*Journal of Roman Studies*
JSNT	*Journal for the Study of the New Testament*

JSNTSup	Journal for the Study of the New Testament Supplement Series
JSOT	*Journal for the Study of the Old Testament*
JSPSup	Journal for the Study of the Old Testament Supplement Series
JTS	*Journal of Theological Studies*
LCL	Loeb Classical Library
LNTS	Library of New Testament Studies
LSJ	Liddell-Scott-Jones Greek lexicon
NCB	New Century Bible Commentary
NICNT	New International Commentary on the New Testament
NIDB	*New Interpreters Dictionary of the Bible*
NIGTC	New International Greek Testament Commentary
NTD	Das Neue Testament Deutsch
NTL	New Testament Library
NTS	*New Testament Studies*
NovT	*Novum Testamentum*
NovTSup	Supplements to Novum Testamentum
NRTh	*La nouvelle revue théologique*
OTL	Old Testament Library
RevExp	*Review and Expositor*
RHPR	*Revue d'histoire et de philosophie religieuses*
SBLDS	Society of Biblical Literature Dissertation Series
SBLMS	Society of Biblical Literature Monograph Series
SBLSBS	Society of Biblical Literature Sources for Biblical Study
SBT	Studies in Biblical Theology
Scr	*Scripture*
SE II	*Studia Evangelica II*
SemeiaSup	Semeia Supplements
SNTSMS	Society for New Testament Studies Monograph Series
SP	Sacra Pagina
SUNT	Studien zur Umwelt des Neuen Testaments
TDNT	*Theological Dictionary of the New Testament*
TF	*Theologische Forschung*
THKNT	Theologischer Handkommentar zum Neuen Testament
TU	Texte und Untersuchungen
TZ	*Theologische Zeitschrift*
WMANT	Wissenschaftliche Monographien zum Alten und Neuen Testament
WUNT	Wissenschaftliche Untersuchungen zum Neuen Testament
ZNW	*Zeitschrift für die neutestamentliche Wissenschaft und die Kunde der älteren Kirche*
ZTK	*Zeitschrift für Theologie und Kirche*

Bible translations

CCB	Christian Community Bible
CEB	Common English Bible
CJB	Complete Jewish Bible
ESV	English Standard Version
JB	Jerusalem Bible
KJV	King James Version
LEW	Agnes Smith Lewis trans. of Peshitta
NAB	New American Bible
NASB	New American Standard Bible
NEB	New English Bible
NET	New English Translation
NIV	New International Version
NJB	New Jerusalem Bible
Phillips	J. B. Phillips New Testament (1959)
Rheims	Douay-Rheims translation
RSV	Revised Standard Version
RV	Revised Version
TEV	Today's English Version
Tyndale NT	Tyndale New Testament

Introduction: Enigma in Two Volumes

The 'Gospel Acts' of Luke: Hellenistic History as 'Biblical' Theology

> The best historians often possess a "majesty of diction" (to quote Cicero) that enables them to arouse and persuade their readers. Put another way, one might paraphrase Dionysius of Halicarnassus and say that the main difference between historian and historian lies "in the aptness with which they arrange their words."
> [Stephen Vaughn, "History as Rhetoric: Style, Narrative, and Persuasion," *The Journal of American History* 82 {1996} 1595]

The Luke-Acts Conundrum

Throughout the long history of the reception of his Gospel the Third Evangelist has seldom been charged with an 'infelicity of style' or slackness in the ordering of his narrative. "The most beautiful book ever written" was Ernst Renan's assessment in the 19th century,[1] and already before the Italian renaissance of the late 14th to 16th centuries, Luke was claimed as the patron of painters by the guilds of artists, especially in the Low Countries. Rogier van der Weyden's "Saint Luke Drawing the Virgin," ca. 1435–40, is emblematic and probably the best known of a series of illuminations by a variety of medieval artists in which Luke is privy to special 'sittings' of the Virgin and Child and thus portrayed as *the artist* par excellence of the Gospel. We could also mention Luke's opening canticles and Septuagintal hymns which formed the liturgical bases of the earliest celebrations of the great feasts of the church[2] that served to etch Luke *the poet* into the very psyche of early Christian worship, not to mention other such examples of Luke the *littérateur* of the New Testament.[3]

---

[1] Ernst Renan, *Les Evangiles et la seconde génération chrétienne* (Paris: Calmann Lévy, 1877), 283; see below Part I "The 'Gospel Acts' of Luke and the Genre of the Gospels," and Chapter One § 1.
[2] "As the hearer comes to the birth of Jesus [in Luke], he sees in the nativity of Jesus the source for all the great feasts in the church catholic: Easter, the ascension and Pentecost" (Chrysostom), quoted and trans. by ed. Arthur A. Just, Jr. in *Luke*, Ancient Christian Commentary on Scripture (Downers Grove, IL: InterVarsity Press, 2003), 35.
[3] Cf., e.g., Robert J. Karris, *Luke: Artist and Theologian: Luke's Passion Account as Literature* (New York: Paulist Press, 1985).

But then there is his second volume. "*The Acts of the Apostles is a strange new dish ... strange, I say, and not strange. Not strange, for it belongs to the order of Holy Scripture; and yet strange, because peradventure your ears are not accustomed to such a subject,*" marvels Chrysostom already in the 4th century.[4] When Acts comes into the picture, sentiments about Luke the writer become a bit blurred. What is Luke trying to do with Acts as a second volume? Is Luke followed by Acts to be read as one continuous narrative story? If so, why did the earliest church communities not read 'Luke-Acts' that way? Why in the several lists of an emerging canon of newly authoritative or "new testament" scripture texts does Acts never follow Luke?[5]

A sentiment ascendant in the first decades of the 21st century is that Luke's Gospel is closest to or actually represents a *bios*/biography of Jesus whereas Acts looks more like a short historiographical sketch of the days following a famous teacher whose fate led to an ongoing movement of "disciples" that succeeded in penetrating even the hearing of the Roman Emperor (see Part One).[6]

Is Luke's 'Gospel Acts' then a *tertium quid*, indeed a "strange new dish," an enigma with no precedents or parallels? Is the problem with Luke's Acts that a gifted writer can no longer persuade or convince his audiences of the main purposes of a second volume because of a deficiency in '*the aptness with which he arranges his words*?' Or is the conundrum of Acts a problem rather of failing to discover Luke's literary-rhetorical strategy such that Acts appears at best a 'stepchild' of the New Testament? Rather than an integral part of Luke's message

---

[4] Cited from a now classic introduction to the reception of Acts and its canonical acceptance, Henry J. Cadbury, *The Book of Acts in History* (New York: Harper and Bros., 1955), 159. The quote is from Chrysostom's *Homiliae in Principium Actorum* [iii, p. 54] and continues "Certainly there are many to whom this book is not even known, and many again think it so plain that they slight it. Thus to some men their ignorance, to others their knowledge is the cause of the neglect." See further, David E. Smith, *The Canonical Function of Acts: A Comparative Analysis* (Collegeville, MN: The Liturgical Press, 2002), "John Chrysostom's Commentary on Acts," 83–89.

[5] See Cadbury, *Acts in History*, Chapter VI "Subsequent History," 136–164; cf. 143–44 on the "Cheltenham Canon," one of very few placements of Luke as the last of the listed Gospels (ca. 360 CE – northern Africa): Matt.–Mark–John–Luke–Paulines!–Acts. In the stichometry of Codex Claromontanus Luke is placed as the last of the Gospels, but Acts is not listed until the very last book of the New Testament (n. 18, p. 162); cf. Codex Claromontanus-Acts following Revelation; cf. syr^{cur}--Luke last of four Gospel codex, no Acts; Theophilus of Antioch-Matt, John, Luke, epistles, Acts. Cf. also the discussions in Mikeal C. Parsons and Richard I. Pervo, *Rethinking the Unity of Luke and Acts* (Minneapolis, MN: Fortress Press, 1993), esp. 1–44; Andrew Gregory, *The Reception of Luke and Acts in the Period before Irenaeus: Looking for Luke in the Second Century*, WUNT 2/169 (Tübingen: Mohr Siebeck, 2003); Smith, *The Canonical Function of Acts*, esp., 11–18.

[6] See below, Chapters One and Two.

that can *not* simply end with the resurrection and ascension of Jesus, are we as postmodern readers left to hear Acts dangling somewhere between the worlds of the evangelists and the world of Paul, both bodies of which seem to diffuse and confuse and indeed marginalize the value of Luke's 'second volume?'[7] If Luke does possess some "majesty of diction," is it all but exhausted when he reaches his second 'book'?

Events, Fiction, and the Hermeneutics of Luke's Narrative Persuasion

> *Fiction 'fills in' the causal relations between historical events which are immutably 'given' by the past to the present but which can never be sufficiently complete to provide their own qualification.*
> [Wesley Trimpi, *Muses of One Mind*, 351[8]]

Ancient Greek narrative rhetoric supplies the manner and rationale for Luke's 'filling in the gaps' between and within his two volumes to compose a persuasive narrative presentation. The thesis of *Luke the Historian of Israel's Legacy, Theologian of Israel's 'Christ.' A New Reading of The 'Gospel Acts' of Luke* is that Luke's literary intentions emerge clearly when his two volumes are viewed through the narrative-rhetorical lenses of Greco-Roman literary theory and practice. We argue that Luke's Acts continues "all that Jesus began to do and to teach" (Acts 1:1) as an intended continuation of the *presence* and *impact* of Jesus of Nazareth of the Gospel volume (see Chapter Seven below for fullest elaboration).[9] By reading

---

[7] For Richard Pervo's illuminating discussion of the issues, see Richard I. Pervo, "Israel's Heritage and Claims upon the Genre(s) of Luke and Acts: The Problems of a History," in *Jesus and the Heritage of Israel: Luke's Narrative Claim upon Israel's Legacy*, vol. 1, *Luke the Interpreter of Israel*, ed. David P. Moessner (Harrisburg, PA: Trinity Press International, 1999), 127–43; cf. Andrew F. Gregory and Christopher M. Tuckett, "Reflections on Method: What Constitutes the Use of the Writings that Later Formed the New Testament in the Apostolic Fathers? in *The Reception of the New Testament in the Apostolic Fathers*, ed. Andrew F. Gregory and Christopher M. Tuckett (Oxford: Oxford University Press, 2005), 61–82, esp. 79; for a reading of Acts attune to cultural markers of the 2nd century, see esp. Todd Penner, "Reading Acts in the Second Century: Reflections on Method, History, and Desire," in *Engaging Early Christian History: Reading Acts in the Second Century*, ed. Rubén R. Dupertuis and Todd Penner (Durham: Acumen, 2013), 1–15.
[8] Wesley Trimpi, *Muses of One Mind: The Literary Analysis of Experience and Its Continuity* (Princeton, NJ: Princeton University Press, 1983).
[9] I do not address directly in this collection of essays the reception and use of Acts in the 2nd-4th centuries and the obvious question, 'Why do we have no explicit evidence that Acts was read as

Luke's 'Gospel Acts' from the conventions of the narrative hermeneutics of multi-volume works of the Hellenistic period, Luke's second volume does begin to fill in the "causal relations" and to construct critical contexts that do make sense of the "events" of one longer narrative story such that they "provide their own qualification." When we let Luke speak on his own terms *vis-à-vis* the elaborate narrative culture of the Greco-Roman period, we discover that "the aptness of the arrangement of his words" do indeed continue to persuade as he communicates his larger vision which he will more than once title "the plan/will of God."[10]

What is needed, therefore, is a method of reading narrative that is historically critical to the hermeneutics of narrative epistemology at the time when Luke was writing. As a 'modern' method of reading ancient narrative, 'redaction criticism' (or its cousin, 'composition criticism') and various 'audience' criticisms flounder for the evangelists Matthew and Luke (and John) precisely because the shape and content of the various written sources for each author and the settings of each writer are basically unknown and thus, not surprisingly, still much in dispute. We do not know what written texts Luke had at his disposal nor who more precisely "the many" (Luke 1:1) were and whether or to what extent Luke was dependent on any of them as a reliable accounting of "all the traditions" to which he, for instance, refers in his prologue (Luke 1:1, 3).

Mark is surely the most likely candidate to be an important written source. But then again, it is unclear whether Luke relies on 'Markan' oral traditions that have been written down slightly differently than our canonical Mark (as reflected in the inexact Lukan 'parallel') and whether the obvious parallels in content with Mark are taken from a text whose overall arrangement corresponds closely to our

---

an ongoing presence of Jesus's actions and words?' But the evidence of the 2nd and 3rd centuries cuts both ways: When Acts is first described in Irenaeus (*Adv. Haer.* III.1; cf. esp. III.12; 18, the book is not disputed and functions simply to interpret what is, and what is not 'apostolic' by understanding Jesus's words of Luke 24:44–49 as the lens by which to read and use Acts in the life of the church. And although Chrysostom in the 4th century laments that Acts is not more vitally known and used (see n. 4 above), he does in fact write a *homiletical* commentary that illustrates again that Acts is an authoritative sourcebook for the ways Jesus himself continues to define the life and character of the church. My intent is to continue pursuing this question in future publications, especially the references to Acts in the 2nd and 3rd centuries.

10 Luke 7:30; Acts 2:23; 4:28; (5:38); 13:36; 20:27; (27:42–43). Cf. Robert W. Wall and Eugene E. Lemcio, *The New Testament as Canon. A Reader in Canonical Criticism*. JSNTSup 76 (Sheffield: Sheffield Academic, 1992), 125: "The title [Acts] calls the hermeneutist to take a particular, aretological stance when reading this narrative ... Such an interpretation of the founding apostles also actualizes the authority of the apostolic witness to God's salvation in Christ Jesus which the canon itself transmits in the corpus of letters which follow."

canonical Mark such that comparison between individual units of both 'Markan' traditions might be legitimately carried out. Just as pertinent, recognizable parallels from Mark or Matthew or possibly even John do not look anything like a two-volume focus on one person followed by stories of his followers' movements to various points throughout the northeastern expanses of the Roman empire. Reading Luke as the 'Gospel of the Differences from Mark' simply does not do justice to the influences of multiple and fluctuating resources nor to the seemingly anomalous 'Gospel' continued by an 'Acts.'

Unfortunately much of the narrative rhetorical criticism applied in the last decade to Gospel narratives is taken from ancient rhetorical treatises that articulate authorial intention and compositional strategies for *specific oral deliveries* and not for written genres whose primary audiences are *not* the recipients of specific speeches. For instance, whether the rhetoric of a text is primarily 'forensic,' 'deliberative,' or 'epideictic' reflects categories inappropriately applied to the *narrative* of the New Testament Gospels and Acts, whether in whole or larger parts.[11] Rather, this threefold taxonomy, attributed to Aristotle, does not pertain to narrative writing nor multi-volume historiographical works but to types of speeches first developed for the law courts and assemblies of the Greek city-state.[12] Certainly it is legitimate to take speeches in the New Testament such as in Acts or

---

[11] The influence of Prof. George Kennedy in the North American context has been significant and most salutary. Too often, however, his discussions of the *tria genera causarum* of speeches conceived originally either for the law courts or assemblies of a Greek city-state have been misunderstood and simply applied by NT scholars to all sorts of writing, including narrative. Similarly, Theon's categories of the *pro-gymnasmata* or exercises in grammar and writing for middle–school age students (cf. Michel Patillon, *Aelius Théon: Progymnasmata* [Paris: Les Belles Lettres, 1997]) are applied indiscreetly to various genres of the NT. Theon's literary form or "idea" of *diēgēma* does not represent narrative works but short stories or shorter episodes that a school boy would write for grammar assignments (§§ 78–96 according to the Greek text of Patillon). The Gospels and Acts as longer narrative works are more often and accurately described as *diēgēseis* according to Greek literary usage (cf. Luke 1:1), though Hellenistic Greek does not enforce a strict denotation for each term. It is telling that Theon uses particular scenes or smaller episodes within larger narrative historiographical works to illustrate what he means by a *diēgēma* well told (e.g., the "Cylonian pollution" of the 7th cent. BCE in both Herodotus and Thucydides [its role in the larger development of Athens]; the Plataeans and Thebans in Thucydides [*War* 2.2–6]). The Four Gospels and Acts can *not* be legitimately categorized as strings of *chreiai* or expanded *diēgēmata* bunched together. Furthermore, a single *diēgēma* according to Theon cannot be conceived as simply a string of *chreiai* (84.2; 96.15). For a valid and instructive application of Theon's 'form' of *diēgēma* to Luke's narrative composing, see Mikeal C. Parsons, *Luke: Storyteller, Interpreter, Evangelist* (Peabody, MA: Hendrickson, 2007), esp. 22–32.

[12] See, e.g., "Rhetorical genres" in *The Westminster Dictionary of New Testament & Early Christian Literature & Rhetoric*, ed. Davie E. Aune (Louisville, KY: Westminster John Knox, 2010), 418–20.

epistolatry discursive writing where a direct delivery by the author is envisioned by the purpose of the writing and ask whether they are primarily forensic, deliberative, or epideictic. But the blanket appropriation of these categories of persuasion to the *narrative* composers of the New Testament suffices only to *occlude* rather than reveal the rich array of meanings delivered by a carefully crafted narrative.

Consequently a hermeneutic must be enlisted that conveys what ancient Greek and Roman writers actually understood about the ways *narrative/diegesis* should be ordered, how various topics and convictions should be communicated through appropriate poetic tropes, and what strategies should be employed to persuade targeted audiences. Fortunately the production of Greek narrative before and during the Hellenistic period was prolific, and it is especially ancient Hellenistic historians who reflect self-consciously on the purpose and means by which they communicate and persuade their audiences to specific ways of thinking about reality. A good number of these narrative writers 'break frame' to tell their readers what they intend to do through their specific undertaking and just how they will partition the sections and arrange the sequences of their account so that it delivers the discrete meanings they intend their audiences to grasp. Parts II and III below introduce various trajectories of the narrative criticism of this period to see if any of the treasures of this rich but neglected rhetorical trove might unlock the intentions and strategies of Luke's 'Gospel Acts.' We discover, in fact, within a rigorous and extensive narrative-rhetorical criticism a precedent for understanding the relation of Acts to Luke that yields an entirely new reading of Luke's two volumes.

Biblical Texts and Intertexts as Narrative 'Arranging' and Intratextual 'Sequencing' for Luke the Hellenistic Historian and 'Biblical' Theologian

> When the literary structures are taken on their own terms, it is finally Jesus who holds his own predicates together in the story, not they him; just as it is finally he who bestows meaning on the titles the story uses to describe him, rather than the reverse.
> [George Hunsinger and William C. Placher on Hans Frei's contributions in "Theological Reflections on the Accounts of Jesus' death and Resurrection" in Frei's *Theology and Narrative: Selected Essays*, 45[13]]

---

13 Oxford University Press, 1993.

We conclude in Parts IV and V that Luke is an able Hellenistic historian whose arrangement and 'way with words' continue to fascinate and to arouse readers' imaginations generation after generation. As such his two volumes, when coordinated through his narrative-rhetorical scheme, produce the first 'biblical' theology precisely through his historiographical ordering of the overarching "plan/counsel/will of God" now decisively fulfilled in Jesus of Nazareth, Israel's "Christ." It is Luke who cites, dovetails, mimics, and echoes the scriptures of Israel to conceive a proto-Christian, proto-orthodox Jewish-Christian scriptural collection that will later emerge in the incipient forms and manuscripts of the Vaticanus and Sinaiticus codices of the first Christian Bible in the 3rd and 4th centuries.

To be sure, Luke's rationale for 'arranging' and his 'methods of elaborating' more generally along the lines of his biblical script–methods that derive from narrative-rhetorical theory of Hellenistic composers–do not finally explain all the content and contours and cultural extra-texts of his two volumes. Luke's reading and interpreting the scriptures do *not* add up by any means to the total array of oral traditions, written sources, and cultural *topoi* that Luke has at his disposal that might have influenced the ways he organizes his narrative.[14] But as Parts IV and V below demonstrate, Luke reconnoiters much of his "plan of God" as already scripted in the Jewish scriptures and filled out in the sending, rejection, violent death, and enthronement of "the Christ of God," the Messiah of Israel's heritage. Thus it should be no surprise that much of his plotting of the career of Jesus which continues in the Acts through his "witnesses" fills *in* as well as fills *out* the *suffering anointed figures* of the scriptures such that Jesus both reenacts as well as consummates *as new* those actors of Israel's sacred texts.[15] Therefore Luke can say at the outset that he is configuring and re-configuring "events that

---

[14] For a rich and provocative reading of Acts within the philosophical/cultural categories of life under empire and Luke's challenge to those priorities, see C. Kavin Rowe, *World Upside Down: Reading Acts in the Graeco-Roman Age* (Oxford: Oxford University Press, 2009), esp. 17–51; cf. now, Karl Allen Kuhn, *The Kingdom according to Luke and Acts: A Social, Literary, and Theological Introduction* (Grand Rapids, MI: Baker Academic, 2015).

[15] As Stephen D. Moore observed, "'Then he opened their minds to understand the scriptures' (24:44–45; compare 24:25–27). Jesus opens his disciples' minds not to the self-sufficiency of his word but to its intertextuality. Far from being self-evident or self-disclosing, his word signifies only in so far as it circulates through the arteries and veins of a written corpus, a body in which it constantly runs the risk of death. Acts ends with a Jesus-in-the-text once again rejected by a nation of poor readers ... 'trying to convince them about Jesus both from the law of Moses and from the prophets' (28:23 ...)," *Mark and Luke in Poststructuralist Perspectives* (New Haven, CT: Yale University Press, 1992), 100–101. For the new dynamic of interpretation that a precursor and successor text set in motion, see esp. Dale C Allison Jr., *The Intertextual Jesus. Scripture in Q.* (Harrisburg, PA: Trinity Press International, 2000) 211–12.

have come to full flowering among us" (Luke 1:1). At the heart of this figuring are central characters and events of Israel's scriptural legacy that both prefigure and are re-figured in the light of the words and actions of the "Christ" who figures at the center of "all that stands written."

In our summary *Conclusion* we shall profile Luke as both Hellenistic *historian* and 'biblical' *theologian*. Ironically, in our search for the interpretation of a 'whole' for two enigmatic volumes we have determined that Jesus the Christ is not only the central character of the whole work, but that he also is indeed the one who *bestows meaning on the titles the story uses to describe him, rather than the reverse*. In the midst of Luke's secondary introduction to his sequel, Jesus becomes again the primary speaker-actor of the new volume. Through a sudden *metaleptic* shift, Jesus defines who he is and who he will be for the remainder of the work. We shall see in a new way how Luke's "aptness in the way he arranges his words" re-defines this puzzling yet ever intriguing work we are calling Luke's 'Gospel Acts.'

Acknowledgments:

I am especially grateful to the Board of the esteemed BZNW series of De Gruyter for their invitation to put together a collection of my essays on Luke and Acts. I have had to learn anew the meanings of 'configuring' and 're-configuring!' Each essay of this collection has appeared previously in part or in full in journals and multi-authored publications. I have tried to indicate at the beginning of each 'chapter' how I have changed or supplemented or shortened its predecessor. I have not attempted to update footnotes or bibliography, now so vast, it would make each chapter a poor semblance of its original.

I want to give special thanks to my assistant, Ms. Lindsey Trozzo, Assistant to the Bradford Chair, a budding New Testament scholar in her own right, and concurrently completing her Ph.D. dissertation at Baylor University, for her indispensable, remarkable help along every step of the way of preparing this manuscript. She, along with her student assistant, Ms. Kyra Fry, have provided a gracious, effective, wonderfully helpful presence through the entire process.

— A word of explanation about my use of quotation marks: Single quotes indicate a quotation within a quotation circumscribed by double quotation marks. Single quotes are also used for technical terms, common idioms and axioms, and for allusions to the same words and phrases discussed previously in the context. Arrows indicate the movement of the plot from one point to a later point in a synchronic progression through the text; they cannot be replaced simply by a comma or semi-colon. I have restrained from blotting out all such phrases as "Son of Man" or "fathers," et al. that appear in my earlier works, allowing my exegetical sensibilities and learned nuances to develop historically as, hopefully, I have made progress through continual study and research through the many years.

Through all of this reprising and revising, it has become clear, at times painfully, how words take on a different aspect in new and unanticipated literary contexts. By introducing each cluster of essays as a Part of a larger whole, I endeavor to promote an *overarching thesis* through the entirety of the book, an understanding of Luke's 'Gospel Acts' that has emerged only after many years of research and writing and re-writing. While this has been rewarding personally, my goal has been to figure this new understanding in a way that rewards all readers of Luke's inimitable volumes. To echo a commentator from the late 19th-early 20th century, "Reader ... if you come to love the evangelist and the book a little more than you ever did before, we shall have our reward" (D. A. Hayes, *The Most Beautiful Book Ever Written* [New York: Eaton & Mains, 1913], vii).

Fort Worth
The Feast of St. Patrick, March 17, 2016

Part I:
Luke's 'Gospel Acts' and the Genre of the Gospels

Only Luke among the authors of the New Testament has composed two long narrative 'books' to claim pride of place as the most prolific of New Testament contributors (ca. 28%), even more than the indefatigable Paul and the corpus of letters attached to his name (ca. 23%). Whether referred to by the traditional names of "the Gospel of Luke" and "the Acts of the Apostles," or by the more urbane "Luke-Acts"–first coined in the post-War period of the previous century by historical critics–Luke's two volumes remain both puzzling and intriguing, controversial yet compelling for a wide spectrum of readers. Why did the church never align Acts as a second volume to Luke in their emerging canon, even though Luke would seem to invite his readers to read the two together as one narrative work in two parts (see Luke 1:1–4 and Acts 1:1–5)? Are both "Luke" and "Acts" of the same genre or type of writing such that they 'fit' together in relating one larger story? What is missed if Luke and Acts are not read in light of one another?

These enduring questions in the interpretation of two beloved books form the heart of *Luke the Historian of Israel's Legacy, Theologian of Israel's Christ*. As the title suggests, Luke is both historian and a committed reader of the Jewish scriptures, combining his skill in configuring a coherent historical narrative with his considerable knowledge and reverence for the God of Israel's scriptures. As the thesis unfolds, we shall argue that the central thrust of our author's comprehension of a 'whole'–what Luke will refer to more than once as "the plan–or counsel of God"–is that Jesus of Nazareth is both the "Christ" of the Jewish scriptures and the one who inhabits his two-volume portrayal as the *raison d'être* of those scriptures.

The two chapters of Part I introduce a reading that takes both volumes together, arguing that Luke writes a short, monograph-length history in two books. This history concerns a movement within Judaism that claimed to incarnate the principle figure of its scriptures and presented itself as the continuing embodiment of the "goal" (τέλος) of those scriptures, manifest especially in the church's rapid spread into the very centers of Mediterranean culture and of Roman empire.

Chapter One, "How Luke Writes," highlights characteristic themes and contours of Luke and Acts when read in the shadow of the canonical 'four' Gospels as well as in the light of each other. Both Luke and Acts retain their individual contributions to the whole of the New Testament as distinct books, even as both take on an unmistakable set of authorially-crafted 'family' resemblances and intra-textual dependencies when read in tandem. The second chapter, "Re-reading Talbert's Luke: The *Bios* of 'Balance' or the 'Bias' of History?," sets out the case why the Gospel of Luke, taken by itself, does not exhibit the distinctive marks of the Hellenistic βίος or 'biography' but rather those of ἱστορία or 'historiography.' Of course the focus of the Gospel plot is upon its central character, Jesus of Nazareth. Yet, there is no presentation of the "life," or the "character" Jesus, apart from his role in Israel's life and character. The very fact that "Messiah" is a central moniker for Jesus shows how critical the calling and legacy of Israel through its "Christ" is for the author who will continue to speak of Israel and "Israel's hope" to the very end of his second volume (for example, Acts 28:20). But even more than that, all the attention upon Jesus as the Christ of Israel and upon Israel's legacy is placed at the service of the all-encompassing embrace and dynamic of the kingly Reign of God that extends back before "the foundation of the earth" and forward to the "consummation of all things." Truly Luke and Acts, read as one sweeping story, parades the emerging Christian "movement" as a world-wide enterprise beheld as the *phe-nomen*al consequence of a comprehensive "plan of God."

Chapter One: How Luke Writes[1]

"This Gospel is represented fittingly by the calf, because it begins with priests and ends with the Calf who, having taken upon himself the sins of all, was sacrificed for the life of the whole world."[2] Thus Ambrose (333–397 CE), bishop of Milan, describes the "Gospel according to Luke" which, in the subsequent years, has become perhaps the most beloved of the church's four Gospels. "The most beautiful book in the world" was Renan's estimate.[3] Indeed, the Third Gospel portrays uniquely some of the most loved of Jesus's miniatures of the Kingdom of God in "The Good Samaritan," "The Prodigal (Lost) Son," "The Friend at Midnight," "The Persistent Widow,"[4] and others, not to mention one of the most dramatically and beautifully narrated 'short stories' in all the Bible, the walk to Emmaus, where the suspense breaks only as Jesus "is recognized"–finally–"in the breaking of the bread."[5]

Yet Luke's Gospel was not apparently the first to be recognized by the church in the century when written "gospels according to" an apostle or follower of an apostle first emerged. As far as Eusebius reports, Papias (in his interviews of the followers of the apostles toward the beginning of the 2nd century) does not refer to Luke's Gospel as he compares Matthew's with Mark's,[6] though Luke's more felicitous narrative arrangement may be implicit in that comparison.[7] When the Third Gospel emerges clearly in the 3rd-century commentary of Origen,[8] it has

---

[1] Excerpted from pp. 149–64, with some changes and additions, from David P. Moessner, "How Luke Writes," in *The Written Gospel*, ed. Markus Bockmuehl and Donald A. Hagner [FS Graham Stanton] (Cambridge: Cambridge University Press, 2005): 149–70. Used by permission.
[2] Ambrose, "Exposition of the Gospel of Luke 1.4.7," in *Luke*, ed. Arthur Just, ACCS, NT III (Downers Grove, IL: InterVarsity, 2003): 2.
[3] Ernst Renan, *Les Evangiles et la seconde génération chrétienne* (Paris: Calmann Lévy, 1877), 283.
[4] Luke 10:25–37; 15:11–32; 11:5–8; 18:1–8, respectively.
[5] Luke 24:13–35.
[6] Eusebius, *Hist. eccl.* III.39.14–16.
[7] Bo Ivar Reicke, *The Roots of the Synoptic Gospels* (Philadelphia, PA: Fortress Press, 1986), 166–67; David P. Moessner, "The Appeal and Power of Poetics (Luke 1:1–4): Luke's Superior Credentials (παρηκολουθηκότι), Narrative Sequence (καθεξῆς), and Firmness of Understanding (ἡ ἀσφάλεια) for the Reader," in *Jesus and the Heritage of Israel*, ed. David P. Moessner, vol. 1, *Luke the Interpreter of Israel* (Harrisburg, PA: Trinity Press International, 1999): 114–19.
[8] Origen, *Homilies on Luke, Fragments on Luke*, trans. Joseph T. Lienhard, FC 94 (Washington, DC: Catholic University of America Press, 1996). The first explicit reference to Luke's "gospel" among the "fathers" of the church is disputed but appears to be Irenaeus toward the end of the second century in his *Against the Heresies*, 3.1.1, who aligns Luke's message with Paul's "gospel." See further, e.g., Joseph A. Fitzmyer, *The Gospel according to Luke I–IX*, AB 28, vol. 1 (New York: Doubleday, 1981), 37–41.

already established itself as foundational in the celebration of the church year. In subsequent patristic exegesis and lectionary readings, Luke becomes the favorite during the Christmas season because of its infancy narratives (Luke 1–2) and at Easter through its vivid resurrection accounts (Luke 24).[9] Though not cited as frequently as Matthew or John in the subsequent writings of the fathers, Luke seems to be preferred for much of the church's admonitions for alms for the poor,[10] especially as Luke's special material[11] matches catechetical emphases of the Lenten season.[12]

Our emphases upon "How Luke Writes" will be illumined through: 1. "The Character of the 'Third Gospel' among 'Four' in the Light of the 'Acts' that Follow," and 2. "The Distinctive Contour and Content of Luke and Acts among 'the Four.'"

1 The Character of the "Third Gospel" among "Four" in the Light of the "Acts" that Follow

In the section that follows, we will consider various ways in which the Third Gospel distinguishes itself among the canonical four. The present section considers first the most obvious of these distinctions–its place (according to its inscribed author[13]) as the first volume[14] of a two-volume work, Luke-Acts.[15] But,

---

[9] See esp. Just, ed., *Luke*, xviii–xix, who cites Hughes Oliphant Old, *The Patristic Age*, vol. 2, *The Reading and Preaching of the Scriptures in the Worship of the Christian Church* (Grand Rapids, MI: Eerdmans, 1998), 147–58, 277–99.
[10] Compare the opening prayer for the Feast of St. Luke in the *Sacramentary of the Roman Missal*: "Father, you chose Luke the evangelist to reveal by preaching and writing the mystery of your love for the poor [...] and let all nations come to see your salvation [...] through our Lord Jesus Christ, your Son [...] one God, for ever and ever."
[11] The passages unique to Luke ("L"): e.g., Luke 12:47–48; 16:1–13,14–15,19–31; 17:7–10; 18:9–14.
[12] Just, ed., *Luke*, who cites William Harmless, *Augustine and the Catechumenate* (Collegeville, MN: Liturgical Press, 1995) and Augustine, *Sermons on Various Subjects*, sermons 341–400, trans. Edmund Hill, vol. 10, *The Works of Saint Augustine: A Translation for the Twenty-first Century* (Hyde Park, NY: New City Press, 1995).
[13] "It seemed good to me also" (ἔδοξε κἀμοί, Luke 1:3a).
[14] For the emerging titles of the Gospels, compare, e.g., Reicke, *Roots*, 150–55; Martin Hengel, *The Four Gospels and the One Gospel of Jesus Christ: An Investigation of the Collection and Origin of the Canonical Gospels* (Harrisburg, PA: Trinity Press International, 2000), 48–56; Dieter Lührmann, *Die Apokryph Gewordenen Evangelien: Studien zu neuen Texten und zu neuen Fragen*, NovTSup 112 (Leiden: Brill, 2004), 29–47.
[15] For a brief survey of modern approaches to "Luke–Acts," see David P. Moessner and David L. Tiede, "Two Books but One Story?" in *Jesus and the Heritage of Israel*, ed. David P. Moessner, vol. 1, *Luke the Interpreter of Israel* (Harrisburg, PA: Trinity Press International, 1999): 1–4; com-

to our knowledge, the church never paired the Gospel according to Luke with the Acts of the Apostles as one narrative movement in two parts.[16] Instead, Luke's Gospel was aligned alongside the other three, and among the varying sequences of canonical lists–even in the few instances when Luke is listed last among the four–Acts never follows the Third Gospel![17] Beyond the obvious physical separation of two "books" necessitated by the maximum length of a single papyrus scroll, the emerging church was also apparently forced to sift through a variety of "Gospel" portrayals of the ministry of Jesus to authenticate those accounts that squared with apostolic oral traditions, a process that Luke himself may be hinting at in his Gospel prologue (Luke 1:1–4): [the] "many [who] have undertaken to compose a narrative account of events come to fruition in our midst [...] concerning those traditions of which you have been instructed" (περὶ ὧν κατηχήθης λόγων). It is clear that what Luke had joined together formally and materially through the two coupling prologues (Luke 1:1–4→Acts 1:1–2),[18] the church has rent asunder.

Nevertheless, it has become equally clear, given the passel of historical-critical and poststructuralist tools available to the (post)modern exegete, that the significance of events in Luke's Gospel is greatly enhanced when viewed through their construal in Acts and that, conversely, our understanding of Acts is significantly impoverished without a fundamental grasp of its prequel ("all that Jesus began to do and to teach," Acts 1:1). Each volume completes and comments directly upon the other.[19]

---

pare, e.g., Luke Timothy Johnson, "Luke–Acts, Book of," *ABD* 4:403–20; Christopher M. Tuckett, *Luke: New Testament Guides* (Sheffield: Sheffield Academic Press, 1996), esp. 11–32, 111–17.

16 Compare the so-called "Anti-Marcionite Prologue," circa end of 2nd century: "Luke was a Syrian of Antioch, by profession a physician, the disciple of the apostles, and later a follower of Paul until his martyrdom [...] he was prompted by the Holy Spirit and composed this gospel entirely in the regions about Achaia [...] Later the same Luke wrote the Acts of the Apostles." See further, Fitzmyer, *Luke I–IX*, 37–41.

17 Compare, e.g., the "Cheltenham Canon" (circa 360 CE–northern Africa): Matt–Mark–John–Luke–Paulines!–Acts; Codex Claromontanus–Acts following Revelation; cf. syr^{cur}–Luke last of four Gospel codex, no Acts; Theophilus of Antioch–Matt, John, Luke, epistles, Acts; see Henry J. Cadbury, *The Book of Acts in History* (New York: Harper and Bros., 1955), 143–44.

18 See below Part II, "Luke's Prologues and Hellenistic Narrative Hermeneutics."

19 See, e.g., the volume of the 47th Colloquium Biblicum Lovaniense (1998) devoted to this issue: Joseph Verheyden, ed., *The Unity of Luke–Acts*, BETL 142 (Leuven: University/Peeters Press, 1999).

1.1 Luke's Gospel: Beginnings and Endings

The very different beginning and ending of Luke's Gospel *vis-à-vis* the other three set this volume apart in both scope and impact. Following his formal *prooemium*,[20] Luke places the action of John the Baptist's and Jesus's callings squarely within the history of Israel ("in the days of Herod, King of Judea," Luke 1:5) and its priestly orders at the center of Israel's worship in the Jerusalem Temple ("a certain priest named Zechariah").[21] The choices of images and cadences of these first two chapters, in fact, echo Septuagintal (LXX) synchronisms[22] as well as the call stories of famous patriarchs and matriarchs, judges and prophets of Israel. The callings of Abraham and Sarah (Gen 16:7–16; 17:1–22; 18:1–15), Menoah, his wife, and Sampson (Judg 13:2–25), Hannah and Samuel (1Kgdms 2:1–10), and even Daniel (Dan 8:15–26; 9:20–27[23]) continue to shimmer in the radiant appearance of the archangel Gabriel to Zechariah and Mariam (Luke 1:8–20, 26–38) who announces God's raising up of a prophet and a savior to "come to the aid of Israel, his [God's] servant" (Mariam, 1:54) and "to visit and make ransom for the redemption[24] of his people Israel" (Zechariah, 1:68b). This unexpected angelophany of Gabriel would appear to herald a most sensational prophecy. It was

---

20 See Part II below, "Luke's Prologues and Hellenistic Narrative Hermeneutics."
21 "This Gospel is represented fittingly by the calf, because it begins with priests and ends with the Calf who, having taken upon himself the sins of all, was sacrificed for the life of the whole world" (Ambrose, *Exposition of the Gospel of Luke* 1.4.7).
22 E.g., the Septuagintal idiom: "It happened in the day(s) of [...]" ([καὶ] ἐγένετο ἐν ταῖς ἡμέραις): Judg 14:15,17; 18:31; 19:5; Ruth 1:1; 1Kgdms 3:2; 4:1; 13:22; 28:1; 2Kgdms 21:1; 3Kgdms 9:9, *inter alia*; compare several other analogous idioms.
23 Gabriel appears to Daniel "at the time of the evening sacrifice" (Dan 9:22), that is, the same time as the *Tamid* offering in Luke 1:5–23; cf. Exod 30:7–8.
24 My rendering of the unusual phrase "make redemption" which is not found in the LXX. But what is consistent from the LXX's usage of the verb λυτρόω and its noun λύτρωσις is the requirement of either animal sacrifice or ransom money/goods (λύτρον) to make redemption a reality. In conjunction with God "visiting" his people to effect release from slavery and/or sin (Luke 1:68b), "make redemption" denotes the unspecified means through which God's presence for release is accomplished (compare LXX Ps 110:9 ["send redemption"]). Cf. Fitzmyer, *Luke*, 1:383: "The combination of the noun *lytrōsis* with the verb *poiein* is strange [...] it describes Yahweh's activity on behalf of his people in terms of ransom or release;" cf. Luke Timothy Johnson, *The Gospel of Luke*, SP 3 (Collegeville, MN: Liturgical Press, 1991), 46: "In contrast to the 'liberation' of the people from Egypt under Moses, however (Acts 7:35), Luke here defines it in apolitical, cultic terms." For God's visitation as gracious deliverance, see esp. LXX Exod 4:31; Ruth 1:6; Pss 79:14; 105:4; for "to redeem/make ransom" and its noun, see e.g., LXX Exod 6:6; 13:13, 15; 15:13; Lev 19:20; 25:25; 27:31,33; Num 18:15, 16; Pss 48:7, 8, 9; 129:8 (from sin); Isa 63:4, *inter alia*.

in fact Gabriel long before who had appeared to Daniel to interpret his dream of "the ram and goat" (Dan 8:1–27) as "a vision for the time of the end" (8:17b) and to "give understanding" of his dream of the "seventy weeks of years" (9:1–27) as the "final days" that "bring in everlasting righteousness" (9:24), climaxing in an "anointed one" (χριστός) who "is cut off" (9:26). Now Gabriel announces that this "coming of God" is about to enact something final and definitive "forever" (cf. Luke 1:33, 55): John will be "a prophet of the Most High" (1:76a) who will prepare a repenting people (1:16–17) and go before the Lord (1:76b), while Jesus will be "Son of the Most High," "the Savior, the Messiah, the Lord" ("angel/messenger of the Lord," 2:11) "who will reign over the house of Jacob," "on David's throne" "forever" (1:32–33).[25]

With these rich resonances of Israel's Scriptures, it would appear that the promises to the ancestors of the "Lord's Christ" like those to Hannah of old are now on the verge of fulfillment to the Hannah and Simeon who eagerly anticipate Israel's "consolation,"[26] Jerusalem's "redemption" (Luke 2:22–38). The birth of Jesus as the "Christ of the Lord" (ὁ χριστὸς κυρίου, Luke 2:26) will not only bring "judgment to the ends of the earth" (compare αὐτὸς [κύριος] κρινεῖ ἄκρα γῆς [...] καὶ ὑψώσει κέρας χριστοῦ αὐτοῦ [Hannah in 1Sam 2:10 = LXX 1Kgdms 2:10]), but this child will also become "a sign that is continually opposed" (Luke 2:33–35) as God's "saving action" streams "a light of revelation to the Gentiles and glory to your people Israel" (τὸ σωτήριόν σου [...] φῶς εἰς ἀποκάλυψιν ἐθνῶν καὶ δόξαν λαοῦ σου Ἰσραήλ [Simeon in Luke 2:29–32]).[27]

More than this, both Mariam and Zechariah prophesy of God's mercy executing great reversal in the socio-political bondage of oppressive "enemies." Patron-client relations will be reversed;[28] those of the peasant-servile statuses

---

25 In Codex Vaticanus (early- to mid-4th century) Daniel appears as the final book of the prophets and thereby in this format comprises the last book of the early church's "Old Testament."
26 Luke 2:25 (παράκλησις) echoes the "consolation"/"comfort" (παρακαλεῖτε, παρακαλεῖτε, Isa 40:1) announced in the call of the prophet in Isa 40:1–11 (cf. esp. Luke 2:32 and Isa 42:6; 46:13; 49:6,9). Isa 40–55 is often referred to as the "Book of the Consolation of Israel."
27 All OT citations are from the Old Greek (LXX).
28 See, e.g., Halvor Moxnes, "Patron-Client Relations and the New Community in Luke-Acts," in *The Social World of Luke-Acts: Models for Interpretation*, ed. Jerome H. Neyrey (Peabody, MA: Hendrickson, 1991): 241–68; Jerome H. Neyrey, "The Symbolic Universe of Luke-Acts: They Turn the World Upside Down," in *Social World of Luke-Acts: Models for Interpretation*, ed. Jerome H. Neyrey (Peabody, MA: Hendrickson, 1991): 271–304; Joel B. Green, *The Theology of the Gospel of Luke* (Cambridge: Cambridge University Press, 1995), 76–121; Peter Esler, *Community and Gospel in Luke-Acts* (Cambridge: Cambridge University Press, 1987).

like Mariam herself will be exalted over the proud and mighty;[29] the rich will be stripped of power and possessions;[30] and Israel will reign over all its enemies as in the glory days of David, with God's strength manifest in unprecedented "peace and holiness,"[31] just as God had promised Abraham and just as all the prophets had re-sounded in looking to the time when God would fulfill "His holy covenant." Are these images of liberation and salvation to be taken literally?[32] Is the "reversal" envisioned to be "spiritual" only?

The end of Luke's Gospel certainly confirms a scriptural "end"-scape of God's promises to Israel. The crucified but resurrected Jesus "appears" to continue God's raising up of witnesses to Israel's eschatological salvation that has been "prepared" for all peoples of the world. But in Luke 24:44–49 the apostles' "recognition" of Jesus can only ensue once they comprehend the fulfillment of all that stands written about him as "the Christ" (24:44b). Their minds first have to be "opened" to understand (24:45) that the whole of Israel's Scriptures centers upon and points forward to Jesus as "the Christ": Jesus as "Messiah must suffer, rise from the dead on the third day, and through his name release of sins be proclaimed into all the nations" (εἰς πάντα τὰ ἔθνη) (24:46–47). This dynamic goal of Scripture thus forms their new identity as "witnesses"[33] (μάρτυρες, 24:48) and transforms "all that Jesus began to do and to teach [...] until the day he was taken up" (Acts 1:1–2) into the culmination of the one two-volume narrative. What is to be proclaimed to all peoples, beginning from Jerusalem (Luke 24:47), is this sweeping hermeneutic of Moses, the Prophets, and the Psalms that finds its

---

29 See, e.g., Robert C. Tannehill, *The Sword of His Mouth: Forceful and Imaginative Language in Synoptic Sayings*, SemeiaSup 1 (Philadelphia, PA/Missoula, MT: Fortress/Scholars Press, 1975).

30 See, e.g., Hans-Joachim Degenhardt, *Lukas Evangelist der Armen: Besitz und Besitzverzicht in den lukanischen Schriften: Eine traditions- und redaktionsgeschichtliche Untersuchung* (Stuttgart: Katholisches Bibelwerk, 1965).

31 See, e.g., Ulrich Mauser, *The Gospel of Peace: A Scriptural Message for Today's World* (Louisville, KY: Westminster John Knox, 1992), 83–103.

32 See, e.g., the debate in Joseph B. Tyson, ed., *Luke–Acts and the Jewish People: Eight Critical Perspectives* (Minneapolis, MN: Augsburg Publishing, 1988); cf. esp. David L. Tiede, "'Glory to Thy People Israel': Luke-Acts and the Jews," in *ibid*.: 21–34, with David P. Moessner, "The Ironic Fulfillment of Israel's Glory," in *ibid*.: 35–50; Robert C. Tannehill, "Rejection by Jews and Turning to Gentiles: The Pattern of Paul's Mission in Acts," in *ibid*.: 83–101, with Joseph B. Tyson, "The Problem of Jewish Rejection in Acts," in *ibid*.: 124–37.

33 On the importance of both "witness" and "eyewitness" in Luke and Acts, see, e.g., Richard J. Dillon, *From Eyewitnesses to Ministers of the Word*, AnBib 82 (Rome: Biblical Institute, 1978); cf. Samuel Byrskog, *Story as History, History as Story: The Gospel Tradition in the Context of Ancient Oral History*, WUNT 123 (Tübingen: Mohr Siebeck, 2000), 228–53.

τέλος in Jesus as "the suffering and raised up Messiah" (cf. Luke 22:37b: τὸ περὶ ἐμοῦ τέλος ἔχει). It would appear that this teleological center of "all that stands written" forms the crux of what it means that Jesus "will reign on David's throne" "forever" (Luke 1:32–33).

Luke ends his Gospel volume with Jesus "blessing" his disciples and "being taken up into heaven" (Luke 24:50–51) along with their mirroring response of worship and joy and "blessing God" continually in the Temple (24:52–53). Different, then, from Jesus commissioning the "eleven" in Galilee in the "name" of the triune God in Matthew (28:16–20), or from the "fear" of the women at the empty tomb in Mark (16:1–8), or from the "beloved disciple's" "testimony" for future generations in John (21:20–25), Luke concludes his first "book" in the same place he began, at the center of Israel's worship. This *inclusio* thus lends completeness to volume one; Jesus has finished his "exodus" journey of "death" and "taking up" from Galilee (Luke 9:31,51) to Israel's central place and its "place of the skull" and beyond "into his glory" (19:41–44; 23:26–33; cf. 24:26b). Yet this concluding event of ascension and doxology does not conclude the plot of the one narrative unity.

1.2 Luke's Acts: Beginnings and Endings

Luke begins his second volume (cf. Acts 1:1–2) with extensive syn-chronological overlapping with the first. With such a "linking"[34] passage, Luke re-configures chronologically one day of resurrection (Luke 24:1–51) into "forty days"[35] of teaching and appearances of the resurrected Christ (Acts 1:3–14). "Power from the exalted place" of the first volume (ἐξ ὕψους δύναμιν, Luke 24:49b) is now translated as "baptized by/in the Holy Spirit not after many days" (Luke 24:49→Acts 1:4b–5). In contrast to John who "baptized with water," the characteristic mark of the apostles' witness will be a baptism by the Holy Spirit. Moreover, this power of the Holy Spirit is aligned with the "living one's" teaching about "the

---

34 Compare the "linking passages" at the beginning of each new volume in Hellenistic general or universal histories such as Diodorus Siculus's *Library of History* through which he ties disparate events of various peoples into one ongoing narrative as though they were the affairs of one great "mētr-opolis" (= mother-city) or global village (I.1.3; I.3.6): II.1.1–3; III.1.1–3; IV.1.5–7; V.2.1; VI.1.1–3; [VII–X]; XI.1.1; XII.2.2–3; XIII.1.1–3; XIV.2.4; XV.1.6; XVI.1.3–6 [compare XV.95.4!]; XVII.1.1–2; XVIII.1.5–6; XIX.1.9–10; XX.2.3; [XXI–XL]; square brackets indicate fragmentary books without extant linking passages.
35 "Forty days" is a biblical idiom of an indefinite period of time, neither particularly long nor short in duration.

Kingdom of God"–"after he suffered" (Acts 1:3). To be "my [Jesus's] witness" in the "power of the Holy Spirit" (Acts 1:8) encompasses the resurrected, crucified Christ's "opening" of and fulfilled presence in the Kingdom of God through his authoritative opening of the Scriptures (παρέστησεν ἑαυτὸν ζῶντα [...] ἐν πολλοῖς τεκμηρίοις [...] λέγων τὰ περὶ τῆς βασιλείας τοῦ θεοῦ, Acts 1:3a).[36]

Consequently in Acts the one who has proclaimed the "Kingdom" in Luke does not become the "proclaimed" but rather the "proclaimed proclaimer."[37] Whether Jesus or his "name" or his Spirit[38] be the primary speaker and actor, the plot of Acts entangles the character and work of God into one "necessary will" or "plan" as already "scripted" in Israel's Scriptures.[39] What is only provisionally anticipated in Luke 24:49 has therefore been augmented into a leitmotif of the "sym-phony" of both volumes. To "recognize" Jesus as the resurrected, crucified Christ of God's reign must now entail the empowering presence of the "Holy Spirit" as the Scriptures are opened to Jews, Samaritans, and all the nations of the "end of the earth" (Acts 1:6–8). It is not by accident that the giving of the Spirit at Pentecost by the exalted-crucified One attends Peter's witness of opening the scriptures (LXX: Joel 3; Pss 15[16]; 109[110] in Acts 2:16–21, 25–28, 33–35, respectively) and crowns his explanation of just how it is that the resurrected-crucified Jesus of patriarch David's offspring "reigns on David's throne, forever" as "Lord and Christ" in God's comprehensive "plan" (2:23–24, 33, 36). It is this overarching "plan" or "counsel" of God that binds Luke and Acts together as one plotted narrative in two parts.

---

36 For a fuller treatment, see David P. Moessner, "Ministers of Divine Providence: Diodorus Siculus and Luke the Evangelist on the Rhetorical Significance of the Audience in Narrative 'Arrangement,'" in *Literary Encounters with the Reign of God: Studies in Honor of R. C. Tannehill*, ed. Sharon H. Ringe and H. C. Paul Kim (New York: T&T Clark International, 2004): 304–23, esp. 318–23.

37 Cf. those passages where Jesus is referred to either as Lord and Christ or his "name" is present and active: Acts 2:21, 24, 32, 33, 36, 38, 47; 3:6, 16, 20, 22, 26; 4:2, 7, 10, 12, 17, 18, 26, 30, 33; 5:14, 28, 40, 41, 42; 8:12, 16, 25, 35; 9:4–6, 10–16, 20, 27–28, 31, 34; 10:13–16, 43, 48; 11:20, 21, 23, 24; 13:10–12, 30–33, 34–39, 44, 47–49; 14:3, 23; 15:11, 17, 26, 35, 36, 40; 16:7, 14–15, 18, 31–32; 17:3, 7, 18, 31; 18:5, 9–10, 28; 19:4–5, 10, 13–14, 17, 20; 20:32; 21:13–14; 22:7–10, 14–16, 17–21; 23:11; 26:14–18, 23; 28:23, 31.

38 Τὸ πνεῦμα Ἰησοῦ, "the Spirit of Jesus," Acts 16:7. The Spirit as character/actor is not included in the references above since the Spirit is distinguished in "name" from "Jesus" or "God" et al.; yet it is also clear that the referent under these several descriptions is the presence or identity of the one God.

39 See David P. Moessner, "The 'Script' of the Scriptures in Acts: Suffering as God's 'Plan' (βουλή) for the World for the 'Release of Sins,'" in *History, Literature and Society in the Book of Acts*, ed. Ben Witherington III (Cambridge: Cambridge University Press, 1995), 218–50.

Acts 1:6–8 therefore re-constellates the Jerusalem-oriented message ("remain in this city," Luke 24:49b) into the emplotment of witness to and through Israel "to the end of the earth." Israel's kingdom of God's rule must not first be re-constituted according to some scheme of "times and seasons" announced by Gabriel to Daniel so that the nations of the earth might participate in Israel's witness (Acts 1:6–7; cf. Dan 9:25–27[40] and Luke 1!). Rather, Israel's witness to God's rule must first be taken to Israel and all the nations through the authenticated witness of the (symbolic) twelve apostles "opening" the scriptures of the "crucified, living one." Again it is no accident that Book Two commences with the restoration of the "twelve" witnesses-apostles rather than the restoration of the kingdom to the nation (ἔθνος) of Israel (Acts 1:15–26).[41]

2 The Distinctive Contour and Content of Luke Together with Acts among "The Four"

When viewed in the light of its canonical configuration, the Gospel of Luke indeed stands out from Matthew and Mark through its structure of a Jesus who journeys. When the journeying framework of Acts is read in tandem as a sequel, the variations of plot movement *vis-à-vis* the first two Gospels are striking. Only John with its multiple journeys of Jesus to Jerusalem and Jesus's subsequent activity in Galilee bears some resemblance to the dynamic of Luke and Acts.[42]

---

40 Both translations of Daniel of the Old Greek and Theodotian speak about a "Christ" in conjunction with "times and seasons."
41 It is curious that Diodorus in his short depiction of the "Jews" in *Library of History* XL.3.1–8 finds it important to include the number of their tribes as twelve (regarded by them, he says, as a "perfect" number and corresponding to the number of months of the year) as definitive of them as a distinct "people"/"nation" (ἔθνος).
42 Interestingly, both Luke and John have Jesus journey four times to Jerusalem (see John 2:13–3:21; 5:1–47; 7:10–10:39; 12:1–20:29); in Luke, Jesus's fifth journey continues the goal of the great (fourth) journey to be taken up/journey into heaven (cf. Luke 9:51). In John Jesus interacts with his disciples in Galilee after his resurrection (John 21), while in Matthew, though Jesus appears in Galilee after his resurrection (Matt 28:16–20), the overall amount of narrative space devoted to Jesus's intentional movement toward Jerusalem is relatively small (Matt 19–20).

2.1 The Journeys of Jesus in the Gospel of Luke

Luke divides his Gospel material into five such journeys, although only two represent Jesus's own decision to move toward a determined goal (signified by *):

1) Luke 2:22–40. Jesus's parents fulfill "the law of Moses" for "the purification" of a new mother and "sanctification of the firstborn" *à la* Lev 12:2–4 and Exod 13:1–16, respectively (Luke 2:23–24). The entire encounter with the pious worthies Simeon and Hannah, however, mimics more the "presentation of Samuel" in Eli's temple at Shiloh than straightforward fulfillment of Torah *halakah*.[43] Does the sacrifice of redemption of the "firstborn" in Exod 13, which recalls and thus re-figures Israel's redemption through the Passover, together with Zechariah's prophecy of "making redemption" (ποίειν λύτρωσις) in the "Lord's" "visitation of his people" in Luke 1:68b, adumbrate perhaps Jesus's self-sacrifice when he will signify his voluntary death "for them" as the sealing of a "new covenant" at the Passover with his "apostles" (Luke 22:19–20 in 22:14–38)?[44]

2) Luke 2:41–52. Jesus journeys again to the Temple under the tutelage of "his parents" (2:41), this time as a boy (παῖς) of twelve for the Passover. Jesus's questions and answers to the "teachers" of the Temple "astound" "all" as well as confound "your father" and "mother" (2:47–48, 50–51). Might the greater tutelage and "concerns of his Father" (2:49) point forward to a future Passover when Jesus in the Temple will again teach and "astound the teachers"[45] of Israel (compare Luke 19:47–21:38)?

3) Luke 4:9–14.[46] Jesus is "led" by "the devil/slanderer" into Jerusalem and onto the pinnacle of the Temple even though the Holy Spirit has been leading him in the wilderness since his baptism in the "region of the Jordan" (4:1; 3:3). The Slanderer casts doubt whether Jesus could be the "Son" or "please" his "father" like Abraham's Isaac or the Lord's "servant" (παῖς) in Isaiah just as the voice from heaven has echoed (3:22[47]) and as Luke's narrator re-echoes immediately in Jesus's genealogy ("[...] son of Adam, son of God," 3:23–38). If

---

43 See esp. LXX 1Kgdms 1:24–2:10,20; cf. Luke 2:22b, "to present him to the Lord."
44 Compare n. 21 and also the opening quote of Ambrose at the beginning of this article.
45 E.g., Luke 20:26, 39–40.
46 Though this "third" temptation, similar to the second, would seem to transcend normal notions of time and space and thus not be a journey like others, still Jesus is presented as allowing himself to be transported by the devil from one temporal-spatial moment to another, and in 4:14 Jesus "returns," again in the "power of the Spirit" (cf. Luke 4:1), to Galilee.
47 Cf. Gen 22:2 ("your [Abraham's] beloved son") with Isa 42:1: "[Israel] my servant, my chosen/elect [son], in whom my soul (I [Yahweh/the Lord]) delights. I have put my spirit upon him."

so, the Devil reckons, Jesus's privileged status must be showcased in a psalm of trust like LXX Ps 90 "concerning" the "you" whom "the Lord" will not allow to be harmed (Ps 90:11–12).[48] Does the Slanderer's 'logic' anticipate here an even greater temptation Jesus will undergo in Jerusalem when the "chief priests and scribes" will "lead" Jesus into their "council" to challenge his identity: "So you, then, are the Son of God!" (22:66, 70)? Does the Devil's subsequent reappearance "at an opportune time" (compare 4:13b–ἄχρι καιροῦ) foreshadow the more humiliating denials of Jesus' "Sonship" (22:63–65; 23:11, 18–23, 35–39; compare 22:3, 6–εὐκαιρία!) when, from the cross, Jesus will cry the lament of a "suffering righteous" as he "entrusts" his spirit to his "Father" (23:46 [LXX Ps 30:5])? In any case, Luke's reconfiguring of "every temptation" of Jesus (4:13) as Israel's "son"[49]–who must re-enact the wilderness trials of Israel's exodus[50] before the "conquest" of the land of inheritance[51] is climaxed in true worship of the Lord at the "central place" (compare Deut 26:1–11; contrast Matt 4)–prefigures Jesus's great journey from Galilee to Jerusalem to "cleanse"[52] "my house" (Luke 19:46) and become the "head stone which the builders have rejected" (20:17 [Ps 118:22]).

*4) Luke 9:51–19:44. Luke's great journey of Jesus from Galilee to Jerusalem, occupying nearly 40 percent[53] of the Gospel narrative, stands in singular relief to the short journey of Mark 10:1–11:10 and the slightly extended version of Matt 19:1–21:9.[54] Consequently much of the material that Matthew and Mark place in Galilee Luke places in this journey.[55] What is Luke trying to signify?

First, the sonorous solemnity of Jesus's decision in Luke 9:51 strikes a contrasting chord to his "being led" previously by others. Now re-sounding the resolve

---

48 Ps 90:11: "concerning you" (sg.), that is, the psalmist who trusts in the Lord; the LXX title attributes the psalm to David.
49 See n. 47 on Gen 22 and Isa 42; cf. also Hos 11:1.
50 Jesus recites Deut 8:3 in Luke 4:4; cf. Deut 6:13 and 10:20 in Luke 4:8.
51 Luke 4:5: Jesus has been "led up" to view "all the kingdoms of the world" under the Devil's "watch" on a scale grander than "all the lands" from Mount Nebo that Moses is shown as the fulfilled promise to "Abraham, Isaac, and Jacob" (Deut 34:1–4).
52 See Mal 3:1–4 and Luke 7:27.
53 That is, when the journey's introduction (Luke 9:1–50) is included; see David P. Moessner, *Lord of the Banquet: A Literary and Theological Investigation of the Lukan Travel Narrative* (Minneapolis, MN/Harrisburg, PA: Fortress/Trinity Press International, 1989/1998), esp. 46–79.
54 John's Gospel, which divides Jesus's public ministry into four journeys to Jerusalem, is closer to Luke's portrayal in its overall form as well as its emphasis upon Israel's feasts but still quite divergent in content and tone from the "syn-optic" construal; see n. 42.
55 Cf., e.g, Moessner, *Lord of the Banquet*, 1–20; Reicke, *Roots*, 63–65, 171–73.

of Ezekiel (priest, "son of humankind"[56]) to declare God's judgment against an idol-sated Jerusalem and the flint-like purpose of the prophet-"servant" (παῖς) of Isa 50:4–11[57] to accept humiliation from his own people as he announces good news, Jesus himself exhibits "unbending determination" to complete his "taking up" by moving resolutely towards Jerusalem. Jesus now unflinchingly embraces the journey of his "exodus/death/departure" (ἔξοδος) that had been discussed by Moses and Elijah and Jesus on a mountain with lightning and cloud and voice from heaven (Luke 9:31 in 9:28–36; compare 10:38;[58] 13:22, 31–33; 14:25; 17:11; 18:31; 19:11, 28, 37, 41).

Second, though Luke provides neither itinerary nor map of Jesus's movement, nor any geographical locale for the vast array of "Q" and "L" sayings of Jesus, he still fashions a journey unparalleled by the other three Gospels.[59] Whether references to Jesus's being received in towns and inns along some "way" or stories of Jesus "receiving tax collectors and sinners" or alternatively acting as host when invited by others to a meal, all of these meal settings and parables which reflect a journeyer and hospitality as well as the several "notices" that Jerusalem is still Jesus's destination all combine to form Luke's "travel narrative." Passages like 13:31–33, 34–35 undertone the whole of the journey with the certitude that Jerusalem is the God-ordained, scripturally-intended destination for Jesus,[60] since he journeys as a prophet who must be pressed with the fate of the long line of prophets sent, rejected, and even killed by their own people in Israel's central place (compare especially 11:47–51; 19:41–44). Whether journeying primarily through Samaria, trans-Jordan, or even Galilee,[61] Jesus journeys as a persecuted prophet from the "Horeb" mountain of theophany to his "departure," like

---

[56] See esp. LXX Ezek 21:2: "Son of man/humankind/mortal, set your face resolutely (υἱὲ ἀνθρώπου στήρισον τὸ πρόσωπόν σου) toward Jerusalem and admonish against their holy sanctuaries" (Codex Vaticanus–B); cf. the same "setting of the face" or unbending resolve of Ezekiel, "son of humankind/mortal," to declare judgment in Ezek 6:2; 13:17; 20:46; 25:2; 28:21; 29:2; 38:2; cf. 14:8; 15:7 of God's "face."

[57] Isa 50:4: "set the face as a solid rock."

[58] For the emphasis upon πορεύομαι and cognates as the linking vocabulary of "the journey notices," see, e.g., David Gill, "Observations on the Lukan Travel Narrative and Some Related Passages," HTR 63 (1970): 200–205.

[59] See Moessner, Lord of the Banquet, 91–288.

[60] See esp. 13:35 with LXX Ps 117:26 and Jer 12:7; 22:5.

[61] In Luke 17:11 Jesus is "passing along corresponding to the middle of Samaria and Galilee"; it is not clear whether this route is through the middle of the land between Samaria and Galilee or along the boundary of the two regions outside of the two in the Decapolis. Commentators are likewise divided whether from 9:51 Jesus is presented primarily in Galilee and/or Samaria or in the trans-Jordan (the Decapolis and Perea).

Moses,⁶² and to his "taking up," like Elijah,⁶³ in order to fulfill in Jerusalem the scriptural mandate of "Moses and/or all the prophets" (Luke 16:29, 31; 18:31; 24:27, 44; compare Acts 26:22; 28:23).⁶⁴

Third, as Jesus progresses toward his goal, more and more of the throngs of Israel press upon him and join him in his journey (11:29; 12:1; 13:34; 14:25). Accordingly Jesus intensifies his warnings to a people (λαός) he perceives to be an increasingly "faithless generation" who, like the synagogue congregation of his home town Nazareth (4:16–30), demand "a sign" of his authority ("evil generation," 11:29; "killers of the prophets," 11:49–51; "hypocrites," 12:56; 13:15; "workers of iniquity" who bemuse Jesus's "eating and drinking and teaching in their streets," 13:26–27). These prophetic rebukes are laced with pronouncements of judgment upon a "hardened," intractable folk (10:12, 14–15; 11:31–32, 42–52; 12:45–48, 57–59; 13:3–5, 24–30, 35; 14:24; 16:27–31; 17:26–30; 19:27, 41–44) "on account of whom," like Moses in Deuteronomy,⁶⁵ Jesus must die. Indeed, as Jesus presses on toward the city that stones the prophets, his anointed consciousness of the "divine necessity"⁶⁶ to be delivered over to death (3:22; compare already 5:35) comes more and more to expression (12:49–50; 13:33–35; 14:27; 17:25; 18:31–33; 19:42; compare 9:22, 23–24, 44). Gazing down from the Mount of Olives upon the city of Israel's destiny, Jesus weeps for a nation that has failed to recognize their "exodus visitation" of deliverance from God (ἐπισκοπή, 19:44; Exod 3:16!; 13:19; compare Gen 50:24). Thus, Luke's great journey plots Jesus's journey to receive the 'prophet's reward.'⁶⁷

But as Luke's fifth and final journey of Jesus suggests (below), the death of the prophet in Jerusalem ushers in a new, eschatological release from Israel's 'interminable' disobedience of God's life-giving words through Moses and their violent rejection of God's mediators of redemption. Though the relation of a journey

---

62 Moses "is completed/dies" "through the word of the Lord" (Deut 34:5); cf. "this word" in Deut 1:37; 3:26–27; 4:21–22.
63 4Kgdms 2:1, 11 (2:1–14).
64 Cf. Luke 1:70; 4:24; 6:23; 9:8, 19; 10:24; 11:47, 49, 50; 13:28, 33, 34; 16:16; 24:25; Acts 3:18, 21, 24, 25; 7:42, 52; 10:43; 13:15, 27, 40; 15:15; 24:14; 26:27; cf. Moessner, *Lord of the Banquet*, 47–56.
65 Deut 1:37; 3:26–27; 4:21–22.
66 Cf. the impersonal verb, δεῖ, "it is necessary," as expressing a divine point of view or plan that Jesus must die, in 9:22; 13:33; 17:25; cf. 22:37; 24:7, 26, 44.
67 Hans Conzelmann, *The Theology of St. Luke* (New York: Harper and Row, 1960) stressed that Luke's "journey" was a portrayal of Jesus's "consciousness" that he must suffer; because Conzelmann's development of "redaction criticism," however, relied too heavily upon modern conceptions of an individual author working with discrete written sources and with Mark as a definitive template, Luke's "own" emphases resemble more the 'Gospel according to the Changes of Mark' rather than the poetics of a Hellenistic narrative οἰκονομία epistemology; cf. David P. Moessner, *Ancient Narrative Hermeneutics and the Gospels*, in preparation, and see n. 15.

'form' to sayings 'content' in Luke 9:51–19:44 remains disputed,[68] it may just be that Luke was inspired by Deuteronomy's retrospect of Moses's 'words' framed by Israel's exodus journey and 'travel notices' of the unfinished journey, and by his prospect for Israel's life once they have crossed over the Jordan into the promised inheritance. For Moses foresees that Israel will continue to disobey God's commands even after they have established a central place of worship. God will judge them into exile, but they will return—ultimately through a journey that consummates their first exodus[69] and features a "prophet like me" to whom Israel must "hearken" (Deut 18:15–19). It is curious that Luke introduces Jesus's "exodus" with the voice from heaven at the Horeb mountain, "hearken to him" (Luke 9:35b) and, after Jesus has crossed over the Jordan, climaxes this journey with "this generation" not recognizing the fulfilled time of their "exodus visitation" from God.[70]

*5) Luke 22:54–24:51. At the Passover meal in the "guest room" with his apostles (Luke 22:11–14), Jesus declares that a betrayer "at table" will "deliver over" "the Son of Humankind" "to go (πορεύομαι)[71] just as it has been ordained" (22:22). But before he embarks on this journey he also indicates he will go willingly to "suffer" and "give" his "body" and "pour out" his "blood" "for their sake" (22:15–20). He will undertake such suffering "in order that you might eat and drink at my table in my kingdom and sit upon thrones, judging the twelve tribes of Israel" (22:30). Through this sealing of a "new covenant," Jesus bequeaths his apostles "the kingdom" which his Father has already bequeathed to him (22:28–30). What is more, this time his apostles will not be able to "go" (πορεύομαι, 22:33) with him since they will betray, deny, and all fall away such that "this that stands written must come to its finale with respect to me (τοῦτο τὸ γεγραμμένον δεῖ τελεσθῆναι ἐν ἐμοί): 'he was reckoned among the lawless' (Isa 53:12). For indeed, what is written concerning me is now coming to its intended goal (γὰρ τὸ περὶ ἐμοῦ τέλος ἔχει)" (Luke 22:37). Like the "servant" of Isaiah, Jesus must suffer alone the fate of those "without law."

---

68 See, e.g., Adelbert Denaux, "Old Testament Models for the Lukan Travel Narrative: A Critical Survey," in *The Scriptures in the Gospels*, ed. Christopher M. Tuckett, BETL 131 (Leuven: Leuven University/Peeters, 1997), 271–305; cf. Richard B. Hays, foreword to the paperback edition of David P. Moessner, *Lord of the Banquet: A Literary and Theological Investigation of the Lukan Travel Narrative* (Harrisburg, PA: Trinity Press International, 1998), xi-xv; Moessner, preface to the paperback edition of *Lord of the Banquet* (Harrisburg, PA: Trinity Press International, 1998), xvii–xxxi.
69 E.g., Deut 29–30, et al.
70 Cf. the retrospect in Acts 7:37–38.
71 See n. 58.

From the Mount of Olives Luke now describes Jesus once again "being led" by others–"into the house of the chief priest," "[...] the council chamber," "to Pilate," to "Herod,"[72] and to the place of "the skull" "with two evil doers."[73] But now Jesus actively embraces this humiliation as his divine calling and utters one final judgment upon an unrepentant Israel before he is crucified and "laid" by others in a tomb (22:42; 23:28–31, 52–53). His journey, however, is not over. In fact, when the "women from Galilee" are perplexed to find the tomb empty, they are reprimanded by two "men in white" for not "remembering" that they could not find the "living among the dead," since Jesus had told them he would "rise up on the third day" (24:1–7). Jesus is still actively journeying ahead with the scripturally "scripted" plan of his "Father" (compare Luke 3:22; 9:22–26, 31–35, 44; 18:31–34; 22:29, 42; 23:[34],46). As he continues (πορεύομαι, 24:13,15) "on the way,"[74] he (again) scolds two of his disciples for "not believing" what "Moses and the prophets" had declared that he as "the Christ had to suffer (ἐδεῖ παθεῖν) before entering into his glory" (24:25–27). And after "appearing" and "opening" "the law of Moses, the prophets, and the Psalms" to his authenticated "witnesses" (Luke 24:36–43→Acts 1:3–5), Jesus, the crucified and living Christ, completes his great journey from a mountain in Galilee (9:51) by "being carried up" and by actively "journeying into heaven"[75]–but not before he discloses the promise of his "Father" for his continuing witness among them (Luke 24:49→Acts 1:4–5, 8).

In sum, these journeys organize Jesus's public career into three main divisions: Galilee 'Release' 4:1–8:56; 'Exodus' Journey 9:51–19:44; 'Lord' of the Temple 19:45–21:38, with the births of John and Jesus and John's baptism introducing (1:5–3:18) and the final journey of the passion and his "taking up" consummating Jesus's calling (22:54–24:51). Jesus's anointing[76] and genealogy (3:19–38), his

---

[72] Only Luke attributes some participation of Herod in effecting Jesus's death; this Herod is the Antipas who "beheads" John the Baptist (Luke 9:9) and is said by Pharisees to be out "to kill" Jesus (13:31). Pilate and he become "friends" after their collusion in Jesus's execution (23:12; cf. Acts 4:27!). For the view that Herod was a prime instigator of Jesus's death à la Luke's presentation, see Pierson Parker, "Herod Antipas and the Death of Jesus," in *Jesus, the Gospels, and the Church: Essays in Honor of William R. Farmer*, ed. E. P. Sanders (Macon, GA: Mercer University Press, 1987): 197–208.
[73] ἤγαγον, ἀνήγαγον, and ἀπήγαγον, Luke 22:54, 66; 23:1, 26, 32; cf. Luke 4:1, 9; cf. 2:22; 4:5, 29; 21:12.
[74] Cf. Luke 24:32, 35.
[75] ἀναφέρω (Luke 24:51); ἀνελήμφθην (Luke 9:51; Acts 1:2,11); ἐπήρθην (Acts 1:9); ὑπολαμβάνω (Acts 1:9); πορεύομαι (Acts 1:10,12).
[76] Cf. Acts 10:38.

appearing "in glory" on a mountain⁷⁷ (9:1–50), and his 'last' Passover meal and 'temptation' on the mountain (Olives) (22:1–53) form watersheds [← →] in the developing plot. Together these major sections "divide" the narrative into a fivefold "arrangement."⁷⁸ See Figure 1:⁷⁹

Figure 1

Prologue: 1:1–4
I. Preface: 1:5–3:18
{Two childhood journeys}
←3:19–38→
II. Galilee 'Release' 4:1–8:56
{One journey}
←9:1–50→
III. 'Exodus' Journey 9:51–19:44
{One journey}
IV. 'Lord' of the Temple 19:45–21:38
←22:1–53→
V. Consummation of Jesus's 'Exodus' Release to the 'Central Place' and his 'Taking Up':
22:54–24:51
{One journey}
Epilogue: 24:52–53

2.2 The Journeying Witness of Jesus in Acts⁸⁰

Luke correlates the plot of his five main sections of the first volume with five sections in its sequel. By such narrative arrangement, a "ring composition" is formed which mnemonically facilitates the aural "following" of the narrative's

---

77 Cf. Exod 24:16–17; Deut 5:24–25; Luke 9:31–32; 24:26; Acts 7:22, 55; 22:11.
78 For "arrangement" as a function of Hellenistic narrative rhetoric, see Parts II and III of *Luke the Historian* below.
79 The two childhood journeys are to Jerusalem (see above).
80 See, e.g., Daniel Marguerat, "Voyages et voyageurs dans le livre des Actes et dans la culture gréco-romaine," *RHPR* 78 (1998): 33–59; Loveday Alexander, "'In Journeyings Often': Voyaging in Acts of the Apostles and in Greek Romance," in *Luke's Literary Achievement*, ed. Christopher M. Tuckett, JSNTSup 116 (Sheffield: Sheffield Academic Press, 1995), 17–49.

substantive claims,⁸¹ as well as reflecting the dominant role that rhetoric plays in Luke's composition.⁸²

Luke 1:5–3:18 is paralleled (≈) by Acts 1:3–26. The "Lord God's" "appearances" through Gabriel "who stands in the presence of God"⁸³ to announce preparations for Israel's anointed salvation is paralleled by the "appearances" and announcements of the resurrected "Lord" Jesus (Acts 1:6) to prepare for the extension of the Kingdom of God beyond Israel by the coming Holy Spirit through the empowered twelve witnesses–apostles.

Luke [←3:19–38→] 4:1–8:56 ≈ Acts 2:1–5:42. In Luke, Jesus is tempted and sent as an eschatologically anointed but rejected prophet (compare Luke 4:1–14,15–30 and Isa 61) who brings God's reign and the healing and release from sin and evil (the demonic) to the environs of his home town, narrowly escaping death.⁸⁴ This parallels the anointed (Acts 2) apostles-witnesses who display their authority as the emerging leaders/judges of "the people" in powerful preaching, "signs and wonders" in "the name/presence of Jesus," and rejection by the Temple authorities that nearly leads to death (Acts 2–5). The church emerges⁸⁵ as the "fulfilled,"

---

81 On "ring composition" in Hellenistic rhetoric, esp. as applied to historiography, cf., e.g., Ian Worthington, *A Historical Commentary on Dinarchus: Rhetoric and Conspiracy in Later Fourth-Century Athens* (Ann Arbor, MI: University of Michigan Press, 1992), 36–37, 339–55; Albert B. Lord, *Epic Singers and Oral Tradition* (Ithaca, NY: Cornell University Press, 1991); Peter Toohey, "Epic and Rhetoric," in *Persuasion: Greek Rhetoric in Action*, ed. Ian Worthington (London: Routledge, 1994): 153–75, esp. 154–62. For the role of a developing writing culture during the rise of the influence of rhetoric, see, e.g., Richard L. Enos, *Greek Rhetoric before Aristotle* (Prospect Heights, IL: Waveland Press, 1993), esp. 1–40; Donald A. Russell, *Criticism in Antiquity* (Berkeley/Los Angeles, CA: University of California Press, 1981), 114–47; Tony M. Lentz, *Orality and Literacy In Hellenic Greece* (Carbondale, IL: Southern Illinois University Press, 1989), esp. 109–44.
82 Cf., e.g., Carol G. Thomas and Edward Kent Webb, "From Orality to Rhetoric: An Intellectual Transformation," in *Persuasion: Greek Rhetoric in Action*, ed. Ian Worthington (London: Routledge, 1994): 3–25; Enos, *Greek Rhetoric Before Aristotle*, esp. 41–140; Walter J. Ong, "Writing is a Technology that Restructures Thought," in *The Written Word: Literacy in Transition*, ed. Gerd Baumann (Oxford: Clarendon, 1986): 23–50; Heinrich Lausberg, *Handbook of Literary Rhetoric*, ed. David E. Orton and Dean Anderson (Leiden: Brill, 1998); Kenneth S. Sacks, "Rhetorical Approaches to Greek History Writing in the Hellenistic Period," in *SBL 1984 Seminar Papers* (Atlanta, GA: Scholars Press, 1984): 123–33.
83 Luke 1:19.
84 Fourteen miracle stories are located in this Galilean section, Luke 4:16–8:56, whereas the great journey primarily summarizes Jesus's "mighty deeds": e.g., Luke 10:13 (flashback); 11:20; 19:37; but cf. Luke 11:14–15; 13:10–17; 14:1–6; 17:11–19; 18:35–43.
85 Luke uses ἐκκλησία for the first time in Acts 5:11 in the sense of "those called out," that is, from the rest of Israel; ironically, this "rest" will be "cut off" from "the people" unless they submit to the authority of Messiah Jesus represented by the twelve apostles (3:22–26). Acts 5:1–11

eschatological people of Israel whose "unity of heart and soul"[86] and possessions[87] is fortified against the temptations of "the Satan" (4:32–5:11).

Luke [←9:1–50→] 9:51–19:44 ≈ Acts 6:1–12:25. Jesus's exodus to "cleanse"[88] and teach in Israel's central place by calling both crowds and disciples to "repent" and sending out "seventy" other disciples into areas of the former ten "tribes" (for example, Samaria, trans-Jordan),[89] as well as his lifting food restrictions and thus proleptically initiating the Gentile mission is mirrored by Stephen's vision of Jesus in glory, Son of Humankind,[90] not bound by land or Temple, by Philip's preaching of "the word" in Samaria and Gaza, and by Peter's and John's subsequent sending to the Samaritans so that the latter might receive the Spirit.[91] Moreover, Luke links Peter's vision of "unclean" food to Jesus's commissioning of the apostles "to the end of the earth" and even farther back to their witness of Jesus's "eating and drinking" with "unclean" tax collectors and sinners (Acts 11:3→10:41→1:4→Luke 24:36–49→15:2→7:34). The apostles' stance toward "unclean" Gentiles thus recalls their attitude to Jesus's "release" for the "little ones" like the handicapped, the infirm, tax-collectors, and sinners and therefore to Jesus's sending to "seek and to save" the "lost."[92] Peter's sending to Cornelius brings Acts 1:8 to a new stage of completion, while Paul's sending to "this people Israel and the nations," sandwiched between the "Pentecosts" of Samaria and Cornelius's house,[93] propels the fulfillment of Jesus's witness "to the end of the earth" through his witness Paul.[94]

Luke 19:45–21:38 ≈ Acts 13:1–19:20. Jesus's confrontation with the chief priests and the leaders of the people (λαός) and his "opening of the scriptures" as David's

---

demonstrates the new apostolic authority to execute discipline, that is, as "judges" (Luke 22:30) among this emerging "church."

86 Cf. Deut 30:1–10.

87 Cf. Deut 15:7–11. Luke presents the first Jesus-Messiah believers as indeed fulfilling certain scriptural injunctions and promises of future life together. While these fulfillments do not result in any great reversal within society itself according to the literal referents of, e.g., Mariam's prophecies (Luke 1:46–55), yet for Luke there are clearly more subtle ways in which society is being confronted/transformed at every level (cf. Acts 17:6); cf. nn. 84 and 85.

88 Cf. Mal 3:1–3; Isa 56:7–8 (56:7a cited in Luke 19:46b).

89 Luke 10:1–24.

90 Acts 7:55–56.

91 Acts 8:4–40.

92 Luke 19:10.

93 Acts 8:14–17 (9:1–30); 10:44–48.

94 Note how Cornelius as the centurion of an "Italian cohort" (Acts 10:1) stationed in "Judea" recalls "visitors from Rome" (2:10) among the Pentecost/First Fruits pilgrims in "Jerusalem"; in Acts 28:17–31 Paul is a "visitor in Rome" announcing "the Kingdom of God" to "all."

"Lord" and the "beloved Son" of Israel's vineyard to the many of Israel ignites an even greater determination by the Sanhedrin to put Jesus to death and will spur on the people who, though "hanging on his every word" now, will become split between those who are persecuted or those who fall away before the final judgment. Paul's "opening of the scriptures" in the "houses of prayer" from city to city of the diaspora leading to the dividing of the people between "those who are persuaded" and those enraged to terminate his life[95] mirrors this dynamic of the rejection of Messiah Jesus, even while Paul continues to "turn to the Gentiles."[96] As Paul journeys twice to Jerusalem before returning to Antioch,[97] the church of Jerusalem is becoming increasingly divided over "the door of faith for the Gentiles" (14:27)–even Paul's own entourage becomes divided–and when a "we" journeys with Paul, the "witness" to Israel and the nations is extended toward Rome, the great pagan power controlling the "ends of the earth" (Isa 45:22).[98]

Luke [←22:1–53→] 22:54–24:51 ≈ Acts 19:21–28:31. Jesus's Passover meal becomes his passion meal as he signifies his voluntary death as vicariously life-giving "on behalf" of the twelve (tribes) (22:17–20), even as all of them will fall away (22:31–38). Paul's gathering between Passover and Pentecost with the Ephesian elders in Miletus (Acts 20:6→16) becomes his passion meal when he predicts his own persecutions and death as he finishes his course, bound for Jerusalem, declaring to them "the whole plan of God" and through the Holy Spirit modeling for them the shepherding of "the church of God which he [God] purchased through the blood of his Own" (Acts 20:28 [25–27]).

Jesus's "going" and "being led away" according to God's plan, his death at the hands of Herod the tetrarch, of the Roman governor, the Temple and lay leaders, even the "people" (λαός) as a whole,[99] as well as his "taking up" from death are re-enacted to a striking degree in the burgeoning rage against Paul which consolidates in Jerusalem in the Temple precincts with the Sanhedrin, Jews from the diaspora, and the λαός of Israel as a whole gathered for the feast of Pentecost to demand his death. But at this point the parallels of plot begin to dissipate. Rome now becomes the instrument by which Paul is "led away" not to execu-

---

95 See, e.g., Moessner, "'Script' of the Scriptures," 245–48.
96 Isa 49:6 in Acts 13:46–47 and 18:6; cf. 11:21; 14:15; 15:19; 26:20; 28:27–28.
97 Acts 15:1–30; 15:36–18:22.
98 For "the end of the earth" symbolizing the nations controlled by a great pagan empire used by God to judge/destroy Israel, see Isa 5:26 (Assyria); Jer 6:22 (Babylonia); Isa 48:20 (Persia); PsSol 8:15 (Rome!); cf. Isa 42:10 and 45:6: Cyrus enables those from "east and west" to know the Lord; 45:13 and 48:20: Cyrus used to liberate Israel; 52:10: the great godless power and all the nations will themselves begin to "turn to the Lord" through the "witness" of the "servant."
99 Luke 23:13–23.

tion but to arrest and testimony as the "Lord's" own "witness" to Caesar at the center of empire (Acts 23:11[100]→27:24), the great God-less rule used by God, not only for judgment against Jerusalem but also for the preaching of the Kingdom which will enable the "isles and nations" even "at the end of the earth" to "turn and be saved."[101] Paul's final journey to Jerusalem (Acts 19:21–21:16), announced and depicted in ways parallel to Jesus's final journeys (Luke 9:51–19:44; 22:54–24:53[102]), and his voyage through the abyss of the sea from which he is rescued out of death[103] (Acts 27) secure for Paul his chief status as "the servant and witness."[104] For it is Paul who actually fulfills Acts 1:8 and "through many afflictions" (Acts 14:22→Luke 14:26–27) accomplishes Jesus's servant mission of release "to the end of the earth," proclaiming "nothing except what the prophets and Moses said must come to pass, that there would be a suffering Messiah, and being the first of those resurrected out of the dead, he [the Messiah] would proclaim light to this people and to the nations" (Isa 42:6; 49:6; 51:5; Luke 2:32; 24:47; Acts 1:8; 13:47; 26:16–18, 22–23).

In sum, through the intertextuality with Israel's scriptures and the intratextuality of Luke and Acts, Luke's two-volume narrative configures a transhistorical "plan of God" enacted through the history of Israel as promised and provoked by those scriptures and re-enacted[105] and consummated in the witness of Israel's Messiah. The corresponding 'ring composition' emerges. See Figure 2:

---

[100] Note in Acts 23:11, "the Lord" appears and tells Paul in a Jerusalem prison that he must "bear testimony" in Rome of the "things concerning me" (τὰ περὶ ἐμοῦ; cf. Luke 22:37; 24:27, 44, 48!).

[101] Acts 27:1–28:10 describes how the "islands" "at the end of the earth" receive the apostolic witness of the "servant" Paul and his companions: cf. Isa 42:10; 45:16–"keep a feast" (cf. the "barbecue" on the isle of Malta! [Acts 28:2,7]); Isa 49:22.

[102] See esp. Acts 20:17–35 par. Luke 22:14–38; cf. Henry J. Cadbury, *The Making of Luke–Acts* (London: SPCK, 1968), 231–32; Walter Radl, *Paulus und Jesus im lukanishen Doppelwerk: Untersuchungen zu Parallelmotiven im Lukasevangelium und in der Apostelgeschichte*, EHST 49 (Bern: Theologischer Verlag, 1975); David P. Moessner, "'The Christ Must Suffer: New Light on the Jesus-Peter, Stephen, Paul Parallels in Luke-Acts," *NovT* 28 (1986): 220–56 [see Chapter Nine below]; William S. Kurz, "Luke 22:14–38 and Greco-Roman and Biblical Farewell Addresses," *JBL* 104 (1985): 251–68.

[103] See esp. Charles H. Talbert and J. H. Hayes, "A Theology of Sea Storms in Luke-Acts," in *Jesus and the Heritage of Israel*, ed. David P. Moessner, vol. 1, *Luke the Interpreter of Israel* (Harrisburg, PA: Trinity Press International, 1999): 267–83.

[104] Acts 26:16.

[105] Cf. Joel B. Green, "Internal Repetition in Luke–Acts: Contemporary Narratology and Lucan Historiography," in *History, Literature and Society in the Book of Acts*, ed. Ben Witherington III (Cambridge: Cambridge University Press, 1995): 283–99; Garry W. Trompf, *The Idea of Historical Recurrence in Western Thought: From Antiquity to the Reformation* (Berkeley: University of California Press, 1979), esp. 116–78.

Figure 2

Luke 1:5–3:18	≈	Acts 1:3–26
Luke [3:19–38] 4:1–8:56	≈	Acts 2:1–5:52
Luke [9:1–50] 9:51–19:44	≈	Acts 6:1–12:25
Luke 19:45–21:38	≈	Acts 13:1–19:20
Luke [22:1–53] 22:54–24:51	≈	Acts 19:21–28:31

3 Conclusions and Implications for the Genre of Luke's Gospel and Acts

We can now make the following observations about the genre of Luke and of Acts:

3.1. The Third Gospel cannot be properly construed as "biography." All the depictions of Jesus's character/ἦθος[106] are subsumed and integrally, intertextually interwoven with the characters and events of Israel's past, with the continuing presence of Jesus through his witnesses in the sequel volume, and with the past, present, and future hopes of God's eschatological reign. Though thoroughly biographical,[107] as indeed many biblical and Greco-Roman histories are, Luke is

---

[106] See Chapter Two, below.
[107] Cf., e.g., Arnaldo Momigliano, *The Development of Greek Biography* (Cambridge, MA: Harvard University Press, 1993), esp. 101–4; Loveday Alexander, "The Preface to Acts and the Historians," in *History, Literature, and Society in the Book of Acts*, ed. Ben Witherington III (Cambridge: Cambridge University Press, 1995): 73–103; Daryl Schmidt, "Luke's Preface and the Rhetoric of Hellenistic Historiography," in *Jesus and the Heritage of Israel*, ed. David P. Moessner, vol. 1, *Luke the Interpreter of Israel* (Harrisburg, PA: Trinity Press International, 1999): 2–60; Richard I. Pervo, "The Problems of a History," in *Jesus and the Heritage of Israel*, ed. David P. Moessner, vol. 1, *Luke the Interpreter of Israel* (Harrisburg, PA: Trinity Press International, 1999): 127–43; Albrecht Dihle, *Die Entstehung der historischen Biographie* (Heidelberg: Universitätsverlag, 1987), esp. 7–22, 64–80; David Aune, *The New Testament in Its Literary Environment* (Philadelphia, PA: Westminster, 1987), 29–31; Willem C. van Unnik, "Luke's Second Book and the Rules of Hellenistic Historiography," in *Les Actes des Apôtres: Traditions, rédaction, théologie*, ed. Jacob Kremer, BETL 48 (Gembloux: Leuven University Press, 1979): 37–60; Eckhard Plümacher, "Die Apostelgeschichte als historische Monographie," in *Les Actes des Apôtres: Traditions, rédaction, théologie*, ed. Jacob Kremer, BETL 48 (Gembloux: Leuven University Press, 1979): 457–66; David P. Moessner, "Re-reading Talbert's Luke: The Bios of 'Balance' or the 'Bias' of History?," in *Cadbury,*

intent to signify the interconnections, including cause and effect,[108] of Jesus's "words and deeds" with the events and mediators of God's salvation in Israel's scriptures, as well as with the extension of that salvation through Messiah's witness-mediators in Acts. To be sure, Greco-Roman multi-volume succession narratives display the ongoing influence of a famous person;[109] yet, the dense intra-text of Acts with Luke, and Acts's continued intertext with the scriptures transcends in form and content any extant exemplars.[110] The closest parallel, rather, would appear to be the biblical succession of the Deuteronomistic History with its singular focus upon Moses (Deuteronomy), a prophet unlike any other (Deut 34:10–12), succeeded by Joshua and a long host of judges, kings, and prophet-mediators who enact the continuing impact of God's words and actions through Moses in Israel's exodus (Joshua–2[4] King[dom]s).[111]

Knox, and Talbert: American Contributions to the Study of Acts, ed. Joseph B. Tyson and Mikeal Parsons (Atlanta, GA: Scholars Press, 1991): 203–28 [see the second chapter of *Luke the Historian* below]; contra biography, e.g., Richard A. Burridge, "About People, by People, for People: Gospel Genre and Audiences," in *The Gospels for All Christians: Rethinking the Gospel Audiences*, ed. Richard Bauckham (Grand Rapids; MI: Eerdmans, 1998): 113–45.

108 E.g., Luke 11:29–32; 12:57–59; 13:1–5,34–35; 17:1–3; 18:9–14; 19:41–44; cf. Polybius, *The Histories*, I.4–5; III.6.7; IV.28.3–4, *passim*; Diodorus Siculus, *Library of History* V.1.1–4; XVI.1.1–3; Dionysius of Halicarnassus, *de Thucydide*, 10–11; Lucian, *How to Write History*, § 55; cf. O. Wesley Allen, *The Death of Herod: The Narrative and Theological Function of Retribution in Luke-Acts*, SBLDS 158 (Atlanta, GA: Scholars Press, 1997); Daniel Marguerat, *The First Christian Historian: Writing the 'Acts of the Apostles'*, trans. Ken McKinney, Gregory J. Laughery, and Richard Bauckham, SNTSMS 121 (Cambridge: Cambridge University Press, 2002), 85–108.

109 See esp. Charles H. Talbert, "Succession in Luke-Acts and in the Lukan Milieu," in *Reading Luke-Acts in Its Mediterranean Milieu*, NovTSup 107 (Leiden: Brill, 2003): 19–55; Charles H. Talbert, *What Is a Gospel? The Genre of the Canonical Gospels* (Philadelphia, PA: Fortress, 1977); cf. David P. Moessner, "Suffering, Intercession, and Eschatological Atonement: An Uncommon Common View in the Testament of Moses and in Luke-Acts," in *The Pseudepigrapha and Early Biblical Interpretation*, ed. James H. Charlesworth and Craig A. Evans (Sheffield: JSOT Press, 1993): 202–27.

110 Talbert (*What is a Gospel?*) singled out Diogenes Laertius's *Lives of the Philosophers* as a close parallel to Luke-Acts, but the successor volumes lack an ongoing narrative plot with the great "founder" of the first volume; successor lists and anecdotes portray the "succession" very differently from the one "plan of God" plotted in Luke-Acts in which the founder continues to act through his witness-agents. Talbert treats "plot" only as a formal or generic category ("Succession in Luke-Acts," esp. 50–55).

111 See, e.g., Moessner, *Lord of the Banquet*, 325; note how Luke and Acts portray Moses, all the prophets, righteous sufferers of the Psalms, Jesus (Luke 3:21; 4:42; 5:16; 6:12; 9:18, 28; 10:21–22; 11:1; 22:39–46 [23:34]; 23:46), Peter (and the eleven), Stephen, and Paul as mediators on their knees before God on behalf of Israel; see Moessner, "Suffering, Intercession, and Eschatological Atonement," 216–22.

3.2. Luke writes in the same vein as a Hellenistic historian. We can outline a few of the characteristic traits and tropes:

i) Central to Luke's historiographical way of arranging his various materials that include both characters and events is his subordinating and molding all of these traditions to a "divine scheme" or "plan." Luke understands his two volumes to be unfolding "the plan of God" as contained in Israel's scriptures. This way of organizing a vast array of disparate material covering a longer period of time was well known to Jewish audiences through the narrative histories of their scriptures and to non-Jewish auditors through the principle of 'divine' or 'providential' steering of people and events as represented through Hellenistic historiography. Luke figures his two volumes as an epitome of the fulfillment or τέλος of the whole of the Jewish scriptures and of Israel's "anointed" as enacted by Jesus "the Christ" in a "plan of God" ([ἡ] βουλὴ τοῦ θεοῦ: Luke 7:30; Acts 2:23; 4:28; 5:38 [ironically]; 13:36; 20:27; compare 27:42–43). With such a formulation, Luke follows the pattern of Hellenistic historians who cover the rise and fate of various individuals and peoples under a grand control or influence of the divine, such as:

a) **πρόνοια**: For example, Josephus, *Antiquities* II.332; IV.47, 114, 128, 185; V.277; Diodorus Siculus, *Library of History* I.1.3; compare 3Macc 4:21; 5:30; 4Macc 9:24; Wis 6:7; 14:3.

b) **γνώμη**: For example, Josephus, *Antiquities*, I.14, 46; II.174, 209; V.277; X.177; XI.327; et cetera.

c) **τύχη**: For example, Polybius, the *Histories* I.4.1–5; I.7.4; Diodorus Siculus, *Library of History*, I.1.3; XIII.21.4–5; XVIII.59.6; XXVI.15.3; XXXIV/XXXV.27.1; et cetera; Dionysius of Halicarnassus, *Roman Antiquities* I.4.2; 5.2; III.19.6; VIII.32.3; XI.12.3; et cetera; Josephus, *War*, III.387–91; IV.238; V.78, 120–22; VI.14, 44; et cetera; Arrian, *Anabasis*, V.1.2 ("the divine principle").[112]

d) **δεῖ**: Luke's own preference for indicating the more comprehensive "divine steering" of events in Israel's history is to employ the impersonal verb δεῖ ("it is necessary"): Similar to τύχη ("fate") or πεπρωμένη ("it is/has been fated/destined"), Luke uses δεῖ especially to register the scriptural "necessity" that Israel's Christ "must suffer" and as a "suffering Messiah" be "raised up" *and*

---

112 For "fate"/"chance"/"necessity" (εἱμαρμένη/πεπρωμένη/ἀνάγκη [*inter alia*]), cf., e.g., Diodorus (*Lib. Hist.* XV.63.2; III.15.7, 19.2; X.21.3; 10.21.3; etc.); Josephus (*Ant.* XVI.397–98; *War* II.162–64; etc.); Dionysius (*Rom. Ant.* III.5.2, XI.1; V.8.6; IX.8.1; X.45.4; etc.); Lucian of Samosata (*Zeus Catechized*). See also John T. Squires, *The Plan of God in Luke-Acts*, SNTSMS 76 (Cambridge: Cambridge University Press, 1993), 15–77, 164–71.

that Jesus is that Messiah: Luke 9:22; 13:33; 17:25; 22:37; 24:7, 26, 44;[113] Acts 1:16, 22; 3:21; 4:12; 9:16; 14:22; 17:3; 19:21; 23:11; 27:24; compare Luke 2:49; 4:43; 13:16; 15:32; 19:5; 21:9; 22:7; Acts 9:6; 10:6; 25:10; 27:21.

Except for the Jewish historian, Josephus, who provides the closest parallel of God's "will" as pervasively programmatic, the "Sicilian" Diodorus is probably the most vocal in insisting that apart from such interweavings of divine and human agencies, history cannot be adequately recorded to serve as inspiration and direction for future generations.[114] He even devotes the first six of his forty books to the "deeds and myths of the earliest times,"[115] since for Diodorus, a nation's cultic-religious life provides the most telling template for many of its later achievements and cultural characteristics.[116]

ii) Luke cites and alludes to the scriptures and mimics them through composing re-enacted plots of Israel's divine figures as "fulfilled" at some stage in the calling of Jesus and/or the church,[117] or "the Day of the Son of Humankind."[118] Such 'imitation' and 'reenactment' is endemic to Hellenistic historiography.[119]

iii) Luke imitates both Jewish (LXX) and Hellenistic convention in his ascending genealogy (Luke 3:23–38; compare Tob 1:1).[120] Jesus is descended from David (through some rather obscure and lowly offspring) and Abraham and yet is God's "son," of the same line as "Adam, son of God" (Luke 3:38) and in this 'descent'

---

113 The "thus" (οὕτως) of Luke 24:46 is the epexegetical link with the δεῖ of 24:44.
114 Good historiography must conjoin both vertical divine dimensions with horizontal cultural forces as though they were the interlocking affairs of "one human city" (Diodorus, *Library of History* I.2.2–a "global village"!). The narrative itself functions as the "herald of the divine voice" (I.2.1, 3), and a good historian serves as a "minister of divine providence" (πρόνοια) (I.1.3); see n. 34.
115 *Library of History*, IV.1.1.
116 "For very great and most numerous deeds have been performed by the heroes and demigods [...] who, because of the benefits they conferred which have been shared by all men, have been honoured by succeeding generations with sacrifices which in some cases are like those offered to the gods [...] and of one and all the appropriate praises have been sung by the voice of history for all time" (Diodorus, *Library of History* IV.1.4 [Oldfather, LCL]).
117 See esp. David L. Tiede, *Prophecy and History in Luke-Acts* (Philadelphia, PA: Fortress, 1980).
118 Luke 17:30; 21:27, 36 *inter alia*; see esp. Chapters Nine and Eleven below; cf., e.g., the imaginative interpretation of OT passages in Luke-Acts in John Drury, *Tradition and Design in Luke's Gospel: A Study in Early Christian Historiography* (Atlanta, GA: John Knox, 1976), 44–81.
119 See, e.g., Part III and the Conclusions, below; cf. no. 105 above.
120 William S. Kurz, "Luke 3:23–38 and Greco-Roman and Biblical Genealogies," in *Luke-Acts: New Perspectives from the Society of Biblical Literature Seminar*, ed. Charles H. Talbert (New York: Crossroad, 1984): 169–87.

crowns the whole human race as "God's offspring" (for example, Paul in Acts 17:28 [Aratus, *Phaenomena* 5]; compare Luke 1:32, 35!). As Moses's calling to liberate the people (Exod 3) is grounded in the lineage of God's previous working (Exod 6:14–27) before Moses leads out the Israelites (Exod 7–12), so Jesus's calling as obedient "Son and Servant" (Luke 3:21–22) will span all of God's dealings with the world through Israel (3:23–38) as Jesus is poised to bring "release" to Israel's "captives" and to announce liberation for the whole human race (4:16–30 [24–26]).[121]

iv) Synchronisms likewise combine both Hellenistic and Jewish historiographical practice:[122] Similar to the synchronisms of "multiple accessions and deaths" or "sea crossings" or "auxiliary events" featured later in the narrative which for Polybius illustrate "Fortune's" (τύχη) unprecedented intertwining of world events to effect the rise of Rome,[123] so Luke joins Roman hegemony to the birth, calling, and expansion of the messianic witness of Israel to demonstrate its unparalleled, recurring, and far greater significance for the whole of humankind (Luke 1:5; 2:1–2; 3:1; Acts 11:28; 18:2, 12; compare "this did not occur 'in a corner,'" 26:26!). Of special intertextual, scriptural interest are the "completions" of a period of time which themselves introduce a new stage of fulfillment in Israel's festal calendar or Torah observance or promises of the prophets: for example, Luke 2:21, 22–24, 34; 3:3–6, 15–16; 4:16–21; 9:28–31, 51; 10:23–24; 12:49–53; 13:31–35; 17:22–35; 18:31–34; 19:41–44; 22:14–18, 28–30, 35–38; 24:25–27, 44–49; Acts 1:20–22; 2:1; 3:22–26, et cetera.

In brief, the core of the 'divine plan' for Luke is the systemic conviction that "the Christ" of the scriptures is Jesus, that Jesus himself interpreted the whole of the scriptures in relation to himself as the suffering and raised Messiah, and that through this messianic script Jesus promulgated Israel's apostolic witness for all time and place.

In conclusion, the resulting form and content of Luke and Acts comprises the single largest contribution of one author to the New Testament, with the Gospel of Luke forming the longest single book, circa 31–32 feet (1151 verses), and with

---

[121] See James A. Sanders, "From Isaiah 61 to Luke 4," in *Luke and Scripture: The Function of Sacred Tradition in Luke-Acts*, ed. Craig A. Evans and James A. Sanders (Minneapolis, MN: Fortress, 1993): 46–69.
[122] See, e.g., William S. Kurz, "Promise and Fulfillment in Hellenistic Jewish Narratives and in Luke and Acts," in *Jesus and the Heritage of Israel*, ed. David P. Moessner, vol. 1, *Luke the Interpreter of Israel* (Harrisburg, PA: Trinity Press International, 1999): 147–70.
[123] Polybius, *The Histories*, I.3.3–4; see Part III, chapter Five below, cf. Adele C. Scafuro, "Universal History and the Genres of Greek Historiography" (Ph.D. diss., Yale University, 1984), 155–204.

Acts a close second, circa 31 feet (1006 verses).[124] Together the Luke and Acts narrative work configures the basis for the liturgical church year, binds the career of Jesus to his followers' subsequent movements, and engrafts many of the church's apostolic traditions of Jesus and the church more integrally into the history of God's dealings with Israel and the Jewish peoples than any other book of the New Testament.[125]

Consequently the Gospel of Luke and his Acts that follow can be read like no other. There is no indication that 'what' Luke wrote, according to his *prooemium* to both volumes (Luke 1:1–4), was to be anything other than what the church would eventually entitle "the Gospel according to [...]." Notwithstanding the canonical separation of the two, the Third Gospel points inescapably to its sequel in which the Christ of volume one remains instrumental through the second: the church exists and thrives only from the "witness" of the risen-crucified one, empowered by the Holy Spirit. Church and Christ are inseparable; thus Acts is the only book of the New Testament that "narrates" the ongoing presence of Christ in God's church and world.

---

124 See esp. Kurt and Barbara Aland, *The Text of the New Testament: An Introduction to the Critical Editions and to the Theory and Practice of Modern Textual Criticism*, trans. E. F. Rhodes, 2nd ed. (Grand Rapids, MI/Leiden: Eerdmans/Brill, 1989), 26–31; Cadbury, *Acts in History*, 138–46.
125 For the resulting Luke followed by Acts as parallel in scope and function to several Jewish-Hellenistic historians, see esp. Carl R. Holladay, "Acts and the Fragments of Hellenistic Jewish Historians," in *Jesus and the Heritage of Israel*, ed. David P. Moessner, vol. 1, *Luke the Interpreter of Israel* (Harrisburg, PA: Trinity Press International, 1999): 171–98.

Chapter Two: Re-Reading Talbert's Luke: The *Bios* of "Balance" or the "Bias" of *History*?[1]

More than any other scholar of the modern postwar period, Charles H. Talbert has shed light upon the Lukan writings by placing them within the larger world of Greco-Roman antiquity. In so "opening up the scriptures" of Luke-Acts, he has forced us as readers to ask, How would this or that notion in Luke-Acts be perceived by persons living in the Mediterranean basin of the first century CE? The texts he has marshaled and the comparisons drawn in his own responses have not only illuminated smaller sections or ideas in Luke or Acts; they have also opened up the entire field of Lukan studies by demanding that interpreters come to terms with the overall phenomenon–Luke-Acts–*as one work* and ask precisely how this unity would be construed generically within Greco-Roman literary history. It is indeed in his genre studies of Luke-Acts and the Gospels as a whole that Talbert has distinguished himself as one of the most important modern scholars in Gospel studies and as one who will continue to occupy a leading place as an interpreter of Luke-Acts in the 20th and 21st centuries.

In *Cadbury, Knox, and Talbert: American Contributions to the Study of Acts*,[2] Mikeal Parsons has provided a very fair and insightful appraisal of Talbert's work. Though I shall take issue with Parsons on one basic point, my main critique will focus on Talbert's contribution.

1 Talbert's Definition of the Greco-Roman *Bios* Genre

Talbert's clearest, most forceful arguments that the Gospels, and Luke-Acts in particular, share the features of the Greco-Roman *bios/vita* more constitutively than any other genre is in a 1988 *Semeia* article in which he states:

---

[1] Used with permission, with minor alterations, from David P. Moessner, "Re-reading Talbert's Luke: The *Bios* of 'Balance' or the 'Bias' of History," in *Cadbury, Knox, and Talbert: American Contributions to the Study of Acts*, ed. Joseph B. Tyson and Mikeal Parsons (Atlanta, GA: Scholars Press, 1991): 203–28. I have retained the title "Luke-Acts" to reflect the conceptions and terms of the genre debate in the last decades of the twentieth century.
[2] Mikeal Parsons, "Reading Talbert: New Perspectives on Luke and Acts," in *Cadbury, Knox, and Talbert: American Contributions to the Study of Acts*, ed. Joseph B. Tyson and Mikeal Parsons (Atlanta, GA: Scholars Press, 1991): 133–71.

*Biography is concerned with the essence of the individual [...]. Biography is interested in what sort of person the individual is, his involvement in the historical process being important only insofar as it reveals his essence. Whereas history attempts to give a detailed account in terms of causes and effects of events, biography presents a highly selective, often anecdotal account of an individual's life with everything chosen to illuminate his essential being.*³

Based on both the discussions of ancient writers and upon his own inductive analysis of many texts, Talbert draws the distinction between what is "essential" to biography, namely to set forth the "essence" (φύσις) or "character" (ἦθος) of the individual, and what is "accidental," such aspects as the extent of the life covered, the style of narration, the use of myth, primary social function, lack of sequential or organic development, and so forth. In my response to Talbert in that same *Semeia* issue, I argue that, on the contrary, according to Talbert's own instructive formulation, Luke-Acts looks far more like history than his essential biography.⁴ I do not intend here to repeat all that I have said there. Rather, I want first to highlight certain fundamental disagreements between Talbert and myself in assessing his categories before looking briefly at Talbert's genetic theory of gospel composition. Although certain of the following points *may* apply to other canonical gospels as well, in keeping with the theme of this book I shall keep my focus on the Luke-Acts narrative.

2 Points of Disagreement

2.1. In echoing a phrase from Graham N. Stanton that "it is difficult to believe that on first acquaintance the canonical gospels, at least, would not have been considered biographical by Mediterranean readers/hearers,"⁵ Talbert strikes a chord to which most readers could chime in. Certainly a book that focuses on one individual for a significant part of his or her career *looks like* a biography and is surely biographical in its content. On this score, yes, to readers on first acquaintance, the Gospels look like *lives* of a distinguished person. But the reason for pause–

---

3 Charles H. Talbert, "Once Again: Gospel Genre," *Semeia* 43 (1988): 53–74 (55–56).
4 David P. Moessner, "And Once Again, What Sort of 'Essence?' A Response to Charles Talbert," *Semeia* 43 (1988): 75–84.
5 Talbert, "Once Again," 55, 60–61, citing Graham N. Stanton, *Jesus of Nazareth in New Testament Preaching*, SNTSMS 27 (Cambridge: Cambridge University Press, 1974), 135. Stanton himself, it should be pointed out, does not agree with this "first acquaintance" *conclusion* for Gospel genre (117–36, 186–91).

why in fact scholars like Karl Ludwig Schmidt[6] and Rudolf Bultmann could not accept the *bios* theory–is that upon greater familiarity, one is struck with the way in which the singular life of Jesus of Nazareth is subsumed to an even greater process, the Kingly Rule of God. All of Jesus's sayings and actions appear to be subordinated to a concluding event of rejection and vindication that reveals most sublimely the "essence" and "character" of this process for the entire career of this great individual, particularly in the case of Luke (and Acts) in which all of history is subsumed to an overarching "plan of God." Talbert himself says clearly, "Whereas history focuses on the distinguished and significant acts of great men in the political and social spheres, biography is concerned with the essence of the individual."[7] He goes on to illustrate this distinction by using Dio Cassius's appropriation of biographical material about Augustus into his *Roman History* (45–56) in order to change the "aim" of this material "from concern with Augustus' individual essence to his place in a social and political process." Talbert further argues, "Biography is interested in what sort of person the individual is, his involvement in the historical process being important only insofar as it reveals his essence."[8]

It is difficult to believe that upon further reading one could conclude that the canonical Gospels and Luke, in particular, are so concerned with Jesus's individual essence that his relation to the Jewish people in the setting of 1st-cen-

---

6 Talbert, "Once Again," 60, rightly concludes that a *bios* for Schmidt is impossible given Schmidt's categorization of the canonical Gospels as *Kleinliteratur* (folk literature) and not primarily the products of individual *literary* personalities. But *contra* Talbert, redaction criticism did not overturn Schmidt's fundamental insight that the *"Kultlegende"* background for the formation of the Gospels includes self-conscious editors (that is, the evangelists) linking individual units into a biographically-oriented order and overall format. After all, Schmidt found the closest parallels to the canonical Gospels to be the Dr. Faust collections, medieval legends of the *chasid*, and certain ecclesiastical "lives of the saints." See Karl Ludwig Schmidt, "Die Stellung der Evangelien in der allgemeinen Literaturgeschichte," in *Eucharisterion: Studien zur Religion und Literatur des Alten und Neuen Testaments: Hermann Gunkel zum 60.*, ed. Hans Schmidt (Göttingen: Vandenhoeck & Ruprecht, 1923), 2.68–75, 79–124. The main reason K. L. Schmidt, *contra* Talbert, rejected the literary Greco-Roman *bios* hypothesis is that all the smaller forms of the canonical Gospels show a process of growth and formation from worshipping communities who, *along with* the evangelists, are convinced that God through the death and resurrection of Israel's Messiah has appeared on earth to establish the eschatological people of old and new covenants ("Jesus Christus," *RGG*[2] [1929] 3.110–51, esp. 110–15). That is to say, both process and final form are explicable only as all the Jesus material is subsumed to cultic and kerygmatic contexts which place Jesus into a larger historical and meta-historical process. Focus on Jesus's *individual* essence is simply not endemic to the canonical gospels.
7 Talbert, "Once Again," 55.
8 Talbert, "Once Again," 55–56.

tury Galilee and Judea, his role in the larger history of this people Israel, and his ultimate significance in the larger process of the events of God's salvation for the whole world are at best external framework, an outer husk which serves the greater purpose of allowing telling glimpses into the enduring character traits (ἤθη) of Jesus. More than that, it is difficult to believe, upon careful scrutiny, that the development of opposition crescendoing through all the four canonical Gospels, the growing division of the people of Israel, tension with their leaders and misunderstanding of the disciples, all of which lead to a climax in which eschatological salvation is offered to the whole world–in short, what most literary critics would call the *plot* of these gospels–that all of this material is immaterial to the presentation except as it might reveal "what sort of person" Jesus was. And that "insignificant gestures or passing utterance" (Plutarch, *Alexander* 1; *Demosthenes* 11.7) might have sufficed just as well in exposing "the essence" of Jesus of Nazareth is likewise suspect.[9] For as Talbert insists, the critical quality which determines the *bios* character of the gospels is what they share with other "lives," that "what is revealed in the narratives about Apollonius, or Pythagoras, or Moses, or Jesus is the same–their distinctive nature."[10]

2.2. That the events and words of the featured individual are clearly secondary to the ongoing, unchanging character traits, and that both deeds and sayings are in fact *via media* to the enduring essence of the individual is emphasized in Talbert's use of Plutarch's discussion. As is well known, during the Hellenistic period interest in the roles of individuals within their historical setting increased significantly from the classical period in which writers like Herodotus and Thucydides were far more concerned to trace trans-personal forces and causes of the events they were describing.[11] Yet this growing biographical interest within Greek history writing[12]

---

9 Talbert, "One Again," 56; cf., e.g., Albrecht Dihle, "Die Evangelien und die biographische Tradition der Antike," *ZTK* 80 (1983): 38: "Eben deshalb aber ist es für den Leser einer Alexanderbiographie wichtiger zu wissen, wie er sich räusperte und spuckte, als seine weltbewegenden Taten erzählt und erläutert zu erhalten."
10 Talbert, "Once Again," 61.
11 See, e.g., Arnaldo Momigliano, *The Development of Greek Biography* (Cambridge, MA: Harvard University Press, 1971), esp. 65–104; Dihle, "Die Evangelien," 37–40; Albrecht Dihle, *Die Entstehung der historischen Biographie* (Heidelberg: Universitätsverlag, 1987), esp. 7–22, 64–80; David E. Aune, *The New Testament in Its Literary Environment* (Philadelphia, PA: Westminster, 1987), 29–31; David L. Barr and Judith L. Wentling, "The Conventions of Classical Biography and the Genre of Luke-Acts: A Preliminary Study," in *Luke-Acts: New Perspectives from the Society of Biblical Literature Seminar*, ed. Charles H. Talbert (New York: Crossroad, 1984), 63–88 (67–71).
12 Dihle, "Evangelien," 37, points to Theopompus's *Philippika* (mid-4th cent. BCE) as representative.

did not lead to a self-contained biographical sub-genre in which the famous individual becomes an epitome of an entire period or culture so that the individual essence of the person becomes representative. Rather, the events themselves and the way the individual illuminates the significance of those events remain uppermost.[13] It is within this larger context of a growing overlap of biographical and historical interests that Plutarch makes his observations.

Do not expect a thorough account of even one, let alone of the many significant events in the lives of Alexander and Caesar that I am writing in this book, since I am not writing histories (ἱστορίαι) but lives (βίοι) [...]. Accordingly, just as painters get the likenesses in their portraits from the face and the expression of the eyes, wherein the character (ἦθος) shows itself, but make very little account of the other parts of the body, so I must be permitted to devote myself rather to the signs of the soul in men, and by means of these to portray the life of each, leaving to others the description of their great contests (Alexander 1.2, 3).[14]

Ironically, a biographer will research the commonplace events and sayings of an individual to glean significant glimpses into the individual's distinctive character, whereas an historian is interested in the distinctive private life and details in order to gain insight into the significant events associated with that person's time period (for example, Plutarch, *Pompey* 8.6). Indeed, given the extensive overlap of biography and history in the period in which the canonical Gospels were written, it is no wonder that they, and Luke-Acts in particular, exhibit marked interest in both the significant events in which Jesus participates and through these "what sort of person" Jesus was. I am in complete agreement that the canonical Gospels are thoroughly *biographical*.[15] But when it comes to the crucial benchmark in

---

13 E.g., Dihle, "Evangelien," 38: "Genau an diesem Punkt aber, nämlich der Erklärung denkwürdiger, in die Gegenwart fortwirkender Taten durch Informationen über Charakter und Lebensumstände der Akteure, liegt nach griechischer Auffassung der Unterschied zwischen Biographie und Geschichtsschreibung"; cf. Momigliano, *Greek Biography*, 64: "Before Aristotle, I would say that there were experiments of a biographical and autobiographical kind which normally were kept outside political historiography as transmitted to the fourth century in the models of Herodotus and Thucydides."
14 Plutarch, *Alexander*, vol. 7, *Lives*, trans. Perrin, LCL (London: Heinemann, 1967), 225.
15 Talbert himself points to Dio Cassius's use of "Augustus" biographical material in Books 45–56 in which, for instance, we learn of his parents (45.1.1), of visions, divinations, prophecies, and signs attending Augustus's birth (45.1.2–2.7), his patrician education in oratory, military service, and politics (45.2.8), and at the end of his public career, of his death and omens attending his burial and rumors of his ascending to heaven (56.46)–in short, the same formal categories as in the Gospel of Luke, and like Luke-Acts, subsumed to the larger story or history (that is, of the

genre between biography and historiography, Talbert comes down decidedly on the side of the "eyes," to use Plutarch's image, rather than on the full body of the portrait. By doing so, Talbert commits a wide and diverse body of writing to this Plutarchan definition and relegates the "history-like narrative" that many biographies utilize to a non-essential, "accidental" status.[16]

It is just here that Talbert's definition will not work for Luke-Acts:

(i) Luke states in his proemium (Luke 1:1–4) that he is writing in a particular order or sequence (καθεξῆς, 1:3) in order to lend "certainty" or "assurance" to the narrative (διήγησις, 1:1) of events (πρᾶγμα, 1:1) that he is relating.[17] In light of the fact that "many" others already before him have set their hand to the same task using the same eyewitness traditions/material (παρέδοσαν ἡμῖν, 1:2), one should probably conclude that he is not fully satisfied with their accounts and that, in fact, his new or different *sequence* will distinguish his account and give it greater credibility. In any case, Luke is saying to Theophilus and to all his readers, "If you want to understand the significance which I am assigning to the material that follows, you must read with the sequence of the text,[18] lest you miss precisely the connections I am trying to make and, in particular, the greater clarity or certainty of those events." Now this kind of comment, coming as it does at the beginning of

---

rise and reign of Rome). In other words, the kind of material found in Luke could be, generically speaking, equally "at home" in either historiography or biography.

16 Talbert's use of the Plutarchan distinction to encompass a vast array of works which focus on one person will not work, e.g., for Tacitus's *Agricola*, where the historical framework and conditions are crucial in describing Agricola's *life* in a way in which Agricola becomes a mirror or representative of a period in Roman history. Chapters 39–42, for instance, portray a considerable amount of information about life in the last years of Domitian's reign not only to illuminate what Agricola was like but also what Rome was like and Agricola's role in that period. Cf., e.g., Dihle, *Entstehung*, 31: "Diese Erwägung erweist Tacitus's 'Agricola' als historische Biographie im mittelalterlich-neuzeitlichen Sinn, als Werk also, in dem eine geschichtliche Epoche im Spiegel eines individuellen Lebens dargestellt wird, ein individuelles Leben aber eine Epoche repräsentiert."

17 Cf., e.g, Aune, *Literary Environment*, 116: "By substituting the term 'narrative' for Mark's 'gospel,' Luke indicated his intention to write history." Cf. Aune, *Literary Environment*, 121: "The 'events completed among us' indicates a historical rather than biographical focus." Although *pragmata* can (obviously) be used with many different referents in any genre of writing, including the 'events'/'affairs' of an individual in a *bios*, it is telling that it is a stock term for *historians* precisely in their *preface* or in digressions where they discuss the purpose and scope of their work (e.g., Polybius, *The Histories*, 1.3.9; Diodorus Siculus, *Library of History*, 1.4; Dio Cassius, *Roman History*, 1.2; Dionysius of Halicarnassus, *Roman Antiquities*, I.3; cf. Lucian, *Historia [How to Write History]* 47; 55). Moreover, they avoid using the term *bios/vita* in those contexts (see below, n. 20).

18 I.e., a "synchronic," not chronological, reading.

a work, runs counter, as we have seen, to Plutarch's comments in his introduction to *Alexander* and *Caesar*. Though Plutarch utilizes Alexander's deeds and follows overall a rough chronological order in his history-like narrative, no significance at all is attached to one *event* per se as compared to another, much less to any sequence of events. Luke, on the other hand, is taking to heart what Lucian says should be the aim of every good *historian* in writing up the material one has at hand:

Let the narrative (διήγησις) be arrayed with the virtues proper to narrative, progressing smoothly [...] let its clarity appear brightly, achieved both by style, as I have said, and by the inter-weaving of the events (πρᾶγμα) [...]. When he has finished the first event, he will introduce the second, attached to it and linked with it like a chain, so as to avoid breaks and a multiplicity of narratives lying juxtaposed to one another; rather always the first and second events must not only be adjacent, but must also have common material and overlap (Historia, 55).[19]

However successfully Luke has carried out his own objective and met Lucian's expectations, it is clear that if the choices for Luke's intent be closer either to biography or history, the answer must fall squarely on the latter. Luke is indicating that the sequence (and significance) of the events is part and parcel of the larger story of "fulfillment" (1:1b) that he is configuring and in no way ancillary or convenient scaffolding for a more essential elucidation of Jesus's essence.[20]

(ii) Like Matthew, Luke is interested in a biographical expansion of the Markan outline which gives his Part One (Gospel) the fuller profile of a "life" (according, for example, to Theon's proprieties [*Progymnasmata* 8]). Yet this fuller sketch is, generically speaking, equally "at home" in biography or in historiography, depending upon the larger context and literary aims into which the source

---

19 Translation mine, from the Greek text of Lucian, *How to Write History* (Kilburn, LCL), 66.
20 Terrance Callan, "The Preface of Luke-Acts and Historiography," *NTS* 31 (1985): 576–81, has shown that *if* a biography has a preface where the purpose and scope of the work is discussed, then invariably the term *bios* or *vita* is used to categorize its genre (with eight examples from four authors, 581 n. 10). Even when Luke in Acts 1:1 summarizes the first half of his work, which has focused almost entirely on the career of one person, he does not refer to volume one as the "life" of Jesus but rather as "all the things/events (πάντα, Luke 1:3, viz., the πράγματα of Luke 1:1) of which Jesus began to do and to teach until the time he was taken up." Volume Two is thus going to relate more things/events that continue the events of fulfillment (Luke 1:1) that Jesus began and which his witnesses are to continue within the overarching story of the Kingdom of God through Israel (Acts 1:3, 6–8; 28:31); see n. 29 below.

material is placed.[21] That Luke dovetails his birth narratives of Jesus *and* John, his description of Jesus's childhood and relation to parents, and the genealogy of Jesus all into the greater story of the fulfillment of Israel's salvation for the whole world illustrates again the subordination of biographical details into a larger story–a sequence in which the events themselves are revelatory, pregnant with meaning, not only for the identity or essence of Jesus but for the story of Israel and the whole human race as well. Announced by heaven as both son of David and Son of the God of Israel in the longed for fulfillment of the oath to Abraham, Luke indicates that the historic line of David and the eschatological reign of God are merging in unprecedented fashion. Portents and signs divulge that this "Son" and "Lord" will bring about the hoped for glory of the people Israel, even as he is a light of revelation of the one God to all nations. But he will be a "sign" of this God's world-saving act as one contradicted and rejected and the cause of the people of Israel to be torn into division (Luke 1:26–38, 39–56, 67–79; 2:8–14, 25–38). In other words, Luke is announcing from the beginning that his story of fulfillment of salvation has a distinctive plot in which the events of rejection and of falling and rising are constitutive of the character or essence of Jesus.

"What sort of person" Jesus is cannot be revealed apart from this larger story and interface with the responses of an historical people. The truth is that Luke, according to Talbert's description of an historian,[22] is interested in *cause* and *effect* in events. Thus, he emphasizes the judgment that awaits Israel *because of* their repeated rejections of the one sent to them for their liberation (for example, Luke 10:13–16; 11:47–52; 13:34–35; 17:22–35; 19:41–44; 21:20–24).[23] Indeed, it is hard to conceive of an essence for Jesus apart from this involvement in the social and political process of Israel, to use Talbert's definition of the focus of history.[24] Nor, judging from the denouement of Part One in which Jesus commands

---

[21] See n. 6 above. Cf., e.g., Aune, *Literary Environment*, 65: "By adding background material, genealogies and birth narratives [...] and resurrection appearances [...] Matthew and Luke have moved closer toward the *biographical and historiographical* expectation of pagan readers" (emphasis mine). Cf. Dihle, "Evangelien," 36: "Die Biographie Jesu als Aufgabe für den Schrifsteller in der christlichen Literatur des 1. und 2. Jahrhunderts zunehmende Bedeutung gewann." But for Dihle neither Mark nor Matthew nor Luke exhibit the overall concerns of the *bios*: "Dieser biographische Rahmen widerum gehörte aber von vornherein in einen mit der Tradition des Volkes Israel vorgegebenen heilsgeschichtlichen Zusammenhang" (46).
[22] Talbert, "Once Again," 56.
[23] The fact that Israel's rejection is part of a larger plan or necessity of God's salvation does not excuse Israel's rejection on the level of human responsibility: e.g., Acts 3:18–19, "What God proclaimed in advance through the mouth of all the prophets--that the Messiah must suffer--God thus fulfilled. Repent *therefore* and turn in order that your sins might be removed."
[24] Talbert, "Once Again," 55–56.

the disciples to take the eschatological salvation to Israel and the nations (see below), can it be the case that Luke is simply choosing a history-like or connected interaction of Jesus with Israel as one of several, in principle equally good, modes for presenting an essential nature that is more fundamental than any particular interaction in time and space with Israel. No, for Luke, *there is no character Jesus nor exalted Christ apart from his role in Israel's life and character*: "Today this Scripture is fulfilled in your hearing" (Luke 4:21).

(iii) Albrecht Dihle has shown how integral to Plutarch's (and thus Talbert's) definition of a *bios* genre 'human nature' is as a static, unchanging composite of virtues and vices based on the individual's own choices in developing character traits (ἤθη) which together build a person's "character" or "essence."[25] The aim of biography, then, whether explicitly didactic or not, is to let the various actions, sayings, and general behavior patterns divulge the unchanging character that transcends all temporal and historical contingencies. Whether an Agesilaus or a Pompey, a Demosthenes or a Cicero, an Alexander or a Caesar, meaningful comparisons of persons from totally different backgrounds, times, and situations can be made since fundamental character traits are trans-personal and trans-historical and are in principle achievable (whether good or bad) by any person of any status or station. The Plutarchan (and Talbert's) definition of the aim of all biography, then, is a description of "what sort of person" an individual is *with respect to these traits*.

How striking by contrast is Luke's interest in Jesus' character:

(1) The Third Evangelist intends to show that Jesus appears in the public arena in a specific time and under particular political conditions: "In the fifteenth year of the reign of Tiberias Caesar […] in the high priesthood of Annas and Caiaphas, the word of God came to John" (Luke 3:1–2). That this *synchronism* is not merely narrative decoration becomes evident when Luke ties the heavenly annunciation of Jesus as "Son" through the historical baptizing movement of John to the genealogy of Jesus that ascends all the way to Adam "son of God" (3:21–22,23–38).[26] The "mightier one" announced by John who is "coming" upon the historical scene is the Son of God whose own baptizing with Holy Spirit and fire will spark the eschatological division and judgment of "all flesh," even as foretold long ago by Israel's prophets (3:15–17, 4–9). Moreover, this Son of God is

---

25 Dihle, "Evangelien," 40–42; Albrecht Dihle, *Studien zur griechischen Biographie* (Göttingen: Vandenhoeck & Ruprecht, 1956), 57–103.
26 For the Lukan genealogy, see William S. Kurz, "Luke 3:23–38 and Greco-Roman and Biblical Genealogies," in *Luke-Acts: New Perspectives from the Society of Biblical Literature Seminar*, ed. Charles H. Talbert (New York: Crossroad, 1984): 169–87.

himself the "Savior" (2:11, 30), the "Anointed One, the Lord" born in the days of Caesar Augustus when Quirinius was governor of Syria (2:1–2, 10–14).[27] By tying Messiah Jesus's public ministry to Israel through these historical synchronisms at the beginning of his two volumes,[28] Luke is demonstrating that "the sort of person" Jesus is can be grasped only through his connection to a unique and unrepeatable set of world geo-political circumstances.[29]

(2) Luke again demonstrates his historical interest in the character of Jesus in his statements about Jesus's *development* (Luke 2:40, 52; compare 1:80). Such growth in "wisdom, stature, and favor before God and humankind" anticipates and prepares Jesus for his sending as the beloved Son of this God (3:22; 4:1–14) and as one eminently qualified to bring salvation to all flesh (3:6) through a mission of "release" to all nations (24:47 and Acts). Again, Talbert's delineation of biography having "virtually no interest in tracing development" since the "essence of a person was not examined in its chronological development but only as a fixed constituent in a 'life'"[30] does not comport with Luke's portrayal. Rather, as the Deuteronomic historians subsumed the many biographical details of Samuel including his "continuing to grow in stature and in favor with the Lord and humankind" (1Sam 2:26; compare Luke 2:21b!) to the "anointed" David's significance in the historical events of the reign of God over Israel through the monarchy, so Luke has done with the Jesus material. Luke shows not the slightest interest in divulging some character trait of Jesus as Son of God that somehow supersedes his historical mission as a more eternal, transcendental quality: "If you are the Son of God, command this stone to become bread [...]. A human shall not live by bread alone" (4:4)!

(3) It seems that whenever the question of "what sort of person" Jesus is breaks open as a public issue, Luke has Jesus "correct" the expectations of his disciples and the crowds with a presentation of Jesus's understanding of his own *mission to Israel*. For instance, in the opening scene of his public activity (4:16–30), Jesus perceives that the "fame" that has already preceded him (4:14–15) has framed certain expectations of his identity that do not square at all with

---

27 See, e.g., Willem C. van Unnik, "The Purpose of Luke's Historical Writing," in *Sparsa Collecta*, NovTSup 29 (Leiden: Brill, 1973): 1:6–15, esp. 9.
28 I am indebted to Prof. James H. Charlesworth who in private correspondence first pointed out Luke's way of emphasizing his historiographical intent by placing the synchronisms at the *beginning* of his two volumes.
29 See, e.g., Dihle, "Evangelien," 45, on Luke-Acts: "Die sorgfältigen Datierungen und andere Details [...] rücken das berichtete Geschehen in einen geschichtlichen Zusammenhang, der die ganze Heidenwelt einschliesst." Cf. esp. Chapter Five below.
30 Talbert, "Once Again," 56.

the Isaianic promises of the anointed prophet-Servant's role that he has come to fulfill (4:18–19). "Is this not Joseph's son?" is answered by the "beloved Son" (3:22, 23; 4:18) who, like rejected prophets before him, must go "outside" Israel with God's salvation (4:23–27).[31] Or again after a significant amount of the Galilean activity is recounted, the one who served to introduce Jesus to the public as "the Christ" (3:15–17) is now questioning Jesus's identity precisely because of that activity (7:18a, 18b–23). As in Nazareth, Jesus indicates who he is, his "essence," by pointing solely to the nature of his calling *with Israel* and again in the language and demonstration (7:21!) of the Isaianic expectations of the final salvation (7:22; ἐμοί, v. 23).[32] Moreover, Luke once again has Jesus define himself in light of Israel's history of the reception of its prophets sent by Wisdom/God, this time by contrast (and continuity) with the mission of John (7:24–35, especially vv. 27–28). Numerous other examples could be cited (for example, 9:18–36; 10:21–24; 15:1–2, 3–32; 22:66–71, etc.) which illustrate that the "character" that emerges from the Gospel of Luke is totally absorbed in Jesus's sending to Israel.

It is not by accident that the author organizes much of his plot in the journeying of Jesus to Jerusalem and its Temple and places Jesus under a divine compulsion to complete the "exodus" of God's salvation to Israel (and the nations) there (9:31; 24:47).[33] Nor is it "accidental" that the author in the finale has Jesus lift the veil of mystery that has enshrouded his own identity among the people from the very beginning by having Jesus point to the whole of Israel's scriptures as the clue to "what sort of person" he is: The story of Israel has come to its crowning point in its suffering Christ (24:25–27, 44–47; compare 22:37 and 24:19–21; see § 2.1-3 below).

It is certainly true that in all of this Lukan sketch of Jesus we do learn a great deal about the sort of person Jesus was: for example, his compassion for the ill or grieving (for instance, 5:13; 7:13; 13:12); his predilection for "tax collectors and sinners" (5:27–35; 7:34–35, 36–50; 15:1–2; 19:1–10) and the "poor" (as examples, 6:20; 7:22); and his apparent enjoyment of the company of women and treatment of them as disciples (for example, 8:1–3; 10:38–42; compare 24:6–11). But in every instance this quality is not linked to a particular moral essence or structure of virtues but rather to the presence or "reign of God" that gives shape and drive to

---

31 Note how Luke's *narrator's* description of the Holy Spirit "upon him" (ἐπ' αὐτόν) in 3:22a is reaffirmed by Jesus in 4:18 using the words of Isa 61:1. Both "voices" thus attest to the "voice from heaven" (3:22b) that Jesus is the "beloved Son/Servant" in whom God delights (Isa 42:1).
32 Notice how Luke's narrator conjoins "Lord" with John's "coming one" in 7:19 as in 3:4, 16; see also 7:27–28. Cf. προσδοκάω in 3:15 and 7:19, 20.
33 See § 2.3 below.

Jesus's mission to Israel. Even when his "character" *vis-à-vis* the Law is assailed, Jesus's response is "characterized" by his understanding of his *presence among Israel* (for example, 5:33–39; 6:1–5, 6–11; 7:29–35; 11:37–52).

2.3. Is then Luke-Acts or even Part One by itself historiography? Yes, but certainly not of the usual variety. As van Unnik pointed out, Polybius's definition holds true for the entire Greco-Roman period: "An historian may include anything he deems necessary, but it has to serve his main theme: the history of the state(s)."[34] Luke or Luke-Acts certainly does not sound or feel like the usual political history; although the fulfillments of the hopes and promises of much of Israel's past form the central plot of both volumes (for example, Luke 1:32–33, 54–55, 68–79; 24:44; Acts 1:6–8; 3:24–26; 26:6–8; 28:20, 26–28), all interest is focused upon the movement begun by one Jew from Nazareth with very little given about the workings of the Jewish Sanhedrin, Jewish relations with Rome, events leading to the Jewish War, et cetera. Nor does the center of Jesus's preaching, the Kingdom of God, sound like the usual state rhetoric representing the origins and aspirations of a national consciousness.

Nevertheless, Luke-Acts fits into the broad generic classification of "general history" (for example, Albrecht Dihle; David Aune) in two ways:

(i) Luke never loses his focus upon the people or λαός of Israel as a whole, even in Part Two (Acts) where corporate Israel is increasingly "deaf" and even hostile to the "sect" of Christians (Acts 28:20–22). Luke sounds the hopes of pious Israelites for the fulfillment of ancient promises (Luke 1–2) through the vivid frame of an angelophany at the central shrine where the λαός are gathered (1:5–23) and the precocious young Jesus teaching the teachers of this people in the Temple at the Passover (2:41–52). He then depicts the interactions of Jesus with the λαός who follow and eventually journey with him to another Passover in Jerusalem where, gathered in the Temple-precincts (19:46–21:38), they will join with their leaders in crying out for the death of this prophet-teacher (23:13–25) who was "to have redeemed Israel" (24:19–21). Because of the people's rejection of their "king" (compare 23:3), God will "rain" destruction upon them (for example, 11:47–51; 13:34–35; 19:41–44; 21:20–24). Here then is a description of an approximately thirty-year period purporting to relate a significant national figure to the origins, character, and ultimate fate of that entire people. In Part Two, irrespective of how final Paul's closing judgment upon Israel may or may not be (28:25–28), Luke continues with another approximately thirty-year period in which the messianic

---

[34] Willem C. van Unnik, "Luke's Second Book and the Rules of Hellenistic Historiography," in *Les Actes des Apôtres: Traditions, rédaction, théologie*, ed. Jacob Kremer, BETL 48 (Gembloux: Leuven University Press, 1979): 39.

salvation of Israel is taken first to the λαός of Israel before it is extended through Israel to the nations of the earth. As the chief figure of this second part exclaims to fellow Jews in the closing scene, "It is because of the hope of Israel that I am bound with this chain" (28:20).

(ii) At the same time that a history of a people is being described, Luke depicts a division within this people through which a "sect" or group of Israel begins to take on its own identity[35] and to propagate its own legitimation to outsiders or non-Israelites. The great concentration of Paul's defense speeches before Roman procurators and his deliverance from the wrath of δίκη ("Justice," 28:4) through the sea voyage scenes at the end all make it clear that the "Christian" movement (11:26; 26:28!) is something that "has not taken place in a corner" (26:26). Luke, then, writes something new, a history of the beginnings of a trans-national, trans-political "religious" movement.[36] In this sense, we can speak of a new kind of "writing" or sub-genre within ancient historiography.[37]

Yet by the use of obvious *historiographical* literary forms and conventions such as speeches, travel accounts (περιηγήσεις), dramatic episodes, sea voyages (περίπλους), letters, summaries, synchronisms, digressions (ἐκβάσεις), and parallelisms,[38] Luke is deliberately presenting this movement to a larger audience in a clearly understandable form in order to show the world-wide significance of a group which claims its origins in an ancient people and professes its relevance for all of human history.[39] As in general histories, it is no wonder that Luke is intent to show the impact of fulfilled Israelite ideology/Scripture on leading intellectual

---

35 Notice how in Acts 15:14; 18:10 λαός clearly denotes non-Israelites or Gentiles as incorporated into the λαός of God. In 18:10 it may be that λαός designates largely Gentile converts, though incorporated into the first Jewish believers in Corinth as the eschatological or fulfilled *people* of God.

36 See van Unnik, "Second Book," 39. This observation, of course, does not mean Christianity is apolitical or necessarily does not have a profound impact on "politics," e.g., Acts 17:5–9.

37 Cf. Aune, *Literary Environment*, 139: "Luke, rather than Eusebius, should be credited with creating the 'new' genre of church history." If the circa sixty-year period and length of text were determinative, then Luke-Acts would be closer to the historical monograph; on this point see, Eckhard Plümacher, "Die Apostelgeschichte als historische Monographie," in *Les Actes des Apôtres: Traditions, redaction, théologie*, ed. Jacob Kremer, BETL 48 (Gembloux: Leuven University Press): 457–66.

38 See esp. Eckhard Plümacher, *Lukas als hellenistischer Schriftsteller*, SUNT 9 (Göttingen: Vandenhoeck & Ruprecht, 1972), 32–137; Aune, *Literary Environment*, 120–31.

39 Cf., e.g., Plümacher, *Lukas*, 79, on the speeches in Acts: "Wollte Lk dieses apostolische Wort als geschichtswirkendes Movens charakterisieren, so konnte nichts nützlicher sein, als bei einer bestimmten hellenistischen historiographischen Tradition Anleihen zu machen, die mit ihren Reden etwas Ähnliches auszudrücken gesucht hatte."

and commercial centers with successes among leading social groups and stretching to the center of the Empire–all directed by an overarching, supra-historical "will" of the God of Israel, the one God of the universe.

But how does the canonical separation of Luke-Acts affect this evaluation? Should each volume be considered on its own, perhaps each belonging to a separate genre as, for instance, Mikeal Parsons argues? Parsons speaks of "authorial unity" as a false criterion and of an author's potential to write in more than one generic vein.[40] But the fact is that neither Talbert nor others like Aune *assume* generic unity because of *de facto* authorial unity, nor do they subsume one book to the other, but rather to a larger whole. As they and I have tried to show, Luke himself states his intention to write a specific work and refers to volume (λόγος) one as he subordinates the subsequent volume (Acts) to a larger program/format of the whole work and not to the Gospel by itself. Part One contains "all[41] the deeds and teaching which Jesus began" (Acts 1:1–2)[42] within a scheme which the apostles will continue as authenticated witnesses to the significance of these deeds and words *within the Kingly Rule of God* (1:3). The apostles' question in Acts 1:6, whatever their understanding, clues the readers in advance through Jesus's response how volume two will continue. The "living one" "after his time of suffering" (ζῶντα μετὰ τὸ παθεῖν αὐτόν, 1:3a) enacts and teaches the "matters concerning the Kingdom of God" through authenticated witnesses empowered by the gift of "the Father" and sent to Judea and Samaria and to the rest of the world (1:6–8),

---

40 Parsons, "Reading Talbert," 163.

41 "All," though standard rhetorical hyperbole, may well be another indication of Luke's goal to write history. See, e.g., Plutarch (*Alexander*, 1.1–3); Cornelius Nepos (*Pelopidas*, 16.1.1); Lucian (*Historia*, 55); and Diodorus Siculus (*Library of History*, 16.1), who refer to history being a "fuller" or "complete" account. πάντων (Acts 1:1a) refers back to the πᾶσιν (neut.) of Luke 1:3, that is to the "fulfilled" πράγματα of Luke 1:1b. Luke it seems was intent on giving a fuller version than his predecessors (Luke 1:1) who he *may* have felt did not give an extensive enough account and thus did not render sufficient clarity or import to the events for a wider readership. His fuller account certainly entails the continuation of the fulfilled πράγματα in his *second* volume (see nn. 11, 12, 13 above).

42 Luke operates with three critical "beginnings": (i) the scriptures, including all the prophets who announce or interpret in advance the events of Luke-Acts, e.g., ἄρχομαι (Luke 24:27; Acts 8:35; cf. ἀρχαῖος in Luke 9:8,19); (ii) Jesus's public ministry, which is the decisive "beginning" of fulfillment and which "begins" with the baptism of John and Jesus's teaching in Galilee, e.g., ἄρχομαι (Luke 23:5; Acts 1:22; 10:37) and with witnesses to this "beginning," e.g., ἀρχή (Luke 1:2; cf. Acts 1:22); (iii) the coming of the Holy Spirit at Pentecost which "begins" the world mission in fulfillment of Jesus's final injunctions before his "taking up" which end the "beginning" of "all that Jesus *began* to do and to teach" (Acts 1:1), e.g., ἀρχή (Acts 11:15); ἀρχαῖος (Acts 15:7); ἄρχομαι (Luke 24:47). This concern for linking different eras and time periods is constitutive of *historiography*, not of biography. See also nn. 12, 26 above.

even as Luke will end the two volumes with Paul in Rome "preaching to all the Kingdom of God" and "the matters concerning the Lord Jesus Messiah" (28:31).[43]

Since Parsons, like Talbert and others, ties reader expectation through genre to at least some level of *authorial intent,* one cannot because of *de facto* canonical separation suddenly switch the terms of the argument to make a canonical reading the basis of generic disunity. How did Luke intend his readers to relate both parts to each other? What expectations did he set for the reader when he tied the two together? These are the primary questions when addressing genre *within the parameters of authorial intent.* At the *different level* of a canonical reading, however, clearly the Gospel of Luke "looks" more biographical as a part of a fourfold sketch of one central figure. Yet again, as we have seen, Luke is distinctive among the four in the extent to which this one figure is subordinated to the great events of the Kingdom of God, on the one hand, and is tied to the reigns and conditions of Roman and Jewish governments and to a genealogy spanning universal history on the other. By itself, the Third Gospel is closer to, for example, Tacitus's *Agricola,* that is to biographical history or historical biography.[44]

2.4. Luke's use of an "omniscient mode of narration"[45] for most of his two volumes needs to be pursued further, particularly in light of the distinctive use of this mode in the great biblical histories spanning Genesis to 2 Kings and Lucian's injunction that an historian should be

[...] like Homer's Zeus, looking now at the land of the horse-rearing Thracians, now at the Mysians' country–in the same way let him look now at the Roman side in his own way and tell us how he saw it from on high [...] let him hurry everywhere [...] to avoid missing any critical situation (Historia 49).[46]

We can, however, observe briefly:

(i) Though our author introduces himself as a "me," "us," "I," and "we," he, unlike his Greco-Roman counterparts, remains anonymous. Rather, this anonymity parallels *Hebrew historiography*, especially Joshua–2 Kings, and more immediately the Septuagint rendering of this large section of the Jewish scriptures.

---

43 See below Chapter Nine § IV.
44 See nn. 9, 11, 13 above; Mikeal Parsons, along with Richard I. Pervo, develop these generic questions further in their volume, *Rethinking the Unity of Luke and Acts* (Minneapolis, MN: Fortress/Augsburg, 1993).
45 Robert Alter, *The Art of Biblical Narrative* (New York: Basic Books, 1981), 155–77; Meir Sternberg, *The Poetics of Biblical Narrative* (Bloomington, IN: Indiana University Press, 1985), 84–128.
46 Lucian, "History," 6.60–63.

(ii) In Part One, after the initial "me" (Luke 1:3) and "us" (1:1, 2) in the preface, our unidentified author "Luke" slips behind the narrator in 1:5–24:53 to a consistent third person mode. He quickly establishes his viewpoint "from on high" as he freely moves his readers from one locale to another (for example, from the Temple to Judea to Galilee, etc.), reveals angelic pronouncements (for example, 1:11–23,26–38), "quotes" private thoughts and desires (for example, 1:25; 2:19), and cites prophetic interpretations of "interior" and supraterrestrial events (for example, 1:41–45, 46–55, 67–79), et cetera. In Acts 1:3 after again inserting himself as an "I," our author retreats behind an omniscient mode and remains a "third person" narrator until a surprising re-surfacing in 16:10–17 in the first of the famous "we" passages.[47] After such extended lengths of omniscient third person narration, this emergence is not only startling but also gives the distinct impression that the "I" of our author is now part of the "we" as an actual participant in the narrated events (see below).

(iii) In Part One, our narrator conjoins his omniscient mode with the divine omniscient perspective of the Lord God of Israel and fuses this perspective with that of the main character, Jesus of Nazareth. For example, "the word of God" to John (Luke 3:2) is pronounced by the *narrator* (3:4–6) as a fulfillment of the prophet Isaiah's oracle (Isa 40:3–5), that is, the narrator is declaring directly what the essence of the "word of God" to John was, is "speaking" for God (compare already 1:6; 2:25, 40, 52, etc.). Then the narrator as omniscient witness fuses the direct "voice" of God from "heaven" in 3:22 with Jesus's point of view in 4:1–13 where Jesus now speaks "directly" for the Lord God (4:8, 12) within the narrator's omniscient frame (4:1, 13). In Part Two the narrator wastes no time. After he links the "I" of authorship to Part One (Acts 1:1) and reasserts this omniscient perspective, he has Jesus (compare 1:1) interrupt the third person narration of verses 3–4a by abruptly *taking the words out of the narrator's mouth*!– "the promise of the Father which 'you heard from *me*.'" Through this amazing "intervention," Luke asserts the fundamental *narrative unity* of the two volumes by fusing their divine omniscient point of view, linking "the promise which 'you heard from *me*'" (1:4b) to the words of Jesus in "the promise of *my* Father" in Luke 24:49c.[48] In full accord with this transition, the narrator continues on in third person, relating the omniscient speech of the "two men in white" who give "heaven's" perspective (Acts 1:11) on Jesus's words to the apostles in 1:7–8.

---

47 Cf. Acts 20:3–15; 21:1–18; 27:1–28:16; on this whole issue, see Jürgen Wehnert, *Die Wir-Passagen der Apostelgeschichte: Ein lukanisches Stilmittel aus jüdischer Tradition* (Göttingen: Vandenhoeck & Ruprecht, 1989).

48 See esp. Chapter Seven below.

In short, it would appear that the only parallels to such lengthy uninterrupted stretches of *divine* omniscient narration are the biblical histories.⁴⁹

(iv) Not only does Jesus speak directly for God in Part One (for example, Luke 5:23–24; 6:20; 10:16, 22–24, etc.), but also in the many speeches in Part Two, the apostles-witnesses proclaim the mind or will of God directly to the people (for example, Acts 2:16–36; 3:13–26; 4:10–12; 5:29–32, etc.). Unlike Greek or Roman historiography in which roughly half of narrated speech is *indirect*, Luke consistently relates *direct* speech similar to the preferred direct speech of Hebrew historiography.⁵⁰

(v) In Luke's relatively few digressions in Part Two (for example, 1:18–19; 17:21; 23:8), he avoids a "first person" comment or speculation, unlike his Greco-Roman counterparts⁵¹ but consistent with the omniscient mode of Hebrew historiography.

To sum up, in terms of sheer uninterrupted length it would appear that Luke's anonymous, divine omniscient mode most closely parallels Hebrew/Septuagintal historiography.

Here it is curious that Lucian's remarks about an omniscient vantage point (§ 49)⁵² come in the middle of his discussion about the *credibility* of the historian's account (§§ 47–51):
- the necessity of *"examining the events in a strenuous and painstaking fashion"* (φιλοπόνως καὶ ταλαιπώρως πολλάκις περὶ τῶν αὐτῶν ἀνακρίναντα, 47); compare Luke 1:3a–"as one who has a thoroughly informed familiarity with all of them that go back way back" (παρηκολουθηκότι ἄνωθεν πᾶσιν ἀκριβῶς, that is, "all the πράγματα" of 1:1–2);
- *"and if at all possible to be present as an eyewitness"* (καὶ μάλιστα μὲν παρόντα καὶ ἐφορῶντα , 47), but if not, *"to pay attention to those who recount the most unbiased version"* (τοῖς ἀδεκαστότερον ἐξηγουμένοις προσέχοντα, 47); compare Luke 1:2–"just as those eyewitnesses and attendants of the oral word/tradition passed on to us" (καθὼς παρέδοσαν ἡμῖν [...] αὐτόπται καὶ ὑπηρέται γενόμενοι τοῦ λόγου);
- and *"once he [the historian] has collected all or most of the data, let him first sort the material into collected notes, thus letting him compose a body of material that is as yet without beauty or coherent arrangement. Then once they [the data/events] are*

---

49 See, e.g., Sternberg, *Poetics*, 72–83.
50 See, e.g., Willem C. van Unnik, "The Book of Acts: The Confirmation of the Gospel," *NovT* 4 (1960): 53: "The speeches in Acts are in the *oratio recta* and not *obliqua*, as often in pagan historiography; they are not a record of the message only, but a direct message itself"; Plümacher, *Schriftsteller*, 32–38; Aune, *Literary Environment*, 91–93, 107–8; Martin Dibelius, "Die Reden der Apostelgeschichte und die antike Geschichtsschreibung," in *Aufsätze zur Apostelgeschichte*, ed. Heinrich Greeven, FRLANT 42 (Göttingen: Vandenhoeck & Ruprecht, 1951): 120–25.
51 On digressions in Greco-Roman historiography, see, e.g., Aune, *Literary Environment*, 93–95.
52 See n. 34 above.

placed into a narrative order, let him give it beauty [...]." (ἐπειδὰν ἀθροίσῃ ἅπαντα ἢ τὰ πλεῖστα, πρῶτα μὲν ὑπόμνημά τι συνυφαινέτω αὐτῶν καὶ σῶμα ποιείτω ἀκαλλὲς ἔτι καὶ ἀδιάρθρωτον· εἶτα ἐπιθεὶς τὴν τάξιν ἐπαγέτω τὸ κάλλος [...], 48);
compare Luke 1:3–"it seemed good to me also to arrange for you a narrative sequence" (ἔδοξε κἀμοὶ [...] καθεξῆς σοι γράψαι; compare 1:1a–πολλοὶ [...] ἀνατάξασθαι διήγησιν);
- all for the *"purpose of showing the skill necessary to put together the more persuasive account"* (κἀνταῦθα ἤδη καὶ στοχαστικός τις καὶ συνθετικὸς τοῦ πιθανωτέρου, 47);

compare Luke 1:4–"in order that you [reader/Theophilus] might have a more certain grasp of those traditions of which you have been taught" (ἵνα ἐπιγνῷς περὶ ὧν κατηχήθης λόγων τὴν ἀσφάλειαν).

Thus it is also curious that Luke employs an eyewitness "we" in Part Two in the midst of an extensive omniscient narrative mode (Acts 16, *passim*). This trope is most unusual unless, of course, the purported "eyewitness" account divulges the distinctive practice and pursuit of credible, persuasive historiography rather than of biography.

3 Talbert's Genetic Theory of Gospel Composition

Talbert argues that the canonical Gospels (and Acts) are *balanced* composites in *bios* form of four different conceptions of divine presence in Jesus, each of which derives from a distinct type of Jesus tradition/material (display of power [miracles]; moral guidance for living [sayings of the wise]; secrets of one's ultimate origin/destiny leading to repentance [apocalyptic revelations]; forgiveness of sins and faith [passion narrative]). He suggests that "the canonical gospels appear to be attempts to avoid the reductionism of seeing the presence of God in Jesus in only one way and attempts to set forth a comprehensive and balanced understanding of both the divine presence and the discipleship it evokes."[53]

Talbert speaks of the new "wholes,"[54] "inclusive reinterpretation,"[55] their "controlling context,"[56] and "the order and connection" of the narratives[57] as safeguards against misunderstanding the nature of "the God who was manifest in Jesus."[58] Yet he never develops nor discusses narrative poetics in any way that makes it clear just how a new connected whole organizes the different types of

---

[53] Talbert, "Once Again," 66–67.
[54] Talbert, "Once Again," 68; Charles H. Talbert, "The Gospel and the Gospels," *Interpretation* 33 (1979): 361.
[55] Talbert, "The Gospel and the Gospels," 361–62.
[56] Talbert, "Once Again," 64, 67.
[57] Talbert, "Once Again," 69.
[58] Talbert, "Once Again," 68.

divine presence into any *coherent* divine presence.[59] One gets the impression, rather, that the Gospels force the reader to confront the different types of presence all within the framework of the *bios* of one figure in a way that ensures that no one presence will unduly assert itself over the others.[60] So, for example, in Luke-Acts, "Luke designed a picture of Jesus that would show him not only in terms of power, morality, and knowledge–all of which emphasize authority over the world–but also in terms of suffering and death. He enters into his glory only *after* experiencing his suffering (Luke 24:26)."[61]

Yet as we look more closely at Talbert's notion of divine presence in Luke-Acts, we confront a basic contradiction in his "composite plus passion narrative" model.[62] On the one hand, Luke gives his passion narrative no soteriological significance, and throughout the two volumes, asserts Talbert, "only Luke fails to speak of the connection between Jesus' death and the forgiveness of sins."[63] (His passion narrative amounts to a "grand rejection story [...] the human NO to God's messenger.")[64] Yet on the other hand, in following "the order and connection" of the narrative of Luke-Acts, "it comes clear" that it was not until after Jesus's death-resurrection-ascension-exaltation-gift of the Spirit that the disciples were effectively attached to him and the kingdom:

---

59 For instance in Charles H. Talbert, *Reading Luke: A Literary and Theological Commentary on the Third Gospel* (New York: Crossroad, 1982), one searches in vain for the role that, e.g., summaries, flashbacks, synchronisms, repetitions, etc. might play in tying various parts of the narrative together. On these and the notion of plot and story utilized below, see, e.g., Norman Petersen, *Literary Criticism for New Testament Critics* (Philadelphia, PA: Fortress, 1978), esp. 33–48.

60 For example, Talbert, "Once Again," 68: "A certain type of biographical narrative (composite plus passion narrative) was admirably suited to express the wholeness and balance of the good news about Jesus"; or in Talbert, "The Gospel and the Gospels," 358: "The canonical gospels are not so much kerygma as reflections of the controversies about the legitimacy of the various forms of proclamation in the ancient church. They come into their present shape not so much as the result of a gradual attraction of Jesus tradition around the core magnet of a passion narrative but rather as the result of a conscious and deliberate composition related to a clear-cut theological stance about the nature of God and the nature of discipleship" (cf. also Talbert, "Once Again," 67).

61 Talbert, "The Gospel and the Gospels," 357–58; Talbert, "Once Again," 66. In his *What Is A Gospel? The Genre of the Canonical Gospels* (Philadelphia, PA: Fortress, 1977), 119–20, Talbert speaks of Luke's stages of salvation history as a "controlling context, in order to indicate the legitimate hermeneutical use of the earthly Jesus" (119) and finds precedent in Paul in, e.g., 1Cor 15.

62 Talbert, "The Gospel and the Gospels," 356; Talbert, "Once Again," 65, 68.

63 Talbert, "Once Again," 66; Talbert, "The Gospel and the Gospels," 357.

64 Talbert, "Once Again," 66; Talbert, "The Gospel and the Gospels," 357.

From the order and connection of Luke's biographical narrative, one sees first that the kingdom is not so much a moral as a christological reality [...] and second that the experience of the kingdom [...] is mediated not so much by the language of Jesus as by what happened to him–death, resurrection, ascension, exaltation, receipt of the promise from the Father–and as a consequence of what happened to him.[65]

Is it conceivable that with Talbert one can read Luke-Acts in sequence (compare Luke 1:3) and conclude that the "consequence of what happened" to Jesus in his rejection and death at the hands of his own people Israel has no soteriological significance in establishing the effective christological reality of the Kingdom of God where the presence of God is experienced as the forgiveness of sins? Has Luke actually relegated the total development of opposition and rejection that culminates on the cross only to a negative foil for the suddenly new and now saving events of resurrection, ascension, et cetera? Could we not with Talbert's interpretation conclude that Jesus's suffering has no integral bearing on the kingdom at all, that it is a function of human sin and its "No" to God, so that now, after the resurrection, exaltation, and the gift of the Spirit one looks only to the *real saving* effective divine presence of God in Jesus through *those* events for the triumphant, even realized life of the forgiveness of sins, the experience of power, revelations of ultimate destiny, and so forth? Does not Talbert's interpretation of suffering and cross actually work directly against the kind of situation of over-realized eschatology that Talbert claims Luke is correcting in his two volumes?[66] As Parsons has pointed out, Talbert unfortunately has neither operated from an overall literary model nor moved very far from his redaction-critical method in which small tradition units are compared from

---

[65] Talbert, "Once Again," 69.

[66] If, as Talbert agrees, the resurrection, ascension, exaltation, and gift of the Spirit have eschatological import, then his argument–that Luke in fighting an over-realized eschatology places emphasis on Jesus remaining in the world and enduring suffering *before* these eschatological, soteriologically effective events in order to show his readers that they must also bear the same conditions; that is, Jesus's passion "does not take one immediately out of the world" ("Once Again," 66)–is void of all parenetic not to mention soteriological power. The same *conditions no longer apply*. According to Peter's first speech, quoting Joel, those who receive the Spirit are already living in the last/final days (Acts 2:17). Would Luke's audience after reading about the sufferings and death of the apostles-witnesses in Acts come to Talbert's conclusion: "[...] Luke, just as the other canonical Evangelists, does not tell his story of Jesus merely as a passion narrative. Rejection, suffering, and death are not the essence of the Christian's life, even though a Christian still experiences them" ("Once Again," 66)?

one Gospel to the next;[67] so, for example, if Luke does not contain the parallel to Mark 10:45, nor the phrase, "for the forgiveness of sins" in Matt 26:28, then, somehow these "omissions" become telling for the whole "order and connection" of Luke's story.[68]

Within the limits here we obviously cannot launch into a fuller treatment of all that Luke understands by the death of Jesus. Nevertheless, consider the following ways that Luke has organized his plot around the events of death *and* resurrection at the end of Part One:

3.1 Simeon's double oracles (Luke 2:29–32, 34–35) reveal that Jesus's reign as son of David, Son of God, in which the Lord God, Savior of Israel has "put down the mighty from their thrones" (Mary) in "remembering his holy covenant, the oath which he swore to Abraham" (Zechariah) is effected only as Jesus is himself a "controverted sign" who spurs the "falling and rising of many" in Israel as God's "saving act" to all nations.[69] What the pious of Israel are expecting as the "divine presence" of their liberator (for example, 2:38) is going to look different indeed (for example, 2:35–Mary).[70]

3.2 At the beginning of the Galilean ministry, Jesus's rejection at Nazareth serves as a template for the whole mission of "release"/"forgiveness" that Jesus came to fulfill. The eschatological mission of the anointed prophet and Servant of Isaiah is being fulfilled in the very rejection of Jesus by his own country folk (4:21–30). Like the prophets of old, sent with redemptive gestures but rejected out

---

67 Parsons, "Reading Talbert," 161.
68 E.g., Talbert, "The Gospel and the Gospels," 356–57. Talbert in the same connection finds it soteriologically significant that Mark has the rending of the Temple curtain (he mentions nothing of Luke's account of this event [23:45]) and the centurion's confession (again silent on Luke's account [23:47]). Talbert also apparently finds no special soteriological significance to Jesus's words of forgiveness from the cross to the one malefactor (Luke 23:40–43), though with Mark's centurion Talbert states, "That God gives his presence to those who rejected his Son is the equivalent to saying that God forgives sinners" (!) ("The Gospel and the Gospels," 357). See also Charles H. Talbert, "The Contribution of the View of Martyrdom in Luke-Acts to an Understanding of the Lukan Social Ethic," in *Political Issues in Luke-Acts*, ed. Richard J. Cassidy and Philip J. Scharper (Maryknoll, NY: Orbis, 1983): 99–110, where Luke 22:19–20 and Acts 20:28 are somehow devoid of atonement or soteriological significance, even though "both speak about the death of Jesus as the seal of the new covenant" (109n2).
69 See further, David P. Moessner, "The Ironic Fulfillment of Israel's Glory," in *Luke-Acts and the Jewish People: Eight Critical Perspectives*, ed. Joseph B. Tyson (Minneapolis, MN: Augsburg, 1988): 35–50; David L. Tiede, "'Glory to Thy People Israel': Luke-Acts and the Jews," in *Luke-Acts and the Jewish People: Eight Critical Perspectives*, ed. Joseph B. Tyson (Minneapolis, MN: Augsburg, 1988): 21–34.
70 Quite differently apparently from Talbert, who in his *Reading Luke* does not treat the Simeon oracles.

of hand by their own people, Jesus's eschatological mission to Israel (and eventually to those "outside the land" [Acts]) is depicted in solidarity with Israel's past *history* of its stubborn rejection of the prophets (4:24–27).[71] Again this depiction is not the kind of "divine presence" that sits well with pious, worshipping folk. And that Luke links Israel's rejection of Jesus already during his public ministry to a *mediation of salvation/release* is made clear by Jesus's preaching good news of release to the poor of Israel, the "sinners" and "tax collectors," the ill and handicapped and women who hear "today" the "forgiveness of your sins"; while at the same time this divine bearing of salvation causes growing opposition by the leaders of the populace and the towns and villages as a whole to refuse Jesus's "good news" of repentance ("release"/"forgiveness" [ἀφίημι: 5:20–24; 7:47–49]; "today" [σήμερον: 13:32–33; 19:5, 9; etc.]; refusal to "repent" [μετανοέω, Galilee: 10:13–15; Journey: 11:29–32; 13:1–5; 15:1–2, 7, 10; 16:29–31; compare 11:47–52; 12:54–59; 13:34–35; 19:41–44]).

3.3 Nearly 40 percent of Luke's Gospel is devoted to a long journey to Jerusalem (9:51–19:44) and is characterized as a fulfillment of Jesus's "exodus"/"departure"/"death," which he discusses with the scorned and persecuted prophets of the Exodus-Horeb theophanies and covenant, Moses and Elijah (9:28–36, especially 9:31). From 9:51 all movement in both words and deeds of Jesus is fixed upon Jerusalem, where Jesus will receive the prophets' "reward" (13:33).[72] Though the "poor" continue to receive eschatological release, the crowds as a whole continue to increase in their opposition to heeding the voice from the mountain as is punctuated by Jesus's pronouncements of judgment upon an obdurate people (for example, 11:29–32, 50–51; 12:57–59; 13:24–30, 35; 14:24; 17:26–30; 19:27, 41–44). The journey, then, not only leads to Jesus's rejection in Jerusalem, it is itself a journey of rejection.

But is this rejection devoid of saving significance in the larger movement of Luke-Acts? (a) Jesus first announces a denouement in Jerusalem once the disciples utter the fact of his messianic status. But this christological reality involves a "necessity" (δεῖ) of Jesus as Son of Humankind "to suffer many things," "be rejected and killed" by the Sanhedrin in Jerusalem, and "on the third day to be raised up" (9:22). (b) Moreover, Jesus announces that his journey there necessitates the continual bearing of a cross with him by all who would "save" (σῴζω)

---

[71] See further, David P. Moessner, "The 'Leaven of the Pharisees' and 'This Generation': Israel's Rejection of Jesus according to Luke," *JSNT* 34 (1988): 21–46.
[72] For a fuller treatment, see David P. Moessner, *Lord of the Banquet: The Literary and Theological Significance of the Lukan Travel Narrative* (Minneapolis, MN: Fortress, 1989), esp. Part III, 81–257.

their life. The journey therefore is corporate in nature, entailing the "following" of Israel of their crucified Messiah. And by calling upon the verdict of the final court of God (9:26), Jesus clearly signifies this "saving" and "forfeiting" life as an eschatological reality. (c) Furthermore, Jesus connects this journey of saving and forfeiting (compare falling and rising) to the reality of the Kingdom of God (9:27). By Luke linking "these words" (9:27–28) with the revelation on the mountain of the *glory* of Jesus and of Moses and Elijah, Jesus's journey becomes an eschatological fulfillment of Moses and Elijah, rejected prophets who by their death (Moses)[73] and "taking up" (Elijah)[74] anticipate the death and taking up (9:31, 51) of the Christ, who "alone" (9:36) is the "Chosen One" of the final Reign of God (9:35). It is no wonder again that this kind of "divine presence" remains mystifying (9:33, 40–41, 44–45) and unthinkable (9:45, 46–48, 49–50). (d) The journey is laced with "passion predictions" by Jesus and bound up in his own messianic consciousness with the whole history of Israel's rejection of God's messengers, on the one side, but also with God's overarching plan or necessity to effect salvation *precisely through this rejection*, on the other (11:47–54;[75] 12:49–53; 13:31–33; 14:27; 17:25; 18:31–34; compare 19:14). In 18:31–34 as the journey nears its end (compare 18:35), Jesus summons the Twelve, those representative of the whole nation, to emphasize that his rejection *and* raising up in Jerusalem is a completion of *all* the things written by the prophets. As in 4:16–30, Israel's Scriptures are in some way a telling template for Jesus's rejection and resurrection. It would appear then that the entire journey of rejection, death, and being raised up has soteriological significance, in some sense a recapitulation, but more importantly, a consummation of *Israel's* history of salvation.

3.4 At table with the Twelve (22:14–38) before Jesus's "suffering many things" (9:22; 17:25) reaches its conclusion (22:15), Jesus interprets his rejection as a voluntary *giving* and *shedding* of his body and blood "on behalf of"/"for the sake or benefit of" the Twelve. To be sure, this rejection does not go unjudged (22:15b), but already forgiveness is promised to the disciples who, though they are "ashamed of Jesus and his words" (9:26a; 22:34!) when the Son of Humankind comes (9:26b; 22:22, 54–62), "turn" from their own participation in his rejection (22:32). Not only is forgiveness thus linked to repentance, as it will be again in the preaching in Acts, but it is tied to the pivotal voluntary, vicarious giving over to death on Jesus's part as a culmination of this rejection. Moreover, Jesus gives peculiar stress to the

---

[73] Deut 1:37; 3:26; 4:21–22; 31:2, 14; 34:1–6.
[74] Cf. ἀναλαμβάνω (and cognates) in Luke 9:51; Acts 1:2,11,22 and 4Kgdms 2:9, 10, 11.
[75] Luke's comment in Luke 11:53–54 connects Jesus's comments about his own generation being held accountable for the death of all the prophets to Jesus's own death.

fact that his rejection by his own people is a necessary crowning and bringing to its intended goal the fate of the righteous suffering Servant of Isaiah who by his own folk "was reckoned as one unrighteous/without the Law" (Isa 53:12; Luke 22:37). It is totally beside the point that the Servant's voluntary giving up of his life for the sins of the many is not quoted by Jesus. Jesus has already signified his coming death in those terms, and the analogous situation of Jesus to the Servant of Isaiah is obvious enough. By placing the quote at the end of Jesus's public ministry and having Jesus point to that passage as its *summation*, Luke places Jesus's *death* at the center of the entire "saving act of God" (compare 2:29–35).

3.5 Luke ends Part One with two scenes (24:13–35, 36–49) which summarize "all that Jesus began to do and to teach" (Acts 1:1), even as they launch the events and preaching (speeches) of the one continuing history of Israel's salvation in Part Two. (a) The two disciples of the Emmaus journey recount what will become the essence of the preaching in Acts: Jesus a mighty prophet, crucified by Israel's leaders is now alive (24:19–23). Yet though they were hoping he would redeem/liberate Israel (24:21a), they do not "see" the living Jesus journeying in their midst (compare 24:24b). Jesus points to "*all* the things spoken by the prophets" and singles out two particular necessities (δεῖ)[76] of scriptural fulfillment: "the Messiah must suffer (many) things (plural) and/so as to enter into his glory" (24:25–26). The entire rejection culminating in Jesus's death is coupled with resurrection/entering glory. As at table with the Twelve, Jesus's *rejection/ death* becomes programmatic for the life that will accrue to Israel (and to the nations).

Far from being a negative foil that must be overcome through the resurrection, Messiah's suffering many things and death stands at the center of the positive *whole* of the scriptures. If read with "open eyes" (24:31, 32b), the scriptures divulge a divine necessity which forms a subject and object of faith/belief (24:25). Yet these scriptures "are not opened" for the Emmaus disciples until their "eyes are opened" "through/in the breaking of the bread" (24:31a, 32b). Already "on the road" their sluggish "hearts" were being "fired" by Jesus' "opening up" to them the central thrust of all the Scriptures (24:25, 32b). But it was not until they heard and saw Jesus "*break* and *give* the bread" that they "*remembered* him" (see 24:8– μιμνῄσκομαι), just as Jesus had told the apostles at table when he signified his broken body "for you" "to remember me" (ἀνάμνησις, 22:19b). Messiah's death "for you" is the key that unlocks and "opens up" the significance of the entire plot

---

[76] See further, Charles H. Cosgrove, "The Divine *Dei* in Luke-Acts," *NovT* 26 (1984): 168–90; John T. Squires, *The Plan of God in Luke-Acts*, SNTSMS 76 (Cambridge: Cambridge University Press, 1993), esp. 228–77.

of Jesus's rejection, suffering, and exaltation to glory.⁷⁷ (b) In 24:36–49 the divine necessity (δεῖ) of Messiah Jesus's suffering *and* resurrection is linked explicitly by Jesus in another "opening" of the scriptures to the "release of sins" and the "preaching of repentance" to Israel and the nations. By God's necessity *both* the suffering/death and resurrection of Messiah must be enacted in line with the scriptures in order for the soteriological-christological life of God for the whole world to become reality.⁷⁸

4 Conclusion

To sum up: 1.) The entire movement of the Gospel of Luke is directed to Jesus's death and resurrection in such a way that Jesus's rejection, suffering, and crucifixion are especially highlighted as soteriologically significant in the overall plan of God. It is difficult to conceive how one reading with the "order and connection" of the narrative can possibly disconnect Jesus's death from the forgiveness of sins. 2.) Talbert's genetic theory of the Gospels as "composite plus passion narrative" in guarding against subversion and reductionism in divine presence is not borne up by Luke's Gospel nor by Acts. Luke subsumes all of the Jesus traditions to the peculiar divine presence of a rejected, suffering, dying, and exalted Messiah of Israel which effects a fulfillment of salvation for and to Israel and through Israel to the nations. Whatever problems and perversions of the gospel Luke may be addressing, he does *not* do so by coordinating and balancing different notions of divine presence. Instead, in both volumes Luke relates the whole career of Jesus to his cross and resurrection, both backward and forward in the history of Israel

---

77 Notice the strong link in language with Luke 22:37!
78 One may wonder why more scriptures are not explicitly cited in Luke and Acts in describing Jesus Messiah as fulfilling a suffering and exalted figure. The main reason can be explained by Luke's emphasis on the larger historical pattern of the rejection of Israel's prophets being repeated in eschatological fashion in the events of Jesus and of the early church. This larger pattern encompasses the whole of the scriptures, especially "Moses and the prophets" (that is, the Pentateuch and the former [the histories] and the latter prophets). See esp. Stephen's articulation of this pattern in "his" commentary on the whole movement of events in Luke-Acts in Acts 7. And on this pattern, see further, David P. Moessner, "'The Christ Must Suffer': New Light on the Jesus–Peter, Stephen, Paul Parallels in Luke-Acts," *NovT* 28 (1986): 220–56 (See esp. Part IV and Chapters Nine and Ten of this volume); Moessner, *Lord of the Banquet*, 294–315, 322–25; on the Psalms as integral to the *whole* of scriptural witness (Luke 24:44), David P. Moessner, "'The Christ Must Suffer,' the Church Must Suffer: Rethinking the Theology of the Cross in Luke-Acts," in *Society of Biblical Literature 1990 Seminar Papers*, ed. David John Lull (Atlanta, GA: Scholars Press, 1990): 165–95, esp. 183–91 (see Chapter Eleven below).

and through that history to the whole world. 3.) Jesus's place and the divine presence represented by him in the history of Israel are not "accidental" to a greater narrative concern of Luke-Acts to expose a deeper "essence" as in biography. In short, there is no "life," no "character" Jesus, apart from his role in Israel's life and character.[79] This observation means, then, that Luke exhibits the concerns associated with the historian and not those of the biographer. Luke's choice of a connected *narrative* for "fulfilled events" may also suggest a special theological concern to tie the Messiah of Israel to the narratives of Israel (see Parts IV and V of this book).

[SHORT EXCURSUS: Richard Burridge's *What are the Gospels? A Comparison with Graeco-Roman Biography,* Cambridge University Press, 1992]

Professor Burridge's provocative conclusions that the canonical gospels exhibit those characteristics that define Greco-Roman *bioi* (lives/biography) and should therefore be regarded as *bioi* or biographies of Jesus have been widely accepted. His first major work is a masterpiece in thoroughness, clarity of method, and precision in execution. I cannot in this present collection properly (and certainly not *adequately*) address his overall conclusions. But a more comprehensive criticism applies to his assumptions in the same way that I have argued above against Professor Talbert's points of departure and corresponding conclusions. Burridge reads the ancient *bioi* narratives as composites of what he terms "generic features" and summarizes them as,

mostly in prose narrative and of medium length; their structure is a bare chronological framework of birth/arrival and death with topical material inserted; the scale is always limited to the subject; a mixture of literary units, notably anecdotes, stories, speeches and sayings, selected from a wide range of oral and written sources, displays the subject's character indirectly through words and deeds rather than by direct analysis [p. 140].

What is entirely missing in his larger work is a discussion and application of ancient Greek narrative hermeneutics in which the 'mind' or 'intent' (*dianoia*) of the narrative composer is 'entangled' or embedded within the dynamic interactions between plotted sequences and audience apprehension through the deliberate means or tropes of rhetorical 'methods of elaboration' (*exergasiai*). Ancient Greek narrative rhetoric describes in detail how 'narratives' (*diēgēmata/diēgēseis*) convey meaning and how sub-genres of narrative result as a function of the discrete triadic synergy of 'authorial intent'-'narrative arrangement'- 'methods of elaboration' (*dianoia–oikonomia–exergasiai*) of every narrative text [to use the rubrics of but one version of the commonplace of a trialectic hermeneutic of *diēgēsis*]. Thus what is missing is that which is most distinctive of all *narrative* qua *narrative*–whether history, biography, tragedy, epic, the novel, comedy, et al.–namely, 'plot'

---

[79] It is remarkable that nowhere in Talbert's discussion of the Gospels as *balanced* views of divine presence in Jesus ("Once Again") does he mention *Israel*.

(*mythos/praxeis*) and the resulting 'continuity of the narrative' (*to tēs diēgēseōs syneches*) that ensconces the rhetorical tropes or the 'methods of elaboration' that guide the audience to the main emphases and messages of the author's *dianoia* or overall *goal* (*telos*). Only by analyzing the dynamic distinctive to narrative hermeneutics can one begin to determine what the genre or sub-genre of that particular narrative might be [see below, esp. Chapters Five, Six, and Seven].

Part II:
Luke's Prologues and Hellenistic Narrative Hermeneutics

If the Gospel of Luke and the Acts that follow portray a universal movement unfolding according to providential steering, Luke writes as one who has the rhetorical training of a skilled narrative writer, even if he should not attain the higher levels of the classical or the Hellenistic littérateur. In his opening *proemium*, our inscribed author ("Luke," [Luke 1:3: ἔδοξε κἀμοί [...] γράψαι]) asserts his qualifications to write good narrative, not only concerning the impact it will have upon his audience (Luke 1:4: "in order that you gain a firm grasp ..." [ἵνα ἐπιγνῷς (...) τὴν ἀσφάλειαν]) but also with respect to the acknowledged repertoire of the narrative-hermeneutical standards of the Hellenistic era. How is it that Luke can propose a new narrative arrangement of the events of Jesus of Nazareth when he cannot claim for himself a critical qualification for authentic writers of recent or near contemporary events, namely, that of "eyewitness?" Since Luke openly acknowledges that he was not privy to firsthand experience of the important "matters" (πράγματα) he relates (Luke 1:2–3), by what authority does he write up yet another account of "events come to fruition among us" amidst the "many" other narrative treatments of the same (Luke 1:1)?

Chapter Three, "The Author 'Luke': 'As one who has a thoroughly informed familiarity (παρηκολουθηκότι [...] ἀκριβῶς) with all the events from the top' (Luke 1:3a)," provides a crucial piece of evidence to Luke's seeming audacity. With the perfect participle of παρακολουθέω, the author of the Gospel and of the Acts asserts that he has the credentialed, authenticated knowledge to offer his own version of these "matters" of consequence. In fact, Luke is so confident of his qualifications that he assures his readers that they too will gain a firm understanding of the events which have come to "full flowering" in his and his auditors' own time (Luke 1:1b). Moreover, given Luke's standing, he indicates by implication that his narrative "arrangement" or "sequence" will be an improvement upon the "many" others. And finally in Chapter Four, "The Meaning of καθεξῆς in Luke's Two-Volume Narrative," Luke styles himself a narrative composer who, by placing the rhetorical dispositional term καθεξῆς in strategic locations in both his volumes, including his opening prologue, lures his audience into the finer intonations and cadences of his mimetic orchestrations in order to register for them a new 'key' of understanding.

Chapter Three: The Author 'Luke': "As One Who Has a Thoroughly Informed Familiarity with All the Events from the Top" (παρηκολουθηκότι ἄνωθεν πᾶσιν ἀκριβῶς, Luke 1:3a)[1]

The meaning of παρηκολουθηκότι, the perfect active participle of παρακολουθέω (literally, "to follow along[side]"), in Luke's preface (Luke 1:3a) is notoriously difficult to render. Luke appears to be offering an important qualification of his decision to write his Gospel. Why, more exactly, did it "seem good" to the author to write for Theophilus (Luke 1:3b)? Should we 'follow' a now classic translation that introduces Luke "as one who has investigated/inquired/traced/informed himself about all the events/matters [...]" so that he can write a reliable account concerning them?[2] If so, Luke is situating himself as one far enough removed from the events he draws up that he needed to employ the stock-in-trade tools of an historian to discover the details of the 'how and the who and the what' transpired in order to deliver an account of their significance.

This understanding of Luke as essentially an historian who investigates written and oral sources to compose his own version of events treated in part by others has become standard in interpreting the author of Luke and Acts. Closely aligned but not necessarily causal in connection is the view that Luke must be, at the least, a "third" generation or more removed from the first followers of Jesus of Nazareth, a movement the author himself will depict more expansively in time and space as "the way."[3] Yet whatever Luke's more precise identity, it is at least clear that the author of the Third Gospel was neither directly associated with the apostles nor a member of the apostles' immediate followers. Indeed, he specifies two groups in relation to a "beginning"[4]–"eyewitnesses" and "attendants/

---

[1] A shorter version of "Luke as Tradent and Hermeneut: 'As one who has a thoroughly informed familiarity with all the events from the top' (παρηκολουθηκότι ἄνωθεν πᾶσιν ἀκριβῶς, Luke 1:3)" first published in *Novum Testamentum* 58 (2016): 259–300, used by permission.
[2] See, e.g., Joseph A. Fitzmyer, *The Gospel according to Luke I-IX*, AB 28 (Garden City, NY: Doubleday, 1981), 287–302.
[3] E.g., in vol. 1 of Jesus's "way": Luke 3:4; 9:57, etc.; vol. 2: Acts 9:2; 18:26; 19:9, 23, etc.
[4] The two groups–οἱ αὐτόπται καὶ ὑπηρέται–may overlap if ὑπηρέτης retains its sense of one who serves or is subservient to someone or something else; some of those who were present for various events of Jesus's public activity became at some later point "attendants/assistants" or "ministers" or "servants" of the messages or words of explanation that developed out of witness-

servants of the word/message" (οἱ ἀπ' ἀρχῆς αὐτόπται καὶ ὑπηρέται γενόμενοι τοῦ λόγου)–upon whom he and the "many" are dependent for vital information "delivered over" (παρέδοσαν) concerning the very "events" or "matters" "just as" (καθώς) he[5] and others among an "us" (ἡμῖν), are attempting to signify[6] (Luke 1:1–2). Though he is dependent on the eyewitness of the apostles and the information from the "servants of the word," he is not himself to be reckoned as one of those followers "from the beginning."

Scholars readily acknowledge that the interpretation of παρακολουθέω is critically significant for understanding the distinctive contribution of Luke's two-volume enterprise. For instance, Joseph Fitzmyer calls παρηκολουθηκότι "the crucial word in the modern interpretation of the Lucan prologue."[7] Or again as Loveday Alexander observed, "The participial clause, as commentators have recognized, brings forward some sort of epistemological claim about the status

---

ing Jesus firsthand, as Peter describes, for instance, in his address to Cornelius's house (Acts 10:36–39–"the word/message [ὁ λόγος] that was sent [...] through Jesus Messiah [...] of all these things Jesus did we are witnesses [...] and he commanded us to preach and to bear witness to the people [...]," vv. 41–42). On the other hand, since Luke mentions two ὑπηρέται in Acts who have become associated with the eyewitness group of apostles, namely "Mark" and "Saul" with Barnabas ("from the group of the apostles," Acts 4:36), ὑπηρέτης can refer to those instructed or who had become associated with the eyewitnesses without themselves having witnessed directly any of the words or deeds of Jesus. Nor is there the suggestion that a ὑπηρέτης must have literally "followed" or accompanied the apostles for a requisite period of time; rather, "attendants" may derive their information or content of the "word/message" from the eyewitnesses, "just as" "the us" (Luke 1:2) receives their information from the two groups in a way analogous to the apostles themselves receiving a summary of the tradition from Jesus (e.g., Luke 24:46–48). *Paul, however, is a notable exception*. Though not of the apostolic group per se, though clearly associated with them–as, for instance, a fellow proclaimer of the word with Barnabas–according to Luke, Paul does not receive his primary information from the apostles but rather revelation directly from the risen Christ (Acts 9:1–9–repeated twice, Acts 22:6–11; 26:12–18; cf. Gal 1:13–17). Thus when Paul is called by the risen Christ himself to become both a ὑπηρέτης καὶ μάρτυς "of those things Paul has just seen" [of the Christ] (Acts 26:16, 22–23), Luke grants him the status tantamount to both the "eye-witnesses" and the "attendants of the word."

5 The gender of the perfect participle παρηκολουθηκότι, Luke 1:3, indicates an inscribed male writer.

6 The aorist of ἐπιχείρω of Luke 1:1 indicates that the multiple attempts to render a connected narrative (sg.!) account have already been launched (literally, "many have set to hand"/"set out to"). That some if not most of those "many" narratives are available in more or less complete form to assess can be assumed from Luke's initiation of his own narrative composing. Particularly in light of his comment in Luke 1:4 that his account will provide a "firm(er) understanding" (ἀσφάλεια: literally, "safety"/"security"), Luke strongly suggests that he is not fully satisfied with the accounts of these others; see conclusions below.

7 Fitzmyer, *Luke*, 296.

of the material presented ... Secondly, what kind of claim is Luke making about the presentation of his work?"⁸ Paddling against the stream of the prevailing reading ("having investigated"), Henry J. Cadbury argued in several articles that Luke must be asserting a "basic familiarity with" the traditions he treats. In his detailed commentary on the prologue of Luke in his *Beginnings of Christianity*, volume 2, he showed how the understanding of several terms as well as the whole of the preface is dependent on the more precise meaning of παρηκολουθηκότι.⁹

Is Luke claiming direct contact with either or both the "eyewitnesses" and "attendants?" To what extent is Luke "following" his literary precursors? Is he announcing one more narrative account of the same ilk as the "many," or is he signaling that his will be superior to these others since it will deliver a "certainty" of understanding that the others apparently do not possess (ἵνα ἐπιγνῷς περὶ ὧν κατηχήθης λόγων τὴν ἀσφάλειαν, Luke 1:4)? Notwithstanding the *idola theatri* of this 'received' interpretation,¹⁰ the thesis of this study is that παρηκολουθηκότι in Luke 1:3 can *not* have the sense of "one who has inquired about," "conducted research on," "informed oneself about," or "investigated" "matters" or "events" (πράγματα) as one who needs to acquire information or basic familiarity with the 'facts.' Rather, παρηκολουθηκώς has almost the opposite sense of "one who is (already) thoroughly familiar with" or "steeped" in certain traditions or texts, whether through firsthand experience or through training or being informed by

---

8 Loveday Alexander, *The Preface to Luke's Gospel*, SNTSMS 78 (Cambridge: Cambridge University Press, 1993), 133–34.
9 Henry J. Cadbury, "Commentary on the Preface of Luke," Appendix C of *The Beginnings of Christianity: Part I, The Acts of the Apostles*, ed. F. J. Foakes-Jackson and Kirsopp Lake, 5 vols. (New York: Macmillan, 1920–33), 2:489–510; cf. also Henry J. Cadbury, "The Knowledge Claimed in Luke's Preface," *The Expositor* 8 (1922): 401–20; Henry J. Cadbury, "The Purpose Expressed in Luke's Preface," *The Expositor* 8 (1922): 431–41; Henry J. Cadbury, "'We' and 'I' Passages in Luke-Acts," *NTS* 3 (1956–57): 128–32.
10 Among many who hold to the now "classic" "investigate": Richard J. Dillon, "Previewing Luke's Project from His Prologue (Luke 1:1–4)," *CBQ* 43 (1981): 218–19; I. I. du Plessis, "Once More: The Purpose of Luke's Prologue (Luke I 1–4)," *NovT* 16 (1974): 266–67; A. J. B. Higgins, "The Preface to Luke and the Kerygma in Acts," in *Apostolic History and the Gospel*, ed. W. Ward Gasque and Ralph P. Martin (Grand Rapids, MI: Eerdmans, 1970): 79–82; F. H. Colson, "Notes on St. Luke's Preface," *JTS* 24 (1923): 304, 309; M. Devoldère, "Le prologue du troisième évangile," *NRTh* 56 (1929): 714–19; Vinzenz Hartl, "Zur synoptischen Frage: Schliesst Lukas durch 1,1–3 die Benutzung des Matthäus aus?" *BZ* 13 (1925): 334–37; Ernst Haenchen, "Das 'Wir' in der Apostelgeschichte und das Itinerar," *ZTK* 58 (1961): 363–65; J. Kürzinger, "Lk 1,3: ... ἀκριβῶς καθεξῆς σοι γράψαι," *BZ* 18 (1974): 253–54; Walter Grundmann, *Das Evangelium nach Lukas*, THKNT (Berlin: Evangelische Verlagsanstalt, 1961), 44; I. Howard Marshall, *The Gospel of Luke*, NIGTC (Exeter: Paternoster, 1978), 42–43; Eduard Schweizer, *The Good News according to Luke* (Atlanta, GA: John Knox, 1984), 12; etc.

others. Indeed, on the basis of this claim of credentialed authority, Luke ventures to render yet another account of momentous occurrences to which he himself could not "bear witness" nor discuss *firsthand*.

Our own 'investigation' will be interested especially where παρακολουθέω appears in prefaces to 'narrative' (διήγησις, compare Luke 1:1) or where the poetics and rhetorical impact of παρακολουθέω upon audiences of extended diegetic performance are discussed. In particular, we shall see that when a reader's/auditor's ability "to follow" the argument or connected presentation of a text is engaged–contexts which have not been sufficiently investigated–the perfect participle παρηκολουθηκότι in Luke 1:3 illumines the author's opening statements quite remarkably and removes the stubborn inconsistencies and in-concinnities of the other interpretations. Moreover, given the very thin threshold between acquiring knowledge and knowledge already attained–between new experiences that add to one's knowledge of some person or event and basic knowledge already in place before new information is received–it will be necessary to present enough of the immediate literary contexts of each occurrence examined to sort out those finer distinctions and to nuance the various tenses used to make those distinctions. Our conclusion will be similar to Cadbury's in rejecting the notion of "one having to acquire knowledge" not previously attained, yet we shall see that Cadbury went too far in aligning παρακολουθέω with physical "eyewitness" presence. Actual presence at events as they unfold is not *necessarily* entailed by παρακολουθέω.

1 The Role of Παρηκολουθηκώς for Discerning Luke's Intention

It will be helpful to examine the structure of the one Atticizing period of Luke's preface to see what role παρηκολουθηκώς might play in adjudicating the reasons Luke intends yet another rendition *vis-à-vis* the "many." Interpreters have noticed a balance between the two "halves" of the *prooimion* (vv.1–2–3–4).[11] We can discern a balance of three parallel phrases, in substance as well as form, between the dependent clauses of the *protasis* (vv. 1–2) and the main clause and its final clause in the *apodosis* (vv. 3–4):

a) Since <u>many</u> *have undertaken to compile* **a narrative** (v. 1a)
    b) Concerning **the events/matters** *which have been fulfilled* <u>in our midst</u> (v. 1b)
        c) Just as <u>those from the beginning eyewitnesses and attendants of the word</u> *delivered over to* <u>us</u> (v. 2)

---

[11] E.g., Fitzmyer, *Luke*, 288.

    a') It seemed good to <u>me</u> also [...] *to write you* **in sequence** (v. 3a,b)
        b') As <u>one who has a thoroughly informed familiarity with</u> **all these events/ matters** *from the top* (v. 3b)
            c') So that <u>you may gain a firm grasp</u> *of the significance* **of the events/ matters of which** <u>you have been taught</u> (v. 4)

The pertinent question for our analysis: Is there any significance in this balance for interpreting παρακολουθέω? If we pair each parallel phrase in form and content with its counterpart, it is easier to discern the 'comparison' (σύγκρισις) between Luke and his predecessors, with the tradents and/or recipients <u>underlined</u>, the development of the tradition in *italics*, and the resulting shape of the tradition in **bold**:

a)   Since <u>many</u> *have undertaken to compile* **a narrative** (v. 1a)
      [causal clause]
a') It seemed good to <u>me</u> also ... *to write you* **in sequence** (v. 3a, b)
      [main clause]
    b) Concerning **the events/matters** *which have been fulfilled* <u>in our midst</u> (v. 1b)
        [participial clause as obj. of preposition]
    b') As <u>one who has a thoroughly informed familiarity with</u> **all these events/ matters** *from the top* (v. 3b)
        [participial {παρηκολουθηκότι} clause dependent on indirect object of main verb of main clause]
        c.) Just as <u>those from the beginning eyewitnesses and attendants of the word</u> *delivered over to* <u>us</u> (v. 2)
            [secondary adverbial clause dependent on causal clause]
        c') So that <u>you may gain a firm grasp</u> *of the significance* **of the events/ matters of which** <u>you have been taught</u> (v. 4)
            [secondary final clause dependent on main clause]

The question that immediately emerges from this parallelism is how the author Luke differs from the many who have the same resources and are likely to be included as part of the "us" who have, like the author, experienced a certain fulfillment or "flowering" of events in their own time and place (περὶ τῶν πεπληροφορημένων ἐν ἡμῖν πραγμάτων, Luke 1:1b). Is Luke comparably suited in his ability to write up a narrative, or is he better situated than the "many" to produce a 'certainty' of understanding through his own narrative arrangement? Clearly παρηκολουθηκότι holds the answer. The parallel c/c' also raises the corollary question whether a larger goal of the author is to give the "you,"

Theophilus, and Luke's audience more generally, a "firmness of understanding" that approximates or can even be compared to those who actually experienced or were "attendants" taught by the eyewitnesses of the events of Jesus of Nazareth. It should be remembered that "Theophilus" (Luke 1:3b), whoever he might be, has already received instruction from tradents (Luke 1:4) whose own understanding must stem at least formally from traditions "delivered over" from the two groups specified in Luke 1:2. How strong are Luke's own qualifications that seem to reside in the significance of the perfect passive participle παρηκολουθηκώς?

In sum, it is readily apparent that one cannot come to a settled conclusion about the nuances of any one balanced pair apart from understanding the ways all three pairs relate to each other. The pregnant παρηκολουθηκώς forms the fulcrum *between* the experiences of "fulfilled events" rendered by the eyewitnesses and attendants (Luke 1:1–2) *and* the attempts to tender a narrative account that does justice to their significance (Luke 1:3–4).

2 Determining the Sense and the Referent of Παρηκολουθηκώς

As a method for determining the sense and referent of παρηκολουθηκώς in Luke 1:3, we will examine the entire spectrum of senses and referents for παρακολουθέω exhibited by the Liddell-Scott-Jones *A Greek-English Lexicon* (LSJ) and by Bauer's *A Greek-English Lexicon of the New Testament* (3rd edition, BDAG) in order not to miss any possible subtlety in Luke's self-presentation. This scope will facilitate both a wide purview of possible meanings both before and after the time of Luke's writing, as well as provide workable limits to our discussion.

2.1 Liddell-Scott-Jones

Liddell-Scott-Jones lists two discrete senses for παρακολουθέω, one literal and one metaphorical. The *literal* sense is divided between transitive and intransitive referents, with the intransitive split between the literal senses "*accrue*" and "*make a succession* of growths." The *metaphorical*, on the other hand, evinces five distinct referents.

Literal:
1. "*follow* or *attend closely, dog one's steps; accrue*"
2. "*make a succession*"

Literal sense 1: LSJ lists six referents for the transitive, two referents for the first intransitive sense, one for the second.

1. Transitive sense:
1) Physical following (behind) (a) person(s) by (an)other person(s)

Aristophanes, *Ecclesiazusae* [ἐκκλησιαζούσαι]
(*The Women's Collectives*) 725 (719–27)[12]:

Praxagora: δῆλον τουτογί·
ἵνα τῶν νέων ἔχωσιν αὗται τὰς ἀκμάς.
καὶ τάς γε δούλας οὐχὶ δεῖ κοσμουμένας
τὴν τῶν ἐλευθέρων ὑφαρπάζειν Κύπριν,
ἀλλὰ παρὰ τοῖς δούλοισι κοιμᾶσθαι μόνον,
κατωνάκην τὸν χοῖρον ἀποτετιλμένας.
Blepyrus: φέρε νυν ἐγώ σοι παρακολουθῶ πλησίον,
ἵν' ἀποβλέπωμαι καὶ ταδὶ λέγωσί με·
"τὸν τῆς στρατηγοῦ τοῦτον οὐ θαυμάζετε;"

Praxagora: *It is manifest concerning these [free women]:*
that they may enjoy the peak performances of our young males.
Those painted hookers shall no longer
poach upon the love nests of the free,
No, let them lie with slavish rogues, alone shack up with vile slaves,
plucked bare in their swinish fluflus.
Blepyrus: *My advice–lead on my dear, I will* follow *close behind,*
that the men may stare and ogle in sheer derision:
"There goes the husband of our Guardianess!"

Comment: In this comedic parody in lyric poetry–probably first performed in Athens in BCE 392 or 391–Aristophanes lampoons the ideal society of Plato's *Republic* by having Praxagora, otherwise social conservative, promote a new society where women are in total control and private ownership as well as marriage is abolished. In this farcical scene, Aristophanes caricatures the equality of this new society where slave and free, male and female know no social nor sexual boundaries, poking fun to the absurd at the liberating role of Plato's 'Guardians'! A literal "following" of one person by another is obvious.

---

[12] All translations are my own from the Greek text of the Loeb Classical Library unless otherwise indicated.

2) Reflection, shadow, image that accompanies an object or entity

Plato, σοφιστής (*The Sophist*) 266c:
Ξένος: Τά τε ἐν τοῖς ὕπνοις καὶ ὅσα μεθ' ἡμέραν φαντάσ-
ματα αὐτοφυῆ λέγεται, σκιὰ μὲν ὅταν ἐν τῷ πυρὶ σκότος
ἐγγίγνηται, διπλοῦν δὲ ἡνίκ' ἂν φῶς οἰκεῖόν τε καὶ ἀλλότριον
περὶ τὰ λαμπρὰ καὶ λεῖα εἰς ἓν συνελθὸν τῆς ἔμπροσθεν
εἰωθυίας ὄψεως ἐναντίαν αἴσθησιν παρέχον εἶδος ἀπεργάζηται.
Θεαίτητος: Δύο γὰρ οὖν ἐστι ταῦτα θείας ἔργα ποιήσεως,
αὐτό τε καὶ τὸ <u>παρακολουθοῦν</u> εἴδωλον ἑκάστῳ.

<u>Stranger</u>: *The appearances that are said to spring up of themselves*
whether in dreams or those during the day,
such as a shadow when a dark object interferes with the light of a fire,
or when a twofold light of its own source and from outside
comes together as one on bright and smooth surfaces
producing an image contrary to our ordinary perception of sight.
<u>Theaetetus</u>: *Yes, for there are these two works of divine making,*
the thing itself and its image which in each case <u>accompanies</u> it.

Comment: Plato's *Sophist* continues the discussion of his *Theaetetus* on the nature of knowledge and compares a sophist to the image of a real object, as one who does not really "know" but only "imitates" knowledge. In the exchange above, the image "follows" or "attends" the reality as it appears.

3) Staying in close physical proximity in a way that harasses, 'dogs,' stalks, et cetera (an)other person(s)

<u>Demosthenes, κατὰ Μειδίου (*Against Meidias*) Oration 21 (14.69)</u>:
ὑμεῖς μέν, ὦ ἄνδρες Ἀθηναῖοι, πάντες
ἀμφότερ' ὡς οἷόν τε μάλιστ' ἀπεδέξασθε, τήν τ' ἐπαγγελίαν
τὴν ἐμὴν καὶ τὸ συμβὰν ἀπὸ τῆς τύχης, καὶ θόρυβον καὶ
κρότον τοιοῦτον ὡς ἂν ἐπαινοῦντές τε καὶ συνησθέντες ἐποιήσατε,
Μειδίας δ' οὑτοσὶ μόνος τῶν πάντων, ὡς ἔοικεν, ἠχθέσθη,
καὶ <u>παρηκολούθησε</u> παρ' ὅλην τὴν λητουργίαν
ἐπηρεάζων μοι συνεχῶς καὶ μικρὰ καὶ μείζω.

You Athenians, all of you, welcomed with open arms both my willing offer and my fortunate turn of events; and your cheers and enthusiastic applause showed how much you were approving of my actions and showing sympathy with my cause. But there was, or so seems to have been, one exception out of the whole lot, namely this man Meidias, who <u>dogged</u> my whole time of service by relentlessly hurling abuse against me, whether trivial or more substantial.

Comment: Meidias, a wealthy Athenian with considerable political influence, was a long-time enemy of the upstart orator-politician Demosthenes. During the Great Dionysia festival of circa 351–350 <u>BCE</u>, he came up to Demosthenes, who was seated as one of the judges of the chorus competition, and punched him in the face. Later before the Assembly, Demosthenes entered a formal complaint against Meidias and won a unanimous vote against his assailant. This oration was apparently never delivered and seems to have been composed before the hearing, in anticipation of a different set of results. The aorist παρηκολούθησε states a fact or looks at the whole of the relationship as unremitting abuse by Meidias as one determined "to follow" Demosthenes's every move.

4) Physical accompanying/following alongside (an)other person(s)
<u>Philemon 124 (from a fragment cited in Clement of Alexandria's *Paedagogus* 3. 11. 73)</u>:[13]

>Clement: Ἐγὼ μὲν οὐδὲ τὰς θεραπαίνας ἀξιῶ
>τὰς <ἐπ'> ἀρισ-<τερᾶς> ταῖς γυναιξὶν <ἢ> τὰς ἑπομένας αὐταῖς
>αἰσχρολογεῖν ἢ αἰσχροεργεῖν, σωφρονίζεσθαι δὲ αὐτὰς πρὸς τῶν
>δεσποινῶν· σφόδρα γοῦν ἐπιτιμητικώτατα ὁ κωμικὸς
>Φιλήμων φησίν·
>[Philemon]: Ἐξιὼν
>γυναικὸς ἐξόπισθ' ἐλευθέρας βλέπω
>μόνην θεράπαιναν κατόπιν ἀκολουθεῖν καλὴν
>ἐκ τοῦ Πλαταιικοῦ τε <u>παρακολουθοῦντά</u> τινα
>ταύτῃ κατιλλώπτειν.
>Ἀναστρέφει γὰρ ἐπὶ τὴν δέσποιναν ἡ τῆς θεραπαίνης
>ἀκολασία [...]. "Οἵα γὰρ δέσποινα,"
>φασὶν οἱ παροιμιαζόμενοι, "τοιάδε χἀ κύων."

>Clement: *For my part, I maintain that maids
>who serve at 'the left hand' of their mistresses or
>who are part of their retinue should neither speak nor act unseemly;*

---

[13] For text, see Claude Mondésert, Chantal Matray, Henri-Irénée Marrou, eds., *Clément D'Alexandrie: Le Pédagogue*, Livre III Texte Grec (Paris: Cerf, 1970), 142–43; cf. J. M. Edmonds, *The Fragments of Attic Comedy* IIIA (Leiden: Brill, 1961), 70–73.

rather they should act restrained when they are with their mistresses.
At all events, the comic poet Philemon expresses it rather censoriously:
[Philemon]: *When I go out and look about I see the good-looking maid*
of a free woman following alone behind her,
making leering glances at those from Platea
<u>*who are following alongside her.*</u>
Clement: *For the intemperance of the maid*
recoils upon her mistress [...]. As the sententious idlers say,
'*Like mistress, like dog.*'
Comment: This text speaks for itself. What is particularly intriguing is the way παρακολουθέω parallels the familiar ἀκολουθέω as a simultaneous physical "following," whether "alongside" as here or from "behind" as in the first referent.

5) In close physical proximity to (a) person(s) with a negative or irritating influence

Demosthenes, περὶ τοῦ στεφάνου (*Concerning the Crown/De Corona*) Oration 18 (162):

καὶ περὶ τῶν ἄλλων πολλάκις ἀντιλέγοντας
ἑαυτοῖς τοῦθ' ὁμογνωμονοῦντας ἀεί. οὓς σὺ ζῶντας μέν,
ὦ κίναδος, κολακεύων <u>παρηκολούθεις</u>, τεθνεώτων δ' οὐκ
αἰσθάνει κατηγορῶν· ἃ γὰρ περὶ Θηβαίων ἐπιτιμᾷς ἐμοί,
ἐκείνων πολὺ μᾶλλον ἢ ἐμοῦ κατηγορεῖς, τῶν πρότερον ἢ
ἐγὼ ταύτην τὴν συμμαχίαν δοκιμασάντων.

Concerning this matter [good relation between Athens and Thebes]
they [Aristophon and Eubulus] *were always of the same opinion,*
in spite of their continually disagreeing with each other
on those other matters of policy [how to relate to Philip's threatening power].
When those [statesmen] *were still alive, you, sly fox* [Aeschines], <u>*pestered them*</u>
<u>*with flattery*</u>; *now that they are dead you accuse them without understanding; for*
what you blame me regarding the Thebans would have had much greater force if
you had been accusing those who approved of a Theban alliance before I did.

Comment: Demosthenes charges Aeschines of "dogging" or continually "attending" his rivals with shameless flattery. The relation of the aorist παρηκολούθεις, describing a whole period of time, to the action of the repeated flattering of the present participle κολακεύων is that of simultaneity.

6) Coursing along a parallel path, intertwined, interrelated, et cetera

<u>Aristotle, τῶν περὶ τὰ ζωία ἱστοριῶν</u>
(*The History of Animals/Historia Animalium*) 496a29:[14]
Φέρουσι δὲ καὶ εἰς τὸν
πλεύμονα πόροι ἀπὸ τῆς καρδίας, καὶ σχίζονται τὸν αὐτὸν
τρόπον ὅνπερ ἡ ἀρτηρία, κατα πάντα τὸν πλεύμονα
<u>παρακολουθοῦντες</u> τοῖς ἀπὸ τῆς ἀρτηρίας.

Ducts also lead into the lung from the heart and split off
in the same manner as the windpipe, coursing throughout the lung,
<u>accompanying</u> those which come from the windpipe.

Comment: [hardly needed here].

2. Intransitive sense.
The literal meanings as "accrue," "result":

1) PSI 3.168.24:[15]
καὶ ἐκ τοῦ τοιούτου τρόπου ἔλυσαν τὸ δηλούμενον χῶ[μ]α
ὥστ' ἀναβροχήσαντας τὸ πεδίον οὐ κατὰ μικρὸν ἐλάττωμα
<u>παρακολουθεῖν</u> τοῖς βασιλικοῖς

and in such a manner they destroyed the dyke that was exposed
so that the footpath became engulfed in water,
<u>resulting</u> in no small disadvantage for the royal party [...].

---

14 Text: Aristotle, *Historia animalium*, vol. 1, *Histoire des animaux*, ed. Pierre Louis (Paris: Les Belles Lettres, 1964).
15 Papyrus 168 (2nd century BCE) of the Società italiana per la ricerca dei papiri greci e latini in Egitto. Pubblicazioni 45/52, *Papiri greci e latini*, vol. 3 (Rome: Firenze F. Le Monnier, 1914).

2) PRein. 18.15:[16]

Ασκληπιαδει συγγενει και στρατηγωι
πάρα Διονυσ[ι]ου του Κεφαλα βασιλικου γεωργου
των εκ κωμ[η]σ Τηνεωσ τησ και Ακωρεωσ
του Μωχιτου • Δια τασ επι του πραγματοσ υπο-
5 δειχθησομε[ν]ασ αιτιασ γραψαμενου εμού τε
και τησ μη[τρ]οσ μου Σεναβολλουτοσ Αδμη-
τωι τωι και Χεσθωτηι των εκ τησ αυτησ
κωμησ συ[γγρ]αφην δάνειου δια του μνημο-
νειου πυρων (αρταβων) ρν εν τωι θ L., ου μόνον
10 δ', αλλα και εθεμην αυτωι εν πιστει καθ' ων
εχω ψιλων το[π]ων συγγραφην υποθηκησ •
ο εγκαλουμενοσ εγκρατησ γενομενοσ
των συναλλαξ[ε]ων ουθεν των διασταθεντων
μοι προσ αυτ[ο]ν επι τελοσ ηγαγεν, ων
15 χαριν ουκ ολι[γα] μοι βλαβη δι' αυτον <u>παρη-
κολουθησεν</u> • [και] νυν δ' επ' άδικου στασεωσ
ισταμενοσ, συνορων με περι την κατα-
σποραν ησ γεω[ρ]γω γησ κατασχολουμενον,
καταδρομασ μ[ο]υ ποιουμενοσ ουκ εα προσ
20 τηι γεωργια γινεσθαι, παρα τα περι ημων
των γεωργων δ[ια] πλειονων προστετα
γμένα •

To Asklepiades, kinsman and praetor
from Dyonysios son of Kephalas, royal farmer
from the village Tenis and Akorios
in Mochites • On account of the matter concerning which
5 the causes will be indicated in the record, we signed, both I
and my mother Senabollous, to Admetus
and to Chesthotes from the same
town, a contract for a loan according to the record for
150 [artabes] of wheat in year 9. Not only that,
10 but also I deposited to them in [good] faith according to which
I laid down cultivated land I own for the contract.

---

16 *Papyrus grecs et démotiques. Recueillis en Égypte et publiés* [Pap.18.15 {2nd bce}], ed. Théodore Reinach, MM. W. Spiegelberg, S. de Ricci (Paris: 1905; Reprint, Milan: Cisalpino-Goliardica, 1972).

> *My accuser, having possession* [of these terms],
> *has still reconciled to none of the orders expressed*
> *to me for him when he began, here at the end.*
> *15 On account of which no small amount of harm, because of him,*
> *has accrued to me. And now raising this unjust issue,*
> *perceiving that I am sowing*
> *the land I'm engaged in farming,*
> *he has made an inroad to my*
> *farm land, and will not let me be*
> *regardless of the rules*
> *we farmers have prescribed many times.*[17]

Literal Intransitive Second Sense: "make a succession":

> Theophrastus, περὶ φυτῶν ἱστορίας (*Enquiry into Plants*) 6.4.8:
> παρακολουθεῖ δὲ μέχρι τοῦ θέρους τὸ μὲν κυοῦν τὸ δὲ
> ἀνθοῦν τὸ δὲ σπέρμα τίκτον

It [sow-thistle] *burgeons in a succession up to the summer, producing part blooms, part flowering of the blooms, part seeds.*

Metaphorical:[18] *"follow closely, attend minutely to, trace accurately, follow all"*
   Five categories of referents are listed. We shall provide one example for each:
1) of events, persons, behavior; times and dates; et cetera;
2) of/by an audience: *"follow with the mind, understand, become familiar with, to be conscious/self-conscious"*;
3) of things: *"keep company with, keep close to"*;
4) of rules: *"hold good throughout"*;
5) of a logical property: *"inseparably connected, constant attribute, to be proper to"*

---

17 Special thanks to Lindsey Trozzo, Ph.D. candidate, Baylor University, and Assistant to the Bradford Chair, for the translation from the Greek and French (see previous note).
18 All translations are my own unless indicated otherwise; Greek text from the Loeb Classical Library.

Referent 1) of metaphorical sense: of events, persons, behavior; times and dates; et cetera: *"follow closely, attend minutely to, trace accurately, follow all"*

> Demosthenes, περὶ τοῦ στεφάνου
> (*Concerning the Crown/De corona*) Oration 18 (172):
> ἀλλ', ὡς ἔοικεν, ἐκεῖνος ὁ καιρὸς καὶ ἡ ἡμέρα
> 'κείνη οὐ μόνον εὔνουν καὶ πλούσιον ἄνδρ' ἐκάλει, ἀλλὰ καὶ
> <u>παρηκολουθηκότα</u> τοῖς πράγμασιν ἐξ ἀρχῆς, καὶ συλλελογισμένον
> ὀρθῶς τίνος εἵνεκα ταῦτ' ἔπραττεν ὁ Φίλιππος καὶ
> τί βουλόμενος· ὁ γὰρ μὴ ταῦτ' εἰδὼς μηδ' ἐξητακὼς πόρ-
> ρωθεν, οὔτ' εἰ εὔνους ἦν οὔτ' εἰ πλούσιος, οὐδὲν μᾶλλον
> ἔμελλ' ὅ τι χρὴ ποιεῖν εἴσεσθαι οὐδ' ὑμῖν ἕξειν συμβουλεύειν.
> ἐφάνην τοίνυν οὗτος ἐν ἐκείνῃ τῇ ἡμέρᾳ ἐγὼ

> *But, as it seems, the call of the crisis on that critical day was not just*
> *for the wealthy advocate but indeed for <u>one who had closely kept track</u>*
> *<u>of</u> the events from the beginning, and who had correctly discerned*
> *what Philip was up to and what it was he was desiring to accomplish;*
> *for anyone who did not know those purposes nor had studied them*
> *for a good while back—however patriotic or however well-disposed he might be—*
> *was not the person who was going to declaim what needed to be done*
> *nor the one to offer you* [the people] *counsel. Such being the case, then,*
> *it became manifest that, on that day, I was the man!*

Comment: The perfect participle παρηκολουθηκώς refers to the necessary credentials for one to step forward and lead the Athenians against the military encroachment of Philip II of Macedon. If one had not followed Philip's "purposes and desire" as an informed contemporary, then one could not be qualified to speak for Athens when recent news of Philip's capture of Elatea came to the Athenians more than twelve years after Philip had begun his "aggression" toward Greece. One simply could not *reckon* (συλλογίζομαι) the "needs of the hour" as a "second-hand" critic, no matter how concerned or *how informed one might have been of the latest developments* of Philip's conquests. Nor could one respond to the recent news by undergoing a quick "study" (ἐξετάζω) to try to comprehend the whole series of developments and thus bring oneself up to the proper level of knowledge of the current crisis. Rather, one had to have "informed oneself" and "kept oneself informed" for some time in order to be able to discern the significance of Philip's most recent conquest of Elatea. In fact, the stock phrase "from the beginning" (ἐξ ἀρχῆς) expresses the criteria for the scope and depth of knowledge required for one who, previously informed of the earliest developments, was thus in a position to relate the more recent events to the larger whole.[19]

In a 1922 article, "The Knowledge Claimed in Luke's Preface," Henry J. Cadbury[20] correctly observed that Demosthenes had excluded any candidate from stepping forward who had not lived through the lengthy, extensive machinations of Philip as a keen observer and evaluator of those events. Yet as Demosthenes continues in the following paragraphs (173–180), he was qualified only because he had been engaged as an *observer and as an actor in Greek politics* and not because he was actually present at the battles of Philip's conquest nor a participant on the front lines. Παρακολουθέω in the *perfect* tense thus refers to one who has sometime in the past become informed and who has followed events as they continue to unfold so that a person has become familiar or trained in a particular phenomenon or historical movement. Cadbury overstated this basic grasp of the sense and referent of παρακολουθέω by placing too much emphasis on actual *eyewitness* observance. "Eyewitness" participation may, of course, be a component of "informed familiarity" but is not necessary to the import of παρακολουθέω.

Referent 2) of metaphorical sense: of/by an audience: "*follow with the mind; understand*":

Polybius, ἱστόριαι (the *Histories*) I.12.7 [12.5–9]:

We shall provide more of the context to make Polybius's argument clearer of how his audience can "follow" his performed/audible written text (of forty long volumes!). Of special interest with regard to Luke 1:1–4 is this citation from a *prologue* to Polybius's entire narrative work:

Ἡ μὲν οὖν πρώτη Ῥωμαίων ἐκ τῆς Ἰταλίας
διάβασις μετὰ δυνάμεως ἥδε καὶ διὰ ταῦτα (καὶ) κατὰ

---

19 According to *Thesaurus Linguae Graecae* (TLG) the perfect participle, παρηκολουθηκώς, occurs four times in Demosthenes's *Orations*: *De falsa legatione* 257.9 (with ἀκριβής); *In Aristocratem* 187.2 (with εἰδὼς ἀκριβῶς in parallelism with παρηκολουθηκώς); *De corona* 172.3 (with τοῖς πράγμασιν ἐξ ἀρχῆς!; see discussion above under LSJ) and *In Olympiodorum* 40.4 (with "exact [ἀκριβῶς] knowledge" in parallel with "who had followed the events [πράγματα] from the beginning [ἐξ ἀρχῆς]"); the only instance of the perfect finite παρηκολούθηκε is in *Contra Polyclem* 13.3, with ἀκριβῶς and dative object τοῖς [...] πράγμασιν, and the sense: "to have followed closely the course of events" for a long period of time and thus to be knowledgable of the circumstances of the trial.
20 Cadbury, "Knowledge Claimed," 401–20 (see n. 9).

τούτους ἐγένετο τοὺς καιρούς, ἣν οἰκειοτάτην κρίναντες
ἀρχὴν εἶναι τῆς ὅλης προθέσεως, ἀπὸ ταύτης
ἐποιησάμεθα τὴν ἐπίστασιν, ἀναδραμόντες ἔτι τοῖς
χρόνοις τοῦ μηδὲν ἀπόρημα καταλιπεῖν ὑπὲρ τῶν
κατὰ τὰς αἰτίας ἀποδείξεων. τῷ γὰρ πῶς καὶ πότε
πταίσαντες αὐτῇ τῇ πατρίδι Ῥωμαῖοι τῆς ἐπὶ τὸ
βέλτιον ἤρξαντο προκοπῆς καὶ πότε πάλιν καὶ πῶς
κρατήσαντες τῶν κατὰ τὴν Ἰταλίαν τοῖς ἐκτὸς ἐπιχειρεῖν
ἐπεβάλοντο πράγμασιν, ἀναγκαῖον ὑπελάβομεν
εἶναι <u>παρακολουθῆσαι</u> τοῖς μέλλουσι καὶ τὸ
κεφάλαιον αὐτῶν τῆς νῦν ὑπεροχῆς δεόντως συνόψεσθαι.
διόπερ οὐ χρὴ θαυμάζειν οὐδ' ἐν τοῖς
ἑξῆς, ἐάν που προσανατρέχωμεν τοῖς χρόνοις περὶ
τῶν ἐπιφανεστάτων πολιτευμάτων. τοῦτο γὰρ ποιήσομεν
χάριν τοῦ λαμβάνειν ἀρχὰς τοιαύτας, ἐξ ὧν
ἔσται σαφῶς κατανοεῖν ἐκ τίνων ἕκαστοι καὶ πότε
καὶ πῶς ὁρμηθέντες εἰς ταύτας παρεγένοντο τὰς
διαθέσεις, ἐν αἷς ὑπάρχουσι νῦν. ὃ δὴ καὶ περὶ
Ῥωμαίων ἄρτι πεποιήκαμεν.

I.12.5 *Such then were the circumstances and motive of this the first crossing of the Romans from Italy with a powerful force, an event which I take to be the most natural beginning point of this whole work. I have therefore made it my critical base, but went also somewhat further back in order to leave no possible obscurity in my statements regarding basic causes. To <u>follow out</u> this previous history–of how and when after the destruction of their home city the Romans themselves began to make progress to a better future, and, again, when and how after conquering the land of the Italians they set out on a course of foreign engagement–seems to me necessary for anyone who hopes to gain a proper overview of their present supremacy. My audience need not therefore be surprised if, in the further course of this work, from time to time I give them some of the earlier history of the most famous states; for I shall do so for the sake of establishing such fundamental beginning points as will make it clear in the sequel starting from what origins and how and when they severally reached their present position. This is precisely what I have just done concerning the Romans.*[21]

---

[21] Some modifications of Paton's (LCL 128) translation and F. W. Walbank's and C. Habicht's revisions (2010).

Comment: In this preface of his two introductory books to his larger 40-volume history, Polybius is justifying the scale, the starting point, and the sequence of his composition for his listening audience. In order for the auditors to gain an overall grasp/synopsis (συνόψεσθαι) of Rome's supremacy–that is, the main purpose of Polybius's enterprise–they will have "to follow" (παρακολουθῆσαι) the earlier events of Rome's rise by integrating them into the sequel (ἐν τοῖς ἑξῆς)[22]–that is, the reader must follow (παρακολουθέω) the sequence of Polybius's lengthy narrative (διήγησις). Only so will a clarity of understanding (σαφῶς κατανοεῖν)[23] emerge which Polybius asserts is required and which motivates him to write in the first place. Παρακολουθέω thus refers to the audience's "following with their mind" *as the text unfolds* in their hearing to comprehend the larger purposes of the author and thus be enabled to relate smaller parts (for example, events) to the larger whole. Παρακολουθῆσαι (aorist infinitive) in this prologue thus signals a noetic principle of *diegesis*: the author's intent for the larger purposes of the work can only be realized through the audience's ability to "follow" the narrative as it unfolds through its entirety.[24] Again, the basic sense of παρακολουθέω is to "follow" or "accompany" some-one/thing as he/she/it develops or occurs.

The best commentary on this narrative hermeneutic, however, is Polybius's own narrative aside (παρέκβασις[25]), later in *the body of his work*, Book III.32:

> Ἧι καὶ τοὺς ὑπολαμβάνοντας δύσκτητον εἶναι
> καὶ δυσανάγνωστον τὴν ἡμετέραν πραγματείαν διὰ
> τὸ πλῆθος καὶ τὸ μέγεθος τῶν βύβλων ἀγνοεῖν
> νομιστέον. πόσῳ γὰρ ῥᾷόν ἐστι καὶ κτήσασθαι καὶ
> διαναγνῶναι βύβλους τετταράκοντα καθαπερανεὶ
> κατὰ μίτον ἐξυφασμένας καὶ <u>παρακολουθῆσαι</u> σαφῶς
> ταῖς μὲν κατὰ τὴν Ἰταλίαν καὶ Σικελίαν καὶ Λιβύην
> πράξεσιν [...] ἢ τὰς τῶν κατὰ μέρος
> γραφόντων συντάξεις ἀναγινώσκειν ἢ κτᾶσθαι;
> [...] ἀκμὴν γάρ φαμεν ἀναγκαιότατα μέρη τῆς
> ἱστορίας εἶναι τά τ' ἐπιγινόμενα τοῖς ἔργοις καὶ
> τὰ παρεπόμενα καὶ μάλιστα τὰ περὶ τὰς αἰτίας

---

22 Cf. καθεξῆς, Luke 1:3.
23 Cf. ἐπιγνῷς [...] τὴν ἀσφάλειαν, Luke 1:4
24 For παρακολουθέω in prefaces, see further, e.g., Archimedes, *Arenarius*; Artemidorus, *Oneirocritica*; Strabo, Theophrastus; cf. also David P. Moessner, "The Lukan Prologues in the Light of Ancient Narrative Hermeneutics. παρηκολουθηκότι and the Credentialed Author," in *The Unity of Luke-Acts*, ed. Joseph Verheyden, BETL 133 (Leuven: Peeters Press, 1999): 399–417.
25 Cf., e.g., I.33.1.

> [...] ταῦτα δὴ πάντα διὰ μὲν τῶν
> γραφόντων καθόλου δυνατὸν ἐπιγνῶναι καὶ μαθεῖν,
> διὰ δὲ τῶν τοὺς πολέμους αὐτοὺς
> οἷον τὸν Περσικὸν ἢ τὸν Φιλιππικόν, ἀδύνατον[...].

Owing to this I must deem those ignorant who think that this work of mine is difficult to come by and difficult to read because of its many, lengthy volumes. For how much easier it is to acquire and to read forty volumes as connected by a single thread, as it were, and thus <u>follow</u> clearly those events involving Italy and Sicily and Libya [...] than it is to read or to acquire those works whose scope consists of limited periods [...]. For I still assert that by far the most indispensable part of a history is its dealing with those things that proceed from, or are more remote consequences of events and, most importantly, those that concern their causes. All these things one can perceive and learn through general histories, but are not at all possible through those historians of the discrete wars, such as the war with Perseus or that with Philip.

Comment: Polybius takes on his "despisers" by referring back to the basic argument of his prologue in Book I: "Following" (παρακολουθῆσαι) Polybius's particular narrative sequence by an audience, even when it involves forty volumes, will instill greater clarity and be easier to read (in the long run!) than particularized accounts whose scope or vantage point is too limited. The reason is this: Polybius interweaves nexuses of events in one part of the world with those of another part in order to illustrate a larger force or "guiding" process of "Fate" or the divine providence which is bringing about Rome's unparalleled rise to world domination. For Polybius only a "general" or "universal" history that intermeshes the causes of one series of events with those of other series can do justice to the larger pattern of fate that is taking shape. The narrative configuration or emplotment must itself lead audiences mimetically to this comprehension.

Polybius claims that his universal history is a great improvement on other accounts whose scope is too limited, whereas his particular entanglement of events provides just what the readers need "to follow" what is "indispensable" to the larger significances of Rome's unprecedented ascent to power. Παρακολουθῆσαι provides the key narrative-rhetorical term of "following with the mind" that must be met if his audiences are to grasp the overall goal for his work.

Referent 3) of metaphorical sense: of things: "*keep company with, keep close to*"; of rules: "*hold throughout*":

> Xenophon, περὶ ἱππικῆς ("On the Art of Horsemanship") 8.14:
> καὶ ἔστι μὲν τοῦτο ἐν βραχεῖ εἰπεῖν, δι' ὅλης δὲ
> τῆς ἱππικῆς <u>παρακολουθεῖ</u>. καὶ γὰρ χαλινὸν μᾶλλον ἂν
> λαμβάνοι, εἰ ὁπότε δέξαιτο ἀγαθόν τι αὐτῷ ἀποβαίνοι·
>
> *and this* [rule/maxim] *can be stated briefly but it <u>holds</u> for the whole art of horsemanship. It* [the horse] *is more likely, for instance, to receive the bit if it is rewarded as soon as it takes it.*

Comment: Παρακολουθέω in the present tense refers to that which "accompanies" or "holds throughout" a process, observance of life, truism, habit, rule of thumb, principle, et cetera as that "rule" is observed or exercised.

Referent 4) of metaphorical sense: of a logical property: for example, also of the genus; of notions *"inseparably connected"* one with another; of cause and effect; *"constant attribute"*; *"to be proper to"*:

> Aristotle, τοπικῶν (*Topica*) 125b.28–34
> Ἐνίοτε δὲ καὶ <u>τὸ παρακολουθοῦν</u> ὁπωσοῦν ὡς γένος
> τιθέασιν, οἷον τὴν λύπην τῆς ὀργῆς καὶ τὴν ὑπόληψιν τῆς
> πίστεως· ἄμφω γὰρ τὰ εἰρημένα <u>παρακολουθεῖ</u> μὲν τρόπον
> τινὰ τοῖς ἀποδοθεῖσιν εἴδεσιν, οὐδέτερον δ' αὐτῶν γένος ἐστίν.
> ὁ μὲν γὰρ ὀργιζόμενος λυπεῖται προτέρας ἐν αὐτῷ τῆς
> λύπης γενομένης· οὐ γὰρ ἡ ὀργὴ τῆς λύπης ἀλλ' ἡ λύπη
> τῆς ὀργῆς αἰτία, ὥσθ' ἁπλῶς ἡ ὀργὴ οὐκ ἔστι λύπη.
>
> *Sometimes also they* [people] *explain as genus <u>that which attends</u> in any manner* [the species], *for example, 'pain' the genus of 'anger' and 'conception' the genus of 'belief'; for both in a manner of speaking accompany the species that have been designated, but neither of them is its genus. For when the angry person experiences pain, the pain has already occurred in the person prior* [to the anger]. *For the anger is not the cause of the pain, rather the pain is the source of the anger; so that 'anger' simply is not* [a species of] *'pain.'*

Comment: Although certain phenomena "accompany/attend" (παρακολουθέω) certain basic sources of behavior or grounds for a number of responses, it does "not follow" that the accompanying behavior or phenomenon "follows" as a species from a genus. Attendant responses or "species" of behavior may or may not "follow logically" (παρακολουθέω) from a particular genus. It is obvious that παρακολουθέω in the present tense describes either a simultaneous or near-parallel development or an occurrence that "follows" directly as a *logical consequence* of or *alignment* with something else.

We may sum up the range of senses and referents treated from LSJ:
παρακολουθέω:
1.... in the *present tense* always refers to a parallel or simultaneous phenomenon, movement, development, or consequence. Whether transitive with dative object or intransitive, παρακολουθέω suggests something or someone as "accompanying" or "aligning" or "developing" or "resulting" *contemporaneously* with that which is "followed."

2.... in the *aorist tense* refers to a larger period of time or to a fact or reality that holds true for a phenomenon, movement, development, or consequence that attends, accompanies, or follows something or someone else *contemporaneously*.

3.... in the *perfect tense* refers to someone who has become "informed," "trained," or perhaps "schooled" in some matter or development that was "followed" so that one can respond to new developments of that matter as one who is *already* knowledgeable and can make judgments without having to go back and retrace developments or conduct research or learn basic elements of the particular matter or movement in question, et cetera. Hence the perfect participle παρηκολουθηκώς designates "one who has already traced, become informed or familiar with, or trained" in some matter, and, depending on context, could be translated "follower."

4. There is no occurrence of a positive literal following of one person by another; rather there are at best only 'neutral' or decidedly 'negative' examples of physical accompaniment ("dogging with insults," "pestering," etc.). No instances of famous teachers or healers or charismatic leaders or others are said to have adherents follow (παρακολουθέω) them.

2.2 W. Bauer (Danker, Arndt, Gingrich)[3]

The revision of Walter Bauer's *A Greek-English Lexicon of the New Testament*, 3rd edition, 2010 (BDAG) lists four discrete senses with multiple referents for each. We shall treat at least one referent for each sense:

1.) "to be closely associated w. someone viewed as an authority figure: *follow* lit. of direct discipleship."

Only two referents are listed, both from the Papias fragments cited in Eusebius, *Hist. eccl.* III.39.4 and 39.15:

Eusebius, ἐκκλησιαστικῆς ἱστορίας (*Ecclesiastical History*) 39.4
εἰ δέ που καὶ <u>παρηκολουθηκώς</u> τις τοῖς πρεσβυτέροις ἔλθοι,
τοὺς τῶν πρεσβυτέρων ἀνέκρινον λόγους, τί Ἀνδρέας ἢ τί Πέτρος **εἶπεν**
ἢ τί Φίλιππος ἢ τί Θωμᾶς ἢ Ἰάκωβος ἢ τί Ἰωάννης ἢ Ματθαῖος ἢ τις
ἕτερος τῶν τοῦ κυρίου μαθητῶν ἅ τε Ἀριστίων καὶ ὁ πρεσβύτερος Ἰωάννης,
τοῦ κυρίου μαθηταί, **λέγουσιν**. οὐ γὰρ τὰ ἐκ τῶν βιβλίων τοσοῦτόν με ὠφελεῖν
ὑπελάμβανον ὅσον τὰ παρὰ ζώσης φωνῆς καὶ μενούσης [emphasis mine]

For if ever any of those <u>who had followed</u> the elders would come,
I [Papias] would begin to inquire about the words of the elders,
what Andrew or Peter or Philip or Thomas or James or John or Matthew or any
*other of the disciples of the Lord **had said**, as well as those which Aristion and*
*'the elder' John, disciples of the Lord, **were continuing to say**. For I did not*
suppose that such traditions/words taken from books would be of benefit to me so
much as those words coming from a living and enduring voice.[26]

<u>39.15</u>
καὶ τοῦθ' ὁ πρεσβύτερος ἔλεγεν· Μάρκος μὲν ἑρμηνευτὴς Πέτρου γενόμενος, ὅσα
ἐμνημόνευσεν, ἀκριβῶς ἔγραψεν, οὐ μέντοι τάξει, τὰ ὑπὸ τοῦ κυρίου ἢ λεχθέντα
ἢ πραχθέντα. οὔτε γὰρ ἤκουσεν τοῦ κυρίου οὔτε <u>παρηκολούθησεν</u> αὐτῷ,
ὕστερον δέ, ὡς ἔφην, Πέτρῳ·

And this the elder was saying:[27] *"Mark who had become Peter's interpreter/*
translator wrote down with understanding/accurately all of whatever he
remembered, though not, to be sure, in an ordered narrative sequence,[28] *the*
things said or done by the Lord. For he had neither heard the Lord nor <u>followed</u>
him, but at a later time, as I have said, [followed] Peter [...].

---

26 Translation mine, from LCL Greek text: Eusebius, *The Ecclesiastical History*, LCL 153 (Cambridge: Harvard University Press, 1975), 1.292–93.

27 This translation of the imperfect, ἔλεγεν, harks back to the same use in III.39.4 of the progressive sense of λέγω in the present tense, λέγουσιν, thus echoing what John the Elder "was saying" to Papias when Papias was conducting interviews of the "elders," rather than the iterative, what John "used to"/"would say" from time to time during his preaching career.

28 Compare F. H. Colson, "Τάξει in Papias: The Gospels and the Rhetorical Schools," *JTS* 14 (1913): 62–69, on the narrative rhetorical significance of τάξις: "Rhetorical considerations had more to do than we usually realize, if not with the formation, at any rate with the acceptance of our Gospels."

Comment: This is the earliest instance of παρακολουθέω with the sense and referent of physically "following" or "attending" the activity of a famous teacher, et cetera, by an adherent or "disciple" of that person. And BDAG lists only these two passages for this positive sense of a literal following.

The finite aorist παρηκολούθησεν in section 15 is the best commentary on the perfect participle παρηκολουθηκώς of section 4: Though Mark had never "followed" Jesus as an eyewitness "apostle" or "disciple," he had "followed" Peter in Peter's later period of itinerant preaching, including especially his teaching in Rome.[29] This strong sense of παρακολουθέω referring to an adherent who follows the teaching of a movement serves, of course, Eusebius's larger purpose in citing this Papias tradition to argue for an undiluted stream of tradition stemming from Jesus himself. By relating Papias's inquiry toward the turn of the 1st to 2nd centuries of two of the "elders" concerning what the elders (as the broader authoritative group) were teaching as "words of the apostles," Eusebius can consider Papias to be passing on directly the words of those two elders (Aristion and the "elder" John) who had overlapped in physical presence and teaching authority with the period of Jesus himself. That the present tense of λέγω ("to speak," 39.4) continues to utter the words of *the apostles* (now 'factual'/'taken as a whole') aorist, εἶπεν (39.4) is necessitated by the specific intent of Papias's procedure–interviewing elders who had not necessarily physically "followed" apostles in their preaching ministry but rather who had been instructed in the teachings of the "elders" and thus could relate what the "elders" *were continuing to speak* up to the time of Papias's interview of them.

Mark's Gospel, therefore, while criticized for its insufficient and confusing "order," is defended precisely because Mark, like Peter, passes on the words and deeds of the "Lord" as one who has been trained in the tradition by the elder Peter. Consequently the perfect participle παρηκολουθηκώς in 39.4 refers to *those followers of the elders* who had been schooled in the tradition over a stretch of time and by virtue of that training "were intimately familiar with" the "words of the elders" concerning the "things said or done by the Lord." A period of literal physical "following" of the elders is *not* necessarily implied.

2.) "to be attendant upon, *follow, accompany, attend* w. dat. of pers."

Similar to LSJ's literal intransitive sense of "accrue," "result" as "a logical consequence of" or "to be proper to" a phenomenon, event, movement, et cetera, BDAG lists ten examples as diverse as "Fortune attending" a person (Demosthenes, *Against Phaenippus*, 42.21) to the behavior "proper to" a person who

---

[29] *Hist. eccl.* II.15.2.

is ambivalent in faith toward God (Philo, *The Sacrifices of Abel and Cain* 70). A typical biblical (LXX) instance of inevitable consequences for disobedience against God is 2Macc 8:11:

μακκαβαίων Β΄ (2Macc) 8:11

εὐθέως δὲ εἰς τὰς παραθαλασσίους πόλεις ἀπέστειλεν
προκαλούμενος ἐπ᾽ ἀγορασμὸν Ἰουδαίων σωμάτων ὑπισχνούμενος ἐνενήκοντα
σώματα ταλάντου παραχωρήσειν οὐ προσδεχόμενος
τὴν παρὰ τοῦ παντοκράτορος μέλλουσαν <u>παρακολουθήσειν</u> ἐπ᾽ αὐτῷ δίκην

> *So immediately he [Nicanor] sent to the towns on the seacoast, announcing to them the sale of Jewish persons/slaves by promising to hand over ninety slaves for a talent, not expecting the vengeance that was about <u>to follow</u> upon him from the Almighty.*

3.) "to conform to someone's belief or practice by paying special attention, *follow faithfully, follow as a rule.*"

μακκαβαίων Β΄ (2Macc) 9:27

πέπεισμαι γὰρ αὐτὸν ἐπιεικῶς καὶ φιλανθρώπως <u>παρακολουθοῦντα</u>
τῇ ἐμῇ προαιρέσει συμπεριενεχθήσεσθαι ὑμῖν

> *For I [Antiochus IV] am persuaded that since he <u>understands the way my mind thinks</u>, he [son of Antiochus IV] will accommodate himself favorably and graciously to your wishes.*

Comment: In this letter to rally support for his named successor shortly before his death, the tyrant Antiochus IV assures his supporters from the Jewish peoples that his son will treat them kindly since Antiochus V 'adheres to' his father's way of understanding and the commitments he has made in the past. His supporters need not fear because Antiochus V "follows" his father's priorities "as a rule." Παρακολουθέω entails both the understanding of his father's mind, having been associated with the family's political control for a longer period of time, and the regularity or consistency of Antiochus V's following his father's policies of governance.

πρὸς τιμόθεον Β΄ (2Tim) 3:10–11 (3:10)

Σὺ δὲ <u>παρηκολούθησάς</u> μου τῇ διδασκαλίᾳ, τῇ ἀγωγῇ, τῇ προθέσει,
τῇ πίστει, τῇ μακροθυμίᾳ, τῇ ἀγάπῃ, τῇ ὑπομονῇ,[11] τοῖς διωγμοῖς, τοῖς
παθήμασιν, οἷά μοι ἐγένετο ἐν Ἀντιοχείᾳ, ἐν Ἰκονίῳ, ἐν Λύστροις, οἵους
διωγμοὺς ὑπήνεγκα καὶ ἐκ πάντων με ἐρρύσατο ὁ κύριος.

You have followed my teaching, my way of life, my public commitments, my faith, my forbearing, my love, my patient endurance, my persecutions, my sufferings–the kinds of things that happened to me in Antioch, Iconium, Lystra–what persecutions I endured and how the Lord rescued me from all of them.

Comment: In this ostensible letter of "Paul an apostle of Christ Jesus" to "Timothy my beloved child" (2Tim 1:1–2), the author asserts that Timothy had adhered to the movement represented by Paul for a period of time, including the apostle's way of life and what Paul had stood for throughout his public career. The import of the finite aorist παρηκολούθησας becomes more precise in 3:14 when Timothy is singled out for all that he had learned and observed faithfully as he had been instructed by others in the same movement over the years, with Paul setting the standard "testimony" for that teaching (μαρτύριον, 1:8). Furthermore, since Timothy had been schooled in the sacred writings from his childhood (3:15), he is one who had not only become steeped in the scriptural traditions that Paul himself had taught and Timothy had "followed," but who also is entrusted with those teachings as a leader of others that imitate Paul's own legacy (for example, 4:2–μακροθύμια καὶ διδαχή; compare 2:1–3, *passim*). Παρηκολούθησας therefore functions in effect as a character description: Timothy was a model "follower" of the Pauline movement.

πρὸς τιμόθεον Α΄ (1Tim) 4:6
   Ταῦτα ὑποτιθέμενος τοῖς ἀδελφοῖς καλὸς ἔσῃ διάκονος Χριστοῦ Ἰησοῦ,
   ἐντρεφόμενος τοῖς λόγοις τῆς πίστεως καὶ τῆς καλῆς διδασκαλίας ᾗ
   παρηκολούθηκας·

If you teach these things to the brothers and sisters, you will be a good servant of Christ Jesus, seeing that you continue to be schooled in the words of the faith and in the solid teaching that you have already followed.

Comment: Different than 2Tim 3:10, the perfect finite παρηκολούθηκα ties the training Timothy has already experienced as a learned adherent of Paul's teaching (1Tim 1:1–2) to his status as one who *continues to be* schooled in the same tradition. It is clear that παρηκολούθηκα cannot suggest that Timothy has only recently been introduced to that teaching and has performed a rapid study of those traditions in order quickly to qualify himself. Rather, the context suggests just the opposite. Timothy is already qualified and recognized as a credentialed teacher. Παρηκολούθηκα depicts one who had been an adherent of the specifics of this "faith" over a longer period of time, thus making Timothy thoroughly qualified to pass the tradition on as a *trained representative* of that teaching (for example, 1:3,18; 6:12b, 20).

4.) "to pay careful attention to someth. in a segment of time, *follow a thing, follow a course of events, take note of* w. dat. of thing."

BDAG lists two types of referents: (i) events/personages/movements, et cetera over a period of time; (ii) reading/hearing of written texts as "to have a thorough grasp of certain writings." Luke 1:3 is described under this broader sense "to pay careful attention to" as: "*with a firm grasp of everything from the beginning."*

(i) Events/personages/movements, et cetera

BDAG lists Demosthenes *De Corona* 18.172 (see above for LSJ under "Metaphorical Sense: of events, persons, behavior; times and dates," etc.). BDAG also cites Demosthenes *Oration* 19.257 with its curious juxtaposition of ἀκριβέστατης ("most accurate") and the perfect participle παρηκολουθηκώς:

<u>Demosthenes, περὶ τῆς παραπρεσβείας
(*On the Dishonest Embassy/De falsa legatione*)
Oration 19</u> (257)
ἀλλὰ καὶ κατηγορῶν ἐκείνου
κακῶς λέγειν προείλετ' ἐμέ, καὶ πάλιν ἐν
τῷ δήμῳ γραφὰς ἀποίσειν καὶ τοιαῦτ' ἠπείλει. ἵνα τί;
ἵν' ὡς μετὰ πλείστης συγγνώμης παρ' ὑμῶν ὁ τὰ τούτου
πονηρεύματ' ἀκριβέστατ' εἰδὼς ἐγὼ καὶ <u>παρηκολουθηκὼς</u>
ἅπασι κατηγορῶ.

What is more, by accusing him [Timarchus] *he* [Aeschines]
*made it his point to speak evil of me, and again at the assembly he
declared he would hand deliver an indictment against me along with other
such threats. But why? So that I might receive the greatest forbearance from
you when I, who have come to have the most accurate knowledge of his evil deeds
and who* <u>have followed</u> *all his doings* <u>closely</u>, *become his accuser.*

Comment: The citizens of Athens were greatly divided over the efforts of the ten ambassadors who were sent to arrange a peace with the encroaching war machine of Philip II. Both Demosthenes and his foe Aeschines were a part of the ten, and both gave very different accounts of what took place at the first and second "embassies," each accusing the other of malfeasance and even betrayal. Demosthenes's account of the second embassy lays out the case of a treasonous Aeschines who, misleading the Athenians by a hidden desire to appease Philip, pushed for a treaty which allowed Philip to have his will against Athens's ally the Phocians. The *perfect* of παρακολουθέω is best defined by the perfect participle εἰδώς in the preceding parallel phrase: The one who has *already come to know* all about Aeschines's alleged malevolent deeds over a longer period of scrutiny is therefore "one who has followed" his misdeeds and thus is already *fully abreast* or *thoroughly informed* of Aeschines's behavior. As Aeschines's prosecutor, Demosthenes does *not* need to "conduct research" or "investigate" the charges in order to obtain crucial information.

(ii) Reading/hearing of written texts

While BDAG lists two Josephus passages in succession from *Against Apion*,[30] one for the following of events (I.53), the other for the ability to comprehend a text while it is being read (I.218), each text is important in clarifying the more precise meaning of the other:

> Josephus, περὶ ἀρχαιότητος Ἰουδαίων (*On the Antiquity of the Jews/Contra Apionem*) I.53–54.1
> Φαῦλοι δέ τινες ἄνθρωποι διαβάλλειν μου τὴν ἱστορίαν
> ἐπικεχειρήκασιν ὥσπερ ἐν σχολῇ μειρακίων γύμνασμα προκεῖσθαι
> νομίζοντες κατηγορίας παραδόξου καὶ διαβολῆς, δέον ἐκεῖνο γιγνώσκειν,
> ὅτι δεῖ τὸν ἄλλοις παράδοσιν πράξεων ἀληθινῶν ὑπισχνούμενον
> αὐτὸν ἐπίστασθαι ταύτας πρότερον ἀκριβῶς ἢ <u>παρηκολουθηκότα</u>
> τοῖς γεγονόσιν ἢ παρὰ τῶν εἰδότων πυνθανόμενον. ὅπερ
> ἐγὼ μάλιστα περὶ ἀμφοτέρας νομίζω πεποιηκέναι τὰς πραγματείας·

> *There are certain base persons who have attempted to slander my history, regarding it as if it were a prize set for a competition among school boys; a bizarre and twisted calumny this; certainly they are obligated to recognize that one who promises others to deliver a narrative of true events must necessarily first have an accurate knowledge of these events, either by <u>having an informed familiarity with</u> the things that happened or by inquiring from those who were in the know about them—the very requirements I consider that I more than amply met for both of my works.*

Comment: *Contra Apionem* 53 is part of a larger argument (§§ 6–56) against critics of his *War* and of his *Antiquities* where Josephus asserts that Greek history writers show much less regard for historical records and historical accuracy than other peoples, especially when compared with the Jewish people. In §§ 44–56 he expounds at length how it is that he is a more qualified writer of the history of the war with Rome than others of late who have published their histories "who neither went out to the places of battle nor traveled anywhere near the actions that took place" (I.46). Josephus, on the contrary, has "composed a true account" as

---

[30] In Greek: *On the Antiquity of the Jews*.

"one present in person at all the events" (τοῖς πράγμασιν αὐτὸς ἅπασι παρατυχών, § 47).³¹ So confident is Josephus of his final narrative account (ἐποιησάμην τῶν πράξεων τὴν παράδοσιν, § 50) that, in countering his critics, he can call as his witnesses (μαρτυρεῖς, § 50), if need be, no one less than Vespasian or Titus, commanders in chief of the war. Other notables who have read Josephus's *War* have already "borne testimony" (ἐμαρτύρησαν, § 52) to its "safeguarding of the truth" (§§ 49–52).

Does Josephus imply that he was "one who had followed" (παρηκολουθηκώς) the occurrences by being physically present at all the battle sites he describes? Does he suggest that he was at each site while the battles were still being fought, or does he mean subsequent visits after the war was over? Moreover, is he linking his "following" with the *War* and the "inquiring from those in the know" (παρὰ τῶν εἰδότων πυνθανόμενον) with his *Antiquities* since he obviously could *not* have been an eyewitness to the vast majority of Israel's history?³²

This explanation runs afoul, however, when Josephus proceeds in §§ 54–56 to describe his qualifications for each work:

τὴν μὲν γὰρ ἀρχαιολογίαν, ὥσπερ ἔφην, ἐκ τῶν ἱερῶν γραμμάτων
μεθερμήνευκα γεγονὼς ἱερεὺς ἐκ γένους καὶ μετεσχηκὼς τῆς
φιλοσοφίας τῆς ἐν ἐκείνοις τοῖς γράμμασι· τοῦ δὲ πολέμου τὴν ἱστορίαν

---

31 For discussions of Josephus's motives, "objectivity," and critics of his *War*, see, e.g., Henry St. John Thackeray, *Josephus: The Man and the Historian* (New York: Ktav, 1967), 23–50; Shaye J. D. Cohen, *Josephus in Galilee and Rome* (Leiden: Brill, 1979); Giorgio Jossa, "Josephus' Action in Galilee during the Jewish War," in *Josephus and the History of the Greco-Roman Period*, ed. Fausto Parente and Joseph Sievers (Leiden: Brill, 1994): 265–78; Martin Goodman, "Josephus As Roman Citizen," in *Josephus and the History of the Greco-Roman Period*, ed. Fausto Parente and Joseph Sievers (Leiden: Brill, 1994): 329–38; Per Bilde, *Flavius Josephus between Jerusalem and Rome*, JSPSup (Sheffield: JSOT, 1988), 191–206; Helgo Lindner, "Eine offene Frage zur Auslegung des Bellum-Proömiums," in *Josephus-Studien*, ed. Otto Betz, Klaus Haacker, Martin Hengel (Göttingen: Vandenhoeck & Ruprecht, 1974): 254–59; Menahem Stern, "Josephus and the Roman Empire as Reflected in *The Jewish War*," in *Josephus, Judaism, and Christianity*, ed. Louis H. Feldman and Gohei Hata (Detroit, MI: Wayne State University Press, 1987): 71–80; Heinz Kreissig, "A Marxist View of Josephus' Account of the Jewish War," in *Josephus, the Bible, and History*, ed. Louis H. Feldman and Gohei Hata (Detroit, MI: Wayne State University Press, 1988): 265–77; Mireille Hadas-Lebel, *Flavius Josephus: Eyewitness to Rome's First-Century Conquest of Judea*, trans. Richard Miller (New York: Macmillan, 1993); Louis H. Feldman, *Josephus and Modern Scholarship (1937–1980)* (Berlin: de Gruyter, 1984), 117–20.

32 Cadbury, "Knowledge Claimed," 404n12, assumes that by Josephus's mention of his *two* works of history in the discussion of the *two* means of acquiring historical knowledge, Josephus is providing an illustration of "each method." The larger context, however, tells against this inference.

ἔγραψα πολλῶν μὲν αὐτουργὸς πράξεων, πλείστων δ' αὐτόπτης
γενόμενος, ὅλως δὲ τῶν λεχθέντων ἢ πραχθέντων οὐδοτιοῦν ἀγνοήσας.
πῶς οὖν οὐκ ἂν θρασεῖς τις ἡγήσαιτο τοὺς ἀνταγωνίζεσθαί
μοι περὶ τῆς ἀληθείας ἐπικεχειρηκότας, οἳ κἂν τοῖς τῶν
αὐτοκρατόρων ὑπομνήμασιν ἐντυχεῖν λέγωσιν, ἀλλ' οὔ γε καὶ τοῖς
ἡμετέροις τῶν ἀντιπολεμούντων πράγμασι παρέτυχον.

With regard to my Antiquities, *as I have said, I have translated from the sacred scriptures, since I am a priest from priestly stock and have been steeped in the philosophy of those writings; with respect to the* War, *I wrote the history since I had been an actor in many of the events and an eyewitness through most of them. Overall, nothing of whatever was said or done escaped my knowledge. How then can one but not regard as brazen those critics who challenge its authenticity, even if, as they claim, they have read the reminiscences of the imperial commanders yet certainly do not have any first-hand knowledge of those things that happened in our camp across the way?*

As Josephus sets out to write his *Antiquities*, rather than "inquire" (πυνθάνομαι) into the meaning of the scriptures from people such as priests who were the authoritative interpreters of the sacred books, he *translates* them since he is already well-versed in their meaning! He has already from his youth been schooled in the meanings of the sacred writings and therefore can "follow" (παρακολουθέω) them with "informed familiarity" when he reads them.

Later in the same Book (I.213–18), Josephus says as much:

οἱ πολλοὶ δὲ τῶν
εἰρημένων ἀνδρῶν τῆς μὲν ἀληθείας τῶν ἐξ ἀρχῆς πραγμάτων
διήμαρτον, ὅτι μὴ ταῖς ἱεραῖς ἡμῶν βίβλοις ἐνέτυχον, κοινῶς μέντοι
περὶ τῆς ἀρχαιότητος ἅπαντες μεμαρτυρήκαν, ὑπὲρ ἧς τὰ νῦν
λέγειν προεθέμην. ὁ μέντοι Φαληρεὺς Δημήτριος καὶ Φίλων ὁ
πρεσβύτερος καὶ Εὐπόλεμος οὐ πολὺ τῆς ἀληθείας διήμαρτον.
οἷς συγγιγνώσκειν ἄξιον· οὐ γὰρ ἐνῆν αὐτοῖς μετὰ πάσης
ἀκριβείας τοῖς ἡμετέροις γράμμασι <u>παρακολουθεῖν</u>.

The majority of these authors are in error in their utterances concerning the truth of our events that go way back to the beginning,[33] *since they had not read our*

---

[33] The rendering of the stock phrase "from the beginning" is interpreted a bit more literally here since Josephus places considerable emphasis on the fact that Hebrew "history" begins with the creation of the world and the first human beings and continues on uninterrupted through many

sacred books, although all are in agreement in documenting our antiquity, concerning which point I am at present attempting to demonstrate. To be sure, Demetrius Phalereus, the elder Philo, and Eupolemus have not strayed far from the truth–for which they are worthy of our pardon; indeed, these historians lacked the ability to <u>follow</u> our scriptures with greater accuracy.

Comment: Although a Demetrius, Philo, or Eupolemus have taken the time to "inquire" into Israel's scriptural records, they do not possess the ability to comprehend more fully the Scriptures when they read them, though Josephus must *not* be referring foremost to their lack of ability to understand Hebrew, since Josephus himself appears at times to rely on a Lucianic version of the Old Greek.[34] Rather, a Demetrius or Philo and others may "be excused" for their lack of "insider" knowledge since they do not have the long years of training of one "schooled" in the way of life of these sacred writings. By contrast, Josephus possesses the requisite credentials to *follow* (with his mind) the meaning of these texts since he, as he says in introducing his qualifications (I.42–46), by "instinct (σύμφυτον) with every Jew, from the day of his birth has come to regard them as the decrees of God, to adhere closely to them, and, above all, if necessary, gladly to die for them" (§ 42). In effect, Josephus is saying that his whole life is tantamount to an "inquiry" of Israel's past through immersion in their Scriptures, and therefore he has an immediate ability to "follow with his mind the meaning" of those ancient events by "following" (παρακολουθεῖν) the sequence of the texts.

To return to the *War* and the significance of Josephus's claim to have "followed" everything: Obviously he could not have "kept abreast" of every major event either as an "actor" or as an "eyewitness." In I.49–50, however, Josephus goes out of his way to show how he could "know" what was going on, even while he was a prisoner:

> ἐν ᾧ χρόνῳ γενομένην τῶν πραττομένων οὐκ ἔστιν ὃ τὴν ἐμὴν γνῶσιν
> διέφυγεν· καὶ γὰρ τὰ κατὰ τὸ στρατόπεδον τὸ Ῥωμαίων ὁρῶν ἐπι-
> μελῶς ἀνέγραφον καὶ τὰ παρὰ τῶν αὐτομόλων ἀπαγγελλόμενα μόνος
> αὐτὸς συνίειν. εἶτα σχολῆς ἐν τῇ Ῥώμῃ λαβόμενος, πάσης μοι τῆς

---

centuries in contrast to the "carefree" attitude of the Greeks, especially regarding the earliest times.

34 See, e.g., Thackeray, *Josephus*, 73–99; Sid Z. Leiman, "Josephus and the Canon of the Bible," in *Josephus, the Bible, and History*, ed. Louis H. Felman and Gohei Hata (Detroit, MI: Wayne State University Press, 1989): 50–58; Steve Mason, "Josephus, *Jewish Antiquities*," in *The Eerdmans Dictionary of Early Judaism*, ed. John J. Collins and Daniel C. Harlow (Grand Rapids, MI: Eerdmans, 2010): 834–38.

πραγματείας ἐν παρασκευῇ γεγενημένης [...] οὕτως ἐποιησάμην
τῶν πράξεων τὴν παράδοσιν.

During the time that I was [a prisoner] *there was not anything that went on that escaped my knowledge. For I would keep a careful record of those things that went on under my watchful eye in the Roman camp, and I myself was the only one who could comprehend the information that was being brought in by those who were deserting. Then in the period of leisure that I received in Rome, when all of my materials were ready at hand [...] in this way I began to compose my narrative of the events.*

Comment: Similar to Demosthenes's monitoring of the rising tsunami of Philip's military might,[35] so Josephus has kept informed throughout the war with Rome through a variety of informants and written communications. When new information from reliable participants comes his way, he is already an "informed follower" of the progress of the war and thus is duly qualified to take in any new information and integrate it with all the rest of the developments.

Josephus's response to his critics, then, is to argue that he is a qualified "follower," whether of staying informed of the events of the war as they were unfolding or of the flow of the Scripture texts as they were unrolling through reading. He clearly distances himself from those who, not "in the know," need through "inquiry" to become "knowledgeable." Thus what παρακολουθέω does *not* indicate is one who, at whatever point, whether in the midst of a longer series of events or absorbed in the extended argumentation or plot of a longer text, has to go back and 'investigate' or 'figure out' or 'become informed' about all the essential matters before one can understand the present context and communicate the larger complex to others. This "reading" of Josephus is confirmed in the prologue to his *Antiquities* I.4–5 where, again presenting his credentials and comparing the present undertaking to his earlier *War*, Josephus states that he himself will "translate" (μεθερμηνεύω) the "Hebrew writings" (I.5). He is doing this work, he says, in order "to benefit" an "ignorant" public (I.4), whereas with his *War*, as one "who had learned by experience" (πείρᾳ μαθών) in the actual battles, he was "forced to narrate it in detail because of those history writers who were inflicting abuse upon the truth" (I.4).

---

[35] See above under *De Corona* 172; both Demosthenes and Josephus claim they are the most *qualified* to render an authentic, truthful account.

We may sum up the range of senses and referents treated from BDAG:
παρακολουθέω:

1.... in the *present tense*, similar to LSJ, refers to a simultaneous or contemporaneous movement, development, alignment with, or consequence from some parallel movement, development, or alignment, including the "following" of another person's "way of thinking" (for example, Antiochus V of Antiochus IV), whether in real time or in the unfolding points of view in a written text (for example, Josephus of the Jewish Scriptures).

2.... in the *aorist tense*, similar to LSJ, can refer to a period as a whole during which time a person may be characterized as a disciple of a teacher (Peter with Jesus) or the follower of a disciple of a famous teacher (Mark with Peter, Timothy with Paul), though only context determines whether this "following" implies a literal physical accompaniment.

3.... in the *perfect tense*, again similar to LSJ, may refer to those who have been immersed or schooled or trained in a tradition for some time. Consequently, the perfect participle, depending on context, may be translated as "one who has an informed familiarity or knowledge of" a particular movement, famous teacher, developing thought, or sequence of texts. Rhetorically it may signal "one who has the necessary informed familiarity to understand rightly" and is therefore properly credentialed to assume a particular responsibility.

4. The only occurrences up to the end of the 2nd century CE of παρακολουθέω as a positive following of a teacher or revered leader are in the Papias fragments of Eusebius in Book III, where physical accompaniment is included by virtue of the context (Mark following Peter in his itinerant preaching). The Pastorals instance the first occurrence of "following" a religious movement as a whole, with a proven "faith" or "trust" as a mark of the loyalty of that "following." Curiously, the Pastorals also adduce the "following" of an apostle by an adherent of "the faith" (Timothy with Paul) in a way which continues the following of the master (Jesus) who is still perceived to be present. Evidently the early Christian claim of Jesus's resurrection from the dead facilitates the unparalleled semantic expression of two generations "following" one who, though previously acknowledged as having died, is still present "to rescue" the "follower," as 2Tim 3:10–11 indicates and 1Tim 4:6 probably suggests.

3 Conclusions

Our conclusions do not square with the commonly translated "after investigating everything carefully from the very first" (NRSV)[36] for Luke 1:3a or similar renderings as "one who has gone back and traced everything carefully ...," et cetera.[37]

---

[36] For "investigate," see, e.g., also NASB; CEB; NAB; NIV; CJB; LEW (Lewis Trans. of Peshitta, 1896); *contra* KJV: "having had perfect understanding of all things from the very first"; RSV: "having followed all things closely from some time past"; Rheims: "having diligently attained to all things from the beginning"; ESV: "having followed all things closely for some time past"; NET: "because I have followed all things carefully from the beginning"; George M. Lamsa, trans., *Peshitta* (San Francisco, CA: Harper & Row, 1933), 1012: "because I was near and considered them all very carefully"; cf. James Hope Moulton and George Milligan, *The Vocabulary of the Greek Testament* (Grand Rapids, MI: Eerdmans, 1930), 486: Luke had such familiarity with the traditions and kept abreast of them "that his witness is practically contemporary witness"; for various renderings in German *exegesis*, see Michael Wolter, *Das Lukasevangelium*, HNT 5 (Tübingen: Mohr Siebeck, 2008), 64–67, citing my article on Josephus's use of παρακολουθέω, who argues himself against "investigate," (e.g., "allem nachgegangen") and translates: "der ich mich an alles von Anfang an genau gehalten habe."

[37] Cf., e.g., RV: "having traced the course of all things accurately from the first"; NEB: "as one who has gone over the whole course of these events in detail"; Tyndale NT: "as soon as I had searched out diligently all things from the beginning"; J. B. Phillips (1959): "since I have traced the course of these happenings carefully from the beginning"; TEV (1966): "because I have carefully studied all these matters from their beginning"; JB: "after carefully going over the whole story from the beginning"; NJB (same as JB); CCB: "after I myself had carefully gone over the whole story from the beginning"; etc. Cf. commentators, e.g., Luke Timothy Johnson, *The Gospel of Luke*, SP (Collegeville, MN: Liturgical Press, 1991), 27: "since I have examined everything carefully from the start"; I. Howard Marshall, *The Gospel of Luke*, NIGTC (Exeter: Paternoster Press, 1978), 42: "thoroughly investigated all the facts"; Darrell L. Bock, *Luke*, BECNT (Grand Rapids, MI: Baker, 1994), 1:60: "his [Luke's] ability 'to follow' the events carefully can result only from investigation"; Frederick W. Danker, *Jesus and the New Age* (Philadelphia, PA: Fortress Press, 1988), 24: "must refer to his investigation of, not merely involvement in, these events" (Danker would change his mind when he edits the third English edition BDAG [2000], see above); Charles H. Talbert, *Reading Luke* (New York: Crossroad, 1984), 8: "The term *parakolouthēkoti* [sic] should be translated 'investigated' (as in Demosthenes, *De Cor.* 53)" (but see n. 19 on Desmosthenes above); Ernst Haenchen, *The Acts of the Apostles* (Oxford: Blackwell, 1971), 97: "was obliged to gather and sift the 'sources' [...] and immerse himself in the psychological climate of past history. He [Luke], had [...] to overcome the historical remoteness of this bygone life with the methods of the historian"; A. R. C. Leaney, *The Gospel according to Luke*, 2nd ed. (London: A.C. Black, 1966), 77: "having given minute attention to everything from the beginning"; Eduard Schweizer, *The Good News according to Luke*, trans. David E. Green (Atlanta, GA: John Knox, 1984), 12: "the author's studies must be meant"; etc. *Contra*: David L. Tiede, *Luke*, Augsburg (Minneapolis, MN: Augsburg Publishing, 1988), 36: "this author claims intimate acquaintance with the beginnings or reliable accounts of the beginnings [...] these stories have been told and retold in the interim;"

Much of the justification of these and similar translations in which Luke takes on the project of an historian to research and figure the significance of the "fulfilled events"–before he too compiles a narrative account–stems from Walter Bauer's fifth German edition (1958), especially as it was known in the English speaking world through the translation and augmentation of F. Wilbur Gingrich and Frederick W. Danker in the second English edition of 1979.[38] The third of three senses is listed there as *"follow a thing, trace or investigate a thing* w. dat. of the thing," with Luke 1:3a rendered: "having investigated everything carefully from the beginning." More than that, this same English edition lists Demosthenes's *De corona* 18.172, *De falsa legatione* 19.257, and the two passages from Josephus's *Contra Apionem* Book I (all treated above) as instances of "to investigate." But as our analysis above shows, these examples simply *cannot* be pressed to mean "to inquire after" (the meaning/significance) of anything.

What then do our investigations suggest is the sense and referent of παρηκολουθηκότι in Luke 1:3 for the author of Luke and Acts? We can rule out the possibility that Luke claims to have *physically accompanied* or "followed" (παρηκολουθηκότι) "all" (πᾶσιν, dative plural masculine) of "the attendants" (οἱ [...] ὑπηρέται) or even "eyewitnesses of the word/message" (οἱ [...] αὐτόπται [...] τοῦ λόγου) who formed the first stage in developing the oral and written traditions that hark back to "a beginning" of Jesus's public career (οἱ ἀπ' ἀρχῆς [...] γενόμενοι τοῦ λόγου, Luke 1:2–3). The credibility of "all/every" (πάντα, Luke 1:3) becomes stretched even beyond acceptable rhetorical exaggeration if Luke is indicating that he has followed many or, at the least, some of the significant characters who "from the beginning" had been privy to the words and deeds of Jesus in his public career. Since Luke has Peter define "the beginning" as "the whole time in which the Lord Jesus went in and out among us, beginning (ἀρξάμενος) from the baptism of John until the time he was taken up from us" (Acts 1:22a) and calibrates this time frame to the "first volume I composed" with "all the things that Jesus began to do and to teach until the day he was taken up" (τὸν μὲν πρῶτον λόγον ἐποιησάμην περὶ πάντων [...] ὧν ἤρξατο ὁ Ἰησοῦς ποιεῖν τε καὶ διδάσκειν ἄχρι ἧς ἡμέρας [...] ἀνελήμφθη, Acts 1:1), the late appearance of a "we" group (Acts 16:10–18; *passim*) who do accompany the ὑπηρέτης, Paul (compare Acts 26:16) falls too late and fulfills too little to constitute a credible "claim" for

---

Wolter, *Das Lukasevangelium* (see previous note); J. T. Carroll, *Luke: A Commentary*, NTL (Louisville, KY: Westminster John Knox, 2012), 18–21: "carefully attended to (followed) all the important events" (p. 21) [the type of 'attending' not spelled out].
38 F. Wilbur Gingrich and Frederick W. Danker, eds., *A Greek-English Lexicon of the New Testament and Other Early Christian Literature*, 2nd ed. (Chicago, IL: University of Chicago Press, 1979).

literally following "all."³⁹ When we see also that the one other instance in which Luke employs ἄνωθεν, he does so by coordinating the span of time again with a "beginning," this time the beginning of Paul's life. Already "from my youth from the beginning" (τὴν ἐκ νεότητος τὴν ἀπ' ἀρχῆς), the credibility of Paul living his life according to the "strictest party of our religious devotion," namely the Pharisees (Acts 26:4–5), can be "attested" (ἐὰν θέλωσι μαρτυρεῖν). Thus, following the precedent in Luke 1:2–3, Luke has Paul assert that "all the Jews have known *for a long time/from the start* [...] that I have lived as a Pharisee" (προγινώσκοντές με ἄνωθεν [...] ἔζησα Φαρισαῖος, Acts 26:5). And thus Luke cannot be said literally to "have followed" "all," if even some, of the "eyewitnesses/attendants" "for a long time"/"from way back" relative to "the beginning"–"beginning from the baptism of John."

Consequently πᾶσιν as the direct object of παρηκολουθηκότι must be the neuter dative plural⁴⁰ and refer to "all" the "matters/events" (πράγματα) that characterize the scope of the traditions "delivered over" by eyewitnesses/attendants of the first stage to the "us" of the second stage, the writers of a narrative account such as the "many" and our author himself (Luke 1:1–3). This "all" (πάντα) thus forms the greater pool of "matters" and "events" from which Luke composes his "first volume concerning all (πάντα) that Jesus began to do and to teach" (Acts 1:1→Luke 1:3) and corresponds also to the events and matters treated in Luke's second volume that will give a Theophilus a greater "certainty" regarding those "events/matters that have come to fruition in our midst" (Luke 1:1→1:4). But what more precisely does Luke mean that "he has followed" "all" of these traditions? How, if at all, does this credential of "following" qualify him as a second level tradent to write his own version of these occurrences of consequence?

The closest parallels to Luke's task that requires considerable expertise in conveying information about a movement that stretches back to a "beginning" time–for which Luke himself had no direct "eyewitness" knowledge–are the situations of the writers Demosthenes (*de Corona* 18.172) and Josephus (*Contra Apionem* I.53 and 218):

---

39 This literal following was of course the view of some patristic exegetes (e.g., Irenaeus, *Haer.* 3.10 [Luke is a *sectator et discipulus apostolorum*], a "follower and disciple of the apostles"). Proponents of this interpretation are quick to point out that the "we sections" of Acts attest to this very meaning–the author as one who accompanies Paul (but see above, esp. n. 4). One would have to provide other evidence to establish that the "we" refers to the author of Luke and Acts [but see Conclusions Chapter below for added discussion].

40 If every other consideration were equal, the lack of a definite article for πάντα [πᾶσιν] in Luke 1:3 on grammatical grounds, in and of itself, would give a nudge to "events"/"matters" over "persons."

1. Neither Demosthenes nor Josephus could claim to have unmediated knowledge of the beginnings of Philip's maneuvering against Athens or of the many battles of the Jewish War against Rome, respectively (especially when Josephus was incarcerated!). Like Luke, neither writer pretended to experience directly what had happened nor claim to know the immediate significance of those events perceived and formulated by those involved in the events as they were unfolding. Rather, both relied on direct participants, oral informants, letters, legal documents, formal charges, public gatherings, et cetera in order to "stay abreast" of the larger movement as it continued to develop. And precisely because each had had an ongoing, firsthand involvement in the larger chain of events "from the beginning" of that movement–Demosthenes already at age 27 when Philip began his encroachment[41] and Josephus as one of the leaders of the outbreak of Jewish military resistance against Rome[42]–neither actor had to become trained or re-schooled in these affairs when new impulses came or potentially significant developments occurred. Both could legitimately claim to be "one who has an informed familiarity" (παρηκολουθηκώς) with the whole process.

But if Luke cannot claim temporal overlap of his own experience with the 'events *of the beginning*,' what force does this analogy actually possess? To be sure, Luke does claim "for a long time," "from way back" to have been "one who has followed" this movement (παρηκολουθηκότι ἄνωθεν) relative to a much longer process–even if literal physical following is excluded. Is this "following," like that of Demosthenes and Josephus, primarily noetic in character, as his intent to deliver a "greater certainty concerning the traditions from which you [Theophilus] have already been instructed" might suggest (Luke 1:4)?

2. The relation of the perfect of παρακολουθέω in 1Tim 4:6 to the aorist in 2Tim 3:10 and Timothy's purported relation to Paul is particularly instructive here. Whatever the actual setting(s) of the compositions of 1 and 2 Timothy, the message of 1Tim 4:6 is that since Timothy has been "trained" (ἐντρέφομαι) for some time in the past and continues to be "schooled" in the "messages/words/content" (λόγοι) of "the faith" which goes back to Paul, he not only has the epistemological qualifications to pass the content on to others, but he has also been trained in a way in which his relation to this knowledge is one of *adherence*. This 'track record' of observance over a longer period makes Timothy admirably suited to be a tradent of this "faith." Thus in the ostensively later correspondence of

---

41 See esp. *De Corona* 295–296.
42 See *Contra Apionem* I.48: "I was leading the opposition among those whom we call Galileans as long as resistance was possible" (that is, before his capture; cf. *War* III.408).

2Tim 3:10,[43] Paul looks back at Timothy's long record and pronounces him a faithful "follower."

Luke too presents his "following" as particularly noteworthy *vis-à-vis* others who are reportedly attempting something similar in offering epitomes of the larger enterprise of "fulfilled events" (Luke 1:1). Since the author of the Third Gospel is tooled with traditions that go back "to the beginning" and has "followed" these traditions "for a long time" in a way in which he can apparently present them in a narrative summary that delivers a "firmer grasp" of their significance, Luke also presents himself as "one who has an informed familiarity" (παρηκολουθηκώς) with them all. Clearly at some point in the past, Luke began to be instructed in the import of these traditions such that when he "sets to hand" to re-configure these events, he has already been appropriately trained to be their interpreter. Hence, though the noetic dimension is uppermost, faithful adherence cannot be entirely removed from Luke's "familiarity."

3. Luke's claim as one temporally and spatially removed from the critical events marked by "a beginning" and yet qualified to represent in summary fashion their true significance has an intriguing parallel in Josephus's framing of his special qualifications to write *both* of his histories. This Jewish freedom fighter turned Roman informant grounds his credentials "to follow" both *events* and *texts* upon the *same foundation*: sustained immersion in the traditions of Israel, whether through active engagement in matters of more recent times or by being thoroughly "steeped" in the classic recordings of Israel's formative events that go back to "a beginning" (τῶν ἐξ ἀρχῆς πραγμάτων, *C. Ap.* I.213). Consequently, whether in reciting new experiences of Israel's rebellion against Rome or in explaining the God of Israel's unique rescues and judgments of this people throughout their ancient history, Josephus is one who has been saturated in "all" of these traditions. His more recent entanglements in the Jewish opposition are *of a kind* with his intimate knowledge of the philosophy of the Jewish religion that establishes and motivates his adherence to its scriptural laws and ethical demands. By contrast, competent, even gifted historians "do not have it in their power to follow with greater accuracy the meaning of our sacred scriptures" (οὐ γὰρ ἐνῆν αὐτοῖς μετὰ πάσης ἀκριβείας τοῖς ἡμετέροις γράμμασι παρακολουθεῖν, *C. Ap.* 218) since they lack the requisite training essential to this task. Josephus, on the other hand–doubly suited by his engagement and schooling–"has an informed familiarity" (παρηκολουθηκώς) like no other to represent the nation of Israel in both past and present.

---

[43] Paul is now in prison, looking back over many years of his teaching and contemplating his own death (e.g., 2Tim 1:3–7,13–14; 4:6–8).

Similarly, Luke describes himself as situated and saturated in more recent "events of fulfillment" stamped by "a beginning" and "passed on to *us*" (περὶ τῶν πεπληροφορημένων ἐν ἡμῖν πραγμάτων, καθὼς παρέδοσαν ἡμῖν οἱ ἀπ' ἀρχῆς) (Luke 1:1–2a, emphasis mine). The passive voice of πληροφορέω, "to bring to fruition, to fill fully, bring full measure," suggests that the experiences of the author in the midst of an "us" and of a larger implied audience are *filling out* or *complementing* or even *bringing to their intended goal* the larger series and sum of events that go back to "the beginning" and that will culminate in defining the whole "party" or group (ἡ αἵρεσις) of an old yet new religious movement (Acts 28:22). Παρηκολουθηκώς would thus explain how it is that Luke can vie with "many" for re-configuring and re-defining this entire movement. His own experienced training, like Josephus's, gives him special credentials to "write for you a new narrative sequence" (καθεξῆς σοι γράψαι) that elaborates and extends the significances and ramifications from earlier stages, even from the origins of the movement, of "matters" that have continued to develop "in our midst" (Luke 1:1–3).

4. The qualification of παρηκολουθηκότι by the adverbial ἀκριβῶς (Luke 1:3a) sits comfortably with the rendering "informed familiarity." Ἀκριβῶς often modifies verbs of perception and cognition with the sense of "strict conformity to a standard or norm, w. focus on careful attention, *accurately, carefully, well*" (BDAG *ad loc*): to "see" (βλέπειν[44]), "hear" (ἀκούω),[45] "pay close attention to" (προσέχειν),[46] "know" (γινώσκειν[47]/εἰδέναι[48]), "perceive" (κατανοεῖν),[49] "scrutinize"/"examine" (ἐξετάζειν),[50] "inquire"/"do research" (ἱστορῆσαι),[51] et cetera. LSJ delineates "to a nicety, precisely" with verbs of perception (εἰδέναι, ἐπίστασθαι, καθορᾶν, μαθεῖν, etc.), approximating a meaning the opposite of ἁπλῶς ("in one way," "in one sense," "simply, plainly," "generally") or of τύπῳ ("in outline, roughly"), thus suggesting the sense "in detail," "fully," "thoroughly," "accurately."

Dionysius of Halicarnassus provides the curious sense and referent of "following" (παρακολουθεῖν) (with the mind) a *written text* ἀκριβῶς ("with understanding," "fully," "reliably"). In his critique of Thucydides's "narrative arrangement" (ἡ οἰκονομία), he complains that the Achaean historian confuses his audience by his jumbled and half-completed sequences of events:

---

44 E.g., POxy 1381.
45 E.g., Thucydides 1.34.1.
46 E.g., Barnabas 7:4.
47 E.g., Diodorus Siculus 11.41.5.
48 E.g., Epictetus 1.27.17
49 E.g., Hermas (Shepherd) 9.6.3
50 E.g., Demosthenes 6.37; Josephus, *Antiquities* 3.70
51 E.g., Stephanus Byzantius, see under Χαράκμωβα.

> *As we would now expect, we wander around here and there, finding it difficult to follow the events that have been described* (δυσκόλως τοῖς δηλουμένοις παρακολουθοῦμεν), *because our mind is confused by the scattering of the events* (ἐν τῷ διασπᾶσθαι τὰ πράγματα) *and cannot easily* (ῥᾳδίως) *or reliably/with understanding* (ἀκριβῶς) *remember the half-completed references which it has heard* [...]. *For none of the historians who succeeded him divided his narrative by summers and winters, but all followed the well-worn paths which lead to a clarity of understanding* (ἡ σαφήνεια) (*de Thucydides* 9).[52]

"To follow" ἀκριβῶς leads to a *clearness of understanding* what the author is intending to convey and suggests a *fuller* or *more thorough comprehension* enabled by this "following" of the overall "arrangement." In the case of the second Papias citation,[53] Mark "writes" his gospel as an "accurate" or "reliable" "remembering" (ὅσα ἐμνημόνευσεν ἀκριβῶς ἔγραψεν) of Peter's teaching, notwithstanding the allegation that Mark's "mistake" makes it difficult essentially to "follow" Mark's sub-standard narrative sequence (τάξις).[54]

To be sure, Luke can use ἀκριβῶς with verbs of cognition in the sense of "accurately" or "reliably," as, for example, in Acts 18:25–26 when Pricilla and Aquila give special instruction (ἐκτίθεσθαι) to Apollos, who is thereby changed from one who teaches "accurately/reliably" to one who now expounds "the way" "more accurately" or "more reliably" (ἀκριβέστερος).[55] But in Acts 23:15, 20 ἀκριβῶς takes on the sense of "thorough" or "fully": "Jews from Asia" who are spearheading opposition to Paul want the leaders of the Sanhedrin to feign a "more thorough" or "fuller inquiry (διαγινώσκειν ἀκριβέστερον) into the charges against him" (compare ἀκριβέστερον πυνθάνεσθαι, 23:20). This latter sense fits the context of Luke 1:3 quite well: "*it seemed good to me also as one who has a thoroughly informed familiarity with all the events from way back/from the top* [...]." Luke has had sufficient training and experience for his task. He does not need a Priscilla or Aquila to import more instruction, whether more "thoroughly" or more "accurately."

---

[52] My translation from the Greek text of the LCL, *Dionysius of Halicarnassus: The Critical Essays* 1.484 [emphasis mine].
[53] Eusebius, *Hist. eccl.* III.39.15; see above.
[54] It is simply not the case that the range of senses and referents for ἀκριβῶς must favor the cognitive function of inquiry as in "to investigate," "to research" for Luke 1:3 as Ernst Haenchen argued: "Das 'Wir' in der Apostelgeschichte und das Itinerar," *ZTK* 58 (1961): 363–65.
[55] See also Acts 24:22 where governor Felix is "quite well-informed (ἀκριβέστερον εἰδώς) about the way."

More than that, again it is both Demosthenes and Josephus who adduce the conjunction of ἀκριβῶς with the perfect παρηκολουθηκώς precisely with the association we are discovering for Luke 1:3. In addition to *De corona* 18 (172.3), where the perfect participle employs the dative direct object τοῖς πράγμασιν ἐξ ἀρχῆς and qualified by πόρρωθεν, a synonym for ἄνωθεν,[56] Demosthenes in *Against Aristocrates* 187.1–3 links both terms by paralleling εἰδώς ἀκριβῶς ("knowing thoroughly/in detail") with παρηκολουθηκώς ("having kept informed") of certain misdeeds of one Charidemus, a leader of mercenary troops at times aligned against Athens, such that, when Demosthenes opposes the Senate's action of "inviolability" for Charidemus, Demosthenes alone is uniquely qualified to present the charges against him. Or again, in *Against Olympiodorus* 40.1–7, Demosthenes refers to the defendant who refuses to engage witnesses "who had a *thorough* knowledge of every one of these matters as indeed those who had kept an informed familiarity of these matters from the beginning" (τοῖς εἰδόσιν ἀκριβῶς ἕκαστα ταῦτα τὰ πράγματα ὡς ἔχει καὶ παρηκολουθηκόσιν ἐξ ἀρχῆς).[57]

Josephus asserts against recent attempts to interpret the Jewish War against Rome that these writers lacked a "thorough" or "fuller knowledge" unlike his own "knowing these things *thoroughly* from the top by having an informed familiarity with those things that had taken place" (ἐπίστασθαι ταύτας πρότερον ἀκριβῶς ἢ παρηκολουθηκότα τοῖς γεγονόσιν) (*C. Ap.* I.53.5).[58]

To sum up, all three writers Demosthenes, Josephus, and Luke engage the perfect participle of παρακολουθέω to situate themselves and nuance their qualifications precisely when an entire historical process has to be re-signified so that the larger public may understand and take appropriate action or make a proper response to the new state of affairs. Παρηκολουθηκώς conveys both 'experienced familiarity with' as well as 'informed competence in' the larger movement in question.

5. Finally, eyewitness presence *may* be the means or part of the means by which a person has become and stays knowledgeable, as the context allows. Παρηκολουθηκώς is particularly adept at indicating both the cognitive knowledge that produces an informed person as well as the knowledge gained through personal involvement and hence overall *familiarity*. Luke 1:3a *may* be Luke's way of anticipating the time when his eyewitness engagement in the "we" passages of Acts 16 and *passim* joins and complements the cognitive knowledge attained through instruction and adherence to a movement over a longer period of time.

---

56 See above under the discussion for LSJ.
57 See further above, n. 19.
58 See above under the discussion for BDAG.

Then again, Luke may have selected παρηκολουθηκώς precisely because it best nuances his long-standing involvement in "the way" such that he is particularly qualified to interpret recent developments "among us" (Luke 1:1b) as significant for the movement as a whole, whereas the "we" passages incorporate a special source and are *not* meant to indicate his eyewitness experience. More work on these "we" passages will need to be carried out.[59]

---

[59] See the discussion of Cadbury's work on "eyewitness" above under the discussions of LSJ; cf. also Chapter Nine as well as the review of possibilities of the use of "we" in the Conclusions Chapter summary.

Chapter Four: The Meaning of ΚΑΘΕΞΗΣ in Luke's Two-Volume Narrative[1]

Our inscribed author "Luke" divulges a wealth of information in his opening balanced, Atticizing period (Luke 1:1–4).[2] Through the dependent clauses of the first half (Luke 1:1–2), the writer includes himself among an "us" who have had "events" or "actions" (πράγματα) "fulfilled" or "brought to fruition" in their midst (1:1). Yet Luke also includes himself among an "us" who have received information from eyewitnesses and attendants of occurrences that have apparently preceded the events of the first group of "us." Though the relationship between the two groups of "us" is not clear, what is certain is that our author links himself to the same (καθώς) general pool of sources of tradition available to the "many" (πολλοί) who have already "set out to compile a narrative summary" (διήγησις) concerning these events that have arrived at some developed stage of fulfillment. But in the last half of the sentence through his *independent* clause, completed with a clause of purpose (ἵνα) (1:3–4), Luke separates himself noticeably from the "many" by his own program. He also is going to arrange a narrative with a particular "order" (καθεξῆς), and, since he "has a thoroughly informed familiarity with all the events from the top" or from the period of "the beginning" (1:3),[3] he can unabashedly commend his account as worthwhile for those like Theophilus who might desire more knowledge about the "events come to fruition" (compare 1:1→1:4).

---

[1] A shortened and slightly revised version, used with permission, of David P. Moessner, "The Meaning of καθεξῆς in the Lukan Prologue as a Key to the Distinctive Contribution of Luke's Narrative among the 'Many,'" in *The Four Gospels, 1992: Festschrift Frans Neirynck*, ed. Frans van Segbroeck, C. M. Tuckett, G. Van Belle, J. Verheyden (Leuven: Peeters/University Press, 1992): 2:1513–28.

[2] See Chapter Three § 1. Cf., e.g., Willem C. van Unnik, "Once More St. Luke's Prologue," *Neotestamentica* 7 (1973): 7–26; Loveday Alexander, "Luke's Preface in the Context of Greek Preface-Writing," *NovT* 28 (1986): 48–74; Vernon K. Robbins, "Prefaces in Greco-Roman Biography and Luke-Acts," *Perspectives in Religious Studies* 6 (1979): 94–108.

[3] See Chapter Three, Conclusions.

1 The "Narrato-Logical" Sense of ΚΑΘΕΞΗΣ

> The common mistake of unoriginal students, in our day as in his, has been to dissect a poem—a complete organism—without regard to the meaning and purpose of the whole. It is the mistake of pedants who divide a masterpiece, and do not rejoin the parts in living union; and thus their pupils, who love life, come to hate the work—of Milton, say—that they are "studying"
> (Lane Cooper, *The Poetics of Aristotle: Its Meaning and Influence*, 11⁴).

What then distinguishes Luke's account from the "many" others? Is it likely that he considers many of the "many" others' attempts to be inaccurate or significantly flawed in their presentation of persons and events? Perhaps, although from the brevity of the prologue it may not seem probable that Luke would extol the eye-witness quality of the resources that he shares with the "many" only to diminish the latter in the next breath. But in light of Luke's use of καθεξῆς in other parts of his narrative, especially in Acts 11:4, and the conjunction in the prologue of this term with the purpose of lending greater "certainty" or "credibility" (ἀσφάλεια) to the events for his readers (1:4), it does seem likely that Luke is writing up the events in a particular sequence that he is commending as peculiarly illuminating. We shall have to suspend judgment on Luke's assessment of the others' narratives until we come to our conclusions below. In any case, it appears that Luke's distinctive ordering or emplotment of the events—including undoubtedly his second "volume"—marks his narrative as unique among the others' and provides an explanation why Luke would attempt yet another compilation in light of "many" others.

Liddell, Scott, and Jones (LSJ)[5] indicate that καθεξῆς is synonymous with ἐφεξῆς "in order, in a row, one after another." Similarly Bauer states that the basic sense in the New Testament and sub-apostolic literature remains "succession": "*in order, one after the other* of sequence in time, space, or logic."[6] Of the total of seven occurrences in the literature exhaustively covered by this lexicon, five are found in Luke and Acts. Especially given this curious Lukan predilection, the only reliable method is to determine what Luke could mean by καθεξῆς in his prologue (Luke 1:3) by investigating the way he employs the word in the rest of his narrative Luke and Acts in conversation with other occurrences in Greco-Roman

---

[4] New York: Cooper Square Publishers, 1963.
[5] Henry George Liddell and Robert Scott, eds., *A Greek-English Lexicon*, rev. Henry Stuart Jones, Roderick McKenzie, and Eric A. Barber (Oxford: Clarendon, 1925/1968); see, e.g., Plutarch, *Moralia* 2.615c; Aelianus, *Varia Historia* 8.7.
[6] Frederick W. Danker, ed., *A Greek-English Lexicon of the New Testament and Other Early Christian Literature*, 3rd ed. (Chicago, IL: University of Chicago Press, 2000); see *T. Jud.* 25:1; *Apoc. Mos.* 8; IGR IV, 1432, 9.

usage. We shall see that Luke's choice of καθεξῆς in the Cornelius episode (Acts 11:4 in 10:1–11:18) sheds special light upon the meaning Luke attaches to it in his *proemium*.

Certainly for Luke καθεξῆς may refer primarily to *chronological* ordering as in Luke 8:1 when "afterwards" or "in the following sequence" (of Jesus's words and deeds) "he himself [Jesus] went on through cities and villages" accompanied by the twelve and certain women. Or again in Peter's speech in Acts 3, the apostle mentions that "all the prophets who have spoken from Samuel and those on down (οἱ καθεξῆς) have also proclaimed these days" of the fulfillment of the prophet like Moses (Acts 3:24; Deut 18:15–19 and Lev 23:29 cited in Acts 3:22–23). Even in these instances, however, logical "order" or "coherence" is not completely absent since, for example, in Acts 3 *all* the prophets including Samuel spoke the same basic message proclaimed by Moses of the coming of the days of the prophet "like him." The prophets after Samuel are not only his chrono-logical but his logical "successors" as well. By invoking the message of all the prophets "in order," Peter is referring not just to an interesting historical sequence; he is also making sense of events of Jesus the prophet like Moses in the "signs and wonders" of the "last days" that are taking place in the very midst of his own audience (for example, Acts 3:1–26;[7] compare 2:17–21).

A *spatial* or *geographical* sense can also be primary for Luke as in Acts 18:23. After spending some time in Antioch, Paul departs to "pass through the region of Galatia and Phrygia from place to place in sequence (καθεξῆς), strengthening (ἐπιστηρίζω) all the disciples." This re-tracing of his itinerary albeit in reverse order (see Acts 16:6!) is, however, hardly unprecedented. Already in Acts 14:21–28 Paul and Barnabas retrace in reverse order the cities that they have just visited– Lystra, Iconium, Antioch of Pisidia, Perga of Pamphilia, and Antioch of Syria– "strengthening (ἐπιστηρίζω) the disciples, exhorting them to remain in the faith" (14:22a). And again in 15:36, following the apostolic assembly, Paul (and now Silas) go back over the same route as on the "first journey" through Syria and Cilicia, including the towns of Derbe and Lystra (compare 14:8–20) and other cities (compare "the cities," 16:4). This return is prefaced by Paul to Barnabas: "Come, let us return and visit the brothers and sisters in every city (κατὰ πόλιν) in which we proclaimed the word of the Lord to see how they are doing" (15:36). So

---

7 "The times of refreshment" (καιροὶ ἀναψύξεως, Acts 3:20) of release of sin brought through Jesus's rejection/execution and resurrection (Acts 3:13–19) echo the deliverance through "signs and wonders" (cf. Acts 2:22, 43) from the plagues of slavery in Egypt (LXX Exod 7:9: σημεῖον ἢ τέρας; 8:11: ἀνάψυξις) as Jesus fulfills Moses's and "the from of old holy prophets'" prophecy of a prophet "like me" (Moses; Deut 18:15–20 and Lev 23:29 in Acts 3:21–23).

when in 18:23 our narrator states that Paul, after spending time again in Antioch of Syria, passes through Galatia and Phyrgia καθεξῆς–part of the new regions covered after the "first" journey (16:6)–and then adds the phrase "strengthening the disciples," we now discern a geographical-sequential rationale consistent with the "order" of Paul's previous movements. Καθεξῆς in Acts 18:23, then, is dynamically equivalent to "corresponding to each city" (κατὰ πόλιν, 15:21,36; 20:23) or "the one city after the other" in the same basic sequence in which Paul had earlier visited that region. Καθεξῆς thus inserts an important logical component into the rationale of Paul's spatial or geographical movement, thereby implicating Paul's itinerancy within a larger coherence of meaning of the Luke-Acts narrative.

Given both the chronological and geographical logic, what are we to make of the contribution of καθεξῆς in Acts 11:4 where the narrator introduces Peter's "speech" to "those of the circumcision" (11:4–18) with Peter's "explaining" or "laying out" his experiences with Cornelius in Caesarea "in order" (καθεξῆς)? Is καθεξῆς primarily chronological or geographical or even of a different logical "order"?

First, we should notice that the *linear sequence* or *order* of the incidents in Peter's recounting of his encounter with Cornelius is not the same as the order in the narrator's presentation, Acts 10:1–48. For example, the narrator begins with Cornelius in Caesarea at prayer and the recipient of a visitation of "an angel/messenger of God" "in a vision" (10:1–3). Peter, on the other hand, begins with the vision that came to him while praying in Joppa (11:5); only later, in 11:13, will he mention the "man's" vision. This difference says nothing, of course, about which vision is represented in the text as having occurred "first" in the chronological time of the narrative. Rather, as we would expect, Peter presents the past encounter from his own vantage point, and as we learn further in his "own" version (for example, 11:12), it is his vision of the sheet with unclean food which unlocks for him the whole purpose and significance of his journey to Caesarea. He simply "begins" with the initial incident of significance from his *point of viewing* the past experience with Cornelius. The narrator, however, has already told us that Cornelius's vision took place almost a full day earlier than Peter's (10:3,9). Clearly, then, καθεξῆς in 11:4 does not mean a recounting concerned to present a *detailed chronology* of events. Perhaps more importantly, neither does it mean an "order" intending to clarify the rather complex, even confusing sequence of dreams and movement of characters in the narrator's account. Peter's rehearsal, 11:4–18, is not simply a distilled version of 10:1–48.

Secondly, some of the events in Peter's shorter version are, as we should expect again, given considerably less space in their recounting. Cornelius's vision is given two verses compared to twelve (11:13–14; 10:1–8,22,30–32), his emissaries' journey one verse compared to five (11:11;10:7–9, 17–18). Καθεξῆς in Acts 11:4 thus does not indicate an expanded, supplemental version or order of certain occurrences. It is interesting to note, however, that Peter's vision is given five verses in his recounting to the narrator's eight (11:5–10; 10:10–16, 28). This discrepancy in the ratio of relative narrative space may be a clue to the significance of καθεξῆς in 11:4.

Thirdly, the material re-description of particular incidents is in some cases significantly different. For instance, in the narrator's account of Cornelius's vision the angel/messenger of God tells Cornelius that his "prayers and alms have ascended as a memorial offering before God" and that he is to send for Peter (Acts 10:3–6). Later in the same account Cornelius repeats the gist of the narrator's presentation by making explicit the rationale for Peter's visit: "We are all here present before God to hear all the things that have been commanded to you by the Lord" (10:33). In Peter's account, on the other hand, we learn of "the man's" (Cornelius's) vision only after Peter has entered his house when the centurion recounts the angel's words: "Send to Joppa and bring Simon called Peter; he will speak a message to you by which you and all your household will be saved" (11:14).

Whose account is correct? Did the angel tell Cornelius that Peter would proclaim a message of salvation, as Peter's version says, or did Cornelius await with great expectation the message Peter would bring but not knowing the exact import of the visit, as the narrator's account suggests? What is curious in this regard is also the question of Peter's knowledge after his own vision. In both accounts it appears that Peter does not know why he has been sent until after he arrives ("I ask then for what reason/purpose have you sent for me?" [10:29b]; "As I began to speak, the Holy Spirit fell on them just as on us at the beginning and I remembered the word of the Lord [...]" [11:15–16]). Yet in both versions already before Peter arrives, the Spirit has begun to interpret the meaning of Peter's vision for Peter in light of the arrival of Cornelius's messengers in Joppa. In the narrator's version, the Spirit tells Peter–"while he was pondering the meaning of the vision"–to go down and accompany the messengers "without hesitation" (μηδὲν διακρινόμενος [middle voice]) "because I have sent them" (10:19–20). In Peter's version there is a slight but substantive change in the phrase μηδὲν διακρίνομαι from the *middle* to the *active* voice: "The Spirit told me to go with them without making a distinction/judging them" (μηδὲν διακρίναντα, 11:12). In other words, neither version is concerned to give a precise record of who knew what and when they knew it!

Peter's version, rather, is pointing back to the narrator's account and giving the reader, as well as "those from the circumcision," an understanding of what was especially significant in the Cornelius-Peter encounter. 'What happened,'

Peter in effect declares, is that since God brought "the same gift [the Holy Spirit] to them" (the Gentiles, 11:18) "as upon us at the beginning" (believers from the circumcision), "who was I to be able to hinder God?" (11:15–17). Seen from the "end" of the event, Peter's vision has become for the leading apostle among the Jewish peoples[8] the critical revelation of God's purposes for the gift of salvation to the Gentiles: Peter and the Jerusalem believers had been "withstanding" God in assuming that God had not cleansed the Gentiles but that they were still "common," "un-clean" non-candidates for the messianic salvation (10:15; 11:9).

Καθεξῆς in Acts 11:4 therefore appears to be neither primarily chronological nor geographical in its "ordering" *sense*. Rather, it suggests a sequencing of Peter's account in which the "logic" of the Cornelius encounter at that particular juncture in the narrative of Acts is illuminated for the significance of the entire Luke and Acts narrative. How is Luke's audience, as well as the Jerusalem believers, to understand Peter's visit to Caesarea in light of the much larger story of "the word of God" (11:1) in the plot that has been unfolding? Peter elaborates the significance of narrating καθεξῆς by disclosing the 'narrato-logical' sense of the larger understanding of Israel's messianic salvation through the larger ordering of the plot. It was especially his vision of unclean food that had opened up the significance of Cornelius's vision and Peter's journey to Caesarea within the developing portrayal of Israel's eschatological salvation.

2 ΚΑΘΕΞΗΣ as a Key to Understanding the Fulfillment of the "Way of the Lord"

> [I]t *must be shown that from what precedes or follows the document* (ex superior et ex inferior scriptura) *the doubtful point becomes plain. Therefore, if words are to be considered separately by themselves, every word, or at least many words, would seem ambiguous* (ambigua); *but it is not right to regard as ambiguous what becomes plain on consideration of the whole context* (ex omni considerate scriptura)
> (Cicero, *De inventione* 2.40.117 [Hubbell, LCL]).

We can see further how καθεξῆς in Acts 11:4 points to a significant contribution of the Acts 11:1–18 passage within the larger movement of the story from the way in which Peter's rehearsal and the narrator's in 10:1–48 function as hermeneutical lenses for construing earlier significances plotted within the Luke-Acts narrative. We have seen how Peter relates his version to the Spirit's injunction to go with the arriving messengers, making no negative distinction of their Gentile

---

[8] See esp. Acts 1:15–2:42.

or supposed "unclean" status (11:12→10:28). Peter's visitation of a Gentile home is in turn linked to *no distinction* in the "same gift" of the Holy Spirit given to Cornelius's family (11:17→10:45, 47b). This "falling" of the Spirit upon them (11:15→10:44) causes Peter to "remember the word (ῥῆμα) of the Lord when he had said, 'John baptized with water, but you shall be baptized with the Holy Spirit'" (11:16→10:48a). But where in the Luke and Acts narrative did Jesus utter this word, and why now in the middle of Acts is Peter speaking about John the Baptist whom Luke's audiences have encountered way back at the beginning of the two volumes? What could John the Baptist's baptism with water possibly have to do with Cornelius and Peter?

Jesus's utterance as it is re-sounded by Peter actually goes all the way back to the beginning of the second volume, Acts 1:5, where the risen Jesus speaks out the narrator's summary of a forty-day period by taking over the "mouth of the narrator": "and while eating with them he [Jesus] charged them not to depart from Jerusalem but to await the promise of the Father which [narrator speaking] 'you heard from me [Jesus speaking], for John baptized with water but not after many days as these you will be baptized with the Holy Spirit'" [Jesus still speaking]. But Jesus's words here not only point forward to the Pentecost event (Acts 2) but also backward to the end of the first volume to Luke 24 where Jesus tells the gathered disciples–while *eating* before them–"Look, I am sending the promise of *my* Father upon you but stay in the city until you are clothed with power from on High" (24:49). Consequently Peter's citation of Jesus's words to "those of the circumcision" in Acts 11:16 transports the reader back to the beginnings of volume two and to the end of volume one (compare the πρῶτος λόγος, Acts 1:1). But even more remarkably when we as auditors hear Acts 1:5 and Luke 24 sounding again, we are now ushered back to the beginnings of volume one, namely, to Luke 3:16, and to none other than to John the Baptist. There it is John who states, "I myself baptize with water [...] but he [the Christ] will baptize you with (the) Holy Spirit and fire."

It appears then that Peter's explanation καθεξῆς in Acts 11:4–18 figures the Cornelius visitation as a critical development in a larger process, an encounter which pulls together much of the two-volume coherence as it points back to certain *beginnings*.

2.1 Pentecost as a *Beginning* (ἀρχή, Acts 11:15) of the Word of God to the Nations through Messiah's Witnesses

Peter describes the falling of the Holy Spirit upon Cornelius and his household "as also upon us at the beginning" (ἐν ἀρχῇ, 11:15). By remembering Jesus's words (Acts 1:5), Peter now perceives the fuller meaning of "what God has cleansed you shall not call common." There is to be no distinction among those who may receive eschatological *salvation*, as Peter proceeds to make explicit in 11:17: "the same gift to them as He gave to us when we came to believe in the Lord Jesus Messiah." That God has established Jesus as both *Lord* and *Messiah* by culminating Jesus's public career through death and resurrection, was the main thrust of Peter's Pentecost speech (Acts 2:36) in laying out the basis for Israel's repentance leading to "forgiveness of sins," baptism "into the name of Jesus Messiah," and the receiving of the *promise* of the "gift of the Holy Spirit" (2:38–39). This "promise," Peter had declared back at that beginning, had been made for Israel *and* for "all (πάντες) who are far off, for everyone whom the Lord our God summons" (2:39b). Now at last Peter had learned that God had summoned the far-off Gentile when he states as an *inclusio* in his address to Cornelius and his family, "Truly I am perceiving that God is not one to show partiality [...]." "Everyone (πᾶς) who believes in him receives forgiveness of sins through his name" (10:34b, 43b; compare 10:36–"Jesus *Messiah* who is *Lord* of all" [πάντες]). "The gift of the Holy Spirit" was proof enough of this salvation, as even those of the circumcision in Jerusalem are now forced to admit after hearing Peter's 'narrato-logically ordered' account: "Then even to the Gentiles God has given repentance leading to life!" (Acts 11:18).

2.2 John's Preaching of a Baptism as the *Beginning* of Witness to the Word of God through Jesus Messiah

Peter's rehearsal in Jerusalem of his Cornelius visit also carries the discerning reader back to the beginning of Jesus's career as Messiah and to the essential distinction between his and John the Baptist's role in Israel's eschatological salvation. We have seen that even in Peter's shortened form, his own vision of unclean animals is highlighted. And we have seen that this emphasis is not incidental but is critical to understanding the Cornelius episode καθεξῆς within the larger narrative configuration. This conclusion is supported all the more when we see how the image of "unclean food" is woven into the beginnings of Jesus's public presence. By echoing to Cornelius the voice of God in Peter's vision (Acts 10:28b) and beginning his address with the main point of that vision (10:34), Peter is re-construing his own understanding of messianic salvation for the "unclean" in the light of this vision: The word or message of good news which God was proclaiming through Jesus Messiah to Israel throughout all Judea *began* (ἄρχομαι) in Galilee after the baptism which John proclaimed (κηρύσσω) (10:37). That Peter is referring to the heart of John's preaching in Luke 3:16 as Jesus's anointing by the Holy Spirit (Luke 3:18–22) is not only clear from Peter's citation in Acts 11:16 (compare Acts 1:5) but also from what immediately follows in 10:38–42. John's baptism *message* was fulfilled in God's proclamation of "good news through Jesus" by God's "anointing (χρίω) him with the Holy Spirit and power" (Acts 10:38).

More than that fulfillment, Peter and other especially appointed "witnesses" witnessed this "messianic"/"anointed" activity of the Holy Spirit through Jesus from that *beginning* in Galilee all the way to Jesus's "hanging on a tree" and his "raising up" in Jerusalem (10:38–42). The distinguishing qualification for that special status of witness beginning after John's preaching was "not granted to all the people but to us [...] who *ate and drank* with Jesus after he had been raised up from the dead" (10:41b). But as we have already seen from Peter's rehearsal in Acts 11:16, Acts 1:5 points to the resurrected Jesus's final *meal* with the gathered disciples as decisively revelatory for the sending of these witnesses (Luke 24:36–49). There the risen Jesus showed his crucified hands and feet and *ate* before them in *opening up* for them the meaning of all the Scriptures ("the law of Moses and the prophets and the psalms"): that Jesus as Israel's "Messiah must suffer and rise up from the dead on the third day and that repentance leading to the release of sins must be proclaimed in his name to all the nations/Gentiles beginning from Jerusalem, these things of which you are *witnesses*" (24:44–48). The command to Peter to *eat unclean* food finally *opens up* for him the significance of that earlier setting–when Jesus had been *eating with him*–that Peter should proclaim release of sins to *unclean* Gentiles.

Nor is this connection between "unclean food" and "eating and drinking" with Jesus a clever mnemonic prompt recalling for the reader, as well as for Peter, the *formal* setting only of the mission charge. Rather, the criticism of "those from the circumcision" against Peter matches the growing chorus of discontent in the Gospel volume against Jesus: "This man receives sinners and eats with them!" (Luke 15:2; compare 5:30→7:34 [Galilee]→15:2 [Journey]→19:7 [near Jerusalem] "this man has entered a house to lodge with a sinner")→"Why have you entered a home to be with uncircumcised folk and to eat with them?!" (Peter with Cornelius, Acts 11:3). Peter is under the same duress for eating with unclean Gentiles as Jesus was for eating with unclean "sinners." And it was *at table* that Jesus had linked the apostles themselves with those who would deny association with him (Luke 22:31–38; especially 22:34; compare 9:23,26), betray him into the "hands of sinners," and "fall away" when their loyalty came to a crucial showdown (22:21–23,31–32; compare 24:7). Consequently, Jesus's greeting of peace and "eating before them" in Luke 24:36–49 constitutes not only a meal of restoration for the disciples with Jesus as forgiven sinners. That next-to-the-last scene with them in the first volume is also that same meal of solidarity that commissioned them to proclaim forgiveness to the unclean "sinner" Gentiles.

The narrator's use of διακρίνω in Acts 10, 11, and 15 nuances this material link between Peter and Jesus further. The Spirit tells Peter to go with Cornelius's messengers "without doubting/hesitation" (διακρίνομαι, present, middle voice, 10:20), but upon his return those of the circumcision "began to dispute" with him (διεκρινόμην, imperfect, middle voice) because of that decision (11:2). But Peter responds that the Spirit had told him not to "make a distinction/discriminate" (διακρίναντα, aorist, active voice, 11:12) between him and them, and, finally, at the apostolic assembly he draws the theological and practical consequences from his vision of *unclean* (ἀκάρτον, 11:8; 10:14b) food and his lodging with Cornelius's family: "God made no *distinction* (διέκρινεν, aorist, active voice) between us and them, since he had *cleansed* (καθαρίζω) their hearts by faith (Acts 15:9 [that is, by "giving them the Holy Spirit just as to us," 15:8→11:15→ 10:47])–"What God has *cleansed* (καθαρίζω) you must not call common or unclean" (11:9b→10:15b!). This paronomasia with διακρίνω draws special attention to the indispensable role that the mission to Gentiles entails in the narrative logic of the larger plot, and, given the fact that διακρίνω occurs only these four times in the whole of Luke and Acts, this semantic "play" can hardly be unintended.

To be a "witness" therefore means to be classified among those who could "bear testimony" to Jesus's *eating and drinking* with *unclean tax collectors and sinners, beginning* after the baptism which John proclaimed. The whole course of Jesus's messianic activity had led to the beginning of the messianic mission to the nations as a fulfillment of John's message. It is indeed no surprise that our narrator has Jesus as the risen crucified Messiah state that he himself ("I") will send the promise of "my Father" upon his witnesses (Luke 24:49→Acts 1:5) just as John had declared in Luke 3:16!

Reading the Cornelius story narrato-logically (καθεξῆς) in Acts 11 means to understand its critical role in relation to the "fulfilled events" whose illumination our author has indicated is the overarching purpose for his two-volume enterprise (Luke 1:1–4). It is therefore appropriate for us to enquire whether the functional significance of καθεξῆς in Acts 11:4 might not also be an important clue to its semantic sense in the author's prologue in Luke 1:3. What is the import for interpreting Luke and Acts if our author announces he intends to write an account καθεξῆς?

3 Paul's *Beginnings and Witness to the "Way Of The Lord"* as a Key to the Meaning of *ΚΑΘΕΞΗΣ* in Luke's Prologue

> The main point is that authorial intention is always the product of critical reconstruction. We cannot know an author's mind directly; it is not a bit of evidence independent of the process of interpretation.
> (Mark Brett, "The Future of Reader Criticisms?" in *The Open Text: New Directions for Biblical Studies?*, 15–16[9]).

We find a curious cluster of three of the words that appear in the prologue of Luke 1:1–4 in Acts 26:4–5. Paul, on trial for representing a party or "sect" (αἵρεσις) of Judaism known as "the Way" (Acts 24:22), claims that he is accused for having the same hope as the twelve tribes of Israel. Yet he has been living, he says, as none other than a devout Pharisee, which "all the Jews have been aware of from the beginning/for a long time" (ἄνωθεν, 26:5a; compare Luke 1:3). This "knowing" is linked, on the one hand, to his life from his youth "spent among my nation in Jerusalem from the beginning" (ἀπ' ἀρχῆς, 26:4; compare Luke 1:2), and to his life lived that whole time as a Pharisee–that is, "according to the most exact (ἀκριβέστατης, 26:5; compare Luke 1:3) sect/school (αἵρεσις) of our religion" (26:5). What is more, if they would but "bear witness" (μαρτυρέω), "all the Jews" would have to confirm that this fact was so. What is especially interesting in light of our question is that "from the beginning" is not defined strictly chronologically but 'begins' with a period (his youth), which is significant for understanding the *course* and *character* of his whole life (compare Acts 22:3–at the feet of Gamaliel in Jerusalem). If any of the Jews were to retrace that course ἄνωθεν–"from the top/beginning" or "for a long time" (that is, back to his roots)–they would see that this circumstance was firmly the case and could therefore be witnesses to Paul's life *from that beginning*.

What we have in Paul's trial in Acts 26, then, is a formal parallel to our author's opening prologue: (i) Like "most excellent (κράτιστε) Theophilus," who is in a situation requiring reliable or more accurate information in order that his understanding (ἐπιγινώσκω) of the fulfilled events be grounded more firmly (ἀσφάλεια, 1:4), so the "most excellent (κράτιστε) Festus" (26:25) has been thrust into circumstances demanding more accurate information in order to rule on the charges against Paul. Since he is at a loss how to proceed with his investigation (25:20a), he needs "firmer" or "more certain facts" (ἀσφαλές) "in order to write" (γράφω, 25:26; compare Luke 1:3!) his superior; (ii) The procurator in Caesarea, then, is in a situation not unlike the tribune in Jerusalem who earlier, "desiring

---

9 Ed. Francis Watson (London: SCM Press, 1993).

to know the true facts/the truth (τὸ ἀσφαλές, 21:34) about the charges brought by the Jews" in order to adjudicate the case against Paul (21:33–34), determines he must turn Paul over to the Sanhedrin for their counsel in this matter (22:30).

But the parallels are clearly more than formal. In the final trial scenes of Acts, Paul twice links his loyalty as a Pharisee Jew to the appearance and mandate of the Lord Jesus, Israel's Messiah (22:3–21; 26:4, 23). Out of his great zeal for God, he persecuted "the Way" (ἡ ὁδός, 22:3–4). But this Way (26:13; compare 9:17, 27) actually led to repentance and turning to God and a proclamation, which says "nothing more than what the prophets and Moses said would come to pass" (26:19–23). Paul the chief opponent of the Way becomes this Way's chief proponent! With Paul on trial, the "way of the Lord" is on trial. Between the tribune's and Festus's attempts to learn the facts comes "most excellent (κράτιστε) Felix" (23:26; 24:3) who realizes that the high priest's and elders' accusations against "the Way" are not accurately represented. In fact, the narrator states that since "Felix knew (οἶδα) the things concerning this Way (ὁδός) more accurately" (ἀκριβέστερον, 24:22; compare Luke 1:3) (that is, than Paul's accusers), he was able to "put off" the high priest's entourage and delay the investigation. This playing with time allows Felix ample opportunity to learn from Paul even more reliable information about this "Way" (24:26b), concerning which Paul in his defense has declared he is on trial (24:14). But "desiring to do the Jews a favor," Felix leaves Paul in prison (24:27).

Paul's trial settings illustrate the importance of obtaining and discerning the certainty of a body of information or facts about the movement called "the Way." Getting these facts "straight" would in fact seem to go a long way in establishing a necessary basis upon which to judge the validity or credibility of this particular messianic movement, not to mention the fate of certain of its adherents. But what does *certainty* about a number of facts concerning "the Way" have to do with recounting an episode καθεξῆς, as, for example, with Peter's retelling of the Cornelius episode (Acts 11:1–14) or Luke's audiences following καθεξῆς his two volumes (Luke 1:3)?

First, it is noteworthy that when Paul is given opportunity to convey information about "the Way" in his two major defense speeches before the people (λαός) of Israel in Jerusalem (Acts 22:3–21) and before Festus and King Agrippa in Caesarea (Acts 26:2–23)–in each instance just after a Roman official has expressed his need to have "more accurate" (ἀκριβέστερον) information–Paul recounts his *beginnings*, trained as a youth in Jerusalem in the strictest party of Israel's religious devotion! More significantly, each rehearsal of his absolute loyalty to the God and hope of Israel leads to the critical "defense" of Paul's authority. He is an authenticated "witness" of the messianic way of Israel because Israel's resurrected Messiah, Jesus himself, has authorized him. Rather than explaining the intricacies of the Jesus messianic movement in relation to Roman law and religious practice or legitimating Paul's beliefs in light of acceptable Roman views, Paul's whole concern is to orient the people and then the governor and "king" of Israel to his relation to Israel's Messiah and the relation of Messiah Jesus to the ongoing eschatological hopes of Israel. Even with Felix who has already some accurate (ἀκριβῶς) information, Paul stresses his relation to the resurrection hope, to that "fact" of Israel's (the Pharisees'!) hope which "the Way" has in common and which especially legitimates Paul as a witness to that Way. In short, to understand Paul and the accusations against him, the people of Israel and the Roman rulers must be able to "figure out" his relation to the way of Jesus Messiah. Accordingly, in no less a manner must Luke's hearers be able to con-figure the accusations against Paul with significant events in Luke's narrative world–most notably the resurrection and appearances of the persecuted, suffering Messiah Jesus. This epistemological requirement, of course, means that, as with the Cornelius episode, the narrative must be allowed to define those relationships through its own unique configuration.

Secondly, and in some ways even more intriguing, is the case of Apollos. He "had been instructed" (κατηχέω, Acts 18:25, compare Luke 1:4!) in "the way of the Lord" and knew "the things concerning Jesus *accurately*" (ἀκριβῶς, compare Luke 1:3). He would seem then already to have achieved the ideal that our author has set for Theophilus! But along came "Priscilla and Aquila" who "laid out/ expounded the way of God to him *more accurately*" (ἀκριβέστερον, Acts 18:26). Just when we think that Apollos may "have the story straight," friends of Paul link up with him to make the story even straighter! What is our narrator doing here? The clue comes with the disclaimer in 18:25b: "Burning with zeal he [Apollos] was speaking and teaching accurately the things concerning Jesus, although he knew only (μόνον) the baptism of John." Here again in the middle of the Acts narrative we find John and his baptism! Then, after his encounter with Priscilla and Aquila, Apollos passes through to Achaia where in public he "completely confuted the Jews, demonstrating through the Scriptures that the Messiah was Jesus" (18:28). The verb διακατελέγχομαι (a *hapax legomenon*) emphasizes the "complete or full refutation" of others' arguments. Certainly the nuance of "powerful" refutation is present (RSV–"powerfully confute") since he buttresses those local believers by his arguments (18:27b), probably by the effective demonstration to (other) Jews that Israel's Messiah was actually Jesus (18:28b). But the narrator has already described Apollos as eloquent and "powerful (δυνατός) in the Scriptures" (18:24b) *before* his meeting with Priscilla and Aquila. What has changed? How has he come to know "the way of the Lord/God" "more accurately?"

Though there seems to be no straightforward answer, the immediately following narrative entanglement would appear most illuminating of Apollos's situation. There in Ephesus (Acts 19:1-7) "approximately twelve disciples" who "had been baptized" into "John's baptism" (and not into "the name of the Lord Jesus," 19:5) had never even heard of the Holy Spirit (19:2b)! Both Apollos and "the about twelve" apparently have no knowledge of Messiah's baptism of the Holy Spirit. Thus once again, now in Acts 18:25b, the narrator points Luke's audience back to Luke 3:15–16 and 7:29–30. Furthermore, in Acts 19:4 Paul himself echoes these same passages on *water versus Spirit baptism* when he conflates the essence of Luke 3:3 (narrator's summary of John's *preaching* a baptism) with Luke 3:16 and 7:29–30, harking back to his earlier words on John in his speech to Pisidian Antioch in Acts 13:25. Curiously there in Pisidian Antioch and in Peter's speech before Cornelius are the only other places where Jesus's *movement* ("coming," 13:25) or "beginnings" (10:37) is specified as occurring "after" (μετά) John.

Once again, therefore, Apollos, like "those of the circumcision" in Jerusalem in Acts 11–in order to have a reliably *accurate* knowledge of the Way–must "go back" to the relationship between John's baptism and Jesus's messianic baptism and sort out the decisive difference. Time and again the narrative re-directs the readers back to Luke 3 and the beginnings of the fulfillment of the way of the Lord heralded there by Isaiah (chapter 40) and highlighted by Messiah's baptism of the Spirit. The fact that Apollos now for the first time *fully/completely* refutes fellow Jews through the Scriptures and that his basic argument is only now described to be the same as Paul's in Corinth–"that the Messiah was Jesus" (18:28; compare 18:5)–itself argues that Apollos needed greater clarity regarding Messiah Jesus's fulfillment of Israel's scriptures as the "way of the Lord." Only after being consulted by Paul and his disciples can Apollos correctly configure Jesus's messianic way to "all flesh" through Messiah's gift of the Spirit (Isa 40:3–5 in Luke 3:4–6). Whatever the new understanding of Apollos may be in greater detail, what has become certain is that Apollos, like Theophilus, becomes symbolic of the role that Luke's audiences must also take on by correlating various events from the larger biblical panorama with those of the way of Messiah Jesus as channeled through the narrato-logical sense of Luke's two-volume arrangement. Even as late as the closing chapters of the second volume, Luke is still instilling 'narrato-logical' sense into his audiences as they follow his narrative καθεξῆς.

4 Conclusions

> Given a fairly intricate and intelligible literary structure which, taken as a whole, conveys a coherent message, our first assumption with regard to individual parts within that structure should not be that they point to a specific community problem, but that they are in service to the larger literary goal of the author.
> (Luke Timothy Johnson; cited by Stephen C. Barton, "Early Christianity and the Sociology of the Sect," in *The Open Text: New Directions for Biblical Studies?*, 155).

We have discovered important clues to the meaning of καθεξῆς in Luke 1:3 and thus to Luke's entire undertaking in our investigation of Peter's *recounting* of his Cornelius visit in Acts 11 and of Paul's relations to the *beginnings* of the Jesus messianic way of the Lord through the baptism of the Holy Spirit in Luke 3. To read καθεξῆς is to 'get Luke's story straight,' to become 'narrato-logically correct' by following Luke's two narrative volumes in sequence from the top (ἄνωθεν [...] καθεξῆς). Only by understanding the relation of the parts to each other and their relation to the whole narrative can one begin to appreciate Luke's distinctive contribution among "the many." The implication of the last half of his *proemium* is that he is not fully satisfied with the many others' narrative versions, though in the first half, he is fully appreciative of their eyewitness sources. Precisely in this setting, Luke asserts that his way of con-figuring the fulfilled events of the "way of the Lord" will lend a greater "certainty" or "firmer grasp" (ἀσφάλεια) of the true significance of this movement which he himself "has followed with a thoroughly informed familiarity from the top" (παρηκολουθηκότι ἄνωθεν πᾶσιν ἀκριβῶς καθεξῆς, Luke 1:3–4).[10]

We have also discovered by following Luke's narrative connections the remarkable way he has ordered and balanced his account to reflect his sense of the 'weight' or import of the various events of this 'Way.' For instance, the beginning of volume two is construed toward the midpoint and even end of Acts as itself a critical 'beginning' in messianic fulfillment within a larger 'way' or plan of God. Beginning, middle, and end of the Acts in turn point to the beginning and end of volume one as yet another and in certain ways even more foundational 'beginning' and 'end' of a larger scheme.[11] To gain a firm grasp, then, of the significance of any event along or within this scheme, one must be able to con-figure it in relation to these 'beginnings' according to the narrato-logical sense or order (καθεξῆς) which Luke has provided through his narrative connections. To

---

10 See above, Chapter Three.
11 On *mimesis* as narrative re-configuration, see further Paul Ricœur, *Time and Narrative* (Chicago, IL: University of Chicago Press, 1984), 1:31–87.

miss these connections is to miss the 'clear certainty' (ἡ ἀσφάλεια), the greater illumination of the events, which sums up Luke's over-arching purpose for his writing. In short, to read Luke's two-volumes καθεξῆς is to become narrato-logically informed or "gain a firmer grasp of the true significance of those events of which you have been instructed" (Luke 1:4).

Part III:
Luke among Hellenistic Historians

If Luke maintains that his way of writing endows his readers with a narrative logic that illumines the lasting significance of crucial events, how do his two volumes compare with other Hellenistic historians who also allege great improvement over others' attempts? If Luke asserts his qualifications as a trustworthy bearer and re-shaper of apostolic traditions, how successful is he in writing a history that educated Greco-Roman auditors would grasp and appreciate? Is Luke's strategy of two "beginnings" guided by sequential markers readily understandable to aural audiences within a wider Mediterranean ambience?

But what if Luke's claims are a bit overblown? Given the fact that his work does not even arouse notice by any Second Sophistic authors, Greek or Latin, by what right can Luke be considered a "Hellenistic historian?" How could educated Hellenistic audiences be led to comprehend the messages and weighted connections that Luke is intending to communicate? Do his short two-volumes about an obscure Jewish group surfacing in a distant, backwater province merit the moniker '*historia*'?

Since Luke begins with a claim to compose a narrative that sheds greater light than rival versions on events of consequence, what narrative-rhetorical techniques does he actually enlist that can accomplish this ambitious goal? It is apparent that it will be expedient for us to compare Luke's rhetorical 'methods of elaboration' and stylistic tropes of signification with recognized historians of the Hellenistic and Augustan periods. When we place Luke and Acts within the frame of historians like Polybius or Diodorus, is there anything *compar*able to a 'family resemblance'?

We shall not attempt to address the full number of narrative-rhetorical methods and categories treated in such works as Aristotle's *Poetics*, Cicero's *De inventione* and *De Oratore*, Horace's *Ars poetica*, Quintilian's *Institutio Oratoria*[1] or the anonymous *Rhetorica ad Herennium*, though we shall summarize important components of *mimetic* narration as illustrated in the *Poetics* that were then taken up by these later works. Nor do we intend to treat fully the status of Luke as littérateur in the context of a highly sophisticated narrative enterprise developed long before the time that Luke composes his own work. Rather, our approach will be to let three historians of the Hellenistic period speak on their own terms concerning their narrative poetics and strategies and bring Luke alongside in

---

[1] Especially Book 7 on "Arrangement."

comparing his own techniques of 'arranging' and sustaining his narrative as he conveys his emphases to his listeners.

We begin Chapter Five by outlining a conventional epistemology of narrative rhetoric utilized and developed throughout the Greco-Roman world by a diverse group of authors, whether "Jew or Greek," "Greek or barbarian."[2] On the basis of this standard poetics we shall illustrate how both Polybius and Luke employ 'synchronisms' to facilitate 'the continuity of the narrative' for their audiences ("'Listening Posts' along the Way: 'Synchronisms' as Metaleptic Prompts to the 'Continuity of the Narrative' in Polybius' *Histories* and in Luke's Gospel–Acts"). In Chapter Six we turn to the 'organization' of 'completed narrative' including 'speeches' as 'methods of elaboration' in developing a sustained '*plot*' by comparing Diodorus Siculus's musings on his poetics of continuity with Luke's utilization of the same ("'Managing' the Audience. Diodorus Siculus and Luke the Evangelist on Designing Authorial Intent"). Finally we close Part III (Chapter Seven) by rehearsing the categories of 'narrative arrangement' in Dionysius of Halicarnassus's critique of Thucydides and applying this narrative-rhetorical 'disposition' to Luke's determination to impact his readers with a "clearer certainty" *vis-à-vis* the events he recounts ("*A New Reading of Luke's 'Gospel Acts'*: Acts as the 'Metaleptic' Collapse of Luke and Dionysius of Halicarnassus's Narrative 'Arrangement' (οἰκονομία) as the Hermeneutical Keys to Luke's Re-Visioning of the 'Many'"). This chapter presents the fullest arguments for Luke's own understanding of the relation of Acts to his first volume.

In our Conclusions Chapter we shall pull together all our findings for Luke as a Hellenistic historian.

---

[2] To use Paul's taxonomy of humankind in Rom 1:14 and Gal 3:28; cf. Acts 28:2, 4.

Chapter Five: 'Listening Posts' Along the Way: 'Synchronisms' as Metaleptic Prompts to the 'Continuity of the Narrative' in Polybius's *Histories* and in Luke's 'Gospel Acts'[1]

For the authors Polybius of Megalopolis and Luke the Evangelist, both writing in Greek during the Greco-Roman era of widespread, pervasive Hellenistic culture, the one Divine Reality/true God has brought together unprecedented historical circumstances that have coalesced into a new and unrivalled state of affairs.

> *Previously the happenings of the world had been, so to speak, scattered, as they were held together by no unity of initiative, results, or place; but ever since this date history has conjoined to become an organic whole* (σωματοειδῆ συμβαίνει γίνεσθαι τὴν ἱστορίαν), *and the affairs of Italy and Africa have been interwoven* (συμπλέκεσθαί τε τὰς [...] πράξεις) *with those of Greece and Asia, all leading up to one result* (τέλος).[2]
> [*The Histories* I.3.3–4]

> *But what God proclaimed in advance through the mouth of all the prophets, that his Christ would suffer* (παθεῖν τὸν χριστὸν αὐτοῦ), *he has thus fulfilled. Change your whole way of thinking, therefore, and turn around in order that your sins might be blotted out so that times of refreshment might come from the presence of the Lord and that he might send to us Messiah Jesus–whom he had appointed beforehand–whom heaven must [now] receive until the times of the restoration of all things* (χρόνων ἀποκαταστάσεως πάντων) *which God spoke through the mouth of his holy prophets from the earliest times.*[3]
> [Acts 3:18–21]

---

[1] A slightly revised version, used with permission, of David P. Moessner, "'Listening Posts' along the Way: 'Synchronisms' as Metaleptic Prompts to the 'Continuity of the Narrative' in Polybius' Histories and in Luke's Gospel–Acts: A Tribute to David Aune," in *The New Testament and Early Christian Literature in Greco-Roman Context: Studies in Honor of David E. Aune*, ed. John Fotopoulos, NovTSup 122 (Leiden: Brill, 2006): 129–50.
[2] Polybius, *The Histories* I.3.3–4. Translations are my own from the Greek text of the LCL unless otherwise indicated.
[3] All translations of New Testament texts are my own.

The narratives of each author, then, must make clear how these pattern-shattering,[4] 'eschatological' events of a divine 'plan' took place in a manner in which Hellenistic auditors can comprehend. Accordingly, each composer must work with a set of narrative-poetic building blocks and rhetorical devices which will lead their audience to the same points of viewing and conclusions that they themselves as convinced authors wish to purvey.

1 The Conventions of Hellenistic Narrative Poetics

Ancient narrative (*diegesis*) was conducted in the Hellenistic period through a standard, though highly developed and differentiated, poetics.[5] As posited in Aristotle's *Poetics* and reflected in the rhetorical school debates of the Hellenistic period (for example, Dionysius of Halicarnassus's *Literary Treatises*;[6] Lucian of Samosata's *How to Write History*[7]), ancient narrative theory integrated a tria-lectic hermeneutics or triadic synergy of authorial intent (purpose) ↔ narrative structure (poetics) ↔ audience impact (comprehension). All three components are dynamically interdependent such that no single component can operate

---

4 For Polybius's view of "the cycle of political forms" (πολιτειῶν ἀνακύκλωσις; *Histories* VI.9.10), see Frank W. Walbank, "Polybius and the Past," in *Polybius, Rome and the Hellenistic World: Essays and Reflections* (Cambridge: Cambridge University Press, 2002): 185–87. Rome's "mixed constitution" retarded the "revolving wheel" of this "social development." Compare *idem*, "The Idea of Decline in Polybius," in *Polybius, Rome and the Hellenistic World* (Cambridge: Cambridge University Press, 2002): 193–211: "'*Tyche*' is frequently little more than a verbal elaboration, a way of speaking or a rhetorical flourish; but in the case of Rome's rise to power he [Polybius] seems, exceptionally, to have invested the process with a teleological character and to have treated the popular Hellenistic goddess as something akin to the Stoic Providence" (195); G. W. Trompf, "Polybius and the Elementary Models of Historical Recurrence in the Classical Tradition," in *The Idea of Historical Recurrence in Western Thought: From Antiquity to the Reformation* (Berkeley; CA: University of California Press, 1979): 60–115: "Appeals to recurrent configurations or operative principles afforded a way of disclosing 'the meaning of history'" (112).
5 "Literary prose first emerges in the middle of the fifth century BCE in writings in the Ionic dialect, including the *Histories* of Herodotus, then in the Attic dialect in the oratory of the Sicilian Gorgias and the Athenian Antiphon, and is seen at the end of the century in Thucydides's History," in George A. Kennedy, "The Evolution of a Theory of Artistic Prose," in *The Cambridge History of Literary Criticism*, ed. George A. Kennedy (Cambridge: Cambridge University Press, 1989): 1.184.
6 See esp. Chapter Seven below.
7 Cf. Gert Avenarius, *Lukians Schrift zur Geschichtsschreibung* (Meisenheim/Glan: Hain, 1956), esp. 165–78; Helene Homeyer, *Lukian: Wie man Geschichte schreiben soll: Griechisch und Deutsch* (München: W. Fink, 1965), esp. 239–81.

without the concurrent enabling engagement of the other two. This threefold synergy formed narrative's distinctive epistemology; the three-dimensional, tria-lectic interaction rendered the various claims of a text.[8]

In the course of expounding the distinctive features of poetic *mimesis* in tragedy and epic in his *Poetics*,[9] Aristotle lays out the familiar fundamentals of a standard narrative poetics in chapter 6.

Of the six ingredients of poetic *mimesis*, the three most constitutive and defined as "objects" of the "poet's" *poiesis* are 'plot' (μῦθος/πράξεις), 'character' (τὰ ἤθη), and 'thought' (διάνοια). These three then comprise the structural rudiments of composed orality, whether of dramatic presentation or narrative performance.

The most important of these is the 'arrangement of the incidents' (ἡ τῶν πραγμάτων σύστασις) *[...] and the end aimed at is* [the representation] *not of qualities of character* (τὰ ἤθη) *but of some action [...] they* [characters] *do not therefore act to represent character traits or qualities* (τὰ ἤθη μιμήσωνται), *but characters are included for the sake of the action* (διὰ τὰς πράξεις) *[...]. The plot* (μῦθος) *then is the first principle and as it were the soul of tragedy*[10]: *character comes second [...]. Third comes 'thought'* (διάνοια) *[6.15–40].*

According to Aristotle, every good tragedy or epic represents a "single action" with a unique sequence of *beginning, middle, and end* in which a main actor undergoes a major turn of events (μετάβασις) from good to bad or the reverse (the

---

8 See further Chapter Seven below.
9 Cf., e.g., Stephen Halliwell, *The Poetics of Aristotle: Translation and Commentary* (London: Duckworth, 1987); Lane Cooper, *The Poetics of Aristotle: Its Meaning and Influence* (New York: Longman, Green and Co., 1927), esp. 15–62; S. H. Butcher, *Aristotle's Theory of Poetry and Fine Art* (New York: Dover Publications, 1951), esp. 121–27; Manfred Fuhrmann, *Aristoteles Poetik* (München: Heimeran Verlag, 1976), esp. 25–31; G. M. A. Grube, *The Greek and Roman Critics* (London: Methuen, 1965), 70–92; D. A. Russell, *Criticism in Antiquity* (Berkeley, CA: University of California Press, 1981), 99–113; Kathy Eden, *Poetic and Legal Fiction in the Aristotelian Tradition* (Princeton, NJ: Princeton University Press, 1986), 69–75; Wesley Trimpi, *Muses of One Mind: The Literary Analysis of Experience and Its Continuity* (Princeton, NJ: Princeton University Press, 1983), 50–63; Malcolm Heath, *Unity in Greek Poetics* (Oxford: Clarendon Press, 1989), 38–55; Paul Ricoeur, *Time and Narrative* (Chicago, IL: University of Chicago Press, 1984), 1:31–51.
10 Or as Aristotle himself states in 9.25–29, "The poet (ποιητής) must be a 'maker' (ποιητής) not of verses but of plots/stories (μῦθοι), since he/she is a poet by virtue of [his/her] 'representation' (μίμησις), and what he/she represents (μιμεῖται) are actions/events (πράξεις)" (trans. mine; numeration according to Aristotle, *Poetics* [Halliwell, LCL]).

latter as in comedy[11]). Every character, event, or action is arranged with all the other characters, actions, or events for the sake of this single action into a unique and dynamic causal nexus of a balanced, beautiful whole, namely, 'plot,' all for the specific purpose of eliciting the emotive reaction or '*katharsis*' of the audience as one of "pity and fear."[12] The extent to which this audience impact (compare modern reader response) is integral to the very *raison d'être* of the poet's undertaking cannot be overemphasized. The goal that the poet must keep vividly before his or her mind for every dimension and section of the drama or narrative epic is the *kathartic* response of the audience:

For the plot (μῦθος) should be so structured (συνεστάναι) that, even without seeing it performed, the person who hears the events that occur experiences horror and pity at what comes about [...]. And since the poet should create the pleasure (ἡδονή) which comes from pity and fear through mimesis, *obviously this should* be built into the events *(ἐν τοῖς πράγμασιν ἐμποιητέον, 14.1–13) [emphasis mine].*[13]

Here we encounter two core components of what we have termed a *triadic synergy* of Hellenistic poetics: (1) the particular form of the actions *(plot)* which (2) is structured by the "poet" toward a specific impact upon the audience. The third component is already implicit, namely, the author's/poet's *intention of the mind* (διάνοια) to compose a plot which issues in the intended audience result. But to describe this authorial intention more directly, we must turn to Aristotle's more nuanced development of the third object of *mimesis*, namely, 'thought' (διάνοια).

As is commonly agreed, Aristotle employs διάνοια in two different sense-referents:[14]

(i) On the one hand, διάνοια "appears wherever in the dialogue they [that is, the characters] put forward an argument (ἀποδείκνυουσι) or deliver a general view on matters (καθόλου τι ἀποφαίνονται)" [6.{1450b}10–11]. Thus διάνοια in this more focused sense is constitutive of character development, which in turn

---

11 The discussion of the latter was either lost or never completed in the *Poetics*; see Halliwell (LCL), on 6, 21 (p. 47 n. e).
12 Aristotle, *Poetics*, 6–8, 13–14, 17 (Halliwell, LCL).
13 Aristotle, *Poetics* (Halliwell, LCL). For the debate on the role and meaning of "*katharsis*," see, e.g., Stephen Halliwell, *Aristotle's Poetics* (Chapel Hill, NC: University of North Carolina Press, 1986), 168–201, 350–56; Leon Golden, *Aristotle on Tragic and Comic Mimesis*, American Classical Studies 29 (Atlanta, GA: Scholars Press, 1992), 5–39; Gerald Frank Else, *Plato and Aristotle on Poetry*, ed. Peter Burian (Chapel Hill, NC: University of North Carolina Press, 1986), 152–62.
14 E.g., Halliwell, *Poetics of Aristotle*, esp. on chapter 6 of the *Poetics*.

is determinative of the quality of action. (ii) Διάνοια, however, may also refer to the poet's own point of view or orientation to the whole of the work, which is expressed through the overall form and content of the work itself. Διάνοια in this wider sense is essentially the rhetoric of the text, because the expression of an author's intent always entails selected language, arranged in specific ways for the purpose of desired effects upon an audience.

Consequently, for any writer to be effective argues Aristotle in chapter 19, she or he must follow the principles (ἰδέα) laid down by the master art, whether involving persuasion, emotional effect, or perspectives on the relative importance of anything. Accordingly, it is ultimately the author's/poet's control of the overall ideological 'thought' of the composition through control of the intermeshing actions, characters, and characters' points of viewing or understanding (διάνοια) that produces a coherent composition (ποίημα) with distinct significances for the audience. Aristotle can even appeal to the formal arrangement of the events (πράγματα) (that is, μῦθος) through the διάνοια of the poet such that the *overall* impact will be the same on any observer or reader. Indeed, speeches or dialogue should be included only when the emplotted action *itself* does not create the desired effect upon the audience of pity and fear, "For what would be the point of the speaker, if the required effect were evident even without speech?" (19.7–8). So tightly interwoven is authorial intention (διάνοια in the broader sense) with the structured plot and its impact upon the audience that Aristotle argues the poet can commit an "incidental error"–such as an impossible detail in depicting life–as long as the larger action becomes more life-like or convincing in producing the desired impact of fear and pity: "It [the error] is justifiable if the poet thus achieves the object (τέλος) of *poiesis* [...] and makes that part or some other part of the poem more striking" (25.23–24).

To sum up, the *Poetics* distills the state of the art of narrative epistemology through a triadic synergy of 'composed orality' consisting of authorial intention (διάνοια), the arrangement of the actions or events (μῦθος), and the impact upon the audience (κάθαρσις).[15]

When the later writers of the church's first Gospels set pen to papyrus, therefore, they were utilizing a genre with norms and expectations of its epistemology and social function widely shared by authors and "literate" audiences alike throughout the Greco-Roman world. Since, according to Aristotle, every proper,

---

15 Cf. Russell, *Criticism in Antiquity*, 99–113, esp. 170, on Aristotle's contribution: "Practically the whole of ancient literary theory–that is to say the search for principles which might form a framework for critical judgment, and set 'literature' in an understandable place among other human activities–turned on the significance and aptness of this notion of *mimesis*."

complete narrative plots a 'single action' of the poet or 'the whole of a certain period of time' of the historian, a single passage isolated from the distinctive plotting of a particular Gospel could become a distortion, a non-'event,' or even misleading 'sayings' of Jesus. This standard narrative hermeneutic thus helps explain the outrage of the proto-orthodox, incipient catholic church when their own Gospels were "dissected," "re-arranged," or their "one Christ" "dismembered."[16]

(Post)modern hermeneutical approaches to narrative of both redaction criticism and reader-oriented criticisms unfortunately as a whole have disabled this finely synchronized, ancient narrative hermeneutic by dis-engaging the dynamic 'components' from each other. In neither of these more recent approaches have the three narrative horizons[17] of author, formal poetics, and audience impact been properly blended and coordinated as equal, co-dependent members in one integrated enterprise.

Whereas long before the 4th century BCE, the composed orality of Homeric epic had pervaded the earliest attempts at writing,[18] whether of the pioneering historical accounts of the Ionic logographers or of the later written versions of sophistic oratorical performance so creatively eschewed in Plato's prose 'dialogue.'[19] Precisely because the earliest traces of Greek oral literature cannot possibly be explained apart from their preoccupation with 'audience impact,' suasive

---

16 "They alter the scriptural context and connection, and dismember the truth [...] with their specious adaptations of the oracles of the Lord. It is just as if there was a beautiful representation of a king made in a mosaic by a skilled artist, and one altered the arrangement of the pieces of stone into the shape of a dog or fox, and then should assert that this was the original representation of a king" (Irenaeus, *Against Heresies* I.7.5, 9.3). The Gospel of Thomas is a good example of a collection of the sayings of Jesus whose utterances have been dislodged or left unconnected with the historical deeds or settings of his public career, that is, a proper narrative construal. For instance, the words of Jesus that find parallels in the canonical Gospels take on a wholly different import in the sayings context of Thomas. For an example of different narrative contextual meanings for a unit of tradition based on Luke's alleged use of Q as a written source, see, e.g., François Bovon, "Tracing the Trajectory of Luke 13, 22–30 back to Q: A Study in Lukan Redaction," in *From Quest to Q: Festschrift James M. Robinson*, ed. J. M. Asgeirsson, K. de Troyer, M. W. Meyer; BETL 146 (Leuven: Leuven University Press/Peeters, 2000): 285–94.
17 I am indebted to Anthony Thiselton for the illuminating use of this term in his synthesis of NT and philosophical hermeneutics, *The Two Horizons: New Testament Hermeneutics and Philosophical Description* (Grand Rapids, MI: Eerdmans, 1980), esp. 293–326.
18 See esp. Carol G. Thomas and Edward Kent Webb, "From Orality to Rhetoric: An Intellectual Transformation," in *Persuasion: Greek Rhetoric in Action*, ed. Ian Worthington (London: Routledge, 1994): 3–25.
19 The extent to which writing was primarily an aide to persuasive speech is striking in Plato's dialogue *Phaedrus*, where Socrates casually refers to a taxonomy of "souls and corresponding discourses" (271d, e).

forms of expression for all sorts of communication had been developing centuries before Aristotle.[20]

Thus through the burgeoning discipline of oratory in the 4th century BCE, rhetorical techniques were already being codified and applied to a variety of forms and genres of both oral and written performance. As Richard Leo Enos has so well documented,

Democracy provided the context that made rhetoric a source of social power. This force of rhetoric prompted a blossoming of attention to discourse that moved from the poetic to the practical [...]. Rhapsodes, historians, orators and logographers demonstrated a compatible and correlative relationship between oral and written composition long before systems of rhetoric were formalized.[21]

This means, then–to employ Aristotle's wider notion of 'thought' (διάνοια)[22]– that an author's overall purpose for impacting an audience and the selection of a written genre appropriate to that impact had become the basis for the coherence of a text rather than Aristotle's more rarefied notion of the 'unity of causality' of the poets. Later composers and literary critics, for instance, did not follow Aristotle's rather idiosyncratic privileging of the poet's 'one action plot' over against the "looser" unity of the single "period of time" of the historians, et cetera.[23] In fact, it is not long after the time of Aristotle before writers of history like Polybius (c. 202–120 BCE), Diodorus Siculus (*floruit* Julian period), or Dionysius of Halicarnassus (*floruit* Augustan period)–each thoroughly immersed in the culture of suasive speech–will conceive their own narrative histories as persuasive, diegetic *poiesis*.[24]

---

20 "Greek literature was already formed when it was first written down" (Albert B. Lord, "Words Heard and Words Seen," in *Epic Singers and Oral Tradition* [Ithaca, NY: Cornell University Press, 1991], 19).
21 Richard L. Enos, *Greek Rhetoric before Aristotle* (Prospect Heights, IL: Waveland Press, 1993), 136, 139.
22 On the role of the author in embedding his/her 'thought' into a re-scripted form of the oral traditions, see esp. Walter J. Ong, "Writing is a Technology that Restructures Thought," in *The Written Word: Literacy in Transition*, ed. Gerd Baumann (Oxford: Clarendon, 1986), 23–50, esp. 37–45.
23 Cf. Russell, *Criticism in Antiquity,* 17: "The Aristotelian insight that imaginative literature uses discourse in a fundamentally different ('mimetic') way from oratory is either forgotten or set aside as not relevant to the business of reading, judging and reproducing the classical texts"; see esp. 114–47 on the influence of rhetoric.
24 See, e.g., Dionysius of Halicarnassus, *Pompeius,* § 3; cf., e.g., Heath, *Unity,* 151: "Aristotle seems to have regarded chronological closure as the equivalent in history to the unified action

1.1 Polybius of Megalopolis

Polybius's *Histories* offers an illuminating link in tracing the triadic synergy of composed orality from the *Poetics* of Aristotle to the unabashedly rhetorically-charged history-narratives of the 1st century BCE.

To be sure, Polybius does not refer to his narrative composing as poetic *mimesis* à la Aristotle, but rather he is the first (extant) composer of multi-volume narrative (*diegesis*) to appeal to his narrative organization as an 'arrangement' (οἰκονομία) specifically designed to lead his audience to the proper (that is, authorially intended!) understanding of the events which he recounts. Similar, then, to Aristotle's formulation, the historian should portray events of a specific time period as they are known to have occurred in order to provide a reliable picture of "all the events in their contiguous relationships that happened to one or more persons" (ὅσα ἐν τούτῳ συνέβη περὶ ἕνα ἢ πλείους, ὧν ἕκαστον ὡς ἔτυχεν ἔχει πρὸς ἄλληλα, *Poetics* 23.22–23). Yet contrary to Aristotle, Polybius will compose his narrative history like Aristotle's well-constructed epic, as "converging to the same goal" (*History* I.3.4 [πρὸς ἓν γίνεσθαι τέλος τὴν ἀναφορὰν ἁπάντων]; compare *Poetics* 23.26 [πρὸς τὸ αὐτὸ συντείνουσαι τέλος]). For it is his bold assertion that never before in the history of the world had events coalesced in this most unusual way to link the world as one and thus produce a 'common history' (καθόλου πραγμάτων, I.4.2[25]). Polybius must, he contends, construct a narrative that reflects this unity through its own 'economy' or 'arrangement' (οἰκονομία[26]):

---

of epic and drama, the structural *sine qua non* of good order. Later rhetorical theory does not follow him in this."

[25] See Adele C. Scafuro, "Universal History and the Genres of Greek Historiography" (Ph.D. diss., Yale University, 1984), 102–15; Polybius refers to his work as τὰ καθόλου, in contrast to historians who concentrate on limited geographical areas of (a) specific nation(s), who thus write κατὰ μέρος, e.g., *Histories* I.4.2; III.23.3; V.31.3; VII.7.6; VIII.2.11; XVI.14.1; XXIX.12. Scafuro contends that Polybius's critique of Ephorus, Theopompus, Kallisthenes, and especially Timaeus as "universal historians" (Bk. 12) extends only to the events that are contemporary with the time of their own writing; only on that basis can he attack their own lack of "autopsy" or shoddy interrogation of other αὐτόπται. In essence, then, Polybius is re-defining the categorization of their "universal histories" (from the beginnings of recorded civilization to their own day) to the status of "monographs" of limited scope, whereas his own work, though concentrating on one period of history, is the true *universal* history since it weaves together the events that for the first time were truly "common" to the peoples of the whole (known) world. Cf. Scafuro, "Universal History," 111: "Rather than invent a new name–one that represented the fact that its universality was 'horizontal' (synchronic) rather than 'vertical' (diachronic)–he kept the old names of *koinē historia* and *hē katholou*."
[26] See esp. *History* I.13.9; all translations of Polybius's *The Histories*, LCL, are my own unless otherwise indicated.

1.5 *For who is so worthless or indolent as not to wish to know by what means and under what system of polity the Romans in less than fifty-three years have succeeded in subjecting nearly the whole inhabited world to their sole government—a thing unique in history?* [...]. 4.1 *For what gives my work its peculiar quality, and what is most remarkable in the present age, is this. Fortune having guided almost all the affairs* (πράγματα) *of the world in one direction* (πρὸς ἕν) *and having forced them to incline toward one and the same end* (πρὸς ἕνα καὶ τὸν αὐτὸν σκοπόν), *a historian should bring before his readers under one synoptical view* (σύνοψις) *the operations by which Fortune* (χειρισμὸν τῆς τύχης) *has accomplished her general purpose* (πρὸς τὴν τῶν ὅλων πραγμάτων συντέλειαν, 4.2).

This great unifying act of Fortune must be re-presented by a narrative 'continuity' (ὁ συνεχές; compare especially I.5.5[27]) which reflects this unprecedented interweaving of events. Even through forty long volumes, Polybius must create a narrative 'road' that will lead all those who take the journey to comprehend this unparalleled convergence of peoples and affairs. Rather than the tightly-knit 'necessary or probable causality' of the one-action plot of tragedy or epic, the unity of Polybius's composition will be established through a *continuity* of narrative performance (τὸ συνεχές[28]) which leads the audience to this 'one result' (τέλος). Again, our trialectic hermeneutic undergirds and ensconces Polybius's enterprise: Polybius's goal (authorial intent) to reflect for his audience the harmonious workings of Fortune will be represented through a continuity of narrative poetics (form of-/formal text) through which the audience will comprehend Fortune's one result (audience impact/understanding).

One of the many such rhetorical-poetics ploys of Polybius is his 'synchronisms.' Though historians like Ephorus of Cyme[29] before him had already utilized 'chronological conjunctions' to coerce audiences to view in tandem what would otherwise be widely disparate if not historically impossible events to link together,[30] Polybius is the first extant historian to employ synchronisms as critical "listening posts" for his audience. By bringing together syn-chronically within his narrative widely separated and ostensibly unrelated happenings in different parts of the world, the Achaean historian prompts his audience to hear

---

27 ὁ συνεχὴς λόγος, ("the message/text that continues on ...", that is, to its overall goal [τέλος]).
28 Cf., e.g., *Histories* IV.1.8; VI.2.1.
29 See below under Polybius's use of synchronisms of main events with auxiliary events that are treated somewhat later in the ongoing continuity of his narrative.
30 "Synchronisms were already a recognized feature of Hellenistic historiography. Duris [of Samos], for instance, opened his work with the synchronous deaths of Amyntas of Macedonia, Agesipiolis of Sparta and Jason of Pherae" (Walbank, "Polybius and the Past," 182).

this most unusual convergence of nations and events as the machinations and orchestrations of divine fate and of Fortune which produced Rome's mercurial ascendancy to world domination. As Frank W. Walbank puts it, "in describing her handiwork in detail he [Polybius] is at pains to underline the clues which *Tyche* distributed in the form of synchronisms [...] not simply as a *Hilfsmittel* for the reader, but as a sign that *Tyche* is actively effecting a change in human affairs."[31]

1.2 Luke the Evangelist

Luke, too, develops synchronisms beyond any of his synoptic co-compositionists. By conjoining Roman and Jewish rulers with his prime actors and events, Luke leads his audience to comprehend the most unlikely, ironic development of 'God's' will that Israel would actually reject their own Savior, Messiah Jesus. But precisely through this unprecedented, indeed 'un-orthodox' means, Israel would realize its own eschatological calling to be a light of salvation to the rest of the world.

To accomplish this larger narrative purpose, Luke intends to compose a narrative better suited than his predecessors' in illuming his audience of those momentous yet difficult "events come to fruition in our midst" (Luke 1:1), and to do so, he will configure "all these events" in two interlocking volumes[32] subsumed to an overarching "plan of God."[33] In comparing his narrative 'arrangement' to "many others,"[34] Luke distinguishes his "sequence" as one that will lead

---

[31] Walbank, "Polybius and the Past," 182.
[32] ≈ [=] "corresponds to": Luke 3:21–24:53≈Acts 1:1–2; Luke 24:13–43≈Acts 1:3; Luke 24:36–49≈Acts 1:4–5; Luke 24:50–51≈Acts 1:6–11; Luke 24:52–53≈Acts 1:12–14. Moreover, the opening address to "Theophilus" in the second volume (Acts 1:1–2) appeals directly to the same Theophilus of the first volume (Luke 1:3) and indicates that this "new" volume is a continuation of the "first" (Τὸν μὲν πρῶτον λόγον [...] ὧν ἤρξατο ὁ Ἰησοῦς ..., Acts 1:1).
[33] Cf. Luke 7:30; Acts 2:23; 4:28; (5:38); 13:36; 20:27; (27:42–43). For an illuminating treatment of this notion in several Hellenistic writers, including Diodorus, Dionysius of Halicarnassus, Josephus, and Luke, see John T. Squires, *The Plan of God in Luke-Acts*, SNTSMS 76 (Cambridge: Cambridge University Press, 1993), esp. 15–52. Squires compares the formulations of providence and divine control over history in the various writers but does not treat the narrative epistemology which shapes the more comprehensive narrative configurations of those formulations; for the comparison of Josephus's notion of divinely motivated history with Polybius's, see, e.g., A. M. Eckstein, "Josephus and Polybius: A Reconsideration," *Classical Antiquity* 9 (1990): 175–208: e.g., on *Tuchē*, "certainty as to the Greek source of this Josephan motif cannot be achieved [...] but given the similarities between the Polybian and Josephan concepts of Tyche, and the similar focus on Tyche's role in Rome's supremacy, Polybius is the obvious candidate" (202).
[34] πολλοὶ ἐπεχείρησαν [...] ἀνατάξασθαι διήγησιν.

the likes of a Theophilus on the paths to "certain clarity" (καθεξῆς σοι γράψαι, κράτιστε Θεόφιλε, ἵνα ἐπιγνῷς περὶ ὧν κατηχήθης λόγων τὴν ἀσφάλειαν, Luke 1:3b–4). Whatever else καθεξῆς σοι γράψαι may mean in detail, Luke certainly ties its "sense" directly to the "referent" of intended impact on his audience, especially since ἡ ἀσφάλεια combines both the *senses* of "clarity" (σαφήνεια) and "security" (ἀσφαλής). The *peroratio* of Acts 2:36, for instance, makes this double-edged thrust unmistakable as Peter clinches the argument in Luke's arrangement of his speech by appealing to the "whole house of Israel": "Let the whole house of Israel know therefore with *clear certainty* (ἀσφαλῶς οὖν γινωσκέτω πᾶς οἶκος Ἰσραήλ)[35] that God established him as both Lord and Christ, this Jesus whom you crucified."[36] Something, then, about the narrative arrangements of the "many" Luke finds wanting; Luke's goal to effect a "firmer grasp" thus becomes a telling clue to his own motivation to write (Luke 1:4).[37]

2 Syn-Chronisms as Metaleptic Prompts in Polybius's *Histories*

Undoubtedly one of Polybius's greatest contributions to the more traditional region-by-region format of history writing (κατὰ μέρος / κατὰ ἰδίαν / κατὰ γένος) is his innovative employment of synchronisms in Books I–VI which become much

---

35 Cf. the only other instance of ἀσφάλεια in Luke-Acts in Acts 5:23 with its literal sense and referent, "the securely locked" prison gates! Cf. BDAG on ἀσφαλῶς in Acts 2:36: "know beyond a doubt"; RSV: "know assuredly"; cf. adjectival senses linked with verbs of "understanding" and "writing" just as with "His Excellency, Theophilus" in Luke 1:4: e.g., Acts 25:26–Festus ("His Excellency,"! Acts 26:25) does not have anything "firmly grasped" about the accusations against Paul "in order to write" his superior (ἀσφαλές τι γράψαι). He therefore needs further illumination from those who are competent to judge Paul's case; cf. Acts 21:34; 22:30.
36 Thus, unlike the direct criticism of other Hellenistic historians who in their *prooimia* promote their own strengths over against alleged weaknesses of their rivals, Luke presents only an oblique critique of his predecessors.
37 Luke's propensity to link the events of Jesus and of the church to "fulfillments" of Israel's events and prophecies according to their scriptures is well documented and embodies a 'wholeness' of events ensembled like no other narrative account: e.g., the "completions" of a period of time which themselves introduce a new stage of fulfillment in Israel's festal calendar or Torah observance or promises of the prophets: Luke 2:21, 22–24, 34; 3:3–6, 15–16; 4:16–21; 9:28–31, 51; 10:23–24; 12:49–53; 13:31–35; 17:22–35; 18:31–34; 19:41–44; 22:14–18, 28–30, 35–38; 24:25–27, 44–49; Acts 1:20–22; 2:1; 3:22–26, etc.; see esp. William S. Kurz, "Promise and Fulfillment in Hellenistic Jewish Narratives and in Luke and Acts," in *Jesus and the Heritage of Israel*, ed. David P. Moessner, vol. 1, *Luke the Interpreter of Israel* (Harrisburg, PA: Trinity Press International, 1999): 147–70.

more than the decorative bookends or mnemonic devices of his predecessors.[38] Though the world is not yet united through Fortune's maneuverings (compare Books VII–XL), Polybius wants his auditors during these earlier periods to anticipate the new era after 218 BCE when the discrete affairs of individual nations will have issued in a "common result" (τέλος/συντέλεια). Such synchronisms become undisguised "listening stations" to lure his auditors to the author's way of hearing what would otherwise sound like totally coincidental occurrences.

2.1 Synchronisms of the Main Event with an Auxiliary Event Treated Later in the Narrative

A synchronism utilized already by one of his predecessors, Ephorus of Cyme, but augmented significantly by Polybius is the alignment of a main event of the 'continuity of the narrative'[39] with an auxiliary event that, in some fashion, will be featured later. Because in Books IV and V Polybius laces each year with two synchronisms of this type, the reader is being prepared to view these earlier events in light of the later "auxiliary" occurrences, as well as to discern parallels in theme and historical development when the synchronically-webbed narrative takes over in Books VII–XL.[40]

---

38 See esp. Scafuro, "Universal History," 155–204; on scope, setting, and purpose of Polybius's history writing, see, e.g., Frank W. Walbank, *A Historical Commentary on Polybius*, 3 vols. (Oxford: Clarendon Press, 1957, 1967, 1974); Kenneth S. Sacks, *Polybius on the Writing of History* (Berkeley: University of California Press, 1981); Shaye J. D. Cohen, "Josephus, Jeremiah, and Polybius," *History and Theory* 21 (1982): 366–81.
39 "Continuity of the narrative" (τὸ συνεχὲς τῆς διηγήσεως, cf. *Histories* I.5.5; I.13.8; III.2.6; IV.1.8; VI.2.1; XXXVIII.5.3) is tantamount to Aristotle's notion of "plot" (μῦθος / πράξεις) for tragedy and epic as the dynamic organization or "structuring of events" (ἡ τῶν πραγμάτων σύστασις, e.g., *Poetics* 6 [1450a].15, 32) to produce a coherent story with a "beginning," "middle," and "end" issuing in a "new state of affairs" (μετάβασις /μεταβολή); see further, David P. Moessner, "'Ministers of Divine Providence': Diodorus Siculus and Luke the Evangelist on the Rhetorical Significance of the Audience in Narrative 'Arrangement,'" in *Literary Encounters with the Reign of God: Studies in Honor of Robert Tannehill*, ed. Sharon H. Ringe and H. C. Paul Kim (New York: T&T Clark, 2004): 308–18.
40 As Scafuro, "Universal History," 178, observes, "[the reader] begins to think that the intrusive international events of the synchronism may subsequently have something to do with the narrative he is presently reading." Book VI is an account of republican Rome's constitution which serves in the narrative as a bridge between the two poetics schemes κατὰ μέρος vs. συμπλοκή) of Books I–V and Books VII–XL respectively.

IV.28.1–*Philip V wages war with certain members of the Aetolian and Achaean Leagues at the time that Hannibal attacks Saguntum.*

Polybius tells his audience why he asserts this syn-chronous relationship:

IV.28.1–3 *Now had there been any connection at the outset between Hannibal's enterprise and the affairs of Greece it is evident that I should have included the latter in the previous Book, and following the chronology, placed my narrative of them side by side in alternate sections* (ἐναλλὰξ [...] κατὰ παράθεσιν) *with that of the affairs of Spain. But the fact being that the circumstances of Italy, Greece, and Asia were such that the beginnings of these wars were particular to each country* (τούτων ἰδίας), *while their ends were common to all* (συντελείας κοινάς) [...].[41]

Unparalleled by any known Hellenistic historian, Polybius places a synchronism in the middle of a Book (IV). The effect would be arresting for the auditor; a "loudspeaker announcement" has just been sounded which must be "heard." Consequently, Polybius's prompting in the middle of Book IV has the impact of pointing to one authorial motive: to bring proper focus upon the Second Punic War–as Polybius continues on, "so that the whole narrative may not only be easy to follow (εὐ-παρακολούθητος) but may make a due impression on my auditors/those paying attention" (τοῖς προσέχουσιν, IV.28.6!). For Polybius's audience is not only led back to the end of Book III where Hannibal is poised to conquer Rome itself but is also prompted forward to Book IX when the Carthaginian general will occupy many of the towns in central Italy and bring the great city to its knees.[42]

2.2 Synchronisms of the Main Event with (an) Auxiliary Event(s) Not Treated Later

I.6.1: *"The Gauls Occupy Rome Nineteen Years after the Battle of Aegospotami, Sixteen Years before Leuctra, the Same Year as the Spartans Make the Peace Known as Antalcidas with the King of Persia, and the Year in which Dionysius the Elder Besieges Rhegium"*

Polybius makes no secret of the reason for this synchronism that comes so early in the whole work. The Gauls' occupation of Rome in 387–86 BCE marks the pre-beginning (πρώτη) of the crucial beginning point (ἀρχή) of Rome's

---

41 Some modifications of W. R. Paton's (LCL) translation.
42 See, e.g., B. L. Hallward, "The Roman Defensive," in *The Cambridge Ancient History*, vol. 8 (Cambridge: The University Press, 1930): 57–82.

ascendancy to world domination and thus of Polybius's whole enterprise (ἐπιβολή):[43]

By "beginning" at an even earlier event in Rome's history, at a point symbolic of the very antithesis of her rise to dominion–when Rome herself is under foreign domination–the historian can poignantly illustrate the paradoxical, even "miraculous" 'turn-around' (περιπέτεια) of affairs guided by Fortune. Polybius intends the reader to 'follow' (παρακολουθέω) a 'synoptic' account of these earlier events to establish a pattern in their minds: there is a rhythm to the rise and fall of empires. But Rome can be seen to fit into this pattern only up to a point. When *historia*'s workings would seem to indicate otherwise, Rome manages to break this pattern.[44]

I.12.6–7, I.13.6, 10–11: *To follow out (παρακολουθῆσαι) this previous history–how and when the Romans after the disaster to Rome itself began their progress to better fortunes, and again how and when after conquering Italy they entered on the path of foreign enterprise–seems to me necessary for anyone who hopes to gain a proper general survey (συνόψεσθαι) of their present supremacy [...]. Now to recount all these events in detail is neither incumbent on me nor would it be useful to my readers (τοῖς ἀκούουσι) [...]. I shall, however, attempt to narrate somewhat more carefully the first war between Rome and Carthage for the possession of Sicily; since it is not easy to name any war which lasted longer [...] with more battles, and greater 'changes of fortune' (περιπέτεια).*[45]

The synchronism of I.6.1–with the Gauls' conquest of Rome in tandem with the rising and falling of other empires–throws down a gauntlet to the reader to make sense of Rome's rising 'from the dead.' By comparison (σύγκρισις) with the actions and traits of other nations, Rome's singular character can now become more vividly portrayed.[46]

---

43 *The Histories* I.5.1–5; V.31.8–32.5.
44 Even the inevitable phase of decline after the zenith, according to Polybius's 'cycle of political/cultural development' (πολιτειῶν ἀνακύκλωσις), seems to be arrested significantly or at least delayed for Rome; cf. Walbank, "Polybius and the Past": "At Rome [...] the setting up of the mixed constitution had acted as a brake on the revolving wheel" (185), and yet paradoxically, "Rome does seem to have been the one and only state for which the anacyclosis worked" (187); see further above n. 4.
45 Some modifications of Paton's (LCL) translation.
46 Scafuro, "Universal History," 155–65, suggests that Polybius has formulated a response to Aristotle's arguments in *Poetics* 9 and 23. Aristotle lampoons historians like the later Timaeus who try to impute "marvelous" workings of Fortune/Fate by linking similar happenings in different

Synchronisms like I.6.1, then, provide *aural-prompts* into the sequence of the 'arrangement' and thus sound the way "to follow" (παρακολουθῆσαι) "the continuous character of the narrative" (τὸν τρόπον συνεχοῦς [...] τῆς διηγήσεως, 1.13.9). Moreover, in this 'following,' the "starting point" of the whole narrative (ἡ ἀρχή) provides the crucial hermeneutical key to the configuration of all the subsequent events:

For the ancients, saying that the beginning (ἡ ἀρχή) is half the whole, advised that in all matters the greatest care should be taken to make a good beginning (ὑπὲρ τοῦ καλῶς ἄρξασθαι) [...]. One may indeed confidently affirm that the beginning (ἡ ἀρχή) is not merely half of the whole, but reaches as far as the end (πρὸς τὸ τέλος διατείνειν) [...]. How is it possible to sum up events properly without referring to their beginning (μὴ συναναφέροντα τὴν ἀρχήν), and understanding whence, how, and why the final situation of the events was brought about (πόθεν ἢ πῶς ἢ διὰ τί πρὸς τὰς ἐνεστώσας ἀφῖκται πράξεις)? So we should think that beginnings (τὰς ἀρχάς) do not only reach half way, but reach to the end, and both lectors (τοὺς λέγοντας) and those who hear (τοὺς ἀκούοντας) [that is, writers and readers] of a general history should pay the greatest attention to them (V.32.1–5).

Auditors should therefore not be surprised that in Book II Polybius will begin weaving Roman engagement of the Carthaginians with the Romans' defeats of the Gauls, a foreshadowing of their later war with the Carthaginians who will have to rely upon the Gauls as critical allies.

2.3 'Synchronisms' as Sounding Boards to 'Following' (παρακολουθῆσαι) 'The Continuity' of the Author's Narrative 'Plan'

We have just seen that in his extended prologue Polybius employs παρακολουθέω to link his auditors to the narrative 'arrangement' that unfolds his own grasp of Fortune's manifold orchestrations. Like a fulcrum, παρακολουθέω also pitches his readers towards Polybius's special credentials to narrate this 'master plan.' Several times throughout his forty volumes, Polybius draws attention to his keen

---

parts of the world but which have no putative relationship of cause and effect: "What is being likened [by Aristotle] is [...] the lack of unity in history and in 'improper' epic [...] due to the inclusion of events that are not causally related" (164). Aristotle cites Herodotus, not Thucydides, as his standard for exemplifying events that occurred at the same time but yet "do not converge to a common result" (οὐδὲν πρὸς τὸ αὐτὸ συντείνουσαι τέλος, *Poetics* 23.26).

study of the rise of Rome both through his *first-hand witness of many of the events themselves* and through careful *study* or *inquiry* of government documents and earlier histories. For instance in III.4–5, in the course of composing the history from the Second Punic War to the end of the Third Macedonian War (220–168 BCE), Polybius learned through his own experiences of turbulent times following "the last conquest" of 168 ("*I not only witnessed most but took part in some of the events*" [τὸ τῶν πλείστων μὴ μόνον αὐτόπτης, ἀλλ᾽ ὧν μὲν συνεργός]) that he must continue his narrative to describe the aftermath of Rome's rule, as well as to have his readers "follow" (παρακολουθέω) back to the earlier "beginning" of 264 BCE to bring this new state of affairs into proper perspective. He goes on to argue:

III.32.1–2: *For this reason I must pronounce those to be much mistaken who think that this my work is difficult to acquire and difficult to read* (δυσανάγνωστον) *owing to the number and length of the Books it contains. How much easier it is to acquire and peruse forty Books, all as it were connected by one thread, and thus to follow clearly* (παρακολουθῆσαι σαφῶς) *events in Italy, Sicily* [...] *than to read or procure the works of those who treat of particular transactions* (κατὰ μέρος) [...]. *For I maintain that far the most essential part of history is the consideration of the remote or immediate consequences of events and especially that of causes* (μάλιστα τὰ περὶ τὰς αἰτίας) [...]. *All this can be recognized and understood from a general history, but not at all from the historians of the wars themselves, such as the war with Perseus or that with Philip.*

Polybius's active *engagement* both as *eyewitness* and as an *informed contemporary follower*[47] of the rise of Rome produced his special qualifications to compose a narrative. Polybius can lead his readers to *follow* his narrative construal precisely because of his "mind's own ability to follow" the course of Rome's preeminence. As one "steeped" in the history of Rome's rise, Polybius assumes that his readers will also become so engaged. All the emphasis, therefore, in his use of παρακολουθέω in Books I and III is upon the effective "following of the mind" into new vistas of understanding which will occur through "following" the distinctive scope and sequence of his narrative road. Παρακολουθέω thus ties the *readers' ability to follow to the author's peculiar competence to lead.*

To sum up, Polybius's 'synchronisms' function as 'aural aids' sounding the way to 'follow' Polybius's 'arrangement' so that his auditors might grasp Polybius's own grand sweep of the multifarious performances of Fortune that converge in 'one result' (τέλος / συντέλεια).

---

47 See Chapter Three above on the similar meaning of παρηκολουθηκότι in Luke 1:3.

3 Synchronisms as Metaleptic Prompts in Luke's 'Gospel Acts'

What does Luke want his auditors to hear with his deployment of synchronisms at the beginnings of his two volumes[48] as well as, like Polybius, in the middle of his volumes? Luke's synchronisms point over and over again to the powers and 'powerful players' that coalesced to cause the "peoples" of Israel, along with the "kings of the earth" (Ps 2:1–2[49] in Acts 4:25b–26) to "*align against*" Israel's "Messiah" and *reject* Israel's "glory as a light of illumination for the nations" (Luke 2:32).

If this characterization is correct, then Luke's synchronisms would thrust his readers into the dynamic of the 'continuity of the narrative' that points to Jesus's *death* as a crucial 'turning point' in the larger plot of the 'end' (τέλος) of the narrative of the "eschatological release of sins." It may be that Jesus's *rejection* plays a far greater role in the "witness" of proclamation into all the nations for the forgiveness of sins than a popular view of Luke's theology of the cross will allow (for example, Luke 24:44–49; Acts 1:6–8).[50] Might it be that the very phrase "the Messiah must suffer,"[51] functions as metaleptic prompting to the larger causal

---

48 In Acts 1:21–23 (cf. 10:37), Luke's narrator describes the "beginning" (ἀρξάμενος) of Jesus's public calling as "from the baptism of John," while later in Acts 11:15 Luke will have Peter point back to the coming of the Spirit at Pentecost as a secondary "beginning." The "beginning" of Pentecost fulfills John's own prophecy of a "mightier one who will baptize with Holy Spirit and fire" (Acts 2:33!) when John's own baptizing was heralding the anointing baptism of the Beloved Son by the Holy Spirit (cf. Acts 10:38) as the primary beginning for both volumes (Luke 3:15–17, 21–22). For secondary beginning points of the continuity of plot at the textual beginnings of each new volume of a multi-volume narrative, see, e.g., Polybius, *Histories* I.5.1, 6.1, 12.5–9; IV.28.4, etc.; Diodorus Siculus, *Library of History* II.1.1–3; III.1.1–3; IV.1.5–7; V.2.1; VI.1.1–3; [VII–X]; XI.1.1; XII.2.2–3; XIII.1.1–3; XIV.2.4; XV.1.6; XVI.1.3–6 [cf. XV.95.4!]; XVII.1.1–2; XVIII.1.5–6; XIX.1.9–10; XX.2.3; [XXI — XL]; [] indicate fragmentary books without extant linking passages.
49 All citations of the OT are from the LXX unless otherwise indicated.
50 A majority view of critical scholarship is that Luke himself lacks or avoids an understanding of Jesus's death as atoning, or, at the least, mutes such significance to a marginal note. See, e.g., Hans Conzelmann, *The Theology of St. Luke* (New York: Harper and Row, 1960), 201; Ulrich Wilckens, *Die Missionsreden der Apostelgeschichte*, WMANT 5 (Neukirchen-Vluyn: Neukirchener Verlag, 1974), 216; Ernst Haenchen, *The Acts of the Apostles*, (Oxford: Blackwell, 1971), 91–92; Werner Georg Kümmel, "Current Theological Accusations Against Luke," *Andover Newton Quarterly* 16 (1975): 134, 138; I. Howard Marshall, *Luke: Historian and Theologian* (Grand Rapids, MI: Zondervan, 1970), 172; Ernst Käsemann, *Essays on New Testament Themes*, SBT 41 (London: SCM, 1964), 92; Joel B. Green, *Theology of Luke* (Cambridge: Cambridge University Press, 1995), 124–25; H. Douglas Buckwalter, *The Character and Purpose of Luke's Christology*, SNTSMS 89 (Cambridge: Cambridge University Press, 1996), 231–72; Peter Doble, *The Paradox of Salvation: Luke's Theology of the Cross*, SNTSMS 87 (Cambridge: Cambridge University Press, 1996), 235–37; etc.
51 Luke 24:26, 46; Acts 3:18; 17:3; 26:23; cf. Luke 9:22; 17:25; 22:15; Acts 1:3; 9:16.

connection of Jesus's crucifixion to the "change of fortune" in the offer of the "forgiveness of sins" to Israel and the nations in Luke's overarching "plan of God" (ἡ βουλὴ τοῦ θεοῦ)?[52]

i) Luke 1:5: "And it happened in the days of Herod, King of Judea, that there was a certain priest, from the order of Abijah, whose name was Zachariah, and his wife, from the daughters of Aaron, and her name was Elizabeth."

Why is Herod–and not the Roman governor or emperor or high priests or other Judean officials–named alone at the pre-beginning (πρώτη)[53] of the plot? Is it not because another Herod of the same power dynasty, Herod Antipas, will figure prominently in John the Baptist's career, whose fate in turn prefigures the lot of Jesus who will meet this Herod again at the 'end' during the process of his "trial" that results in his crucifixion (compare especially Luke 3:19–20→3:21–22→9:9→23:8–11)? Are we perhaps to hear that, above all, Israel's own "king" was instrumental in fulfilling the plot of Israel's own "suffering" Messiah? Is this king in some way symbolic of the whole nation who are eager "to see" Jesus but who refuse to "repent" (compare Luke 9:9→13:31–35→23:8–11)?

ii) Luke 2:1: "And it happened in those days [that is, those of John's birth, Luke 1:57–80] that an edict from Caesar Augustus was sent forth, declaring that the whole inhabited world [of Rome] should be registered. This landmark registration took place around the time when Quirinius was serving as governor of Syria."

Luke's auditors were well aware that Augustus at that time was the most powerful ruler on earth, who according to, for instance, the Priene inscription, was hailed in eastern provinces like Asia or Syria as "savior for us and for our descendants [...] the beginning of the message of peace (εὐαγέλια)."[54] Luke wants his readers to know of another "Savior" and "Lord," "the Christ" of the royal line of David (2:4–14) whose humble origins become a "sign" of God's saving act "for the whole people" (2:10–12) and herald "peace" for "all humanity of God's gracious plan (εὐδοκία)" (2:14). Does not Jesus's birth by conception of the Holy Spirit augur a Savior far greater than the adopted son of Julius Caesar and a "peace" more momentous than the *Pax Romana* (compare 1:26–38)?

iii) Luke 2:21: "And when the eight days before he was to be circumcised were fulfilled, he was given the name 'Jesus' [that is, ὁ κύριος σῴζει], the name given by the angel [Gabriel] before he was conceived in the womb."

---

52 See n. 8 above.
53 For the relation of the πρώτη to the ἀρχή in narrative plotting, see above on *The Histories* I.6.1.
54 See, e.g., Hans-Josef Klauck, *The Religious Context of Early Christianity: A Guide to Graeco-Roman Religions* (Minneapolis, MN: Fortress Press, 2003), 298.

Jesus's "parents" follow the "law of Moses" as Torah-adherent Jews. Does Luke perhaps wish to underscore that the Savior already named in heaven before his birth was reared as an Israelite, "of the house and line of David," and that his life was geared to follow the rhythms and customs of faithful Jews as an elect son[55] of Israel (compare Luke 23:35!)?[56]

iv) Luke 2:22–24: "And when the days of their cleansing according to the law of Moses were fulfilled, they ['the parents,' compare 2:27] brought him up into Jerusalem in order to present him to the Lord, just as it stands written in the law of the Lord, 'Every male that opens the mother's womb [firstborn] shall be declared "holy" for the Lord' [Exod 13:2,12,15], and to offer a sacrifice according to what is spoken in the Law of the Lord, 'a pair of turtledoves or two young pigeons' [Lev 12:8; 5:11]".

Jesus's parents fulfill "the law of Moses" for "the purification" of a new mother and "sanctification of the firstborn" *à la* Lev 12:2–4 and Exod 13:1–16, respectively. The entire encounter with the pious worthies Simeon and Hannah, however, mimics more the "presentation of Samuel" in Eli's temple at Shiloh than straightforward fulfillment of *halakah*.[57] Does the sacrifice of redemption for the "firstborn" in Exod 13 which reenacts Israel's redemption through the Passover, together with Zachariah's prophecy of "making redemption" (ποιεῖν λύτρωσις)[58] in the "Lord's" "visitation of his people" in Luke 1:68b, perhaps adumbrate

---

55 E.g., [LXX] 2Kgdms 7:8–17.
56 See, e.g., Joel B. Green's illuminating presentation of Luke's intertextuality with the LXX, "Internal Repetition in Luke–Acts: Contemporary Narratology and Lucan Historiography," in *History, Literature, and Society in the Book of Acts*, ed. Ben Witherington III (Cambridge: Cambridge University Press, 1996): 283–99, esp. 290: "Luke inscribes himself in scriptural tradition, showing his debt to this previous story, and inviting his auditors to hear in this story the resounding continuation of that story."
57 See esp. 1Kgdms 1:24–2:10,20; cf. Luke 2:22b: "to present (παραστῆσαι) him to the Lord."
58 My rendering of the unusual phrase "make redemption," which is not found in the LXX. But what is consistent from the LXX's usage of the verb λυτρόω and its noun λύτρωσις is the requirement of either animal sacrifice or ransom money/goods (λύτρον) to *make* redemption a reality. In conjunction with God "visiting" his people to effect release from slavery and/or sin (Luke 1:68b), "make redemption" denotes the unspecified means through which God's presence for release is accomplished (cf. LXX Ps 110:9 ["send redemption"]). Cf. Joseph A. Fitzmyer, *The Gospel according to Luke*, 2 vols., AB 28 (New York: Doubleday, 1981/1985), 1.383: "the combination of the noun *lytrōsis* with the verb *poiein* is strange [...] it describes Yahweh's activity on behalf of his people in terms of ransom or release"; cf. Luke Timothy Johnson, *The Gospel of Luke*, SP 3 (Collegeville, MN: Liturgical Press, 1991), 46: "In contrast to the 'liberation' of the people from Egypt under Moses, however (Acts 7:35), Luke here defines it in apolitical, cultic terms."
For God's "visitation" as gracious deliverance, see esp. LXX Exod 4:31; Ruth 1:6; Pss 79:14; 105:4; for "to redeem/make ransom" and its noun, see e.g., LXX Exod 6:6; 13:13,15; 15:13;

Jesus's self-sacrifice when, after "cleansing" the Temple, he will signify his voluntary death "for them" as the sealing of a "new covenant" at *the Passover* with his "apostles" (Luke 22:19–20 in 22:14–38; compare 2:7–Jesus as the "firstborn"!)? Luke would seem to be prompting his audience to hear the promises of "redemption" of Israel's founding *release* and *covenant* with the Lord God as coming to a new and definitive stage of realization in the career of Jesus.

v) Luke 2:27b–28: "And when the parents brought the child Jesus in [that is, into the Temple] in order that they might do according to what was customary under the law concerning him, then he himself [that is, Simeon] received it [the infant] into his arms and blessed God, saying, [...]."

Luke presents this "presentation" with considerable aural fanfare:

(a) Simeon's arrival at the Temple "by the Spirit" at the very moment that the "Lord's Christ" is also present (2:26–27a) is a God-ordained occurrence. What could appear as a marvelous "accident" of an aged "righteous" person, who had been waiting year after year for Israel's "consolation," is actually part of a grander scheme of the Lord's "saving action" (2:30a), disclosed to Simeon in advance by the very same "Holy Spirit" (2:26).

(b) Like Melchizedek blessing Abraham, the "greater" Spirit-led Simeon blesses Mariam (and Joseph) and reveals to her what role her child will play in God's "pre-ordained plan" (κεῖται, 2:34) and even her own experience of this plan. Now she must learn that her child, called "Son of the Most High" who "will reign on David's throne forever" (1:32–33), will do so only as a "sword of discernment" cuts conflict right through the "heart" of the "many" in Israel and does not spare even her "own soul" (2:34–35). As a 'character' in the 'plot,' clearly Simeon is endowed with omniscient-like understanding that can declare directly what God's 'plan' specifically entails.[59]

(c) Hence, whatever temptations there might be for Luke's audience to regard Mariam's and Zachariah's prophecies as "triumphalistic" oracles of a political nationalistic messianic reign–to destroy literally Israel's enemies (compare Luke 4:1–13!)–are transmuted into nearly the opposite, namely, an "anointed" "king," whose rule consists of being greatly opposed by his own people and thus of creating deep division among Israel itself. A number of terms and expectations from the "Servant of the Lord's" calling in Isa 40–55 are clustered in Luke's *poiesis*

Lev 19:20; 25:25; 27:31, 33; Num 18:15, 16; Pss 48:7, 8, 9; 129:8 (from sin); Isa 63:4, *inter alia*.

59 For the relation within the plot of various characters' understanding (διάνοια) of the larger plot in conjunction with the plotted understanding (διάνοια) of the composer-author, see Aristotle, *Poetics*, esp. chaps. 6, 19, and 25.

here; Simeon himself looks to be one of the "righteous" of Isaiah, who are linked corporately as "the servant" (ὁ δοῦλος) with a righteous one depicted more in individual characteristics as "the servant" (ὁ παῖς). Moreover, even as God's "saving action" in the child Jesus will engender "glory to your people Israel," the "light" of this salvation will be dispersed "among the nations" (2:30–32).[60]

(d) "Hannah," who is reminiscent of her namesake's role in a presentation at a temple, and mirroring the qualities of Simeon, including her ordained appearance "at that very hour" (2:38a), confirms Simeon's oracles by offsetting and re-defining the expectations for all those "awaiting the redemption (λύτρωσις) of Jerusalem" (2:38b).

In sum, Luke places particular emphasis upon Simeon's and Hannah's oracles by hoisting a mega-phone of three 'synchronisms' of the special calling of Jesus that Jesus will fulfill as "God's saving act." "Savior," "Lord," and "the Christ" all take on transformed roles through the prophecies of these two elderly righteous of Israel: Jesus's circumcision actually involves a particular "naming" for his special "calling," his "presentation to/for the Lord" is in reality a dedication to his unprecedented task of causing the "falling" as well as the "rising" of the "many," and his reception in the Temple by the righteous of Israel is a preview not only of the "rising" of Israel, but also of those who will be enlightened "among the nations."

By fusing these early scenes of Jesus's childhood with the requirements of "the law of Moses," Luke would have us *hear* that a special *type* of fulfillment, as well as a special *time* of fulfillment, is truly taking place. All emphasis upon the "saving act" is upon Jesus as a *sign of opposition*; the "redemption" of Jerusalem will actually take place through a great conflict of judgment within the very soul of Israel. Clearly this 'continuity of the narrative' is not what Greco-Roman auditors would be anticipating. As Luke completes his frontispiece (πρώτη) to the 'beginning' (ἀρχή) of his narrative, it would appear that the "good news" consists in the ironic, if not unbelievable, message that salvation for Israel will come to its decisive goal in the rejection of "Messiah the Lord" (compare Isa 53:1).

vi) Luke 3:1: "In the fifteenth year of the rule of Tiberias Caesar, when Pontius Pilate was serving as governor of Judea, and Herod [as] Tetrarch of Galilee, and

---

60 Notice the cluster of images, phrases, and terms from Isaiah, esp. chaps. 40–55, in Luke 2:29–32: e.g., Isa 40:5; 42:6; 46:13; 49:6, 9; 52:10; see now further, David P. Moessner, "Luke's 'Witness of Witnesses': Paul as Definer and Defender of the Tradition of the Apostles–'from the Beginning,'" in *Paul and the Heritage of Israel: Paul's Claim upon Israel's Legacy in Luke and Acts in the Light of the Pauline Letters*, ed. David P. Moessner, Daniel Marguerat, Mikeal Parsons, and Michael Wolter, vol. 2 *Luke the Interpreter of Israel* (London: T&T Clark, 2012): 117–47, esp. 138–47.

Philip, his brother, Tetrarch of the regions of Ituraea and Trachonitus, and Lysanius, Tetrarch of Abilene, at the time when Annas and Caiaphas were high priest, the word of God came in the wilderness to John, son of Zachariah."

This sixth synchronism adumbrates the 'beginning' (ἀρχή) point of both volumes by linking John's calling to be the "voice in the wilderness" of Isa 40 ff. (Luke 3:4–6) with the geo-political control of Palestine and portions of Syria and Trans-Jordan:

(a) We meet "Herod" again, now presented as "Tetrarch" over Galilee rather than "King of Judea." Now Pontius Pilate "is governing" Judea. Power has shifted, as have also the characters. Even Augustus Caesar has changed to Tiberias. Yet God's promises to Zachariah and Elizabeth fulfilling Israel's scriptures continue unbroken and according to a set pace. The "word of God" happens "just as it stands written in the book of the oracles of the prophet Isaiah, 'A voice crying in the wilderness [...].'"

(b) Is it simply fortuitous that "Herod" follows "Pilate" after the one who rules over them both is mentioned? Are we to hear already near 'the beginning' of the plot that these two figure prominently "during the whole time that the Lord (κύριος!) Jesus went in and out among them" (Acts 1:21)? Are we not also to think of them as decisive at the 'end,' who as former "enemies" link *hands* to become "friends" and put the 'Son of sinful humankind' to death (Luke 9:7–9→9:44→23:12→24:7→Acts 4:25–28). According to the thought of the "gathered servants (δοῦλοι)" in Acts 4, Pilate's and Herod's becoming friends–to join "the arrogant machinations of the nations" with "the vain schemes of the peoples of Israel against your holy servant (παῖς) Jesus whom you anointed"–follows exactly "whatever your [God's] *hand* and *plan* (βουλή) had ordained in advance to accomplish" (fulfilling Ps 2 regarding the κύριος and his χριστός, Acts 4:25b–26). Pilate and Herod are synchronized in the "plan of God" even as they are set in place to stamp '*the beginning.*'

(c) "Release of sins" (ἄφεσις ἁμαρτιῶν) is the goal of John's "preparing the way of the Lord" of Isa 40:3 (Luke 3:3). John's proclaiming of a "baptism of a change of mind/repentance" results in (εἰς) that "release," as radical 'turn abouts' will be effected through John's preaching; what was once crooked will become straight, valleys are to be filled and mountains leveled as "all flesh shall see this saving act of God" (Isa 40:4–5 in Luke 3:4c–5). John's "baptism of a change of mind" will certainly be instrumental in the "saving act" of God (Luke 3:6) through his Christ.

But why is the "baptism for a release of sins" (Luke 3:3) tied to the calling of the prophet in Isa 40? Is it because the prophet-herald of good news (ὁ εὐαγγελιζόμενος) of Isa 40 and 51 "prepares" the way for the Lord's own coming to the restored exiles: "Look, your God; look, the Lord [...] is coming" (Isa 40:9b–10 ['Ιδοὺ ὁ θεὸς ὑμῶν. ἰδοὺ κύριος [...] ἔρχεται ...; compare 52:7)? Is the Christ the "Lord" whose way John is preparing (Isa 53:1–2; compare Luke 1:43; 2:11 and others)? Is then this Lord the individual servant figure of Isaiah 40–55 whose ignominious rejection and violent death from his own people is itself regarded as an atonement like a 'scapegoat' who "bore the sins of the many" (αὐτὸς ἁμαρτίας πολλῶν ἀνήνεγκεν, Isa 53:12b)? Will the high priestly duty of the Day of Atonement of a Caiaphas be evacuated by the death of God's "Christ" (Luke 23:45b–46: "And the veil of the sanctuary was split down the middle [...] when he breathed his last breath")? It would seem that the decisive 'turn about' (μεταβολή / μετάβασις) of Jesus's rejection at the 'end' by all the peoples of Israel and the nations is already being "figured" here as 'the beginning point' is being shaped by "the kings of the nations" who "lord it over them" (Luke 3:1→22:24–25!).

vii) Luke 3:21–22: "And it happened during the time all of the people were baptized that when Jesus was baptized and was praying, the heaven opened up and the Holy Spirit descended in bodily form like a dove upon him, and a voice from heaven sounded, 'You are my beloved Son, in you I take delight'" (compare Gen 22:2; Isa 42:1).

This seventh synchronism, which introduces 'the beginning' (ἡ ἀρχή) of the narrative, presents "the baptism of John" as the telling 'beginning' for all of Jesus's calling. The two figures of John and Jesus are fused together in one plan through their synchronized fulfillment of scripture. The "saving act" which John prepares will be accomplished through the "beloved Son" and chosen Servant of Israel's great redemption as figured by the 'sacrifice of Abraham' and the sacrifice of the 'sin offering' and 'scape goat' of the Lord's anointed Servant (see Gen 22:2; Isa 42:1; 53:6, 10, 12). It now also becomes clear why our narrator has seemingly "jumped ahead" of the plot by announcing already in Luke 3:20 that Herod "locked up John in prison," while Jesus's baptism, presumably by John, is not described until 3:21–22. John's own fate as a rejected prophet by the "Herod" of the "peoples of Israel" embodies the "sign of opposition" against Israel's "anointed Son and Servant." We are reminded of Polybius's comments on the significance of 'the beginning.' John thus "goes before the Lord to prepare his way" both in life and in death: "And Herod said, 'John I beheaded. Who then is this about whom I am hearing these things?' And he was seeking to see him [Jesus]" (Luke 9:9b→23:8: "because of all that he [Herod] was hearing about him [Jesus], he had been hoping to see some sign performed by him"). "But no sign shall be given to this generation, except 'the sign of Jonah' [that is, sign of impending judgment, as Jonah was to Nineveh]" (Luke 11:29–32). John's death, not his ultimate vindication, is that quintessential 'sign.'

viii) Luke 13:1–5: "Now there were there at that very time certain ones who began to tell him [Jesus] about the Galileans whose blood Pilate had mixed with their sacrifices. And answering he said to them, 'Do you think that these Galileans are worse sinners than all the rest of the Galileans, because they experienced these things? No!, I tell you, but unless you all change your way of thinking/repent (μετανοέω), you will likewise perish. Or those eighteen upon whom the tower at the Siloam fell and killed–do you think that they were worse transgressors than all the rest of those who live in Jerusalem? Not at all! I say to you, that unless you all turn around in your way of thinking, you will all likewise perish!'"

Will Pilate mix Jesus's blood with Jesus's sacrifice (compare Luke 11:50–51→22:20→Acts 5:28→20:28→22:20)?

ix) Acts 11:27–28: "In those days [that is, when Barnabas and Saul were teachers in Antioch] prophets came down from Jerusalem to Antioch. And one of them with the name of Agabus stood up and indicated by a sign through the Spirit that a great famine was about to come upon the whole of the inhabited world, which [in fact] happened during the reign of Claudius."

The time of "signs" is not over. The prophetic powers of the Holy Spirit relate to the whole of the inhabited world and not just to a Jewish sect in an obscure part of the earth (compare Acts 26:26!). The "Christian" movement (11:26) impacts the fate of the whole of humanity whose ruler is Claudius. Does the mention of the Caesar suggest that Saul/Paul himself will reach as far as Rome with his preaching of the good news? Is Rome the goal of the resurrected Jesus's commission in Acts 1:8 to extend the "witness to/of" Jesus "to the end of the earth" (compare Isa 49:6)?

x) Acts 18:1–2: "After these things, departing from Athens, he [Paul] came to Corinth. And finding there a certain Jew by the name of Aquila, a native of Pontus who had recently come from Italy with his wife, Priscilla–because Claudius had given the edict that all the Jews must leave Rome–he [Paul] paid them a visit."

This notice of the negative treatment of Jews by Rome during the mid-fifth decade of the 1st century raises the question about the status of Jews like Paul who are convinced that Jesus is Israel's Messiah. Caesar is still in control of "the inhabited world" (οἰκουμένη, Luke 2:1), or so it appears, and would seem to dictate the fates of all peoples, notwithstanding whatever was accomplished by the Christ in Jerusalem (Luke 19:45–24:49). Will Caesar and his representatives treat Paul similarly?

xi) Acts 18:12–13: "When Gallio was pro-consul of Achaea, the Jews with one accord attacked Paul and led him to the tribunal, declaring, 'This man persuades people to worship God contrary to the law.'"

Echoing Pilate's disdain for such matters as the laws and customs of 'foreigners,' Gallio tells the Jews that since "it [the complaint] involves questions of words and names and of your own law, see to it yourselves!" (Acts 18:15). Paul has incited fierce opposition from the Jews almost in every city that he has visited and yet was favorably received in Cyprus by the Roman pro-consul, Sergius Paulus, who "believed, as he was astonished by the teaching of the Lord (ἐπὶ τῇ διδαχῇ τοῦ κυρίου)" (13:4–12). When Paul enters Jerusalem for the last time and is nearly killed by the throngs of "the people" (ὁ λαός) gathered for Pentecost but is protected by the Roman tribune, "the Lord stood by him that night, saying, 'Take courage, for just as you have been bearing witness to those things concerning me here in Jerusalem, so also you must bear witness in Rome'" (23:11).

"Rome" can both embrace the spreading good news of Jesus the Christ and act menacingly indifferent. What is more, since the Christian "way" can be confused by Roman officials as Jewish propaganda (for example, Acts 16:19–24), Paul's predicament is placed all the more in the ambiguous shades and shadows of Jewish antagonism and Roman brute force. Will Roman authority welcome him when he "bears testimony in Rome?"

Our composer Luke would lead us to believe–as Paul faces the "governors" of Judea, Felix and Festus in Caesarea, and is taken "in chains" to Rome–that the dynamics of the plot will lead Paul into the hostile, threatening crowds of Jews as well as foreshadow indifferent, if not looming, neglect by the Romans. Instead, Luke is silent about Roman reactions, except for Paul's ability to speak openly about the "things concerning Jesus" within his "rented quarters," and our author subverts every expectation of Jewish reaction (Acts 28:21–22,25).[61] Instead of a typical violent second meeting with Paul (compare Acts 13:42–52), the Jewish leaders in Rome simply "take their leave" while "being in disagreement" (28:25).

Like Polybius's grand sweep of Fortune which overturns and shatters the normal patterns of history, so Luke places Paul as "witness" in the city that controls "the end of the earth" (compare Isa 45:22), "proclaiming the reign [kingship] of God and teaching the things [from the scriptures] concerning the Lord Jesus Christ with entirely unhindered openness" to both Jew and Gentile (28:31). In Caesarea, Paul had summarized the message he had conveyed all along his calling: "bearing testimony to both small and great alike, declaring nothing except those things which the prophets and Moses had said would take place, that there would be a suffering Messiah, and that being the first of the resurrection from the dead, he [suffering Messiah] would proclaim light to this people and to the nations" (26:23). By the conclusion of Luke's two volumes, there is no doubt that Paul's sending, like the Servant's, to "bear witness" "to nations and

---

61 On the "ending" (τελευτή) of Acts as the "end" (τέλος) of Acts, see further, David P. Moessner, "'Completed End(s)ings' of Historiographical Narrative: Diodorus Siculus and the 'End(ing)' of Acts," in *Die Apostelgeschichte und hellenistische Geschichtsschreibung: Festschrift für Eckhard Plümacher*, ed. Cilliers Breytenbach and Jens Schröter, AGAJU 57 (Leiden: Brill, 2004): 193–221.

kings and the sons and daughters of Israel" within God's all-embracing "plan"[62] has been fulfilled (Acts 9:15→28:31; compare Isa 52:15–53:2).

To *summarize*, Luke would have us hear, from the very frontispiece of the beginning, that the whole inhabited world of Jews and Gentiles–the peoples of Israel and the rulers of the nations–will collaborate to put Jesus to death. Both the ordinances of Moses and edicts of Rome will converge in the overarching plan of God that epitomizes "all" that the scriptures declare must take place concerning Israel's "Christ." Pre-figured and pre-saged by the cluster of synchronisms in the pre-beginning and beginning of the narrative, it is the Messiah's rejection by his own people in concert with the authority of "all the kingdoms of the world" (Luke 4:5) that will radically transform the world in ushering in the new beginnings of "the saving act of God." Paul's own calling is choreographed with Rome's power in such a fashion that the plan of God vouchsafes Paul's witness of–and to–the "suffering Christ" "*to* the end of the earth" at the center of the great supra-ethnic power that controls the nations "*at* the end of the earth" (Acts 1:8; Isa 45:22; 49:6).

4 Conclusion

Both Polybius and Luke 'arrange' their narratives so that their audiences may grasp a 'providential plan' that has been enacted among and through the nations of the world:

1. Rome's divinely orchestrated ascendancy to control of the nations brings opportunity and benefaction for untold populations in a fashion in which all previous analogies are found wanting. By comparing and contrasting the events that propelled Rome into power with the patterns of events of other world powers, Polybius's synchronisms steer his audience to comprehend Rome's unrivalled rise to world domination.

The suffering rejection and rising from the dead of Israel's Messiah effects a universal release of sin and unparalleled blessing that inaugurates the very 'end' of God's 'saving plan,' unlike any for which Israel or any other people had ever prepared or even reckoned. Luke's synchronisms guide his readers to see how both the great power of the nations as well as the leaders of Messiah's own people cluster in historically unique ways to produce the crucifixion of Jesus.

---

[62] Isaiah 40–55 stresses God's comprehensive plan for the whole world for all time through Israel and "His servant" who become "the Lord God's" "witnesses" (Isa 43:10,12; 44:8: μάρτυρες; cf. 55:4; cf. e.g., βουλή – Isa 45:26; 46:10; 55:8).

2. Polybius aligns the working of providence with Fortune and Fate and yet does not attribute any direct causation or intervention of these "divine" forces to the events themselves in their causal interactions. At most, any hint of a more *im*-mediate explanation of Rome's success emerges by highlighting Rome's unusual balance of courage and equanimity of spirit *vis-à-vis* other peoples.

Luke, on the other hand, writes in the biblical tradition of the Jewish writers of scripture and their LXX in which God himself has "visited his people"–but now in an unparalleled, eschatologically definitive way. To be sure, signs and omens, 'mighty works' and wonders, prophets and kings,[63] and theophanies and angelophanies prepare the way for the conception of the very "Son of God" in a lowly female human being. Nevertheless, the words and deeds of "all that Jesus began to do and to teach" become the events that spark such devoted misunderstanding, on the one hand, or hostile reception, on the other, which ironically contrive together to enact the providentially-intended rejection of that "Son." It is also highly ironic that only when Jesus's followers begin looking for him "among the dead" does the magnitude of God's enfleshed life among human beings begin to be re-discovered and unraveled into the ongoing story of all that this Jesus continued to do and teach through his Spirit-empowered flesh and blood witnesses "to the end of the earth" (the Acts).

3. However different providence's workings may be for these two Hellenistic historians, both use the metaleptic allure of synchronized events to draw their audiences into the strange conjunctions of human actors and divine players that characterize such unprecedented historical developments. Through the rhetorical-poetics ploy of synchronisms, both authors insert finely tuned listening posts to sound the way along their authorially-designed 'continuity of the narrative' and consequently lead their audiences to the greater 'end' of their grand narrative 'schemes.'

---

63 Cf., e.g., Luke 10:24.

Chapter Six: 'Managing' the Audience: Diodorus Siculus and Luke the Evangelist on Designing Authorial Intent[1]

If the reader has become part of the action, is caught up by the language, the question of what the passage 'means' does not arise. Once the desired effect has been achieved, there is no need, or room, for interpretation.

So declares Jane Tompkins about the 'reader' in 'classical antiquity.'[2] In this most influential essay of 1980, Professor Tompkins maintains that "interpretation" is a modern, post-Renaissance endeavor and has very little to with the ancients' impact of a literary performance upon an audience:

The concept of language as a force acting on the world, rather than as a series of signs to be deciphered, accounts for the absence of a specificity in ancient descriptions of literary response [...]. The text as an object of study or contemplation has no importance in this critical perspective, for literature is thought of as existing primarily in order to produce results and not as an end in itself. A literary work is not so much an object, therefore, as a unit of force whose power is exerted upon the world in a particular direction.[3]

Accordingly she adduces Aristotle's well-known "pity and fear" as two emotions "proper to tragedy" and yet illustrating a force of impact rather than specific cognitive-affective understandings elicited by the form or structure of the tragedy itself: "In other words, it is not the *nature* of the impact that concerns him [Aristotle], but the degree."[4]

---

[1] Abbreviated and with minor changes, used with permission, from David P. Moessner, "'Managing' the Audience: Diodorus Siculus and Luke the Evangelist on Designing Authorial Intent," in *Luke and His Readers: Festschrift A. Denaux*, ed. Reimund Bieringer, Gilbert Van Belle, and Joseph Verheyden, BETL 182 (Leuven: Peeters/University of Leuven Press, 2005): 61–80.
[2] Jane P. Tompkins, "The Reader in History: The Changing Shape of Literary Response," in *Reader-Response Criticism: From Formalism to Post-Structuralism*, ed. Jane P. Tompkins (Baltimore, MD: Johns Hopkins University Press, 1980), 203.
[3] Tompkins, "Reader in History," 203–4.
[4] "Aristotle, although he speaks of pity and fear as the emotions proper to tragedy, judges the merit of poetic production in general on 'vividness of impression,' and 'concentrated effect,' and says that the end of the art is to be 'striking'" (Tompkins, "Reader in History," 203).

Tompkins's larger point is, of course, correct that in antiquity "words were a power loosed,"[5] that even during the critical cultural transition from orality to orality *and* literacy in the Greece of the 5th–4th centuries BCE, literature was still perceived as primarily oral impact and not an 'object' of scrutiny. On the whole, her essay is a brilliant survey of the role of the audience throughout the entire history of literary criticism.

Her lasting contribution notwithstanding, I would like to suggest that she overstates the dichotomy between "effect" and "interpretation." It is simply not the case that ancient literature, written as primarily oral impact upon an audience, does not concern itself with specific content that can be rightly or wrongly interpreted. To be sure, the "degree" of impact is of paramount concern during the Hellenistic period as rhetoric flourishes into a discrete, self-conscious discipline;[6] yet so is the "nature" of this impact. There are ample discussions of the relation between specific form of the text and its authorially intended impact of specific understanding *upon* or *for* the auditor. This fact becomes significant especially in the rather extensive Hellenistic narrative enterprise that transcends and transforms traditional genres, as well as forms the literary-cultural milieu for the production of the church's Gospels.

When the Evangelist Luke claims that auditors of his narrative will "gain a firmer grasp of the traditions taught" to "Theophilus" (ἔδοξε κἀμοὶ [...] σοι γράψαι, κράτιστε Θεόφιλε, ἵνα ἐπιγνῷς περὶ ὧν κατηχήθης λόγων τὴν ἀσφάλειαν) (Luke 1:3–4), he is not simply asserting that the performance of his narrative (*diegesis*) will elicit poignant, proper emotive responses such as "fear" or "pity" or empathic "folk-feeling" *vis-à-vis* "tragic" or wronged parties or even triumphant figures of the narrative story. Rather, by comparing Luke with the historian Diodorus Siculus, who, a century or more earlier, was concerned to craft rhetorical strategies to produce particular understandings of the events he narrates, we can appreciate how Luke also designs his narrative presentation to convey "certain" knowledge about events alleged to have "come to fruition" (Luke 1:1b). We shall see, for example, that the third evangelist goes out of his way to ensure that his auditors comprehend the substantive theo-logical significance of Israel's mandate to extend their messianic salvation "to the end of the earth."

---

5 See Robert S. Reid, "When Words Were a Power Loosed: Audience Expectation and Finished Narrative Technique in the Gospel of Mark," *Quarterly Journal of Speech* 80 (1994): 427–47.
6 See esp. Richard L. Enos, *Greek Rhetoric Before Aristotle* (Prospect Heights, IL: Waveland Press, 1993).

I A Shared Epistemology of the 'Composed Orality' of Narrative (διήγησις)

Before we examine Diodorus in greater detail, it is important to recall a commonly shared epistemology of *diegesis*, whether of the 'composed orality' of tragedy, epic, historiography, and novelistic romances of the earlier periods, or of the Hellenistic developments of these narrative sub-genres in the 4th to 1st centuries BCE. Aristotle posits the rudiments of this widely accepted–if not uncontested–standard of poetics of the composed orality of narrative (*diegesis*)[7] in his *Poetics*, notwithstanding the possibility that he intended his expositions of *poetic mimesis* to be an indirect rebuff of his teacher, Plato![8]

II Narrative 'Arrangements' (οἰκονομίαι) Designed to Convey Specific Messages to Targeted Audiences

It is understandable, then, that when Diodorus announces that he intends to improve upon his predecessors' treatments of the history of the world, he engages the triadic synergy of this standard hermeneutic in order to show his audience just how his particular narrative arrangement will have a superior impact in comprehending the events he describes. In light of Tompkins's contention, we shall be most interested in those passages in which Diodorus reveals the ways that his choices of rhetorical forms and tropes of elaboration will determine the specific understanding and evaluative significance that his audience will attain.

---

[7] Aristotle's treatment of comedy was either lost or never completed in the *Poetics*; see Aristotle, *Poetics* 6.21 (Halliwell, LCL [47 n. e]).
[8] For these conventions, see above, Chapter Five, 128–33. Cf., e.g., Stephen Halliwell, *Aristotle's Poetics* (Chapel Hill, NC: University of North Carolina Press, 1986), 1: "It may be no more than fanciful, and it is certainly chronologically difficult, to suppose that when near the end of his *Republic* Plato issued the challenge which forms the epigraph to this chapter [that is, *Republic* 10,607d], he had already encountered resistance to his view of poetry from the young Aristotle [...]. The Platonic challenge as such goes unmentioned, but the absence of Plato's name is undisturbing: Aristotle often argues against his predecessor without drawing explicit attention to the fact."

1 The Lessons of Providence Revealed through the Mimetic Diegetic Interconnections of All Human Affairs.

According to Diodorus, historiography is the grandest of all genres of human composing because, when rightly conceived and executed, the universal history narrative mirrors forth the moral patterns that Providence (πρόνοια), together with Fate (τύχη), has bestowed to human life. When the historian faithfully reflects these interworkings, humans are inspired through the narrative vehicle to that true morality:

In general, then, it is because of that commemoration of good deeds which history accords human beings that some of them have been induced to become the founders of cities [...] and that many have aspired to discover new sciences and arts in order to benefit the race of humankind. And since complete happiness can be attained only through the combination of all these activities, the foremost title of praise must be awarded to that which more than any other thing is their cause, that is, to history (ἰστορία) [...] [that] herald of the divine voice (διαβοώμεναι τῷ θειοτάτῳ τῆς ἰστορίας στόματι) *(Library of History I.2.1,3).*[9]

Diodorus goes on to hail ἰστορία as "guardian of the high achievements," "witness [...] to the evil deeds of the wicked," and the "benefactor of the entire human race [...] the mother-city (μητρ-ό-πολις) of philosophy as a whole" (I.2.2). It is indeed as a mouthpiece for "Fate" and "Providence" and their interweavings of the whole inhabited world "as though the affairs of one city/state," that he, Diodorus, sets out to be the true universal historian and serve "most sublimely" as a "minister of Providence" (ὑπουργοὶ τῆς θείας προνοίας, I.1.3) "to all humanity who love and seek the truth" (πασῶν εὐχρηστοτάτην συντάξαιτο τοῖς φιλαναγνωστοῦσιν, 1.3.6).

But when Diodorus surveys past ensembles of the workings of Providence, he becomes convinced that the narrative arrangements themselves have not lived up to their task:

When we turned our attention to the historians before our time, although we approved their purpose without reservation, yet we were far from feeling that their works had been composed so as to contribute to human welfare as much as might have been possible (οὐ μὴν ἐξειργάσθαι πρὸς τὸ συμφέρον κατὰ τὸ δυνατὸν τὰς

---

[9] Slightly revised from C. H. Oldfather's translation, LCL 1; unless specifically marked, all other translations of Diodorus are my own.

πραγματείας αὐτῶν ὑπελάβομεν). *For although the benefit which history affords its readers* (γὰρ τοῖς ἀναγινώσκουσι τῆς ὠφελείας) *lies in its embracing a vast number and variety of circumstances, yet most writers* (οἱ πλεῖστοι) *have recorded no more than discrete* (αὐτοτελεῖς) *wars waged by a single nation* (ἔθνος) *or a single state* (πόλις) *and but few have undertaken* (ὀλίγοι δ' [...] ἐπεχείρησαν), *beginning with the earliest times* (ἀρχαίων χρόνων ἀρξάμενοι) *and coming down to their own day, to record the events connected with all peoples* (τὰς κοινὰς πράξεις)*[...] (Library of History* I.3.1–2).[10]

Two main types of deficient history narratives stand out as he continues: 1) "Isolated" or "self-contained" (αὐτοτελεῖς) wars of a single people or city as the sole focus (I.3.2); 2) More recent universal sweeps which fail to relate: past civilizations to some major nation or city/state; the momentous developments of Roman hegemony during Diodorus's own time; proper chronology; the myths or "ancient legends" of the "barbarians;" or, finally, the intended conclusion because of the untimely death of the author (I.3.2).

In both categories–whether insufficient scope or chronology–what is missing are the interconnections among peoples and events both "vertically" through time and "horizontally" through the cause-effect nexuses of the interweavings of Providence. Hence, it is not the case *à la* Tompkins that Diodorus complains about the degree of impact upon the audience or even that the readers of these earlier historians are vicariously experiencing the wrong emotions. Rather, insufficient knowledge is conveyed through the narrative connections themselves such that Diodorus assails the *nature* of the impact. It is extremely toilsome, he says, for any reader to learn why events have transpired in specific ways: "For this reason, because both the times of the events and the events themselves are strewn about in numerous accounts and in diverse history writers, attaining knowledge of them becomes difficult for the mind to coordinate and for the memory to retain" (δυσπερίληπτος ἡ τούτων ἀνάληψις γίνεται καὶ δυσμνημόνευτος, I.3.4).

Thus Diodorus constantly keeps his audience's grasp of specific relationships and causal explanations in the forefront of his own compositional endeavors: "Consequently, once we had examined the compositions of each of these other historians, we decided to compose a history according to a plan which would reward its readers with the greatest of benefits but, at the same time, inconvenience them the least" (μὲν ὠφελῆσαι δυναμένην, ἐλάχιστα δὲ τοὺς ἀναγινώσκοντας ἐνοχλήσουσαν, I.3.5).

---

[10] Diodorus Siculus, *Library of History* I.3.2 (Oldfather, LCL, with slight alterations in translation).

Diodorus in fact climaxes his own decision to write by summarizing the greater benefit of his new narrative configuration; from first to last the reader must be more illumined in the ways of Providence through the paths the history writer creates:

The reason for this is that, in the first place, it is not easy for those who propose to go through the writings of so many historians to procure the books which come to be needed and, in the second place, that, because the works vary so widely and are so numerous, the recovery of past events becomes extremely difficult to comprehend and to secure (ἔπειτα διὰ τὴν ἀνωμαλίαν καὶ τὸ πλῆθος τῶν συνταγμάτων δυσκατάληπτος γίνεται τελέως καὶ δυσέφικτος ἡ τῶν πεπραγμένων ἀνάληψις); *whereas, on the other hand, the account which keeps within the limits of a single narrative* (ἡ δ' ἐν μιᾶς συντάξεως περιγραφῇ πραγματεία) *and contains a connected account of events* (τὸ τῶν πράξεων εἰρόμενον ἔχουσα) *facilitates the reading and contains such recovery of the past* (τὴν μὲν ἀνάγνωσιν ἑτοίμην παρέχεται) *in a form that is perfectly easy to follow* (τὴν δ' ἀνάληψιν ἔχει παντελῶς εὐπαρακολούθητον, compare Luke 1:3) (I.3.8).

Both the sheer chronological sweep and the wide swath of inter-connections are impossible for *the reader to grasp* ("follow" [παρακολούθητος]) unless both dimensions are fused together through the interwoven poetics (plot) of the one narrative. In improving upon his predecessors, Diodorus's "single narrative" (μιᾶ σύνταξις, I.3.3) will "begin with the most ancient times and record to the best of his ability the affairs of the entire world down to his own day, so far as they have been handed down to memory, as though they were the affairs of some single city" (ὥσπερ τινὸς μιᾶς πόλεως, I.3.6). It is this synoptic inter-calating of happenings as *one larger process of a larger force unfolding* which constitutes the "greater" benefit purportedly lacking in the other histories. Both form and content must inhere in order to cohere!

In contrast to the narratives of his precursors, then, Diodorus's history narrative will combine both linear chrono-logical trajectories with lateral syn-chrono-logical networks to "ensemble forth" the finely meshed workings of the "one global village."[11] Diodorus argues that the impact of history narratives can be lacking in the proper *interpretation* of their wholes or of larger movements

---

[11] Adele C. Scafuro, "Universal History and the Genres of Greek Historiography" (Ph.D. diss., Yale University, 1984), 116–54, 205–62, is one of the few to treat these critical epistemological aspects of the poetics of narrative historiography in any detail; see esp. her discussion, 205–62.

of Providence, not just in the ability of the narrative to move the reader to experience the moralities or actions of various characters. As Diodorus goes on to say,

A history of this nature [that is, Diodorus's narrative] *must be held to surpass all others to the same degree as the whole is more useful than the part* (χρησιμώτερόν ἐστι τὸ πᾶν τοῦ μέρους) *and continuity than discontinuity* (τὸ συνεχὲς τοῦ διερρηγμένου), *and, again, as an event whose date has been accurately determined is more useful than one of which it is not known in what period it happened* (πρὸς δὲ τούτοις τὸ διηκριβωμένον τοῖς χρόνοις τοῦ μηδὲ γινωσκομένου τίσιν ἐπράχθη καιροῖς, I.3.8).

Such entwinements and details only make sense when, as the primary aims of the narrative emplotment executed through the mind or 'thought' of an author, they become "useful" for proper *interpretation*, as well as for emotive response. Moreover, in the transition in Book I from his *prooemium* to the forty volumes of the main body (I.1–5), Diodorus states directly that certain content must be narrated in order to "be heard," lest the auditor miss substantive connections and explanations of other parts within the larger unified whole. Again, comprehension through discrete interpretation is central to Diodorus's enterprise:

Concerning the various conceptions of the gods [...] and [...] the myths [...] although we shall refrain from narrating most of the parts in detail (τὰ [...] πολλὰ συντάξασθαι [...] κατ' ἰδίαν), *since such a procedure* (ὑπόθεσις) *would require a lengthy account, yet whatever concerning these subjects we feel to be pertinent to the several parts of our projected history* (ὅσα δ' ἂν ταῖς προκειμέναις ἱστορίαις οἰκεῖα δόξωμεν ὑπάρχειν) *we shall present in summary fashion* (ἐν κεφαλαίοις), *that nothing of those things worth hearing may be missed* (ἵνα μηδὲν τῶν ἀκοῆς ἀξίων ἐπιζητῆται) (I.6.1).

2 Improperly Balanced 'Arrangements' (οἰκονομίαι) Hinder Authorial 'Management' (οἰκονομικόν) of the Audience's Interpretation and Overall Response.

It is most intriguing in answering the question, "What for Diodorus 'is worth hearing?'" to note the rhetorical ploys or patterns of history writing which Diodorus argues deflect or even "drown out" the specific content the readers are intended by the author to "hear." Our limited scope restricts us to two illustrations of the diegetic-rhetorical poetics that Diodorus, by contrast, himself employs to "manage" his audience to the right interpretations:

i) An exemplar of proper "balance" within his 'arrangement' of a universal history would seem to be Diodorus's predecessor Timaeus–except, that is, for one fatal defect:

Some historians indeed, although they are worthy objects of praise in the matter of style (κατὰ τὴν λέξιν) *and in the breadth of experience derived from the events which they record* (κατὰ τὴν πολυπειρίαν τῶν ἀναγραφομένων πράξεων), *have nevertheless fallen short in respect of the way in which they have handled the matter of arrangement* (κατὰ τὴν οἰκονομίαν), *with the result that, whereas the effort and care which they expended* receive the approbation of their readers (ἀποδοχῆς τυγχάνειν παρὰ τοῖς ἀναγινώσκουσι), *yet the order* (τὴν δὲ τάξιν) *which they gave to the material they have recorded is the* object of just censure. *Timaeus, for example, bestowed, it is true, the greatest attention upon the precision of his chronology and had due regard for the breadth of knowledge gained through experience, but he is criticized with good reason for his untimely and lengthy censures, and because of the excess to which he went in censuring he has been given by some men* [thus] *the name Epitimaeus or Censurer*[12] (V.1.2).

Although Diodorus considers Timaeus's choice of words and their arrangement, along with his chronological ordering, to be most effective in eliciting empathic experience of the events as the audience is drawn into the sequence of Timaeus's narrative, yet the 'ordering' or 'arrangement' of the lateral, synchronic connectors with the diachronic developments is defective precisely because his "censures" interrupt the proper connections and thus "sense" which the audience is to make of the larger picture. Overall, his 'order' (τάξις)[13] does not serve his larger pur-

---

12 "Epi-timaeus" (= "Censurer") is the paronomastic obloquy for Timaeus's predilection for lengthy and "untimely" "censures" Diodorus Siculus, *Library of History* (Oldfather, LCL), emphasis mine.
13 For the role of τάξις in a more theoretically developed system of 'arrangement' (οἰκονομία) in the younger contemporary Dionysius of Halicarnassus, which includes 'division'/'partitioning' (διαίρεσις), 'order'/'sequence' (τάξις), and 'method or effectiveness of development' (ἐξεργασία), see Robert S. Reid, "'Neither Oratory nor Dialogue': Dionysius of Halicarnassus and the Genre of Plato's Apology," *Rhetoric Society Quarterly* 27 (1997): 63–90, esp. 67–83; David P. Moessner, "Dionysius' Narrative 'Arrangement,'" in *Paul, Luke and the Graeco-Roman World: Essays in Honour of Alexander J. M. Wedderburn*, ed. Alf Christopherson, Carsten Claussen, Jörg Frey, and Bruce Longenecker, JSNTS 217 (London: Sheffield Academic Press, 2002): 149–64, esp. 151–53 (see Chapter Seven below). Diodorus appears to be working with a very similar formal poetics, emphasizing the 'effectiveness of development' in engaging the reader by making sure that the 'order' (τάξις) has a well-balanced emplotment or entanglement of both linear and lateral connectors in promoting the 'continuity of the narrative'. "Most" of his predecessors in writing universal

poses (V.1.3), which, for Diodorus, can only mean the intent to convey the proper interpretation of the narrated events. Contrary to Tompkins's argument regarding only the *degree* of the "effect" of the performed text, Diodorus lauds Timaeus for his success in this very dimension of impact but still finds the more comprehensive "effect" of meaning to be fundamentally flawed and hence Timaeus's larger enterprise a failed experiment. Timaeus failed to "manage" his audience through the diachronic and synchronic webbings such that his auditors' interpretation of the events is wanting. A telling contrast is Ephorus, who elicited the well-deserved reputation of a successful writer of "universal history" since both his 'style' and his 'arrangement' (οἰκονομία) were skillfully conceived and executed and the reader duly rewarded with the specific moral instruction Ephorus was intent to communicate through those discrete connections (οὐ μόνον κατὰ τὴν λέξιν, ἀλλὰ καὶ κατὰ τὴν οἰκονομίαν ἐπιτέτευχε, V.1.4).[14]

Diodorus describes his method for procuring proper 'arrangement' to be the same technique utilized by Ephorus, namely, composing volumes "complete in themselves" (αὐτοτελεῖς[15]). "Complete" volumes consist of the full scope of the nexuses of cause and effect of important events of a given period surrounding a ruler or actions of a city/state, which in turn are related to other key movements and developments within the larger work. The rationale for composing in this way is again, as in Book I, based upon the audience's ability to comprehend the knowledge intended by the author.

A book "complete in itself" enables readers to "remember" what is presented because the chains of earlier causes developed through medial influences and leading to specific outcomes are "clear" (σαφῆ) and uninterrupted "for the readers" (τὴν ἱστορίαν εὐμνημόνευτον καὶ σαφῆ γενέσθαι τοῖς ἀναγινώσκουσιν) (XVI.1.1).

---

history, he contends, have "not developed their narrative presentations as effectively as possible for the greatest benefit [to the reader] (οὐ μὴν ἐξειργάσθαι πρὸς τὸ συμφέρον κατὰ τὸ δυνατὸν τὰς πραγματείας αὐτῶν)" (I.3.1). This 'arrangement' is, in turn, much like Dionysius', wholly contingent also upon the proper 'beginning' and 'ending' points of major sections, referred to as 'division' by the Halicarnassan; see esp. Dionysius of Halicarnassus, *De Thucydide*, 9–20.

14 Ephorus apparently earned Didodorus's critique because he did not extend his chronology far enough into the time period of Ephorus's own setting.

15 The referent here is not to be confused with the referent in Book I.3; in Book XVI "self-completed" refers to individual volumes or books of the larger work, whereas Diodorus's criticism in Book I is directed against history writers who confine their entire scope to one nation or war (cf., e.g., Thucydides?!). Such description thus results in "isolated" or "independent" events, unrelated to the larger workings of Providence and Fate.

For incomplete accounts of actions (ἡμιτελεῖς πράξεις) in which the culminating events exhibit no continuity with the beginning events (οὐκ ἔχουσαι συνεχὲς ταῖς ἀρχαῖς τὸ πέρας) interrupt the interest even of avid readers (μεσολαβοῦσι τὴν ἐπιθυμίαν τῶν φιλαναγνωστούντων), whereas those accounts which do exhibit the continuity of the narrative (τὸ τῆς διηγήσεως συνεχές) up to the very conclusion of the events (μέχρι τῆς τελευτῆς) produce a narrative account which is well-roundedly complete (ἀπηρτισμένην τὴν τῶν πράξεων ἔχουσιν ἀπαγγελίαν) (XVI.1.2).

Such balance within a manageable, mnemonic whole recalls Aristotle's depiction of well-proportioned plots that produce predictable effects upon the audience.[16]

ii) We should expect the role assigned to speeches (λόγοι) by Hellenistic historians especially illuminating (or devastating!) for our argument. If speeches are designed solely or even primarily to effect an audience's emotive response such as praise or blame and *not* to lend important interpretive commentary to the events described, then Tompkins would certainly be right for this significant sub-genre and focus of the 'master art' during the Hellenistic age. In Book XX, Diodorus opines:

One might rightly censure those who in their histories insert lengthy public orations (δημηγορίεις) or employ frequent speeches (ῥητορείαι). For not only do they break up the continuity of the narrative (τὸ συνεχὲς τῆς διηγήσεως [...] διασπῶσιν) because of the poorly timed insertion of speeches, but also they interrupt <u>those who are wanting to press on to a fuller knowledge of the events</u> (πρὸς τὴν τῶν πράξεων ἐπίγνωσιν μεσολαβοῦσι τὴν ἐπιθυμίαν). Yet certainly there is opportunity for those who desire to display rhetorical skill to compose separate public discourses or speeches for ambassadors, or speeches of praise or blame and the like [apart from histories]; for by employing and developing both occasions for speech writing (χρησάμενοι καὶ τὰς ὑποθέσεις χωρὶς ἑκατέρας ἐξεργασάμενοι κατὰ λόγον) <u>through proper arrangement of the speeches</u> (τῇ γὰρ οἰκονομίᾳ τῶν λόγων) in each of two discrete settings, they might reasonably expect to acquire a reputation in both areas of literary endeavors. But, as it is, some writers, by multiplying to excess the number of rhetorical passages, make the whole of history writing into an appendage of rhetorical performance. Not only does that which is composed poorly give offense, but also that which seems in certain respects to be effectively written <u>ends up altogether missing the mark of the themes and occasions proper to their</u>

---

[16] See, e.g., *Poetics* 8.30–35: "the various components of the events should be so structured that if any is displaced or removed, the sense of the whole is disturbed and dislocated [...]."

ordered sequence (ἀλλὰ καὶ τὸ δοκοῦν [...] ἐπιτετεῦχθαι, τόπων καὶ καιρῶν τῆς οἰκείας τάξεως διημαρτηκός). *Thus, even among those who read such works, some skip over the rhetorical passages–even if they should seem to be entirely effective–while others, wearied by the sheer length and poor taste of the historian, abandon their reading entirely. But this frustration is not without reason; for the genre of history is straightforward and coherent to itself* (τὸ γὰρ τῆς ἱστορίας γένος ἁπλοῦν ἐστι καὶ συμφυὲς αὐτῷ) *and as a whole is like a living organism. If it is distorted, it is stripped of its vital charm; but if its necessary integrity is propitiously maintained, then the harmony of the composition functioning as a whole offers a delightfully clear reading* (ἐπιτερπῆ καὶ σαφῆ παρίστησι τὴν ἀνάγνωσιν).

Nevertheless, though disapproving of speeches crafted solely for rhetorical effect, we do not ban them totally from historical works [...]. For one could find no small number of reasons for which on many occasions the aid of rhetoric will necessarily be enlisted. For when many things have been said effectively and felicitously, one should not out of contempt [for rhetorical effect] *pass over what is worthy of remembrance and possesses a benefit nicely blended for history; nor when the subject matter is great and momentous should one allow the speech* [of characters] *to appear inferior to the deeds themselves. Moreover, there are occasions when an event turns out contrary to expectation such that we should be forced to engage words that are appropriate to the subject for the sake of explaining what appears to be inexplicable* (χάριν τοῦ λῦσαι τὴν ἀλογίαν) (XX. 1.1–2).[17]

First of all, we note again the importance of an 'arrangement' (οἰκονομία) which delivers the intended content of significance to the audience; when speeches are placed improperly or appear too frequently in the narrative, the 'continuity of the narrative' meaning is disturbed and thus robbed of its epistemological as well as emotive power. The author's ability to 'manage' the "delivered" interpretation of the events is destroyed. The carefully coordinated links among characters and events are broken since the careless 'disposition' (τάξις) of the speech interrupts the reader's attentive abilities to make the proper connections.

Secondly, even when the author has arranged the narrative in such a way to manage the intended construal of the events, certain events are too momentous not to have an accompanying rhetorical affirmation of their significance. Again, Diodorus is highlighting the critical role that speeches play in *interpreting* events within the larger narrative whole. The *nature* as well as the *degree* of their impact

---

17 Emphases (as well as translation) mine.

is certainly in Diodorus's purview here. Their noetic function is too great not to incorporate speeches into contexts of prime significance!

Finally, as if to drive home the point beyond any pale of doubt, Diodorus mentions certain events that would seem to cut against the grain of narrative expectation. Given previous cause and effect patterns, some developments would seem to defy all logic. In those cases, a speech becomes critically necessary in order to bring some cognitive "resolution" of the relation of this event to the rest of the events. Though history, by and large, should prove "straightforward and coherent to itself," there are, nevertheless, those happenings that demand special "words" (λόγοι) of explanation.

In short, speeches in universal history writing are to be composed not solely or even primarily for their rhetorical function to "move" audiences to certain responses. Rather, speeches are critical in rendering a composition that functions harmoniously–for the reader!–as an epistemological whole.

Space does not permit treatment of Diodorus's transition "linking" passages[18] toward the beginning of each new book which summarize the main content of the volume just completed and relate that material to what will be accomplished in 'the continuity' of the new volume. Such rhetorical devices are designed to "manage" the readers' comprehension and steer it along the appropriate lines of interpretation for both part and whole. With these and other means of both intra- and extra-textual cross-referencing, it becomes patently clear that Diodorus intends and actually thinks that he will be successful in imparting the specific significance of content to the events he configures.[19] Parallel to Aristotle's depiction of a discrete plot as embedded with specific meaning and responses for its targeted audiences, Diodorus appeals to the same tria-lectic hermeneutic of, a) authorial intent, b) ensconced in a plotted narrative to produce, c) a realized

---

18 *Library of History* II.1.1–3; III.1.1–3; IV.1.5–7; V.2.1; VI.1.1–3; [VII – X]; XI.1.1; XII.2.2–3; XIII.1.1–3; XIV.2.4; XV.1.6; XVI.1.3–6 [compare XV.95.4!]; XVII.1.1–2; XVIII.1.5–6; XIX.1.9–10; XX.2.3; [XXI – XL]; [] indicate fragmentary books without extant linking passages.

19 Diodorus's synchronic abilities have generally been regarded as at best "second rate," though Kenneth S. Sacks (*Diodorus Siculus and the First Century* [Princeton, NJ: Princeton University Press, 1990], esp. 3–8) has gone a long way in "rehabilitating" Diodorus's contribution both in the treatment of his sources as well as his own compositional skills. Cf., e.g., P.J. Stylianou, *A Historical Commentary on Diodorus Siculus Book 15* (Oxford: Oxford University Press, 1998), 1: "For the cardinal fact about Diodorus is that he was a second-rate epitomator who generally used first-rate sources;" Anne Burton, *Diodorus Siculus Book I: A Commentary* (Leiden: Brill, 1972), 1: "The very title of the work indicates that little more is to be expected than a convenient compilation of earlier historical writings. And in spite of the noble declarations in his introduction, Diodorus seems generally to have achieved little more than this."

interpretation on the part of the audience.[20] Contra Tompkins, then, for Diodorus the question of what the passage 'means' does indeed arise over and over again.

III Luke's 'Arrangement' Vouchsafes Gentile Inclusion as Central to the Fulfillment of Eschatological Salvation through Israel's "Christ"

The operative narrative hermeneutic engaged by Diodorus is evident in Luke's opening statement. Luke's decision "to write" a narrative sequence to a targeted audience (καθεξῆς σοι γράψαι) (Luke 1:3), even though there are already "many" (πολλοί) such "accounts" (διήγησις) (Luke 1:1), signals (a) his intention to communicate content (ἔδοξε κἀμοὶ [...] γράψαι, 1:3) (b) composed in a distinctive narrative arrangement (καθεξῆς [...] γράψαι, 1:3; compare ἀνατάξασθαι διήγησιν, 1:1a), (c) for the purpose of securing for his readers a firmer understanding of the significance of the traditions in which his readers have already been taught (ἵνα ἐπιγνῷς [...] κατηχήθης λόγων τὴν ἀσφάλειαν, 1:4). Luke's intent is revealed only through the epistemological dynamic of managing the comprehension of his audience through the formal arrangement of his new narrative enterprise. But as we have seen, such a dynamic is hardly idiosyncratic among Hellenistic historians.

That Luke's intent focuses to a great extent upon conveying specific knowledge to his audience rather than eliciting primarily empathic approbation or rejection becomes clear from his use of the ἀσφαλ- word group in his second book. At the end of the first major speech (λόγος, compare Acts 2:41) and second longest of volume two, Luke has Peter conclude his address, "Let the whole house of Israel know therefore with *clear certainty* (ἀσφαλῶς) that God had established him as both Lord and Christ, this Jesus whom you crucified" (Acts 2:36). Not only does this summary climax the entire import of the speech (compare 2:37–"What shall we do?"), but the use of both "Lord" and "Christ" also suggests that the essence of the argument is being summarized as well, since extensive scripture has been cited and all three quotations include a "Lord" figure,[21] while the last two refer

---

20 Only once (*Library of History* XXVI.1.1) does Diodorus admit that certain individual auditors are incorrigible solipsists who will never be satisfied with the content that the author wishes to convey. Yet even here it is not a question of the audience not understanding what the author has structured his/her narrative to mean but rather a refusal to accept or be satisfied with the conveyed content.

21 I am, of course, not suggesting that every use of "Lord" in the citations *must* refer to Jesus (Acts 2:20, 21–Joel 2:31, 32; Acts 2:25–[LXX] Ps 15:8; Acts 2:34b–[LXX] Ps 109:1); rather the texts

David's words (Psalms) to "Jesus of Nazareth" or "this Jesus" whom David himself had "foreseen" and "spoken about" as "the Christ"[22]. Are we to surmise that the "clear certainty" on the part of Peter's (Luke's) audience is integrally connected to the comprehending of this scriptural argument? Moreover, the three occurrences of the adjective/substantive ἀσφαλές (Acts 21:34; 22:30; 25:26) are linked with verbs of "understanding"[23] and/or "writing." Acts 25:26 curiously combines the need for a "firmer grasp" of the events around Paul in order that his "most excellent" Festus,[24] after a more thorough examination of Paul, might write his superior with specific content (περὶ οὗ ἀσφαλές τι γράψαι τῷ κυρίῳ οὐκ ἔχω [...] ὅπως [...] σχῶ τί γράψω)! It therefore appears that ἀσφάλεια combines both the *senses* of "clarity" (σαφήνεια/σαφῆ) and "security" (ἀσφαλής) and has as its referent "certain knowledge."[25]

Our scope will confine us to only one further example among many of Luke's diegetic structures designed to convey specific, "certain" knowledge.

At the conclusion of the first book, Luke 24:44–49, the apostles' new recognition of Jesus is first linked to the *fulfillment of all that stands written* about Jesus as "the Christ" (24:44b). In fact, their "mind" has first to be "opened" to "comprehend" (24:45) that the whole of Israel's scriptures focuses upon Jesus as "the Christ who suffers, rises from the dead on the third day, and in/by his name a release of sins is proclaimed into all the nations" (24:46–47). This "topic" of Scripture forms their new identity as "witnesses of these things" (μάρτυρες τούτων, 24:48) that they have witnessed in Jesus of Nazareth. What is to be proclaimed, then, to all the nations, beginning from Jerusalem (24:47), is this new understanding, this sweeping hermeneutic of "Moses, the prophets, and the Psalms" (24:44) that finds its τέλος in Jesus as the Christ (compare Luke 22:37b: τὸ περὶ ἐμοῦ τέλος ἔχει). It would appear that the "opening of the scriptures" to all the peoples of the world forms the crux of what it means to be "witnesses of

---

which speak of "Lord" beg for explanation in light of the affirmation in Acts 2:36 that Jesus is "Lord."

22 Acts 2:25a: "For David speaks concerning him" (that is, "Jesus of Nazareth," 2:22); 2:34a: "For David did not ascend, but he himself says" (in the following citation of Ps 110:1, David can therefore not be speaking about himself but about another, viz., "this Jesus," Acts 2:32a, whom he speaks about in advance as "the Christ," Acts 2:31).
23 Both Acts 21:34 and 22:30–γνῶναι τὸ ἀσφαλές–involve the Roman tribune who wants to know more of the "certain facts" surrounding such opposition to Paul.
24 Acts 26:25–κράτιστε Φῆστε; cf. Luke 1:3–κράτιστε Θεόφιλε.
25 Cf. the only other instance of ἀσφάλεια in Luke-Acts in Acts 5:23 with its literal sense and referent, "the securely locked" prison gates! Cf. Bauer on Acts 2:36: "know beyond a doubt"; RSV: "know assuredly"; cf. also Acts 16:23.

these things" (24:48) and would thus articulate the central "topic" or "continuity" of the ongoing narrative.

Luke's transition "linking" *prooemium* at the beginning of his second volume (Acts 1:1–14) confirms this observation. In particular, Acts 1:4–5 frames and fuses Luke 24:44–49 to the narrative continuity of Acts in a most extraordinary way. The risen Jesus who opens the scriptures and gives the charge in Luke 24:44–49 breaks into and takes over the voice of the narrator in Acts 1:1–4a→1:4b–5. A striking message is delivered: Jesus the resurrected-crucified Christ, the "living one" present as the goal of all the scriptures, the authoritative voice of volume one—not the author's narrator—prophesies to apostolic witness and reader alike the manner of divine presence through which the apostles' legacy as his witnesses will be fulfilled. "Power from the most High (Place)" is now interpreted as their being "baptized by/in the Holy Spirit not after many days" (Luke 24:49→Acts 1:4b–5). In contrast to John who "baptized with water," the characteristic mark of the apostles' witness will be a baptism *by* the Holy Spirit. Thus, unlike any of Diodorus's transition passages,[26] the *prooemial* voice of this linking passage has shifted from the narrator to the main actor and speaker of the previous volume (compare Acts 1:1b). It would appear that Luke is vouchsafing a narrative continuity (compare τὸ συνεχές)[27] for his two "books" and thus providing a hermeneutic bellwether for his readers.

The narrative threads of Acts 1:1–14 thus characterize the emplotment that must proceed to the announced goal of "witness in Jerusalem, in all of Judea and Samaria and all the way to the end of the earth" (Acts 1:8). The linear developments of the apostles' proclamation must reach "the end of the earth." The lateral developments must include empowerment by the Holy Spirit in order for the plotted momentum to be motivated and ultimately achieved. Moreover, the "Kingdom of God" (Acts 1:3b) appears to be a pithy moniker for the preaching of a "change of mind" (μετά-νοια, Luke 24:47) concerning the center and goal of Israel's scriptures.

But just as clearly, Peter and the eleven apostles do *not* fulfill the Christ's mandate to "be his witnesses [...] to the end of the earth."

(i) Acts 11:1–18 ≈ Acts 10:1–48[28]

As late as Acts 10, and only under special circumstances, have Peter and John visited Samaria once (Acts 8:14–25), and Peter is still preoccupied with itinerant

---

26 See n. 17 above.
27 For "continuity" in *Library of History*, see esp. I.3.8; XVI.1.2,6; XVII.1.2; XX.1.1.
28 For further elaboration, see above Chapter Four § 2.2 "John's Preaching of a Baptism as the Beginning of Witness to the Word of God through Jesus Messiah."

preaching and healing in Judea (Acts 9:32–43). Rather, Peter must be granted a special audition of a voice from heaven in order for him and the rest of the church–centered in Jerusalem under apostolic authority–to break out of this stubborn non-compliance (Acts 10:9–16 in 10:1–48; compare 11:5–10 in 11:1–18).

In Acts 11:15, as Peter tells the murmuring discontents from the Jerusalem church about the "falling of the Holy Spirit" upon Cornelius's household–"just as I began to speak"–Peter utters this stunning confession: "The Holy Spirit fell upon them just as upon us in the beginning (ἐν ἀρχῇ[29]) and I remembered the word of the Lord, how he had said, 'John baptized with water, but you shall be baptized with the Holy Spirit'" (Acts 11:15b–16→1:4b–5).[30] Peter reverberates the *prooemial* voice of the risen Christ! It is that "beginning," linking voice of the transition between Luke's two books that now (finally!) provides the divine sanction for Peter's eating with and preaching to "unclean" peoples of the nations/Gentiles (τὰ ἔθνη, Acts 10:45; 11:1, 18). We have just seen that this inbreaking voice functions to pull the two volumes together into one plot of the words and actions of the risen-crucified one and his apostolic witnesses. Curiously, Luke's narrator has the "Holy Spirit" fall upon Cornelius's household just as Peter begins to proclaim (ἔτι λαλοῦντος τοῦ Πέτρου τὰ ῥήματα ταῦτα, Acts 10:44a)[31] that "all the prophets bear witness (μαρτυέω) that a release of sins is to be received through his name" (Acts 10:43→Luke 24:47). When the scriptures are "opened," the power of the Spirit grants a "change of mind/orientation" to the risen-crucified one, "leading to life" (Acts 11:18b). Thus Luke, like Diodorus, uses lateral, syn-chronic descriptors, such as the re-hear-sal of Acts 10:1–48 in 11:1–18, not only to advance the forward motion, but also to endow new, even unprecedented developments to and within the significance of 'the continuity of the narrative' itself: "If then God

---

29 Acts 11:15b (ἐν ἀρχῇ, refers to Pentecost, Acts 2, as anticipated by the *prooemial* voice in Acts 1:5, echoed in Acts 11:1, and re-sounded in Acts 15:7 (see below for Acts 15:1–35).
30 For elaboration, see David P. Moessner, "The Appeal and Power of Poetics (Luke 1:1–4): Luke's Superior Credentials (παρηκολουθηκότι), Narrative Sequence (καθεξῆς), and Firmness of Understanding (ἡ ἀσφάλεια) for the Reader," in *Jesus and the Heritage of Israel*, ed. David P. Moessner, vol. 1 *Luke the Interpreter of Israel* (Harrisburg, PA: Trinity Press International, 1999): 84–123, esp. 100–105.
31 Cf. Eckhard Plümacher, "The Mission Speeches in Acts and Dionysius of Halicarnassus," in *Jesus and the Heritage of Israel*, ed. David P. Moessner, vol. 1, *Luke the Interpreter of Israel* (Harrisburg, PA: Trinity Press International, 1999): 253–54, (n. 30), who cites this connection as telling evidence for Luke of the catalytic function of speeches in advancing and not simply recapitulating the plot, similar to Dionysius of Halicarnassus's explicit understanding of their role (see below, Chapter Seven). Acts 10:44 exemplifies Diodorus's categorgy of events which "turn out contrary to expectation" (XX.2.2).

gave them the same gift just as He had given to us who had come to believe in the Lord Jesus Christ, who was I of any power to withstand God" (Acts 11:17)!

(ii) Acts 15:1–35 (15:7–11 ≈ 11:1–18 ≈ 10:1–48)

At the "apostolic assembly" of Acts 15, one of the "elders," James, delivers a clinching judgment upon the status of "those from the nations who are turning to God (τοῖς ἀπὸ τῶν ἐθνῶν ἐπιστρέφουσιν ἐπὶ τὸν θεόν)" (15:19). But it is the *apostle* Peter who passes the apostolic mantle of *witness* to the nations to the non-apostle[32] Paul (and Barnabas) by first addressing the gathering,

You yourselves know that from the days of the beginnings (ἀφ' ἡμερῶν ἀρχαίων) *God chose among you that through my mouth the nations* (τὰ ἔθνη) *should hear the message of the good news and come to believe. And God who knows the heart bore witness* (ἐμαρτύρησεν) *to them by giving to them the Holy Spirit just as also He gave to us. And by cleansing* (καθαρίσας) *their heart through faith, He made no discrimination between us and them [...]. Rather, we believe that it is through the grace of the Lord Jesus that we are saved just in the same way that they are"* (Acts 15:7b–9, 11)!

The echo of Acts 1:8 as well as the voice from heaven "not to call what God has cleansed (ἐκαθάρισεν) unclean" (Acts 11:9b→10:15) ring together as one. Now Peter has merged the days "in the beginning" of the falling of the Spirit upon themselves at Pentecost with "the days of the beginnings" of the falling of the Spirit upon the nations through Peter's preaching! Now instead of the Jewish believers' receiving the Spirit as the paragon for the salvation of the Gentile nations, Peter flips the encounter around to make the receipt of the Spirit by Cornelius's household the touchstone for the "grace of the Lord Jesus" among the *Jewish* believers. Peter has himself undergone a "turning" almost as radical as the "turning of the nations." He had had to learn that his prior "mindset" toward the nations as "unclean" was, in God's mind, "discrimination" against them in defiance of the risen Christ's command to be His witnesses to them (Acts 1:8).

This message in Luke's different 'arrangement' from "the many" is hard to miss. Luke 'manages' his audience to the "clear certainty" (ἀσφάλεια) that the apostolic-messianic witness to the nations is part and parcel of the scriptural

---

[32] The two uses of ἀπόστολος for Paul (and Barnabas) (Acts 14:4, 14) refer to their being sent out by the (Antioch) church in the more generic sense of "one who is sent" (cf. Luke 11:49 with Acts 13:31); although Barnabas is linked with the twelve apostles as part of a larger apostolic circle from the early days in Jerusalem (Acts 4:36), Luke neither ties Paul directly to this group nor names him an "apostle" with the same status or import.

mandate "opened" by Messiah himself. Though it is also certain that Luke's audience would "be caught up by the language"[33] of Peter's "discrimination" and respond with ringing rejection of such behavior, it is unmistakably clear that a specific interpretation of the theo-logical rationale for the transformation of Peter's mindset is rendered by the epistemological contours of the narrative itself. Luke arranges his 'continuity of the narrative' such that Peter's *peripeteia* cannot be simply understood as a change of Peter's own empathy for the Gentiles or of anecdotal circumstances *vis-à-vis* the non-Jewish peoples geared to elicit the emotive responses of Luke's auditors. Rather, the 'arrangement' itself coerces Luke's audiences to this understanding. It may even be that this concrete content symbolizes certain of the "events come to fruition among us" (Luke 1:1) that motivated our "inscribed" author to re-configure and thus, for the likes of Theophilus, to re-manage the "witness" of the church's "opening of the scriptures."

---

[33] From the quotation of Tompkins, cited above at the beginning.

Chapter Seven: *A New Reading Of Luke's 'Gospel Acts'*: Acts as the 'Metaleptic' Collapse of Luke and Dionysius of Halicarnassus's Narrative 'Arrangement' (οἰκονομία) as the Hermeneutical Keys to Luke's Re-Visioning of the "Many"[1]

The author of Luke and Acts is intent in his[2] opening *prooemia* to explain why he should attempt yet another construal and why he especially–as neither "eyewitness" nor "attendant from the beginning" of traditions that have now "come to fruition"–should present himself qualified to re-configure these traditions and change their overall format in a radically new narrative proposal (Luke 1:1–4→Acts 1:1–2). Consequently, rather than legitimate his undertaking by stereotyped appeals to his audience's familiarity and his own competence with recognized genres of narrative production,[3] Luke uses his opening statement to situate his work within the ambiance of a conventional narrative poetics–a Hellenistic standard complete with its own logic of legitimation. Thus Luke's narrative enterprise has less to do with the 'type' or sub-genre of narrative than with commending the specific scope and sequence of his *diegesis vis-à-vis* the 'many' other accounts that are already 'at hand' (Luke 1:1, 3; compare Theophi-

---

[1] As a whole this chapter presents a new reading of Luke and Acts. Parts 1 and 2 are amalgamations of my "Dionysius' Narrative 'Arrangement' (οἰκονομία) as the Hermeneutical Key to Luke's Re-vision of the 'Many,'" in *Paul, Luke and the Graeco-Roman World: Essays in Honour of Alexander J. M. Wedderburn*, ed. Alf Christophersen, Carsten Claussen, Jörg Frey, and Bruce Longenecker, JSNTSup 217 (Sheffield: Sheffield Academic Press, 2002): 149–64 and of my "The Triadic Synergy of Hellenistic Poetics in the Narrative Epistemology of Dionysius of Halicarnassus and the Authorial Intent of the Evangelist Luke (Luke 1:1–4; Acts 1:1–8)," *Neotestamentica* 42 (2008): 289–303; Part 3 develops new observations from my earlier work on *metalepsis* published in the journal of the Chicago Society of Biblical Research: "Diegetic Breach or Metaleptic Interruption? Acts 1:4b–5 as the Collapse between the Worlds of 'All that Jesus Began to Enact and to Teach' (Acts 1:1) and the 'Acts of the Apostles,'" *Biblical Research* 56 (2011): 23–34.

[2] Παρηκολουθηκότι (masc. perf. participle, Luke 1:3) indicates a male author, inscribed by a "me" (Luke 1:3), who came to be identified in Christian tradition as "Luke."

[3] Cf., e.g., Loveday C. A. Alexander, "The Preface to Acts and the Historians," in *History, Literature, and Society in the Book of Acts*, ed. Ben Witherington III (Cambridge: Cambridge University Press, 1996): 73–103, with the essays by Daryl Schmidt, "Rhetorical Influences and Genre: Luke's Preface and the Rhetoric of Hellenistic Historiography," and Richard I. Pervo, "Israel's Heritage and Claims upon the Genre(s) of Luke and Acts: The Problems of a History," both in *Jesus and the Heritage of Israel*, ed. David P. Moessner, vol. 1, *Luke the Interpreter of Israel* (Harrisburg, PA: Trinity Press International, 1999): 27–60 and 127–43, respectively.

lus's 'instruction' [ὧν κατηχήθης λόγων], Luke 1:4). That is to say, rather than hazard a guess from nuanced distinctions of genre why Luke would include such specific references as his 'scope' (πάντα [all] the πράγματα/traditions, Luke 1:1, 3) and 'starting point' (οἱ ἀπ' ἀρχῆς αὐτόπται καὶ ὑπηρέται γενόμενοι τοῦ λόγου, Luke 1:2) and distinctive 'arrangement' of his narrative as especially important for his readers (καθεξῆς σοι γράψαι [...] ἵνα ἐπιγνῷς περὶ ὧν κατηχήθης λόγων τὴν ἀσφάλειαν, Luke 1:3–4), Luke, instead, would have his audience be assured from the outset that their aspirations and expectations of a quality *narrative* performance will indeed be met. But more than that, by such strategy, Luke signals not only that his narrative will be rhetorically rewarding but that also his two-volume rehearsal will fundamentally change the way audiences hear the traditions of Jesus "just as they have been handed down to us" and are being interpreted in the communities of "the many." When read in tandem with his opening words in his sequel volume, Luke stakes no less a claim than that his own two-volume version is a worthy and authentic and indeed more illuminating re-configuration than the "many" other attempts.

The first point of our thesis argues that the 1st-century BCE teacher of rhetoric, historian, and literary critic Dionysius of Halicarnassus (*floruit* ca. 60–8 BCE), in his critique of Thucydides's 'arrangement' (οἰκονομία) of the *Peloponnesian War*, presents narrative-rhetorical categories closely parallel to the later thought and rationale of Luke's opening assertions. This contention can be demonstrated not simply by pointing to similar technical narrative-rhetorical terms–a cluster which turns out to be closer to Luke's narrative categories than any other–but, more importantly, to a commonly shared epistemology of narrative that informs both passages. This epistemology of *diegesis* is articulated in its essentials in Aristotle's *Poetics*[4] before, in the next two centuries BCE, more elaborate schemes of poetic 'management' (οἰκονομία) will be developed from within this broad consensus.

[For the 'state of the art' of narrative rhetoric during Aristotle's time, see Chapter Five above, § 1.]

'Management' of the limited scope of this essay, however, dictates that we treat in detail only one focal passage in Dionysius, although it will become apparent that we have already encountered several of these common categories of narrative poetics in Polybius of Megalopolis and Diodorus of Sicily (see Chapters Five and Six, respectively, above).

---

4 Undoubtedly a compendium by Aristotle's students of the master's lectures, the *Poetics* elaborates the distinctive elements and dynamics of tragedy and of epic as models for Aristotle's more comprehensive discussion of the "mimēsis of enactment." See Aristotle, *Poetics* (Halliwell, LCL). See esp. *Poet*. 1–5 and Halliwell's Introduction, 3–20.

1 Dionysius's 'Management' of Narrative 'Arrangement' Elaborated

When Aristotle appeals to the powerful effect of the enactment of action (μίμησις [...] πράξεως) (or 'plot'–μῦθος) of a tragedy, even when this plot is heard rather than seen enacted on stage, it is easy to see how the narrative-rhetorical theory of the *Poetics* could be applied to all narrative such as historiography and biography and not simply to epic or comedy.[5] This appropriation of theory would be especially tempting when history writing attains the self-conscious goal of imparting a morality for living based upon the patterns of *persona* and events configured through the arrangement of the history narrative itself.[6] And although Aristotle draws a sharp distinction between the object of the history writer and that of the poet as between the presentation of particular facts (τὰ καθ' ἕκαστον) over against the re-presentation (ποίησις) of general truths (τὰ καθόλου) (*Poetics* 9.3) (historiography is 'casual,' treating subjects and events over a particular period of time, whereas tragedy and epic are 'causal,' treating a single action of one particular person or family), scholars such as Frank W. Walbank have shown that Aristotle's distinction was idiosyncratic to the Hellenistic period and never did gain wide acceptance (compare a notable exception, Lucian in *How to Write History*).[7] In fact, Walbank, along with others, has argued that a narrative poetics formed the epistemological basis for varieties of more 'tragic' history well before the time of Aristotle.[8] In any case, regardless of how and when the earlier developments of narrative poetics evolved, for our purposes in understanding Luke's claims for his own *diegesis*, we need move only to Dionysius, who flourished in Rome roughly one century before Luke, to see how the triadic synergy of narrative poetics showcased in the *Poetics* functions as the commonly assumed basis for Dionysius's critique of Thucydides's historical narrative.

---

[5] The discussion of the latter was either lost or never completed in the *Poetics*; see Halliwell (LCL), on 6.21 (47 n. e). See above for the audience impact of a well-ordered plot, Chapter Five § 1.
[6] According to Kenneth S. Sacks, Diodorus Siculus, elder contemporary of Dionysius, is the first historian so explicitly to formulate the historiographical task, though he is apparently echoing Ephorus as his source (*Diodorus Siculus and the First Century* [Princeton, NJ: Princeton University Press, 1990], esp. 23–54).
[7] Compare G. M. A. Grube's assessment (*The Greek and Roman Critics* [London: Methuen, 1965], 333–38): "Lucian, unlike Polybius, also discusses the kind of style appropriate to history, a subject treated only very incidentally by other critics, so that we have in this essay the fullest discussion of historiography as a literary genre from antiquity" (quoting 338).
[8] Frank W. Walbank, "History and Tragedy," *Historia* 9 (1960): 216–34. Walbank, however, rejects the notion of any distinct sub-genre or species of "tragic historiography."

In two of the extant texts of Dionysius's Literary Treatises or *Scripta Rhetorica*,[9] in his *Letter to Gnaeus Pompeius (Pomp.)* and his *On Thucydides (Thuc.)*, Dionysius turns his attention to a composer's ability to arrange prose sequence (τάξις/οἰκονομία) in larger blocks of material, and, with but one exception, restricts his analysis to writers of history. In the present form of the former work, written most likely not long after the completion of his *On Demosthenes (Dem.)*, Dionysius spends the first two chapters rebutting Gnaeus Pompeius's charges of Dionysius's unfair comparison of Demosthenes's style as superior to Plato's (compare *Dem.* 5–7), before comparing Herodotus with Thucydides (*Pomp.* 3) and Xenophon with Philistus (chapters 4–5), and finally identifying Theopompus as Isocrates's "most illustrious pupil" (chapter 6).[10]

That Dionysius's defense of Demosthenes's superior style to Plato's in chapters 1–2 of the *Letter to Gnaeus Pompeius* forms the exception to his otherwise singular examination of Greek *historians* proves to be telling. For as is well known, Demosthenes is Dionysius's master *par excellence* in his incomparable ability to impact audiences. But given Dionysius's all-controlling concern to revive the craft of the orator "to bewitch [γοητεύειν] the ear" by unleashing the magic of persuasion (ψυχαγωγία) of Attic dialect (*Words* 12), this choice is hardly surprising. In fact, this appeal of Dionysius to reprise the period when Attic "words were a power loosed"[11] sounds the keynote of Dionysius's entire career. Or as Dionysius states in *On Demosthenes* 18, "After all, the most potent weapon for a political

---

[9] Cf., e.g., Stanley Fredrick Bonner, *The Literary Treatises of Dionysius of Halicarnassus: A Study in the Development of Critical Method*, Cambridge Classical Studies 5 (Cambridge: Cambridge University Press, 1939); W. Rhys Roberts, *Dionysius of Halicarnassus: On Literary Composition* (London: Macmillan, 1910); W. Kendrick Pritchett, *Dionysius of Halicarnassus: On Thucydides* (Berkeley, CA: University of California Press, 1975); David L. Toye, "Dionysius of Halicarnassus on the First Greek Historians," *AJP* 116 (1995): 279–302; G. M. A. Grube, "Dionysius of Halicarnassus on Thucydides," *The Phoenix* 4 (1950): 95–110; David L. Balch, "Two Apologetic Encomia: Dionysius on Rome and Josephus on the Jews," *Journal for the Study of Judaism* 13 (1982): 102–22.

[10] These latter chapters on the historians, however, are quoted excerpts from one of Dionysius's lost treatises, which Dionysius cites himself as "Essays which I addressed to Demetrius on the subject of imitation" (περὶ μιμήσεως), a survey in three books of model poets and prose writers for students of rhetoric. This work must precede *De Oratoribus Antiquis*, the earliest extant work, given internal cross-references within the entire corpus and an epitomator's summary of Book II (Papyrus Oxyrynchus VI).

[11] See Robert S. Reid, "When Words Were a Power Loosed: Audience Expectation and Finished Narrative Technique in the Gospel of Mark," *Quarterly Journal of Speech* 80 (1994): 427–47; Robert S. Reid, "Dionysius of Halicarnassus' Theory of Compositional Style and the Theory of Literate Consciousness," *Rhetoric Review* 15 (1996): 46–64.

speaker or a forensic pleader is to draw his audience into an emotional state of mind."¹² In this, Demosthenes excelled like no other, even besting the great *composers* Herodotus and Plato, whose words were not always "achieving the appropriate force of expression" (compare *Pomp.* 1–2; *Dem.* 41–42).

It is this latter comparison of an orator with composers representing a variety of *written* genres, including narrative historiography, which may seem the most surprising. To be sure, Dionysius's treatment of Demosthenes's compositional arrangement was either lost or never completed; yet what is found in the extant *On Demosthenes*, as well as numerous references to Demosthenes throughout the *Scripta Rhetorica*, indicate clearly enough what his supreme achievement was. His ability to raise the persuasive potency of Attic Greek to new heights through the 'arrangement'/'management' (οἰκονομία) of 'subject matter' (πραγματικοὶ τόποι)–whether in the conjunction of periods or relation of larger sections to a whole–qualifies Demosthenes as the most admired model of Greek oratory. Paradoxically, Dionysius's treatment of Demosthenes's *oratorical* rhetoric adduces the poetics of *narrative* as a standard well ensconced before the dawn of the Common Era.

These assertions can be nuanced in several ways.¹³ In his *On Demosthenes* 51, Dionysius divulges his reasons for applying the current system of *prose arrangement* to the persuasive craft of the *rhetor*:

> [Demosthenes] *observed that good organization* (διαίρεσις) *of a speech depends on two factors, selection of <u>subject-matter</u>* (πραγματικὸς τόπος) *and <u>style of delivery</u>* (λεκτικός), *and that these two are each divided into two equal sections, subject-matter into <u>preparation</u>* (παρασκευή), *which the early rhetoricians call <u>invention</u>* (εὕρεσις), *and distribution of the prepared subject matter, which they term <u>arrangement</u>* (οἰκονομία); *and that of style into <u>selection of words</u>* (τὴν ἐκλογὴν τῶν ὀνομάτων), *and <u>composition</u>* (σύνθεσις) *of the words chosen. <u>In both of these sections the second is the more important, arrangement in the case of subject-matter and composition in the case of style</u>.*¹⁴

From his elevation of the second element over the first in both categories, we see that it is precisely the craft of good *prose* arrangement that most effectively

---

12 Dionysius, *Dem.* 18 (Usher, LCL).
13 I am indebted to Robert S. Reid for his pioneering observations on Dionysius's treatment of prose arrangement (οἰκονομία) ("'Neither Oratory nor Dialogue': Dionysius of Halicarnassus and the Genre of Plato's *Apology*," *Rhetoric Society Quarterly* 27 [1997]: 63–90).
14 Trans. and emphasis mine.

unleashes the powers of persuasion.¹⁵ We are already reminded of the goal in the *Poetics* of *structuring* plots to impact the audience as poignantly as possible.

2 Dionysius's *On Thucydides* and Luke's Rationale for Re-'Arranging' the "Many"

It is, however, Dionysius's last and critically most mature literary-critical essay, his *On Thucydides*, which deals most extensively with prose arrangement. In chapter 9 Dionysius begins to apply this 'arrangement' system to Thucydides's *Peloponnesian War*, offering the remarkable statement:

One aspect of his [Thucydides's] compositional organization (κατασκευάση) is less satisfactory, and because of which some have criticized him. It concerns the more technically-skilled (τὸ τεχνικώτερον)¹⁶ side of subject-matter (τὸ πραγματικός), that which is called arrangement *(τὸ οἰκονομικόν),* which is required in every kind of writing, *whether one chooses philosophical or rhetorical subjects. It consists of* division *(διαίρεσις),* order *(τάξις) and* method of elaboration *(ἐξεργασία) [Thuc. 9].*¹⁷

What is clear again from the far-ranging scope and probative value of the poetics of prose *arrangement* (οἰκονομία) in the 1st century BCE is how much a matter of convention, or 'matter of fact' status, this system enjoys for all sorts of composition. There is no need for Dionysius to urge the categories *per se*; he takes for granted that his readers aspire to the same standards. More than that, Dionysius appears to be employing virtually the same categories of prose criticism, whether from the earlier or later periods of his literary career.¹⁸

Given the limited scope of this study, however, I shall draw comparisons with Luke only on the first two of the three categories of the οἰκονομία schema (that is, διαίρεσις and τάξις).

Like a skilled surgeon, Dionysius applies the critic's knife to the first category of "division"/"partitioning" (διαίρεσις):

---

15 Cf. Reid, "'Neither Oratory nor Dialogue,'" 71: "It is adroit 'arrangement,' whether of subject matter (οἰκονομία) or words (σύνθεσις), that is the true 'potency' in the Dionysian art of rhetoric."
16 Cf. "technical" (Pritchard), "artistic" (Usher).
17 Trans. and emphasis mine.
18 Whether in *Comp.* (21–24), *Dem.* (37–42), or *Thuc.* (9–20).

Wishing to follow a new path, untraveled by others, he [Thucydides] *divided* (ἐμέρισε) *his history by summers and winters. This decision produced an outcome contrary to his expectations: the seasonal <u>division</u> by time periods* (ἡ διαίρεσις τῶν χρόνων) *did not lead to greater <u>clarity</u>* (σαφεστέρα) *but to <u>greater difficulty in following the narrative</u>* (δυσ**παρακολουθητοτέρα**)*. It is rather amazing how he failed to realize that a narrative (***ἡ διήγησις***) that is broken up into small sections, which taken together are to describe the many events* (πολλῶν **πραγμάτων**) *that took place in many different places, will not catch that "pure light" that "shines from afar"*[19] *as becomes obvious from* [the following of] *the events themselves. As an example from the third book* [...] *he <u>begins to write</u>* (ἀρξάμενος **γράφειν**) *about the Mytileneans, but before <u>completing</u> this whole section of the narrative* (ὅλην ἐκπληρῶσαι **τὴν διήγησιν**)*, he withdraws to the affairs of the Lacedaemonians. And he does not even round these events off before relating the siege of Plataea. What is more, even this he leaves <u>unfinished</u>* (ἀτελῆ) *in order to recount the Mytilenean War. Then from there he switches his narrative* (ἄγει **τὴν διήγησιν**) *to the affairs of Corcyra* [...]*. He then leaves this account, too, <u>half-finished</u>* (ἡμιτελῆ) [...]*. What more do I need to say? The <u>whole</u>* (ὅλη) *of the book is chopped up in this way, and <u>the continuity of the narrative</u>* (τὸ διηνεκὲς τῆς ἀπαγγελίας) *is destroyed. As we would now expect, we wander around here and there, <u>finding it difficult to follow the events</u> that have been described* (δυσκόλως τοῖς δηλουμένοις **παρακολουθοῦμεν**)*, because our mind is confused by <u>the scattering of the events</u>* (ἐν τῷ διασπᾶσθαι **τὰ πράγματα**) *and cannot easily <u>or reliably</u>* (**ἀκριβῶς**) *remember <u>the half-completed references</u>* (τὰς ἡμιτελεῖς [...] ἀναφερούσης) *which it has heard. Rather, a history narrative should be a flowing and uninterrupted written account* (τὴν ἱστορικὴν πραγματείαν εἰρομένην εἶναι καὶ ἀπερίσπαστον)*, especially when it is concerned with a considerable number of events that are difficult to learn about. It is manifest that Thucydides' principle is neither right nor appropriate to the writing of history. For none of the historians who succeeded him <u>divided</u>* (διεῖλε) *his narrative by summers and winters, but all followed the well-worn paths which lead to a clarity of understanding* (σαφήνειαν) [*Thuc. 9*{**bold** = Lukan parallels}].[20]

In one shorter period, Dionysius combines three technical terms that Luke will employ in his short prooemial period (Luke 1:1–4) approximately one century later. Moreover, four other terms or cognates of the Lukan prologue are key components in Dionysius's immediate context (γραφή; διήγησις; σαφήνεια/ἀσφαλής;

---

19 Allusion to Pindar, *Pythian Odes*, iii.75 (so Usher, et al., LCL 1.483).
20 Trans. and emphasis mine.

ἐκπληρόω/πληροφορέω). Even more important are the shared assumptions concerning the role a plotted narrative plays in effecting the intent of an author for the desired impact upon his or her audience:

2.1 Plotted 'Sequence' that Conveys the Author's Intended Meaning is a Function of Proper 'Dividing' or 'Partitioning' of the Narrative

DIONYSIUS: The sequencing and hence connections of the events to each other do not lead Thucydides's readers to a reliable (ἀκριβῶς) understanding of their significance. The blame for this confusion lies with Thucydides's faulty 'partitioning'/'dividing up' (διαίρεσις) of the subject matter (the πράγματα of the war). Without the proper relationship between larger series of events and other such series, the interconnections between single events and other specific events become unintelligible. Operative in Dionysius's model of 'management' is the co-relative, integrating relationship between proper 'division' (διαίρεσις) and good 'sequence' (τάξις). Without proper 'divisions' (διαίρεσις) defining the whole, no 'ordering' (τάξις) of the material can render a clarity of the whole. In other words, 'sequence' is a function of 'division,' which together are constitutive of proper 'arrangement' (οἰκονομία). Again, it is the overarching conception of 'emplotment' of a narrative that is decisive. Impact on the audience is tied directly to the structuring of the events or plot itself which, in turn, is tied directly to the author's deliberate choice in the art or craft of 'managing' the material of his narrative. Thus according to the operative tria-lectic poetics of Dionysius, Thucydides would have accomplished his desired outcome much more effectively if he had 'arranged' (ᾠκονομῆσθαι, chapter 12) his 'narrative' (διήγησις) differently.

At the heart of Dionysius's critique of Thucydides's 'management'/'arrangement' of his narrative material, then, is the resulting lack of a unified whole: "The continuity of the narrative is destroyed" (chapter 9). Dionysius had formulated this same complaint earlier in his *Pomp.* 3, when he compared the arrangement of Thucydides to Herodotus who "did not break the continuity of the narrative" (οὐ διέσπασε τὴν διήγησιν): "Whereas Thucydides has taken a single subject and divided the whole body into many parts, Herodotus has chosen a number of subjects which are in no way alike and has made them into one harmonious whole." 'Fragmentation' of the narrative is the result of an ill-conceived organization which issues in 'un-completed' (ἀτελῆ) or 'half-completed' (ἡμιτελῆ) descriptions of events. Thucydides's descriptions are not 'unfinished' simply or even primarily because he neglects to come back to scenes which he has abruptly interrupted–although he is certainly 'guilty' of that failure in Dionysius's estimation.

Rather, more destructive of the narrative wholeness which good 'arrangement' should vouchsafe is the absence in Thucydides of a bodying forth of the total ensemble of events through which alone a reader can make the proper causal connections, discern significances of specific events, and draw the proper moral and pragmatic conclusions regarding actions and characters connected together in this particular way. Unless a reader is able to 'move' from one section of the narrative to another and 'follow' (παρακολουθέω) a developing plot or complication and resolution of a whole series of events, the author has failed to imbue the reader with "the pure light shining from afar." Wholeness, therefore, is not just a function of scope, although we shall see that the proper 'beginning' and 'ending' points are critical to good οἰκονομία. Central, rather, to the 'arrangement' of a narrative that effectively impacts its audience is its 'division,' which necessarily entails its resulting sequence.

LUKE: Luke also is comparing his narrative *arrangement* to "many" others' and distinguishing his *management* as one which will lead the likes of a Theophilus on the paths to certain clarity (καθεξῆς σοι γράψαι, κράτιστε Θεόφιλε, ἵνα ἐπιγνῷς περὶ ὧν κατηχήθης λόγων τὴν ἀσφάλειαν, Luke 1:3b–4). Whatever καθεξῆς σοι γράψαι may mean in more detail, Luke certainly ties its 'sense' directly to the 'referent' of intended impact on his audience, especially since ἡ ἀσφάλεια combines both the *senses* of 'clarity' (σαφήνεια) and 'security' (ἀσφαλής). Acts 2:36 makes this double-edged sense unmistakable as Peter clinches his argument in Luke's arrangement of his speech by appealing to the "whole house of Israel": ἀσφαλῶς οὖν γινωσκέτω πᾶς οἶκος Ἰσραήλ ("Let the whole house of Israel know therefore with *clear certainty*[21] that God had established him as both Lord and Christ, this Jesus whom you crucified").

On the other hand, unlike the direct criticism of a Dionysius,[22] or of other historians in their προοίμια (prefaces) who promote their own strengths *vis-à-vis* alleged weaknesses of their rivals, Luke presents only an oblique critique of his predecessors. He has "followed" (παρακολουθέω) "reliably"/"with understanding" (ἀκριβῶς) the whole scope of "all" the "events" (πράγματα, Luke 1:1) from "the top"/"the beginning" (ἄνωθεν) of the sequence of the narrative (παρηκολουθηκότι ἄνωθεν πᾶσιν ἀκριβῶς, 1:3) "compiled" or "ordered" by the "others" from the oral accounts and traditions (πολλοὶ ἐπεχείρησαν ἀνατάξασθαι διήγησιν [...] λόγων, 1:1a,4); but now he must "write" his own "narrative sequence" (καθεξῆς [...] γράψαι, 1:3b). *Something* about these other narrative arrangements

---

21 Cf. BDAG on Acts 2:36: "know beyond a doubt" (147); RSV, "know assuredly."
22 Dionysius of Halicarnassus, *Ant. rom.* I.1.2–4.

of the whole is found wanting: Luke's purpose with his audience is a telling clue to his own motivation to write (1:4).[23]

The distinct 'divisions' of Luke's Gospel (and Acts) among the Gospels are well known.[24] Furthermore, Luke's propensity to link the events of Jesus and of the church to 'fulfillments' of Israel's events and prophecies according to their scriptures is well documented and embodies a 'wholeness' of events ensembled like no other narrative account.[25] Most especially, Luke's *synchronisms* are salient instances of his insistence that a "firmness of understanding" of the "events that have come to fruition" will result for the reader, not only through the many rich and varied interconnections to be made with the larger story of Israel but also with worldwide events within the theatre of Rome's control.[26]

Luke's emphasis upon the continuity of the fledgling Jesus-Messianic movement with Israel's history is nowhere more obvious than in the overlapping partitioning (διαίρεσις) of his two volumes to create one ongoing narrative account (διήγησις). The technique of 'indirect' to 'direct speech' within a short, secondary *prooemium* is most unusual (Acts 1:4b) and delivers a striking message: In Luke's 'arrangement' (οἰκονομία), 'all' (πάντα) the traditions (Luke 1:3, compare λόγοι) that Luke has so judiciously 'followed' are not exhausted by Jesus's ascension at the end of the first volume. "All [πάντα] that Jesus began to do and to teach" (Acts 1:1b) continues on through the διαίρεσις (partitioning) of one narrative work, interrupted only by Jesus himself who breaks in to the narrator's recapitulation of volume one to assume the *'prooemial* voice' of the inscribed author ("I" [author], Acts 1:1 → "me" [Jesus], Acts 1:4b). Jesus broadcasts to apostolic witness and reader alike the plot of the continuing *diegesis* as the fulfillment of his own prophecy and legacy in the 'Kingdom of God' ("receive power [...] my witnesses [...] to the end of the earth," Acts 1:3–8 → Luke 24:48–49). The further fact that the closing events (πράγματα) of the 'Gospel' volume are repeated and

---

23 See esp. Chapters Three and Four above.
24 See esp. Chapter One above.
25 Cf., e.g., Luke 1:5, 80; 2:1–2; 3:1–2; Acts 11:27–28. Of special interest are the 'completions' of a period of time which themselves introduce a new stage of fulfillment in Israel's festal calendar or Torah observance or promises of the prophets: e.g., Luke 2:21, 22–24, 34; 3:3–6, 15–16; 4:16–21; 9:28–31, 51; 10:23–24; 12:49–53; 13:31–35; 17:22–35; 18:31–34; 19:41–44; 22:14–18, 28–30, 35–38; 24:25–27, 44–49; Acts 1:20–22; 2:1; 3:22–26; etc.; see William S. Kurz, "Promise and Fulfillment in Hellenistic Jewish Narratives and in Luke and Acts," in *Jesus and the Heritage of Israel*, ed. David P. Moessner, vol. 1, *Luke the Interpreter of Israel* (Harrisburg, PA: Trinity Press International, 1999): 147–70.
26 See Chapter Five above.

re-figured as the opening events of the continuing volume,[27] moves the reader to one inescapable conclusion: Luke's 'management' is significantly different than the "many's" such that he creates a new 'whole' (and) a whole 'new' emplotment of "the events that have come to fruition" (Luke 1:1b).

2.2 'Beginning' and 'Ending' Points Determine the 'Partitioning' and Hence 'Sequencing' of the Narrative Plot that the Author Wishes to Convey to Targeted Audiences

DIONYSIUS: Dionysius moves immediately (chapters 10–11) from his critique of Thucydides's muddled 'arrangement' to link the faulty 'divisions' (and 'sequence') of the text to Thucydides's *beginning* and *ending* points of his narrative under the rubric 'sequence'/'order' (τάξις). Because both the ἀρχή and the τέλος of the narrative are inappropriate to the stated purpose and scope of Thucydides, the whole *arrangement* (οἰκονομία) of various parts and their sequences is jumbled. The reader cannot connect causal factors that issue in later events to a seminal event and thus to the fundamental forces that had eventually coalesced to produce *the beginning* (ἀρχή) of the conflict:

Some critics also find fault with the <u>sequence</u> (τάξις) of his narrative, complaining that he neither chose the right <u>beginning</u> (<u>ἀρχή</u>) for it nor the proper ending (τέλος). They say that by no means the least important aspect of good arrangement (οἰκονομίας ἀγαθῆς) is that a work should have as its <u>beginning</u> (ἀρχή) the point where nothing necessarily be perceived as preceding it, and that the account should end (τελέω) where it appears that nothing further need follow. Because of these considerations, they claim that he [Thucydides] has not paid proper attention to either of these aspects. The historian himself has provided them sufficient grounds for this charge. For after he states right from the start that the Peloponnesian War was of far greater magnitude–both in terms of length and the amount of suffering from the multitude of misfortunes–than any war that preceded it, he begins to conclude his prooimion by wanting first to state the causes [of the War] from which he had determined its <u>beginning</u> (<u>ἀφ' ὧν τὴν ἀρχὴν</u> ἔλαβε). He lays out two, the true cause, which is not generally spread about (the growth of the Athenian war machine), and that which is not true, the one fabricated by the Lacedaemonians

---

27 Luke 3:21–24:53 corresponds to Acts 1:1–2; Luke 24:13–43 corresponds to Acts 1:3; Luke 24:36–49 corresponds to Acts 1:4–5; Luke 24:50–51 corresponds to Acts 1:6–11; Luke 24:52–53 corresponds to Acts 1:12–14.

(the sending of the allied forces to aid the Corcyreans against the Corinthians). *Indeed, he does not <u>begin his narrative</u> (τὴν ἀρχὴν πεποίηται τῆς διηγήσεως) from the true cause, the one which he himself believes, but from that other point [Thuc. 10; underline = Lukan parallels].*[28]

'Starting points' organize basic causes which justify the telling and hence the arranging of the plot in the first place. Emplotment without proper causal connections is epistemologically impotent in effecting the proper response from the audience.

This improper beginning point, then, would have been sufficient in itself to prove that his own <u>narrative</u> is not arranged (ᾠκονομῆσθαι <u>τὴν διήγησιν</u>) in the most competent way by him, by which I mean that it does not begin at the natural <u>starting point</u> (τὴν κατὰ φύσιν ἔχειν <u>ἀρχήν</u>). Added also to this is the observation that his <u>history</u> does not come to a head at the proper point of completion (ἔδει κεφάλαια τετελευτηκέναι <u>τὴν διήγησιν</u>). For although the war lasted twenty-seven years and he lived the whole time right up to its conclusion (τῆς καταλύσεως), he carried his history down only to the twenty-second year by extending the eighth book through the Battle of Cynossema, even though he says in the prooimion that he intends to cover <u>all</u> (πάντα) the events which taken together made up the war (κατὰ τόνδε τὸν πόλεμον)[29] *[Thuc. 12; underline = Lukan parallels].*

Earlier in his *Letter to Gnaeus Pompeius*, Dionysius had opined:

The matters that are treated in the concluding section (ἐν τέλει) of his narrative are replete with even more difficulties. In spite of the fact that he says he was <u>present in person</u> (παρεγένετο) during the whole war [...] it would have been better, after going through <u>all</u> (πάντα) the events of the war, to close his history with a climactic ending (τελευτῆς)–one that was most wondrous and especially gratifying to his audience–the return of the exiles from Phyle, which constituted <u>the beginning</u> (ἡ πόλις <u>ἀρξαμένη</u>) of the city's recovery of freedom [Pomp. 3; underline = Lukan parallels].[30]

---

28 All translations of Dionysius's *Literary Treatises* are my own.
29 Usher in his LCL translation appears to pass over entirely the more precise meaning of the Greek phrase κατὰ τόνδε τὸν πόλεμον when he translates: "having expressed his intention in his introduction to include all the events of the war." He does, however, point out in a note that Thucydides does refer to the larger scope of all the events earlier in *War* 5.26.
30 Trans. and emphasis mine.

With both ἀρχή and τέλος inappropriately selected, the whole arrangement lacks the requisite power to move audiences to the suitable moral lessons from the whole simply because the whole plot itself is structured unsuitably. When the scope does not comprehend sufficient πράγματα to build to a climax through a properly sequenced beginning, middle, and end, the overall impact is destroyed. The *Poetics'* prescription for the proper magnitude of 'beginning, middle, and end' which breaks open into a new state of 'resolution' (λύσις) of affairs[31] is the assumed rationale for Dionysius's criticism of Thucydides's inability to lead the audience along the path of clarity.

LUKE: In Acts 11:4 Peter "lays out" 'in a narrative sequence'/'arrangement' (καθεξῆς)[32] the story of his visit to Cornelius when some believers from among "the circumcision" "dispute with" him, accusing him of "eating" with "those of the uncircumcision" (Acts 11:1–3). By comparing Peter's narrative accounting in 11:4–18 with the narrator's much longer version in 10:1–48, we can observe that καθεξῆς denotes the 'narrato-logical' sense of the Cornelius visit within the larger 'divisions' and 'sequence' of meaning created by the οἰκονομία of the two-volume Luke and Acts. In light of the "many's" "ordering" (ἀνατάξασθαι, Luke 1:1) of their "narrative," Luke's καθεξῆς signals a sequence which is 'logical' but within the very different configuration of his diegetic emplotment, including especially the span of two discrete volumes instead of apparently the *one* of the "many." We have seen, in fact, that Peter's *relecture* in Acts 11:1–18 of the baptism of the Holy Spirit upon Cornelius's household pinpoints two distinct and decisive 'beginning' points: the seminal ἀρχή of the one two-volume work–Jesus's baptism (of the Spirit) by/through John–and the derivative 'beginning' or ἀρχή of the extended plot of the baptism of the Spirit upon the apostolic witnesses at Pentecost in the opening of the sequel volume (Acts 2).[33]

Does Luke re-configure and extend his narrative account of the others because each lacks a sufficient scope of events to deliver the proper comprehension of "all that Jesus began to enact and to teach" (Acts 1:1)? Correlatively, is Luke convinced that particular events in his second volume are necessary to entangle with those of the first in order to communicate the proper significance of Jesus's appearance and fate in that first volume? Is it possible, for instance, that the announce-

---

31 See esp. *Poetics* 7 and 18.
32 See esp. Chapter Six, § III., above. BDAG (490) emphasizes 'succession' "in order, one after the other of sequence in time, space or logic." Of the complete listing of seven occurrences in the New Testament and sub-apostolic literature treated by Bauer, five are in the New Testament and all occur in Luke and Acts!
33 See above Chapter Six §III.

ment of a messianic salvation to the whole world anticipated in Isaiah (compare Luke 2:29–32; 3:4–6; 4:17–19) requires in Luke's world of comprehending Jesus an enactment of those prophecies through an advance to the "ends of the earth?" Must Jesus's followers somehow be intricately interwoven with the "actions and teaching" of Jesus in such a fashion so as to profile a more accurate picture of Jesus's messianic salvation as dramatized in advance in the Jewish scriptures? Is Luke perhaps convinced that the 'organization' of others' accounts exhibits the wrong 'starting' and 'ending' points? In short, is Luke, similar to a Dionysius, 'following' the attempts by "many" to compose a narrative and concluding that their storyline is inadequate, even misleading?

My contention is that through the sequence of Acts 1:4a to 1:4b, Luke collapses the world of Jesus's followers after the resurrection/ascension of Jesus into the world of the activities and presence of Jesus of the first volume (Gospel of Luke). Master–disciple, disciple–Master co-figure and thus con-figure each other. Luke thus 'partitions' his narrative sequence in such a way that his audiences are compelled to hear about Jesus in light of the impact he had had upon his followers, and, conversely, the significance that his followers' words and deeds provoke among their audiences must be discerned through the illumination of Jesus's own words and deeds. Through *metaleptic* transumption, the movement of the narrative level of Acts 1:4a to 1:4b transfers Luke's audiences into the one new world of fulfilled salvation.[34] The period of Jesus and the time of the church are narrated as *one era*, as one new reality; the Messianic activity of Jesus (Gospel) and that of Messiah through his disciples (Acts) must be grasped as *the one new reign and realm of God*: the Kingdom of God present and active on earth.

3 Acts 1:4a–5 as the Metaleptic Transference of Messiah Jesus of Nazareth to the Messianic Kingdom of God that Extends to 'the End of the Earth'

Of the many notable 'oddities' of Luke's sequel volume—naked exorcists, magical handkerchiefs, dangling vipers in an Maltese-island barbeque to name but a few—none is stranger than the reference to John's baptizing with water in Acts 1:4*b*–5: "And while he was eating with them [narrator speaking], he charged them not to

---

[34] See esp. the role of Isaiah in framing this fulfillment as God's "saving actions" (σωτήρια) through Israel's entire history that culminates in the rejection, taking up, and enthroned "witness" (Luke) of the Servant's "witnesses" to the center of Empire that controls the "end(s) of the earth" (Acts): Luke 3:4–6 → Luke 22:35–38 → Acts 1:8b → Acts 13:45–52 → Acts 28:25–28.

depart from Jerusalem but rather to await the promise of the Father which *you* have heard from *me* [Jesus speaking]." As the sudden, unexpected intrusion of this first person singular, genitive pronoun "my" (μου) alleges, the resurrected Jesus himself addresses the apostles in first person direct speech ("for John baptized with water but *you* shall be baptized by the Holy Spirit not after many days as these"). But the resurrected Jesus has already uttered this command at the end of the first volume: "Stay in this city until you receive power from the exalted Place" (Luke 24:49b). In effect, the main character of the previous volume who had already closed the story by "being taken up into heaven" (Luke 24:51b) interrupts and takes over the voice of the familiar sounding narrator who has begun the second volume in the same way as the first.³⁵ And like the first prologue, the narrator will again, without notice, slip behind a 'third person' voice at the beginning of volume two (Acts 1:1–2→1:3; compare Luke 1:1–4→1:5).

Are we to continue hearing Jesus *speak* as though the first volume continues uninterrupted ("all of the things which Jesus began to enact and to teach" [ὧν ἤρξατο ὁ Ἰησοῦς ποιεῖν τε καὶ διδάσκειν]) as Acts 1:1 reprises, even though we have just witnessed Jesus's ascension into heaven (Luke 24:50–51)? Luke strangely interrupts his narratorial voice with the voice of the leading character of the previous volume to address other major characters of that same narration: "For John [as Jesus goes on to say] baptized with water, but you (plural) will be baptized with the power of (the) Holy Spirit not after many days as these" (Acts 1:5). Once again the narrator speaks, but more diplomatically now that Jesus's direct speech is finished, "And when they had gone out together, they began to ask him, 'Lord, will you at this time restore the kingdom to Israel?'" (Acts 1:6). Jesus, *deus ex machina*-like, continues "to act and to teach" as he did in volume one.

3.1 The Complex Narrative Overlap between Volumes 'One' and 'Two'

The narrative *poiesis* between the volumes, however, is more complex than a simple breaking of narrative boundaries. Immediately before this voice takeover, the narrator has suggested that Jesus actually gave special appearances and teachings over a more or less longer period of time ("forty days," Acts 1:3–4a; compare 13:31, "many days") before he was finally "taken up" (ἐπήρθη, Acts 1:9), with his apostles and a larger group of disciples looking on (compare Acts 1:9–11 ≈ Luke 24:50–51). Are the "forty days" of live presentations and teachings on the Kingdom of God a hermeneutical lens for comprehending an ascended Christ,

---

35 λόγος πρῶτος, Luke 24:50–51.

or are the "forty days" rather a way of extending the deeds and words of "all that Jesus began to do and to teach" of the prequel beyond the resurrection event before Jesus is finally removed from the *diegetic* action of his public ministry in Acts 1:9–11? Are perhaps both of these rationales combined in Luke's mind? Most importantly, do we have any historical-literary precedents to make sense of what Luke himself might be *trying "to do and to teach"* with this rhetorical maneuver?

The surprising slippage *of* the narratorial voice with the audience ("O Theophilus [...] to whom he presented himself alive [...] charged them [...] to await the promise of the Father, Acts 1:1a, 4a) *to* the address by the main actor of the previous volume from within that prior narrated world ("which you heard from me"– Jesus to the apostles) can be illuminated by Luke's use of the trope *metalēpsis* (μετάληψις). By designating in Acts 1:3–14 an 'in-between temporal space' (that is, between resurrection and ascension) as well as a liminal physical space for the resurrected Jesus (between earth and heaven)–that is, between intra-diegetic and extra-diegetic plotting and between intra-diegetic and extra-diegetic universe– Luke collapses the two worlds of 'the narrated' and 'the narrator's.'[36] By such metaleptic juxtaposing and overlapping, Luke would have his audience understand that the two volumes intermesh to narrate *one story* or 'narrative continuity' of Israel's Messiah Jesus who composes the one 'subject matter' or πραγμάτικος τόπος of Luke's 'work,' what we can more aptly term his 'Gospel Acts':

καὶ συναλιζόμενος παρήγγειλεν αὐτοῖς ἀπὸ Ἱεροσολύμων μὴ χωρίζεσθαι ἀλλὰ περιμένειν τὴν ἐπαγγελίαν τοῦ πατρὸς ἣν <u>ἠκούσατέ</u> **μου** ὅτι Ἰωάννης μὲν ἐβάπτισεν ὕδατι ὑμεῖς δὲ ἐν πνεύματι βαπτισθήσεσθε ἁγίῳ, Acts 1:4a-b.

In utilizing the narrative-rhetorical *metalepsis*, "Luke" in the face of his non-eye-witness, non-apostle status[37] enhances his *authority* to narrate an authentic interpretation of the Kingdom of God as he blends the temporal and spatial universes of Israel's "Christ" and "the church" and thus in his narrating breaches the conventional barrier between 'the world narrated' and the 'world of his own.' We attain the following schema "between" Luke and Acts:

---

[36] For the use of these terms, see Gerard Genette, *Narrative Discourse: An Essay in Method*, trans. Jane E. Lewin (Ithaca, NY: Cornell University Press, 1980).
[37] Luke 1:2.

Acts		Luke	* = *metalepsis*
1:1–4a	≈	3:21–24:53	[inscribed author, "I": vol. 1 summarized and expanded by a '40' day period]
1:3	≈	24:13–43	["K of G announced" to apostles for '40' days after Jesus "suffering": 3rd pers. Narrative resumes from Luke 24:53]
1:4a	≈	24:36–49	[at a meal: apostles told by resurrected Jesus to "stay in this city" {Jerusalem}]
*1:4b–5	≈	24:49	[Jesus speaks directly out of narrator's mouth as diegetic first level narration of Acts: "await the promise which you heard from me!"]
1:6–11	≈	24:50–51	[witness to "end of the earth" answer to "restoring the Kingdom to Israel" with Jesus analempsis]
1:12–14	≈	24:52–53	[apostles/disciples re-gather in the Temple]
1:15ff	≈		[resumption of plotted time from Luke 24:53!]

3.2 Literary-Historical Precedents

Quintilian treats *metalepsis* among the various tropes (*tropus*) of proper style for persuasive presentation in Books 8–9 of his *Institutio Oratoria*. After discussing metaphor, synecdoche, metonymy, autonomasia, onomatopoeia, and catachresis, according to this great teacher of rhetoric[38] *metalepsis* provides:

> *a transition [transumptio] from one trope to another [...]. It is the nature of metalepsis to form a kind of intermediate step between the term transferred and the thing to which it is transferred, having no meaning in itself, but providing a transition. It is a trope with which to claim acquaintance, rather than one which we are ever likely to require to use* [Institutes, 8. 6. 37–38].[39]

Quintilian had already prefaced his comments by pointing out that *metalepsis* is a 'Greek thing,' "not infrequently used" by them, but rarely so in Latin, except for comedy (8.6.37). He gives as example the use of the apocopated "cano" for "canto" (to repeat), and since "canto" is a synonym for "dico," "cano" therefore forms a trope as a middle term-synonym for "dico" (8.3.38). Quintilian immediately adds, "We need not waste any more time over it [*metalepsis*]. I can see no use in it except, as I have already said, in comedy" (8.3.39, Butler's translation).

In modern-postmodern narratology, however, *metalepsis* has become much more than an auxiliary trope for nuanced signification. In his seminal *Discours*

---

38 Quintilian taught in Rome from CE 68 into the 90s.
39 Quintilian III, *The Institutes* (Butler, LCL), 323.

du récit [*Narrative Discourse*], first published in English in 1980,[40] Gérard Genette adopts and applies the ancient notion of transumption or transference to characterize the breaking of narrative boundaries or "levels," as he calls them, in order better to explain narrative significations rendered through the novel forms of the 'novel' in such delineations as 'narrator,' 'the narrated,' and 'narratee.' In his chapter on "Voice," Genette defines *metalepsis* as "any intrusion by the extradiegetic narrator or narratee into the diegetic universe (or by diegetic characters into a metadiegetic universe, etc.), or the inverse [...] [that] produces an effect of strangeness that is either comical [...] or fantastic."[41]

According to this definition, if the level of narrating be defined as *a first level* event, then the events narrated are "inside" the narrative produced by the narrating and can be depicted as "intra-diegetic," while the actual narrator/author is "extra-diegetic" to the narrated story or *diegesis*. But how are we to understand the not uncommon situation in modern novels in which the presumed author as narrator introduces his or her act of narrating within the narrative itself to form a second narrative within the first level narrative? Genette calls this second narrative "metadiegesis" since it presumes to hover somehow above or exterior to the primary narration, though contained within it. Accordingly, the narrator's location or world is "less a distance than a sort of threshold represented by the narrating itself, a difference of *level*."[42]

Genette enumerates two main types of "metadiegesis" that he discovers in classical Greek literature:

1) Summoning Homer's *Odyssey*, Books 9–12, he portrays Odysseus's recounting to the assembled Phaeacians of what had happened earlier to him within the first-level narrative (namely in Book 5) as a *"direct causality"* type of *metadiegetic* narration that answers the question, "What events have led to the present situation?"[43] The benefit for the audience of the performance is obvious, since much of the previously narrated material is summarized and re-contextualized and thus re-signified into the ongoing intra-diegetic sequential world. *Prima facie* the two re-iterations of Paul's calling with the character Paul himself as nar-

---

40 Genette, *Narrative Discourse*.
41 Genette, *Narrative Discourse*, 235.
42 Genette, *Narrative Discourse*, 228. Genette is quick to add that when the author-narrator of the first narrative-narration (whether of fiction or non-fiction) introduces him- or herself into that *diegesis* by addressing the audience (a ploy he terms "homo-diegetic"), then "they are at the same narrative level as their public–that is, as you and me" (229). Similarly, we should wonder how Luke's audience would understand the rhetoric of "I"/"me"/"us" in his two prologues, particularly as they relate to the sudden "we" in Acts 16:10, etc.
43 Genette, *Narrative Discourse*, 232.

rator in Acts 22:1–21 and 26:2–23 of what was narrated about him by the first level narrator in Acts 9:1–19 appears to be this type of metadiegesis; in addition, Peter's own account to his Jerusalem critics of the events he had experienced earlier with Cornelius (Acts 11:1–16) as depicted by the narrator of Acts 10 would appear to be the same type of 'direct causality' metadiegesis.

2) The second sort of metadiegesis in metaleptic transference Genette describes as "telling as if it were diegetic [...] something that has nevertheless been presented as metadiegetic in its principle or, if one prefers, in its origin." He refers to Plato's *Theaetetus* in which Socrates's conversation with Theodorus and Theaetetus about the nature of knowledge is later told by Socrates to his friend Eucleides who then writes it down. When Eucleides relates his account to Terpsion at a still later date, Eucleides tells Terpsion that "to avoid in the written account the tiresome effect of bits of narrative interrupting the dialogue, such as, 'and I said' or 'and I remarked' [referring to Socrates's own speaking and answering in the second narration to Eucleides],⁴⁴ the conversation has been reworded into the form of 'a direct conversation between the actual speakers'" [*Theaetetus*, 143B–C]. Genette types this form of *metalepsis* as "reduced metadiegetic" where "the metadiegetic way station, mentioned or not, is immediately ousted in favor of the first narrator, which to some extent economizes on one (or sometimes several) narrative level(s)."⁴⁵ It is perhaps telling that already in Luke 5:14 through indirect speech the narrator's voice slips almost imperceptibly into the direct speech of the main character Jesus:

καὶ αὐτὸς παρήγγειλεν αὐτῷ μηδενὶ εἰπεῖν

ἀλλὰ ἀπελθὼν δεῖ**ξον** <u>σεαυτὸν</u> τῷ ἱερεῖ καὶ <u>προσένεγκε</u> περὶ τοῦ καθαρισμοῦ [...].

The grammatical structure is strikingly parallel to Acts 1:4:

καὶ συναλιζόμενος παρήγγειλεν αὐτοῖς ἀπὸ Ἱεροσολύμων μὴ χωρίζεσθαι

ἀλλὰ περιμένειν τὴν ἐπαγγελίαν τοῦ πατρὸς ἣν <u>ἠκούσατέ</u> **μου** ὅτι Ἰωάννης [...].

Is this narrativizing trope of metaleptic economizing perhaps at work in Acts 1:4b–5, where the metadiegetic 'way station' of 1:1–4a of the author-narrator's second level address to his audience as "I" and "you"–"O Theophilus"–is abandoned quickly for the first level narration where Jesus speaks directly to his apostles? Might such a move recast the sequel volume of the "doing and the teaching" of the followers of Jesus as organically *first level* narration, even though the entire

---

44 Plato, *Theaetetus*, 143B-C (Fowler, LCL).
45 Genette, *Narrative Discourse*, 237.

volume has been introduced (to quote Genette) as "metadiegetic in its principle or, if one prefers, in its origin" (compare Luke 1:1–2)?[46]

3.3 Jesus as the 'Proclaimed Proclaimer' and 'Enacted Actor' of Acts

More than simply an intrusion of Jesus's direct address into the new narrative world where the events and teachings of Jesus might now be viewed primarily from within the perspective of the church, to the contrary, the metaleptic shift provokes a 'reduced metadiegetic' narrating in which the originating source of action and primary speech continues unabated. The result is that *all of the shorter episodes and emplotted sequences of Acts must now be read and heard through the lens and sounding box of the ever-present suffering enthroned, yet active Christ.* Indeed, already the events of sending, blessing, ascending, re-gathering, and worshiping that conclude the Gospel account (Luke 24:47–53) receive a striking make-over within the "overlap" of Luke with Acts:

i) Jesus's "Taking Up" (Luke 9:51→24:51b).

Jesus's "being taken up into heaven" (Luke 24:51b) now ushers in the special opportunity of "witness"[47] to God's rule in this "Kingdom" as this reign is now re-defined and re-constituted by demonstrations of Messiah's suffering and ongoing, living *presence* (Acts 1:3, 6–8, 9–11; compare Luke 24:13–53; 24:48, "witnesses of these things" → Acts 1:6, "Lord, at this time will you restore the Kingdom to Israel?").

ii) Jesus's Sending and Final Blessing (Luke 24:47–51a).

The final *blessing* of the first volume, after which Jesus becomes invisible to their physical sight (Luke 24:50–51), is transformed into a *world-wide sending of Messiah's witnesses through Jesus's continuing presence* empowered by the eschatological coming of the Holy Spirit (Acts 1:3–8).

---

[46] It is curious here that Genette, though commenting on the postmodern novel, remarks, "The most troubling thing about *metalepsis* indeed lies in this unacceptable and insistent hypothesis, that the extradiegetic is perhaps always diegetic, and that the narrator and his narratees–you and I–perhaps belong to some narrative" (*Narrative Discourse*, 236).
[47] Luke 21:13 can now begin to be realized.

iii) Worshiping God in the Temple (Luke 24:52–53).

The re-gathering in the Temple to praise God that forms an inclusio to volume one (Luke 1:5–23 ↔ 24:52–53) is re-formed into the gathering of the eleven apostles together with women disciples, the mother of Jesus, and Jesus's kinsfolk[48] *in a discrete place* where they are devoted to prayer. *Worship of the one God* of Israel is reconceived as *gathered devotees of the crucified-risen one*, whether in Temple or in private 'houses' (Acts 1:12–14).

3.4 The Doing and Teaching of Jesus the Crucified-Enthroned Christ through His Witnesses in Acts

If this redirecting of point of viewing–this change of comprehending (μετανοία, Luke 24:47)–is correct, a major implication of this shift would be that any temptation to conceive of the crucified-resurrected-ascended Christ as somehow removed from the acts of the apostles' witness, who no longer continues to figure as the major character of the narrative world–supplanted perhaps by the Holy Spirit–is ill-conceived and misses a prime significance of Luke's extended, re-'arranged' narration different from the "many." Accordingly, the command to be "my witnesses" (μου μάρτυρες) in Acts 1:8 is pregnant with both objective and subjective referents of the genitive "my" (μου): the apostles are to *bear the presence* of the one concerning whom they bear testimony ("witnesses of/to *me*") as well as *re-present the authority* of the one for whom their witness is given ("witnesses of *mine*"). This would mean that for Acts the apostolic authority explicitly anchored in Jesus's "choosing" (ἐξελέξατο) and "commanding (ἐντειλάμενος) through the Holy Spirit" (Acts 1:2) and linked to a future judging/governing of the twelve tribes in Jesus's Kingdom (Luke 22:28–30, "my kingdom" [βασιλεία μου, 22:30]) becomes constitutive for the plotted second volume: the ones "sent" continue to "act and teach" (Acts 1:1) for the one *who continues to be present as the one who acts and speaks*. This emphasis would explain, in part, the priority given in the first level *diegesis* to the replacement of Judas and the re-fulfilling of the mandate of apostolic eyewitness tradition *before* any other acts are configured (Acts 1:15–26; compare Luke 1:2, "just as they handed on to us" [καθὼς παρέδοσαν ἡμῖν]).

If this notion of "witness" is correct, then the crucified–enthroned Christ becomes in essence the 'proclaimed proclaimer' who 'acts' through witnesses *of* and *by* the church in the world. The following list is partial but suffices to indicate

---

48 Cf. Luke 4:16–30!

that the enthroned Jesus of Nazareth continues his active presence of "doing and teaching" through his re-presentatives, of whom Paul becomes chief protagonist:

1) Acts 1:15–5:42.
Jesus is present primarily through his "name" (τὸ ὄνομα) (continuing LXX usage): He speaks through various agents, healing, for example through the apostles; "faith" can be said to be directed toward Jesus's active presence:

Acts 2:38–39→2:47: "Baptized into the name of Jesus Christ" is *aligned* with a "call" from "the Lord our God": "Lord" (κύριος) is ambivalent in referent, following the two "Lords" of LXX Pss 15 and 109 and echoing Joel 3:5, τὸ ὄνομα κυρίου, Acts 2:21; and "the κύριος adding daily to the whole," 2:47b.

3:1–26: 3:6, Peter to paralytic: "*in/through the name of Jesus Christ of Nazareth*, get up and walk" (ἐν τῷ ὀνόματι Ἰησοῦ Χριστοῦ τοῦ Ναζωραίου [ἔγειρε καὶ] περιπάτει) → 3:16, "and by means of faith/trust in his name, his name *itself* has strengthened this one, and the faith *which is through him* has given him [the paralytic] this wholeness of health" (ἐπὶ τῇ πίστει τοῦ ὀνόματος αὐτοῦ τοῦτον [...] ἐστερέωσεν τὸ ὄνομα αὐτοῦ, καὶ ἡ πίστις ἡ δι' αὐτοῦ ἔδωκεν αὐτῷ τὴν ὁλοκληρίαν ταύτην) → 3:26, "Since God raised up his servant, *he sent him first to you to bless you* by each of you turning away from your wicked deeds" (ὑμῖν *πρῶτον ἀναστήσας ὁ θεὸς τὸν παῖδα αὐτοῦ ἀπέστειλεν αὐτὸν εὐλογοῦντα ὑμᾶς ἐν τῷ ἀποστρέφειν ἕκαστον ἀπὸ τῶν πονηριῶν ὑμῶν*).

4:1–22: Peter and John are taken in custody before the Sanhedrin: 4:7, "*by what power or by what name* have you done this thing [healed the paralytic]" (ἐν ποίᾳ δυνάμει ἢ *ἐν ποίῳ ὀνόματι* ἐποιήσατε τοῦτο ὑμεῖς;) → 4:10, "[...] that *by the name of Jesus Christ of Nazareth* [...] *through this one* he [the paralytic] stands before you in good health" (ὅτι *ἐν τῷ ὀνόματι Ἰησοῦ Χριστοῦ τοῦ Ναζωραίου* [...] *ἐν τούτῳ* οὗτος παρέστηκεν ἐνώπιον ὑμῶν ὑγιής) → 4:12, "for there is no other *name under the heaven*" (οὐδὲ γὰρ *ὄνομά ἐστιν ἕτερον ὑπὸ τὸν οὐρανὸν*) → 4:17–18, "neither to speak to anyone *by this name* [...] nor to teach *by the name of Jesus*" (μηκέτι λαλεῖν *ἐπὶ τῷ ὀνόματι τούτῳ* μηδενὶ [...] μηδὲ διδάσκειν *ἐπὶ τῷ ὀνόματι τοῦ Ἰησοῦ*) [compare Acts 1:1!].

4:23–33: Peter and John return to "their own gathered" disciples, called "servants" (4:29): 4:30, "*signs and wonders* occur *through the name of your holy servant Jesus*" (σημεῖα καὶ τέρατα γίνεσθαι *διὰ τοῦ ὀνόματος τοῦ ἁγίου παιδός σου Ἰησοῦ*) → 4:33, "with great power the apostles were providing witness *of the resurrection of the Lord Jesus*" (δυνάμει μεγάλῃ ἀπεδίδουν τὸ μαρτύριον οἱ ἀπόστολοι *τῆς ἀναστάσεως τοῦ κυρίου Ἰησοῦ*).

5:12–42: The Twelve are arrested and appear before the Sanhedrin: 5:12, "*through the hands* of the apostles many *signs and wonders* were being per-

formed" (διὰ δὲ τῶν χειρῶν τῶν ἀποστόλων ἐγίνετο σημεῖα καὶ τέρατα πολλά) →
5:14, "Yet more than ever those exhibiting faith *were being added to the Lord*"
(μᾶλλον δὲ *προσετίθεντο πιστεύοντες τῷ κυρίῳ*) → 5:28, "We charged you not *to
teach by/through his name* [...] you have filled Jerusalem with your *teaching* [...]
you are determined *to bring upon us the blood of this man*" (παρηγγείλαμεν ὑμῖν
μὴ *διδάσκειν ἐπὶ τῷ ὀνόματι τούτῳ* [...] πεπληρώκατε τὴν Ἰερουσαλὴμ τῆς *διδαχῆς
ὑμῶν* [...] βούλεσθε *ἐπαγαγεῖν ἐφ᾽ ἡμᾶς τὸ αἷμα τοῦ ἀνθρώπου τούτου*) → 5:41–42,
"they went on their way with joy [...] to be considered worthy to receive dishonor
for the sake of the name [...] *not ceasing in their teaching* and their proclaiming the
good news *that Jesus is the Messiah*" (ἐπορεύοντο χαίροντες [...] κατηξιώθησαν
ὑπὲρ τοῦ ὀνόματος ἀτιμασθῆναι [...] *ἐπαύοντο διδάσκοντες* καὶ εὐαγγελιζόμενοι
τὸν χριστόν Ἰησοῦν).

2) Acts 6:1–8:40.

Stephen is aligned with the Jesus of Nazareth who is capable of destroying the Temple, presumably at any moment. Yet in this transition from the original apostolic witness in Jerusalem (Acts 1:15–5:41) to Paul's more universal mission to both Jew and Gentile alike (9:1 [*passim*] through 28:31), though the enthroned Jesus of Nazareth welcomes Stephen's "witness" before the "standing attendants" as witnesses in the Heavenly Throne Room (see especially Dan 7:9–18), there is *no direct speech or action* of Jesus at the earthly *level* of plotted action.

Before his accusers Stephen claims he can see this Jesus "standing [...] the Son of Humankind standing at the right hand of God":

6:1–15: Stephen, working signs and wonders, is seized and accused before the Sanhedrin: 6:7, "The word of God kept increasing" (ὁ λόγος τοῦ θεοῦ ηὔξανεν) → 6:13, "saying that this *Jesus of Nazareth will destroy* this place [Temple]" (λέγοντος ὅτι Ἰησοῦς ὁ Ναζωραῖος οὗτος καταλύσει τὸν τόπον τοῦτον).

7:1–60: Stephen's Speech and Reaction:

7:55–56: Stephen: "saw [...] Jesus standing [...] 'I see *the Son of Humankind standing at the right hand of God*'" (εἶδεν [...] Ἰησοῦν ἑστῶτα [...] θεωρῶ τὸν υἱὸν τοῦ ἀνθρώπου ἐκ δεξιῶν ἑστῶτα τοῦ θεοῦ).

8:1–40: Philip and Peter and John in Samaria, and Philip in Gaza:

8:12: Philip "proclaiming the good news of the Kingdom of God [...] and *the name of Jesus Christ*" (εὐαγγελιζομένῳ περὶ τῆς βασιλείας τοῦ θεοῦ καὶ *τοῦ ὀνόματος Ἰησοῦ Χριστοῦ*).

8:6,13: Philip an agent of "signs and mighty works taking place" (σημεῖα καὶ δυνάμεις μεγάλας γινομένας).

3) Acts 9:1–30 and Two 'Relectures' of the 'Calling' of Paul with Paul as Narrator (22:4–21→26:9–20).

The direct voice of the risen-crucified Jesus of Acts 1:4b is *heard again for the first time* addressing Paul, "Why are you persecuting me?!" (9:4). But unlike Jesus's commissioning of the Twelve,[49] this voice will continue to speak directly through Paul in a way unattested with the Twelve. In fact, Paul, not the Twelve, will fulfill the proemial voice to be Jesus's witness to the "ends of the earth" (Acts 1:8). Paul becomes *the* witness of witnesses for the Jesus who continues to speak and enact salvation through Paul in unprecedented ways:

<u>9:1–30</u>: Saul/Paul encounters Jesus the Lord who *appears* to him, *speaks* to him, and *sends* him (through Ananias) to Israel and the Nations as one "who must suffer for the sake of my [Jesus's] name": 9:16, "*I myself* will show him how much he will have to suffer for the sake of my name" (ἐγὼ γὰρ ὑποδείξω αὐτῷ ὅσα δεῖ αὐτὸν ὑπὲρ τοῦ ὀνόματός μου παθεῖν).

<u>22:4–21</u> and <u>26:9–20</u>: Paul's *hypo*diegetic commentary progressively heightens the role that the acting and direct speaking of Jesus "the Lord" and/or the "Lord God" play in engaging Paul to "turn around" from being chief antagonist to prime protagonist through Jesus's own presence in the fulfilled reign of God:

22:10: Now Paul extends the conversation with the "Lord" on the Damascus Road (compare 9:5–6; Luke 24:13–35): "But the *Lord said* to me: 'Get up and go into Damascus and there I will tell you about all the things that I have commanded you to do" (ὁ δὲ κύριος εἶπεν πρός με· ἀναστὰς πορεύου εἰς Δαμασκὸν κἀκεῖ σοι λαληθήσεται περὶ πάντων ὧν τέτακταί σοι ποιῆσαι) → 22:17–21: Paul telescopes the later Temple encounter when in a trance he will see *Jesus saying* to him, "Move quickly and get out of Jerusalem in a hurry for they will not accept your witness concerning me"[50] (σπεῦσον καὶ ἔξελθε ἐν τάχει ἐξ Ἰερουσαλήμ, διότι οὐ παραδέξονταί σου μαρτυρίαν περὶ ἐμοῦ [compare 22:20 and 7:55–56: Paul protests, appealing to Stephen's vision]) → v. 26, "Go, for I will send you myself far away into the nations" (πορεύου, ὅτι ἐγὼ εἰς ἔθνη μακρὰν ἐξαποστελῶ σε) → 26:16–18: Now Paul collapses Ananias's role as mediator of revelation into the *voice of the Lord* himself. *Jesus* tells Paul *directly* that he must be both "servant" and "witness" to the things he has seen in the Jesus he has been persecuting and bear witness to all those things through which Jesus himself will appear and reveal to Paul: "For this purpose *I have appeared to you*, to appoint you to be *a servant and witness of those things which you have seen of me and to those things of which I shall disclose to you*, rescuing you from the people and from those of the

---

49 Actually the "Eleven" in Acts 1:4b–8.
50 Acts 9:26–30.

nations to which *I am sending you* to open their eyes, to turn them around from darkness to the light, from the authority of Satan to that of God, *so that they might receive release from their sins and an inheritance among those who have been made holy by means of their faith which is entrusted to me*" (εἰς τοῦτο γὰρ ὤφθην σοι, προχειρίσασθαί σε ὑπηρέτην καὶ μάρτυρα ὧν τε εἶδές [με] ὧν τε ὀφθήσομαί σοι, ἐξαιρούμενός σε ἐκ τοῦ λαοῦ καὶ ἐκ τῶν ἐθνῶν εἰς οὓς ἐγὼ ἀποστέλλω σε ἀνοῖξαι ὀφθαλμοὺς αὐτῶν, τοῦ ἐπιστρέψαι ἀπὸ σκότους εἰς φῶς καὶ τῆς ἐξουσίας τοῦ σατανᾶ ἐπὶ τὸν θεόν, *τοῦ λαβεῖν αὐτοὺς ἄφεσιν ἁμαρτιῶν καὶ κλῆρον ἐν τοῖς ἡγιασμένοις πίστει τῇ εἰς ἐμέ*).

4) Acts 9:31–28:31.

Though Peter's voice predominates in presenting the 'word' and 'name' of the Lord in the first five chapters of Acts, it is Jesus's voice that takes over the narrator's and Paul's own voice in a fashion similar to the metaleptic transumption of Acts 1:4b. Thus Jesus's direct speech takes precedence over any other voice, thereby defining and disseminating in the last two-thirds of Acts the presence of "the Lord" who reigns in the Kingdom of God:

10:1–11:15: Peter tells *Cornelius's household* in 10:43 that "all the prophets *bear witness through this one* (τούτῳ [Ἰησοῦ τῷ ἀπὸ Ναζαρέθ] [...] οἱ προφῆται μαρτυροῦσιν) that release of sins is received *through his name* (διὰ τοῦ ὀνόματος αὐτοῦ)".

10:9–16→11:5–10: Peter in a trance "sees" a sheet with unclean animals lowered from heaven with a *voice* telling him to "kill and eat;" Peter later understands this voice to have been from "the Lord" (10:14; 11:8).

11:16: Peter only later aligns the coming of the Spirit upon the Gentile household with the "word of the Lord" of Acts 1:4b–5!

[15:6–11: Similar to Paul, Peter eventually understands the whole Cornelius episode to be God's own "bearing witness" to the Gentiles through the Spirit].

13:13–52 Paul in Antioch of Pisidia: "to you *through this one* release of sins is being proclaimed" (διὰ τούτου ὑμῖν ἄφεσις ἁμαρτιῶν καταγγέλλεται).

(13:47–49: Paul reports, "'I [the Lord] have appointed you [Paul and Barnabas and entourage] to be a light of the Gentiles, in order that you might be salvation to the end of the earth'" [τέθεικά σε {...} σε εἰς σωτηρίαν {...}] [Isa 49:6 describing the "servant" Israel as both a group of Israel to Israel and an individual who represents that group par excellence, now fulfilling the command given by the "Lord Jesus" to the twelve (eleven) apostles in Acts 1:8 to extend his witness "to the end of the earth."])

14:1–6 Paul in Iconium [of Lycaonia]: Paul and Barnabas "speak openly on behalf of the Lord [Jesus] who himself bears witness to the word of his grace" (παρρησιαζόμενοι ἐπὶ τῷ κυρίῳ τῷ μαρτυροῦντι ἐπὶ τῷ λόγῳ τῆς χάριτος αὐτοῦ).

26:1–29: Paul before Festus and Agrippa [Caesarea]: *Summing up his entire calling*:

Paul has taken his stand "by bearing witness (μαρτυρόμενος) [...] saying nothing other than those things which Moses and the prophets said would take place, namely, that there would be a suffering Messiah, and that being the first of the resurrection from the dead, *he himself* [Messiah] would proclaim light to the people and to the nations (εἰ παθητὸς ὁ χριστός, εἰ πρῶτος ἐξ ἀναστάσεως νεκρῶν φῶς μέλλει καταγγέλλειν τῷ τε λαῷ καὶ τοῖς ἔθνεσιν, 26:23).

We can sum up the metaleptic transfer of Acts 1:4a–5 of Jesus's words and deeds in the Gospel to the reign of the Kingdom of God in Acts:

1) The enthronement of the crucified-living one at the end of Luke and beginning of Acts narrates the continuing active "doing and teaching" of Jesus of Nazareth in the ongoing reign of God in the sequel volume of Acts. While all three scenes of Luke 24 depict the physical absence of Jesus in the midst of his *still*[51] very poignant presence, it is the metaleptic transfer of Jesus's active presence that establishes the entire sequel volume of Acts as the continuing narration of that presence (Acts 1:4a→4b–5).

2) While Peter becomes the chief spokesperson for the "word of the Lord" (Acts 2:41→4:4, and others) of the apostolic word that stems from Jesus himself, he does not utter the voice of the Lord with the same immediacy and thus authority as will be demonstrated many times later for Saul/Paul. As a prime example, Peter must first undergo a major "change of thinking" about the relation of Jesus's active presence to the salvation of the rest of the non-Jewish world as he and the rest of the apostles ignore and thus disregard Jesus's immediate command to take his salvation "to the ends of the earth" (Acts 1:8→10:1–11:18). By contrast, Paul's "change of thinking" takes him from chief antagonist to premier advocate for Jesus's word to Israel and the nations immediately following his first-person encounter on the road to Damascus (see especially 9:19:b–30→22:17–21). By the end of Acts 9, Paul's life is threatened by the very people he had rallied in opposing "the way" of Messiah Jesus. Or toward the end of the narrative, after his arrest and incarceration fueled by fierce opposition from fellow Jews at the feast of Pentecost, "the Lord" Jesus speaks directly to Paul for all of Luke's audiences to hear,

---

51 Cf. esp. by analogy Luke 24:6b and the message of the "two men" that what you [women disciples] experienced before is even more operative now: "Do you not remember how he spoke to you *when he was still with you in Galilee*" (ἔτι ὢν ἐν τῇ Γαλιλαίᾳ)?

"Take courage, for just as you have been bearing witness to those things concerning *me* here in Jerusalem, so also you must bear witness in Rome" (23:11).

3) The almost exclusive concentration of the direct utterance of Jesus within Paul's sending renders Paul the definer and primary defender of the apostolic tradition as articulated by the risen-crucified Jesus himself in the opening prologue of Acts (Acts 1:4b–8). By subsequently inserting the *direct voice* of Jesus only for the first time into Paul's calling, Luke collapses the narrative-historical space of the missions of the "Twelve" and of the "Seven" into the fulfillment of Jesus's command through Paul's journeys. Not only does Paul obey the proemial voice to become a "witness to the ends of the earth," but the metaleptic shift also projects Jesus's ongoing words and deeds into the characteristic words and actions of Paul.[52] Through Paul, Jesus is the 'proclaimed proclaimer' and the 'enacted actor' par excellence. Through Paul, the "things concerning the Lord Jesus Messiah" and "the Kingdom of God" are proclaimed openly at the center of the 'kingdom' that controls "the ends of the earth" (Acts 28:30–31; Isa 45:4–6). It is he who represents the authentic deeds and teachings of Jesus to the Roman world, declaiming not Sebaste Caesar, but Jesus the Christ as Sovereign of the universe. Consequently *through Paul*, Messiah's calling in Israel's scriptures to bring eschatological salvation to Israel *and* the nations is recapitulated and consummated. In short, Luke entangles Paul as *the* witness of all witnesses into the "beginning" of the entire two-volume narration in such a way that his audiences can comprehend neither the continuity nor the goal of Luke and Acts apart from Paul's unprecedented role.

4 Conclusion:

We may now draw together our conclusions:

1. Following Hellenistic narrative-rhetorical conventions, particularly diegetic-historiographical 'partitioning' and 'sequencing' of the narrative 'arrangement' of events for longer periods of time (for example, Dionysius of Halicarnassus, *On Thucydides*), Luke reconfigures the traditions he has received and expands them by adding a sequel 'book' to form a new two-volume narrative work (Acts 1:1). Though Luke does not belong to the group(s) who were eyewitness tradents of the words and deeds of Jesus (Luke 1:1–2; Acts 1:1), he nevertheless undertakes a radical re-visioning of them by bodying forth a new whole through a 'whole' new emplotment of them. This unparalleled ensemble effects a new grasp, a new

---

52 E.g., "Jesus I know and Paul I know, but who are you?!" ["one of the evil spirits" to the "seven sons of the Jewish high priest, Sceva," Acts 19:15].

"firmness of understanding" of the significance of all these "events that have come to fruition in our [the author's] midst" (Luke 1:1, 4). Most likely Luke regarded the scope and arrangement of the events of "the many" to be insufficient and inadequate, respectively. Thus, in order for his audiences to gain a proper understanding of "all that Jesus began to enact and to teach" (Acts 1:1), Luke will co-figure the disciples with Jesus and Jesus with the disciples in such a way that his audiences must hear about Jesus in light of the impact he had had upon his followers (Luke), and, conversely, the significance that his followers' words and deeds provoke in the church must be discerned through the illumination of Jesus's own words and deeds (Acts). Both "books" supplement and comment upon each other.

2. Through the metadiegetic "way station" (Genette) of Acts 1:4–5, Luke collapses the world of Jesus's public words and deeds into the world of his followers by reframing the actions and teachings of his followers through the continuing acting and speaking of Jesus in their presence in the church. Through this metaleptic transumption, the movement of the narrative level of Acts 1:4a to 1:4b transfers Luke's audiences into the one new world of fulfilled salvation. The result is a "reduced metadiegetic" (Genette) that establishes Jesus's presence as actor and speaker as first level narration. Consequently all of the shorter episodes and emplotted sequences of Acts must now be read and heard through the lens and sounding box of the ever-present suffering enthroned, yet active Christ. The period of Jesus and the time of the church are narrated as *one new era*, the new time of eschatological fulfillment, the realized reign and realm of God.

3. Paul becomes the chief mediator of the voice and actions of Jesus. As the crucified-exalted one, Jesus speaks, teaches, acts, and appears more directly to and through Paul than any other character in Acts. In fact, the first time Luke's audiences hear again the *metalepsis* of Jesus's *voice* of the opening prologue is in Acts 9 and the voice to Paul on the Damascus Road. Hence Paul is placed at the center of the apostolic faith that is established and interpreted by Jesus himself. Ironically, then, it is Paul–not the Twelve nor the Seven–the 'witness' who did not witness the deeds and words of Jesus during his public activity–who becomes the chief *hermeneutēs* of the words and works of Jesus of Nazareth in the two volume Luke and Acts. Certainly this poetic emphasis of Luke's arrangement must be a telling clue to one of the main reasons that Luke re-configures even as he expands "all the events that have come to fruition."

By writing "for you a new narrative sequence [...] so that you might grasp [...] the clear certainty" of these events (καθεξῆς σοι [...] ἐπιγνῷς [...] τὴν ἀσφάλειαν, Luke 1:3–4), Luke indicates that his 'partitioning' and 'sequencing' form an 'arrangement' of 'all' the events that both meets Hellenistic expectations and–unlike Dionysius's estimate of Thucydides!–delivers the benefits he desires for his audience.

Part IV:
Luke's *Theologia Crucis*. The Suffering Servant(s) of the Lord: Moses, David, The Suffering Righteous, and Jesus and "All The Prophets"

You foolish folk, sluggish of heart to believe all that the prophets have declared: Was it not necessary that the Christ should suffer these things and thus enter into his glory? [...] and breaking the bread he began to give it to them—and their eyes were opened (Luke 24:25–26,30–31a).

It would seem that much of the thrust of historical criticism's examination of the crucified Jesus in Luke's two volumes would have to fall under Jesus's rebuke to the Emmaus wanderers: Jesus' execution by the Romans was the tragic martyrdom of the prophet par excellence which God in God's providence overcame with the triumph of resurrection. 'Triumph over tragedy,' then—in this conventional view—forms the banner of the good news in Luke–Acts. This gospel of the resurrection must be taken to the ends of the earth, translated to Jew and Greek, Roman and barbarian alike. Accordingly, the speeches of Acts will confirm and proffer this 'gospel of resurrection' which will break the stranglehold of sin and injustice for the whole world as Jesus now reigns "from heaven above."

Part IV offers something very different. If it is true as we witnessed in Parts I–III above that Luke has radically altered the tradition of the *diegesis* of the "many"–known primarily through Mark–by making the Christ of the Gospel the chief actor and speaker in the Acts that follow, then accordingly the reading of Luke's 'Gospel Acts' has also to be substantially transformed. No longer, for example, can the speeches in Acts that are addressed not only to audiences within the unfolding drama, but also as direct speech to Luke's auditors be heard as essentially *prosopopoietic* attempts to disclose the kinds of things said and believed by members of the first witnesses in the church. Rather, Luke has now changed the way we hear the apostolic witness through the Christ who breaks through the voice of the narrator. Especially with Paul, Jesus as the Lord and Christ of the Pentecost "signs and wonders" who distributes the Spirit as Joel and David continue to speak, speaks and acts most directly to and through Paul as early as Acts 9 and on to the end of the narrative (and end of the earth!). Paul is featured through most of Acts as the articulator of Jesus's voice and premier interpreter of Jesus's own apostolic teaching.

But if this metaleptic shift in the prominence of Jesus's active presence is correct, then the intra-textual back-and-forth between Jesus's speaking in the

Gospel and his continued speaking in Acts–including utterances through his witnesses–must be taken seriously in determining how Luke signifies the death and exaltation of this Christ. Only a method which allows the intertextual soundings of Israel's scriptures and the intratextual reverberations of the primary characters in Luke's 'Gospel Acts' can do justice to his theology of the cross. Only a historical-critical, narrative rhetorical approach which takes into account Luke's goal of putting "all the events" of consequence in his and the church's midst into a greater coherence and clarity can do justice to what Luke could possibly intend with his numerous references to the Christ's suffering, his raising up, his exaltation or enthronement, his continued speaking and acting–"all as it stands written" in Israel's scriptures.

Spanning the whole of his 'Gospel Acts,' Luke has structured the economy (οἰκονομία) of his *poiesis* to feature the callings and fates of Moses, David and the suffering righteous, and all the prophets as trailblazers for Jesus the anointed eschatological prophet, the Christ. Jesus's calling through the baptism of the Holy Spirit at the "beginning" during John's baptizing signals the prophet-servant who must consummate the "way" of suffering and exaltation from the rejection and humiliation that Moses, David, and all the prophets had endured at the hands of a recalcitrant Israel. This basic plot of God's sending to render redemption resulting over and over again in resistance and persecution drives the 'continuity of the narrative' as defined by Hellenistic writers of history. Luke looks over the whole of Israel's scriptures and, seeing this repeating pattern, aligns the cohesion of his narrative accordingly. Luke's primary scenario as recapitulated in the Christ is the more comprehensive exodus sending which incorporates not only Moses and the conquest but also the series of prophets sent to call Israel back to the covenant faith of Sinai and to their release from the slavery of their own idolatry, as well as from other nations. David himself is primarily an anointed prophet-king whose suffering from enemies and the promise of life after the grave forges the career-path of suffering for his offspring "the Christ."

This more expansive pattern of exodus release exposes the core of Luke's "plan of God" for the forgiveness of sin and justice for Israel and through Israel for the nations. Precisely the violent rejection of Israel's own Messiah issues in life. Life generated through death defines a new "way" of living, a notion of divine regenerativity diametrically opposed to life defined by Empire, on one side, and ironically–paradoxically, fulfills the 'goal' and 'end' of Israel's hierocratic sacrificial system, on the other: "Today this scripture is fulfilled in your hearing"–to the synagogue folk of Jesus's home-country Nazareth, who attempt to hurl him off a cliff (Luke 4:21); "Today you will be with me in Paradise"–to the penitent criminal on the cross (Luke 23:43); "This cup is the new covenant through my blood being shed on your behalf"–to the Twelve representing Israel and

Israel's calling (Luke 22:20). In short, "the Christ must suffer" (Luke) and "Jesus is that suffering (exalted) Christ" (Acts). Luke must show that this 'partitioning' of his 'arrangement' through the 'sequences' of the suffering righteous servants extends to the apostles and to Jesus's chief witness Paul in the time of witness of the risen-crucified one to the end of the earth. Peter and the Twelve, Stephen, and Paul do indeed fit into the pattern of the suffering righteous as the suffering, exalted Christ continues to speak and act through them in extending his saving death and exaltation to the far reaches of the earth. By transforming the apostolic traditions into two interlocking volumes, Luke provides a complete(d) narrative (αὐτοτελεῖς) that stands on its own while, at the same time, invoking the larger biblical story of God's saving actions.

Chapter Eight depicts Jesus's great journey from Galilee to Jerusalem as the capstone of Israel's exodus from slavery. It is obvious from the end of Deuteronomy and the Deuteronomistic history that God's promise of worshiping the Lord God in Israel's own "place"–without the idolatry of their stubborn resistance– had as yet not been realized. With Israel still under the yoke of the foreign oppressor when the Spirit rests upon Jesus, the anointed prophet setting out as the Christ must now fulfill the path of *life through death* already tread by the Lord's "chosen" "servant" to effect that release. As "the prophet like" but greater than Moses, Jesus must complete Israel's exodus in his journey to Israel's central place to be rejected like Moses and taken up like Elijah and thus unleash the new life of forgiveness and bring true worship in the promised land to fruition ("Luke 9:1–50: Luke's Preview of the Journey of the Prophet Like Moses of Deuteronomy").

"'The Christ Must Suffer': New Light on the Jesus–Peter, Stephen, Paul Parallels in Luke–Acts" (Chapter Nine) elaborates the role of the prophet like Moses for the whole of Luke's two-volume 'arrangement.' Stephen's speech functions as the hermeneutical hinge. His recounting of Israel's history follows the stereotypical Deuteronomistic view of the prophets' sending for which Jesus will play the decisive, dramatic role in bringing this history to its ultimate conclusion. The persecution erupting out of Stephen's charges to the Sanhedrin is spearheaded by none other than Saul who, like Moses and the prophets, Jesus, Peter, and Stephen, will be opposed at every turn by the Jewish peoples as he is "turned around" by the risen-crucified Jesus himself and sent to Israel and the nations under the aegis of "how much he must suffer for the sake of my name" (Acts 9:16→22:17–21). Sent out from the Temple to Israel and the nations far away, Paul undertakes a final journey to Jerusalem toward the end of his prophetic call that both recalls and imitates Jesus's final journey to receive the 'prophet's reward.'

Finally, "Luke's 'Plan of God' from the Greek Psalter: The Rhetorical Thrust of 'the Prophets and the Psalms' in Peter's Speech at Pentecost" (Chapter Ten), argues that Peter's speech at Pentecost unrolls Luke's blueprint for the plotted 'continuity' of the remainder of Acts. While the prophet Joel envisions what is taking place eschatologically through the pouring out of the Spirit by the exalted-crucified Christ (Acts 2:33), it is the prophet David who, in two of his psalms of the suffering righteous, paints the print of Israel's own divided house and opposition to the Lord's selected servants of salvation. Psalm 15's (LXX) revelation of a "Lord" continually at David's right hand develops the exposure of Psalm 109's (LXX) cameo appearance of David's "Lord," "my Lord," who will be exalted "at the right hand of God." This Lord is the Christ of David's "loins," the one whom Israel impaled and the one over whom death could not continue its grip–this "Lord and Christ whom God had appointed" (Acts 2:36). Jesus is the Lord and Christ of David's–and all the suffering righteouses'–path of suffering and exaltation. As such "God's plan" features *both* the rejection and the resurrection of Jesus at its heart; the Acts 2 'speech' broadcasts the "good news" of the saving *death* and *resurrection*. And for the rest of the speeches of Acts, this double beat of glory rendered through suffering orchestrates the sym-phonē of Luke's 'theologia crucis.'

Chapter Eight: Luke 9:1–50: Luke's Preview of the Journey of the Prophet like Moses of Deuteronomy[1]

The problem of an unmitigating dissonance of form from content in the central section (9:51–19:44)[2] of Luke's Gospel has become one of the central problems in Lukan studies.[3] Both the silence concerning any developing journey to Jerusa-

---

[1] Previously in David P. Moessner, "Luke 9:1–50: Luke's Preview of the Journey of the Prophet Like Moses of Deuteronomy," *JBL* 102 (1983): 575–605. Used with permission.

[2] From a literary-thematic point of view, the journey to Jerusalem, beginning at 9:51, continues until Jesus's arrival there, that is, up to 19:45 where he enters the Temple precincts. For discussions of the end of this section, see Johannes Schneider, "Zur Analyse des lukanischen Reiseberichtes," in *Synoptische Studien: Alfred Wikenhauser zum siebzigsten Geburtstag [...] dargebracht*, ed. J. Schmid and A. Vögtle (Munich: K. Zink, 1953): 210–11; James L. Resseguie, "Interpretation of Luke's Central Section (Luke 9:51–19:44) Since 1856," *Studia Biblica et Theologica* 5 (1975): 3n2.

[3] Among the more recent treatments of the central section are Kenneth E. Bailey, *Poet and Peasant* (Grand Rapids, MI: Eerdmans, 1976), 79–85; J. Blinzler, "Die literarische Eigenart des sogenannten Reiseberichts im Lukasevangelium," in *Synoptische Studien: Alfred Wikenhauser zum siebzigsten Geburtstag [...] dargebracht*, ed. J. Schmid and A Vögtle (Munich: K. Zink, 1953): 20–52; Gilbert Bouwman, *Das dritte Evangelium* (Düsseldorf: Patmos, 1968), 70–75; Hans Conzelmann, *Die Mitte der Zeit: Studien zur Theologie des Lukas*, BHT 17, 3rd ed. (Tübingen: Mohr Siebeck, 1960), 53–66; J. H. Davies, "The Purpose of the Central Section of Luke's Gospel," *SE* II (= TU 87; Berlin: Akademie, 1964): 164–69; John Drury, *Tradition and Design in Luke's Gospel* (Atlanta, GA: John Knox, 1976), 138–64; Morton S. Enslin, "Luke and the Samaritans," *HTR* 36 (1943): 294–97; Christopher F. Evans, "The Central Section of St. Luke's Gospel," in *Studies in the Gospels: Essays in Memory of R. H. Lightfoot*, ed. D. E. Nineham (Oxford: Blackwell, 1955): 37–53; Joseph A. Fitzmyer, "The Composition of Luke, Chapter 9," in *Perspectives on Luke-Acts*, ed. Charles H. Talbert (Danville, VA: Association of Baptist Professors of Religion, 1978): 149–52; Helmut Flender, *Heil und Geschichte in der Theologie des Lukas*, BEvT 41 (Munich: Kaiser, 1965), 69–83; W. Gasse, "Zum Reisebericht des Lukas," *ZNW* 34 (1935): 293–99; David Gill, "Observations on the Lukan Travel Narrative and Some Related Passages," *HTR* 63 (1970): 199–221; Louis Girard, *L'Evangile des voyages de Jésus ou La Section 9,51–18,14 de Saint Luc* (Paris: Gabalda, 1951); M. D. Goulder, "The Chiastic Structure of the Lucan Journey," *SE* II (= TU 87; Berlin: Akademie, 1964): 195–202; M. D. Goulder, *Type and History in Acts* (London: SPCK, 1964), 138–39; M. D. Goulder, *Midrash and Lection in Matthew* (London: SPCK, 1974), 465–73; Walter Grundmann, "Fragen der Komposition des lukanischen Reiseberichts," *ZNW* 50 (1959): 252–70; Aileen Guilding, *The Fourth Gospel and Jewish Worship* (Oxford: Clarendon, 1960), 132–39, 230–31; Luke Timothy Johnson, *The Literary Function of Possessions in Luke-Acts*, SBLDS 39 (Missoula, MT: Scholars, 1977), 103–15; R. H. Lightfoot, *Locality and Doctrine in the Gospels* (London: Hodder & Stoughton, 1938), 136–40; Eduard Lohse, "Missionarisches Handeln Jesu nach dem Evangelium des Lukas," *TZ* 10 (1954): 1–13; I. Howard Marshall, *Luke: Historian and Theologian* (Exeter: Paternoster, 1970),

lem[4] and the seemingly chaotic scramble of teaching units that bear no relation to a journey motif[5] continue to baffle scholars.[6] In general, four basic approaches[7] have attempted to clarify the nature of this tension and to that extent to "solve the riddle" of this most intriguing yet confusing contour in the Luke-Acts landscape.[8]

148–53; C. C. McCown, "The Geography of Luke's Central Section," *JBL* 57 (1938): 51–66; Michi Miyoshi, *Der Anfang des Reiseberichts: Lk 9,51–10,24*, AnBib 60 (Rome: Biblical Institute, 1974); Robert Morgenthaler, *Die lukanische Geschichtsschreibung als Zeugnis*, ATANT 14, 2 vols. (Zurich: Zwingli, 1949), 1:156–57; John Navone, "The Way of the Lord," *Scr* 20 (1968): 24–30; George Ogg, "The Central Section of the Gospel according to St Luke," *NTS* 18 (1971): 39–53; J. C. O'Neill, *The Theology of Acts in its Historical Setting*, 2nd ed. (London: SPCK, 1970), 29–73; Peter von der Osten-Sacken, "Zur Christologie des lukanischen Reiseberichts," *EvT* 33 (1973): 476–96; Bo Reicke, "Instruction and Discussion in the Travel Narrative," *SE* I (= TU 73 [1959]): 206–16; Bo Reicke, *The Gospel of Luke* (Richmond, VA: John Knox, 1964), 36–40; Resseguie, "Interpretation," 3–36; William C. Robinson, Jr., *Der Weg des Herrn: Studien zur Geschichte und Eschatologie im Lukas-Evangelium*, TF 36 (Hamburg: Evangelischer Verlag, 1964), 21–43; William C. Robinson, Jr., "The Theological Context for Interpreting Luke's Travel Narrative (9:51ff.)," *JBL* 79 (1960): 20–31; Karl Ludwig Schmidt, *Der Rahmen der Geschichte Jesu: Literarkritische Untersuchungen zur ältesten Jesusüberlieferung* (Berlin: Trowitzsch & Sohn, 1919), 246–71; Schneider, "Analyse," 207–29; Frieder Schuetz, *Der leidende Christus*, BWANT 89 (Stuttgart: Kohlhammer, 1969), 70–86; Frank Stagg, "The Journey Toward Jerusalem in Luke's Gospel," *RevExp* 64 (1967): 499–512; Ned B. Stonehouse, *The Witness of Luke to Christ* (London: Tyndale, 1951), 110–27; Charles H. Talbert, *Literary Patterns, Theological Themes and the Genre of Luke-Acts*, SBLMS 20 (Missoula, MT: Scholars, 1974), 51–56, 118–20, 134–36; Vincent Taylor, *Behind the Third Gospel* (Oxford: Clarendon, 1926), 151–59, 172–75, 246–54; G. W. Trompf, "La section médiane de l'évangile de Luc: l'organisation des documents," *RHPR* 53 (1973): 141–54; J. W. Wenham, "Synoptic Independence and the Origin of Luke's Travel Narrative," *NTS* 27 (1981): 507–15; see also commentaries on 9:51.
4 See esp. McCown, "Geography," 54–64; Blinzler, "Eigenart," 33–41; Schneider, "Analyse," 211–17; the "travel notices" usually include 9:51, 53; 13:22, 33; 17:11, and in addition those outside of the "Great Insertion" (9:51–18:14), 18:31; 19:11, 28, 41.
5 See n. 3. See also Schmidt, *Rahmen*, 271, who concludes "dass der Evangelist Lk beim Ordnen der Einzelgeschichten sichtlich manchmal ermüdet ist [...]. Er tat's dann doch, so gut er konnte, indem er dabei einem inneren oder äusseren Grunde folgte, der für uns nicht mehr feststellbar ist."
6 See I. Howard Marshall, *The Gospel of Luke*, NIGTC (Exeter: Paternoster, 1978), 401–2, "the general themes of the section are hard to define, and it is even more difficult to find any kind of thread running through it."
7 It will become apparent that there is considerable overlap among the four approaches, especially between the first two. In the first category, the concern to place Jesus in the grand scheme of salvation history is primary, while in the second ecclesiastical and ethical interests take the upper hand. The seminal role of Conzelmann's study (*Mitte*) for both approaches is indisputable, and the second is often a development from his watershed conclusion that Luke did not intend a running journey report.
8 We shall restrict our synopsis to current exegetical consensuses; much work is still needed in comparing the role of journeying in the Gospels and Acts to the journey accounts, especially in the popular Greco-Roman biography. See, e.g., Philostratus, *The Life of Apollonius of Tyana*,

I

1. *Theological-Christological.*[9] Luke's intention is to present a particular christological conception of Jesus's ministry within an overall plan of the history of salvation. Whether Jesus's awareness of his suffering or his suffering as a path to glory or the way of Jesus as the outworking of the preordained "way of the Lord" or the authoritative journey of king messiah et cetera is emphasized, the motive is the same: the journey is a viable symbol of a distinctive phase in the unfolding dynamic of the *Heilsgeschichte*. Though from "source," "form," and "traditio-historical" critical points of view the discrepancy between the form and its content persists, yet the significant contribution of this literary redactional approach is the muting of the dissonance by harmonizing this piece upon the stage of its performance in the church rather than in the *mise en scène* of the ministry of Jesus. Given Luke's overall perspective of the movement of salvation from Galilee to Jerusalem and then to the "end of the earth" (Acts 1:8; 10:37, 39), the setting of a journey is not so anomalous after all.

2. *Ecclesiastical-Functional.*[10] Drawing considerably upon the first approach, the proponents of this solution point to the predominantly didactic paraenetic

---

vii.10–16 (Jones, LCL); see also Clyde Weber Votaw, *The Gospels and Contemporary Biographies in the Greco-Roman World*, FBBS 27 (Philadelphia, PA: Fortress, 1970), esp. 8–11, 15–16, 21, 27; David L. Dungan and David R. Cartlidge, *Sourcebook of Texts for the Comparative Study of the Gospels*, SBLSBS 1, 4th ed. (Missoula, MT: Scholars, 1974), 85–94, 291–345; Charles H. Talbert, *What Is a Gospel: The Genre of the Canonical Gospels* (Philadelphia, PA: Fortress, 1977), 38–43; Grundmann, "Fragen," 252–54.

9 E.g., Conzelmann, *Mitte*; Davies, "Purpose"; Evans, "Central"; Joseph A. Fitzmyer, *The Gospel according to Luke I–IX*, AB 28 (Garden City, NY: Doubleday, 1981), 162–71; Robinson, *Weg*; Robinson, "Context"; Schuetz, *Leidende*; Talbert, *Patterns*; see nn. 6, 9.

10 E.g., Flender, *Heil*; Gill, "Observations"; Grundmann, "Fragen"; Lohse, "Missionarisches"; von der Osten-Sacken, "Christologie"; Reicke, "Instruction"; Schneider, "Analyse"; Stagg, "Journey"; a strict demarcation of "theological-christological" from "ecclesiastical functional" is virtually impossible. While the theological emphases usually address the church or churches in a particular situation, the ecclesiastical emphases place the weight more on the practical ordering of church life based on certain of the author's theological themes; see n. 6. A good example of the organic development of this second approach from the first is von der Osten-Sacken, "Christologie," who, building principally upon Conzelmann, stresses the importance of the "ascension" in correcting a false idea of Jesus's messiahship for the church living in the "delay" of the final advent. The church is thus instructed to conduct its life on the pattern of Jesus's journey–a road of suffering that only later leads to glory. See also Flender, *Heil*, 84–98; O'Neill, *Acts*, 29–73. For a critique of the correlation of alleged "community needs" with dominant literary themes, see, e.g., Luke Timothy Johnson, "A Cautious Cautionary Essay," in *SBL Seminar Papers 1979*, ed. Paul J. Achtemeier (Missoula, MT: Scholars, 1979), 1:87–94.

character of the disparate material. Above all, Jesus is a teacher preparing his disciples to be the future leaders of the church as he journeys to his death in Jerusalem. Faithful following amidst rejection, correction of an uncomprehending discipleship, proper orientation to the values of the world, preparations for the Gentile mission, et cetera are all thematic thrusts programmatic to the unity of the whole. In this way Luke engages the journey motif primarily, again as in number 1, at the level of the instruction and edification of the church. In short, the central section coheres because it exhibits a useful parallel between Jesus's journeying and the church's present journey.

3. *Literary Aesthetical.*[11] The amorphous mass of Luke's vast middle section in reality betrays a distinct literary pattern. Whether already in the tradition or through Luke's literary skill, this pattern–and not a form-content tension–is constitutive to the shape of the whole. That is to say, any disparity between the form of a journey and its content subsists only at a level that misses a more fundamental structure. Chiasmus, analogy to Deuteronomy, lectionary cycles, et cetera have been suggested as the telltale templates. Thus, through aesthetic or pragmatic (or a combination of) reasons cohesion is achieved essentially at the level of the use of the central section–whether in its initial writing or its reading–in the church. Jesus still journeys to Jerusalem, to be sure, but he does so to a carefully conceived artistic pattern.[12]

4. *Traditional-Logical.*[13] "Galilee to Jerusalem" is intrinsic to the rudimentary gospel sequence of earlier tradition. That Luke has taken advantage of this chronological fact to insert a great amount of material vital to the church should

---

11 E.g., Bailey, *Poet*; Drury, *Tradition*; Evans, "Central"; Goulder, "Chiastic"; Guilding, *Worship*; Morgenthaler, *Zeugnis*; Johnson's pattern of the "Prophet and the People" coheres at the level of the story of Jesus and thus is not included in any of the four approaches (*Possessions*, 103–15). Though our thesis is–independently–in fundamental agreement with his, it provides a far more specific pattern that purports to resolve the tension between the sayings and the journey theme. See Johnson, *Possessions*, 106–7: "There remains a large amount of material only loosely related to the journey, if at all [...] especially so for the sayings material which for the most part can be related only tenuously to the Journey motif."

12 E.g., Goulder, "Chiastic," 202, on Luke 13:34–35: "The chiasmus has as its intersection a short section [...]. We are, says St. Luke as he gives us the first lament, half way through the Journey."

13 E.g., Blinzler, "Eigenart"; E. Earle Ellis, *The Gospel of Luke*, NCB, rev. ed. (London: Oliphants, 1974), 146–51; Norval Geldenhuys, *Commentary on the Gospel of Luke*, NICNT (London: Marshall, Morgan & Scott, 1951), 291; Marshall, *Historian*; Marshall, *Gospel*; Ogg, "Central"; Karl Heinrich Rengstorf, *Das Evangelium nach Lukas*, NTD 3, 5th ed. (Göttingen: Vandenhoeck & Ruprecht, 1963), 128 (apparently); Stonehouse, *Witness*; Taylor, *Behind* (with qualifications); see also Marshall, *Historian*, 149–50, on the central section: "It is doubtful whether the various recent studies of it have adequately accounted for its nature."

strike no one as unusual. Luke's procedure in the middle part of his Gospel is in principle no different from that in the Galilean phase (4:14–9:50), where Jesus is also an itinerant preacher-teacher. The travel notices may wish to imbue the section with the shades and sheen of Jesus's impending death-exaltation in Jerusalem. But at base no overriding theological motif is at work as the controlling principle throughout. Instead, a logical progression of themes, or an ordering of catchwords or phrases, or polemics with opponents, et cetera, rather than a chronological progression of Jesus's journey-ministry is the prevailing modality. The journey notices then function as a convenient scaffolding for a great mass of heterogeneous traditions.[14] In the final analysis, the dissonance between Jesus the traveler and the content that follows is more apparent than real, more a misreading of Luke's intent and procedure than an actual problem begging solution.

The overlap of these approaches is clear, and the valuable insights of each equally so.[15] In the first group, a unity emerges from the central section's position in a larger whole rather than from an internal coherence of the part itself. Still, this solution–especially in its less static forms[16]–goes a long way in explaining the existence at all of this section in the Lukan corpus: Luke's journeying Jesus seems quite natural given his penchant for the dynamic fulfillment of Old Testament history which moves on into the mission of the church. What unfortunately is left unexplained is the bulk of material included in a travel scheme that at the level of the story[17] of Jesus bears no relation to it and seems after a while to be

---

14 E.g., Ellis, *Luke*, 147–48.
15 See nn. 6, 9. Scholars have, of course, viewed the central section from many different vantage points. Resseguie, "Interpretation," has compiled a useful summary, though his analysis suffers from the lack of a critical center or reference point. What is important are categories endemic to the critical problems themselves and subsumed in the overarching relation of *form* to *content*.
16 See Robinson's critique of Conzelmann (*Weg*, esp. 39–43).
17 By "story" we mean the Russian formalists' delineation of the world of all the events, actions, themes, sayings, etc. of a given text in their temporal or causal order (namely, the "story-stuff") in contrast to the plot or actual sequence of this material. Foremost was Viktor Shklovsky's determination of "plot devices"–which organize indifferent elements or materials of the story-stuff into a dynamically coherent structure–which emancipated form from its traditional static notion of an outer "cover" or "vessel" into which the content is "poured." See, e.g., Boris Mixajlovic Èjxenbaum's assessment of Shklovsky's contribution: "The original concept of form took on the added complexity of new features of evolutionary dynamism, of incessant change" ("The Theory of the Formal Method," in *Readings in Russian Poetics: Formalist and Structuralist Views*, ed. Ladislav Matejka and Krystyna Pomorska [Cambridge, MA: MIT University Press, 1971]: 18). Analysis of the form-content of the central section in current exegetical discussion has ossified into a static "journey" framework into which Luke has poured various sayings of Jesus. Our thesis sug-

piled up willy-nilly without regard for any plan. Here certainly the ecclesiastical functional approach offers some help. With Jesus as a journeying teacher preparing the church for the period after his death, didactic and paraenetic units will seem logical even though their ordering remains illogical. Here, however, the reader is confronted by the embarrassing fact that very little of this teaching is branded with the mark of the cross, let alone with a journey. Right in the midst of this road to death, this teaching is suspended, as it were, without the suspense moving through it to its denouement. In effect, then, in both numbers 1 and 2 Luke's literary skill in crafting the *story* of Jesus's journey-ministry to Jerusalem is sacrificed to grander schemes, on the one hand, or to practical-functional concerns on the other.

In grouping number 3, Luke in certain instances becomes the *littérateur par excellence*. The unity is there if one is perceptive enough to behold it. Nevertheless, however true it may be that a chiastic or "inverted outline"[18] or a lectionary cycle[19] is followed by Luke, his readers are still faced with the uncompromising dilemma that Jesus appears to stand still in the vast wastelands of colorless crowds and faceless foes,[20] this despite Luke's express intention of writing "in ordered sequence" a "narrative of the events that have come to completion among us" (1:1, 3). Here again as in the first two instances–the ingenuity of the writer notwithstanding–unity is accomplished at the price of Luke's own literary aims.[21] The analogy with Deuteronomy would appear to be the most promising of

---

gests that Luke has dynamically structured his story-stuff by integrating his plot devices around a fourfold movement or plot motivation, namely, the calling and fate of Moses in Deuteronomy (see below, Section III). For excellent introductory surveys of the rise, rubrics, and results of the Russian formalists, see *Readings in Russian Poetics*, 3–37; Stephen Bann and John E. Bowlt, eds., *Russian Formalism: A Collection of Articles and Texts in Translation* (Edinburgh: Scottish Academic Press, 1973), 6–19, 26–40, 48–72. For an application to the NT, see Norman R. Petersen, *Literary Criticism for New Testament Critics* (Philadelphia, PA: Fortress, 1978), 24–92, esp. 33–48.
18 Bailey's term (*Poet*, 80) in his expansion and modification of Goulder, "Chiastic."
19 Guilding, *Worship*; Goulder, *Midrash*, 465–73.
20 Esp. from 12:1 to 17:11; see n. 3.
21 For a concise, well-balanced discussion of the issues in Luke 1:1–4 and of the more recent literature, see Marshall, *Gospel*, 39–44. That καθεξῆς (1:3) must refer to a strict chronological order is dubious at best if only for the lack of a precise sequential as well as topographical detail in the Gospel. Yet a general concern for chronology does not rule out a coherent or consistently ordered development conceived within an overall continuous journey or progression. Luke says, in fact, that he has both a story (διήγησις) to tell, that is, "the events (πραγμάτων) that have come to completion among us" (1:1), and that through his judicious effort he has plotted this story, that is, is relating all of his story-stuff (πᾶσιν) in an "ordered fashion" (καθεξῆς) (1:3). The inability of approaches 3 and 4 to engage the specific plotting of the story in the larger literary structures makes them helpful but insufficient solutions. See n. 16; for determining Luke's overall inten-

all the solutions; a great mass of teaching is presented in the form of a journey to the promised land. Yet in the expositions thus far,[22] no attempt has been made to relate the peculiar tension between the teaching and the course of the journey in Deuteronomy to that of the central section.[23] Rather, as in the second approach, Jesus, the "prophet like Moses" of Deut 18:15–19, is essentially a teacher, now delivering a new Torah which in sequence and substance parallels the old (Deut 1–26). A number of the parallels are indeed startlingly close; others consisting of verbal and catchword connections, without substantial similarity in either correspondence or contrast, are tenuous at best.[24] The result as before is either a functional cohesion within the edifice of the church or a literary model that at crucial joints collapses under scrutinizing stress.

The fourth approach is attractive since it appears to ask the right questions by gaining a more balanced perspective of Luke's procedure overall in his adherence to a normative gospel pattern. But from the very outset, this stance sidesteps the crux of the matter. For it is simply not the case that within the Galilean ministry Luke directs his readers' attention to Jesus's resolute determination to climax his prophetic destiny in Jerusalem. Through a solemn declaration and then through intermittent reminders,[25] the story in 9:51 has clearly taken a twist in a different direction; the journey notices have now entered into Luke's thematic development. His procedure is not the same. Readers have every right to ask where in Luke's "connected narrative" of "the whole course of events" Jesus's journeying

---

tion, see Schuyler Brown, "The Role of the Prologues in Determining the Purpose of Luke-Acts," in *Perspectives on Luke-Acts*, ed. Charles H. Talbert (Danville, VA: Association of Baptist Professors of Religion): 99–111; Fitzmyer, *Luke*, 287–90.

22 Evans, "Central," esp. 40–42, 50–53; Drury, *Tradition*, expands Evans's parallels and secondarily uses the sequence of material in Matthew as a clue to the "ordering" of Luke 9:51ff.

23 Neither Evans nor Drury attempts to illuminate the development of the journey or the function of the journey motif within the story of Moses's final delivery and exhortation of the Law to the people at the borders of the promised land. For this reason both our point of departure and our conclusions are substantively different and should in no way be confused with the "Christian Deuteronomy" of Evans. The brilliance of his contribution, however, is not to be gainsaid; see nn. 22, 15.

24 See, e.g., Ellis, *Luke*, 147; see also J. W. Wenham's recent summary of scholarly response to Evans and Drury on Deuteronomy: "The supposed parallels are often tenuous in the extreme, e.g., [...] the command to destroy the foreigners is said to correspond by contrast to the parable of the Good Samaritan, the law about escaped slaves is said to correspond to the parable of the Unjust Steward. The theory is ingenious rather than plausible" ("Independence," 509–10). Yet the unmistakable substantial parallels are rendered fully explicable by our fourfold framework (see below), which would invite such parallels, especially in the mode of comparative midrash.

25 See n. 3.

is taking them.²⁶ Every step forward by this fourth resolution, then, is at the same time a step in reverse. The reader is thrown back at every turn to the same question: Can a writer whose literary capabilities encompass a thrilling journey account of well over a thousand kilometers (Acts 27:1–28:16) do no better here than this?

All four approaches lead inevitably to one conclusion: Either Luke–at his best–has done a mediocre job in fulfilling his desire to give an "ordered" account, or in 9:51 he shifts his aims entirely for grander theological, practical, or aesthetic pursuits. But even with this latter alternative, the central section remains an oddity. Can we be satisfied with an evangelist whose literary felicity does not include a credible picture at the level of the story of Jesus's words and deeds? Can we dismiss the undramatic flair of more than one-third of Luke's storytelling artistry as simply an adherence to a normative unpatterned gospel pattern?²⁷ When all is said and done, is the journey motif merely a convenient silo for a farrago of tradition?

The answer of the present writer is no on all counts. What follows is an attempt to launch a new approach to the present deadlock over the central section. Obviously a study of this scope cannot provide a thorough or comprehensive treatment of the relation of a journey form to an immense expanse of traditional material. Nevertheless it is hoped that a number of incisive lines can be drawn that will point the way forward to a more satisfactory solution. For in the present state of critical exegesis, the hammer lock of disparity between form and content continues to choke the organic cohesion and hence literary function that the central section assumes in Luke's great narration of the events of salvation. The thesis presented here is that in 9:1–50 Luke provides a "window preview" of the journey that follows in 9:5–19:44. Through this lens the reader is able to focus the lights and shadows of the winding contour ahead as that of the journey of the Prophet Jesus whose calling and fate both recapitulate and consummate the career of Moses in Deuteronomy. We have here nothing less than the prophet like Moses (Deut 18:15–19) in a New Exodus unfolding with a dramatic tension all its own.

---

26 See Schmidt, *Rahmen*, 261, on 17:11: "Wo befinden wir uns eigentlich?"
27 It is ironic that, though about one-third of his Gospel is viewed essentially as a convenient dumping ground for dislocated traditions, Luke is still regarded generally by these critical scholars as a master storyteller. See, e.g., G. B. Caird, *Saint Luke*, Pelican New Testament Commentaries (Harmondsworth: Penguin, 1963), 15: "He had something of the poet in his make-up"; but cf. p. 139 on 9:51–19:28. See also Paul Schubert, "The Structure and Significance of Luke 24," in *Neutestamentliche Studien fur Rudolf Bultmann*, ed. Walther Eltester, BZNW 21 (Berlin: Tüpelmann, 1954): 185: "Luke is a littérateur of considerable skill and technique." Of course it is possible that Luke did not live up to his intention to give a coherently connected account; see n. 21.

II

It will be expedient first to paint in broad strokes the career of Moses according to the story of Deuteronomy.[28] Through many "signs and wonders" (see, for example, 34:11–12), Moses has led all Israel[29] out of Egypt to the borders of the promised land in the valley opposite Bethpeor (3:29;[30] compare 34:6). There, shadowed by the funereal slopes of the Nebo massif (32:49–50; 34:1; compare 1:37; 3:27; 4:21–22), he takes the people through a renewal of the covenant that had been established at Mount Horeb. As a prelude to the recounting of the law, he leads the pilgrim tribes back in memory to their momentous experience at that mountain and their ensuing wilderness wanderings of forty years (chapters 1–11). And here (especially chapters 1–5, 9) it becomes clear just what prophetic role Moses was to play.[31]

When at the mountain out of the midst of the fiery cloud God began to speak to the gathered assembly of Israel (4:12–13, 33, 36; 5:4, 22, 24; 9:10; 10:4), the

---

[28] This portrait of his calling is indebted heavily to Gerhard von Rad, *Old Testament Theology*, 2 vols. (New York: Harper & Row, 1962–1965), 1:289–96; Gerhard von Rad, *Deuteronomy: A Commentary*, OTL (London: SCM, 1966), *passim*; see also Eva Osswald, *Das Bild des Mose in der kritischen alttestamentlichen Wissenschaft seit Julius Wellhausen*, Theologische Arbeiten 18 (Berlin: Evangelische Verlagsanstalt, 1962), esp. 254–307; Rudolf Smend, *Das Mosebild von Heinrich Ewald bis Martin Noth*, BGBE 3 (Tübingen: Mohr Siebeck, 1959), esp. 48–61. Our canvas depicts the Moses of the text as a whole in its present configuration (see n. 17). For questions of tradition and redaction, see, e.g., Ernest W. Nicholson, *Deuteronomy and Tradition* (Oxford: Blackwell, 1967), esp. 18–36; Gerhad von Rad, *Deuteronomium-Studien*, FRLANT N. F. 40, 2nd ed. (Göttingen:Vandenhoeck & Ruprecht, 1948); Moshe Weinfeld, *Deuteronomy and the Deuteronomic School* (Oxford: Clarendon, 1972), esp. 179–89, 320–70; Siegfried Mittmann, *Deuteronomium 1,1–6,3: literarkritisch und traditionsgeschichtlich untersucht*, BZAW 139 (New York: de Gruyter, 1975); Norbert Lohfink, "Darstellungskunst und Theologie in Dtn 1,6–3,29," *Bib* 41(1960): 105–34, esp. 107–10.
[29] Deut 1:1; 5:1; 11:6; 13:11; 18:6; 27:9, (14); 29:2, (10); 31:1, 7, 11 (2x); 32:45; 34:12.
[30] For the apparent contradiction between "in the wilderness" and "in the Arabah" in 1:1, see Martin Noth, *Überlieferungsgeschichtliche Studien* I, Schriften der Königsberger Gelehrten Gesellschaft, Geisteswissenschaftliche Klasse 18/2 (Halle: Niemeyer, 1943), 701.3, who attributes the Jordan valley site to the Deuteronomistic history.
[31] Chapters 1–3 as a unit recount the *Heilsgeschichte*, while 4:1–40 is primarily hortatory and appears to bridge the historical retrospect with the presentation of the Decalogue (5:1–21) at Horeb. Noth (*Überlieferungsgeschichtliche Studien*, 54–60, 79–81) argued that 1:1–4:40 was the work of the Deuteronomistic historian(s) to introduce their great history. In agreement with Noth, it is not the least strange that here Moses's calling and fate are telescopically reviewed, a fitting preface to a theologoumenon on Israel's prophetic history; see Lohfink, "Darstellungskunst," 106n2; Nicholson, *Tradition*, 18–22; Mittmann, *Deuteronomium*, 115–28, for redaction in chapter 4.

people were so terrified that they implored Moses to mediate the voice (φωνή) of Yahweh for them (5:4–5,22–31). This then becomes Moses's great calling, to utter the voice of the Lord to the people (for example, 5:27–28, 30–31; compare 30:2, 8 etc.) by teaching them all the commandments that they might live in the land that they were to possess as an inheritance (4:5, 14, 40; 5:31–33; 10:5; 32:46–47 etc.; compare 30:1–20). But though they had promised fidelity to Moses's God-given word (5:27), even while Moses is still on the mountain speaking "face to face" with God (34:10), the people[32] at the base rebel by worshiping an image, the molten calf (9:8–21; compare 4:15–19). The Lord's anger is so overwhelming that only Moses's suffering submission in intercession can appease his wrath sufficiently to save the people from total annihilation (9:18–20, 25–29; 10:10–11).[33]

So the Lord continues his promise to them by sending Moses onward from Horeb at the head of the people to the land of promise (10:11; 1:7). But it would seem to no avail. Despite the searing discipline (4:36) of seeing the very glory of God on the mountain (5:24) and hearing his great voice from the cloud of fire (4:11), the people are intractable in defying Moses's authority. At Kadesh-Barnea, some eleven days' journey (see 1:2), all Israel and especially the "men of war" (2:14–16) spurn the voice of the Lord through Moses and spite Moses's leadership altogether as first they "murmur" against the call to battle and then go up against the Lord's command (1:19–46). With that, two epoch-making judgments fall upon Moses and his egregious entourage: (i) Only the children (παιδίον, 1:39;[34] compare vv. 34–38) of the assembled people at Horeb will become the future possessors of the land; the entire older generation will be wiped out (1:35; 2:14–16). (ii) "On account of"[35] (1:37; 3:26) the people's intransigence, Moses must suffer the anger of the Lord, the anguish of being choked off from the land of promise, and thus ultimately die without the promised deliverance–all because of[36] the

---

[32] See von Rad, *Theology*, 1: 294: "The most impressive corroboration of this all-embracing mediating office of proclamation is of course the fact that the corpus of Deuteronomy is put into the form of words of Moses (and so not of Jahweh) spoken to Israel." See also Lohfink, "Darstellungskunst," 106n4. Deuteronomy consists actually of three addresses by Moses (1:6–4:40; 5:1–28:68; 29:1–30:20).

[33] Von Rad, *Theology*, 1:294: "But this concentration of all Israel's communion with God upon him now had a result which Deuteronomy clearly envisaged–Moses is a suffering mediator" (cf. n. 52).

[34] טפכם; בנים; the former is a colloquial expression, "little ones," rendered in the LXX by παιδίον νέον; see esp. 11:2; 31:13.

[35] 1:37-בגללכם–δι' ὑμᾶς; 3:26- למענכם–ἕνεκεν ὑμῶν.

[36] See Thomas W. Mann, "Theological Reflections on the Denial of Moses," *JBL* 98 (1979): 486: "Nowhere in the deuteronomic explanations does Moses refer to his own responsibility; the blame falls squarely on the people."

sin of his people (1:37; 3:26; 4:21–22; compare 9:18–20, 25–29; 10:10–11; 31:2, 14; 32:50–52; 34:4).

These two themes become the double-beat *leitmotiv* which like a dirge undertones the whole of Deuteronomy. The first is sounded as the relentless, interminable stubbornness of all Israel to heed God's voice through Moses, even from the moment they left Egypt (for example, 9:6, 7, 13, 27; 10:16; 12:8; 29:19; 31:27). They have been "rebellious"[37] (1:26, 43; 9:7, 23, 24; compare 21:18, 20; 31:27) as long as Moses has known them (9:24). They are "wicked" or "presumptuous"[38] (9:4–5, 27; 17:13; 18:20, 22; 19:16; 25:2), "sinful"[39] (5:9; 9:18, 21; 15:9; 19:15; 21:22; 23:21–22; 24:15–16; 30:3), "proud"[40] (8:14; 17:20), slow to believe and "hearken"[41] (9:23; 32:20; compare εἰσακούω, 1:43; 9:23; 21:18), refusing discipline and training[42] (4:10–14, 36; 5:5, 23–30; 8:2–5, 16–17; 9:6–29; 11:2–12) without "understanding"[43] (32:28; compare 4:6; 11:2). They need new "eyes to see and ears to hear" (29:4), or as Moses himself sums up, they are en masse a "stiff-necked," "faithless," and "crooked generation" (32:5, 20; 1:35).

It is only against this strain that the echo of Moses's suffering and death (ii) can be heard as a clarion call to effect deliverance precisely through this means. For it is not the case that the younger generation, the "children" on the mountain who take possession of the land, are blameless while their "fathers," the "men of war," receive the punishment. Rather, it is striking how this generation at the "border" is lumped with its predecessors as one solitary mass of a disobedient, perfidious people, such that their fate is linked to that of their "fathers," on the one side, but also to the necessity of Moses's tragic fate, on the other. First of all, the present generation's distinction as the innocent ones "without knowledge of good or evil" (1:39) is completely nullified by their eyewitness incorporation in "all the great work of the Lord" (11:7b), which had begun in Egypt and had continued through the wilderness period right up "until you came to this place" (11:5). Because they are one with their fathers in experiencing this *Heilsgeschichte* (11:1–7), they are also now without excuse in their responsibility to heed the commandments of the Lord once they have entered the land (11:8–9, 13–25). Second,

---

37 מרה(hiph.); סרר –ἀπειθεῖν, -ής; see Mann, "Denial," 484, on *mrh*: "It seems to have been introduced into the vocabulary of the wilderness theme by the Deuteronomist."
38 רשעה; זדון; סרה; רשׁע; זיד (hiph.)–ἀσέβ-, εια; -ημα; ἀσεβεῖν.
39 עון; חטאת; חטא–ἁμαρτία.
40 רום–ὑψωθῇς.
41 שמע; שׁמה–εἰσακούειν.
42 E.g., 8:5–יסר (pi.) –παιδεύειν.
43 תבונה–ἐπιστήμη.

their stubborn ways, which mimic those of their "fathers," are dovetailed directly into that "evil generation's" rebellion at Horeb and at KadeshBarnea:[44]

Hear, O Israel, you are to pass over the Jordan this day [...] Do not forget how you *incensed the Lord in the wilderness [...] Even at Horeb* you *provoked the Lord to wrath [...] And when the Lord sent* you *from Kadesh-Barnea [...] then* you *rebelled against the commandment of the Lord. [...] Circumcise therefore the foreskin of your heart and do not be obstinate any longer* (9:1a, 7a, 8a, 23; 10:16).

Any distinction in culpability between them and their "fathers" is again obliterated. But, finally, there is one undeniable difference: this generation does enter the land of promise. Yet the story of this imminent fulfillment in its present configuration is at pains to make clear that this salvation is a gracious act of Yahweh that not only does not stem from any conceivable merit on the part of the people (for example, 9:4–6) but also is not conceivable without dire consequences for their leader. At three crucial junctures in the story time,[45] the necessity of Moses's death is woven into the progression and ultimate completion of the present generation's deliverance: (a) Moses's suffering mediation and intercession for the people at Horeb, which allays Yahweh's wrath sufficiently to continue the otherwise aborted exodus redemption, is welded to Yahweh's sentence at Kadesh-Barnea. Moses's cry for relief from the "burden and strife" of a contrary people "at that time" (1:9)[46] is granted–ironically, if not heartlessly–in the subsequent and explicit announcement of his death (1:9,12 → 34–40; compare 9:7–21 → 22–24). (b) As if to dispel any notion that Yahweh's anger was assuaged by the death of the older evil generation or that the exodus continued to the borders of Canaan through the "uprightness" or innocence of Caleb or Joshua or the "children" of the mountain, the narrator has Moses repeat Yahweh's sentence to him "at that time" (3:23)[47] when the possession of the Transjordan area was completed. Moses's plea to enter into the land is met with "anger on your account" (3:26a). Because of the sin of the audience Moses is

---

44 And also at Taberah, Massah, and Kibroth-hattaavah (9:22).
45 See n. 17.
46 Deut 1:6, 19 make it clear that the Horeb episode is meant.
47 For the lapse of time to Moses's present address, see 3:29–4:1. For the interesting suggestion that the three accounts of Moses's denial were added by a redactor during the tumultuous period following the tragic death of King Josiah as a theological statement on the relationship between the leader and the people, see Mann, "Denial," 490–94. Accordingly, Moses and Josiah are linked in their deaths in a way demonstrating that at least one element of the Deuteronomistic school "recognized the ineluctable corporate doom against which even the ideal leader was helpless" (493–94).

addressing, he must die (3:27). (c) The third announcement removes any vestige of the possibility that Moses's death is, after all, merely parallel to the main event of deliverance or that his denial outside the land is simply an example "of the tragic dimension of human experience."[48] After reviewing the affairs at Beth-peor from the time of the second declaration of his demise, Moses harks back to the revelation of Yahweh at Horeb to warn against apostatizing and uses that watershed event with its sequel at Kadesh-Barnea to summarize and typify his audience's present state of affairs "this day" (4:20b). They stand freed from their bondage in Egypt, ready to pass over into the land, to be sure (4:20), but–again–Moses must die, precisely because "on account of you,"[49]

> Yahweh swore that I should not cross the Jordan nor enter into the good land which the Lord your God is giving you as an inheritance. For I[50] must die in this land, I must not cross the Jordan, but rather you shall cross over that you may take possession of that good land (4:21–22).

In short, without Moses's death they would not receive the gracious act of deliverance that Yahweh is now bringing to pass[51] (compare 31:2,14; 32:48–50;[52] 34:4). But they are also forewarned; if they continue their rebellious ways once they have entered the land, they will meet the same fate as their fathers (4:23–28). Thus it is at each of the three critical turns of events in the developing story that Moses's death moves the action of Yahweh's deliverance forward to its climax at the boundaries of the land and enables the people to cross over to their promised inheritance.[53]

---

[48] So Mann, "Denial," 486, referring to Hillel Barzel, "Moses: Tragedy and Sublimity," in *Literary Interpretations of Biblical Narratives*, ed. Kenneth R. R. Gros Louis, James Stokes Ackerman, and Thayer S. Warshaw (Nashville, TN: Abingdon, 1974): 129.
[49] For the three parallel synonymous expressions (1:37; 3:26; 4:21), see S. R. Driver, *Deuteronomy*, ICC, 3rd ed. (Edinburgh: T&T Clark, 1902), 27.
[50] The emphatic "I" is twice sharply contrasted with the emphatic "you."
[51] Driver, *Deuteronomy*, 71.
[52] Usually ascribed to the P account; see, e.g., von Rad, *Deuteronomy*, 201; Mann, "Denial," 483.
[53] We are not suggesting that a developed, theoretical explanation of Moses's death as atoning or redemptive is offered in Deuteronomy. Yet within the plotted dynamics of the story, Moses's death is indispensable to the execution of the exodus deliverance and occupation of the land, an event that must be accomplished according to the divine will and, consequently, an explanation of the *raison d'etre* of Moses's denial. Moses's death vis-à-vis the older generation is vicarious in the sense of a shared participation in their punishment, and it is redemptive for the younger generation as it finally enables or allows their deliverance to be consummated. For "vicarious" in the sense of "substitutionary" and/or "representative," see, e.g., von Rad, *Theology*, 1:294–95; von Rad, *Deuteronomy*, 45, 201; G. Ernest Wright, "Exegesis of Deuteronomy," in *IB*, ed. George

The pen-portrait is now distinct. Moses has emerged as a suffering mediator, sent from Horeb to lead the "faithless" and "crooked generation" of "children" to the promised salvation by dying outside the land. More precisely, we can distinguish a fourfold dynamic to his prophetic vocation: (i) On the mountain Moses's calling to be the mediator of God's life-giving words (the Law) on the exodus journey is revealed most formidably by the voice (φωνή) out of the fiery cloud to the gathered assembly of all Israel. (ii) From the mountain the persistent stubbornness of the people in not hearkening to this voice is divulged through the twisting of this voice in the image of the molten calf; this defiance in turn illustrates the unwillingness of the people to "hear" this voice from the beginning. (iii) Accordingly, while Moses is still on the mountain and as he descends and is sent on the exodus, his calling is disclosed to be a suffering journey to death. (iv) As a result, his calling does not effect deliverance for all those who follow him to the promised land but only for the new people of the land, the "children of the mountain." At the core of this dynamic is the double-stroke of Israel's stiff-necked opposition to the voice of the Lord through Moses and the consequent tragic fate of this prophet. As later generations of the Deuteronomist historians colored his career,[54] Moses's death outside the land was a necessary punishment for the sin of all Israel–even of the "children" who like their fathers proved themselves to be a "stubborn" and "crooked generation."

III

It has long been recognized that Luke's account of Jesus's mountain transfiguration (9:28–36) introduces his subsequent journey (9:51ff).[55] But from a literary standpoint, the whole of 9:1–50 performs such a function through Luke's[56] care-

---

A. Buttrick, 12 vols. (New York: Abingdon, 1951–1957): 2:339–40; for the explicit development in Mosaic tradition (e.g., Isa 53), see von Rad, *Theology*, 2:261–62; Geza Vermes, "Die Gestalt des Moses an der Wende der beiden Testamente," in *Moses in Schrift und Überlieferung*, ed. Henri Cazelles and Fridolin Stier (Düsseldorf: Patmos, 1963): 78–86, esp. 79–80; Louis Ginzberg, *The Legends of the Jews*, 7 vols. (Philadelphia, PA: Jewish Publication Society of America, 1910), 2:302.
54 See nn. 27, 30, 46.
55 So, e.g., Conzelmann, *Mitte*, 51; Davies, "Purpose," 164–65; Gill, "Observations," 218–21; Grundmann, "Fragen," 256–57; Lightfoot, *Localit y*, 136–37; McCown, "Geography," 64–66; von der Osten-Sacken, "Christologie," 482–84.
56 Or perhaps his sources' continuity. For 9:7–50 and especially Herod's perplexity (9:9) as raising the question of Jesus's identity and in 9:10–50 depicting Jesus's authoritative status in preparation for the "Teacher par excellence" of the central section, see Fitzmyer, "Composition," 149–52.

fully carved continuity in audience and scenery. In this way, before the journey is signally announced (9:51), Luke sets forth a fourfold exodus typology of the prophetic calling of Jesus that conforms closely to that of Moses in Deuteronomy as we have outlined it above. This typology in fact becomes the organizing principle for the form and content of the whole of the central section. As the scheme is set out, it is important to bear in mind that the correspondence in "type" is not a function of a mechanical, rote-like parallelism in the sequence of events or description of details. It is not suggested that a one-to-one analogy in the chronology of episodes in Deuteronomy exists in Luke 9:1–50 or that every event or subject in the one has a mirror image in the other. Rather, what we discover is a profound correspondence in the calling, execution, and fate of the calling of the one who is the prophet like Moses (Deut 18:15–19), effecting a New Exodus for a renewed people of God:

(i) Only Luke of the three Synoptists speaks of Jesus's transfiguration taking place "while he was praying" (9:28b, 29a); like Moses Jesus is one who speaks directly with God.[57] As his robes begin to "flash like lightning" (ἐξαστράπτω) and the "appearance" (εἶδος)[58] of his face is altered, suddenly (ἰδοὺ) Moses and Elijah "appear" "in glory" (ἐν δόξῃ, 9:29b–31a) with him. Luke alone would have his readers behold three glowing personages who must have created quite a spectacle for the unwitting spectators. As with the Horeb theophany, the mountain was "burning with fire" (Deut 5:23). Again it is only Luke who states that the three disciples saw Jesus's glory (τὴν δόξαν αὐτοῦ, v. 32b) "and the two men standing with him." They thus become witnesses to the divine glory just as the Israelites are shown this glory on the mountain (τὴν δόξαν αὐτοῦ, Deut 5:24). Peter, dumbfounded and stumbling over every word, suggests that they make three tents (9:33b) when, just "as he was speaking," a cloud[59] comes and "overshadows" them (9:34).[60] The disciples are "frightened" as the cloud engulfs them and a "voice from the cloud" (φωνὴ [...] ἐκ τῆς νεφέλης) declares, "This is my Son, my

---

57 It may be objected that since Luke alone presents Jesus at prayer in other instances (e.g., 3:21; 5:16; 6:12; 9:18) and since Exodus also portrays Moses speaking directly with God (e.g., 19:9–13), this detail does not say very much, if anything at all. But this feature takes on added weight within the interlocking picture of Jesus with the Moses of Deuteronomy (see below) in which the Mosaic portrait is clearly distinguished from the J and E accounts in Exodus (see, e.g., von Rad, *Theology*, 1:291–95). That Jesus is often at prayer merely shows the consistency of Luke 9:28–36 with the rest of the Lukan presentation.
58 Cf. (LXX) Exod 24:10,17–only Luke has this verbal link with the Exodus account.
59 Cf. (LXX) Exod 40:35; Pss 90(91):4; 139(140):7; Prov 18:11.
60 Whether the disciples or Jesus and Moses and Elijah are meant is not decisive for our thesis; see Marshall, *Gospel*, 387.

Chosen One, hearken to him" (αὐτοῦ ἀκούετε, v. 35). Now it is the heavenly voice (φωνή) of Horeb which, Moses reminds the people time and time again, is their life (Deut 4:11–13, 33, 36; 5:22, 23, 24, 25, 26; 8:20; 18:16; for the future, 4:30; 13:4, 18; 15:5; 26:14, 17; 27:10; 28:1, 2, 9,13, 15, 45, 62; 30:2, 8, 10, 20). To hearken is to live, to disobey to die. And not only to this voice in Moses but also in the "prophet like" him who shall "arise" (ἀνίστημι) "among his brethren" after him are they to "hearken to him" (αὐτοῦ ἀκούσεσθε, v. 15b of 18:15–19).[61] Here it is curious that of the three versions of this heavenly voice, only Luke in both vocabulary and word order matches the LXX of 18:15b.[62] Thus, like all Israel, who on the mountain hundreds of years earlier witnessed the authoritative revelation of the divine voice through Moses, so now on the mountain the three disciples, representing the "Twelve" and hence the twelve tribes of all Israel, witness the definitive revelation of the divine voice through Jesus, God's chosen Son. Like Moses Jesus is called to mediate the voice of God.

(ii) It is only Luke of the evangelists who dares mention that while Jesus is transfigured "in glory" with Moses and Elijah the disciples sleep (βεβαρημένοι ὕπνῳ, 9:32a)![63] Only after they have "awakened" (διαγρηγορήσαντες, v. 32b) do they "see" Jesus's glory and the two men. What is more, Luke does not spare Peter and his companions further embarrassment when Peter, astir with "greatness in the air," thinks that in keeping with such a grand occasion the group needs a "booth" for each of the "glorious" figures–"not knowing what he was saying" (9:33b). It is then, "as he was speaking" (9:43a), that a cloud comes and the "voice out of the cloud" commands the terrified disciples to obey the voice of God in Jesus, his elect Son. Like the people of Israel on Horeb, who in their stubborn resistance to obeying the voice of God through Moses had to be disciplined by the shock of the thundering voice from the fiery cloud (Deut 4:36), so the stuporous disciples in their sluggard response to the voice of God through Jesus also have to be overwhelmed by the traumatic voice from out of the cloud. Luke continues (9:36) that "after the voice had spoken Jesus was found alone" and the disciples "were mute," "telling no one in those days[64] anything of what they had seen" (ἑώρακαν). For it was true of them that they had "this day" (ἐν τῇ ἡμέρᾳ ταύτῃ) "seen (εἴδομεν) God speak with man and man still live" (Deut 5:24b)!

---

61 It must not be overlooked that the authority of the prophet like Moses is tied directly to Moses's authority revealed at Horeb (18:16–17).
62 If any direct textual dependence is involved, this parallel would seem to indicate familiarity with the LXX account rather than any "change" of Matthew or Mark, especially given the latters' divergent emphases (see n. 74).
63 For linguistic issues, see Marshall, *Gospel*, 385.
64 Luke 9:36b–ἐν ἐκείναις ταῖς ἡμέραις.

It may be objected already that this second analogy hardly holds together when it is recalled that in fear of their own lives the Israelites eagerly accepted Moses's mediation of the divine voice on the mountain in contrast to the halting ambivalence of the disciples, who do not even comprehend the life-and-death matters in their midst at all. But what we are presenting is a typological correspondence far more fundamental than a specific sequence or episode within a momentous revelation. To penetrate these deeper dimensions, it will be necessary to see how Luke's casting of the disciples on the mountain is, like Deuteronomy, carefully engrafted into the behavior of the crowd below on the plain (9:1–27, 37–50).

In 9:1–6 Jesus "sends" out the Twelve with "power" (δύναμις) and "authority" (ἐξουσία) to continue the same activity in which he himself has been engaged, namely, healing and preaching the kingdom of God (9:2; compare 9:11). Herod's stance to both Jesus's and his emissaries' amazing feats is then dovetailed into this sending out (9:7–9): Herod has "heard of all the things that were being done." Folks are buzzing with speculation that "John the Baptist had been raised" (ἠγέρθη) or that "Elijah had appeared" (ἐφάνη) or that "one of the prophets of bygone days had arisen"[65] (ἀνέστη; compare ἀναστήσω, Deut 18:15, 18). As for Herod, he is at a loss just what to think–he must "see" (ἰδεῖν) this Jesus for himself (9:9; compare 23:6–12)! The disciples' activity here is without doubt identified with Jesus's fame; to hear about their work is to force a decision about Jesus.[66] They appear to be *one* with their master in the power and authority granted them.

The Twelve return (9:10) and report, but no response by Jesus is given except that he takes them "apart" to Bethsaida.[67] "The crowds" (οἱ ὄχλοι, 9:11), however, who have thronged Jesus for some time now,[68] learn where he is going and follow him. While it is not explicitly stated that these crowds represent the same folk who are voicing their opinions about Jesus (9:7–8), yet it is interesting that right at this point, after Jesus has spoken about the kingdom of God, healed,[69] and with his disciples fed these crowds in a desert place (ἐν ἐρήμῳ τόπῳ, 9:12b; compare ἐν τῇ ἐρήμῳ, Deut 8:2), Jesus asks his disciples just what these crowds are thinking about him (9:18). And they report almost verbatim the same sentiments that

---

[65] This phrase is only in Luke.
[66] A vivid illustration of the *shaliah* concept, cf. Luke 9:10–οἱ ἀπόστολοι. See Charles K. Barrett, "Shaliah and Apostle," in *Donum Gentilicium: New Testament Studies in Honour of David Daube*, ed. Ernst Bammel, Charles K. Barrett, and William D. Davies (Oxford: Clarendon, 1978): 88–102.
[67] Contrast this "return" with that of the "seventy(-two)" in 10:17–20!
[68] E.g., 6:17, 19; 7:9, 11, 12, 24; 8:4, 19, 40, 42, 45.
[69] These first two activities match those of the Twelve (9:2).

are troubling Herod's ears (9:19). The popular feeling is that Jesus is a great prophet, comparable to the greatest of the Old Testament figures. The reader is led to believe, then, that these opinions are emerging essentially from the same crowds. Peter, on the other hand, not content to be marked by such commonality, goes beyond this stance, acknowledging Jesus to be God's own "Anointed" (τὸν χριστὸν τοῦ θεοῦ, 9:20). But unlike the other Synoptists, no praise or blessing by Jesus is accorded this insight; no period of private correction and teaching is awarded the disciples' confession.[70] Instead, Jesus, "charging" and "commanding" them to silence and in the same breath (εἰπών)[71] telling them that "the Son of Man must suffer many things [...]," continues on by telling (compare ἔλεγεν,[72] v. 23) all that they too must suffer if they want to save their lives by following him (9:23–26). The sequence here is quite different from that in Mark and Matthew. For Luke presents one continuous scene in which the same crowds remain close by as a theatrical backdrop for the disciples' performance. This lack of interaction of Jesus with his disciples might appear to "level" them with the masses, to join them with the popular currents of the crowds. All must follow Jesus, and all alike must suffer. Yet however different this picture, without Mark and Matthew as foils and stylistic variances notwithstanding, Luke's account is straightforward and intrinsically logical. The disciples are distinguished from the crowds confessionally and spatially by a relative privacy where Jesus is praying "alone," in addition of course to their commissioning (9:1–6) and special assistance in feeding these multitudes (9:12–17).

But as we pursue the advancing lines of the plot, this suspicion is borne out as the disciples' solidarity in power and authority with Jesus takes marked turns in the opposite direction. The divergences in audience and sequence with Mark and Matthew do indeed become signposts of a fundamentally different terrain, which lies ahead. The great tableau of Jesus's following, which extends from 9:10–27, climaxes with Jesus prophesying to all that some among them will not "taste death" before they "see" (ἴδωσιν, v. 27) "the Kingdom of God." "Now about eight days after these sayings, Peter, James, and John–in spite of themselves–see" (εἶδον, v. 32) Jesus's glory on the mountain. "The next day" when they have descended, Jesus is met by a "great crowd" (ὄχλος πολύς, 9:37b) only to learn from one of them (compare ἀπὸ τοῦ ὄχλου, v. 38a) that his disciples "were unable" (οὐκ ἠδυνήθησαν, v. 40) to heal this man's "only son" (compare v. 38b). Jesus responds, "You faithless and crooked generation!" (ὦ γενεὰ ἄπιστος καὶ

---

70 Contrast Mark 8:31–32; Matt 16:17–19, 21, 24–28.
71 See, e.g., Grundmann, "Fragen," 255–56.
72 See Marshall, *Gospel*, 373: "He went on to say"; for this use of the imperfect see BDF § 329.

διεστραμμένη, 9:41a). Here Jesus lumps his disciples together with one solid mass of a disbelieving, perverse people. Indeed just as earlier the people's faithless twisting of God's commandment in the molten calf at the base revealed their stubborn perversity as Moses descends the mountain, so now as Jesus descends the mountain, the disciples' faithless twisting of their divinely bestowed power and authority with the man's only son at the base reveals the stubborn perversity of the whole generation. Moreover, Moses's charge to the people that they are a "stubborn and crooked generation" (γενεὰ σκολιὰ καὶ διεστραμμένη, 32:5) and "a perverse (ἐξεστραμμένη) generation, children in whom there is no faith" (οὐκ ἔστιν πίστις, 32:20) is matched here by Jesus: in both, the zealous anger of the Lord who confronts an obdurate generation "in the wilderness" comes to expression. And Moses's cry of desperation at Horeb, "How can I bear alone the weight and the burden of you and your strife?" (1:12), is echoed remarkably again by Jesus here at the base of the mountain: "How long am I to be with you and bear you?!" (Luke 9:41).[73] Jesus laments that he must endure this faithless mass any longer; even the disciples, who hardly more than a week earlier had confessed his messiahship, are pulled into and identified with this crooked lot. They in fact are the very provocators of this outburst. Their "impotence" at the base of the mountain becomes a striking demonstration of their ambivalence at the top. The whole generation, disciples and all, are like their Horeb counterparts–one disobedient, rebellious mass.

That this portrayal is not happy coincidence is startlingly confirmed as the scene unfolds. Luke moves at a quick pace. While the crowds "marvel" at the "majesty" (μεγαλειότης, 9:43) "of God [...] and all that he was doing," Jesus tells his disciples again in sobering if not stern words, "Let these words sink into your ears (ὦτα) [...]" (9:44). The disciples fare no better this time than with Jesus's first prediction of his passion, as Luke stresses in four different phrases their incapacity to grasp these words: They (a) do not "understand" (b) that which has been "concealed" from them, (c) "in order that they should not perceive," and (d) "they were afraid to ask him about this saying" (9:45). They are like their frightened wilderness predecessors who remain slow to believe and hearken (Deut 9:23; 32:20), a people "without understanding" (32:28), even though they had witnessed the "majestic" (μεγαλεῖος, 11:2–7) deliverance of God. Despite the mighty signs in their midst and the glory on the mountain, they reembody that people to whom Moses so well observed, "You have seen all the things the Lord did [...] the signs

---

[73] The disciples are "at strife" in 9:46–48 (see below); see n. 74 for the different import of this lament in Matt 17:17 and Mark 9:19.

and those great wonders. Yet the Lord has not given you a heart (καρδία) to know or eyes to see or ears (ὦτα) to hear, even to this very day" (29:2b–4).

But as with the Israelites, the disciples' and the whole generation's "crooked" perfidy is not simply summed up by uncomprehending unbelief. For immediately Luke continues on at the same time and in the same crowded arena with the disciples arguing which of them is the "greatest" (9:46–48). That they could squabble about their own importance in the midst of these crowds right when they had failed miserably at casting out a "demon" (δαιμόνιον, v. 42) from one of their children seems almost as if Luke here has resorted to burlesque. With the powerful perception of a prophet, Jesus penetrates all the way to their "hearts" (εἰδὼς [...] τῆς καρδίας αὐτῶν, 9:47a) and places a "child" (παιδίον) by his own side. The point: Unless one can humble a puffed-up heart, and "in my name" associate with, that is, "receive" (δέχομαι) a person as small (μικρότερος) and insignificant as a child, that one will be unable to "receive" Jesus and thus also the One who has "sent" Jesus (9:48). There is no point in being at Jesus's side unless one is humble enough to be at a "child's" side. The rebuke to the disciples could hardly be more scathing. They are failing to obey Jesus's voice through "proud and patronizing hearts."

That this is the pith of the problem in its Lukan context is illustrated by the next pericope, which again continues on uninterrupted in setting. John "answers" that they (that is, the disciples) "saw (εἴδομεν) someone casting out demons (δαιμόνια) in your name"; they "forbade him, because he does not follow with us" (ἀκολουθεῖ μεθ' ἡμῶν, compare 9:11, 23). Not only are the disciples blind and deaf to the true authority of Jesus's voice, but their presumptuousness also makes them numb to Jesus's discipline. What they see in this Jesus who performs mighty works is principally that which makes them mighty as well. That is to say, they cannot recognize and fall in line with Jesus's authority structure but insist that "true following" (compare 9:23–27) requires a "falling in line" with them. The resonance of ἐν τῷ ὀνόματί σου (9:49) with ἐπὶ τῷ ὀνόματί μου (9:48) is loud and clear. Jesus's retort is also equally unequivocal. He forbids them to "forbid" the person who is working "in Jesus's name"[74] since such a one is obviously not "against" the disciples but is "for them" (9:50). Jesus's pointing to the child in verse 48 as an object lesson in submission to his authority has been of no account whatever. The disciples are too caught up in their own "prominence" to stoop to the side of the child. They are like their obstinate antetypes refusing discipline and training (Deut 9:6–29; compare 4:36; 5:23–30; 8:2–5, 14–20; 11:2–7).

---

74 There is no indication by Jesus that his authority is being abused by the "unknown" exorcist.

Their glimpse of Jesus's divine glory on the mountain has revealed their own self "glory" on the plain (Deut 5:24; Luke 9:32).[75]

We are now in a position to see how the incidents at the base of the mountain interpret the behavior on the summit and in fact all that precedes the ascent (9:1–27). The contrast of the disciples with the unknown exorcist could not be starker. He has the power and authority to exorcise demons because he works in Jesus's name, that is, he has submitted to the divine voice in Jesus. This incident (9:49–50), which at first seems to be attached arbitrarily by Luke, indeed renders Jesus's lament and charge in 9:42 fully comprehensible. The disciples are unable to exorcise the demon from the child because they have not submitted to this divine voice, and they cannot because their hearts are bloated beyond response to the child in their midst. They are at base no different from the rest of the twisted, unbelieving generation of the crowds. Thus, what we have is the same fundamental distortion of the divine voice as at Horeb. In both, the command to hearken to the authority of the Lord through his mediator is completely contorted to the authority of their own imagination. As the image of the molten calf divulges the rebellious refusal to obey the voice of God in Moses, so the image of the self-importance of the disciples reveals their stubborn refusal to obey the voice of God in Jesus. The idol of the one is as real as the idol of the other. Thus, in both Deuteronomy and Luke 9 the reluctance and fear of listening to the voice of God on the mountain is truly a foreboding revelation of the "twisted generation" on the plain.[76] And the incomprehension, strife, conceited hearts, imper-

---

[75] A comparison with the portrayal of the disciples in the corresponding Matthean and Markan passages discloses that only Luke reflects a developed complex of exodus motifs that determines the whole tenor and structure of the story of Jesus: Mark 9:14–50–the disciples are bound to Jesus through their confessing, though naive and insufficient, faith and as such are set apart from the unbelieving and in part even hostile crowds; Matt 17:14–18:35–even more than Mark the disciples are distinguished from the unbelieving and perverted crowds (17:17a) by their faith and responsibilities as guardians of that faith. See Ernst Lohmeyer, *Das Markus-Evangelium*, Kritischexegetischer Kommentar über das Neue Testament, 10th ed. (Göttingen: Vandenhoeck & Ruprecht, 1937), 184–97; Julius Schniewind, *Das Evangelium nach Markus*, NTD 1 (Göttingen: Vandenhoeck & Ruprecht, 1963), 90–98; Julius Schniewind, *Das Evangelium nach Matthäus*, NTD 2 (Göttingen: Vandenhoeck & Ruprecht, 1950), 194–203.

[76] Does the desire to be sheltered by a "tent" or "booth" (σκηνή, οἶκος; see Luke 9:33; Deut 5:30) perhaps reflect an early typological explanation of the disciples' reluctance to hearken to the divine voice in Jesus? In both Deut 5:30 and Luke 9:33, the "witnesses" are eager to have this "voice" in their midst but only on their own terms (see also Deut 1:27; 31:14–15; 1Kgs 19:9–15; Luke 16:9; Acts 7:43, 44 and the word play of σκηνή and σκήνωμα with οἶκος in Acts 7:46–50!). In Deuteronomy the "tent" (σκηνή, σκήνωμα, 16:13; 33:18) symbolizes the joy of God's saving pres-

viousness to discipline, et cetera all become salient signs of this generation's crooked unbelief. We can schematize this basic dynamic of response in both Deuteronomy and Luke 9:1–50 as follows: Reluctance and Fear of Hearing the Voice on the Mountain → Stubborn Perversion of this Voice on the Plain → Incomprehension, Strife, Conceit, Rejection of Discipline, et cetera by Whole Generation. What was true of the miraculous signs and feeding in the wilderness for the people (λαός) of God becomes true again for the λαός of God in Luke: "You have been rebellious against the Lord from the day that I knew you" (Deut 9:24; compare 8:3,15–20).

(iii) It is only Luke of the Gospel writers who discloses that while the disciples slumber, Moses and Elijah converse with Jesus about his "exodus" (ἔξοδος) "which he was to fulfill in Jerusalem" (9:31). We have already seen that Luke explicitly links Jesus's words about bearing a cross and losing one's life directly to the mountain glorification (9:23–27, 28). These words are in turn an amplification of the Son of Man's suffering rejection and death at the hands of the "elders, chief priests, and scribes" (9:22), that is, by the Sanhedrin in Jerusalem. Moreover, in the context of 9:51 where "the days (plural) of his taking up" in Jerusalem are (literally) "becoming completely full," that is, "had already arrived,"[77] it is certain that the exodus Jesus fulfills in Jerusalem is also one that he fulfills on his way to Jerusalem, that is through a journey to that city. Hence his exodus is both a "going out" to and "departure" from Jerusalem. *Like Moses, then, Jesus's calling to journey to death is revealed to those on the mountain who would follow behind him to reach the "promised land" of salvation* (Deut 10:11; 1:7; Luke 9:22–25, 32, 51).

As Jesus descends and is met by the crooked generation, his cry of desperation like Moses's lament reveals the palpable necessity of his suffering. "How long must I be with you and put up with you" voices the sentiment not of a normal mortal but of one who is clearly reckoning with a departure from "this generation"[78] in the imminent future. This necessity is suddenly voiced again, this time in the most ironic of settings. As the chorus of the crowds of "men" marvel approval, Jesus tries to shake his disciples from the monolithic snare of sin by warning them of these same "men" into whose hands he is about to be

---

ence when the nation is in an obedient relation to its covenant God (cf. Acts 15:16); see also the "shame" of Luke 9:26–27 and the disciples' behavior in 9:40–50!

77 Cf. Acts 2: 1 for the best analogy; see also Davies, "Purpose," and Schubert, "Structure," 184–85, for clear discussions of the linguistic relation of 9:51 to 9:31.

78 Luke 7:31; 11:29, 30, 31, 32, 50, 51; 17:25; cf. 16:8; 21:32; Acts 2:40; see Martin Dibelius, *Die Formgeschichte der Evangelien* (Tübingen: Mohr Siebeck, 1971), 278.

delivered (παραδίδωμι, 9:44b;[79] compare 9:23–25,18). It is not only the Sanhedrin that is going to kill Jesus, but so is this same twisted generation![80] The base of the mountain again confirms what has already been divulged at the top. And as at Horeb, this warning falls on deaf ears (see Deut 1:43). As Jesus and his following continue from the mountain on the exodus, it becomes all too transparent that the disciples can only think of calling down more of that "glorious fire" (9:29–34) to vindicate their own status as the mighty men of war for their Messiah-Deliverer (9:54–Deut 1:41; 2:16). But for Jesus's stiff rebuke the disciples would "gird on his weapons of war and go up and fight" (Deut 1:41). Even their most noble of Elijahlike intentions is totally askew, "unfit" for the death journey that lies ahead (9:61–62, 53; Deut 1:41a; 1Kgs 19).

The grounding for the death of Jesus is thus the same as for Moses in Deuteronomy. Because of the intransigent sin of the people, a stiff-necked resistance so powerful that even gestures of redemption are spurned with twisted contempt, Moses/Jesus must suffer and die. Though the first "passion prediction" (Luke 9:22) occurs before the ascent while Moses's necessity to suffer is disclosed upon the mountain, yet the plotted portrait in both is intriguingly similar. For as later generations of Deuteronomists came to view Moses's whole calling as one of suffering and dying outside the land, so Luke and the traditionists before him became convinced that Jesus was born to die. Thus, running through the narrative sections, both before and after the large teaching section on the commandments (Deut 12–26),[81] are the notices of Moses's suffering and death (1:12–13, 37; 3:25–28; 4:21–22; 9:18–21, 25–29; 10:10; 31:2, 14, 23; 32:50–51; 34:4). Even as early as 1:9, 12 and explicitly at 1:37 the reader is impressed with the passion of Moses as the signet for the whole. Similarly, in Luke's story the reader is informed of Jesus's tragic but redeeming destiny from the outset (2:34–35; 4:16–30!). But more significant for the central section, the indicators of Jesus's passion are concentrated both before and after a large teaching section (Luke 10:25–18:30), which is buttressed by the Deuteronomic pillars 10:27 and 18:20 on the commandments

---

79 Verses 23–25 along with probable paronomasia on ὁ υἱὸς τοῦ ἀνθρώπου with χεῖρας ἀνθρώπων (see Joachim Jeremias, "*paradeisos*," *TDNT* 5 [1967]: 715) indicate a generic sense of "man," or the generation of Jesus's day. In 17:25 (cf. 9:41) it is expressly stated that "this generation" rejects "the Son of Man" and thus is responsible for Jesus's "suffering." See nn. 76, 80, 106; in 23:13–25 Pilate delivers (παραδίδωμι, v. 25) Jesus over not only to the religious leaders but also to the people (ὁ λαός).

80 Pace Fitzmyer, "Composition," 148, who links "men" only with Jesus's enemies (cf. 9:22); see n. 78.

81 This legal section still possesses a paraenetic character; see von Rad, *Deuteronomy*, 19.

(9:22, 23–25, 31, 41, 43b–45, 51; 18:31–34; 19:47; 20:9–18, 19, 20, 26; but compare 12:49–50; 13:31–33; 17:25). It also becomes clear that Herod's beheading of John the Baptist with his desire to "see" (ἰδεῖν) Jesus (9:9; compare 23:8) is an omen of ill on a par with the "crowds'" (9:11–19) or the "disciples'" (9:20, 27, 28–36, 37–50) ability to "see" Jesus. Already then with Herod symbolizing the devious nation as a whole, the disciples' desire to dismiss rather than feed the λαός in the wilderness is, like the exodus antetype (Deut 8:2–5, 14–17), a poignant demonstration of the whole stubborn generation's refusal to accept discipline and hence the inability to heed the voice of the mountain revelation.[82] Consequently, in Luke 9 as in Deut 1–4, *the necessity of Jesus's suffering and death is first adumbrated and then announced in advance of the fuller manifestation on the mountain.*

(iv) It is only Luke of the Synoptists who links the figure of a child directly to the mountain revelation. Only the childlike can heed the voice of the mountain and receive this Jesus who has been sent by God from the mountain. Already in 9:23–25 Jesus had set forth the indispensable conditions of this receiving, or of this following him on his exodus to Jerusalem. Followers must deny themselves, take up the cross daily and follow him (v. 23), for those who wish to save their lives will in fact lose them (v. 24a). Now what we find in 9:46–47 are the disciples trying desperately to "save" their lives, promoting instead of denying themselves. With the child at his side, Jesus says in effect that such behavior can only lead to destruction of life as it stifles the life-giving liberation of the Son of Man's exodus to death and exaltation. That is precisely why the anonymous exorcist (9:49–50) is for (ὑπέρ) the disciples, since his childlike submission is a powerful promotion for the following Jesus demands.

As Jesus proceeds on his exodus, he is quite adamant that only the childlike will inherit the blessings of the land (10:17–24; 12:32; 13:34; 15:3–7; 17:1–2, 33; 18:14, 15, 17). The seventy(-two),[83] Samaritans,[84] women,[85] the "poor,"[86] the sick and possessed,[87] tax collectors and "sinners"[88] all constitute the renewed "children" of the promise, the λαός whom Jesus gathers and sifts from among the Horeb covenant λαός.[89] Here it is curious that following relatively closely

---

82 Only Luke places Peter's confession immediately following the feeding (9:10b–17).
83 Luke 10:17–24.
84 Luke 10:29–37; 17:11–19.
85 Luke 10:38–42; 13:10–17.
86 Luke 12:13–15, 16–21, 22–32, 33–34; 14:12–14, 15–24, 25–33; 15:11–32; 16:14–15, 19–31; 18:18–30.
87 Luke 10:1–12, 17–20; 11:14–23; 13:10–17, 31–33; 14:1–6, 15–24; 18:35–43.
88 Luke 14:15–24; 15:1–7, 8–10, 11–32; 18:9–14; 19:1–10.
89 See Paul S. Minear, "Jesus' Audiences according to Luke," *NovT* 16 (1974): 81–109, for Luke's use of λαός; Minear, however, does not sufficiently distinguish the λαός as the sinful covenant

in Luke's story is Jesus's terming the seventy(-two) "infants" (νήπιοι, 10:21) as those who in following him to Jerusalem work great exorcisms with "power" and "authority" in Jesus's name (10:17–20).[90] But this is only one of many instances where it becomes certain that only those who hearken to him, who hear the word of God in him and keep it, inherit the life of the new exodus land (10:25–28, 29–37, 39; 11:27–28, 42; 12:43, 47–48; 13:9, 22–30; 14:35; 15:1; 16:3, 4, 8, 9, 29, 31; 18:18–30; compare 12:17–18, 38 [D]; 19:48; 21:38; 23:34).[91]

But alas, as with the first exodus, so now even the "children" become patent representatives of the "faithless and perverse generation" responsible for Jesus's death. For just as the children of Horeb turn away and like their fathers perpetrate the death of Moses in the end, so also the λαός turn away and become with their leaders collaborators in Jesus's death at the fatal end[92] (Deut 1:37; 3:26–28; 4:21; 9:24; 11:1–7; 31:14, 16–22, 26–29; 32:5, 20; 34:4–5–Luke 22:3–6, 24–27, 31–33, 35–38, 54–62; 23:13–16, 18–23, 35; Acts 3:11–16; 4:27; compare Luke 2:34; 13:34–35; 19:41–44; Acts 2:22–23, 40; 10:39; 13:27–28, 41; 28:26–27). Again as in 9:1–50, it is with the greatest irony that those disciples closest to Jesus become active accomplices–wittingly or not–in demonstrating the absolute necessity of Jesus's death in the face of the monolithic repudiation of his sending (see especially 22:47–62).[93] And yet the story is not at an end. *For just as through Moses's death the "children" do enter the land of deliverance, so through Jesus's death the childlike who submit to the prophet like Moses, whom God "raised up from" his "brethren" (Acts 3:22a), do receive the blessing of the covenant promised to Abraham (3:24–25).*[94] "You shall

---

nation from the renewed λαός which Jesus gathers from the former (e.g., 7:29; 3:15, 18). Nor does he pay sufficient attention (83–84) to the whole nation's (people's) role in the death of Jesus (23:13–25; Acts 3:11–26; see n. 78).

90 Cf. ὄφις and σκορπίος (Luke 10:19) in Deut 8:15.

91 ποιέω, ἀκούω, φυλάσσω are the key verbs.

92 We are of course not suggesting that there is a parallelism in the kind of cooperation or in the immediate causes that bring about Moses's/Jesus's death. What is central to both is the Deuteronomistic conception of a monolithic, corporate rejection of Yahweh's messengers in a continuous history of Israel's rebellion against his voice (see below).

93 For the disciples' involvement, see especially Paul S. Minear, "A Note on Luke xxii 36," *NovT* 7 (1964–1965): 128–34; for the λαός, see nn. 78, 88, and, e.g., Jerome Kodell, "Luke's Use of 'Laos,' 'People,' Especially in the Jerusalem Narrative (Lk 19,28–24,53)," *CBQ* 31 (1969): 327–43; see also n. 98.

94 Luke is especially concerned with showing that it must be through Jesus's death and resurrection that the λαός are brought into the consummation of the salvation that fulfills the OT redemption, e.g., 24:7, 19–27, 44–49; Acts 3:18–19, 24; 13:26–30, 32–33, 38–39; 26:22–23, 27; cf. 7:52; see, e.g., Schuetz, *Leidende*, 42–96; Schubert, "Structure," 173–85; Caird, *Luke*, 34–39.

hearken (ἀκούω) *to him in whatever he tells you. But it shall be that every person who does not hearken* (ἀκούω) *to that prophet shall be destroyed from the people* (ὁ λαός)" (Acts 3:22b–23 quoting Deut 18:15b–16a, 19). Though the λαός like their forerunners hundreds of years earlier acted in "ignorance" (Acts 3:17), they now have the unprecedented opportunity–through faith in the powerful presence of Jesus's name (3:6–7, 11–16)–to be released from their wickedness (πονηρός, Acts 3:26–Deut 4:25; 9:18; 28:20; 31:29). "Those days" proclaimed by Moses and "all the prophets" (Acts 3:22–25) have been fulfilled. The monolith of stiff-necked disobedience is at last at an end (3:19).[95]

Luke then would tell his readers in 9:1–50 that the story of the prophet like Moses of Deuteronomy is about to unfold in a New Exodus journey to the "promised land." We can illustrate this Moses-Deuteronomic typology by arranging our results into a literary-functional "cross section" of Luke 9:1–50. Through a tightly-knit progression in audience and scenery, Luke presents two tableaus or, perhaps better, plateaus divided by the mountain of revelation (see Diagram 1).

(1) Each incident on the one side has its mirror image on the other side of the mountain. What the one reveals about God's gathering, training, and disciplining a people through his prophetic "Voice," Jesus, the other reveals about the ignorant, stubborn, and even perverted opposition of a people who make the suffering and death of this "Voice" an absolute necessity. (2) The disciples are patent examples of this "stiff-necked generation." (3) Like Mount Horeb, 9:28–36 forms the apex of God's selection of a special people through his chosen "Voice" and this people's monolithic resistance to this selection. Upon this summit the fourfold career of the Moses of Deuteronomy for Jesus is divulged for the rest of Luke's central section. As in Deuteronomy the mountain manifests most mightily the magisterial authority of the Lord's Prophet-Voice but also the tragic terrain of suffering and death ahead. (4) As Luke's "travel narrative" progresses and the Jerusalem ministry culminates in the death-exaltation and Pentecost of the Acts,

---

[95] It is highly significant that Luke pictures the early Jerusalem community as the fulfillment of Moses's prediction of a restored and consummated covenant people in the land through a New Exodus (Deut 30:1–10): (i) All of the dispersed from every corner "under heaven" are gathered in the land (Acts 2:5–12–Deut 30:1b, 3b–5). (ii) Their stubborn hearts are "cleansed" (Acts 1:5; 2:1–4,37–41; 3:19–LXX Deut 30:6a). (iii) Thus, true obedience to Yahweh's voice through the prophet like Moses is effected (Acts 3:21–24–Deut 30:2, 8, 10). (iv) Their sins are "released" (Acts 2:38) or "removed" (Acts 3:19) in that the ill effects are "cured" or "counteracted" (LXX Deut 30:3a). (v) "Singleness" or "oneness" of devotion to the Lord is fulfilled (Acts 4:32–Deut 30:2, 6, 10). (vi) This unity is manifested by the eating and rejoicing at "the place" that consummates the exodus deliverance of Deuteronomy (Acts 2:46–47a–Deut 26:1–11; 30:9).

the mountain revelation is confirmed as the sending of the prophet like Moses of Deuteronomy (18:15–19) to bring redemption from "wicked" disobedience to the "children of the mountain" who submit to God's "Voice."

Points (1) to (4), therefore, indicate that the "other side" (base) of the mountain divulges the double-beat *leitmotiv* of Deuteronomy, which the first side poses proleptically (see Diagram 2).

In short, points (1) to (4) demonstrate as in Deuteronomy that the mountain of revelation forms the watershed for the plot to follow.[96]

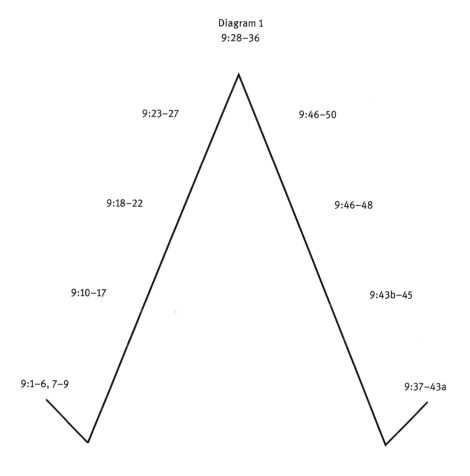

Diagram 1
9:28–36

---

[96] Our findings support in a general way the significance of "the mountain" as the place of revelation in Jesus's ministry as stated by Conzelmann, *Mitte*, 38–39.

Diagram 2

Luke 9:1-50
9:28-36
(Four-fold Moses-Deut Typology)

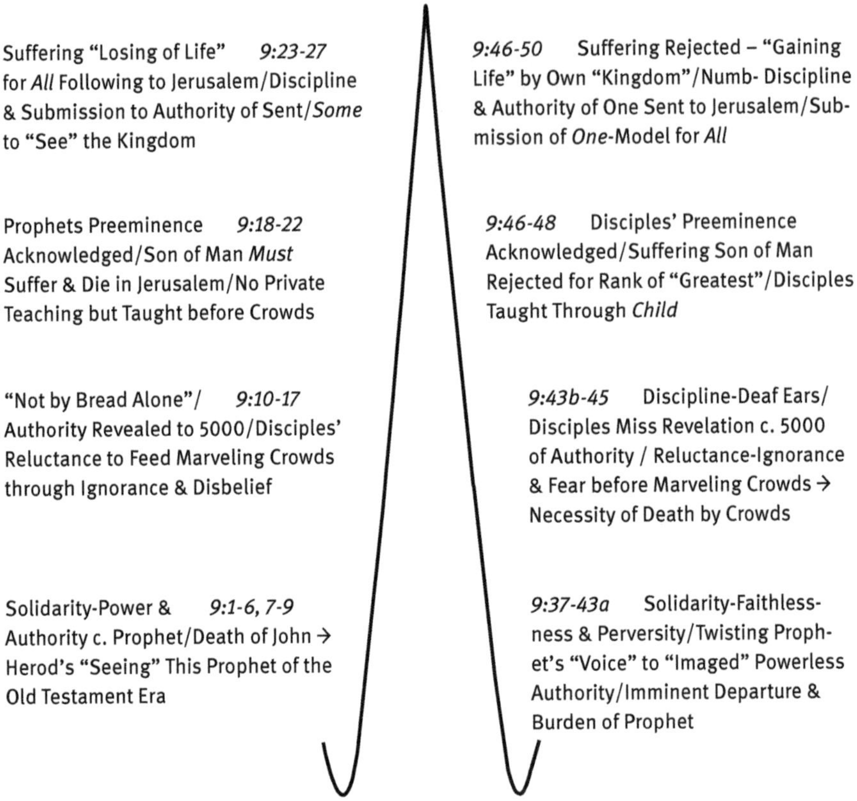

Suffering "Losing of Life"   9:23-27
for *All* Following to Jerusalem/Discipline
& Submission to Authority of Sent/*Some*
to "See" the Kingdom

9:46-50   Suffering Rejected – "Gaining
Life" by Own "Kingdom"/Numb- Discipline
& Authority of One Sent to Jerusalem/Sub-
mission of *One*-Model for *All*

Prophets Preeminence   9:18-22
Acknowledged/Son of Man *Must*
Suffer & Die in Jerusalem/No Private
Teaching but Taught before Crowds

9:46-48   Disciples' Preeminence
Acknowledged/Suffering Son of Man
Rejected for Rank of "Greatest"/Disciples
Taught Through *Child*

"Not by Bread Alone"/   9:10-17
Authority Revealed to 5000/Disciples'
Reluctance to Feed Marveling Crowds
through Ignorance & Disbelief

9:43b-45   Discipline-Deaf Ears/
Disciples Miss Revelation c. 5000
of Authority / Reluctance-Ignorance
& Fear before Marveling Crowds →
Necessity of Death by Crowds

Solidarity-Power &   9:1-6, 7-9
Authority c. Prophet/Death of John →
Herod's "Seeing" This Prophet of the
Old Testament Era

9:37-43a   Solidarity-Faithless-
ness & Perversity/Twisting Prophet's "Voice" to "Imaged" Powerless
Authority/Imminent Departure &
Burden of Prophet

IV

What remains is to delineate briefly several trajectories in Luke-Acts that not only corroborate the thesis above but also point the way to further investigation.[97]

1. *Form-Content*.[98] In his traditio-historical study of the Deuteronomistic conception of the role and fate of the prophets within its comprehensive view of Israel's history, Odil H. Steck[99] concludes that one overriding framework of understanding permeated the Palestinian Judaism of circa 200 BCE to 100 CE.: *A.* The history of Israel is one long and persistent story of a "stiff-necked," disobedient people. *B.* God sent his messengers, the prophets, to mediate his will (the Law), instruct and admonish in this will, and to exhort and warn the people to repent lest they be destroyed. *C.* Nevertheless, Israel en masse rejected all these prophets, even persecuting and killing them. *D.* Therefore, Israel's God had "rained" destruction upon them in 722 and 587 BCE and would annihilate them again if they did not heed his word. Upon closer examination of Luke 9:51–19:44, it is remarkable how the profile of Jesus's activity and reception matches this four-point thrust. A "table of content" conveniently illustrates this (see Table 1).[100]

---

[97] A more extensive treatment of the points in this section appears in Moessner, *Lord of the Banquet*.
[98] See n. 16.
[99] Odil H. Steck, *Israel und das gewaltsame Geschick der Propheten*, WMANT 23 (Neukirchen-Vluyn: Neukirchener Verlag, 1967), esp. 60–80, 317–20.
[100] As would be expected in such a dynamic, extensive overlap occurs within the text. The prophet's activity (B) in fact encompasses the whole of 9:51–19:44. This is true even of the miracles, which do not formally belong to the Deuteronomistic view of the prophets' commissioned sending, but which in the central section are a sign of Jesus's authority vis-à-vis the leaders of Israel in interpreting the Law (see esp. 10:13–15; 11:14–36; 13:10–17; 14:1–6; 19:37–40; see also 7:18–23). The non-Deuteronomistic passion predictions (17:25; 18:31–34) are linked thematically to the tragic fate (C) of the prophet in 13:31–33,34–35 primarily through the travel notices. And since the pronouncement of impending judgment became a function of the prophets in certain strands of later Deuteronomistic thinking (see Steck, *Geschick*, 123n5, 140, 193–95, 218–22), the passages in D have been included in B. At the level of Jesus's ministry, D is, of course, a prophetic prediction rather than an accomplished fact of history. Pericope divisions are based upon Kurt Aland, *Synopsis Quattuor Evangeliorum* (Stuttgart: Württembergische Bibelanstalt, 1964).

A.	B.	C.	D.
"This Generation" = Stiffnecked" like Their Fathers	Jesus Sent as Voice–Mediate Will/Instruct, Admonish/Warn Repentance	"This Generation" Rejects Jesus-Prophet & Kills Him	Therefore God Will Rain Destruction on the Whole Crooked Nation
11:29–32,49–52 12:54–56,57–59 13:1–9,22–30,34 16:27–31 17:25–30 18:8 19:41–42,44b	9:51,52–56,57–62 10:1–12,13,15,16, 17–20,21–24,25–28, 29–37,38–42 11:1–4,5–8,9–13, 14–23,24–26,27–28, 29–32,33,34–36,37–54 12:1,2–9,10,11–12, 13–15,16–21,22–32, 33–34,35–48,49–53, 54–56, 57–59 13:1–9,10–17,18–19, 20–21,22–30,31–33, 34–35 14:1–6,7–14,15–24, 25–33,34–35 15:1–7,8–10,11–32 16:1–9,10–12,13, 14–15,16–17,18,19–31 17:1–3a,3b–4,5–6, 7–10,11–19,20–21, 22–37 18:1–8,9–14,15–17, 18–23,24–30,31–34, 35–43 19:1–10,11–27,28–40,41–44	9:51,52–56,57–58 10:3,10–11,13,16,25 11:14–23,24–26, 29–32,47–54 12:49–50,54–56 13:1–9,14–17,25–30, 31–33,34 14:1,24 15:1–2 16:14–15,16,27–31 17:25–30 18:8,31–34 19:7,14,39–40	(10:12,14–15) 11:31–32,50–51 12:57–59 13:24–30,35 14:24 (16:27–31) 17:26–30 19:27,41–44

The story begins with the sending[101] of the prophet Jesus on his exodus to the historical and symbolic center of the nation of Israel and ends (19:41–44) with the pronouncement of judgment upon the whole people as he looks over the forsaken city. As the table clearly shows, the bulk of the section consists of the words of Jesus in teaching units of the mediation of the divine will, paraenesis, and warnings of judgment and blessing, which correspond closely to the three cat-

---

[101] The travel indicators (see n. 4) form a chain to Jerusalem from Jesus's mountain sending (9:31, 51).

egories of the words of Moses in Deuteronomy.[102] Moreover, as in Deuteronomy, few individual miracles are described; rather they are summed up as a whole, for example, his "mighty deeds" (Luke 19:37; 13:17; 10:13; compare 9:7, 9–10, 11b; 10:9, 17, 19–20; 13:32–Deut 4:34; 6:22; 7:19; 11:3; 13:1, 2; 26:8; 29:3; 34:11).[103]

Thus, like its counterpart, the central section depicts a prophet gathering and leading the covenant people to redemption by teaching them the will of God and faithful obedience to that will. Again as in Deuteronomy, the mountain marks the beginning of an ever-intensifying opposition to the living voice of God by a twisted generation. The Pharisees-lawyers, epitomizing the "fathers"[104] of "this generation,"[105] become the orchestrators of this antagonism as their "eating and drinking" with Jesus only exacerbates their differences and propels Jesus onward rather than tempering the disturbing claims coming from his lips. For as the crowds increase (11:14, 29; 12:1; 14:25), so does the "leaven of the Pharisees" (12:1), forcing Jesus to increase his exhortation of the disciples to be on their guard and to intensify his appeal to the crowds to turn from the coming judgment.[106] Now the pulse that we discover within the dynamic A–C is precisely the same "double-beat" that we traced above in Deuteronomy: the crescendo of rejection of God's voice in Jesus leads directly to his death.[107]

---

102 These three forms cohere closely with the covenant renewal pattern; see von Rad, *Deuteronomy*, 12. In Deut 26:16–30:20 at the borders of the promised land after a long journey the Horeb covenant is renewed; in Luke 22:20 in Jerusalem after a long journey the "new covenant" is instituted. See nn. 94, 96.
103 In Deuteronomy σημεῖα καὶ τέρατα; see Johnson, *Possessions*, 45: "In fact nearly every occurrence of 'signs and wonders' in the LXX refers to the Exodus story" (cf. Acts 2:22, 43; 4:30; 5:12; 6:8; 7:36; 14:3; 15:12).
104 See Luke 11:19–οἱ υἱοὶ ὑμῶν [...] αὐτοὶ ὑμῶν κριταὶ ἔσονται: See 1Pet 5:13; Heb 12:5 for "son" as a "pupil."
105 See nn. 77, 91.
106 E.g., 12:35–48; 12:54–13:9; 13:22–30; 14:25–35; 16:1–13; 17:1–11, 22 through 18:14; 18:15–34; 19:11–27.
107 It is not the case that the Pharisees-lawyers disappear altogether once the Jerusalem ministry and passion narrative are treated. To be sure, "Pharisees" does not occur after 19:39, but the plot to put an end to Jesus's public influence as it is conceived already in 6:7 (climax of 5:17–6:6) and developed through the Pharisees-lawyers' (scribes') resistance in the central section (11:37–54; 12:1; 13:31–33; 14:1–24; 15:1–32; 16:14–31; 19:39–40; cf. 17:20–21; 18:9–14) is continued by the "scribes" (γραμματεῖς) of the Sanhedrin. According to Luke the specific plan that eventually succeeds in arresting and killing Jesus is a scheme of the official council of the leaders of the people and is not divulged until 19:47. Hence the listing of functionaries within this council rather than religious parties should not be unexpected. Nonetheless, Luke takes pains to link these γραμματεῖς to those of the Pharisees in the pre-Jerusalem ministry and to their plot to "watch" Jesus "in order to bring him to court" (6:7; cf. 6:6–11; 11:53–54; 14:1; 15:1–2; pace

By the time Jesus reaches Jerusalem, the resistance of a stubborn, unrepentant people becomes so overwhelming that the nation's "doom" (D) as well as his own death (C) is already sealed (19:41–44, 47–48; compare 13:34–35). These four categories therefore not only confirm the picture of Jesus the prophet independently of the fourfold Moses-Deuteronomic typology–thus rendering the latter *a posteriori* more probable–but they also make this prophet like Moses come alive through the telltale "shades and shadows" of the tragic fate of all of Israel's prophets.[108] Finally, this prophetic profile coheres with the overarching pattern in Luke-Acts of the language and lineage of the prophets, which several recent studies have cogently demonstrated.[109]

2. *The Exodus Pattern.* That the exodus is one of the central patterns, if not the definitive pattern, for the "saving" acts of God in both the Old Testament and New Testament is widely agreed.[110] Further, that "journeying" plays a dominant

---

J. A. Ziesler, "Luke and the Pharisees," *NTS* 25 [1979]: 146–57). The closest links are through the scribes' public reputation, which in 20:45–47 is directly connected back to Jesus's accusations against the Pharisees-lawyers (scribes) at table (11:43, 46; 14:7–11; cf. 18:9–14; 20:47b). As in 20:47 it is the Pharisees' scribes of 11:47–52 who will receive the "greater condemnation" for their detrimental influence upon the people (for fuller evidence, see now the author's *Lord of the Banquet*, 186–211, and cf. nn. 100, 106).

108 See n. 95. The author's thesis is that the Deuteronomistic view of the prophets' calling and fate in general and that of Moses in Deuteronomy in particular converge in the career of Jesus to form one coherent drama for Luke's "travel narrative." Luke's two volumes may in fact be continuing and updating the great Deuteronomistic History of the OT. If this thesis is correct, then two major reevaluations of Luke's thought must be made: (1) The story time at the end of Acts indicates that tenet D had not yet been fulfilled. Unless Luke planned another volume, he would be cavalier in the extreme if he did not draw out the consequences of Israel's disbelief as voiced in the tones of tenet A by Paul in 28:25–28–cf. Luke 21:5–9, 12–24–if Jerusalem and the Temple had already been destroyed. Perhaps then here is a bridge from the "narrative world" to the "author's world" or *Sitz im Leben* (cf. this problematic in Robert J. Karris, "Windows and Mirrors: Literary Criticism and Luke's *Sitz im Leben*," in *Society of Biblical Literature 1979 Seminar Papers*, ed. Paul J. Achtemeier [Missoula, MT: Scholars, 1979]: 47–58). (2) Luke may have a highly developed and pregnant theology of the cross as an atonement by the prophet like Moses, who must die to effect repentance and new life of the forgiveness of sins in the land for a stiff-necked generation (see Luke 24:45–47, 49; Acts 1:5, 8, etc.) (contra prevailing consensuses; see, e.g., Werner Georg Kümmel, "Current Theological Accusations Against Luke," *ANQ* 16 (1975): 134, 138; Charles H. Talbert, "Shifting Sands: The Recent Study of the Gospel of Luke," *Int* 30 (1976): 389.

109 See especially Paul S. Minear, *To Heal and To Reveal: The Prophetic Vocation according to Luke* (New York: Seabury, 1976); Johnson, *Possessions*, 38–126.

110 See esp. David Daube, *The Exodus Pattern in the Bible*, All Souls Studies 2 (London: Faber and Faber, 1963), 12, on patterns of deliverance: "I soon discovered that there was none remotely comparable to the exodus"; Vermes, "Moses," 78. By exodus "pattern" we have been referring specifically to the fourfold picture of Moses's vocation as outlined above. Deuteronomy of course

role in the master plot of Luke-Acts and thereby expresses an important aspect of Luke's theology is also widely acknowledged.[111] Stephen's speech (Acts 7) is especially pertinent here. More than 50 percent[112] recounts the Moses-Exodus journeying in presenting the essential heritage of the church's "fathers" as well as justifying its existence during one of the most critical stages of the community's early history.[113] Such a pattern, then, in the heart of the Gospel that recounts the events "delivered to us by those who from the beginning were eyewitnesses" (Luke 1:2) should come as no surprise.

3. *Promise-Fulfillment.* This scheme in Luke and Acts not only harmonizes with the fourfold Moses-Deuteronomic typology but also resounds the very modulation of the great Deuteronomistic history.[114] That Jesus recapitulates and consummates the exodus drama as the prophet like Moses of Deuteronomy in the central section of Luke's Gospel as it is *previewed* in 9:1–50 is the conclusion reached. The motive for such a program is not hard to find. For in the "journeying Jesus," Luke and his predecessors discovered the Lord himself going before them to restore the λαός to the land–a land now freed from the bondage of a stubborn, rebellious heart: "For this means life to you" (Deut 30:6b, 29; compare Luke 10:25–28, 38–42).

---

combines the older Exodus (deliverance from Egypt and "Reed Sea") tradition with the Sinai covenant tradition, while incorporating material from the conquest traditions of the older tribal league (see esp. Martin Noth, *Überlieferungsgeschichte des Pentateuch* [Stuttgart: Kohlhammer, 1948], 45–58, 62–67; Nicholson, *Tradition*, 38–45, 58–73).

111 See especially Floyd V. Filson, "The Journey Motif in Luke-Acts," in *Apostolic History and the Gospel: Biblical and Historical Essays Presented to F. F. Bruce on His 60th Birthday*, ed. W. Ward Gasque and Ralph P. Martin (Exeter: Paternoster, 1970): 68–77. In Deuteronomy the motif of pilgrimage journeys to Jerusalem for the festivals is already combined with the exodus journey; see esp. 26:1–11.

112 53.8 percent of Stephen's words; 57 percent of his recounting the *Heilsgeschichte* (7:2–50).

113 Note how the journey motif is constitutive of the whole of Acts 7 and follows the pattern of the credo in Deut 26: 1–11. See in addition to the Stephen literature, Johnson, *Possessions*, 70–76; for a comprehensive view of Acts as developing a fulfillment of an Isaianic New Exodus, see David W. Pao, *Acts and the Isaianic New Exodus*, WUNT 2/130. (Tübingen: Mohr Siebeck, 2000).

114 Luke-Acts: see Schubert, "Structure," 165–86; Nils A. Dahl, "The Story of Abraham in Luke-Acts," in *Studies in Luke-Acts: Essays Presented in Honor of Paul Schubert*, ed. Leander E. Keck and J. Louis Martyn (Nashville, TN: Abingdon, 1966): 139–58; for the Deuteronomistic History, see esp. von Rad, *Deuteronomium-Studien*, 52–64; Gerhard von Rad, "Theologische Geschichtsschreibung im Alten Testament," *TZ* 4 (1948): 161–74.

Chapter Nine: "The Christ Must Suffer": New Light on the Jesus – Peter, Stephen, Paul Parallels in Luke-Acts[1]

The strikingly similar features of the central characters in Acts and Jesus in the Gospel of Luke have long been the subject of interest.[2] That Peter and especially Paul perform the same type of healings (Luke 5:17–26–Acts 3:1–10; 14:8–18), raise people from the dead (Luke 7:11–17; 8:40–56–Acts 9:36–43; 20:7–12), preach repentance to Jew and Gentile alike (Luke 24:44–48–Acts 10; 17:16–33), and suffer shame and rejection by their own folk (Luke 22:47–23:49–Acts 4:1–22; 21:27–22:29)[3] in imitation and in the "the name"[4] of their Master have raised fundamental questions concerning Luke's primary literary and theological aims in continuing the ὁ πρῶτος λόγος of Jesus's deeds and teaching in the "second word" of the Acts (Acts 1:1). Stephen, too, in the remarkable parallels between his death and Jesus's passion has generated fascination among critical scholars, though his position within the wider ranging Peter-Paul parallels has often escaped attention.[5] In Part I we shall present a brief overview of critical treatment of these parallels and suggest a historical perspective which comprehends Stephen along with Peter and Paul and provides an underlying pattern of coherence from which to focus the many similarities. In Parts II–IV we shall develop this pattern by applying it respectively to Stephen, Jesus and Peter, and Paul, before summarizing our conclusions.

---

1 First published with the same title in *Novum Testamentum* 28 (1986): 220–56, and reprinted in *The Composition of Luke's Gospel: Selected Studies from Novum Testamentum*, ed. David E. Orton (Leiden: Brill, 1999): 117–53. Used with permission.
2 One of the first critical comparisons of Jesus and Paul was by Bruno Bauer (*Die Apostelgeschichte: Eine Ausgleichung des Paulinismus und des Judenthums innerhalb der christlichen Kirche* [Berlin: Gustav Hempel, 1850]); see the survey of research on the parallels in, Walter Radl, *Paulus und Jesus im lukanischen Doppelwerk* (Bern: Lang, 1975), 44–59.
3 Already in 1845, F. C. Baur listed these and other parallels in detail (*Paulus, Der Apostel Jesu Christi, Sein Leben und Wirken, seine Briefe und seine Lehre*, 2nd ed. [Leipzig: Fues 1866–67; repr., Osnabrück: Zeller, 1968], 1:104–5, 116–17, 179, 218–20, 245–47, etc.).
4 Luke 24:47; Acts 4:7–10; 5:28; 23:13.
5 Especially within the *Tendenz* critique; see Part I below.

I History of Research on the Jesus – Peter, Stephen, Paul Parallels and New Light on the Coherence of Luke's Prophetic Patterning

In 1838 F. C. Baur noted the Peter-Paul parallels within the intention of Acts as part of his evidence of a thoroughgoing Paulinist apologetic to present "Paul as Petrine as possible and Peter as Pauline as possible" in bridging the Paulinist with the Petrine party into catholic Christianity.[6] Shortly thereafter in 1854, Baur's student Eduard Zeller, in taking over Baur's problematic and corroborating Matthias Schneckenburger's Acts as a defense of Paul (1841),[7] introduced Stephen as a link between the Peter-Paul parallels and the Jesus of the Gospel, on the one hand, and between the primitive Petrine Christianity and the Pauline Gentile mission, on the other.[8] Zeller goes on to the curious observation that a common christological conception–namely, a mighty *prophet* who must suffer–underlies the Jesus-Peter/(Stephen)/Paul parallels.

Particularly in the rage that Jesus, Stephen, and Paul experience from the rejection of "the Jews" it is clear that "Luke," the one and same author of both volumes, intends to bind together their common "person and ministry." And yet Zeller backs away from developing this christological cohesion.[9] Indeed, like his contemporaries, the Jesus-Peter/(Stephen)/Paul parallels are used *solely* in illuminating the apologetic character of Acts.

In the years following the demise of the Tübingen School's approach to Acts as a *Tendenzschrift*, scholars either neglected the Jesus-Peter/(Stephen)/Paul parallels altogether or mentioned them generally in conjunction with the principle of the master-disciple.[10] It was not until the flowering of *Redaktionsgeschichte* for Lukan studies in Hans Conzelmann's *Die Mitte der Zeit* that the methodological

---

6 My translation of F. C. Baur, "Ueber den Ursprung des Episcopats in der christliche Kirche," in *Ausgewählte Werke in Einzelausgaben*, ed. Klaus Scholder (Stuttgart-Bad Cannstatt: Frommann, 1963), 462; also cited in Radl, *Paulus*, 44.
7 Matthias Schneckenburger, *Über den Zweck der Apostelgeschichte* (Bern: Fischer, 1841).
8 "Stephen thus forms the proper link between Paul and the primitive church; in character and fate he is the type of the Gentile apostle" (Eduard Zeller, *The Contents and Origin of the Acts of the Apostles, Critically Investigated*, 2 vols. [London: Williams & Norgate, 1875–76], 2:176).
9 Zeller, *Acts*, 2:175–76, 200–1, 227–33; see Franz Overbeck's criticism of Zeller on this point as discussed by Radl *(Paulus,* 48).
10 R. B. Rackham's commentary on Acts is a notable exception (*The Acts of the Apostles*, Westminster Commentaries, 8th ed. [London: Methuen, 1919], xlvii-xlix); see A. J. Mattill, Jr.'s survey, "The Purpose of Acts: Schneckenburger Reconsidered," in *Apostolic History and the Gospel: Biblical and Historical Essays Presented to F. F. Bruce on His 60th Birthday*, ed. W. Ward Gasque and Ralph P. Martin (Exeter: Paternoster, 1970): 113–15.

way was clear to pose again the question of Luke's *own* literary-theological intentions in the Jesus-Peter/(Stephen)/ Paul parallels.[11] In his 1961 commentary on Luke, Walter Grundmann modified Conzelmann's distinction between the *heilsgeschichtliche* epochs of Jesus and that of the church by asserting that Jesus's passion was intrinsically constitutive for the life of the church through the eschatological presence of the suffering Lord in the divinely ordained suffering of his witnesses: "*Dabei wird eine deutliche Parallelität zwischen dem Herrn und seinen Zeugen sichtbar.*"[12] Grundmann's notion was echoed or reverberated with minor modulations in succeeding years[13] until in 1975 Walter Radl drew out the fuller consequences for the *heilsgeschichtliche* approach by making the Jesus-Paul parallels a direct focus of investigation. His conclusions: in both individual detail and the overall structuring of his narrative, the author of Luke-Acts purposely parallels Paul with Jesus to demonstrate to the Gentile, post-apostolic church under duress that its life is presented precisely through the presence of Jesus in the pattern of suffering that Paul and other apostles as well as their Lord himself underwent. Consequently, the period of Jesus and that of the church, though distinguishable, form one inseparable era of the fulfillment of the "good news of the Kingdom of God."[14]

At the same time that Conzelmann's history of salvation perspective had reached a zenith of influence, its redaction-critical foundation was beginning to crack under the weight of literary-critical studies which made the narrative world of Luke-Acts, rather than Mark, the *primary* context for discerning Luke's thematic intentions in one or the other of his two volumes.[15] An important consensus pres-

---

[11] Hans Conzelmann, *Die Mitte der Zeit: Studien zur Theologie des Lukas*, BHT 17, 3rd ed. (Tübingen: Mohr Siebeck, 1960).

[12] Walter Grundmann, *Das Evangelium nach Lukas*, THKNT 3, 8th ed. (Berlin: Evangelische Verlagsanstalt, 1978), 4; see esp. 1–6.

[13] E.g., Gustav Stählin, *Die Apostelgeschichte*, NTD 5, 13th ed. (Göttingen: Vandenhoeck & Ruprecht, 1970), 4–5; cf. Radl, *Paulus*, 54–57; independently of Radl's work but in a similar direction, see Gudrun Muhlack, *Die Parallelen von Lukas-Evangelium und Apostelgeschichte*, Theologie und Wirklichkeit 8 (Bern: Lang, 1979).

[14] Radl, *Paulus*, esp. 375–95. See also Jürgen Roloff's analysis of the Lukan Paul and his discussion of Radl ("Die Paulus-Darstellung des Lukas," *EvT* 39 [1979]: 510–31); though coming to the same basic conclusion, Roloff stresses more the individuality of Paul's historical mission in determining the particular character of the Gentile church. For a more recent, very valuable, and most detailed treatment of the parallels, including narrative hermeneutical considerations, see Andrew C. Clark, *Parallel Lives: The Relation of Paul to the Apostles in the Lucan Perspective*, Paternoster Biblical and Theological Monographs (Carlisle: Paternoster Press, 2001).

[15] Already G. W. H. Lampe in 1955–56, though comparing with Mark and Matthew, emphasized the speeches in Acts as the best point of departure in determining the "peculiarly Lucan portrait

ently arising out of this methodological shift is the prominence given by Luke[16] to "prophetic" notions, whether in the structuring of his narrative around a promise (prophecy)-fulfillment scheme, or the central literary *figure* of the prophet who fulfills earlier prophecies and prophesies new fulfillments within the ongoing historical pattern. Foremost is Paul S. Minear's, *To Heal and To Reveal,* in which he has developed extensively both the prophetic consciousness that pervades Luke-Acts and the special lineage of characters that mediates this world of the invisible but "compresent reality" of God.[17] Central to Minear's findings is the specific type of prophetic model in the "prophet like Moses." Using Peter's and Stephen's explicit identification of Jesus as the prophet of Deut 18:15–18 as strategic commentaries on the whole movement of Jesus and his followers in Luke-Acts, Minear points to the critical role that the suffering of *rejection* from Israel plays in integrating so many of the distinctive Lukan emphases: for example, repentance and forgiveness; fulfillment of all the prophets; the universalism of the covenant to Abraham.[18] It thus becomes clear that, whatever particular purposes Luke has in mind for his audience(s), the *prophetic* parallels between Jesus and the *dramatis personae* of the Acts belong to the very warp and woof of his two-volume story.

More recent literary studies have confirmed independently Minear's picture and elucidated further the prophet like Moses prototype in Luke's narrative technique and overarching plot. For instance, in 1980 David L. Tiede highlighted the Deuteronomic prophetic-historical pattern of Israel's apostasy – punishment → vindication that undergirds Luke's re-interpretation of the prophetic promises of Scripture that are both fulfilled and promised in the ministry of Jesus and the church in Acts. Although Tiede does not treat the Jesus-Peter/(Stephen)/Paul parallels directly, it is manifest that the pattern of rejection of the apostolic emissaries by the Jews in Acts resonates the rejection of Jesus in the Gospel as the prophet like Moses.[19] This "concept of the suffering prophet is [...] established as the framework for telling 'the good news of Jesus.'"[20]

---

of Christ" ("The Lucan Portrait of Christ," *NTS* 2 [1955–56]: 160–75, quoting 160); see further, Radl, *Paulus,* 57–58.

16 In these authors and in the rest of our study, "Luke" is the author of Luke-Acts, irrespective of the identity of the "we" in Acts.

17 Paul S. Minear, *To Heal and to Reveal: The Prophetic Vocation according to Luke* (New York: Seabury, 1976).

18 Minear, *To Heal and to Reveal,* esp. 102–21.

19 David L. Tiede, *Prophecy and History in Luke-Acts* (Philadelphia, PA: Fortress, 1980), esp. 33–63. The Suffering Servant of Isaiah coalesces with the prophet like Moses and serves to justify the mission to the Gentiles as an apologetic for Paul (42–55). Compare nn. 43 and 66.

20 Tiede, *Prophecy and History,* 43.

The force of these prophetic features in both plot and characters is to provide an intrinsic rationale as well as an internal coherence for the Jesus-Peter/(Stephen)/Paul parallels. For it is decisive in this approach that the coherence be distinctively *christological* as over against the *heilsgeschichtliche* perspective. Whereas even in the earlier *Tendenz* critique, as in the salvation-historical, the parallel actions of the actors point away from themselves to a variety of possible mediums or agencies which *guarantee the continuity of salvation* (for example, the Holy Spirit, the "word" of God, apostolic succession, fidelity to the law, etc.), in the christological it is the actions or events of the characters themselves, sc., a messianic pattern inhering in the fabric of the narrative itself, which bind the parallels into an organic whole. Peter, Stephen, and Paul must suffer rejection like their Messiah because that is the very manner in which the fulfillment of the messianic history takes place within the promised plan of God. Therefore it is also the case that this *christological-historical* perspective vouchsafes the continuity of salvation, however the various stages or phases of salvation may be conceived or divided.

Yet in some of the expositions of the prophetic patterns thus far, a lack of precision in clarifying concepts such as "the prophet like Moses" or "deuteronomic history" has tended to mitigate the significance of the parallels and even to make certain scholars wary of the whole prophetic "cast" of Luke-Acts. In what sense, for example, can the suffering of "the prophet like Moses" be tantamount to the motif of the "suffering prophet" of intertestamental Judaism?[21] Does a *deuteronomic-prophetic* dynamic refer to the course of Israel's history as a whole, as in the interaction of human freedom with divine providence, or to only certain salvific events, et cetera?[22] Moreover, are we not in danger of forfeiting the distinctive roles of the various characters in Acts by subsuming them to the status of prophet and then subordinating the various similarities with Jesus to prophetic parallels or "patterns"?[23] How can Peter, for instance, be linked with Paul as a prophet "like Jesus" or "like Moses" when his career never issues in formal charges such as blasphemy nor elicits the kind of rage from larger masses of Israel as we find with both Stephen and Paul?

---

21 E.g., Tiede, *Prophecy and History,* 40–44, esp. 140n37.
22 Tiede, *Prophecy and History,* 30–33; Tiede, however, has done an excellent job in raising the literary issues surrounding Lukan historiography and in pointing to the rich and varied scriptural traditions that inform Luke's presentation of the "definite plan and prescience of God" (Acts 2:23).
23 This is the tendency of Luke Timothy Johnson's study (*The Literary Function of Possessions in Luke-Acts*, SBLDS 39 [Missoula, MT: Scholars, 1977]) of the prophets as "men of the Spirit" (38–121), though his pattern of the Prophet and the People is a penetrating illumination of the overall contour and dynamic of Luke's two-volume story.

The thesis of this study is that the inner dynamic of the christological-historical conception that binds the characters of both volumes as *prophets* is the specific Deuteronomistic view of Israel's history with respect to the reception of her prophets as messengers and mediators of Yahweh's salvation. In his monumental *Israel und das gewaltsame Geschick der Propheten,* Odil Hannes Steck outlined this perspective for the Palestinian Judaism of circa 200 BCE to 100 CE by amassing overwhelming evidence that *one* conceptual canopy of Israel's past and the role and fate of her prophets within that history covered all its literature.[24] He summarizes this basic orientation under four interlocking tenets:[25]

A. The history of Israel is one long, unending story of a "stiff-necked" and disobedient people;
B. God sent his messengers, the *prophets,* to mediate his will (that is the Law/Torah), to instruct and admonish them in this will, and to exhort them to repentance lest they bring upon themselves judgment and destruction;
C. Nevertheless, Israel *en masse* rejected all these prophets, even *persecuting* and *killing* them out of their stubborn "stiff-neckedness";
D. Therefore, Israel's God had "rained" destruction upon them in 722 and 587 BCE and would destroy them in a similar way if they did not hearken to his word.

This understanding encompasses the wide divergences of the multi-hued Judaism of the intertestamental and early New Testament period and is an *inner* Jewish critique of its *own* history that can vary widely in tone and application. For instance, how faithfulness to the covenant law should be expressed or which group in fact in the past may have constituted a faithful remnant, et cetera, are all operative within this unifying view.[26]

---

24 Odil Hannes Steck, *Israel und das gewaltsame Geschick der Propheten: Untersuchungen zur Ueberlieferung des deuteronomistischen Geschichtsbildes im Alten Testament, Spätjudentum und Urchristentum,* WMANT 23 (Neukirchen-Vluyn: Neukirchener Verlag, 1967). We shall not concern ourselves with the *extent* of the Deuteronomistic view in Jewish literature of Palestinian provenance; that Steck has proved his contention for a vast amount of this literature is beyond question (see e.g., John H. Elliott, review of *Israel und das gewaltsame Geschick der Propheten,* by Odil Hannes Steck, *JBL* 87 [1968]: 226–27).
25 Steck, *Geschick,* esp. 60–80; it is particularly characteristic of Hasidic apocalyptic literature that the final judgment include the large portion of Israel that has not joined their repentance movement and spare (in certain cases) Gentile nations/individuals that do repent. In any case, the final judgment is often depicted in terms of 587 BCE (Steck, *Geschick,* 123, denotes this final judgment as *Tenet F2;* to avoid needless confusion we shall refer to an eschatological use of *Tenet D).* See Steck, *Geschick,* 153–89; cf. n. 31.
26 Steck, *Geschick,* 196–222.

The author of Luke-Acts shares this orientation to Israel's past but with a major modification: the cycle of stubborn disobedience has been definitively broken by the coming of the prophet like Moses, the Anointed One, Jesus of Nazareth, whose death for the sinful nation and raising up from the dead ushers in the *final* salvation, promised by the prophets, for the eschatological remnant of Israel. In this fulfillment, Jesus as the prophet like Moses stands unique. None of the apostolic suffering or martyrdom in Acts accomplishes the decisive saving act as the suffering and death and resurrection of the Lord's Messiah.[27] Once the Acts begins, Israel is offered, a second time, through the prophet-apostles, the final redemption sealed through the prophet like Moses and appropriated through repentance for the final forgiveness/removal of sin. At the same time, refusal of this offer by Israel *as a whole* evokes the pronouncement of eschatological judgment, again promised by the prophets, that is to say, the pronouncement of *Tenet D* which is conceived as the final judgment of God upon Israel for rejecting its prophet *par excellence*, the one whom Moses himself prophesied. Therefore Peter and the other apostles, Stephen, and Paul are bound to the fate of the Prophet-Messiah like Moses. Rejection of their message of repentance is a rejection of their prophetic calling and thus of the prophet like Moses himself whose authoritative presence has sent them and propels them onward. Peter, Stephen, and Paul, then, are Deuteronomistic rejected prophets whose sending to Israel (*Tenet B*) ends in persecution and even death (*Tenet C*). It is this fundamental view of Israel's continued disobedience that is the linchpin of cohesion of the Jesus-Peter/Stephen/Paul parallels.

In Part II we shall see how Stephen's speech and tragic fate point both back to the culmination of Israel's rejection of the prophet like Moses, at the end of the Gospel and early Acts community, and forward to the career and fate of Paul. Before tracing this climax in the last section of Acts, however, we shall demonstrate in Part III that Jesus's own sending to Jerusalem as a Deuteronomistic rejected prophet in the Gospel serves as the bedrock for the landscape to follow in the Acts. At no point shall we raise the separate, though closely related and important, question of which particular situation(s) or problem(s) Luke is attempting to address with his vivid portrayal of Israel's reception of her prophets. Such issues lie beyond the scope of the present study.

---

[27] For the view that the cross has atoning significance as Jesus dies as the prophet like Moses, David P. Moessner, "Jesus and the 'Wilderness Generation': The Death of the Prophet like Moses according to Luke," in *Society of Biblical Literature 1982 Seminar Papers*, ed. Kent H. Richards (Chico, CA: Scholars, 1982): 319–40.

II Stephen's Rehearsal of the Deuteronomistic History Now Realized in the Coming of Jesus the "Just One," the Suffering Exalted "Prophet like [but greater than] Moses"

Recent literary criticism has demonstrated the pivotal juncture of Stephen's speech (Acts 7) in illuminating the overarching plot of Luke's two volumes.[28] Stephen first enters the story of Acts in the conflict arising between "Hellenists" and "Hebraists" in the young Christian community (Acts 6). But no sooner is this threat apparently relieved (6:7) than the reader is thrust into the tragic end of Stephen's ministry. Why does Luke give such "short shrift" to Stephen's career which he then concludes, oddly, with a lengthy speech, in fact, the longest speech of the Acts? The reason becomes evident when the content of his speech is read as a commentary on the state of Israel's reception of its messianic salvation. Stephen is a transition figure. His own death marks the beginning of concentrated persecution of the church by the leaders of Israel (8:1–4; 9:1–2; 11:19), even as it foreshadows the growing opposition of the *people* of Israel as a whole that will meet Paul at nearly every turn.[29] Already before this speech is recounted, Luke drops a hint of what is to come. Stephen ignites the fury of diaspora Jews resident in Jerusalem from the synagogue that includes Cyrenians and those from Asia. Luke will tell his readers before long that it was Christian converts from Cyrene dispersed from Jerusalem because of Stephen's persecution who along with men from Cyprus first preached the "Lord Jesus" to non-Israelites at Antioch (11:19–20; see also 13:1). And then somewhat later, Paul himself will be sent out from Antioch on a mission to Israel and the Gentiles in which Jews from Asia will emerge as his chief opponents (13:1–3; 14:27–28; 19:23–20:1, 16; 21:27; 24:18). Thus, opposition to Stephen results in journey missions which carry to the "end of the earth" the messianic salvation prophesied by "Moses" and "all the prophets" (3:18, 21–25; 7:37, 52; 8:28; 10:43; 13:27, 40–41; 15:15–18; 24:14; 26:22–23, 27; 28:23, 25). The plan of Acts 1:8 takes a decisive step forward.

It is in Stephen's defense before the Sanhedrin in 7:2–8:3, however, where Luke fuses the fate of Stephen's reception by Israel to the fate of Jesus in the Gospel. Wearing the mantle of the prophet,[30] Stephen sets out to defend the Jerusalem community's relationship to the God of "our fathers" by recounting Israel's past. The journey motif that pulsates throughout this rehearsal not only serves

---

28 See e.g., Earl Richard, *Acts 6:1–8:4: The Author's Method of Composition*, SBLDS 41 (Missoula, MT: Scholars, 1978), 311–59; Johnson, *Possessions*, 70–76.
29 See below, Part IV (iv).
30 See esp. Minear, *To Heal and to Reveal*, 102–11, 116–21, 133–42; Johnson, *Possessions*, 38–78.

as convenient scaffolding for the leading ideas; it is itself integral to the view of Israel's history that informs the entire presentation:

(i) Upon a revelation of God in Mesopotamia (7:2), Abraham moves to Haran after being commanded to "go out" and "come" to the "land" which God will show him (v. 3). But Haran is not the promised "land" since God "leads him to migrate" to "the land" "in which you are now living" (v. 4). From the outset, then, movement to the "land" of revealed promise is the dynamic pivot of the plot. It appears that by the end of verse 4, Stephen already anticipates the climax by pointing out to his hearers in Jerusalem that they are standing in the very land of the fulfilled promise;

(ii) But the fulfillment did not come so quickly in their journeying history, simply because Abraham himself received no inheritance in the land. Instead, God promised "possession" (v. 5) only after "his descendants" were to become "enslaved" as "strangers" in a "foreign land." Only then after some four hundred years would they "journey out" and come "to worship" "in this place" (τόπος) (v. 7b). That is to say, first another journey is necessary–and indeed a journey to the place in the promised land–before the promised inheritance could be realized;

(iii) But even before this journey, Stephen recounts the journey into slavery (vv. 9–16). First, out of scorn from his brothers, Joseph is sold into bondage in Egypt. But delivered from his afflictions, raised up within the house of Pharaoh, and elevated above all the people of Egypt by God himself, Joseph becomes an anticipation of the exodus deliverer[31] by feeding the "twelve patriarchs," Jacob and his relatives, who are "sent" or later "journey down" to escape a devastating famine. Though unrecognized by his brothers on their first visit, this Joseph who was *cast aside* by his own becomes exalted among them as their "deliverer";

(iv) Since "the time of *promise* was drawing near" (v. 17), this glorious period was not to last for long. Moses, himself one of the brethren of Israel (v. 20) but raised in the house of Pharaoh (v. 21), also goes unrecognized by his own when he visits and "delivers" (v. 25) one of them from the oppression of the Egyptians. On his return to reconcile a feud among his brethren he is spurned and *"cast aside"* (v. 27). Thus he must flee to Midian, an alien in his own "house," as well as a sojourner in a foreign land (vv. 29-34). It is only then that Moses, in the desert of Mount Sinai, trembles in fear at the *voice* of the Lord (φωνὴ κυρίου) in the midst of burning fire and receives a calling to be *sent* (ἀποστέλλω) on a *journey*

---

31 Like Moses, Jesus, and Stephen, Joseph is σοφία, v. 10 (Luke 2:40, 52; Acts 6:3, 10; 7:22; cf. Luke 21:15); like Jesus and Stephen he has χάρις, v. 10, before God and the people (Luke 2:40, 52; Acts 6:8; 7:46; cf. 2:47).

to his people to deliver them from Egypt. So it is as the days of the long-awaited promise to Abraham and the patriarchs are beginning to be completely full that the exodus journey begins (vv. 35–45). But although already repudiated by his people, Moses becomes their "ruler" and *"deliverer"* to *"lead* them out" with "wonders and signs in Egypt, the Red Sea, and in the desert for forty years" (vv. 35–36). It is there on the journey that he prophesies of one whom "God will raise up from your brethren *like me*" (v. 37–Deut 18:15) and receives "living words" "in the desert" "upon the mountain." Yet–despite all of this–he is scorned and *"cast aside"* a second time by his brethren, "our fathers," who "turned in their hearts back to Egypt" (v. 39). This epoch-making rejection is epitomized by the calf to which they sacrificed and "were rejoicing" in the "works of their hands" (v. 41). Thus a perverted rejoicing in the wilderness *at the mountain* forms the quintessence of a froward people whom God not only gave over to idolatrous worship but also to the foreign land of *Babylon* (that is *Tenet D*) "just as it is written in the book of the *prophets*" (vv. 42–43). Consequently, before the promise is fully realized, the pronouncement of the judgment of *Tenet D*[32] falls over the exodus journey "to the *place*" in the land;

---

32 Tenet D often refers to the actual punishment in the past of the Northern kingdom (722 BCE) and/or Babylonian exile and destruction of Jerusalem in 587 BCE (see Steck, *Geschick*, 63n8) In certain strands of later Deuteronomistic thinking, however, the pronouncement of impending judgment became an integral part of the prophetic calling (Steck, *Geschick*, 123n5, 140, 193–95, 218–22). Tenet D is found *inter alia* in Hebrew OT: Deut 28:45a, 46, 48–57, 59–62a, 63b–68 (cf. vv. 45b, 47, 62b); 2Kgs 17:18,20 (cf. vv. 7–17,19); 2Chr 24:23–24 (cf. vv. 18–22); 36:16b–21 (cf. vv. 12–16a); Ezra 9:7b, 9a, 13, 14b (cf. vv.7a, 10b–11,15b); Neh 1:8b (cf. vv. 7–8a); 9:27a, 30b, 32, 36–37 (cf. vv.13–14, 16–17a, 18, 26, 28a, 29–30a, 33b–35); Jer 7:32–34 (cf. vv. 25–28); 25:8–14 (cf. vv. 3–7); 26:6 (cf. vv. 2–5); 29:17–18, 30b (cf. vv. 19–20a); 35:17 (cf. vv. 13–15); 44:2, 6, 11–15 (cf. vv. 3–5, 7–10); Zech 1:2 (cf. vv. 3–4, 6); 7:12c–14 (cf. vv. 11–12b); Dan 9:7b, 11b–14a, 16, 17b–18a (cf. vv. 5–6, 8, 9b–11a, 14b, 15b), Pss 79:1–5, 7 (cf. v. 8a); 106:40–42 (cf. vv. 6–7, 13–14, 16, 19–21a, 24–25, 28–29a, 32–39); *Deutero-canonical* and *Pseudepigrapha*: (see immediate contexts for Tenets A–C): Tob 3:4b; Bar 1:20; 2:1–5a, 6–7, 9, 13–14, 20–26, 29–30; 3:4b, 7a, 8; Pr Azar 4, 5, 8–10, 14, 15; T. Levi 10:4; 15:1–3; 16:4–5a; T. Jud. 23:3–4; T. Iss. 6:2; T. Zeb. 9:6; T. Dan 5:8; T. Naph. 4:2, 5; T. Ash. 7:2, 6; *1 En.* 89:56, 66; 90:25–26; 91:12,14–15; *Jub.* 1:13; *Pss. Sol.* 8:28; 9:1a, c, 2a; 17:20; *As. Mos.* 3:1–6; 8; *Bib. Ant.* 12:4; 13:10; 19:7; *4 Ezra* 3:27; 14:32–33; *2 Bar.* 1:4–5; 4:1; 31:5; 44:5–6, 12b, 15b, 46–46b; 77:4b; Qumran: 4QDibHam 2:11; 3:6–14a; 5:3b–6a,16b–18a; 6:7–8, 11–13; 1QS 1:26; CD 1:3b–4a, 12–13a, *NT and early Patristic*: Matt 22:7; 23:29–31; Mark 12:9; 1Thess 2:16; *Barn.* 5:11; Justin, *Dial.* 16:4; Josephus, *Ant.* 9.13.2 § 266; 9.14.1 § 281; Rabbis: *Pesiq. R.* 138a; 146a.

As is clear from these examples, the language of *Tenet D* is as varied as the literary contexts and backgrounds in which it is expressed. Although many images are stereotyped (e.g., "desolate/deserted land," [Jer 7:34b; 25:11; 44:2, 6; Zech 7:14; 2Chr 36:21b; T. Jud. 23:3; T. Ash. 7:2, etc.] or "scattered/dispersed," [Zech 7:14a; Tob 3:4b; Bar 2:4b, 13, 29; 3:8, T. Levi 10:4; 16:5; T. Jud. 23:3; *Jub.* 1:13, etc.]), *Tenet D* defies strict form-critical delimitations–to be sure, incorporating

(v) The journey, however, continues, led by "the tent of witness" which was with "our fathers in the desert" as it was built by Moses (v. 44). This tabernacle formed the focal point for "our fathers" when God thrust out the nations during the time of Joshua and up to the days of David who "found favor before God." Though David wanted to "find" a "dwelling place" for the God of the house of Jacob, it was his son Solomon who built him a "house" (vv. 45–47). But there is no doubt that this building of the Temple did *not fulfill* the promise to Abraham that his posterity (that is, "house") would "journey" "to this place" to "worship" God (vv. 7 → 17). For Stephen immediately qualifies the importance of the Temple by reminding his hearers that God does not dwell in such "hand" or "man-made" structures "just as the prophet [Isa 66:1] declares: 'Heaven is my throne [...]. What is the *place* (τόπος) of my dwelling? Did not *my* hand make all these things?'" (vv. 48–50);[33]

(vi) The journeying history for the "house of Jacob" was not over; the *coming* of the Righteous One was still to come. But now instead of relating the events of this period, Stephen abruptly changes his tack altogether by lashing into his audience with a most "scandalous" accusation: "You stiff-necked folk (σκληροτράχηλοι), uncircumcised in your hearts and ears! As your fathers did so you yourselves continue to do–you always resist the Holy Spirit" (v. 51). Here the classic indictment of *Tenet A* could not be more forcefully expressed.[34] Stephen's hearers are no different than their stubborn ancestors who continually resisted the redemptive gestures of God.[35] Though mention of the "Holy Spirit" contemporizes the Christian community's understanding of the messianic fulfillment, it is clear that the crowd's resistance continues the *same* unceasing obstinacy that Israel has always shown to the messengers of God's redemptive pleading:[36]

---

various judgment oracles as the prophetic "woe" (*Wehespruch*) (Steck, *Geschick*, 51–53, 63n8), etc.–and thus exhibits less stereotypical formulation as a *whole*. What is crucial in identifying Tenet D is its logical sequence within the dynamic *complex* of the Deuteronomistic view, that is within *Tenets A–C*, which must clearly pervade the literary context. This methodological procedure will be followed for our entire study. **See also n. 25.**

33 Compare Nils A. Dahl, "The Story of Abraham in Luke-Acts," in *Studies in Luke-Acts: Essays Presented in Honor of Paul Schubert*, ed. Leander E. Keck and J. Louis Martyn (Nashville, TN: Abingdon, 1966): 142–48. Dahl comes to a similar interpretation of the Temple polemic within the speech.

34 See e. g., Neh 9:16–17a, 29; 2Kgs 18:14; Jer 7:24, 26; Bar 2:30,33; *Jub.* 1:7,20, etc.

35 E.g., Bar 1:19: "From the day when the Lord brought our fathers out of the land of Egypt until today, we have been disobedient to the Lord our God, and we have been negligent in not heeding his voice."

36 For this obstinate resistance against the *Spirit* of God who spoke the law and warned Israel *through the prophets,* see Neh 9:30; cf. v. 20; Zech 7:12b; 1QS 8:15–16.

"Which *of the prophets* did not your fathers persecute? Indeed, they killed these who proclaimed beforehand the coming of the Righteous One, the one whom you yourselves have now betrayed and murdered" (v. 52). Hence with *Tenet B* implicit, Stephen moves directly from *Tenet A* to *Tenet C*, that is to Israel's persecuting and killing of all the prophets that has now climaxed in the killing of the Righteous One, *the prophet like Moses!*[37] But right at the point when the audience might expect the solemn tones of *Tenet D* to fall once again[38]–but now upon them– the narrative takes yet another surprising turn. Suddenly Stephen is gazing "into heaven" at the "glory (δόξα) of God," seeing "Jesus standing at the right hand of God" and declaring to his audience the majesty of his beatific vision. As these "blasphemous" words enter into ears that are still smoldering from the outrageous assertions of his speech, the crowd's hostility can no longer be contained as they drag Stephen outside the city and stone him.

Before we enumerate the parallels between Stephen's dying moments and Jesus's passion that Luke takes pains to draw, we must take stock of the orientation to Israel's history and sketch the characters that now color Luke's presentation:

Moses. Stephen's speech is dominated by Moses and the *exodus*, for example, verses 17–45 of verses 2–50 or approximately 60 percent of the speech: 1. Moses's calling to lead the people on a journey of redemption issues from the voice of God in brilliant light; 2. This journey sending is to be the fulfillment of the "God of glory's" promise to Abraham that this posterity would worship God in the place (v. 7 → 17), that is, in Jerusalem where the tent of witness had been laid to rest and the Temple built (vv. 44–47);[39] 3. Yet the exodus did *not* fulfill the promise simply because the entire journey was fraught with the perverted repudiation of God's chosen deliverer and mediator of living words and ended with an idolatrous use of the "house" or Temple. What is more, Israel's history from that time forward continued the calloused rejection (*Tenet A*) of the voice of God through his messengers (*Tenet B*) by killing the prophets (*Tenet C*). Thus, God "delivered" them over to Babylon (*Tenet D*). Especially illuminating is the role of the calf in this reconstruction of the past: its idol-

---

[37] For the move from *Tenet A* to *C* with *B* as the historical background, see the immediate contexts of the passages cited in n. 33, esp. Neh 9:26–30 and *Jub.* 1:7–12; cf. Zech 7:8–14.
[38] See n. 31 *fin.*
[39] For the importance of the "central place" in Deuteronomic thinking, see e.g., Ernest W. Nicholson, *Deuteronomy and Tradition* (Oxford: Blackwell, 1967), 53–57; for the Deuteronomistic history, e.g., Frank Moore Cross, *Canaanite Myth and Hebrew Epic* (Cambridge, MA: Harvard University Press, 1973), 278–85.

atry sets the precedent for Israel's entire history of stiff-necked resistance.[40] Therefore, *Tenet D* follows immediately after this seminal perversion of the true worship of God (compare v. 7), though the Babylonian exile be hundreds of years removed[41] (vv. 39–43). Another journey of redemption by the Righteous One must come.

Jesus. Even though there is no direct depiction of Jesus's coming, the whole of Israel's journeying history culminates with him: *1*. No description of a divine authorization of his calling is presented; *2*. Jesus's coming is the consummation of the calling of Moses to lead Israel on the exodus journey to the place in the land of promise for the true worship of God. Already on the exodus, Moses himself prophesied his "raising up" to be a "prophet [...] like me;" *3*. With the spurning of Moses coupled to the tragic fate of the prophets, it is certain that the reception of Moses's "living oracles" of the law, which in Deut 18:15 promises a "prophet like me," is anticipated in the persecution and killing of the prophets before it is fulfilled in Jesus's coming as the Righteous One who is "murdered" by a stiff-necked folk who continually failed *"to keep the law"* (v. 53). That is to say, Jesus is like the prophets quintessentially as the *prophet like Moses*. He brings Israel's journeying history of unrelenting disobedience to God's messengers to its fulfillment.

Stephen. Stephen's speech and vision link him inseparably to Moses and the prophet like Moses: *1*. His recital of Israel's history of disobedience is confirmed by the vision of the "God of glory" whose glory first appeared to Abraham with the promise and now encompasses Stephen's ministry and leads it into the journeying salvation to the "end of the earth;" *2*. Stephen's charge denies the fulfillment of the exodus salvation to *worship God* in Israel's central place in Jerusalem, including his present audience in that "place." They always resist the Holy Spirit and did so by rejecting the coming of Jesus, the Righteous One. By implication it is the Christian community that participates in this fulfillment; *3*. His accusation of a monolithic repudiation and even killing of the prophets and the prophet like Moses is matched by the rage of his audience that kills him as well. Accordingly,

---

40 As for instance in Deuteronomy; see David P. Moessner, "Luke 9:1–50: Luke's Preview of the Journey of the Prophet like Moses of Deuteronomy," *JBL* 102 (1983): 582–87. See above Chapter Eight. See also n. 41.

41 A similar telescoping of Israel's history is found in *Jub.* 1 in which the Deuteronomistic view of Israel's disobedience is programmatic: *A* 1:7–11; *B* 1:12a; *C* 1:12b; *D* 1:13. *Tenet D* follows immediately upon a summary description of the monarchy as one *unending period of idolatry* (vv. 10–12) that continues the idolatry *from Mount Sinai* (vv. 3–9, cf. vv. 21–22). Emphasis on the defilement of the central place in Jerusalem is also pronounced (vv. 10, 27–29).

his vision of Jesus the Son of Man[42] with the glory of God draws him directly into Jesus's fate of rejection as the prophet like Moses.

As Luke concludes his description of Stephen, his legacy in the line of Jesus as the prophet like Moses and of all the rejected prophets is sealed. In his dying breath Stephen utters the words of Jesus on the cross (Acts 7:59–Luke 23:46) but now directly to the "Lord Jesus" himself. Moreover, his echo of Jesus's prayer on the cross for forgiveness (Acts 7:60–Luke 23:34) now takes on the added dimension that the same leaders (Sanhedrin) of Israel are continuing their rejection of Jesus by stoning Stephen. When we join to this continuity the oft-cited parallels between the charges against Jesus and Stephen, the portrait of Stephen as a type of the Deuteronomistic rejected prophets and antitype of the prophet like Jesus (Moses) is poignant indeed: "We have heard him [Stephen] speak blasphemous words against Moses and God [...]" for "this man never ceases to speak words against this holy *place* and the law, for we have heard him say that this Jesus the Nazorean will destroy this *place* and will change the customs which *Moses* delivered to us" (6:11, 13–14). The Temple, the central place of all Israel, has become the center of the contested claims to the true vision of Moses and the worship of the God of glory. For it was Jesus's blasphemous words before the Sanhedrin that "from now on the Son of Man shall be seated at the right hand of the power of God" (Luke 23:9) which sparked the final surge of hostility that ended on the cross. Meanwhile, "Saul was consenting to Stephen's death" (Acts 8:1a).

III Jesus "the Prophet like [but greater than] Moses"

Do the accents of Stephen's stance towards Israel's past resonate with Luke's account of Jesus in the Gospel, or does Stephen stand out as a "singular saint"? Our scope does not permit a rehearsal of the correspondences between the callings of Jesus and of Moses in Deuteronomy that the author has discussed elsewhere.[43] But we can summarize several of the characteristic contours of the Gospel landscape.

---

42 Of the twenty-five previous uses of this phrase in Luke's first volume, fourteen instances are linked *directly* to the "shame," rejection, or suffering/death of this figure.
43 Moessner, "Prophet Like Moses," 583–600 (Chapter Eight above); a comprehensive study of the entire Lukan journey by the author appears as David P. Moessner, *Lord of the Banquet: The Literary and Theological Significance of the Lukan Travel Narrative* (Minneapolis, MN: Fortress Press, 1989 [repr., Harrisburg, PA: Trinity Press International, 1998, with Foreword by Richard B. Hays]).

The Transfiguration

1. Only Luke speaks of Moses, Elijah, and Jesus appearing together "in glory" and the three disciples beholding "his glory" (τὴν δόξαν αὐτοῦ, 9:32). As "all Israel" previously had witnessed this divine "glory" on the mountain (Deut 5:24), so Peter, John, and James, representing the twelve disciples and thus the twelve tribes of Israel are privy to the divine glory now concentrated in Jesus. But before Peter can begin to accommodate the divine glory engulfing Jesus and Moses and Elijah, the latter two disappear and a cloud descends into the brilliant light (vv. 33–34). Again only Luke by following the word order of the LXX emphasizes that the voice from the fiery cloud reverberates the divine command concerning the *prophet like Moses* spoken by the Lord himself to Moses *at Mount Horeb* and repeated by Moses at the borders of the land of promise on the exodus journey (Deut 18:15–20): "hearken to him" (αὐτοῦ ἀκούετε, 18:15b–Luke 9:33b).[44] The glory of the mountain calling of Moses to mediate the life-giving voice to the people on the exodus[45] has been transferred to Jesus as the prophet like Moses. For he it is who utters "living oracles" (compare Acts 7:38b) to Israel and now with "the voice" is "found *alone*" (9:36a).

2. Jesus's calling to be the prophet like Moses is grounded and clarified only in Luke as an "*exodus*" *journey to Jerusalem* predicted already by Moses and Elijah (9:31). When verse 31 is linked back with Jesus's own prediction nearly a week earlier that he as the Son of Man must be rejected and killed by the "elders, chief priests, and scribes" (9:22, 28) and connected forward to verse 51 where "the days of his *taking* up," a euphemism for his death (and exaltation),[46] are already beginning to *be fulfilled*, then it is evident that the "exodus" that Jesus fulfills *in* Jerusalem is one that he fulfills also on his way *to* Jerusalem, that is, on a journey to the center of the nation.[47] Moses and Elijah, the two great prophets of the exodus,[48] are thus pointing ahead to a journey that culminates with the prophet

---

[44] In both the MT and LXX of Deut 18:15–22, it is clear that vv. 16b–20 are a retrospect on the events at Horeb in 5:23–31.

[45] See Moessner, "Prophet Like Moses," 583, 587, 589.

[46] See Joseph A. Fitzmyer, *The Gospel according to Luke I–IX*, AB 28 (Garden City, NY: Doubleday, 1981), 828, for linguistic discussion.

[47] For the connection between 9:31 and v. 51, see J. H. Davies, "The Purpose of the Central Section of Luke's Gospel," *SE II* (= TU 87; Berlin: Akademie, 1964): 164–69, and Paul Schubert, "The Structure and Significance of Luke 24," in *Neutestamentliche Studien für Rudolf Bultmann*, ed. Walther Eltester, BZNW 21 (Berlin: Töpelmann, 1954): 184–85.

[48] See e.g., 1Kgs 19:4–18; Sir 48:7–8; cf. *1 En.* 89:51–52. The Jewish Torah reading of Exod 32:11–33 (golden calf and Moses pleading for the people) is followed by the *haphtorah* reading of Elijah's

like Moses reaching Israel's leaders in the central place of the whole people, that is, the Temple precincts. But as the heavenly voice also declares, Jesus the prophet like Moses accomplishes this uniquely as God's "Chosen Son" (9:35b).[49]

3. Again it is distinctive to Luke's narrative that precisely at the point in which the exodus fulfillment is being discussed, the representatives of the twelve tribes of Israel are "asleep!" (v. 32a). This detail may appear inconsequential at best until it is also noticed that: (i) Luke is interested, too, in the fact that they "wake up" (v. 32); (ii) Upon waking up the disciples' observance of the divine glory leads to a response totally inappropriate to that disclosure–"not knowing what he [Peter] was saying" (v. 33b), leading to (iii) the fear the disciples bear when the cloud overshadows them and the voice commands them to hearken to Jesus (vv. 34b–35). The disciples have missed the divine voice in Moses, Elijah, and Jesus. "Hearken to him" consequently becomes the mandate of the coming journey. Like Moses and Elijah, Jesus is sent to Israel with the voice of God (*Tenet B*). But thus far, reluctance and incomprehension and fear mark Israel's reception.

Luke grafts the behavior of the disciples among the crowds below on the plain to the texture of the disciples' behavior on the mountain in a way that confirms and elucidates further the peculiar features of the transfiguration narrative. After descending and learning that his disciples were incapable of casting out a demon, Jesus immediately denounces the *whole* generation as "faithless and crooked" (v. 41) and decries a prophetic calling which must continue to bear up and bear with such an obstinate folk. Indeed Jesus echoes Moses's cry of lament at the base of Mount Horeb: "How long am I to be with you and bear you" (Luke 9:41–Deut 1:12). And unlike Matthew and Mark, it is the disciples themselves who provoke Jesus's reaction and become patent examples of a froward generation. For in uninterrupted sequence and "crowded" setting, Jesus tells the disciples that the "Son of Man will be delivered into the hands of men" (v. 44b).[50] Not only

---

challenge on Mount Carmel to the worshipers of Baal (1Kgs 18:1–39)! For "Elijah's cup" at Jewish Passover celebrations and the use of Mal 4:5–6 (MT 3:23–24) at the Great Sabbath before the Passover feast, see Aharon Wiener, *The Prophet Elijah in the Development of Judaism: A Depth-Psychological Study* (London: Routledge and Kegan Paul, 1978), 133–35.

49 Resonance with the "voice from heaven" in Jesus's baptism (Luke 3:22, "my beloved/chosen Son") is clear and confirms Jesus's calling on that occasion, esp. for the *disciples*. See e.g., I. Howard Marshall, *The Gospel of Luke*, NIGTC (Exeter: Paternoster, 1978), 388 ("elect one" connects both 9:35 and 3:22 through the Servant's calling to suffer, Isa 42:1); Fitzmyer, *Luke*, 793, 802–3. See also n. 65.

50 Verses 23–25 along with probable paronomasia on ὁ υἱὸς τοῦ ἀνθρώπου ὁ υἱός του ἀνθρωπου with χείρας ἀνθρώπων (see Joachim Jeremias, "παῖς θεοῦ in Later Judaism in the Period after the LXX," *TDNT* 5 [1967]: 715) indicate a generic sense of "man," or the generation of Jesus's day. In

is the Sanhedrin going to "kill" Jesus (v. 22), so is "this generation" that is deaf to the voice of God in their midst: "for they [the disciples] were not comprehending this word and it was concealed from them that they should not perceive it, and they were afraid to ask him about this word" (9:45). Reluctance, incomprehension, and fear again emerge as the salient signs of "this generation." But Luke does not end here. The disciples now begin to argue which of them is the "greatest" (vv. 46–48; compare Deut 1:12 at Mount Horeb!). Jesus sets a child at his side to illustrate the *proper* response to the *authority* of his *sending* (ἀποστέλλω, v. 48). The disciples betray their imperviousness to the voice of God in Jesus yet again as they pride themselves in their "privileged" position, which had prevented one who did successfully exorcise demons "in Jesus's name" (ἐν τῷ ὀνόματί σου, v. 49; contrast vv. 48, 40b). Like their Horeb counterparts in their perverted twisting of the voice of God in the molten calf, so the disciples' glimpse of the divine glory on the mountain reveals their own self-glory on the plain.[51] They are *one* with the "men" of "this generation" as a faithless and stiff-necked lot![52]

Before moving to Luke's "journey section," we can capsulize what has already become strikingly apparent: Stephen's portrayal in the Deuteronomistic tones of the stubborn rejection of the prophets Moses and Jesus has already been anticipated in the Transfiguration: *1.* Like Moses Jesus receives a calling to a journey sending from the *voice* of the Lord in brilliant *light*. But now Jesus is to *fulfill* Moses's sending with "living oracles" as the "prophet like me"; *2.* Jesus's journey is an exodus to the Temple in Jerusalem to consummate Moses's exodus to the central place of all Israel for the true worship of God; *3.* From the very outset the entire journey is characterized as one of suffering the stubborn rejection of the people *as a whole.*

– *Tenet B* stands behind the prophetic conception of a sending as mediators of the redemptive voice of God, number *1* while it is equally clear that *Tenets A* and *C* inform the reception of the prophet, number *3*. Only number *2* stands alone as the callings of Moses and Jesus, the prophet like Moses, on the exodus to the nation's center.

17:25 it is expressly stated that "this generation" rejects "the Son of Man" and thus is responsible for Jesus's suffering.
51 That John (v. 49) leads the disciples' response ties the disciples' behavior here even more tightly to the three disciples on the mountain.
52 For the incomprehension, fear, strife, and imperviousness to discipline as characterizing "all Israel's" response to Moses in Deuteronomy, see Moessner, "Prophet Like Moses," 583–87, cf. 588–95.

The Journey (9:51–19:44)

i) Not only does Luke launch his journey narrative with a resounding rejection of Jesus that recalls the repudiation of Elijah by a Samaritan,[53] but he also ties his sonorous announcement in 9:51 to a string of journey notices which will remind the reader that Jesus's exodus *as* the voice of God from the mountain to Jerusalem is indeed moving forward.[54] More than this, Luke will tell his readers that as Jesus progresses through the "towns and villages of Israel, teaching in their streets" (13:22), the crowds continue to swell around him until these "myriads" become a "multitude of crowds" (11:29 → 12:1 → 14:25). As the prophet like Moses, Jesus gathers all Israel on their exodus to Jerusalem.[55]

ii) Within this dynamic framework at the midpoint, two quarter-points, and at the end of the journey Luke marks in the chilling cadences of the Deuteronomistic prophetic fate the reception accorded Jesus the prophet like Moses:

a) *11:47–51* At the end of a large crowd tableau (11:14–36) in which Jesus levels the four different responses of "marveling" amazement (v. 14b), charge of alignment with Beelzebul (v. 15), "testy" skepticism (v. 16), and naive admiration (vv. 27–28) *to one mass* of an "evil generation" (v. 29), he turns to the Pharisees at table who emerge from the crowd (v. 37) as its leaders (vv. 43–44, 46, 52; 12:1b). Their scholars in the *law* "are witnesses and consent *to the deeds of your fathers*" (*Tenet A*) by "building the tombs of the prophets whom your fathers killed" (*Tenet C*) (vv. 47–48). Indeed, the Wisdom of God had *sent* prophets and apostle-messengers (προφήτας καὶ ἀποστόλους, v. 49) to Israel (*Tenet B*), who had been killed and persecuted in order that "this generation" would now be spattered with "the blood of *all* the prophets shed from the foundation of the world [...] from the blood of Abel to the blood of Zechariah who perished between the altar and the sanctuary [*Tenets C & D*]. Yes, I tell you, it shall be required of this generation (*Tenet D*)"[56] (vv. 50–51). The history of Israel has been one unending stiff-necked rejection of its prophets, reaching from its patriarchal roots all the way to the very heart of the nation in the sanctuary of its Temple! And now as 11:52–12:1 divulge, Jesus the prophet greater than Jonah and wiser than Solomon (11:29–32) has *entered* into this destiny to bring Israel's history for *this generation* to its climax.

---

53 2Kgs 1:2–16; cf. Luke 9:54 (James and John!); cf. also 1Kgs 19:19–21 and Luke 9:61–62.
54 Luke 9:53; 10:38; 13:22, 33; 14:25; 17:11; 18:31; 19:11, 28, 41.
55 See e.g., Luke 9:23, 59–62; 10:1–16; 11:23; 12:32–34; 13:31–35; 14:15–15:32; 18:18–19:40.
56 For blood vengeance "required," cf. Gen 9:5; 42:22; 2Sam 4:11; Ps 9:12(13); for avenging the "blood" of the prophet(s), see 2Kgs 9:7; 2Chr 24:20–22, 25; cf. Ezek 33:6, 8. On the formulation of *Tenet D*, see nn. 24, 31; cf. Deut 18:19. For Luke 11:50–51 as a prophetic *Drohwort*, see Steck, *Geschick*, 52.

b) *13:33–35* Strange as it may seem on the surface, Luke has Jesus pronounce a judgment oracle[57] upon Jerusalem and its Temple long before Jesus ever reaches the nation's center (13:34–35; compare 17:11). But now in light of the prophetic penetration of Israel's stubborn stance already voiced by Jesus in the journey sending, the position of this prophecy of doom is understandable. For Luke has just presented Jesus in the burgeoning crowds (12:1–13:9), in their synagogues (13:10–21), and in their streets (13:22–30) teaching, admonishing, and warning the people of Israel about the "leaven of the Pharisees" which "eats and drinks in the presence"[58] of Jesus and entertains the *signs* of the present time[59] but refuses to repent before the voice of God in their midst: "I tell you, unless you repent you will *all* likewise perish" (13:3, 5). By the time Luke has reached the midpoint of the journey narrative, the crowds of "this generation" have already been fully identified with their leaders as "hypocrites" (11:37–12:1 → 12:56). It is no wonder, then, when Pharisees again emerge from "the crowds" in 13:31 to "engage" Jesus, he responds with the classic Deuteronomistic castigation of a disobedient people and yet simultaneously with the pathos of the prophet like Moses whose efforts to gather the people have gone unrequited: "Jerusalem, Jerusalem, You killer of prophets and stoner of those [*Tenet C*] who are sent (τοὺς ἀπεσταλμένους) to you [*Tenet B*]. How often I have wished to gather your children as a hen gathers her brood under her wings but you have not so wished! Look, your house is forsaken [*Tenet D*]." As in 11:47–12:1 it is clear that Jesus's special prophetic sending to Jerusalem fully recapitulates the tragic fate of all of Israel's prophets, "for it cannot be that a prophet should perish away from Jerusalem" (13:33b). But now it is even clearer that as Jesus goes toward Jerusalem, the whole nation's destiny goes with him.

c) *17:25–30* Farther along the journey (compare 14:25), Pharisees and their scribes once again (15:1–2) demonstrate that "this generation" remains deaf to the special mouthpiece of God in their midst. When a heated exchange ensues (16:14–18), Jesus counters with a parable (vv. 19–31) mirroring Israel's monolithic callousness and the categorical warning, "If they do not hearken to *Moses and the prophets*, neither will they be convinced if some one should rise up from the dead" (*Tenet C*) (v. 31). Tenets *A* and *B* lie behind this articulation of Israel's past here, while it is also the case that Jesus's prophetic commission is tied to that

---

57 With 13:35a cf. Dan 9:17b; Bar 2:26; esp. *T. Levi* 15:1; *Pesiq. Rab.* 138a; 146a; for a similar judgment oracle on the "house" as the palace and "lineage" of the king, cf. Jer 12:7; 22:5. In *1 En.* 89:56 and *2 Bar.* 8:2; 64:6, "God" is described as actively leaving the Temple; see also nn. 24, 31.
58 Luke 13:26.
59 Luke 12:54–56.

refusal of all the prophets and yet stands unique as an eschatological sending. Subsequently, Jesus's encounter with the solid front of unresponsive lepers of the Jewish nation (17:11–19) sets the stage for Jesus meeting yet once more with Pharisees whose blindness to the "sign" of God's effective rule standing in their midst (17:20–21) has become patent for the whole nation. For Jesus immediately warns the disciples against falling prey to "this generation's" demand for proofs of God's redemption to Israel (ἰδοὺ ὧδε, 17:23 → 21 → 11:30,32). "This generation" will, in fact, inflict suffering and rejection (17:25) (*Tenet C*) upon Jesus, the Son of Man, and then continue on unchanged *like the generations of Noah and Lot* (*Tenet A*) to "eat and drink," "buy and sell," totally hardened by the redemptive pleadings of the past (*Tenet B*), and oblivious to the future day of the Son of Man.

d) *19:41–44* As Jesus's entourage nears Jerusalem (compare 18:31–34; 19:11), the large band of disciples fulfills Jesus's prophecy in 13:35b by heralding him as the "king, the one who comes in the name of the Lord" (19:38). Aglow with the "mighty works" they had *"seen"* (v. 37b), they are joined by the many of the crowds who are electric with expectation that Jesus's approach to Jerusalem signals the immediate *"appearance"* of the Kingdom of God (19:11). But given the dynamic of the reception of the prophet on the journey, that Jesus–precisely in the midst of this messianic fervor–both weeps over Jerusalem and prophesies her destruction in the dirge[60] of *Tenet D* seems only fitting: "not one stone upon another will they leave in you" (19:44a); for Jesus knows full well that the time is coming quickly when the disciples will no longer cry out praise but link hands with the multitudes and leaders of Israel who cry out for his death. His final interaction on the journey with the leaders of "this generation," the Pharisees, provides a poignant conclusion: "When the disciples become silent, then [as in Hab 2:11] the toppling stones of ruin will shriek out against the perpetrated evil" (19:40 → 44).[61] Thus Luke ends his journey as it began: Jesus laments a wilderness generation closed to the "living words" that would have made for peace with God (v. 42a → v. 38b). Because it is a "faithless and twisted generation" that "has not known the time of your *visitation*," the *Exodus visitation* (LXX Gen 50:24–25; Exod 3:16) of God must now become his visitation for destruction (for example, Jer 6:15; Isa 29:6).

To sum up ii), Luke's special journey section reveals in both contour and content, dynamics and depiction, a view of Israel's reception of Jesus from the mountain of revelation to the central place that is thoroughly and distinctly Deu-

---

60 Cf. Jer 6:6–21; Isa 29:1–4.
61 See Adolf Schlatter, *Das Evangelium des Lukas: Aus seinen Quellen erklärt* (Stuttgart: Calwer, 1931), 409–10; for the grammatical construction, see BDF §§ 363, 373.

teronomistic. For as Jesus, the Anointed and Chosen Son, is received like all the prophets before him, he brings this persistent history of disobedience to its consummation uniquely as the *prophet like Moses*.

iii) The Temple in Jerusalem is both the focus and the vortex of Jesus's journeying from the mountain in Galilee. Jesus himself determines resolutely (9:51) to consummate (τελειοῦμαι, 13:32b) his prophetic calling to gather Israel and crown their exodus deliverance by journeying to the center of their worship of God. Only at the central place can Israel's destiny be won. But he is also drawn there irresistibly, as if by a mighty whirlwind of intractable disobedience that also must fulminate in Israel's fate at the central place (13:33). In each of the *three* programmatic pronouncements of *Tenet D* on the journey (11:47–51; 13:31–35; 19:41–44), the Temple (οἶκος) becomes the epitome of opposition. In 11:50–51 the long history of the blood of all the prophets has flowed to its penultimate climax "between the altar and the sanctuary!" In 13:35a Israel's "house" is described as "forsaken" in the imagery of the departure of the presence of God from the Temple that will take place in the destruction of Jerusalem![62] And finally in 19:41–44, with the journey coming to a close, Jesus pronounces a final judgment that sums up the whole course of the journey. Although the Temple is not singled out in verses 41–44, Jesus immediately enters the Temple in verse 45, declaring that *"my house* will be a house of prayer, but you have made it a lair of robbers." That is to say, Jesus's journey to Jerusalem culminates in the Temple to lay claim to the *true worship of God*. But it is precisely here, in the atmosphere of the "plundering" of the worship, that the opposition which leads irreversibly to Jesus's death sets in without delay. At once Luke, in an overview (19:47–48) and several episodes (20:1–21:4), describes the authority of the teacher of Israel which provokes a coalition of the people's leaders to seek his death. And Luke will conclude this Jerusalem section with Jesus in the Temple prophesying the destruction and exile of the nation–in strokes reminiscent of 587 BCE[63]–while pointing to the Temple as the omega point of this destruction: "Not one stone upon another shall be left" (21:6 → 19:44 → 19:40). Both the fate of the prophet like Moses and the nation are sealed in Jesus's journey to the Temple.

---

[62] See nn. 56, 31.
[63] See C. H. Dodd, "The Fall of Jerusalem and the 'Abomination of Desolation,'" *JRS* 37 (1947): 47–54; independently, Bo Reicke, "Synoptic Prophecies of the Destruction of Jerusalem," in *Studies in New Testament and Early Christian Literature: Essays in Honor of Allen P. Wikgren*, ed. David E. Aune (Leiden: Brill, 1972): 121–34.

Peter and the Death of Jesus in the Early Acts Community

What again must seem singularly strange is the sudden twist Luke's story takes in chapter 22. It is Judas, one of "the twelve" (22:3), who makes the decisive move to "deliver" Jesus over to the scribes and chief priests–those just portrayed as the plotters of Jesus's demise. But what Jesus at the base of the mountain had pro-leptically perceived about a "crooked generation" and prophetically predicted about "the hands of men" (9:44) has come to pass. Even more ironic is the role Peter plays in the final consolidation of "this generation" to put Jesus to death:

i) At the Passover meal (22:14–38) when Jesus announces that "the hand" of the one who will "deliver him over" is with him *at table*, the disciples once again begin to argue which of them is the greatest (22:24–27 → 9:46–48). They thus not only repeat their behavior at the mountain but also mimic the leaders of this generation by *striving for rank at table* (22:24–27 → 20:46 → 14:7–11 → 11:43). In the midst of this quarreling, Peter is designated the crucible for Satan's sifting that *the twelve* (ὑμᾶς 22:31) must uniquely undergo before ultimately they "eat and drink" and "judge" in the Kingdom of God. Peter's reply of readiness to go to prison and death indicates again that "he was not knowing what he was saying" (22:33–9:33b).

ii) Peter's denial (22:54–62), following upon the *sleeping* of the disciples at the crucial moment of testing in the garden (vv. 40–46), welds the incorporation of the twelve into "this generation" and preludes the monolith that will form around Pilate, "king of the Gentiles" (22:25a). After Jesus is condemned for assenting to be the "Son of God"–as the mountain voice had already proclaimed–and shuttled back to Pilate from Israel's king (23:8 → 9:9), who mocks Jesus's royal-messianic status (23:11 → 2b–3), the crowd now termed "the people" (ὁ λαός) join together with the chief priests and their "rulers"[64] to demand the death of this false prophet and messianic pretender (23:13–25; 24:19–21). The whole people of this generation is assembled, and it is into their hands that Pilate delivers Jesus

---

[64] It is not the case that the Pharisees-scribes disappear altogether once the Jerusalem ministry and passion narrative are treated. To be sure, "Pharisees" does not occur after 19:39, but the plot to put an end to Jesus's public influence as it is conceived already in 6:7 (climax of 5:17–6:6) and developed through the Pharisees-scribes' (lawyers') resistance in the journey section (11:37–54; 12:1; 13:31–33; 14:1–24; 15:1–32; 16:14–31; 19:39–40) is continued by the "scribes" (now functionaries instead of religious party) of the Sanhedrin. The closest links are through the scribes' public reputation, which in 20:45–47 is directly connected back to Jesus's accusations against the scribes at table (11:43, 46; 14:7–11; cf. 18:9–14 and 20:47b). As in 20:47 it is the Pharisees' scribes of 11:47–52 who will receive the "greater condemnation" for their detrimental influence upon the people.

over (παραδιδόναι, 23:25 → 48 → 21–22 → 20:20 → 18:32 → 9:44; compare 24:7,20). Not only has Peter's confession of Jesus's messiahship (9:20) been twisted into its exact oposite by the whole nation, but his calling to *suffer* with Jesus on the journey to Jerusalem, which was *confirmed by the heavenly light* while he and the other disciples were *sleeping* (9:20–27 → 30–32), has also become the very antithesis for him, the disciples, and the whole people (compare 14:25–27).

iii) As Peter was the leader of the disciples in death, so is he also in the new life of the prophet like Moses (24:19, 27). The first to see the risen *glorified* Christ, to whom *Moses* and *all* the prophets had pointed (24:26–27 → 34), it is he who leads the disciples in reconstituting the *twelve* as the authoritative witnesses to Israel of the resurrection (Acts 1:15–26). Moreover, on the day of "First Fruits" it is Peter who represents the twelve and the larger group of disciples by declaring to the gathered people of Israel from all over the world that the eschatological Spirit has been "poured out" by the exalted Jesus (Acts 2:5–36). When approximately 3,000 of his audience repent and are baptized "in the name of Jesus Messiah" (vv. 38, 41), they along with the disciples constitute the "first fruits" of the renewed, eschatological Israel who *worship at the Temple* and gather at the central place to witness to the unrepentant Israel (2:46; 3:1, 11; 5:20, 42; compare Luke 24:53). Accordingly, it is once again Peter who *at the Temple* proclaims that Israel can now become heirs of the *promise to Abraham* by repenting of their killing of Jesus, the prophet like Moses (3:18–26; compare 2:39), and who before the Sanhedrin exclaims that "you" are the "builders" of Ps 118:22 who reject the "stone" "that has become the head of the corner" (4:11, 5–12).

Within this general orientation to what has transpired *with Israel* in the death and resurrection of Jesus, it is intriguing to see that the Deuteronomistic view, through *Peter*, informs the more specific explanation of *how* the fate of Jesus fulfills the final salvation in the overall plan of God for Israel's history:

Tenet A. Israel has remained a "crooked generation" (Acts 2:40–Luke 9:41; compare Deut 32:5) that has out of "ignorance" (3:17) and "wickedness" (3:26b) "denied" and "killed" the "Righteous One" (3:13–14). "Ignorance" and "wickedness" are classic descriptions of culpable disobedience in Deuteronomic language.[65] And that "ignorance" for Peter does not relieve Israel of its responsibility for the killing of Messiah is clear by the juxtaposition of the *demand* for repentance (3:17–19, οὖν!). One must be "rescued" from this "evil" lot (2:40b).

---

[65] E.g., Deut 4:25; 9:18, 27; 13:5, 11; 15:9; 17:13; 18:20, 22; 19:16; 25:2; 32:28; cf. 4:6; 9:4–5; 11:2; see also Moessner, "Prophet Like Moses," 584.

Tenet B. God "sent" (ἀποστέλλω) his servant[66] Jesus to Israel first, after having raised him up (ἀναστήσας, 3:26a). This "raising up" most likely refers to Jesus's earthly mission or sending, that is, to the "raising up" of the prophet in his calling, as in verse 22.[67] In any case, qua the Deuteronomistic conception, a prophet is *sent* to *proclaim* the will of God "in order to bless you in turning every one of you from your wickedness" (v. 26b). To procure the blessing of the law or will of the Lord in the midst of perverse disobedience is the very *raison d'être* of the prophets' calling.[68] But even more significantly, Jesus has already been sent to do this to fulfill Moses's *prophecy* of the "prophet [...] like me (v. 22). You shall hearken to him in whatever he tells you" (v. 22b). Furthermore, this sending brings to fruition the prophecies of *all the prophets*. Thus we find again what we have discovered in Stephen's speech, the transfiguration, and the journey. As a prophet, Jesus is sent to Israel with the living oracles of the prophet like Moses whose coming consummates all the prophets.

Tenet C. "To be rescued" from the "froward generation" of Israel for Peter's hearers means disentanglement through *repentance/turning* from the objective guilt or "wickedness" of killing Israel's Christ (vv. 19, 26b; 2:38a). We do not find the charge that they have killed all the prophets, as in Stephen's speech and Jesus's journey; the tone is considerably less invective here. Nevertheless, we do find the assertion that the stubbornness (*Tenet A*) which led to Jesus's death is the fulfillment of what *all* the prophets (3:18) had forecast, that is, that "God's *Christ* must suffer" (3:18–Luke 18:31–33; 9:20–22; compare 24:26–27; Acts 7:37, 52). From verse 24 it is certain that this fulfillment includes the suffering that the Messiah must undergo precisely as the prophet like Moses (v. 22). Consequently, what in fact has taken place in Jerusalem (v. 14) fulfills what Moses and Elijah in glory on the mountain had prophesied (Luke 9:31) and what Stephen will later recount (Acts 7:37, 52).

Tenet D. The pronouncement of judgment upon Israel as a whole is lacking in the early speeches of Peter in the Acts as well as in Stephen's speech. With thousands responding to the cry for repentance, clearly the eschatological Israel is being formed out of the unrepenting Israel. Peter thus quotes Deut 18:19 (enriched by Lev 23:29) to declare that those individuals who fail to hearken to

---

[66] Analysis of the use of παῖς and Servant of Isaiah christological notions, which function in Luke-Acts to express the *positive* conception of the mission to Gentiles (e.g., Luke 2:32; Acts 13:47; 26:23), lies outside the present scope, and their relationship to the Deuteronomistic rejected prophets must be the subject of a future study (see now Chapter Seven above).
[67] See Moessner, "Wilderness Generation," 338–39.
[68] E.g., Neh 9:26, 29–30.

the voice of the prophet like Moses will be destroyed *from the people*. Gone is Jesus's blanket condemnation and prophecy of doom for the nation as a whole. "Removal of sin" (3:19) and "turning away from wickedness" (v. 26), rather, are the signs of these eschatological times (v. 24).

We can draw together our results for the *Jesus–Peter parallels* that we have discovered are grounded in the Deuteronomistic view: *1*. Peter, representing the twelve tribes of the eschatological Israel, is the authoritative witness of *the glory of God* in Jesus, the prophet like Moses, on the exodus journey from the mountain in Galilee to his raising up in glory in the ascension in Jerusalem (Acts 3:13; Luke 24:26,34). He not only witnesses the calling in great light of Jesus as the prophet like Moses and the disciples' calling to obey him, he also thunders again the heavenly voice in Jerusalem: "hearken to him"; *2*. Peter journeys with Jesus on the exodus to the Temple and becomes the leader of the renewed eschatological Israel that makes the central place of all Israel the center of their worship. And it is there that he declares that the promise to Abraham has been fulfilled in the prophet like Moses whom God sent to "his brethren" and raised up and glorified from the dead; *3*. Peter participates fully in the *crooked* generation that, like their fathers, denied the Righteous One. Yet at the Temple he proclaims that their killing of the prophet like Moses fulfills all the prophets in finally breaking up Israel's monolith of disobedience to God's voice. Thousands of Israel respond to his plea for repentance.

Although Peter becomes one with the prophet like Moses in the suffering and rejection inflicted by the *leaders* of the unrepentant Israel (Acts 4:5–31; 5:17–41, especially v. 26; 12:1–17), his later career of suffering remains outside of Luke's greater interest to trace the prophetic career of Paul, to which we now turn.

IV Paul Uniquely Parallels and Completes Jesus's Calling as "the Prophet like [but greater than] Moses"

We have already met the character who occupies roughly one-quarter of Luke's overall story material at Acts 8:1 where he was "consenting" to Stephen's death along with the other "witnesses" (7:58). After the journeys to Samaria and Gaza (8:4–40) spawned by Stephen's stoning, we meet "Saul" again in 9:1 where Luke picks up the thread of his persecution of the church from 8:3 and weaves together Paul's "conversion" on the Damascus road (9:1–19). Before analyzing Paul's last journey to Jerusalem, we shall see how his calling, expanded by the parallel accounts in 22:6–21 and 26:12–23, develops out of the larger christological-historical pattern that undergirds Luke's narrative.

The Calling

The immediate contexts of all three accounts stress the paramount position of Saul in opposing *to the death* the disciples of "the Way," those bound to the "name of Jesus of Nazareth." Not only that, but Jerusalem had continually been the center for this persecution, even though Saul journeyed to foreign cities under the commission of the guardians of the *Temple* worship, the chief priests (9:2, 14; 26:12), and the leaders of the people, the "whole council of elders" (22:5):

1. Like the mountain transfiguration, a great light from heaven "flashes," and a voice from heaven sends the overwhelmed Paul on a journey mission (9:3–6; compare 22:13–15). Parallel to the curious detail that on the mountain the "trembling trio" actually *see* Jesus in flashing light before *hearing* the heavenly voice is the twofold insistence that Paul was both to *see* and *hear* "Jesus," the "Righteous One" (22:7, 14–15; 26:13–14, 16; compare 9:7, 27–Luke 9:32, 35–36)–now with the difference that the voice is that of the "Lord" Jesus himself. In short, whereas Peter's (the twelve's) and Stephen's callings are directly confirmed by the heavenly light of the glorified Jesus, Paul's calling is *initiated* from the glory of that light (22:11).

2. Like the mountain revelation, so Paul is sent on a journey mission, which eventually will take a decisive turn in the Temple as Paul journeys to Jerusalem for the purpose of worshiping God (20:16; 24:11, 17–18). Now, however, his calling to all peoples–Israel and the nations alike–becomes a sending *away* from Jerusalem, and more particularly *from the Temple,* which is confirmed by a vision of the "Lord" Jesus in that very sanctuary (22:17–21). Once again the fate of Paul like Jesus and Stephen will be settled at the central place!

3. Like the mountain theophany and as in Stephen's vision, Paul's calling is one to suffer rejection by his own people (9:16, δεῖ [...] παθεῖν; 22:18, 21; 26:17). What distinguishes this opposition as the dynamic pivot of his calling in Paul's case is the threefold insistence that his persecution of the Christian Way was in truth the persecution of Jesus–the Righteous One–himself (9:1–2, 4–5, 13–14; 22:4–5, 7–8; 26:9–11, 14–15). This solidarity in suffering is further enhanced by the way Luke has tied Stephen's death to Paul's *calling:* i) Paul is not merely an active witness in Stephen's "murder" (compare 9:1), he himself becomes the representative *par excellence* of the "stiff-necked" generation of Stephen's audience by inflaming the ensuing efforts to extinguish the Christian movement (22:4–5; 26:9–11). After his "about face," Paul becomes a victim of his own ravages, first in Damascus (9:23–25) and then in Jerusalem where the non-believing *Hellenists* try to kill him (9:29; compare 6:1, 8–14); ii) In what Luke undoubtedly intends as a recounting of this Jerusalem visit, Paul, before the lynching crowds at his last Jerusalem visit, relates his calling in the Temple when he had once again seen

the "Righteous One"[69] and had confessed that the fury of the Jews against him was directly related to his own shedding of Stephen's "blood" (22:17–21). Through the heavenly vision of all that "he had seen and heard" of the suffering Righteous One, Paul becomes one with Jesus and Stephen in his mission of suffering (22:14–15, 18, 21; 26:16; compare 9:27).

The Final Journey to Jerusalem

After relating Herod's threat on Peter's life during the *Passover* (12:1–19) and then Herod's own death (vv. 20–24), Luke presents in 12:25–15:35 and 15:36–19:20 two major journey missions of Paul and his cohorts: first from Antioch (compare 11:25–26, 30) to Cyprus and south-central Asia Minor back to Antioch and on *to Jerusalem* for the apostolic assembly; and then from Antioch through Asia Minor, Macedonia, Achaia, and return via *Jerusalem* to Antioch followed by a return to Asia Minor and a long stay in Ephesus. In 19:21–28:31 we encounter the longest journey section[70] and the one in which a number of extraordinary parallels to Jesus's passion journey have long been noted.[71] We shall discuss only those constitutive of the christological-historical pattern:

(i) Only Paul's third and final journey, as in Jesus's third[72] and final journey to Jerusalem, is prefaced by "a resolve in the Spirit" (19:21) / "resolute determination" (Luke 9:51) to reach Jerusalem before passing on to Rome. Again Luke is signaling that the divine order (δεῖ, 19:21b) of salvation[73] is building to a new climax.

(ii) This divinely-directed journey follows a period which initiates a fulfillment of time. As in Luke 9:51, when the days of Jesus's itinerant ministry within

---

69 The αὐτόν in 22:18 has τὸν δίκαιον in v. 14 as its antecedent.
70 For this division of the journey sections, see e.g., Floyd V. Filson, "The Journey Motif in Luke-Acts," in *Apostolic History and the Gospel*, ed. W. Ward Gasque and Ralph P. Martin (Grand Rapids, MI: Eerdmans, 1970): 68–77.
71 See e.g., Rackham, *Acts*, xlvii and *passim*; M. D. Goulder, *Type and History in Acts* (London: SPCK, 1964), 34–51, 60–61; cf. Radl's survey (*Paulus*, 44–59); Mattill, "Schneckenburger," 114–22; A. J. Matill, Jr., "The Jesus-Paul Parallels and the Purpose of Luke-Acts: H. H. Evans Reconsidered," *NovT* 17 (1975): 15–46; David P. Moessner, "Paul and the Pattern of the Prophet like Moses in Acts," in *Society of Biblical Literature 1983 Seminar Papers*, ed. Kent H. Richards (Chico, CA: Scholars, 1983): 203–12.
72 Luke 2:22–28 and 2:41–51; 4:9–12 is not presented as a *journey* account.
73 See Erich Fascher, "Theologische Beobachtungen zu δεῖ," in *Neutestamentliche Studien für Rudolf Bultmann*, ed. Walther Eltester, BZNW 21 (Berlin: Töpelmann, 1954): 228–54.

Galilee come to a close the days of his "taking up" in Jerusalem are *already* being "filled to completion" (συμπληρόω), so in Acts 19:21 as Paul's mission in the eastern Mediterranean has become "fulfilled" (πληρόω) he must press forward to Jerusalem and Rome.

(iii) As in Jesus's journey, so in Paul's a foreboding rejection serves as the frontispiece (Acts 19:23–41–Luke 9:52–56). This scene is followed by intermittent predictions along the journey of suffering and death awaiting Jesus/Paul in Jerusalem (Acts 20:22–25; 21:4, 10–14; compare 20:38; 23:11; 27:10–Luke 12:49–50; 13:31–35; 17:25; 18:31–34).

(iv) As in Jesus's journey, so in Paul's the sense of impending doom in Jerusalem stems from a gathering storm as the journey advances. Already the riot in Ephesus is no isolated incident but a programmatic development within a skein of rejection scenes uncoiling to an explosion in Jerusalem. As the second journey begins (15:36), John Mark–who had dropped out "of the work" (15:38) at Pamphylia (13:13) before the first series of persecutions mostly from "Jews" were inflicted (13:45, 50–51; 14:2, 5–6, 19–20) and had thus not learned firsthand that "we *must* (δεῖ) enter the Kingdom of God *through many tribulations*" (14:22b)–is excluded by Paul for further participation in his calling (9:16; 22:18; 21; 26:17). Paul then circumcises Timothy for the mission "because of the Jews in those places!" who knew "his father *was a Greek*" (16:1–4). Strangely forbidden to preach in *Asia* (16:6), Paul and companions then confront a new series of persecutions largely again by unrepenting countrymen in Macedonia and Achaia (17:5–9, 13–15; 18:6, 9–10, 12–17) who as a whole[74] violently object to Paul's contention that Jesus is the Messiah and precisely so as one who "had to suffer" (τὸν χριστὸν ἔδει παθεῖν, 17:2–3 → 10b–11 → 18:4–5). Now on his return to Jerusalem Paul does stop at Asia where he argues with Jews in Ephesus who, however, encourage him to stay. But again Paul mysteriously leaves Ephesus, promising to return only "if God wills" (18:21 → 16:6). After returning through Galatia and Phrygia from Antioch,[75] Paul eventually arrives again at Ephsus but only after Apollos goes from Ephesus to *Corinth* and there "powerfully confutes the Jews" in demonstrating that "Jesus is the Christ" (18:28). As Paul resumes his arguing in the synagogue, he does meet some "hardening" and "reviling" (19:9),[76] but by the end of his stay the opposi-

---

[74] Beroea (17:10–12) is the only exception; otherwise only "some" Jews repent in the other cities to add to the core or remnant of the repenting eschatological Israel (17:4; 18:4).

[75] This retracing of the cities already visited is the consistent practice of Paul in Acts (14:21; 15:36, 41; 16:1, 4; 18:23); therefore 18:21 stands out all the more in creating narrative *dissonance*.

[76] Notice how Paul is *identified* with Jesus in the *opposition* by the seven sons of a Jewish high priest (19:13–17); the coming opposition to Paul in the Temple by the high priest (22:30–23:5) is adumbrated.

tion of the craftsmen associated with the Artemis temple has been so overwhelming against the "Way" and even against Jews that to all appearances Jewish opposition has paled to insignificance (vv. 23–41). All the stranger, then, that Luke immediately follows with "a plot by the Jews" in Greece (20:3) which forces Paul to return by land to Asia Minor and then has Paul "sail past" Ephesus "so that he might not have to spend time in Asia" while at the same time "he was hastening [...] to be in Jerusalem on the day of Pentecost" (20:16).

The shroud of mystery covering Ephesus and Asia is finally pierced in the final legs toward Jerusalem:

a. *Ephesian Elders at Miletus*: 20:17-38, *Vv. 18–20:* The *whole period in Asia* has been a patient endurance of *persecution* by "plots of the Jews;" *Vv. 22–25:* Paul remains resolutely determined to "complete" (τελειόω) the course given to him by the Lord Jesus by *going to Jerusalem* where "imprisonment," "afflictions," and probable death have been divinely impressed upon him; *Vv. 26–31:* Paul links his fate *in Jerusalem* to the fierce opposition that he has encountered in *Asia* and even to "men" from "the flock" who "will arise" and propound "twisted"/"perverted" things (διεστραμμένα, 20:30; compare Luke 9:41!) after his departure (vv. 29–30). But Paul stands apart from the "blood of all" that will be required from a faithless stance to "the whole will of God" that he has dared to preach and that God has secured "through the blood of his own,"[77] that is through the suffering and death of the Christ (compare v. 21b).[78] As Jesus earlier had linked his arrival in Jerusalem to the *blood* required of the generation that continues to reject God's prophets, and as Paul at his calling had linked his own journey missions to the shedding of Stephen's *blood,* so now Paul joins his own persecution and death to his arrival in Jerusalem on account of the "twisted folk" of "the Jews" in rejecting his mission. He has just summarized his calling to them, that is to Jews and

---

77 The language of "own" (ἴδιος, v. 28b) reflects the filial character of the heavenly message at the baptism (Luke 3:22b, "*my* beloved Son") and transfiguration (9:35b, "*my* Chosen Son"). See e.g., F. F. Bruce, *Commentary on the Book of the Acts*, NICNT (Grand Rapids, MI: Eerdmans, 1954), 416n59 (ἴδιος is equivalent to יָחִיד, "only," as translated by ἀγαπητός, ἐκλεκτός, or μονογενής).
78 Whether or not "Christ" is the more original reading in v. 21b, the larger context of the argument with the Jews in Macedonia and Achaia supports the conclusion that the fierce opposition in Ephesus from the "plots of the Jews" (20:19–20a, 23–25, 26–31) stems from the burning contention that the "Christ" had to suffer and that Jesus is the Christ (see above); furthermore, v. 21b is speaking about "faith" and not the suffering or death of Jesus as the content of preaching. Cf. Steve Walton, *Leadership and Lifestyle: The Portrait of Paul in the Miletus Speech and 1 Thessalonians*, SNTSMS 108 (Cambridge: Cambridge University Press, 2000); Beverly R. Gaventa, "Theology and Ecclesiology in the Miletus Speech: Reflections on Content and Context," *NTS* 50 (2004): 36–52

Greeks, as a messenger of *repentance* (*Tenet B*), including the "typical" tasks of "teaching" and "exhortation" of the prophet. Moreover, his pronouncement of judgment on the "blood guilt" of the Asian audience reverberates this same pronouncement against the Jews in Corinth who had reviled him for "bearing witness [...] that the Christ was Jesus" (18:4–6 → 17:2–5). Before the Ephesian elders, then, *Tenets B* and *D*[79] are explicit, while *Tenets A* and *C* set the tone of the whole farewell address. A monolith of rejection is moving into place (20:38)!

b. *Tyre and Caesarea:* 21:4, 8–14. In "every city" (20:23) the Holy Spirit is "bearing witness that imprisonment and afflictions await" Paul. But though the "brethren," who prophesy "through the Spirit," try to dissuade him, he remains "bound by" or "in the Spirit" (20:22; compare 19:21) to do the "will of the Lord" (21:14b) and thus remains ready "to be imprisoned and to die in Jerusalem" (21:13; compare Luke 22:33!). Like Jesus "the Jews will bind the man [...] and deliver him over into the hands of the Gentiles" (21:11–Luke 18:32).

c. *Paul's Arrival in Jerusalem:* 21:15–36. Paul soon learns that he is known among the "myriads" of believing Jews in Jerusalem as one who teaches *all the Jews* in the *diaspora* to "forsake Moses" (v. 21). With his journey missions once again linked directly to his fate in Jerusalem, it hardly comes as a surprise when we read that Jews *from Asia* are the ones who lay their hands on Paul and place him at the mercy of "the crowd" of "Israel" and of "the whole city and the people" (λαός) who demand his death (vv. 27–28; compare 24:19b–20; 25:24). Nor is it coincidental that they accuse Paul of defiling the worship of the Temple by having taken Trophimus, the *Ephesian* and a *"Greek,"* into its environs. The riot over the temple of Artemis has now culminated in the uproar over "this holy place" (v. 28b).

To sum up, as was true for Jesus, so also for Paul "that it cannot be that a prophet should perish away from Jerusalem" (Luke 13:33b; compare Acts 21:31a).

(v) Accordingly, it is also the case that as with Jesus and Stephen the Temple forms the fulcrum of hostility against those "prophets and apostles sent to" her (Luke 13:34a). For it is Paul's appearance in the Temple that foments the convulsion leading to the charge of blasphemy and despoiling the worship of that place (24:6). Later in his defense before Felix, Paul will declare that he journeyed to Jerusalem in order to worship (24:11), and as a loyal Israelite he went to the central place during the Feast of First Fruits to bring alms and offerings for his nation (24:17; compare 20:16; Deut 16:9–12). And more significantly, before Festus and Herod Agrippa Paul will aver that he is on trial "for hope in the *promise* [...] to the fathers" which has given meaning and purpose to the whole Temple cultus

---

[79] See nn. 32, 56.

and is fulfilled in the raising up of one from the dead (26:6–8). But instead of recounting the events of Jesus's death and resurrection, Paul launches into an account of his own calling to suffer in which he sums up his whole career as one of *proclaiming repentance* to both Jews and Gentiles. Indeed it is because of this message of repentance that "the Jews seized me in the Temple and tried to kill me" (26:21). But, finishes Paul, he is only doing what *"Moses* and *all the prophets* said would come to pass," that is, "that the *Christ must suffer* and, being the first to rise from the dead, he [Christ] would proclaim light both to the people and to the Gentiles" (26:22b–23).[80] As with Stephen, Paul's solidarity with the one who journeyed to Jerusalem to die to fulfill Moses and all the prophets is complete (compare Acts 23:11).

(vi) Thus it is also true that as in Jesus's arrest and trial, so in Paul's, representatives of the *whole* nation–the Sanhedrin, the people (λαός), and Herod, "king" of the Jews–along with their Roman governor and his authorities collaborate to decide his fate (Acts 21:30–32, 36, 39–40; 22:30; 23:1–5, 12–22; 24:1–9; 25:1–12–Luke 22:66–23:25; compare Acts 4:27). And as with Jesus, so with Paul the people and their chief priests and elders demand his death, while the Roman governor three times pronounces his innocence (Acts 21:27–31, 34–36, 40–22:1, 22, 30–23:5, 12–15, 29; 25:2, 15, 18–20, 24–25, 30–31; 28:17–19–Luke 23:1–25).

(vii) But again it is the charges against Paul which encapsulate the christological-historical pattern of the rejection of the prophet like Moses and of all the prophets. He is accused of (a) Teaching all the Jews of the diaspora against "Moses," that is, against circumcision and the "customs" (Acts 21:21; compare 6:14; 26:3; 28:17), and summarized as not "observing the law" in 21:24; (b) Teaching against "the people and the law and this place" and of defiling the Temple with Greeks (21:28; compare 24:6); (c) Creating agitation "among all the Jews in the world" and of being a leader of the "sect of the Nazoreans" (24:5; compare 6:14; Paul and the "Nazorean," 22:8; 26:9); (d) "Offending against" "the law of the Jews, the Temple, and Caesar" (25:8); (e) "Actions against the people and the customs of our fathers" (28:17). These charges can be grouped together as against the law (Moses), the people (nation), and the Temple, as a member of the "Nazoreans"–the same accusations against Stephen–and in addition, against Caesar. Now in Jesus's arrest and trial he also is charged with "agitating the people" (Luke 23:5), "perverting" them with false teaching (23:2, 5, 14), and

---

[80] See n. 66; the seminal role of Isaiah in framing Jesus's and Paul's calling to suffer has been noted by a number of scholars. One more recent portrayal comes independently to conclusions similar to mine: Peter Mallen, *The Reading and Transformation of Isaiah in Luke-Acts*, LNTS 367 (London: T&T Clark, 2008), esp. 201–07.

resisting allegiance to Caesar (23:2). "Law," "people," "Caesar" are precisely the charges against Jesus, especially as they reached a fever pitch in Jesus's teaching in the Temple (19:47–20:47).

(viii) Finally, though Paul unlike Stephen is not killed by the end of Acts, Paul's journey to Rome does fulfill the journeys to "the end of the earth" begun by the stiff-necked rejection of the prophet like Moses and of Stephen in Jerusalem and commanded by the "raised up" prophet like Moses as a fulfillment "that the Christ must suffer and on the third day rise from the dead and that repentance and forgiveness of sins should be preached in his name to all nations, beginning from Jerusalem" (Luke 24:46–47; compare Acts 1:8). This is the reason Paul utters Isa 6:9–10 exactly when and where he does. For his preaching of repentance in the name of the risen Christ who had to suffer at the hands of his own people has progressed to all nations *through* the unrelenting history of rejection of God's messengers to Israel (*Tenets A & C*): "Go *to this people* and say, 'You shall indeed hear but never understand [...]. For this people's heart has grown fat, they have become hard of hearing [...] lest they should *hearken* [...] and *turn* for me to heal them" (Acts 28:26–27). Paul, the great prophetic pleader of repentance to Israel (*Tenet B*), in nearly every city of his journeying had to turn to the Gentiles, "for they will hearken" (28:29b). Now in Rome and thus from there to the "end of the earth" (Isa 49:6; Acts 1:8; Luke 2:32) Paul sounds again the "your fathers" (28:25b) of Stephen (7:51–52) and Jesus (Luke 11:47–48). As the monolith had begun to consolidate against Jesus on the exodus journey to Jerusalem, provoking the pronouncements of *Tenet D*, so along Paul's journeys which culminated in the monolith of rejection in Jerusalem Paul has also uttered *Tenet D* (Acts 13:40–41, compare vv. 46–47; 18:6, compare 20:26).[81] But it is precisely through this christological-historical pattern of the Deuteronomistic rejection of the prophet like Moses and his prophet-apostles that the exodus salvation, the "glory of Israel," is extended as "light to the Gentiles" in "the presence of all peoples" (Luke 2:31-32).[82]

Conclusions

We can now draw together our conclusions with a schematic profile of the three constitutive elements of the pattern of the prophet like Moses and his rejected prophets:

---

[81] See nn. 32, 56.
[82] See n. 66.

1. The calling to a journey sending to Israel is revealed by the voice of the Lord in "glorious" light.

Jesus →	(Peter)/Moses/Stephen →	Paul
(Luke 9:29–35)	(Acts 7:30–32)	(Acts 9:3–15; 22:6–15; 26:13–18)

Peter's (Israel's) calling to journey with Jesus is confirmed in the transfiguration and echoed to the gathered Israel in Jerusalem (Acts 3:22, 26).

The journey missions from *Stephen's* witness are confirmed by the heavenly light (Acts 7:55–56).

2. The journey is the consummation of Moses's sending on the exodus deliverance to the central place, the Temple, in Jerusalem for the true worship of God.

Jesus →	(Peter)/Moses/Stephen →	Paul
(Luke 9:31, 51–19:46)	(Acts 7:7, 17, 35–47, 52b)	(Acts 11:19–30; 13:2–19:20, 21–28:31)

Peter (the twelve) is the authoritative witness of this journey from the mountain in Galilee to the fulfillment of the eschatological Israel at the central place in Jerusalem (Luke 9:32, 35; Acts 3:22–26).

Stephen's witness leads (Acts 8:1–4; 11:19–20) to *Paul's* journeys which extend the exodus salvation to the Gentiles from the Temple (Acts 9:15; 22:15–21; 26:17b–18) and which eventually culminate decisively at the central place of all Israel (19:21–28:31).

3. The journey sending to the central place is a calling to suffering and rejection from the whole people of Israel. But through the persecution and even death of the prophets, Israel's unrelenting history of stubborn resistance is fulfilled precisely as it is broken in the Israel that repents and extends its salvation to the Gentiles, as foretold by Moses and all the prophets.

Jesus →	(Peter)/Moses/Stephen →	Paul
(Luke 9:31, 51–19:46)	(Acts 7:23–43, 51–53)	(Acts 9:15–30; 22:14–21; 26:16–23)

Jesus is the "Christ" as the suffering prophet like Moses who is "raised up" from his violent death to bring the new life ("glory") of the exodus salvation to Israel and the nations (Luke 24:26, 45–47; Acts 26:22–23).

Peter (repenting Israel) suffers rejection by the leaders of the nation before the monolithic rejection of the salvation of the prophet like Moses forms once again (Acts 4:5–31; 5:17–41; 12:1–17).

Stephen suffers rejection and violent death as a transition figure between the opposition of the leaders and the consolidating monolith of the people as a whole (Acts 7:54–8:4).

Paul suffers rejection of the people as a whole as the "glory of Israel" is extended to "all peoples" (Acts 19:21–28:31; Luke 2:31–32).

Chapter Ten: Luke's "Plan of God" from the Greek Psalter: The Rhetorical Thrust of "The Prophets and the Psalms" in Peter's Speech at Pentecost[1]

Luke presents the first and third longest explicit citations of the Jewish scriptures in the church's New Testament in his Acts 2 Pentecost speech. The author of Luke-Acts, in fact, adds a third quotation that, together with the other two, divides Peter's address into three discrete movements. Each division features a prophetic utterance from the Septuagint to structure the *narratio* of Luke's argument: Joel 3:1–5 in Acts 2:14–21 [2:17–21]–"God says" (longest); Ps 15:8–11 in Acts 2:22–28 [2:25–28]–"David says" (third longest);[2] Ps 109:1 in Acts 2:29–36 [2:34–35]–"he himself [David] says." Rather than his characteristic rhetoric of "to fulfill," Luke introduces each citation as "God" or the prophet continuing to speak (present tense) through scripture to interpret what the Pentecost pilgrims are experiencing in the "strong wind," "tongues like fire," and "variety" of foreign "tongues" uttered in their midst (Acts 2:1–4). Ostensibly Peter must explain how the eschatological "pouring out" of the Spirit could be occurring even though the people of Israel ("you") had "crucified this Jesus whom God had established as Lord and Christ" (2:36). How could Israel, together with the "lawless" Romans, violently execute Israel's own "Messiah" and still in some way be enacting "the foreordained plan and prescience of God" (2:23)?

Of the three citations, commentators have the most difficulty in explaining why Luke would quote nine lines of Ps 15 only apparently to find, in two of them, one rather cryptic nugget allegedly predicting the resurrection from the dead of David's future offspring and χριστός (Ps 15:10 in Acts 2:27, paraphrased in 2:30–32). To be sure, Ps 15:10 is echoed in 2:31 as a specific prophecy by David the "patriarch" and "prophet" (2:29–30) who, "seeing in advance," thus spoke

---

[1] First read in slightly different form in the "Greek Bible Consultation" of the SBL annual meeting, 2006; published with the same title in *Scripture and Traditions: Essays on Early Judaism and Christianity in Honor of Carl R. Holladay*, ed. Patrick Gray and Gail O'Day, NovTSup 129 (Leiden: Brill, 2008): 223–38. Used with permission.
The plot of the suffering righteous emerging from the interactive reading of the two psalms, section II below, represents a substantial development of the scriptural exegesis of Luke's 'plan of God' beyond my first attempt at the rhetorical strategy of the Pentecost speech in my "*Two* Lords 'at the Right Hand'? The Psalms and an Intertextual Reading of Peter's Pentecost Speech (Acts 2:14–36)," in *Literary Studies in Luke-Acts: Essays in Honor of Joseph B. Tyson*, ed. Richard P. Thompson and Thomas E. Phillips (Macon, GA: Mercer University Press, 1998): 215–32.
[2] Cf. Heb 8:8–12 (Jer 31:31–34 = LXX Jer 38:31–34)– second longest.

of the resurrection of "the Christ" (ὁ χριστός) of his own "offspring/fruit of his loins" who would "sit" some day upon David's own "throne." This direct application by Peter to Jesus's resurrection builds to the *peroratio* in verse 36: "Let the whole house of Israel know with clear certainty that God has established him as both Lord and Christ, this Jesus whom you *yourselves* crucified." This summary indictment is reason enough–so the standard explanation runs[3]–to cite a greater number of the lines of the Psalm surrounding 15:10. Why did the people not have the presence of mind to realize that in rejecting Jesus of Nazareth, they were actually crucifying this "holy one" of Ps 15 of David's own lineage?![4]

Consequently, in the standard interpretation Ps 15:10 becomes an easy way out of Israel's dilemma. Though the people should have known better than to crucify "the Christ" of David's own loins, God "lowers the crane" to rescue the whole salvation story as Jesus is raised up from the dead. Unlike David, when this "holy one" dies, his "flesh" does not decay in the tomb, just as David foresaw (compare Acts 2:26c [David's flesh]→2:31*b* [the Christ's])! Presumably, then, this difference becomes all telling for the inclusion, in the first place, of Ps 15 with its extensive quotation. This "holy one's" reprieve from bodily decomposition functions as a *deus ex machina* not only for David ("my flesh shall dwell in hope," Ps 15:9c in 2:26c), but also for the whole "foreordained plan and prescience of God" in offering Israel once again salvation in Jesus of Nazareth (compare Acts 2:23–24, 33, 38–40). Instead of dying and rotting in the tomb, this "holy one" is

---

3 See, *inter alia*, William H. Bellinger, Jr., "The Psalms and Acts: Reading and Rereading," in *With Steadfast Purpose: Essays on Acts in Honor of Henry Jackson Flanders, Jr.*, ed. Naymond H. Keathley (Waco, TX: Baylor University Press, 1990): 127–43, esp. 128–36; James D. G. Dunn, *The Acts of the Apostles* (Peterborough: Epworth Press, 1996), 30–31; Jacques Dupont, *The Salvation of the Gentiles: Essays on the Acts of the Apostles*, trans. John R. Keating (New York: Paulist Press, 1979), 103–28; Ernst Haenchen, *The Acts of the Apostles* (Oxford: Blackwell, 1971), 179–82; Joseph A. Fitzmyer, *The Acts of the Apostles* (New York: Doubleday, 1998), 256–57; Beverly R. Gaventa, *The Acts of the Apostles* (Nashville, TN: Abingdon, 2003), 78; Luke Timothy Johnson, *The Acts of the Apostles* (Collegeville, MN: Liturgical Press, 1992), 48–55; Donald Juel, "Social Dimensions of Exegesis: The Use of Psalm 16 in Acts 2," *CBQ* 43 (1981): 543–86; Gerhard Krodel, *Acts* (Minneapolis, MN: Augsburg, 1986), 83–89; I. Howard Marshall, *Acts* (Grand Rapids, MI: Eerdmans, 1980), 73–81; Robert C. Tannehill, *The Acts of the Apostles*, vol 2., *The Narrative Unity of Luke-Acts: A Literary Interpretation* (Minneapolis, MN: Fortress, 1990), 26–42; Ben Witherington III, *The Acts of the Apostles: A Socio-Rhetorical Commentary* (Grand Rapids, MI: Eerdmans, 1998), 146, allows some explanation of the crucifixion although the main focus of Ps 15 is still on the resurrection: "that what happened to Jesus was part of a preordained plan as revealed in Scripture."

4 For a traditio-historical approach, see H. W. Boers, "Psalm 16 and the Historical Origin of the Christian Faith," *ZNW* 60 (1969): 105–10, who comes to the revealing conclusion that an "earlier" function of Psalm 15[16] was to interpret the *death* of Jesus before it became a commentary on the resurrection experiences of the early believers (that is, conventional interpretation).

raised up to allow the whole saving action to continue and to build to the giving of the Spirit and even to redound to the rescue of the likes of a David in Hades.

But why in narrative oral performance would Luke waste rhetorical time and space with insignificant details that would only distract and therefore detract from the building argument? Why have David mention his great "joy" in "continually seeing" "the Lord" "at his right hand," which produces a new confidence that he will not die before his time nor before he has followed the "paths that lead to life" and to "the joy of your [God's?] presence" (Ps 15:8, 11 in Acts 2:25, 28)? What do "paths of life" and a new confidence *vis-à-vis* the intimidation of enemies have to do with resurrection and "the Christ"? Is it possible that suffering and its eschatological outcome in the "release of sins," not "raising up" after death per se, composes the tenor of reference for "your holy one"?

The thesis presented here in gratitude for Professor Carl Holladay's enormous contribution to the understanding of Luke and Acts, to Hellenistic historiography in particular, and to the whole field of Judaism and early Christianity more generally[5] is that each of the three citations of Septuagint Scripture delineates the essential blueprint of the "plan of God"–first articulated by Peter in Acts 2:23 and utilized by Luke some five other times in Luke and Acts[6]–to encapsulate the divine intent of the "Lord" of Israel and the nations in the fulfilled messianic salvation. Indeed, each of the three citations functions as *synecdoche* for this "plan" by circumscribing a critical aspect of the larger movement while, at the same time, implicating the other two *pars pro toto*. It is manifest that the Joel 3 and Ps 109 texts complement each other by interpreting each other; the one "exalted at the right hand" as "my Lord" certainly qualifies to fill the role of "pouring out" the Spirit of "the end days" (Acts 2:17a→2:33). But what about "the Christ?" Why does Peter conclude his argument by claiming that through all these events it had become clear that God had appointed Jesus both "Lord and Christ" (2:36b)? What does the "anointed of the Lord"/"Messiah of Israel" have to do with exaltation and the giving of the Spirit?

One of the hallmarks of Carl Holladay's scholarship is his uncanny ability to sort out varying approaches to the text and to coordinate and integrate the

---

5 See esp. his definitive translation and commentary on the Hellenistic Jewish historians, Carl R. Holladay, *Fragments from Hellenistic Jewish Authors*, vol. 1 *Historians*, vol. 2 *Poets*, vol. 3 *Aristobulus* (Chico, CA/Atlanta, GA: Scholars Press, 1983); see also his lucid comparison with Acts, "Acts and the Fragments of Hellenistic Jewish Historians," in *Jesus and the Heritage of Israel*, vol. 1, *Luke the Interpreter of Israel*, ed. David P. Moessner (Harrisburg, PA: Trinity Press International, 1999): 171–98.

6 "The plan of God" or slight variations in Luke-Acts: Luke 7:30; Acts 2:23; 4:28; 5:38 (ironically through Gamaliel); 13:36; 20:27; (27:12, 42).

methods that are most historically germane and critically fruitful in bringing New Testament texts to life in both their ancient and contemporary contexts.[7] It is hoped that this new approach to the Pentecost speech offered here might in some small measure honor Carl's sterling scholarship.

I The Pentecost Speech: Peter's Outline of the "Plan of God" from "the Prophets and the Psalms"

At the end of the first volume, the risen Crucified had "opened the minds [of the apostles] to comprehend the scriptures," adding "the promise" that "power from the exalted place" would soon "clothe them" (Luke 24:44–49). Now at Pentecost as this promise comes to fruition, Peter–representing the group whose minds had been enlightened by Christ himself–opens up the three scriptures to expound "the plan of God." Thus at the conclusion of his first volume Luke had anticipated Peter's inaugural speech through Jesus's final words. In Luke 24:44–49 Jesus provides a three point summation of the whole of the scriptures regarding Israel's salvation and its χριστός:[8] a. the Messiah must suffer (Luke 24:46a); b. the Messiah must rise from the dead (24:46b); and, c. in Messiah's name the release of sins must be proclaimed to all the nations by the apostles as witnesses (24:47–48). This essential "plan" of the scriptures can be enacted, however, only by the subsequent empowerment of these witnesses "from the exalted place" (ἐξ ὕψους, Luke 24:49).

It is curious that Luke has Peter pick up each of these three points as Peter "opens up" the scriptures, including the Psalms (Luke 24:44c), for the Pentecost pilgrims. As the rhetorical occasion requires, Peter begins with the Joel 3 text to interpret the wind and the fire and the many languages. The basic sequence of texts in Acts becomes perforce c., a., b.:

---

[7] See esp. his magisterial introduction to the writings of the NT, Carl R. Holladay, *A Critical Introduction to the New Testament: Interpreting the Message and Meaning of Jesus Christ* (Nashville, TN: Abingdon Press, 2005).
[8] As one example of the pervasive scriptural hermeneutic that configures as well as figures Luke's two volumes is his phrase, with slight variations, "[all] that stands written." Some twenty-two times Luke cites this summary formula in capturing the import of an event or in providing the basis of the larger narrative sequence of characters and their interactions (Luke 2:23; 3:4; 4:4, 8, 10, 17; 7:27; 10:26; 18:31; 19:46; 20:17; 21:22; 22:37; 24:44, 46; Acts 1:20; 7:42; 13:29, 33; 15:15; 23:5; 24:14). Cf. Luke 1:70; 2:22; 3:4; 4:17; 5:14; 20:37; 24:25; Acts 2:16, 30; 3:22; 7:48; 8:28, 30, 34; 13:27, 39, 40; 15:21; 28:25.

Context:		Acts 2:1–41
2:1–13		Residents and Pentecost sojourners in Jerusalem (all nations of earth) confused and marveling at Galileans speaking their native languages
1. 2:14–21		The Pouring Out of the Spirit Upon "All Flesh" Is the Fulfillment of the Salvation of the End Days as the Scriptures (God speaks [v. 17] through the *Prophet Joel*) Declare
		v. 17c–prophesying (men and women)
		v. 17d–visions and dreams (young and old)
Joel 3 c.		v. 18–men and women "servants" shall prophesy
Luke 24:47–49		v. 19a,b–wonders and signs (heaven and earth)
		vv.19b-20–Cosmic Impact to the Day of the Lord (all space and time)
2. 2:22–28		Jesus of Nazareth's Signs, Crucifixion, and Resurrection Already Inaugurated the End Days of Salvation as the Scriptures (David speaks [v. 25] in *Psalm 15[16]*) Declare
		v. 22–Mighty works, wonders, and signs attested by God
		v. 23–Affixing of Jesus by the Israelites as plan of God
		v. 24–Loosing/freeing from pangs/cords of death by God
Psalm 15 a.		vv. 25–28–David (Ps 15:8–11b) as prophet speaks about Jesus of Nazareth, God's Holy One, as the Lord **"at my right hand"** who is rejected by his own people and yet never decomposes in the grave, even as David himself suffers rebuke from the people of Israel, knows he will die, and be buried, and yet takes comfort that his Lord will not abandon him in death.
Luke 24:46a		
3. 2:29–36		As Exalted Christ and Lord at God's **"right hand,"** Jesus Is Pouring Out the Spirit of the Salvation of the End Days as the Scriptures (David speaks [v. 34] in *Psalm 109[110]*) Declare
		vv. 29–31–the prophet David, whose tomb is still present, saw and spoke of the resurrection and the enthronement of his own offspring, the Christ, whose own "flesh" would not waste away in a tomb (i.e., "Your Holy One," [Ps. 15:10 ~ vv.27b→31b] can not be David)
		v. 32–God did raise up Jesus, of which the apostles are witnesses
Inclusio:		v. 33–Jesus has in fact been exalted and has received the promise of the Father and, thus, is the one who is pouring out what the audience is seeing and hearing
Psalm 109 b.		vv. 34–35–David himself speaks of this "Lord and Christ" when he declares that the "Lord" [God] said to Jesus, "my Lord," "Sit **at my right hand**" **(Ps. 109:1)**
Luke 24:46b		
QED		v. 36–Therefore, God had indeed established the Jesus whom Israel crucified as both "Lord and Christ" [i.e., both David's Lord and "anointed" heir]
Response:		
2:37–41		Through repentance (change of orientation/mind-set) the promise of the Spirit is for Israel and for all those Afar (the plot of Acts according to "the plan of God"); cf. 2:37: "their heart was pricked" –**Ps. 108[109]:16**

c. Joel 3 explains how it is that release of sins is being proclaimed in Messiah's name to all the nations, as those gathered from every nation hear in their own native tongues the preaching of the salvation story fulfilled in Israel's Messiah (Acts 2:5–13)–just as Jesus, at the end of volume one, had foreseen and commanded (Luke 24:47).

b. Psalm 109 then describes how David had also foreseen the enthronement of his "my Lord" to the exalted Place where the "offspring of his womb" (Ps 109:3b) would reign over his enemies. The "my" of "my Lord" must refer to David since he is introduced as the speaker, prophesying about *his* Lord enthroned (Ps 109:1 in Acts 2:34).

Consequently Luke argues through *inclusio*: The wind, flame, and multiple languages are due to the enthroned "Lord and Christ" who is "pouring out the Spirit upon all flesh" (2:33–35) just as Joel had prophesied (Joel 3:5: "Everyone who calls upon the name of this Lord will be saved"–Acts 2:21; compare 2:40b: "be saved from this twisted generation").

a. Psalm 15 then should illumine how it could have happened that the Messiah, David's own progeny, could suffer and be delivered over to crucifixion and still be enacting "the foreordained plan and prescience of God." The long number of lines from Ps 15 holds Luke's (Peter's) answer: David had already prefigured that fate in both his life and death for his future scion, Jesus of Nazareth. Therefore, the people of Israel had been given a powerful demonstration in advance of what their Messiah would be like. But because the people acted in character as a "twisted generation," they must now change their whole way of comprehending their response to David's "Lord and Christ."

If Luke follows the same rhetorical strategy for Ps 15 as he does for the Joel and Ps 109 texts, then Ps 15 will produce an organic connection between the Spirit poured out upon the nations, on the one side, and "my Lord's" enthronement to "the right hand," on the other. We can phrase the issue thus: What does "calling upon the name of the Lord" in Acts 2:21 (Joel 3:5) have to do with "repenting/changing of the mind and being baptized into the name of Jesus Messiah for the release of sins" and thereby "receiving the gift of the Holy Spirit," as Peter indicates to his contrite audience (Acts 2:37–38)?

II The "Plan of God" "Opened" by the Interacting, Intertextual Enriching of [LXX] Psalm 109 by [LXX] Psalm 15

c. The speech opens with Peter's explanation of why the gathered believers could not be "drunk" in speaking all the international languages (Acts 2:7–12). Rather, what is happening is nothing less than the realization of Joel's marvelous vision of Israel's "sons and daughters prophesying, its youth seeing visions and its senior citizens dreaming dreams" (2:17).[9] More than that, this Joel citation forms a template for the rest of the Acts as in each major development of the plot more and more ethnic groups and people from a wide socio-economic spectrum are brought into full inclusion of the "people of God." It is also significant that in Acts 2:18 (Joel 3:2), both men and women[10] who are receiving the end-time Spirit are characterized as "servants" (δοῦλοι καὶ δοῦλαι), a term anticipating a future scenario of the pouring out of the eschatological Spirit in fulfillment of the "plan of God" through God's "anointing" of his "holy servant Jesus" in Acts 4:23–31.[11]

b. The third and final section (Acts 2:29–36) will peak in a "QED" (ἀσφαλῶς οὖν) for the whole of Peter's speech even as it comes back full circle to identify the giver of "the Spirit of the end days" as the one whom David calls "my Lord" and who "sits at the right hand" of "the Lord," making his enemies "a footstool." The rhetorical strategy appears to be augmentation or *probatio* of the *narratio* that has been demonstrated through the citation of Ps 15 in the middle third of the speech, Acts 2:22–28, since 2:29 begins with the declaration that David could not be the one of whom Ps 15 prophesies, seeing that David had died and his tomb is there-

---

[9] See, e.g., Acts 7:55–56; 9:10–16 [11–12]; 10:3–7, 10–16; 11:28. For "signs and wonders" of the Joel text as introducing the "mighty acts of God" as God working through Jesus the mighty acts of salvation, see Robert B. Sloan, "'Signs and Wonders': A Rhetorical Clue to the Pentecost Discourse," in *With Steadfast Purpose: Essays on Acts in Honor of Henry Jackson Flanders, Jr.*, ed. Naymond H. Keathley (Waco, TX: Baylor University Press, 1990): 145–62; in a similar vein, Daniel J. Treier, "The Fulfillment of Joel 2:28–32: A Multiple-Lens Approach," *JETS* 40 (1997): 13–26. For a comparison with Paul's use of the same Joel and Psalm 109 [110] texts, see Richard B. Hays, "The Paulinism of Acts, Intertextually Reconsidered." In *Paul and the Heritage of Israel. Paul's Claim upon Israel's Legacy in Luke and Acts in the Light of the Pauline Letters*, edited by David P. Moessner, Daniel Marguerat, Mikeal Parsons, and Michael Wolter, 35–48, Vol. 2, *Luke the Interpreter of Israel* (London: T&T Clark, 2012).
[10] See, e.g., men who prophesy, Acts 19:6–7; for women, Acts 21:8–9 et al.
[11] Cf. "The holy one, your servant Jesus" (Acts 4:27); "Your plan which you foreordained to take place" (4:28); "let your servants speak your word with boldness as you extend your hand to heal and to perform signs and wonders through your holy servant Jesus" (4:29–30). The link to Joel 3 in Acts 2 is multi-faceted.

fore 'living' proof! Hence, Ps 109:1 appears not to function as a primary proof text for Jesus's resurrection from the dead; its thrust, instead, seems to be contingent upon the force of Ps 15 whose verse 10 in this third section (Acts 2:31–32) forms a metaleptic prompting back to the argument of the second.

But does this pointing back to Ps 15 concern only the two lines of Ps 15:10 in Acts 2:27, as the standard interpretation avows, or does the contrast of the "holy one's" fate in Hades to David's "abandonment" point rather to the larger comparison and contrast of their calling, reception, and fate at the hands of their own people, perhaps then to the larger profile of David (and the 'holy one') in the whole of Ps 15?

Peter's call in his *peroration* to a radically new way of thinking makes the most sense when we see that Luke represents this earliest Jesus-messianist community re-reading their scriptures with the new lens that the resurrected-Crucified himself had given them (Luke 24:44–47). Thus Peter illumines the "plan of God" by reading in tandem the only two psalms in the Septuagint psalter in which the phrase "my lord" occurs, Pss 15 and 109. In both psalms David speaks *to* and speaks *about* two distinct "Lords" whose actions upon earth climax at "the Lord's right hand." These two "Lords" in the two psalms are thus read as two primary characters in one larger plot of "the foreordained plan and prescience of God" (Acts 2:23) that has come to a major fulfillment in the coming of the Spirit upon all nations.

Before we see how this common plot emerges, we must distinguish between HB Ps 16 and LXX Ps 15: Whereas Ps 16 rehearses David's "song of trust," Ps 15 sketches David's self-portrait as a "suffering righteous of the Lord" to produce a very different profile.[12] It will be helpful to place the psalms together in parallel columns. The greatest difference of Ps 15 with Ps 16 occurs in verses 3–6, 3–5 respectively as indicated between the columns. The citation of Ps 15:8–11 in Acts 2:25b–28 is in italics, important differences underlined:

---

[12] For a different view, that the LXX Ps 15 in the ethos of the Hellenistic era brings out rather the fuller eschatological implications of the HB Ps 16, see Armin Schmitt, "Ps 16,8–11 als Zeugnis der Auferstehung in der Apg," *BZ* 17 (1973): 229–48.

Psalm 16 (Hebrew-NRSV trans.)	Psalm 15 (LXX-my trans.)
1 Protect me, O God, for in you I take refuge.	1 Keep me, O Lord; for I have hoped in you.
2 I say to the LORD, "You are <u>my Lord</u>; I have no good apart from you."	2 I said to the Lord, you are <u>my Lord</u>; for you have no need of my goodness
<u>3 As for the holy ones in the land. they are the noble, in whom is all my delight.</u>	3 On behalf of the saints that are in His land he has magnified all His pleasure in them.
<u>4 Those who choose another god multiply their sorrows: their drink offerings of blood I will not pour out or take their names upon my lips.</u>	4 Their afflictions (weaknesses/bodily illnesses) have been multiplied; afterward they hastened.
<u>5 The LORD is my chosen portion and my cup;</u> you hold my lot.	5 I will certainly not assemble their bloody meetings, neither will I make mention of their names with my lips.
6 The boundary lines have fallen for me in pleasant places; I have a goodly heritage.	6 The Lord is the portion of my inheritance and of my cup: you are the one who restores my inheritance to me.
7 I bless the LORD who gives me counsel; in the night also my heart instructs me.	7 The measuring lines have fallen to me in the best places; yes, I have a most excellent inheritance.
<u>8 I keep the LORD always before me; because he is at my right hand. I shall not be moved.</u>	*<u>8 I kept seeing the Lord before me continually in mv presence; for he is at mv right hand, that I should not be shaken.</u>*
9 Therefore my heart is glad, and my soul rejoices; my body also rests secure.	*9 Therefore my heart rejoiced and my tongue exulted; more than that also, my flesh shall rest (dwell) in hope,*
10 For you do not give me up to Sheol, or let your faithful one see the Pit.	*10 Because You will not abandon my life in Hades, neither will You allow Your Holy One to see decomposition.*
11 You show me the path of life. In your presence there is fullness of joy; <u>in your right hand</u> are pleasures forevermore.	*11 You have made known to me the ways of (that lead to) life; You will fill me with joy with Your presence; <u>at Your right hand</u> there are delights for ever.*

What rings through nearly every verse of the Hebrew is the ebullient confidence David has in Yahweh's "goodness" and in his own "good lot" with Yahweh (Ps 16:2). Not even Sheol will be able to hold David's "life." Indeed, at Lord Yahweh's ("your") *"right hand"* are the very "pleasures" of life "forever" (16:10–11). The linkage, however, between "my Lord" and "suffering saints" is absent in Ps 16. By contrast, the David of Ps 15 is in solidarity with "my Lord" and with other saints in the land as they experience great persecution ("You are my Lord [...] on behalf of all the saints [...] their afflictions have multiplied [...] their bloody meetings [...] the Lord before me continually [...] that I should not be shaken," vv. 2, 3, 4, 8). It is this "my Lord" whom David sees in his presence ("at my right hand") and also foresees would one day be exalted at the Lord God's "right hand" ("not see decomposition [...] at your right hand there are delights forever," vv. 10, 11).

The argument from the Psalms in the Pentecost speech now takes on a very different twist. Placing Pss 15 and 109 side by side will facilitate the interactive reading of the two that the early church comprehends as one larger unfolding of the "plan" that David foresaw:

Psalm 15 (LXX) (mv trans.)	Psalm 109 (LXX) (my trans.)
A Writing of David	A Psalm of David
1 Keep me, O Lord; for I have hoped in you.	1 *The Lord said to <u>my Lord</u>. "Sit at <u>my right hand</u>, until I make <u>your enemies your footstool</u>."*
2 I said to the Lord, you are my Lord; for you have no need of my goodness	2 The Lord shall send out for you a scepter of power out of Zion; rule <u>in the midst of your enemies</u>.
3 On behalf of the saints that are in his land, he has magnified all his pleasure in them.	3 With you is dominion in the day of your power, <u>amidst the splendors of your saints</u>. I have begotten you from the womb before the morning.
4 Their weaknesses (illnesses/bodily afflictions) have been multiplied; afterward they hastened.	4 The Lord swore an oath and will not change his mind, "You are a priest forever, according to the order of Melchizedek."
5 I will certainly not assemble their bloody meetings, neither will make mention of their names with my lips	5 <u>The Lord at your right hand has dashed into pieces kings in the day of his wrath.</u>
6 The Lord is the portion of my inheritance and of my cup: you are the one who restores my inheritance to me.	6 He shall execute judgment among the nations, he shall fill up [the number of] corpses, he shall crush the heads of many upon the earth.
7 The measuring lines have fallen to me in the best places, yes I have a most excellent inheritance.	7 He shall drink from the brook on the way; therefore he will lift up his head.
8 *I kept seeing the Lord before me continually in my presence: for he is at my right hand, that I should not be shaken.*	
9 *Therefore my heart rejoiced and my tongue exulted; more than that also, my flesh shall rest (dwell) in hope,*	
10 *Because you will not abandon my life in Hades, neither will you allow your Holy One to see decomposition.*	
11 *You have made known to me the ways of (that lead to) life; You will fill me with joy with your presence*; at <u>your right hand there are delights for ever.</u>	

It should be acknowledged at the outset that there are multiple ways to identify speaker and addressee. The psalms are especially fluid in their ability to address different audiences in different historical settings and in varying periods of Jewish as well as the church's history of interpretation. God may speak, David speaks, the psalmist-narrator speaks, the synagogue speaks, and so on. More importantly for our analysis, it is not possible to determine when one speaker finishes and the narrator or another character in the scenario takes over. For instance, in Ps 109:2 does the David identified as the psalmist in the LXX sub-heading continue to speak (compare "my Lord" in 109:1), or does "the Lord" who is speaking at the end of the verse continue to speak in verse 2, or does a psalmist-narrator now address the worshipping, reading audience? Do these voices overlap? Or who is the "you" (σου [singular]) in verse 2: David? the "my Lord" of verse 1? the general audience? Presumably the "Lord" of verse 2 wields the same type of authority as in verse 1 in granting a shared rule over "enemies" as "Lord" (v. 1 "at my right hand") or in dispatching a "scepter" of rule "in the midst of your enemies" (v. 2).

It would make sense at least at one level to read verse two as David continuing to speak but now more directly to the "my Lord" of verse 1: If in verse 1 David announces to his audience what "the Lord" had said to his ("my") Lord, now in verse 2 David speaks to 'his' Lord about the same granting of power and authority that "the Lord" had declared in verse 1. "The Lord" of verse 2 would then be identical with "the Lord" of verse 1.

Nonetheless, one could undoubtedly make an equally valid case for understanding the speaker of verse 2 to be "the Lord" of verse 1 who continues to speak but now to David as the "you." So the Lord now promises David that his Lord (compare "my Lord," v. 1) will provide David with the Lord's own scepter of power so that David will be able to rule in the midst of his own enemies, et cetera. The point to stress, therefore, is that there is more than one way to construe the developments and dynamics of the psalm(s) as the histories of interpretation have made clear.

Our contention therefore concerning the way that Luke through earlier traditions has interpreted these psalms to refer to Jesus illustrates this versatility of polyvalent referents within early Jewish-Christian exegesis. Yet according to Luke, Jesus himself had provided a very different way of viewing the psalms as he had to "open the minds" of the apostles before they could comprehend that at fundamental points the psalms were "referring" to himself (Luke 24:45–46; compare v. 44b–περὶ ἐμοῦ)!

The logic of the argument of the Pentecost "speech" seems to make the most sense and possess a greater persuasive power when the "the Lord" at David's ("my") "right hand" of Ps 15:8 in Acts 2:25b–c is identified as the same "Lord" at "the Lord's" ("my") "right hand" of Ps 109:1 in Acts 2:34b–35.

We can list the formal parallels of both psalms: 1) "My Lord" occurs (and only in these psalms) (Ps 15:2; 109:1); 2) A "Lord" and/or David is aligned with "saints" (Ps 15:3; 109:3); 3) "My Lord" and/or David has "enemies" (Ps 15:4–5, 8; 109:2, 5–7); 4) A Lord and/or David defeats the enemies (Ps 15:5, 8, 10; 109:1b, 2, 5–7); 5) "My Lord" is enthroned at "the Lord's right hand," or there are wondrous delights at a "Lord's" "right hand" (Ps 15:11; 109:1); 6) David has great hope for a final (eschatological) triumph of a "Lord" over all of the enemies (Ps 15:9b–11; 109:1,4–6).

The emerging plot of the two psalms could be configured thus:

David addresses the Lord of Ps 15:1 as "my Lord" in 15:2. This "my Lord" takes special delight in the saints ("holy ones") that are in this Lord's "land" who are undergoing severe persecution, including physical abuse of some sort ("bodily afflictions" [ἀσθένειαι]; "gatherings resulting in bloodshed" [τὰς συναγωγὰς αὐτῶν ἐξ αἱμάτων]); and the need for secrecy regarding the identities of these saints (οὐδὲ μὴ μνησθῶ τῶν ὀνομάτων αὐτῶν διὰ χειλέων μου). In the midst of this oppression, David avows a special solidarity with this Lord concerning both his inheritance and his "cup" of suffering; through all the opposition, David has learned discipline (παιδεύω) from this Lord, including the experience of his own bodily suffering (Ps 15:7). Thus David remains confident through this whole period of suffering that this Lord will restore his true inheritance (Ps 15:5–6).

Moreover it is David's experience of "continually seeing" this "Lord" "at my [his] right hand" precisely in the midst of this persecution that convinces him that he would not be defeated or die before his time ("that I should not be shaken," Ps 15:8). Even more (ἔτι δὲ καί, Ps 15:9c in Acts 2:26c), through continual solidarity with this Lord, David foresees that he himself would not simply rot in decay after his death; because of this Lord's presence in David's own presence, David boldly announces that "you" ("the Lord"/ God) will not "abandon" him to the tomb because "you" ("the Lord"/God) will not allow the "Lord" at his side, this "holy one," even to decompose in the tomb. This Lord will in fact precede David in final triumph over death (Ps 15:9–10). Consequently it is David's vision at his own right hand that enables him to see the eschatological vision at the Lord God's "right hand" where there will be "delights for ever" (εἰς τέλος, Ps 15:11c). In sum, because of "my Lord's" presence with David in his earthly rule, David has embraced an eschatological hope that already anticipates the final "joy" of the Lord's presence at the Lord God's right hand.

This reading of Ps 15 is emboldened by Ps 109. Indeed, each psalm invites mutual interpretation and enrichment. In Ps 109 David sees in advance that the "my Lord" who is constantly at his side (compare Ps 15:7–9) is invested at the Lord God's right hand with ultimate authority and power (Ps 109:1). The enemies that David, "the saints in the land," and "my Lord" had suffered in solidarity during

David's reign (compare Ps 15:2–4) are indeed defeated by the same "my Lord" who had been at David's side but now is ensconced at the Lord God's "side" (Ps 109:2–3a).

Probably the most straightforward reading of Ps 109:2–4 is for David to resume direct speaking as the psalmist in verse 2 so that David is speaking directly to "my Lord" of verse 1 as "you" (Ps 109:2 [σοι, σου], 3 [σοῦ–3x; σε], 4 [σύ]). Since David has overheard the Lord speak to "my Lord," David is privy to his Lord's calling and fate (compare Ps 15:10): "My Lord" will rule from Zion over all the enemies of God/Israel, while at the same time this rule will be constituted and characterized by a special solidarity with the "splendor of your ['my Lord's'] holy ones" (Ps 109:2–3a; compare Ps 15:3). What is more, David speaks with the divine authority of investiture by declaring, "I have given you birth from the womb before the morning dawn" (Ps 109:3b). "My Lord" is David's own offspring![13] "My Lord" thus qualifies to be both David's "Lord and Christ." With eschatological dominion this Lord and offspring will function as a "priest" in the priestly "order of Melchizedek." Similar to verse 1, David has overheard the Lord God swear an oath to David's "my Lord" and repeats this declaration to his audience (Ps 109:4; compare Ps 15:3).

In Ps 109:5–7 the audience (and speaker) appears to change. Now David could form the primary audience (σου, Ps 109:5) as he is told by a narrator-psalmist that a "Lord" at his "right hand" has already defeated his enemies and in the future will oppose and defeat again any enemy of Israel as this Lord will "judge among the nations" and be acclaimed the universal ruler over all ("he shall lift up the head," Ps 109:7b; compare Ps 15:11).[14] Read in this way, verses 5–7 comment upon Ps 15:8–11. The solidarity David was experiencing with his Lord over against his enemies during his own reign forms the pattern for the ultimate victory of the Lord over Israel's enemies at the end. David's enemies (Ps 15:4, 8; Ps 109:5) are "my Lord's" enemies (Ps 15:4, 8; Ps 109:2, 6–7) and *vice versa*. The saints in solidarity with David are in solidarity with "my Lord" and *vice versa* (Ps 15:3–4; Ps 109:3). As David's "Lord" and offspring, "my Lord" is bound together with David and the saints even as they "defeat" their common enemies. But that is to say, the "Lord at my right hand" of Ps 15:8 is the same "Lord at your right hand" of Ps 109:5.

---

13 This detail is completely absent in HB Ps 110; this difference ties "my Lord" more directly to David's own physical descent and thus opens the psalm and "my Lord" to messianic interpretation. LXX Ps 109 reads like a lullaby of David to his future son (and Lord)!

14 Cf. LXX Exod 15:6b (Song of Moses) as the exodus paradigm for the Lord's deliverance from Israel's enemies: "Your right hand, O Lord (ἡ δεξιά σου χείρ κύριε), crushed the enemies."

In both psalms, therefore, David speaks *to* "my Lord" (Ps 15:[1], 2, 5b; Ps 109:2, 3, 4) and *about* "my Lord" to the congregation (Ps 15:3, 5a, 7–8, 10b, 11; Ps 109:1). In both, David refers to a "Lord" (God) distinct from "my Lord" (Ps 15:[1], 10–11; Ps 109:1, 2, 4). Finally, in both psalms, two Lords interact with David, with enemies, and with saints to carry out the "preordained plan and prescience of God" (Acts 2:25, 34: "for David says ...").

Conclusion: The Prophet David as Messiah's Trailblazer in the "Plan of God" through the Suffering and Rejection by His Own People Israel

The significance of this plot for Peter's (Luke's) argument is now manifest: Like Jesus's words to the Emmaus disciples who are scolded for not knowing "Moses and the prophets" so as to recognize the script of Jesus's messianic suffering right before their eyes (Luke 24:25–27), so Peter chides the gathered Pentecost pilgrims for "crucifying this Jesus" whom God had appointed "Lord and Christ" as spoken by the prophets and the Psalms (Acts 2:36; compare Luke 24:44). They should have known better–not because they failed to understand one obscure little reference to "a holy one" who is raised from the dead but because the pattern of Messiah's rule had already been graphically played out in David's career. Like David, Jesus had divided the "house of Israel" and had thus sparked mounting opposition leading to his rejection and persecution, yet it was clear that "God had performed mighty works, wonders, and signs through him [...] just as you yourselves know" (Acts 2:22–23; compare Acts 10:38).

According to the logic of Pss 15 and 109, then, Jesus's path to life, to the "right hand of the Lord God," had already been blazoned through David's path to life "at his right hand." Jesus's enemies were the enemies to the greater *plan* that God had dramatically staged in advance in the suffering righteous David. David's "holy ones" were the saints who anticipated the "holy servants" of Jesus's career who now gather in the name of the "holy servant Jesus" to recite "our father David concerning your [Lord God's, Acts 4:24] holy servant Jesus whom you anointed (ἔχρισας) [...] to enact whatever your hand and your plan (ἡ βουλή) had foreordained to take place" (Acts 4:23–31). The paths that lead to life "at the right hand" are essentially, quintessentially, the paths of David's suffering and death.[15]

---

15 Cf. [LXX] Ps 17:17: "Let your [the Lord God's] hand be upon the man of your right hand and upon the son of man whom you did strengthen for yourself" and Acts 7:56, where Stephen "sees [...] the son of man standing at the right hand of God."

Peter is identifying the career of Jesus directly from the scriptures–from the suffering prophet David's own psalms "opened" by David's own "Lord and Christ" (Luke 24:44–46).[16]

In a surprising rhetorical twist, then, it is David who pinpoints Israel's responsibility for crucifying their Lord and Christ by pronouncing the unassailable explanation of what is transpiring on the Day of Pentecost ("David says" [present tense], 2:25, 34a)! Though long dead with the 'living proof' of his tomb, it is Israel's patriarch and prophet David who corroborates Peter's charge to the gathered worshippers at the "holy place" that they must "change their whole way of thinking" and be "baptized into the name of this Jesus Messiah" so that their sin might be removed and they receive the "Holy Spirit" from David's "Lord and Christ" at "the exalted place."[17] Ps 15:8–11 in Acts 2:25–28 forms the critical hinge to connect the "pouring out of my [God's] Spirit" of "the last days" to the crucified

---

[16] In the first five chapters of Acts immediately following Luke 24:44, there are sixteen citations or allusions/echoes from fourteen different psalms. After Acts 5 the citations and allusions almost completely disappear; but see, e.g., Ps 15:10 in Acts 13:35: [LXX numeration]–Pss 2; 15; 17; 19; 40; 68; 77; 88; 108; 109; 114; 117; 131; 145. The two cited doubly: Ps 15! and Ps 108. More specifically (Hebrew numeration in parentheses when significantly different in content and/or context): Ps 2:1–2 – Acts 4:25–26; Ps 15(16):8–11 – Acts 2:25–28; Ps 15(16):10 – Acts 2:31; Ps 17(18):4 – Acts 2:24; Ps 19(20):6 – Acts 2:36; Ps 40:10 – Acts 1:16; Ps 68:26 – Acts 1:20; Ps 77:8 – Acts 2:40; Ps 88:4 – Acts 2:30; Ps 108:8 – Acts 1:20; Ps 108:16 – Acts 2:37; Ps 109:1 – Acts 2:34–35; Ps 114(116):3 – Acts 2:24; Ps 117:22 – Acts 4:11; Ps 131:11 – Acts 2:30; Ps 145:6 – Acts 4:24!

[17] David's name appears explicitly five times in Acts 1–5, along with the following epithets: "patriarch" (Acts 1:16; 2:25; 2:29); "prophet" (Acts 2:30); and "servant" (παῖς) (4:25). This last designation is intriguing since David is also called "servant" (παῖς/δοῦλος) ten times in six of the sixteen cited/alluded psalms (see n. 16 above) [LXX-numbering]: Pss 17 [sub-title]; 68:17, 36; 77:70; 88:3, 20, 39, 50; 108:28; 131:10.

David is χριστός in three of the psalms cited (viz. Pss 17:50; 88:38; 131:10), while in two of them David's anointed status anticipates a future χριστός (Pss 88:51; 131:17); in two other psalms a χριστός occurs who appears to be a future "anointed" of David's line (Pss 2:2; 19:6). With both categories, "servant" and/or "Christ," David or an unnamed "righteous" person can be opposed by unrighteous or wicked folk *within Israel*. A basic plot emerges. David or an anointed person is a righteous, Torah-abiding figure, often in solidarity with a larger group of righteous folk, called "saints" or even "servants" (δοῦλοι, i.e., just as Peter describes the first Pentecost believers through the Joel text!). It is ironically, even scandalously God's will that the "anointed," faithful servant be smitten by the unrighteous of Israel (e.g., 68:26; 108:16!). Accordingly, in Acts 1:20, Judas's role in the betrayal of Jesus as the "leader of the arresting party" is portrayed in Ps 68, and the necessity of Judas's replacement in the apostolic ministry is pre-profiled in Ps 108.

In Acts 4:25–26, David is introduced as "patriarch" and "servant" as he prophesies in the utterances of Ps 2:1–2 about a "Lord" and a "Lord's christ." This Christ cannot be David himself but rather points to another, namely to Jesus as the "servant" and the "Lord's christ" through his rejection (crucifixion) at the hands of "the nations and the peoples of Israel" including their

"Lord exalted at the right hand" of God. With equal irony, the reversal of Israel's situation demonstrates that in rejecting Jesus of Nazareth, the people of Israel were unwittingly participating in "the foreordained plan and prescience of God." A "change of mind" or repentance that embraces this 'plan' was now facilitating for them eschatological "release from their sins," as well as forgiveness to their offspring, indeed, even to all those "far away, whomever the Lord our God calls" (Joel 3:5 echoing in Acts 2:39). Therefore the enriched "openings" of Pss 15 and 109 bear the theological *gravitas* of Peter's 'speech' to illumine the rejection and resurrection of Israel's Lord and Christ, and, at the same time, to lay the scriptural foundation for the apostolic "word" of this "witness" according to the new hermeneutic of the resurrected crucified one himself (Luke 24:44–49; Acts 1:3–8, 20–22; 2:32, 41).

---

leaders, "Herod and Pontius Pilate." Thus another psalm of David is cited to explicate the "foreordained plan of God" (Acts 4:28).

Part V:
Luke, the Church, and Israel's Legacy

The rich chorale of the voices of the suffering righteous that Luke blends into the cantata of his Christ continues to reverberate throughout the church's testimony to that Christ. As witnesses from among and to the people of Israel, first the apostles, then Stephen and the Seven, and finally the climactic 'about face' of Paul resound the voice and relive the rejection of the suffering-exalted one to the ends of the earth. Luke shows how the church proceeds out of the presence and actions of the suffering-risen one who continues to call Israel to their God-ordained and select role of bringing the light of God's saving justice to the nations.

By the 'ending' and at the 'end' of Acts, Israel remains a divided people–some change their whole mentality to embrace the Christ who releases them from their stubborn disobedience, while others continue Israel's eschatological role of denying their Lord and Christ ("how well did the Holy Spirit speak through the prophet Isaiah ... !" [Isa 6:9–10 (LXX) in Acts 28:25b–27]). Through a continuum that spans benign apathy all the way to outright hostility toward Jesus's witnesses, Paul still appeals to "the people" of *Israel* and their "Christ" as the basis for God's fidelity to God's "plan" as this chief witness becomes a sojourner-prisoner, chained and yet unfettered to proclaim the "Kingdom of God" and to teach with "with all openness" "the things concerning the Lord Jesus, the Christ" (28:30–31). Thus for Luke, Israel remains Israel throughout Luke and Acts–some obedient and others obstinate–in theory and practice no different than Israel had ever been since God's election of them out of their bondage of slavery. Paul pronounces the telltale judgment of Isa 6 upon the leaders of the Jewish peoples in Rome "while they left discordant" with Paul and his notion of "the things concerning Jesus from the Law of Moses and the prophets" (Acts 28:23–27).

Although it has become popular to debate whether Luke is essentially supersessionist and "writes off the Jews" or has depicted a "repenting Israel alongside an unrepenting Israel"–the latter of which by the end of Acts is no longer eligible to join "the people" for salvation–Luke will have nothing to do with either pole or position. *Israel remains Israel throughout both volumes.* For Luke there is no 'true Israel,' no 'new Israel,' only an Israel split by "the falling and rising of the many" provoked by the Christ. What we demonstrate in the two chapters that follow is that this very dynamic of growing opposition to Israel's Christ by Israel itself *is itself the means and modulation* of the very "counsel of God." This "plan" embraces non-Jewish Gentiles into the heart of "the people" of God's eschatological salvation, on the one side, while holding out to non-repenting Jews "the hope of Israel" that keeps in tension pronouncements seemingly contradictory but ultimately consistent with Israel's prophetic traditions, on the other: the coming eschatological *judgment* of destruction *along with* the undulating, often unspoken *'unless you repent.'* Luke does *not* seem to draw specifically on "remnant" scriptural passages to represent the *ecclesia* that is forming *out of* repentant Israel and believing Gentiles, though the image of a smaller group emerging in the "end time" as an obedient Israel is reminiscent of and functions more or less like a "remnant." Instead Luke calls forth the schema of the 'servant' calling as concentrated in Isaiah 40–55, consistent with the whole of Isaiah, and in Luke's formulation, in concert with "Moses and all the prophets." Israel is summoned and sent and *remains* for Luke the chief instrument of the performing "acts of God's salvation" for the whole world.

In Chapter Eleven, "Paul in Acts: Preacher of Eschatological Repentance to Israel," we argue that Luke not only purposely parallels Paul's final journey to Jerusalem with Jesus's great journey to suffering and death, but that Paul also re-sounds Jesus's eschatological pronouncements of judgment, especially as the final 'movement' within the "plan of God" crescendos to its climax. At strategic points in his sending as the Lord Christ's primary witness *from* Jerusalem *through* Samaria and the diaspora *to* Israel and *to* the nations afar, Paul's message to the Jewish peoples echoes unwaveringly, that Israel's "Christ must suffer and be raised," that "Jesus is that Christ," and that therefore as both Lord and Christ "he [Jesus] commands all human beings everywhere to repent" (Acts 17:30).

Chapter Twelve „Das Doppelwerk des Lukas und *Heil als Geschichte.* Oscar Cullmanns auffälliges Schweigen bezüglich des stärksten Befürworters seiner Konzeption der Heilsgeschichte im Neuen Testament," presents Luke's calling of Paul on the road to Damascus as constitutive for the execution of "the plan of God" and thus of the entire plotting of Luke and Acts. While Hans Conzelmann was correct in understanding Luke's two volumes as an extended narrativizing of the "gospel" proclaimed by Paul and first narrated by Mark, yet Paul's role in the overarching "plan" of Luke is much closer to Paul's self-described calling to the Gentiles via Israel than Conzelmann was willing to acknowledge. Rather than 'historicizing' a much sharper dialectic between the cross of Christ and eschatological decision in Paul (and Mark) à la Conzelmann and the Bultmann school more generally, Luke choreographs Paul's sense of a critical *time of the end* in which the gospel must be proclaimed worldwide by emplotting the various circumstances that lead to Paul's uncompromising insistence that he visit Rome as Christ's chief "witness." Paul's reaching of Rome in Acts (Acts 19:21–28:31) is in fact portrayed similarly to Paul's desire in his letter to the Romans to journey there in order to fulfill in part an eschatological calling of the servant mission of Isaiah of extending the reign of God "to the end of the earth" (compare especially Romans 9–11; 15).

Thus with Paul's arrival in Rome, an eschatological time between times has been completed according to Paul's and Luke's conceptualizations. Utilizing Oscar Cullmann's tension between an "already and not yet" in a "history of salvation" schema derived from Paul's own letters, we delineate the plot lines that connect Acts's narration of "the times of the end" and Paul's own formulations of the unparalleled urgency of his calling. We point out further that had Cullmann argued backward from Luke and Acts to Paul rather than the reverse, he would have had to reckon with the much stronger 'family resemblance' between the two in each writer's formulation of a *Heilsgeschichte* in which Paul becomes the decisive player *after* the public career of the Christ and yet renders this indispensable role precisely *through* the continuing activity of Jesus the Christ himself.

At the end of Part V we draw together our conclusions for the whole of the volume.

Chapter Eleven: Paul in Acts: Preacher of Eschatological Repentance to Israel[1]

The 'enigmatic ending' of Acts continues to baffle the exegetes.[2] Not the least of its difficulties is the status of "the Jews" after Paul's peculiarly solemn pronouncement of Isa 6:9–10 against a "closed" and "hardened" people (Acts 28:26–27). Coming as it does as a climax to the equally ponderous pronouncements of judgment in Acts 13:46 and 18:6, for many scholars the cumulative, three-fold impact of this indictment resounds a note of finality, of foreclosure upon Israel which consequently consummates an era and looks ahead almost exclusively to a Gentile church. The two leading clusters of opinion expressing this understanding are those associated with Ernst Haenchen[3]–that repentance for Israel by the end of Acts is *de facto* now over, with Gentiles replacing Jews as the people of God–or with Jacob Jervell[4]–that a core of repenting Jews constitutes a restored Israel which, along with increasing numbers of Gentiles, by the end of chapter 28 has completed its mission to unrepenting Jews who no longer have a right to the name "Israel" or "people of God."

It is the contention of this investigation that neither "replacement" (Haenchen) nor "restoration-exclusion" (Jervell), neither an "old" nor "Israel alongside"[5] a "new" or "re-newed" people of God, respectively, does justice to a distinctive dynamic of Israel's history that Luke unfolds in his two volumes. To carve the contours of this "historical" profile we shall use as our point of vantage the largely neglected correspondences in the pronouncements of eschatological judgment between Jesus and Paul within the wider-ranging Jesus-Paul parallels.[6] Our task

---

1 Previously in David P. Moessner, "Paul in Acts: Preacher of Eschatological Repentance to Israel," *NTS* 34 (1988): 96–104. Used with permission.
2 For a lucid discussion of the various interpretations, see Paul W. Walaskay, *'And so we came to Rome': The Political Perspective of St. Luke*, SNTSMS 49 (Cambridge: Cambridge University Press, 1983), 18–22.
3 Although Haenchen's delineation between the story time of the narrative and Luke's own time is not always clear, he apparently is convinced that Luke himself believes that by the time of Paul's arrival in Rome, the Pauline mission had "written off" the Jews (Ernest Haenchen, *The Acts of the Apostles*, 14th ed. [Oxford: Blackwell, 1971], 128–29); see n. 10 below.
4 Jacob Jervell, *Luke and the People of God* (Minneapolis, MN: Augsburg, 1972), 41–74; Jacob Jervell, *The Unknown Paul* (Minneapolis, MN: Ausburg, 1984), 26–51, esp. 39–43.
5 Jervell, *Luke and the People of God*, 68.
6 See, e.g., Walter Radl, *Paulus und Jesus im lukanischen Doppelwerk* (Bern: Lang, 1975); A. J. Mattill, Jr., "The Jesus-Paul Parallels and the Purpose of Luke-Acts: H. H. Evans Reconsidered,"

is necessarily restricted to a synchronic analysis[7] of the specific role these utterances play in presenting a perspective on Israel's past and continuing 'reception' of God's messengers of salvation that culminates in Jesus and in the mission of his 'witness' Paul. We thus can only begin to address Luke's larger view of Israel and the church's relation to their history in his two volumes.

1 Book One: The Gospel according to Luke

In his journey section to Jerusalem (Luke 9:51–19:44), Luke sums up the growing opposition to Jesus's message from the burgeoning crowds of Israel (11:29; 12:1; 14:25) at three strategic junctures. In each instance Jesus warns of impending judgment as a result of their failure to repent before the one who brings Israel's salvation to its fulfillment:

1.1. In 11:37–54 at table with Israel's leaders, who together with Jesus (v. 37) have emerged from the throngs of "this evil generation" (11:29), Jesus utters six Old Testament prophetic "woe oracles" (*Weheworte*)[8] in which a distinct pattern emerges. As the builders of the "prophets' tombs" (v. 47), the Pharisees' scribes are continuing the unbroken history of disobedience of "their fathers" who tenaciously persecuted and killed the "prophets and messengers" "sent" to Israel. Indeed, Jesus's hosts are pouring their contribution into the stream of blood that extends all the way back to Abel in Genesis and flows through the whole history of Israel to Zechariah, ben-Jehoida, in the last book of the Writings,[9] but now in a special way. Upon this generation of Jesus's audiences falls the blood guilt of Israel's entire history of disobedience, "that the blood of all the prophets shed from the foundation of the world may be required (ἐκζητέω) of *this generation.*

NovT 17 (1975): 15–46; David P. Moessner, "'The Christ Must Suffer': New Light on the Jesus-Peter, Stephen, Paul Parallels in Luke-Acts," *NovT* 28 (1986): 220–56 [Chapter Nine above].

7 An approach to any narrative text which places a priority on relating various parts of the 'narrative world' of the text *to each other* in establishing the *necessary* literary context *within* which diachronic issues and conclusions concerning tradition and redaction should be addressed. See further, n. 10.

8 E.g., Amos 5:18–20; Isa 5 (*passim*); Mic 2:1–4; Jer 22:13–14; Ezek 34:2; compare *1 En.* 91–104 (*passim*). Compare David E. Aune, *Prophecy in Early Christianity and the Ancient Mediterranean World* (Grand Rapids, MI: Eerdmans, 1983), 96–97; Odil H. Steck, *Israel und das gewaltsame Geschick der Propheten*, WMANT 23 (Neukirchen-Vluyn: Neukirchener Verlag, 1967), 190–94, locates the *Sitz im Leben* of the "woe oracle" in recitations of the "curses" of Deut 27:15–26 in the covenant renewal ceremony. See below for this Deuteronomistic view of Israel's guilt.

9 See Gen 4:10; 2Chr 24:25.

Yes, I say to you it shall be required of this generation" (vv. 47–51). Like Ezekiel in his day, Jesus is a "watchman" who sounds the toll of the blood that is required (compare LXX, ἐκζητέω, Ezek 33:6, 8) of a recalcitrant people. But when Luke adds in verses 53–54 that "as Jesus journeyed on from there the scribes and the Pharisees began to act in a very hostile manner [...] lying in wait [...] to trip him up," and this is combined with one "wiser" than Solomon and "greater" than Jonah whose demands for repentance fall on the deaf ears of Israel just previous to our table scene (11:29–32, 33–36), it is clear that for Luke Jesus regards himself as more than *a* watchman, rather as *the* consummating point of all the prophets' tragic sending. Israel's disobedience to his voice brings about the *final* or *eschatological* judgment upon an unrepentant folk. The pattern that has emerged is this: A. Israel's history is one long unremitting story of a stubborn, disobedient people; B. God has sent his messengers, the prophets, to plead repentance lest Israel bring upon itself the destruction of God's judgment. Jesus is the crowning prophet or messenger in the long line sent to Israel; C. Israel, nevertheless, *en masse* rejected all these prophets, even persecuting and killing them, and rejects Jesus's mission as well; D. Therefore, God will bring upon Jesus's generation the "final judgment" for the whole history of the blood guilt of this disobedience.

1.2. We see the Pharisees next trying to "trip up" Jesus at the midpoint[10] of the journey (13:31–35), again after Jesus has warned the ever swelling crowds of Israel of the judgment that is coming because they will not repent (12:54–13:9, 22–30). The same pattern presents itself again but with the following additions: (1) Jesus now acknowledges explicitly that he is a prophet whose sending to Jerusalem must of necessity end in the tragic fate awarded all their prophets (v. 33). A prophetic *Scheltwort* followed by the *Drohwort*[11] is addressed to this nation's center: "Jerusalem, Jerusalem, you killer of the prophets and stoner of those sent to you.

---

10 The approximate "mid-point" according to a sequential reckoning of the "story-stuff" (*fabula*) in the journey account. For definitions of "story," "plot," "story time," "plotted time," "narrative world," etc., as developed by the Russian Formalists and utilized in the present investigation, see Stephen Bann and John E. Bowlt, eds., *Russian Formalism* (Edinburgh: Scottish Academic, 1973), esp. the essays of Tzvetan Todorov (6–19), Richard Sherwood (26–40), and Viktor Shklovsky (48–72); Norman R. Petersen, *Literary Criticism for New Testament Critics* (Philadelphia, PA: Fortress, 1978), 33–92. For various interpretations of the dissonance of form from content in the Lukan "travel narrative," see David P. Moessner, "Luke 9:1–50: Luke's Preview of the Journey of the Prophet like Moses of Deuteronomy," *JBL* 102 (1983): 575–605 [Chapter Eight above]; idem, *Lord of the Banquet: The Literary and Theological Significance of the Lukan Travel Narrative* (Minneapolis, MN: Fortress, 1989); reprinted with new preface by the author and a foreword by Richard B. Hays (Trinity Press International, 1998).

11 E.g. Isa 3:12; 29:12–14; Jer 16:11–13; Amos 3:2; 4:1–2; 8:4–8; Mic 3:9–12; compare Aune, *Prophecy*, 92; Steck, *Geschick*, 57–58.

Chapter Eleven: Paul in Acts: Preacher of Eschatological Repentance to Israel — **295**

How often I desired to gather you [...] but you did not so desire! Behold, your house is/will be *abandoned* (ἀφίημι)," (vv. 34–35a). (2) Recalling the imagery of Ezekiel 9–11 (especially 9:9) when Yahweh forsakes the Temple or of Jer 7:8–15 and 12:7–13 where Yahweh "abandons" (ἀφίημι) his heritage, "house," by destroying his "house," the Temple, which had become a "lair of robbers" (σπήλαιον λῃστῶν, 7:11), Jesus's oracle now uses this destruction of 587 BCE with its exile to forecast the eschatological judgment awaiting an unresponsive folk. Now it is expressly stated that because Israel has spurned the persistent pleadings of the prophet Jesus, they will be forsaken in a way hauntingly reminiscent of the devastation of 587 BCE.[12]

1.3. At the end of the journey, just after the parable in 19:11–27 of the 'Nobleman Who Went on a Journey to Receive a Kingship' mirrors the entire rejection accorded Israel's journeying Prophet-King, the throng of disciples who hail the "king who is coming" would seem to defy this depiction even if we do find some Pharisees once again trying to throttle Jesus's movement (vv. 37–40). Yet in the measured metre of the dirge (vv. 42–44),[13] Jesus utters a judgment of blanket destruction which not only reverberates the previous oracles of 11:47–51 and 13:34–35 but also transposes the enthusiastic cries of the disciples into the shrill shrieks of crucifixion that will soon be sounded by the whole nation of Israel's leaders (for example, 19:47; 20:19; 22:52, 66), their king (23:6–12), the *laos* (see especially 23:13, 18), and even the "Twelve" (22:3–6, 31–34, 47, 54–62) as they all consolidate to form "this evil generation." As a result, Jerusalem will be "encircled" (περικυκλόω) with "siege-mounds" (χάραξ) "cast up" (παρεμβάλλω) about them, and their inhabitants shall be "dashed" or "razed" to the ground (ἐδαφίζω) (19:43–44). As C. H. Dodd demonstrated already in 1947,[14] this vocabulary clusters around the prediction of the spectre of 587 BCE by the great prophets Isaiah, Ezekiel, and Jeremiah, especially the two former where the LXX is found using χάραξ,[15] παρεμβολή,[16] κύκλος,[17] and ἐδαφίζω.[18] Χάραξ and ἐδαφίζω or any cognates appear only once in the New Testament, here at Luke 19:43–44.[19]

---

12 For the same notion in intertestamental and rabbinic literature of the God of Israel "abandoning/leaving" the Temple, see e.g., Bar 2:26; *T. Levi* 15:1; *1 En.* 89:56; *Pesiq. Rab.* 138a; 146a; compare Dan 9:17b.
13 Compare Amos 5:1–2.
14 C. H. Dodd, "The Fall of Jerusalem and the 'Abomination of Desolation,'" *JRS* 37 (1947) 47–54.
15 Isa 29:3; 37:33; Ezek 4:2; 21:22.
16 Ezek 4:2; compare Jer 27:29.
17 Isa 29:3; 37:33; Ezek 4:2; compare Jer 27:29.
18 Isa 3:25–26.
19 See Dodd, "Fall," 50–52, for detailed discussion; for an instructive history of interpretation and various positions on the situation of Lukan eschatology, see John T. Carroll, *Response to the*

Before we turn to Paul's pronouncements of judgment in Acts we must look briefly at the apocalyptic prospect in Luke 21 which does *not* sever the 'end' from the destruction of Jerusalem either in a qualitative or determinedly quantitative sense. With the framing of the entire apocalyptic 'timetable' inside the Temple within the warnings to Jesus's audience at the beginning in Luke 21:8a and the ending in 21:36– "take heed [...] watch at all times [...] that *you* may have strength to escape *all these things that will take place*" –it is clear that the walls of the "nest of thieves" (σπήλαιον λῃστῶν) of Luke 19:45 (Jer 7:11) will tumble (Luke 21:6) for "this generation" which "will *not* pass away" (v. 32) not only until "the son of Man is first rejected" (17:25) but also not until "*all* has taken place" (21:32).

Even more interesting is the pattern of judgment that unfolds. Unlike Mark and Matthew, Luke follows a period of persecution of disciples by fellow Jews *not* by an intensified "abomination of desolation" (βδέλυγμα ἐρημώσεως, Mark 13:14; Matt 24:15) in the Temple but by an ἐρήμωσις of destruction upon Jerusalem as a punishment upon "this people" *Israel* (21:23b). Though this judgment is not *explicitly* linked to their rejection of Jesus, this rationale becomes manifest in the way Luke intertwines the 'story time' of the 'eschaton' with the 'plotted time'[20] of the mission of Jesus and his disciples:

(*a*) The decimation of the Temple –"no stone upon another" in 21:6–by echoing the οὐκ ἀφήσουσιν λίθον ἐπὶ λίθον of 19:44, depicts *pars pro toto* the razing of Jerusalem and sets this destruction as the eschatological horizon for the penultimate "signs" in verses 8–11 and 25–26 which herald the Final Judgment of the Son of Man (vv. 27–28). "The great distress/calamity (ἀνάγκη) upon the earth/land (ἐπὶ τῆς γῆς)" "in those days (ἐν ἐκείναις ταῖς ἡμέραις)" of verse 23 not only points back as a fulfillment of the "days coming (ἐλεύσονται ἡμέραι)" of verse 6 but also continues uninterrupted the same period of international conflict characterized by the "anguish/terror of the nations (συνοχὴ ἐθνῶν)" "upon the earth (ἐπὶ τῆς γῆς)" of verse 25. For verse 9 speaks of only one period of universal warfare of indeterminate duration that is to precede "the end" (οὐκ εὐθέως τὸ τέλος). The "wrath upon this people," Israel (v. 23), funneled in the devastation of Jerusalem and its Temple (vv. 20–24), is thus sandwiched in the midst of universal strife (vv. 9–11, 20–24, 25–26) that is attended by great "natural" disasters

---

End of History: Eschatology and Situation in Luke-Acts, SBLDS 92 (Atlanta, GA: Scholars Press, 1988), esp. 1–119; cf. Manfred Korn, *Die Geschichte Jesu in veränderter Zeit: Studien zur bleibenden Bedeutung Jesu im lukanischen Doppelwerk*, WUNT 2/51 (Tübingen: Mohr Siebeck, 1993); Michael Wolter, "Israel's Future and the Delay of the Parousia, according to Luke." In *Jesus and the Heritage of Israel. Luke's Narrative Claim upon Israel's Legacy*, edited by David P. Moessner, 307–24. Vol. 1, *Luke the Interpreter of Israel*. Harrisburg, PA: Trinity Press International, 1999.
20 See n. 10.

(for example, σεισμοί, v. 11 [...] ἤχους θαλάσσης, v. 25) and "panic" (πτοέω, v. 9 [...] ἀποψυχόντων [...] ἀπὸ φόβου, v. 26) in the world and by cosmic "terrors" and "signs from heaven" (φόβητρά τε καὶ ἀπ' οὐρανοῦ σημεῖα, v. 11 [...] σημεῖα ἐν ἡλίῳ, v. 25, δυνάμεις τῶν οὐρανῶν σαλευθήσονται, v. 26).

(*b*) "But before all this" the followers of Jesus will be "persecuted" (v. 12a), "brought before kings and governors" (v. 12b), "betrayed" by friends and even family (v. 16a), "hated by all" (v. 17a), and some even "put to death" (v. 16b)–they experience the same fate of suffering and rejection as their Master–all "because of" or "on account of my name" (vv. 12b, 17b). Though it becomes apparent that during this time of "testimony" (v. 13) Jesus is not with them in the same bodily presence as before, nevertheless his solidarity of presence with them is as binding as before. Whether they are to beware of imposters declaring "in Jesus's name," "I am he" (v. 8), or are to rely solely on Jesus personally (ἐγώ) telling them what to say in their defense (v. 15a), it is certain that the same conditions of being with Jesus as disciples now that he has arrived in Jerusalem remain as when he made his great journey to Jerusalem: compare "taking up one's own cross *daily*"/"losing life *for my sake*" (9:23–24); "rejecting" the disciples is tantamount to rejecting Jesus and the Kingdom of God that has still come near in these representatives (10:11, 16) or 14:27–32–"counting" the cost. Consequently, when the disciples are to flee because they see Jerusalem surrounded by foreign armies (21:20–21), there is not the slightest suggestion that Jerusalem is destroyed *only* because of Israel's rejection of Jesus and *not* because of Israel's rejection of his followers. Nor can it be that the Final Judgment is disconnected from Jerusalem's desolation and pushed off to an indefinite future as salvation or rescue for the persecuted disciples.[21] Rather, as verses 25–26 pick up from verses 9–11 with the eschatological signs attending the destruction of Jerusalem and its Temple, the Jesus movement is revealed to be one where master and disciples are bound together in Israel's fate of judgment as the persecuted eschatological remnant.

(*c*) The conclusion of (*b*) is confirmed by verses 22–24 in which the "days of retribution" are characterized in the stereotypical language of death by "sword" and "exile as captives among the nations" (v. 24),[22] all of which occur "in order to fulfill all that is written in the Scriptures" (v. 22b). Within Luke's own 'story time' this fulfillment of judgment must certainly refer back to the Scriptures of Luke

---

[21] So Georg Braumann, "Die lukanische Interpretation der Zerstörung Jerusalems," *NovT* 6 (1963): 120–27.
[22] Dodd, "Fall," 51–52; Bo Reicke, "Synoptic Prophecies on the Destruction of Jerusalem," in *Studies in New Testament and Early Christian Literature: Essays in Honour of A. P. Wikgren*, ed. David E. Aune (Leiden: Brill, 1972): 126–28.

18:31–32 where all that is written in the prophets about Jesus as the journeying Son of Man must be consummated in Jerusalem, especially since this Son of Man who comes to Jerusalem "seeking and saving the perishing" in 19:1–10, immediately tells of the nobleman who, though physically absent, has appointed agents who are called to task when he returns to destroy the whole rebellious people who "do not want this one to reign over us" (19:14). This final judgment in chapter 21 is again certainly the point of the scriptures in the parable of the "Wicked Tenants" (20:9–18) that is precipitated by the challenge to Jesus's authority in the Temple (20:1–8; see 20:19b). The rejected "stone" of Ps 118:22 becomes the stone of "scandal" of Isa 8:14–15 that then turns and crushes a hardened nation (Luke 20:17–18). But even more curious is the phrase ἡμέραι ἐκδικήσεως αὗται (21:22a) which re-sounds the ἡμέρα ἐκδικήσεως of Deut 32:35, where in the LXX a future and final judgment of God upon the people of Israel and *then* upon the nations is prophesied by Moses because of Israel's continued stubborn disobedience to the voice of God through him and through future messengers once they occupy the land (compare Deut 31:14–29). The Song of Moses (Deut 32:1–43), which is utilized by the Deuteronomistic historians as a vivid capsule of the dynamics of Israel's past, presents the classic pattern of persistent disobedience–destruction and exile–repentance–and return/vindication,[23] based upon the events of 587 but set now "in the last days" (ἐπ' ἐσχάτων [ἡμερῶν],[24] 32:20). Now according to Luke Jesus forecasts the fulfillment of this scripture for "this generation" of Israel, with his disciples the remnant that escapes the Gentile destruction of Jerusalem until these "times" (καιροί), and for Luke, "opportunities" "of the Gentiles," are completed by the universal appearance and assize of the Son of Man.

Thus we may combine the pattern of Israel's reception of their prophets with this Deuteronomistic dynamic of history for the following schema:[25]

A: Israel's history continues as one long, unremitting story of a stubborn, disobedient people;

B: God has sent his messengers, the prophets, to plead repentance lest they bring upon themselves judgment and destruction. Jesus, together with his disciples, represents the crowning point of this sending to Israel;

---

23 George W. E. Nickelsburg, *Jewish Literature between the Bible and the Mishnah* (Philadelphia, PA: Fortress, 1981), 9–18; Steck, *Geschick*, 110–95; Gerhard von Rad, *Deuteronomy: A Commentary* (Philadelphia, PA: Westminster, 1966), 195–201.
24 In Codex B.
25 Compare Steck, *Geschick*, 77–80, 137–43, on this dynamic in the Deuteronomistic history.

C: Nevertheless, Israel has *en masse* rejected all these prophets, even persecuting and killing them, and has done so quintessentially with Jesus and his disciples;

D: Therefore, as God had rained destruction upon them in BCE 587, so he will again, but now the final judgment of destruction for an unrepentant people.

2 Book Two: The Acts of the Apostles

It has often been observed that in Luke's narrative world, Paul's arrival in Rome takes place within the period of "testimony" in which, like Jesus himself, his followers are hauled before "kings and governors" (for example, Agrippa, Acts 25:23–26:32; Festus, 25:1–12). The Temple still stands; armies have not surrounded Jerusalem. Yet what has not been carefully observed is the way that Paul's pronouncements of judgment continue to fill in the chronological but especially the conceptual framework of Jesus's eschatological preview.

2.1. Acts 13:40–46 *Pisidian Antioch*.

Paul finishes his detailed explanation of the "word of this salvation" which "has been sent to us" (Acts 13:26), Israel, along with "fearers of God," with a shocking prophetic *Mahnwort*.[26] In quoting Hab 1:5 (LXX)–"look, you scorners, marvel and then be destroyed/perish for I am performing a deed […] that you will never believe, even if one should explain it in detail to you"–Paul takes the warning of the coming disaster in the rise of Nebuchadnezzar and applies it to his Diaspora-Jewish mission. Because they are "judging themselves unworthy of this final salvation" (v. 46b), they bring down upon them the final judgment of Tenet D as viewed through the lens of 587. And thus for Paul, it is not just the death and raising up of the Messiah that fulfills "all that is written" (13:27, 29, 32–35) but, as in Luke 21, the coming judgment upon an obdurate people as well.

---

26 Aune, *Prophecy*, 95.

2.2. Acts 18:6 *Corinth*.

Paul's second pronouncement, in Greece, following as it does one persecution after another from fellow countryfolk throughout south central Asia Minor and then in Macedonia, not only makes the solemnity of the Pisidian Antioch declaration anything but an isolated pronouncement but also articulates what has now become manifestly evident: Paul himself is included among the long line of prophets and apostles rejected and repudiated by a recalcitrant Israel. Consequently, Paul's uttering, "Your blood be upon your head," which resonates Ezekiel's warning of further judgment to Israel because they did not repent at the judgment of 587 (Ezek 33:4–5),[27] is not by accident. As the "watchman" for Israel, Paul sounds once again Jesus's warning that the "blood of this generation will be required" because they refuse to accept God's salvation through Jesus and his messengers. Moreover, here the "blood" of Acts 20:26, 28 is already anticipated where before the Ephesian elders Paul will abruptly declare that he is "innocent of the blood of all" the Jews that will be required of them for their failure to repent (μετάνοια, v. 21) at the "whole will or counsel of God" that is effected "through the blood of his Own" (v. 28). Now as Paul journeys to Jerusalem, knowing that the Ephesians "will see my face no more" (v. 25), Paul's destiny is sealed with the blood of all the prophets from Abel to Zechariah, with Jesus (compare Luke 22:20; Acts 5:28), and with Stephen whose blood Paul will invoke in 22:30 when he recalls his own participation in the growing solidarity of hostility to the messengers of salvation.

2.3. 28:25–28 *Rome*.

Thus at the end of Acts after Paul has been accused by "the whole people of the Jews, both at Jerusalem and here" (25:24, Caesarea) of perverting "all the Jews in the Diaspora" (21:21) or in "the inhabited world" (24:5), or as Paul himself sums it up–the Jews tried to kill him because he had "declared first to those at Damascus, then at Jerusalem and throughout all the country of Judea and to the Gentiles that they should repent and turn to God and perform deeds worthy of this repentance" (26:20)–we find that it is again no accident that Paul pronounces a "final" final judgment against "the people" (τῷ λαῷ), "my nation" (τοῦ ἔθνους μου) of Israel (28:17, 19). In the chilling cadence of Tenet A Paul fulfills Isaiah's calling to

---

27 Walther Zimmerli, *Ezekiel 1*, Hermeneia (Philadelphia, PA: Fortress, 1979), 2, 67.

announce God's inexorable judgment against a calloused folk whose ears have grown "thick," whose eyes are "shut."

Having traced the eschatological framework A.–D. for the last two-thirds of the Gospel and demonstrated not only the intrinsic compatibility but also the organic development of Paul's pronouncements of judgment from within this dynamic, we can formulate the following implications:

Both believing Jews and non-believing Jews constitute and remain throughout Acts the *one* Israel, the people of God;

Believing Jews form the eschatological remnant. This remnant, along with growing numbers of Gentiles, which together comprise the church, functions as the vanguard that calls unbelieving Israel to repentance, and will itself be spared the final destruction of Jerusalem and punishment upon the whole people of Israel.

At the end of the plotted time, some Jews do respond to Paul's proclamation in Rome, as in other cities, and he preaches freely to all. The period of bearing "testimony" before the "days of retribution" is still in force. Therefore to speak of a Lukan vantage point from which repentance or belief for Jews is, for all intents and purposes, over is not only misleading but also has no warrant in the text. Rather, as with the prophets of Israel, along with the pronouncement of certain judgment comes the implicit "Unless you repent." Nevertheless, the third and final pronouncement of final judgment bears an unmistakable force of warning to Israel. Although Tenet D is not uttered explicitly, the fact that Paul announces Tenets A–C *before* any period of preaching in Rome is described leaves the reader with the inescapable impression[28] that, within Luke's narrative world, not only is the plan of Acts 1:8[29] and its prolepsis at Pentecost realizable but also that the "days of retribution" upon an unrepentant people are straining to fulfillment.

---

[28] The *variation* is significant within the threefold *repetition*; for "variation" and "repetition" as poetic devices in the narrative "point of view," see Adele Berlin, *Poetics and Interpretation of Biblical Narrative*, Bible and Literature Series 9 (Sheffield: Almond, 1983), 73–79.

[29] For "the end of the earth" symbolizing the nations controlled by a great pagan empire used by God to judge/destroy Israel, see Isa 5:26 (Assyria); Jer 6:22 (Babylonia); Isa 48:20 (Persia); PsSol 8:15 (Rome! from a probable Palestine-geographical perspective!).

Chapter Twelve: Das Doppelwerk des Lukas und *Heil als Geschichte*: Oscar Cullmanns auffälliges Schweigen bezüglich des stärksten Befürworters seiner Konzeption der Heilsgeschichte im Neuen Testament[1]

Meine These ist mehr eine Frage als eine Feststellung, eher eine erstaunte Beobachtung als eine Schlussfolgerung. Professor Cullmann hat enorm viel geschrieben. Warum hat Oscar Cullmann von seinen zahlreichen Publikationen nicht wenigstens <u>eine</u> größere Studie oder <u>einen</u> längeren Aufsatz dem heilsgeschichtlichen Aufriss und Charakter des lukanischen Doppelwerks gewidmet? Wenn irgendwo unter den Hauptzeugen des Neuen Testaments, dann finden wir doch hier eine ausführliche narrative Darstellung von Heilsereignissen, die sich aus den entscheidenden, eschatologisch definierenden Ereignissen von dem Messias Israels bis hin zum „Endziel" aller Heilsereignisse der Bibel entwickeln – eine Parade von „schon und noch nicht" Ereignissen und von Vorwegnahme von Heil und seiner Vollendung, die eine perfekte Illustration der Hauptthese Cullmanns von der grundlegenden heilsgeschichtlichen Darstellung der Bibel zu sein scheint. Wenn ich mich nicht gänzlich irre, hat Cullmann abgesehen von seiner (verständlicherweise durch die Einschränkungen eines Wörterbuchs beschränkten) Behandlung der Apostelgeschichte im RGG-Artikel über „Geschichtsschreibung," in der dritten Auflage von 1958[2], nie ausführlich über das Wesen der Heilsgeschichte im Doppelwerk des Lukas geschrieben. Sicherlich, Einzelstellen der Apostelgeschichte werden im Zusammenhang ihrer thematischen Verbindung mit anderen neutestamentlichen Schriftstellern behandelt, z. B. die Gütergemeinschaft in Apg 2 und 4 und die paulinische Kollekte als *koinonia* mit

---

[1] First delivered in German at the Symposium, "Zehn Jahre nach Oscar Cullmanns Tod: Rückblick und Ausblick," in Basel, Switzerland, June 5–6, 2009. Special thanks to the translators Karlfried Froehlich, organizer of the symposium, and Jens Schröter for improving both my English and my "ausländisches" Deutsch. I have retained the rhetoric of the lecture format.
First published as "Luke/Acts and Salvation as History: Oscar Cullmann's Strange Silence Concerning the New Testament's Strongest Proponent of His Conception of *Heilsgeschichte*," in *Zehn Jahre nach Oscar Cullmanns Tod: Rückblick und Ausblick*, ed. M. Sallmann, K. Froehlich, Basler und Berner Studien zur historischen Theologie 75 (Zürich: Theologischer Verlag, 2012): 135–45.
[2] Oscar Cullmann, „Geschichtsschreibung. Im NT," in RGG³ 2 (1958), Sp. 1501–1503 (1503): dass Lukas „ein historisches Interesse für die Zeit der Kirche zeige".

den „armen" Heiligen von Jerusalem (vgl. Röm 15), oder die „anderen" (*alloi*) von Johannes 4, 38 und die Hellenisten in Samaria in Apg 8 usw. Aber eine kontinuierliche Behandlung der heilsgeschichtlichen Struktur der Apostelgeschichte oder des lukanischen Doppelwerks als Ganzem sucht man in Cullmanns reichem Werk vergebens.

I Gründe des Schweigens

Lassen Sie mich wagen, einige Gründe für dieses seltsame Schweigen zu nennen. In einer Liste von ansteigender Wertigkeit würde ich drei separate, aber miteinander verbundene Faktoren nennen.

I.1. Seit der Aufklärungskritik, die besonders mit <u>Ferdinand Christian Baur</u> und der sogenannten „Tübinger Schule" verbunden ist, fand man den *logos* des Evangeliums in seiner reinsten Ausprägung im *kerygma* des Paulus, während die Evangelienberichte bestenfalls als Verwässerungen oder Verzerrungen in sub-literarischem, volkstümlichem Erzählungsstil anstelle des „reinen Wortgeschehens" der weitschweifigen Verkündigung betrachtet wurden. Die Apostelgeschichte war in ihrem Wert als Zeuge des Evangeliums sogar noch eine Stufe tiefer eingestuft als die Evangelien. Bestenfalls sah man sie als archivalischen Zusatz zu den Evangelien an, obwohl Baur ohne Zögern auf die Parallelen zwischen dem Lukasevangelium und der Apostelgeschichte aufmerksam machte und die zwei Bücher als Darstellung eines frühkatholischen Anliegens betrachtete, in dem Petrus so paulinisch wie möglich und Paulus so petrinisch wie möglich erscheinen sollte. Schon hier also wurde das lukanische Doppelwerk als ein Ganzes aufgefasst und mit einer bestimmten „Tendenz" innerhalb der sich entwickelnden Orthodoxie des späten ersten und zweiten Jahrhunderts verbunden.

I.2. <u>Rudolf Bultmann</u> und einige seiner Schüler repräsentieren z. T. eine Bewegung, die das grundlegende Missverständnis des Paulus und deshalb auch der radikalen paulinischen Kreuzestheologie durch Lukas betonte. Diese „Haut den Lukas!"-Bewegung, wie einige Gegner sie nannten, argumentierte nicht nur, dass Lukas Paulus falsch darstellte, sondern dass er zumindest eine, wenn nicht sogar mehrere Generationen nach dem Wirken des Apostels schrieb, so dass der nachpaulinische Paulinismus des Lukas nicht mehr in der Lage war, Paulus eigenes Denken und Wirken verlässlich darzustellen. Das dialektische *kerygma* der „Rechtfertigung des Sünders" war in eine „Traditionsreligion" von Formeln, Sakramenten und kirchlichen Ämtern umgewandelt worden, die natürlich weiterhin Spuren ihres religiösen Ursprungs reflektierte, aber in Wirklichkeit den jüdischen Kontext weitgehend hinter sich gelassen bzw. ersetzt hatte.

I.3. Ein Vertreter der Bultmannschule, Hans Conzelmann, so scheint es, hat die definitive Darstellung des Lukas als des Theologen der Heilsgeschichte geschrieben. Cullmann erkennt dies an, wenn er in Heil als Geschichte³ auf Conzelmanns Buch Die Mitte der Zeit⁴ verweist: „Es ist zuzugeben, dass erst Lukas, wie Conzelmann gezeigt hat, eine vollständige heilsgeschichtliche Sicht ausgearbeitet hat, in der nun der Hauptakzent gerade auf der Zwischenzeit, der Zeit des Heiligen Geistes, der Apostel, der Kirche liegt. Diese Akzentverlagerung hängt freilich damit zusammen, dass die Zeit nun gedehnt ist".⁵ Dementsprechend bestand keine Veranlassung für den heilsgeschichtlichen Charakter des lukanischen Doppelwerks Gründe vorzubringen; Conzelmann hatte bereits die überzeugende Interpretation geschrieben. Conzelmanns Beschreibung des Verhältnisses der lukanischen zur übrigen frühchristlichen Literatur wurde rasch Gemeingut der neutestamentlichen Wissenschaftler.

Natürlich kritisierte Cullmann sofort Conzelmanns übertriebene Behauptung, das „letzte Ende" habe für Lukas keinerlei Bedeutung mehr und Conzelmann habe daher die Distanz des Lukas zu Jesus und Paulus im Hinblick auf die fundamentale Spannung zwischen den in Kreuz und Auferstehung „bereits erfüllten" Ereignissen einerseits und der Erwartung des „Endes" andererseits, die dieses eschatologische Geschehen als solches in sich trägt und daher unausweichlich mit sich bringt, übertrieben. Cullmann wies mit Recht auf den Grundfehler in Conzelmanns Gesamtentwurf hin: „Die Unterschiede zwischen Paulus und Lukas beruhen in Wirklichkeit darauf, dass im Zuge der Weiterentwicklung der Aufnahme einer gedehnten Zeit in die Heilsgeschichte bei Lukas eine bewusste theologische Reflexion über diese Aufnahme vorliegt. Aber das ist nicht ein Unterschied zwischen einer existentialistischen Auffassung des Heils und einer heilsgeschichtlichen".⁶

Wenn meine Vermutung richtig ist, hat Cullmann niemals die spezifischen Reflexionen des Lukas über diese ausgedehnte Zeit des Heilsgeschehens im weiteren heilsgeschichtlichen Horizont so beschrieben, dass er beides, die Unterschiede und die grundlegenden Ähnlichkeiten zwischen Lukas und Paulus, aufzeigen konnte. Hätte er dies getan, hätte er die weitaus größere organische Verbindung der heilsgeschichtlichen Kategorien des Lukas mit denen des pau-

---

3 Oscar Cullmann, *Heil als Geschichte: Heilsgeschichtliche Existenz im Neuen Testament* (Tübingen: Mohr Siebeck 1965), 222.
4 Hans Conzelmann, *Die Mitte der Zeit: Studien zur Theologie des Lukas*, 4th ed. (Tübingen: Mohr Siebeck, 1962).
5 Cullmann, *Heil als Geschichte*, 222.
6 Cullmann, *Heil als Geschichte*, 223 f.

linischen *Kerygmas* und mit Paulus' eigenem Kommentar zu diesem *Kerygma* erweisen können, mit dem Paulus es im Rahmen seiner vielfach umstrittenen Rezeption nuancierte und verteidigte. Hätte Cullmann sozusagen „rückwärts" argumentiert, von Lukas zu Paulus, so hätte seine Kritik an der Bultmannschen existentialistischen Paulusinterpretation – und all ihren katastrophalen Folgen, die Cullmann als Resultat einer ernsthaften Verkleinerung der paulinischen Botschaft ansah –, wohl bedeutend mehr Gehör gefunden. Aber im ideologischen Klima dieser Zeit war es kaum vorstellbar, dass „Erzählung" die Epistemologie des unmittelbar („senkrecht von oben"!) empfangenen paulinischen „Worts" erhellen kann. Narrative Epistemologie kann bestenfalls sekundär, abgeleitet sein!

Anscheinend akzeptierte Cullmann Conzelmanns Unterscheidung von drei verschiedenen Zeitabschnitten der Heilsgeschichte als einer lukanischen Erfindung. Es scheint, als habe er nirgendwo im Detail die Auswirkung von Conzelmanns Postulat einer dritten „Zeit der Kirche" in Frage gestellt, ein Postulat, das im Lukasevangelium genau genommen jede Enderwartung von Jesus von einem abschließenden Heilsereignis zerstreute und damit effektiv auch das *sine qua non* des „schon – noch nicht" der Heilsgeschichte enteschatologisierte und leugnete, für das Paulus im zweiten Band des lukanischen Doppelwerks die unentbehrliche Hauptperson darstellte. Stattdessen nahm Cullmann im Großen und Ganzen mit der Bultmannschule an, dass Lukas für die Apologetik der ausgedehnten Zwischenzeit verantwortlich war, wenn der Evangelist, „die Linien konsequent auszieht, indem er über die ‚Periodisierung' bewusst reflektiert,"[7] während er die entscheidenden Merkmale dieser gedehnten Zeit, nämlich die Gegenwart des Heiligen Geistes, der Kirche und der Sakramente, narrativiert und historisiert. Indem er zugesteht, dass Lukas diese Rolle spielte, hat Cullmann in Wirklichkeit ein ausschlaggebendes Argument gegen die existentialistische Interpretation der paulinischen Theologie verloren. Wenn Lukas Paulus erweitert, ist es bedeutend leichter zu schließen, dass Lukas Paulus verfälscht, indem er eine Heilsgeschichte entwickelt, als umgekehrt zu zeigen, dass das lukanische Doppelwerk im Grunde als narrative Parallele die unbestimmte Zwischenzeit erhellt, die die paulinische Theologie in allen ihren Entwicklungen formt und bestimmt.

---

7 Cullmann, *Heil als Geschichte*, 222.

II Vergleich der paulinischen Heilsgeschichte nach Cullmann mit der Einordnung der Berufungsgechichten des Paulus in die Erzählung der Apostelgeschichte

Da ich mich in diesem Beitrag kurz fassen muss, möchte ich nur kurz Lukas' Erzählung der Apostelgeschichte mit der Grundlage der paulinischen Heilsgeschichte vergleichen, die nach Cullmann alle theologischen Überlegungen des Paulus bestimmte. Cullmann unterscheidet zwei Aspekte des einen beherrschenden Grundereignisses: 1. Paulus' Berufung als „Apostel" auf der Straße nach Damaskus, um den Heiden das Evangelium zu predigen, und 2. die Offenbarung (ἀποκάλυψις) der Bedeutung dieser Berufung an Paulus durch den auferstandenen Christus selbst (Gal 1–2).

Aber zunächst noch zwei allgemeine Bemerkungen, die einer näheren Untersuchung bedürfen:

(i) In vielerlei Hinsicht stellt Cullmanns Darstellung der Heilsgeschichte als Zentralelement der Rhetorik der christlichen Bibel eine Vorwegnahme der Aufnahme und Anwendung der „Intertext" und „intertextuellen" Theorie in die Diskussion über den Einfluss von Quellen und Überlieferungen auf biblische Autoren dar, insbesondere auf die Beziehungen zwischen dem christlichen „Alten" und „Neuen" Testament. Cullmanns einleuchtende These, dass neue Ereignisse die ganze Kette von „Offenbarungsgeschichte", in der die Heilserzählungen Israels für die ganze Welt erzählt werden, neu interpretieren und damit neu konfigurieren, hatte bereits die Richtung für Vieles vorgegeben, das gegenwärtig in der intertextuellen Exegese unternommen wird. Ein Beispiel: Die Tatsache, dass sowohl Paulus als auch Lukas die jüdischen Schriften lebten und atmeten und über Christus und das weitergehende Christusgeschehen in der Kirche schrieben, wobei sich ihre „christlichen" Formulierungen an den jüdischen Schriften orientierten, ist inzwischen merklich dabei, sich als die vorherrschende Hermeneutik bei biblischen Exegeten durchzusetzen. Für diesen gegenwärtigen Stand der Entwicklung der Intertextualität sind Cullmann und andere, z. B. Gerhard von Rad, mit ihrer Betonung der Neuinterpretation und Neuformulierung späterer Ereignisse durch frühere in der andauernden Neubestimmung von dem Heil Israels wichtige Wegbereiter gewesen.

(ii) Cullmanns heilsgeschichtliche Konzeption hängt wesentlich von der literarischen Gattung der „Erzählung", der *narratio*, mit der ihr eigenen Poetik und epistemologischen „Entfaltung" (ἐξεργασίαι) ab. Ohne die großen Erzählungen der Bibel würde Cullmanns Heilsgeschichte wenig Sinn machen. Aber wegen seiner Aufnahme und Anwendung der Formgeschichte auf die Evangelienberichte und wegen seines Gebrauchs traditionsgeschichtlicher Kategorien für die Bibel im Allgemeinen, zog er die besonderen hermeneutischen Verfahren und exegetischen Ergebnissen der narrativen Rhetorik nicht in Betracht. Obwohl diese Vernachlässigung ein bedeutendes *desideratum* im Hinblick auf Cullmanns Methodologie darstellt (wie auch für die deutsche Aufklärungswissenschaft ganz allgemein), ist diese Vermeidung angesichts der hermeneutischen Impulse der form- und traditionsgeschichtlichen Methoden in Cullmanns Karriere verständlich. Wenn man die rhetorische Poetik von Erzählungen nicht in Betracht zieht, fällt es bedeutend leichter, Paulus mit „unmittelbarer" Offenbarung zu verbinden und die Evangelisten mit erzählenden oder midraschischen „Erweiterungen", die die Offenbarungsbegegnung verwässern oder sogar entstellen. Aber solche Schlussfolgerungen resultieren wahrscheinlich aus den fehlgeleiteten Vergleichen von diskursiver mit diegetischer Rhetorik, z. B. der Gegenüberstellung paulinischer Briefformulierungen mit narrativen Reden der Apostelgeschichte, wie sie in dem nun klassischen Fall eines solch unpassenden Vergleichs in Philipp Vielhauers berühmten Aufsatz „Zum ‚Paulinismus' der Apostelgeschichte" vorliegt.[8] In dieser Hinsicht war Cullmann ein „Produkt seiner Zeit".

II.1 Paulus Berufung als „Apostel" auf der Straße nach Damaskus, um den Heiden das Evangelium zu predigen

Wenn, nach Aussage Cullmanns, die Berufung des Paulus auf der Straße nach Damaskus (Gal 1–2) das grundlegende Argument für die Notwendigkeit und Bedeutung der Zwischenzeit liefert, nämlich dass es nun eine ausgedehnte Zeit geben muss, in der die Heiden in das erfüllte Heil des Messias Israels aufgenommen werden können („darum gibt es eine Zwischenzeit"[9]), so ist es Lukas, der diese Berufung des Paulus auf der Straße nach Damaskus als den hermeneutischen Schlüssel zum gesamten zweiten Teil seines Doppelwerks und damit zum Zentralereignis für die Gesamtinterpretation des Doppelwerks macht:

Wir können die grundlegende Rolle, die Paulus in der Apostelgeschichte spielt, unter zwei Kategorien verdeutlichen, 1.) Die hellenistische Konzeption von göttlicher Kontrolle oder Herrschaft über den Kosmos, wie sie verschiedentlich ausgedrückt wurde und vorwiegend bei hellenistischen Geschichtsschreibern anzutreffen ist, und 2.) die Einordnung der Berufungsgeschichte in die Erzählung selbst, Apg 9, die Lukas zweimal wiederholt, in Apg 22 und 26:

---

8 Philipp Vielhauer, „Zum ‚Paulinismus' der Apostelgeschichte," *Evangelische Theologie* 10 (1950–51): 1–15.
9 Cullmann, *Heil als Geschichte*, 228.

II.1.1.) Göttliche Kontrolle der Herrschaft über die Geschichte
In einer oralen Kultur, in der Schreiben ein *aide-de-mémoire* zum mündlichen Vortrag darstellt, hat Lukas seine Poetik in solch einer Weise „verwoben", dass seine Zuhörer der grundlegenden Rolle nicht entkommen können, die Paulus in der Heilsgeschichte Gottes für Israel und für die Völker spielt, die das Raum-Zeit-Kontinuum von der Schöpfung bis zur Neuschöpfung oder den „Zeiten der Wiederherstellung aller Dinge" umspannt (Lukas 11,50→ Apg 3,21[χρόνοι ἀποκαταστάσεως πάντων]). Lukas deutet bereits am Anfang die Rolle des Paulus in einem größeren Plan an, wenn er jüdische „Gäste aus Rom" (Apg 2,10) unter denen auflistet, die sich zu Pfingsten versammelten, und er beendet sein Doppelwerk mit Paulus als Besucher in Rom (vgl. ἐνέμεινεν [...] ἐν ἰδίῳ μισθώματι, Apg 28,30), der nichts verkündet außer dem, was das Gesetz des Mose und die Propheten verkündet haben und „Ketten trägt" „für die Hoffnung Israels" (Apg 28,20; 23,25–28). Von diesem „zweiten Anfang" von Pfingsten (von Petrus erkannt anhand der neuen Sicht auf Cornelius! ἐν ἀρχῇ, Apg 11,15), zeichnet Lukas das Panorama „des Planes Gottes " für das Heil der Welt als die messianische Landschaft des Israels „dieser letzten Tage" (ἐν ταῖς ἐσχάταις ἡμέραις, Apg 2,17). Als Bürge der Augenzeugentradition, die bis zu dem ersten „Anfang" „von der Taufe des Johannes" zurückgeht (Lk 1,2→Apg 1,1–2→Apg 1,21–22), erklärt Petrus zuerst „den Plan Gottes" durch den auferstandenen gekreuzigten Messias Jesus, um „das Wort/die Botschaft (von Gott)" zur Sprache zu bringen (Apg 2,41; 4,4 etc.), das/die in der Apg durchgängig gepredigt und von Paulus wiederholt wird (Apg 13,5; 26 etc.), wenn er am Ende der Apg seinen Plan zur Erfüllung bringt.

Dieser Teil des Planes Gottes ([ἡ] βουλὴ θεοῦ) bildet somit das Gerüst für die gesamte narrative Inszenierung „dieser letzten Tage":

Apg 2,23: der gekreuzigte, auferstandene Jesus ist für alle von diesen Endtagen grundlegend – Ps 15 [LXX] wird aufgerufen;

Apg 4,26: Israel und die Völker sind gegen den Knecht Christus versammelt (παῖδά σου ... ὃν ἔχρισας, Apg 4,27) –Ps 2 wird aufgerufen;

Apg 5,38: Gamaliel, der Lehrer von Paulus (Apg 22,3), ahnt möglicherweise, dass sich ein größerer Plan Gottes mit Jesu messianischer Bewegung entwickelt;

Apg 13,36: Im Grundsatz entspricht das Wort des Paulus dem Wort des Petrus, das in dem „Holz" und der Auferweckung von den Toten kulminiert (13,29–30) – Ps 2 und 15 sowie Jes 55 werden aufgerufen, wenn Paulus Hab 1,5 [LXX] zitiert, um vor einem bestimmten „Werk" des Heils „in euren Tagen" zu warnen, das zu einem Ende kommen wird (βλέπετε [...] μὴ ἐπέλθῃ, Apg 13,40);

Apg 20,27: Während der gesamten Dauer seiner Sendung schreckte Paulus nicht davor zurück, den gesamten Plan Gottes zu verkündigen, der sich auf den „Kaufpreis der Kirche" durch „sein (Gottes) eigenes Blut" zentriert (Apg 20,28) – Gen 22,12 und Jes 42,1; 49,1 werden aufgerufen;

Apg 27,12; 42: ein menschlicher „Ratschlag" wird mit dem „Ratschlag Gottes" durch Paulus kontrastiert, wenn Paulus sie durch den Sturm zur „Rettung" steuert, wodurch der „Zeuge" Paulus in die Lage versetzt wird, Rom zu erreichen (vgl. Apg 23,11: οὕτω σε δεῖ καὶ εἰς Ῥώμην μαρτυρῆσαι).

Als Paulus Rom erreicht, verkündet er das gleiche Wort zu einem gespaltenen Israel, wobei er sich wiederum auf die Propheten beruft (Jes 6), um die jüdischen Anführer zu warnen, dass sich „dieses Heil von Gott" stetig auf eine endgültige Abrechnung hinbewegt (Apg 28,23–28). Zum ersten Mal in der Apg wird „dieses Heil" nicht als zu Israel *und* den Völkern/Heiden gesandt erklärt sondern nur zu den Heiden, „die tatsächlich hören werden" (Apg 28,28; vgl. 3,26; 10,36–38; 13,26→46→18,6; 22,21 (Sendung an die Völker von Jerusalem schließt ein, zuerst zu Diaspora-Synagogen zu gehen, wie 13,1ff. deutlich macht); 26,17; (vgl. Cullmanns Betonung von Israels „Verhärtung" und der Rolle des Paulus besonders in dem Bereich der Heilsgeschichte, der Paulus bei Damaskus offenbart wurde, wiederentdeckt durch seine Mission, und dargelegt von ihm selbst in Röm 9–11; vgl. Apg 28,27a [Jes 6,10]): ἐπαχύνθη γὰρ ἡ καρδία τοῦ λαοῦ τούτου).

II.2 Die Offenbarung (ἀποκάλυψις) der Bedeutung dieser Berufung an Paulus durch den auferstandenen Christus selbst (Gal 1–2)

Da, nach Cullmann, Christus sich selbst Paulus in Damaskus offenbart und ihm das wahre Verständnis der Offenbarung seiner Berufung mitteilt (Gal 1–2), muss Lukas die Berufungspassagen so in seine Erzählung einbetten, dass Paulus' Heidenmission ein integraler Bestandteil des gesamten Heilsplans wird, der seine entscheidende Erfüllung in der Kreuzigung und Auferstehung des Messias Israels findet. <u>Jeder der drei Berufungsberichte bringt den Plan der paulinischen Heidenmission weiter, näher an Rom heran, wo das endzeitliche Heil Gottes die „Enden der Erde" (Jes 45,1; 49,6) erreichen kann.</u>

II.2.1.) Die Berufung des Paulus als Strukturierung und innerem Antrieb der Handlung der Apostelgeschichte

Apg 9,1–19 (20–30) ist aus der Perspektive des Erzählers innerhalb der übergreifenden Rhetorik der Erzählung dargestellt (διάνοια). Als das Volk (der laos) von Jerusalem und Judäa beginnt, sich gegen die ersten Jesusanhänger zu wenden und wie ein Mob zur Steinigung von Stephanus aufhetzt, ist Paulus dabei. Er lenkt nicht nur die Gewalt (Apg 7,58; 8,1), sondern er wird auch ein Anführer der folgenden großen Verfolgung der „Versammlung der Gläubigen" (ἐκκλησία), die gezwungen sind, sich nach „Judäa und Samaria" zu zerstreuen (διασπείρω) (8,4).

Als die Apostel Petrus und Johannes den Auftrag des auferstandenen Christus aus Apg 1,8, Zeugen (μάρτυρες) in Samaria zu sein, zu erfüllen beginnen (8,25) und Philippus auf der Straße nach Gaza, die von Jerusalem wegführt, einem äthiopischen Gottesverehrer begegnet (8,26–40), ist Paulus noch als Gegen-Zeuge in Jerusalem und Judäa (7,58–οἱ μάρτυρες), „Drohung und Mord schnaubend" und Jünger „des Weges" gefangen nach Jerusalem zurückbringend (9,1–3; vgl. 4,29).

Es scheint demnach, als habe Lukas bewusst die Berufung dessen, der sowohl zu Israel als auch zu den Völkern gesandt ist (Apg 9,1–30), zwischen die Aussendung der Apostel nach Samaria auf der einen Seite (8,4–25) und Petrus' Bestellung zu dem Heiden Cornelius, auf der anderen Seite (9,31–11,18) eingebettet, um Paulus als denjenigen hinzustellen, der letztendlich den Auftrag des auferstandenen Jesus in Apg 1,8 erfüllen wird. Allerdings wird auch Petrus eine grundlegende Offenbarung empfangen, aufgrund deren er umkehrt und Heiden nicht länger als „unrein" betrachtet und die Bekehrung/den Sinneswandel eines Heiden herbeiführt (11,18); aber er verschwindet nach Apg 12 weitgehend und nach einem kurzen Auftritt auf dem Apostelkonzil (15,7–11) vollständig, nachdem er zuvor das „Öffnen der Tür des Glaubens" gegenüber den Heiden durch Paulus und Barnabas bestätigt hat (vgl. 14,27). Bereits in 11,19 kehrt die Erzählung zu der Nebenhandlung von „Saulus" und der großen Verfolgung zurück, und in Vers 25 taucht der, der darauf aus war, die Kirche zu zerstören, wieder auf. Er wird als von der Jerusalemer Kirche Bestätigter von Barnabas als Lehrer für Juden und Griechen in Antiochia eingeführt, und ist bereit, von Antiochia zu den „Söhnen und Töchtern Abrahams" (13,26) und ebenso zu „den heidnischen Völkern" (13,46) ausgesandt zu werden. Wäre es möglich, dass die Berufung des Paulus, „ein auserwähltes Gefäß" zu sein (vgl. Jes 54,16), um „meinen Namen zu tragen vor den Völkern und den Königen und Söhnen und Töchtern Israels" (vgl. Jes 52,15) und „für meinen Namen zu leiden" (Apg 9,15–16) die Berufung von Israel als Knecht sowohl in kollektiver als auch in individueller Dimension zusammenfasst?

Apg 22,4–21 fügt entscheidende Informationen über Paulus' Berufung aus seiner eigenen, ausgereiften Reflexion hinzu, bewährt durch alles, was ihm in der Zwischenzeit bei seiner Israel- und Völkermission widerfahren ist. Nun erzählt Paulus der rasenden Menge des „Volkes" von Israel, wie er als Zeuge für Israel und die Völker aus Jerusalem selbst berufen wurde (Apg 22,17–21 ≈ 9,26–30). Der Effekt für die größere Leserschaft des Lukas ist, dass Paulus anfängliche Berufung bei Damaskus (9,1–25) mit seiner letzten Verhaftung in Jerusalem (21,15–36) verbunden wird, und auf diese Weise im Gesamtkontext der Erzählung erklärt, warum Paulus „Rom sehen muss" (19,21; vgl. 23,11; 27,24). Wir erfahren, dass Paulus bereits in Damaskus (Kap. 9) von Ananias gesagt wurde, dass Gott Paulus auserkoren habe „den Gerechten (τὸν δίκαιον) zu sehen und zu hören" und auf der

Basis dieses Sehens und Hörens vor allen Menschen ein Zeuge dafür zu sein, was er gesehen und gehört hat (μάρτυς αὐτῷ πρὸς πάντας ἀνθρώπους ὧν ἑώρακας καὶ ἤκουσας, 22,15). Was Paulus gerade gesehen und gehört hat, ist natürlich, dass er, als er „die des Weges" verfolgt hat (z. B. „das Blut deines Zeugen Stephanus" 22,20), er zugleich den auferstandenen Jesus verfolgt hat, den Gerechten selbst! (22,7–8 ≈ 9,4–5). Aber jetzt erfahren wir zusätzlich, dass Paulus, als sein Leben in Jerusalem in Gefahr war (9,29–30), er durch eine Vision des Herrn im Tempel (vgl. Jes 6!) aus Jerusalem weggeschickt wurde. Wiederum hat Paulus den „Gerechten" gesehen und gehört, nunmehr im Tempel, als er zu ihm spricht: „Sie werden dein Zeugnis (μαρτυρία) über mich nicht annehmen [...] Geh, denn ich sende dich zu fernen Völkern" (εἰς ἔθνη μακράν, Apg 22,17–21).

Somit erhält Paulus, wie Petrus und die Apostel, den gleichen Auftrag von dem auferstandenen Christus (Apg 1,6–8) „ein Zeuge all dieser Dinge für alle Völker zu sein, beginnend in Jerusalem" (Lukas 24,47b-48→Apg 22,21). Die Leserschaft des Lukas hat nun erfahren, dass bereits früh in seiner Berufung, Paulus' eigene Leiden denen des „Gerechten" nachgebildet sind, verbunden in der Zurückweisung („Warum verfolgst du mich?!"), die an die Berufung des Knechtes bei Jesaja erinnert (bes. 42,1–6; 49,1–7; 50,4–11; 52,13–53,12). Wie aus Apg 13–20 deutlich wird, ist das Zeugnis des Paulus vor den Völkern als stets heftig zurückgewiesene Aussage charakterisiert, zuerst in den Synagogen, bevor er sich – vergleichbar mit dem Auftrag des Knechtes – an die Heiden wendet. Paulus identifiziert seine Sendung in Apg 13,47 mit der des „kollektiven Knechtes", da Jesus, der Knecht aus Jes 49,1–6, gute Nachrichten <u>durch</u> ihn <u>und</u> seine Mitarbeiter verkündet.

Weiter erhält das „Schließen der Tempeltore" gegen Paulus' Zeugnis (Apg 21,30), das den Höhepunkt seiner fünften (letzten) Reise nach Jerusalem bildet und zu einer gewaltsamen Reaktion führt, nun eine neue Bedeutung. Es wird nunmehr deutlich, dass die Prophezeiung des auferstandenen „Gerechten" in der Tempelvision jetzt in entscheidender Weise erfüllt ist (9,28–29 (≈ Apg 22,18)→21,30). Paulus hat sein Zeugnis in der Zwischenzeit drei Mal nach Jerusalem gebracht (11,30; 15,3–29; 18,22). Nun, bei diesem letztem Besuch, wurde er im Tempelbezirk verhaftet und verlor beinahe sein Leben an das <u>Volk</u> von Israel–vergleichbar dem Schicksal des Stephanus. Nicht nur verhärtete sich das zu Pfingsten versammelte Volk von Israel spontan, um Paulus der Verletzung der Heiligkeit des Tempels anzuklagen (Apg 21,27–30); sogar die große Zahl gläubiger Juden war überzeugt, dass Paulus ein Verräter der Schriften und Bräuche Israels war, so dass sein Leben offen zur Verhandlung stand! (21,20–26). Als die Tempeltore sofort hinter Paulus geschlossen wurden, er nach draußen geschleift und beinahe zu Tode geprügelt wird (21,30), bildet diese Entwicklung ein abschließendes Ereignis von Ursachen und Einflüssen, die sich durch die gesamte Erzählung hindurch verfolgen lassen (Apg 9,15–16; vgl. Röm 15,25–32!).

Paulus' Zeugnis an Israel wurde an diesem zentralen Ort radikal und entschieden zurückgewiesen. Der Hauptfeind des „Weges" wurde der Hauptfeind im Weg von „dem Volk, dem Gesetz und dieser Stätte" (Apg 21,28a). Wie „der Herr" Paulus bald verkünden wird–wiederum in einer Vision–weil er „in Jerusalem von mir Zeugnis abgelegt hat", ist es noch notwendig, auch in „Rom Zeugnis abzulegen (δεῖ [...] μαρτυρῆσαι)" (23,11). Von diesem Zeitpunkt an erscheint nur noch „die Tür des Glaubens zu den Völkern" (14,27) weit offen.

Apg 26,9–23 zeichnet Paulus vor „vielen Völkern" und „Königen", die über seinen Bericht „staunen" und „ihre Münder schließen" (Jes 52,15a). Der Erzähler stattet Paulus' Verteidigung vor Agrippa und Festus mit all dem Glanz und den Umständen einer Voruntersuchung aus, um die „kaiserliche Appellation" (Apg 25,25) vorzubereiten. „König" Agrippa und seine Frau Bernice, militärische Hauptleute und die Vornehmsten von Caesarea kommen mit großem Zeremoniell herein, um Paulus zu vernehmen und das Material für „seine Exzellenz" Festus zu beschaffen, um „dem Herrn", dem Kaiser, „zu schreiben" (Apg 25,26; vgl. 25,13; Lk 1,3–4). König Agrippa staunt über Paulus' fantastische Geschichte von „den Propheten", die versucht, ihn zu überzeugen, während der Statthalter Festus über den Wahnsinn eines verrückt gewordenen Verstandes seinen „Mund schließt"! (26,24–29; vgl. V. 13). „Denn denen nichts davon verkündet ist, die werden es nun sehen, und die nichts davon gehört haben, die werden es merken" (Jes 52,15b).

Darüberhinaus fasst Paulus seine gesamte Berufung im Licht und Schatten der Sendung des Knechtes zusammen und verkündet im Kern, dass seine Mission Apg 1,8 zur Erfüllung gebracht hat. Nun sagt der „Herr" „Jesus" selbst „in der himmlischen Vision", anstelle von Ananias!, zu Paulus, dass er ein „Diener und Zeuge" (ὑπηρέτην καὶ μάρτυρα) sein soll „für das, was du von mir gesehen hast und was ich dir noch zeigen will. Und ich will dich erretten von deinem Volk und von den Heiden, zu denen ich dich sende um ihnen die Augen aufzutun, dass sie sich bekehren (ἐπιστρέφω) von der Finsternis zum Licht und von der Gewalt des Satans zu Gott. So werden sie Vergebung der Sünden empfangen" (26,16–18). Großer Widerstand hat einen Funken entzündet. Des Weiteren schaut Paulus zurück auf seine gesamte Sendung und erklärt sie für erfolgreich: Er hat 1) „zuerst zu denen in Damaskus und dann denen in Jerusalem und all den Regionen von Judäa" (was Samaria einschließt), „und zu denen aus den Völkern/Heiden", 2) eine Sinnesänderung und eine Bekehrung zu Gott verkündet (ἀπήγγελλον μετανοεῖν καὶ ἐπιστρέφειν ἐπὶ τὸν θεόν)" (26,20; vgl. Lk 24,47; Apg 1,8). „Deswegen (ἕνεκα τούτων) haben mich die Juden im Tempel ergriffen und versucht, mich zu töten" (Apg 26,21). Die ganze Zeit dieses Weges hat er die Schriften geöffnet, „Zeugnis ablegend ... und sagend, dass nichts anderes geschehen würde als das, was die Propheten und Mose vorausgesagt haben: dass Christus leiden müsse (εἰ παθητὸς ὁ χριστός), und der erste sein werde, der von den Toten aufersteht und das Licht seinem Volk und den Heiden verkündigt werde (φῶς μέλλει καταγγέλλειν τῷ τε λαῷ καὶ τοῖς ἔθνεσιν)" (26,22b-23; vgl. Lk 24,44–46). Wo auch immer Paulus gesprochen hatte, war es eigentlich der gesalbte Jesus, der, wie der gesalbte Knecht (Jes 42,1–4), Licht für Israel und die Völker verkündet hat!

Daher ist der „Plan von Gottes" Heilsgeschichte erfüllt, als Paulus Rom erreicht und die Erzählung kann zu einem Ende gelangen. Als der symbolische Mittelpunkt der großen heidnischen Macht, die „die Enden der Welt" kontrolliert, übt Rom, vergleichbar dem „gesalbten" Cyrus aus Jesajas Prophezeiung (Jes 45), durchgreifende Macht aus und legt alle Zwistigkeiten zwischen den Völkern bei, indem sie den Auftrag des Herrn erfüllt. Ohne die durchgreifende Macht Roms wäre Paulus „Zeugnis" an „alle" in der Hauptstadt des Reiches, historisch gesprochen, unmöglich gewesen (Apg 28,30–31). Als Paulus in Rom ankam, „alle empfing, das Reich Gottes predigte und lehrte von dem Herrn Jesus Christus, mit allem Freimut ungehindert." (28,31), hatte das Römische Reich den Cyrus vorausgesagten Einfluss auf Israel erfüllt. „Wendet euch zu mir, so werdet ihr gerettet, aller Welt Enden" (Jes 45,22: ἐπιστράφητε πρός με καὶ σωθήσεσθε οἱ ἀπ' ἐσχάτου τῆς γῆς; vgl. Jes 49,6). Die Tatsache, dass Rom in mindestens einem jüdischen, vorchristlichen Text, PsSal 8,15, mit dem „Ende der Welt" in Verbindung gebracht wurde, verleiht Lukas' Verknüpfung von Paulus „Zeugnis" mit dem „Zeugnis" von Jesajas „Knecht" weitere Glaubwürdigkeit.

Zusammenfassung:
1. Lukas' Beschreibung von Paulus unersetzlicher Rolle für die Heilsgeschichte Israels, die das messianische Heil Israels für die ganze Welt hervortreten lässt, stimmt sicherlich mit Paulus' Sicht von seiner eigenen Berufung und von Israels eschatologischer Rolle für die Völker überein, wie Prof. Cullmann sie für Paulus' eigene Briefe beschrieben hat.

2. Die eschatologische Dynamik des „schon–noch nicht" in Cullmanns Paulusentwurf bleibt nach Lukas während der gesamten Mission des Paulus in der Apg bestehen. Paulus' Ankunft in Rom ist ein eschatologisches Ereignis mit der Verkündung eines Urteils gegen ein verstocktes Volk, aber vor dem Hintergrund, dass die Völker Anteil am Heil Israels erhalten. Die Dynamik von Verhärtung und Einbeziehung der Heiden ist sehr eng mit Röm 9–11 verwandt.

3. Vergleichbar mit Cullmanns Betonung, dass neue Ereignisse neue Offenbarungen über vergangene Ereignisse und über die Heilsgeschichte als ganze enthüllen, zeichnet Lukas Paulus als durch die Ereignisse seiner Mission neue Einsichten gewinnend, die ein neues Licht auf das Ganze des „Planes Gottes" werfen. So verleiht Paulus' Offenbarung Jesu Worten im Evangelium eine neue Bedeutung und dies besonders in Bezug auf die Erfüllung von Jesu Befehl in

Lk 24,44–47 und Apg 1,6–8 das erfüllte Heil des auferstandenen – leidenden Christus aus Israels Schriften zu allen Völkern zu bringen. Paulus, nicht die „Zwölf", erfüllt dieses Zeugnis.

4. Lukas erzählerische Deutung argumentiert nicht notwendigerweise in die eine oder andere Richtung bezüglich seines Verhältnisses zu Paulus, ob er zum Beispiel Teil des „wir" der „Wir-Abschnitte" der Apostelgeschichte war oder ob er zu der „dritten" oder „vierten" Generation von Tradenten gehört. Dennoch lässt die starke „Familienähnlichkeit" zwischen den zwei literarischen Corpora, die mehr als 50 % des NT ausmachen, stärkere Kontinuität in der grundlegenden Konzeption des messianischen Heils vermuten, besonders in der jeweiligen Betonung der Rolle Jesajas durch Paulus und Lukas, die deutlich größer ist, als viele Neutestamentler in der Vergangenheit zugestanden haben. Professor Cullmanns Überzeugung, dass Heilsgeschichte die gemeinsame „Währung" für Paulus und Lukas in Bezug auf Israels Heil darstellt, trifft den Kern der Kontinuität. So können wir die Worte dieses Pioniers der biblischen Theologie über Paulus verwenden, um unsere Ergebnisse für den Paulus des Lukas zusammenzufassen: „Paulus ist zugleich der Ausführende dieser Weiterentwicklung des Heilsplans und sein Offenbarer. Beides ist in dem Ereignis auf dem Wege nach Damaskus angezeigt".[10]

---

10 Cullmann, *Heil als Geschichte*, 228 n3.

Conclusion
Luke the Hellenistic Historian of Israel's Legacy, Theologian of Israel's 'Christ'

After our long journey through a variety of Hellenistic texts and the 'Gospel Acts' of Luke,' it is time to weave together our conclusions.

We have compared the narrative rhetoric of Luke with well-known Hellenistic composers of narrative histories. By many counts, Luke is a Hellenistic historian:

I. *Luke is a <u>Configurer</u> (ποιητής) of a pool of oral and written traditions regarding events and matters purporting to have taken place at various times and places in the real world of the author. By 'arranging' a new narrative sequence different from a number of predecessors, Luke imparts a new cognitive and affective understanding of these happenings. His altered epistemological landscape provides its own settings of significance.*

Luke's desire to give his audiences a greater "firmness of understanding" of the matters he relates divulges his primary agenda of sequencing persons, events, and consequences into meaningful, eventful relationships. Invoking the metaphor of "securely locked gates"[1] for his audiences' overall grasp of his carefully coordinated events divulges the basic *modus operandi* of a historian and not that of a poet. Affective responses of anger, delight, zeal, et cetera are woven into the fabric of intellectual comprehension and consent but are subsumed to Luke's rhetoric of intellectual perception, nevertheless.

To be sure, we have seen that certainly by the first decades of the imperial period the distinction between history writing as a more or less factual account of a longer series of events begins to blur with the desire to entertain and inspire audiences to certain points of morality and experiences of life.[2] A writer like Diodorus or the historian Cassius Dio can relate happenings of the gods and weave their 'significance' into the warp and woof of the daily affairs of human

---

[1] ἡ ἀσφάλεια, Luke 1:4; cf. Acts 5:23.
[2] Cf. Frank W. Walbank, "History and Tragedy," *Historia* 9 (1960): 216–34, who points out that the grammarians consistently classified *historia* as the subject matter of both epic and tragedy and distinguished these traditions about events purported to have happened over against "myths"/"legends" (μῦθος/*fabula*) or those of "fiction" (πλάσμα/*argumentum*), the former a mixture of fiction and real events and thus verisimilar to real events, and the latter, events that did not occur and therefore are false to actual history. Walbank also notes that the same divisions also occur with slightly different nomenclature in Asclepiades of Myrleia, the *Ad Herennium*, Cicero, *De Inventione*, and in the Byzantine *Scholia* to Dionysius Thrax (225).

societies without apparently violating literary sensitivities. If Luke configures his narrative well, he can at the same time tell a good story. Hellenistic historiography need not in the least be distanced from the persuasive power of *diegetic performance*.

We have also witnessed the simultaneous ascendancy of *rhetoric* as a discipline in the formulation of all things written, irrespective of genre or public occasion. History writing now bleeds into elaborate story telling.[3] A historian's overall 'point of viewing' reality (διάνοια) forms the epistemological lens for the telling and focuses the manner or particular media through which the narrative story is told. Although *historia/historein* do not yet in the first centuries of the Common Era indicate a theory that views 'history' as an idea abstracted or concept transcendent to the actual events described, historians nevertheless are keen to tell their own story of the how and 'why' certain things have transpired, and they do so by attending to the way that meaning and explanation are built into the very 'organization' or 'economy' of the narrative text they are composing.[4] Though '*historia*' has not yet attained the status of a subsistent grid, 'arranging' a narrative has nevertheless become in the fuller sense a 'managing'[5] of audience perception and reaction.[6]

Luke also is keen to tell his audience what he wishes to accomplish with them through his narrative presentation:

Prooimia. Luke identifies himself at the outset as one who has received reports of "events" or "matters" and intends to configure them into a more meaningful

---

[3] Cf. this observation in Gerald A. Press, *The Development of the Idea of History in Antiquity* (Kingston: McGill-Queen's University Press, 1982), 65–67: "A story is an account of the facts about real things the point of which is to entertain, please, or point a moral" (66).

[4] For a lucid overview of the continuum of 'factual reporting of research,' on one end, to making up details to entertain an audience, on the opposite end, see John Marincola, *Greek Historians*, New Surveys in the Classics 31 (Oxford: Oxford University Press, 2001), esp. 1–8.

[5] Both English metaphors deriving from the one responsibility of "managing a household" (οἰκονομεῖν/οἰκονόμος). Cf. Marincola, *Greek Historians*, 7n18, on Hellenistic historians: "there is a perceptible tension between individual (and, at times, unique) actions on the one hand, and on the other hand larger patterns within which events take place. The larger patterns do not prescribe how or when certain results follow from certain actions; rather, the ways in which the pattern can be fulfilled seem to be limitless, and it is on these contingent specifics that the historian (as opposed to the philosopher or poet or scientist) focuses. The way in which the specific set of circumstances fulfills the pattern then provides another proof of its validity ... history then fulfills the function of both commemoration and instruction."

[6] See especially Lucian's spoof of this wholesale blurring of a historian's "reporting" with the spinning of tales for sheer entertainment or manipulation in his "True Story," *Lucian* 1.247–357 (Harmon, LCL).

whole. His mention of *eyewitness* tradents and attendants and organizers who are responsible for the content and resulting forms of the traditions (ὁ λόγος→λόγοι, 1:2→1:4) makes it clear that, as a historian, Luke is treating matters he believes are more or less factual–affairs that have happened–and that their interrelationships in, through, and among these traditions and incipient narrative constellations are worthy of his re-telling through new poetic strategies. His secondary *prooimion* restates his desire to bring his audiences to a greater clarity of understanding of "all that Jesus began to do and to teach" (Acts 1:1) in accord with his own view of their truth or continuing significance. When he continues in his sequel volume to reprise the 'end' events of the first volume (Acts 1:3–14), the overall goal of his narrative enterprise becomes crystal clear. "Events/matters that have come to fruition in our midst" (Luke 1:1) are of considerable consequence, and the import of these being re-configured into a well-interpreted story is of primary concern to our author.

Two-Volume *Poiesis*. Luke's producing of a narrative (Luke 1:3) in two volumes (Acts 1:1) apparently breaks the mold of the growing tradition's "narrative" (διήγησις, Luke 1:1) account of the traditions (λόγοι, 1:4). In outline fashion we can mention only *three* of the more general and overlapping historiographical *patterns* that Luke follows but at the same time recreates through his unique combinations of narrative-rhetorical elaborations. By breaking from the pattern of the Jesus traditions already in play (Luke 1:1–2), Luke (re)shapes his narrative story *as a historian* to deliver a firmer grasp of the traditions' 'traditional' meaning than the "many" others who are vying for attention (Luke 1:3–4):

1 Patterns of Recurrence from Authoritative Written and Oral Traditions

We have seen that Hellenistic historians re-tell the stories and myths of 'important' persons and actions that are derived from multiple written and oral sources, though to be sure with considerable reformulation and recontextualizing.[7] Nonetheless, the mark of good historians, whether of more limited affairs or of universal histories, is to manifest the ways more recent happenings are both

---

[7] Cf. Lewis R. Donelson, "Cult Histories and the Sources of Acts," *Biblica* 68 (1987): 1–21: "In the collection process he would have followed the public canons of Hellenistic historians; he would have contacted the major cities and churches involved in the story along with as many eyewitnesses as possible (as he notes in his prologue). Acts then would be built upon the memories and chronicles of Christians and churches involved in the events" (20).

're-cycled' *and* yet unprecedented in such a fashion that they may eclipse–or at the other extreme cast only a pale shadow[8] upon–their precursor(s) within the newer narrative scheme crafted by the author. Such patterns of recurrence alert audiences to the significances of the 'new' actors and actions that resemble a more or less 'traditional' set of circumstances and outcomes but which, at the same time, beg a differing interpretation, a necessary re-assembling that only a new alignment can bring.[9]

Like some of his predecessors,[10] Luke draws on the traditional 'material' of the Jewish scriptures that represent Israel's history. The variety of ways as well as the extent to which he does so may be unprecedented, depending on whether Matthew is one of those "many" sources. Regardless of Luke's relationship to synoptic traditions, he tips his historiographical hand in the attention he pays to the 'recurrence of newness':

1) Recurring Patterns in Citations and Allusions to Israel's Scriptures.

i) *"Fulfillment"* language. Luke goes out of his way to emphasize how many of the actions and sayings of Jesus and of his disciples "bring to fruition" prophecies, expectations, promises, ordinances of the Mosaic law, and sayings and actions of the prophets, wise sages, and saints in a long line that have preceded Jesus the Christ. The Jewish scriptures are rife with characters, plots, problems, promises, and crises of human triumph and failure that find some form of resolution and rationale in the coming of the "anointed of God" and of the "anointed" disciples[11] in the Acts that follow. "(The Law of) Moses, the prophets, and the psalms" or individual "books" of scripture or the "redemption of the firstborn," et cetera are cited as only now coming to a fuller, God-ordained purpose. Luke in fact has Jesus encapsulate the whole of his public words and deeds as climaxing in the realization of the servant's calling to be "counted among the lawless" as he is turned over to the Temple and Roman authorities by an arresting party "led by one of the Twelve."[12] Luke punctuates this greatest of ironies for the Jewish

---

[8] Cf., e.g., Frank W. Walbank, "The Idea of Decline in Polybius," in *Polybius, Rome and the Hellenistic World: Essays and Reflections* (Cambridge: Cambridge University Press, 2001): 193–211.
[9] Polybius's *Histories* is an obvious example of this radical re-drafting.
[10] Mark is a most likely candidate.
[11] E.g., Acts 2:33, "pour out [the Holy Spirit] upon" (ἐκχέω).
[12] Isa 53:12 in Luke 22:37.

people with Jesus's pleonastic conclusion, "For indeed what is written about me is now (finally) coming to its intended goal."[13]

ii) Jewish *Feasts and Sacrifices*. Luke entangles the *feasts* and *holy days* and *sacrifices* of the Jewish festival calendar with the significance of Jesus's and of his disciples' movements. Jesus is "presented" at the Temple to fulfill the redemption of the firstborn of the first Exodus Passover, and later he will discuss with Moses and Elijah the "exodus" of his "going out" and "death" and "going away," before he, like Ezekiel, will "set his face resolutely" to head for Jerusalem and encounter the "polluted" priesthood in the Temple precincts. Like an observant Jewish male, Jesus journeys to Jerusalem for the Passover, prepares a Passover feast with his 'family' of apostles, yet announces during the meal that the celebrated paschal [LXX] lamb is now actually the sacrifice of his broken body and shed blood. This great journey from the mountain of revelation to Israel's 'central place' brings Israel's first great exodus to its intended goal, when Jesus will die, like Moses, and be taken up, like Elijah, in bringing the longed-for life of release and redemption and worship in the land of promise to its completion. If Luke opens with the altar of incense preparing the offering of a lamb in the daily afternoon/evening *Tamid* sacrifice, Luke closes his first book again in the Temple where the exodus goal of the true worship of God is finally realized when the disciples return from worshipping Jesus as he ascends to the power of God (Luke 24:49–53).[14] If Luke begins with the priest Zechariah's silence before Gabriel's stunning announcement that the time of the afternoon sacrifice of the final "seventy weeks of years" to "put an end to sin and to atone for iniquity" is about to take place through an "anointed one" (χριστός),[15] Luke ends his Gospel with the followers of this "cut-off" and ascended Christ, this one as a "Son of Humankind,"[16] flowing with words of praise to God in Israel's central place.

---

[13] καὶ γὰρ τὸ περὶ ἐμοῦ τέλος ἔχει, Luke 22:37c.
[14] See esp. Chapters Eight and Nine above.
[15] Dan 9:25: Gabriel comes to Daniel at the time of the evening sacrifice to announce the time of the "end" when an "anointed one shall be cut off [LXX]/destroyed" [Theod.] before the "culmination of sinning and the sealing of sin and expunging of lawlessness and the atoning for iniquity and the bringing of eternal righteousness and the sealing up of the vision and the prophet and the anointing of the holy of holies" [my trans. of Theod.]. In Luke 1, Zechariah's offering of incense on the "altar of incense" (Exod 30:1–10 [closer to the 'holy place']) attends the *Tamid* or *olat tamid* ("daily burnt-offering"), described in the ninth or tenth tractate of the order *Kodashim* in the Mishnah and the Babylonian Talmud. A lamb for the sin of Israel is offered both in the morning and in the afternoon/evening (3 p.m.) on the altar of sacrifice (Exod 29:38–42). Gabriel's appearance there matches the timing of Gabriel's appearance after Daniel's long prayer of intercession for the atonement of Israel's unending sin (Dan 9:3–19).
[16] Dan 7:9–18; 9:20–27; Luke 22:69.

Luke follows a similar pattern of recurrence in his Acts that follow. Israel's Feast of Weeks/First Fruits/Pentecost [LXX] breaks the opening equilibrium of the gathered, expectant followers.[17] But now instead of "betraying" and "denying" and disappearing, Jesus's disciples receive the promise Jesus delivered at the end of Luke 24 and begin to utter praise to God for the gifts of the end-time Spirit as the prophets Joel and David had predicted. The 'first fruits' of Pentecost begin to flow as the Jewish peoples from all over the known world proclaim the "crucified, raised up" Messiah in their own languages, anticipating this end-time salvation of God reaching to the "end(s) of the earth" (Acts 2:5–13). Luke carefully choreographs Paul emulating Jesus's final journey to Jerusalem, replete with passion predictions and obstructions on the part of "disciples."[18] But again it is a 'recurrence of newness' that weaves the poetic thread. Especially between "the feasts of unleavened bread" and of Pentecost (Acts 20:5→20:16), Luke paints Paul as under special obligation to participate in the latter Feast of Firstfruits, despite the intense opposition to his path to Israel's central place foisted on him by "Jews from Asia."[19] Later Paul will assert that he had intended to "present alms and offerings to his nation"[20] as first fruits of his worldwide execution of his calling to both the people of Israel and the nations. Like Jesus, Paul is soundly rejected at a central feast of Israel but now in the way in which the universal sweep to the nations is effectively set in motion.

iii.) Luke is steeped in the *poetics and stylistics of the Old Greek Bible*. He is fond, for instance, of the *topoi* and various tropes of literal and non-literal figuration of characters and events etched in the Greek scriptures, including vintage markers of biblical narrative as "signs" and "wonders," "omens," angelophanies, human-divine appearances, et cetera along with idioms that mimic the translations of the Hebrew texts known by the end of the 1st century CE as the Septuagint/the 'Seventy' [translators]. The opening cadences of the annunciations by Gabriel, for example, and the hymnic responses resonate the chords and modulations of larger narrative portions from Genesis to 4 Kingdoms. Luke is thus an animator of texts that breathe the air of the Greek Bible, accommodating various Greek styles to a larger biblical rhetoric that is consonant with and familiar to Jewish readers of their sacred scriptures. By the end of the 2nd century CE, the Gospel narratives and Luke, separated from Acts, will be heard alongside the Greek translations that eventually became known as the church's "Old Testa-

---

17 Acts 1:15–26.
18 See above, esp. Chapter One 2.2, and Chapter Nine §IV.
19 Acts 20:13–35.
20 Acts 24:17–19.

ment."[21] Luke's Gospel, and possibly to a lesser extent Acts, will have played a major role in spawning early forms of an emerging Christian Bible of "Old" and "New" Testaments. Such compositional *mimesis* of events echoing earlier sacred stories is, *during the Hellenistic period*, the primary prerogative of a historian and not that of a poet.[22]

iv.) Luke *imitates plots* and *scenarios* from the *Jewish scriptures* with a '*parallel of newness.*'

(a.) Childless couples are conscripted by the God or Lord of the scriptures to initiate scenarios of release and redemption. Whether Sarah and Abraham, the mother of Sampson and Menoah, or Hannah and Elkanah with Samuel, a "son" born begins a new period or time when God acts in new and different ways for an Israel that has previously, by and large, been unresponsive and/or ill-equipped to fulfill a divinely intended role. Abraham (and Sarah) in particular bears a special function in prefiguring and provoking the entire story of Israel's salvation that culminates in the births of John and Jesus and continues to all the nations in the sequel of Acts.[23]

(b.) Both John and Jesus receive divine callings as prophets. Jesus especially is compared to one called as an "anointed prophet" of Isaiah who will bring about eschatological "release," whereas John fills the role of the prophetic announcer who must prepare a people to receive this new "anointed one."[24] Both John's and Jesus's callings are reminiscent of Moses's and Elijah's callings, both in the suffering of rejection and in the vindication of an incomparable mediation of God's *torah* as epitomized upon a mountain of revelation.[25] But in the end Jesus stands "alone" by rendering a redemption that brings an 'end' to Israel's stubborn disobedience to their calling to effect salvation for all the peoples of the world. He alone is "taken up" in enthronement to the "exalted place" of God. Peter, Stephen,

---

21 Melito of Sardis is credited with the first extant use (before 170 CE) of the phrase "the books of the old covenant" (τὰ τῆς παλαιᾶς διαθήκης βιβλία) for authoritative Jewish Scriptures known from Melito's trip to the east (Palestine) in a letter referred to as the *Extracts* cited in part by Eusebius, *Hist. eccl.* 4.26.12–14. Melito claims to have made "six books of extracts" (αἱ ἐκλογαί ... ἐξ βιβλία διελών, 4.26.14) from twenty-six books [not including the eleven additional from the "one book of the Twelve"].
22 See esp. Karl Olav Sandnes, "*Imitatio Homeri*? An Appraisal of Dennis R. MacDonald's 'Mimesis Criticism,'" *JBL* 124 (2005): 715–32.
23 Note Luke's summary of this entire Abrahamic history in Acts 3:18–26 in Peter's second speech.
24 Luke 4:16–30; 3:4–6, 15–17, respectively.
25 See esp. Chapters Eight and Nine above.

and especially Paul continue the anointed one's calling in patterns that resound or emulate Jesus's words and actions.

(c.) John and Jesus are both typecast as prophets sent to Israel in a long line of prophetic messengers to proclaim God's *Torah*, call Israel to repentance in the light of their disobedience, and to pronounce God's judgment upon an unremitting, unrepentant people. This Deuteronomistic mold of "Moses and all the prophets," however, is radically broken by the eschatological filling and culminating of this recurrence through John's declaring Jesus to be the anointed "Christ" of the end days, as well as through Jesus's suffering, violent rejection, and rising up from the tomb. As such Jesus is the quintessential prophet (like but greater than Moses) sent to Israel.[26]

(d.) Luke privileges scriptures of 'suffering righteous' servants of the psalms and especially of David to identify Jesus as the suffering righteous figure prefigured in "Moses, the prophets, and the psalms" as God's specially "anointed one, the Christ." As "the Christ who must suffer," Jesus's calling is pioneered in the careers and sufferings particularly of David, of Moses, and of the mysterious "servant" of Isaiah.[27] In Acts, the Messiah-Servant's witnesses launch Isaiah's eschatological servant salvation to the far corners of the world.[28]

(e.) Luke alone comprehends Jesus's anointed status as the sum total of "all that stands written."[29] Not everything in Moses, the prophets, and the psalms speaks about Jesus as the Christ. Yet each and every part of the scriptures points unreservedly, in its entirety and holistically, to a suffering anointed one such that Luke's overarching hermeneutic can be punctuated: "the Christ must suffer and Jesus is that (suffering) Christ."[30]

(f.) Luke's *'recurrence of newness'* stretches beyond many of the more *traditional notions of 'typology'* such as particular objects or actions that call to mind similar objects, situations, and reactions in the "defining days" of a people's history.[31] The childless Elizabeth and Mary clearly conjure up the likes of Sarah and

---

[26] See esp. Chapters Eight and Nine above.
[27] See Chapters Eight, Nine, and Ten above.
[28] See esp. Chapter Nine §§ III–IV.
[29] Luke 18:31; 21:22; 24:44; Acts 13:29; 15:15; 24:14.
[30] Luke 24:26, 46; Acts 3:18; 17:3; 26:23. See esp. Chapters Eight, Nine, and Ten above.
[31] For instance, the use of "sign" language for God's special action or presence in the world points to a 'type' of Israelite narration that now asserts anti-types in the presence of God in Jesus: e.g., Luke 2:12, 34; 11:16; et al.; cf. Josh 2:18; 4:6; Isa 7:11,14, etc. "The sign of Jonah" in Luke 11:29–32 is a good illustration of how Jesus [Luke] transforms the Jewish demand for a "sign" from God to a re-enactment of the "sign of Jonah." Now the recurrence is a pale shadow of the 'precursor' and yet points to an eschatological escalation in a developing plot of God's dealings

of Hannah; yet the ties between those two complexes extend far beyond 'types' or 'scenarios' of 'barrenness' or of old-age births. With the insertion of a divinely guided interpretation by the heavenly messenger Gabriel, for instance, Luke's readers now understand that larger plots and sub-plots of their past are being recalled not merely for the sake of entertainment or to delight their imagination, but that also what was divinely intended in the original occurrences are now *recurring* with more extensive parallels of event and characters that are climaxing those earlier scenarios. Luke's interlacing of the events of Jesus and the disciples in the church with the events and characters of the Jewish scriptures is certainly 'typological' as, in part, a non-literal *poiesis* or trope of narration; yet the resonating of earlier events in those of Jesus and the church is akin to Hellenistic patterns of similarly-shaped events that evince divine control in a much larger working of a 'providence' or 'fate' or 'necessity.'[32] Polybius's extensive parallels of recurrence for multiple peoples over longer periods of time climaxes in Rome's repetitive and yet finally unprecedented climaxing of these 're-enactments.'[33] Diodorus's 'complete(d) narratives' necessarily show how a divine steering enacts its will through scenarios interpreting other series of happenings in diverse parts of the world.[34] Or in order to convince of Rome's superior appropriation of their organically derived Hellenism, a Dionysius must 'arrange' all of the world events into a 'continuity of plotted development' such that Rome alone ends up defining and providing rationale for the superior culture of a Greek way of life.[35]

As a Hellenistic historian, then, Luke coordinates and elaborates the 'inner-relatedness' of the events of Jesus and of the church with their precursors in the larger patterns now discernible in and through Israel's scriptures.[36] Clearly the events of Jesus with his followers and those of God's dealings with the Jewish peoples centuries earlier require semblances in actions and situations in order for a historian like Luke to detect similar patterns in complexes of occurrences that point to a more comprehensive scheme. But equally, as a proper historian, Luke must showcase the organic inter-connectedness and movement of all these

---

with Israel through their "Christ": whereas the god-less Ninevites did repent at the preaching of Jonah, now the Jewish people of Israel refuse to change their way of disobedience even when confronted with their own "Messiah."

32 See also G. W. Trompf, *The Idea of Historical Recurrence in Western Thought: From Antiquity to the Reformation* (Berkeley, CA: University of California Press, 1979), 116–78.
33 See esp. Chapter Five §§ 1–2.
34 See Chapter Six above.
35 See Chapter Seven above.
36 See now Kenneth Litwak, *Echoes of Scripture in Luke-Acts: Telling the History of God's People Intertextually* (New York: T&T Clark, 2005).

events toward this divinely intended goal. This is exactly what Luke is doing in his Gospel Acts: "You foolish and dull of heart to believe in all of those things spoken by the prophets. Was it not necessary that the Christ should suffer these things so that he might enter into his glory?!" (Luke 24:25–26).

In sum, it is already clear that *Luke the historian configures* his traditions to correlate with the biblical patterns of Israel's role in facilitating salvation and that the salvation he highlights through multiple images, types, plots, promises, and fulfillments centers upon a suffering, anointed Christ figure of Israel's scriptures. As a *historian* of Israel's legacy through Jesus of Nazareth, Luke is simultaneously a *biblical theologian of Israel's "Christ."*

2) Patterns of Recurrence from Israel's Scriptures Synchronized with World Events

Luke *synchronizes* the events of Jesus and his followers and biblical precursors with world events against a universal backdrop.[37] By the end of Acts, it is clear that "this [movement of Israel's Christ] has not taken place in a corner" (Acts 26:26) but instead has thrust itself onto the larger world stage.[38] Paul's witness in Rome plants the Jesus movement firmly in the center of empire, sounding Israel's legacy for all nations to hear:

i.) Utilizing Septuagintal sociolect, Luke has major actors like Paul declare the one God of Israel to be *the creator of "all," "the God who made the universe and everything in it, who is Lord of heaven and earth"* (Acts 17:24; compare 4:24; 14:15).[39] This God controls the "periods and seasons" and "times" unique to nations, the "life and breath" of all creatures, the rhythms of nature and the bounty of harvest,

---

37 See esp. Chapter Five above.
38 Cf. Trompf, *Historical Recurrence*, 155: "Gentile history acquires a background importance for Christianity's emergence, even if the Jewish setting counted for more in terms of divine authentication."
39 LXX: Exod 20:11; Ps 145 (146):6; Isa 37:16; 42:5; 4Kgdms 19:15 et al. ring through Paul's speech. For the intertextuality of the Areopagus Speech in Acts 17 and the use of the rhetorical trope "allusive speech" (e.g., Demetrius, *On Style*) in Paul's (Luke's) criticism of Hellenistic and Roman idolatry in Athens, see A. J. Strait, "Gods, Kings and Benefactors: Resisting the Ruling Power in Early Judaism and Paul's Polemic against Iconic Spectacle in Acts 17:16–32," (Ph.D. diss., University of Pretoria, 2015), esp. 420: "In an urban metropolis like Athens where gods were imaged as humans and powerful human benefactors were imaged as gods, Luke's universal polemic against idols articulates a worldview that is incompatible with the representation and purported benefaction of gods *and* deified imperial authority."

as well as the sequences and progression of time itself.[40] Patterns of recurrence are ultimately to be ascribed to God's discreet disbursements. Thus it is not the least surprising that Greek and barbarian cultures speak to these same phenomena as discernible, divinely-given presences or incursions into everyday human life, even "as certain of your own poets have said, 'For we are indeed God's offspring'"[41] (Acts 17:28).

ii) Luke reflects a *two-age theory of time and history*, similar to apocalyptic Jewish and early rabbinic texts, and not the ebb and flow of repetitive cycles or of inter-cataclysmic renewal and destruction through flood and conflagration. Nor does Luke perceive a golden age followed by ceaseless declines and rebirths as represented in various Greek and ancient Near Eastern schemes. "The coming age" (Luke 18:30) clearly overlaps with the age of messianic woes that is already being inaugurated by Jesus and is taking on its emblematic form through Jesus's rejection and violent treatment. Jesus himself forecasts the extension of these sufferings to his followers over an indefinite period leading to the "days of retribution" and the "times of the nations" that culminate in the final reckoning of all humanity who will "stand before the Son of Humankind" (Luke 21:5–36).

As a historian of Israel's history, Luke reckons with a final end to the "times and seasons" that have characterized biblical chronology (Acts 1:5–6; compare, for example, Dan 12). Unlike a Polybius, the ascendant power in history will not be an earthly kingdom aided by Fortune's inscrutable favor but by the collision of the God of the universe with the created world in the "days of the Son of Humankind" (Luke 17:22–37; 21:25–36). Indeed, already in Luke's *genealogy* of Luke 3:23–38, Jesus as "beloved Son," the Servant-Son in whom God "delights" (Luke 3:22), re-constitutes the whole human race as "son of Adam, son of God" (3:38)[42] through the "days of the Son of Humankind" of repudiation, resurrection, and enthronement as Son of God, Son of Humankind (compare Acts 7:55–56→Dan 7:13). Similar to apocalyptic timetables, Jesus even declares that his presence among Israel's leaders catalyzes the reckoning of the "blood of all the prophets, shed from the foundation of the world, from Abel to Zechariah"[43] upon his own ("this generation") people (Luke 11:48–51). The final result, however, will be the "re-constituting of *all things*" (ἀποκαταστάσεως πάντων) into an unprecedented reality or new creation (Luke 3:23–38→Acts 3:21).

---

40 See esp. Acts 17:24–28; 3:20–21; 14:15–17.
41 Opening lines of Aratus's *Phaenomena*.
42 See esp. Chapter One § 3.2.
43 See 2Chr 24:20–22.

But more than that, as a Hellenistic historian Luke also portrays important *patterns of recurrence in Israel's history* that come to a pen-ultimate climax in the destruction of Jerusalem by an unequalled war machine of God's retributive justice. Luke 19:43–44 delineates the "encirclement" along with "siege mounds" "ramped up" against the walls of the Temple that refract uniquely the war 'artillery' developed by the Romans and that match Josephus's graphic reminiscences,[44] while at the same time conjuring up the predictions of the 587 BCE conquest of Jerusalem as the telling precursor. Luke placards distinctive LXX images of both Isaiah's (3:25–26; 29:3; 37:33) and Ezekiel's (4:2; 21:22) prophetic forecasts as coming true once again.[45] Israel's disobedience in rejecting their Messiah is requited with a "wrath" that unleashes a tri-focal funneling of the Final Judgment (587 BCE → 70 CE → End/Final Assize of the Son of Humankind [Luke 21:36]). Acts 7 also exhibits a classic Hellenistic patterning of recurrences both of longer periods[46] or events or promises later fulfilled.[47] But Israel's "killing of those who had announced beforehand the coming of the Just One" has come to its divinely intended, ultimate recurrence through their role as his "murderers" (φονεῖς, 7:52).

iii) "The God who made the world and everything in it" is the same God who has sent "the Lord Christ" into the world *when Augustus was the "lord emperor"* (ὁ Σεβαστός) and the *"whole world" under the imperium of the Julio-Claudian dynasty* (Luke 2:1, 11 [Augustus] → 3:1 → 20:22–25 [Tiberius] → Acts 11:28 → 18:2 [Claudius] → 25:1, 25 ["lord emperor," "Caesar" {Nero}]). With these and other *synchronisms*, Luke carefully coordinates the "good news" of a "Savior" born to a virgin at the same time that Octavian is being heralded as the "Savior and benefactor of all

---

44 "Siege mound" (χάραξ) and "dashed"/"razed to the ground" (ἐδαφίζω) are found in the NT only here in Luke. See Josephus, esp. *War* V.258–274 for the fullest description of the Roman siege works and the terror they could unleash, overwhelming seemingly impregnable fortresses: V.269-χαράκωμα ("palisades/siege works"). For ἐδαφίζω, cf. Isa 3:26; Ezek 31:12.
45 See also Chapter Eleven § 1.(iii) above along with the references to C. H. Dodd, "The Fall of Jerusalem and the 'Abomination of Desolation,'" *JRS* 37 (1947): 47–54, and Bo Reicke, "Synoptic Propecies on the Destruction of Jerusalem," in *Studies in New Testament and Early Christian Literature: Essays in Honour of A. P. Wikgren*, ed. David E. Aune (Leiden: Brill, 1972): 121–34.
46 E.g., relative obedience and true worship: Abraham's calling (7:2–8); Tent and Tabernacle, esp. with David (7:44–46); early Jerusalem community of Jesus worshippers who chose Stephen as one of "the Seven" (6:3–8, 15; 7:55–56). Pernicious idolatry and disobedience and rejecting God's messengers of salvation and redemption: Joseph (7:9–16); Moses (7:23–43); "the prophets" (7:51–52a); "the Just One," "Jesus," "the Son of Humankind" (7:52b–56).
47 E.g., the "glory of God appearing" to Abraham to call him to "the place" where Israel should worship God was fulfilled when Stephen, at "the place" (Acts 6:13–14), looks up into the "opened heaven" and sees "the glory of God" and Jesus "the Just One," the enthroned "Son of Humankind, standing at the right hand of God" (7:2–7 → 7:17 → 7:44–46 → 7:54–56).

humankind,"[48] who in the pastoral lore of the *Eclogues*[49] is born from a virgin to become the "Most Favored One" ("Augustus") for all time and all space.[50]

As a historian and biblical theologian, therefore, Luke is keen to lace world events with the unfolding *dynamis* of the Jesus-Messiah movement to make his case that nothing falls outside of a comprehensive 'plan' or providence of the ultimate Divine will. Hence Roman power appears both overwhelming and impotent, in full control yet utterly at the mercy of the one God of Israel who reigns over all the nations. Whether Rome squashes all forms of uprising or Roman officials move against the Jesus movement, Luke exposes the divine reality of Greeks and Romans and barbarians for what it is, vain and dumb idolatry, "thinking the deity is like an image, formed by the art and imagination of mere mortals" (Acts 17:29b). Luke choreographs the checkered performance of Roman "governors" and "consuls" like an undulating counterpoint that frames the narrative arc in composing his case.[51]

Jesus's *birth* at the time Quirinius was governor of Syria when a great census took place (Luke 2:1–5) recalls the birth of the Zealot uprising attributed to Judas the Galilean, as Gamaliel will later prompt the reader to remember (Acts 5:37). Like a Polybius who early on would synchronize an auxiliary event to undertone all the main developments that would emerge only later in the continuity of the narrative, so Luke associates Jesus's birth with Rome's humiliation of "the Judeans" when Augustus personally oversaw the liquidation of "King" Archelaus's estate, for which Josephus will assign the main cause of the revolutionary resistance movement that fomented into the "Jewish War" of 67–74 CE (*Ant.* 18.26, 29).[52]

Not only a Judas or Theudas[53] will be "crushed and scattered," according to Gamaliel, in line with "the plan of God" (Acts 5:35–39), but so also will Israel's Christ–"the king of the Jews, this one!"–be scourged and debased and violently silenced (Luke 23:6–12, 13–29). Not only in birth but also in *death* a Roman governor will mock the Judean 'king,' Jesus of Nazareth, now *executed in exchange for* an "insurrectionist and murderer" (διὰ στάσιν καὶ φόνον), again, according to

---

48 See the Priene (Ionia) Inscription (9 BCE) in, e.g., Hans-Josef Klauck, *The Religious Context of Early Christianity: A Guide to Graeco-Roman Religions* (Minneapolis, MN: Fortress Press, 2003), 296–98.
49 Virgil, *The Eclogues*, trans. Guy Lee (London: Penguin Books, 1984): *Eclogue* IV.6.
50 See esp. Chapter Five § 2 above.
51 See esp. Chapter Five above.
52 For more details and elaboration, see David P. Moessner, "Quirinius," *NIDB* 4:704–5.
53 Cf. "the Egyptian" in Acts 21:37–40 over against Paul's 'movement.'

a greater "counsel or plan of God."⁵⁴ Whether it be Herod (1:5), Quirinius (2:2), Herod Antipas (23:6–12), Pilate (23:1–25),⁵⁵ Gallio (Acts 18:12–17) or Felix (Acts 23:26–24:26) et al., all, unwittingly, combine to facilitate a very different Lordship and kind of "decree" that issues in the "good news" of "the release of sins to all the nations" (24:44–49 → Acts 2:7–11)–with Paul circling within the vortex of empire, "proclaiming the Reign of God ... openly and without hindrance" as Luke 'closes the book' on his two-volume enterprise (Acts 28:31).

2 Patterns of Recurrence of 'First Person' Participation within the Described Events.

In our look at Luke's Gospel preface, we discovered that παρακολουθέω has a basic sense of "following" something as that thing, person, event, et cetera unfolds, whether in the real time of the participant's world, or of the simultaneous "following with the mind" the world that opens up as one reads a text, whether of discursive argument or narrative story.⁵⁶ Discussions of the significance of the "we" passages in Acts⁵⁷ are usually dovetailed into the discussion of "us," "me," and "I" of the two prefaces (Luke 1:1–4; Acts 1:1–5).⁵⁸ But in truth, the mystery of the "we" passages has still not been fully or thus finally resolved.

Yet our findings suggest some new possibilities. Παρηκολουθηκώς is used for instance by both Demosthenes and Josephus to vouchsafe their own expertise and comprehension of a larger set of events while at the same time allowing them–as they choose and circumstances permit–to include themselves as firsthand participants at various stages of the developing chain. This firsthand 'witness' of some of the events in no way dilutes or compromises their epistemological mastery of the larger movement; 'subjective involvement' is in no way implicated or putatively assumed by the audience. In fact, especially for these two writers, παρηκολουθηκώς is chosen as an active participle in the perfect sense precisely when they want to persuade their hearers that they have the noetic savvy to re-signify an entire historical process in order to convince their

---

54 Ironically, not unlike Pontius Pilate who escaped the silence of history through his role in the passion of Jesus Christ, Publius Sulpicius Quirinius, also a Roman governor, became a figure of lasting significance because of the birth of Jesus.
55 In addition to Pilate's role in Jesus's passion, see Luke 13:1–3; Acts 4:27–28 (entwined with Herod in facilitating the "plan/counsel of God" against Jesus the righteous rejected servant).
56 See esp. Chapter Three above.
57 Acts 16:10–17; 20:3–15; 21:1–18; 27:1–28:16.
58 See Chapter Two above §I.4.

audience to take appropriate action in light of this newly divulged state of affairs. Παρηκολουθηκώς invites both the senses of "informed competence" and "experienced familiarity with" without having to tip its hand apart from its context. Hence παρακολουθέω *may* but does not necessarily entail 'eyewitness' involvement.[59]

If παρηκολουθηκώς can encompass both the cognitive knowledge that produces an informed person as well as the knowledge gained through personal involvement, then it would seem to be an ideal term for credentialing one's authority to generate a new configuration of the whole. Are there any clues in the "we" passages in Acts that would link the "we's" ability to transcend the intra-*diegesis* and speak to the external audiences from a meta-diegetic level[60] like the inscribed author does in his opening prologues?

We have noticed that in Acts 20:7 when Paul and the "we" gather (συνάγω) with disciples in Troas (20:7–12), the narrator speaking as "we" utilizes the perfect tense of the participle of συνάγω (συνηγμένων) rather than the aorist to describe their ("we") practice of the "breaking the bread on the first day of the week." The thrust of the perfect must be something like "when we had the habit of gathering" or "when we [typically] gather" rather than a discrete moment of gathering that would be expressed by the aorist or historic present ("when we were gathered"[61]).

The upshot of the "we" narrator breaking frame to address his audience appears to be the same kind of metaleptic maneuver that the inscribed author makes in Luke 1:1, 2, 3 and Acts 1:1, especially as in both prefaces a Theophilus is singled out as part of Luke's audience and is included in the "us" who have allegedly experienced some of the events or matters that have been brought to fruition and that Luke will re-tell.[62] *In Acts 20:7 the worlds of the narrator and the narratees are collapsed into one,* similar to the way Luke continues Acts 1:4b–5 as a transference of the words and deeds of the Gospel Jesus to the Jesus who continues to speak and act in Acts. Acts 20:7 may thus be an understated clue that connects the inscribed "me" and "I" and "us" of the first volume to the "I" and "we" of the second. Such a possibility begs even more investigation! In any event, the metaleptic slip of Acts 20:7 functions rhetorically like narrative asides (ἐκβάσεις) of Hellenistic historians to lend greater credence to Luke's claims in his prologues to be an admirably qualified tradent and re-configurer of eyewitness Jesus traditions.

---

59 See Chapter Three above.
60 See esp. Chapter Seven § 3.2.
61 E.g., NRSV.
62 See further Chapter Seven § 4.(iv).

3 Patterns of Recurrence Attributed to an Overarching Divine Will, Fate, or Necessity

We have seen that Luke discovers a pattern of an anointed savior or Christ figure in the Jewish scriptures that he attributes to an all-encompassing divine "plan." As we observed especially in Polybius, Diodorus Siculus, and Dionysius of Halicarnassus, it was customary for Hellenistic historians to provide their audiences with a birds-eye viewing of their own meta-physical vantage point. In particular Diodorus, who spends much of the first six volumes rehearsing myths of various deities to illustrate their role in the development of a particular people or ethnic group, is emblematic of Hellenistic historians' intent to include some explanation, albeit partial and often rather vague, of some greater transcendent principle or divine force that steers history in various directions. Polybius was most insistent that "fate" (τύχη) influenced Rome's unprecedented rise to world domination and yet could give no real specifics or ideological underpinnings to this conviction.[63]

We can mention three of the most important terms in historians outside of Luke's usage:[64]

a) **πρόνοια** ("providence, purpose"): E.g., Josephus, *Ant*. II.332; IV.47, 114, 128, 185; V.277; Diodorus Siculus, *Library of History* I.1.3; compare 3Macc 4:21; 5:30; 4Macc 9:24; Wis 6:7; 14:3;

b) **γνώμη** ("foreknowledge, purpose, mind"): E.g., Josephus, *Ant.*, I.14, 46; II.174, 209; V.277; X.177; XI.327; et cetera;

c) **τύχη**[65] ("fate, fortune, chance"): E.g., Polybius, the *Histories* I.4.1–5; I.7.4; Diodorus Siculus, *Library of History*, I.1.3; XIII.21.4–5; XVIII.59.6; XXVI.15.3; XXXIV/XXXV.27.1; et cetera; Dionysius of Halicarnassus, *Roman Antiquities* I.4.2; 5.2; III.19.6; VIII.32.3; XI.12.3; et cetera; Josephus, *War*, III.387–91; IV.238; V.78, 120–22; VI.14, 44; et cetera; Arrian, *Anabasis*, V.1.2 ["the divine principle"]).

---

63 Cf. Walbank, "Idea of Decline," 195: "'*Tyche*' is frequently little more than a verbal elaboration, a way of speaking or a rhetorical flourish; but in the case of Rome's rise to power he [Polybius] seems, exceptionally, to have invested the process with a teleological character and to have treated the popular Hellenistic goddess as something akin to the Stoic Providence."

64 See the end of Chapter One above. Πρόνοια in Acts 24:2: the "foresight of provisions" that Felix provides his province; γνώμη in Acts 20:3: Paul's decision to change his mind for his return route.

65 For "fate"/"chance"/"necessity" (εἱμαρμένη/πεπρωμένη/ἀνάγκη [*inter alia*]), cf., e.g., Diodorus (*Lib. Hist.* XV.63.2; III.15.7, 19.2; X.21.3; 10.21.3; etc.); Josephus (*Ant.* XVI.397–98; *War* II.162–64; etc.); Dionysius (*Rom. Ant.* III.5.2, XI.1; V.8.6; IX.8.1; X.45.4; etc.); Lucian of Samosata (*Zeus Catechized*). See also John T. Squires, *The Plan of God in Luke-Acts*, SNTSMS 76 (Cambridge: Cambridge University Press, 1993), 15–77, 164–71.

We may well ask, did Luke find such a scheme because he was in a Hellenistic milieu of metaphysical speculation that promoted such patterns as in philosophical schools like the Stoics? Was Luke predisposed to 'see' such a plan because he was primarily a historian and expected to subsume events to some cosmic design?

It is of course impossible to probe Luke's mind to solve such a puzzle that perhaps even Luke himself could not fully answer. What we have seen, as we summarized above, is that the events of Jesus themselves–primarily his violent rejection at the historical center of Israel's worship and the claim that he was alive and appearing and ascending before his disciples–forced the first followers to make sense of such a strange, in many ways unthinkable scenario that Israel's Christ must suffer, and through that suffering effect the glory of a universal salvation for Jew and Gentile, Greek and barbarian alike. The new hermeneutic of a suffering Christ seems to have been thrust upon the first Jewish believers who, believing that Jesus was alive, began re-reading their scriptures to see *if* and *how* this could be so. Of the four canonical evangelists, Luke showcases with greatest emphasis that Jesus himself, both before and after his ascension, gave his disciples specific readings of those scriptures to enlighten their understanding, as Luke 24 and Acts 1–2 especially bring to light.

We can draw the conclusion, therefore, that Luke understands his two volumes to be unfolding "the plan of God" as discernible in Israel's scriptures in light of the events of Jesus as Israel's Christ. Luke figures his two volumes as an epitome of the *telos* of Israel's "anointed" as pre-scripted and debuted by Jesus of Nazareth whom "God had designated both Lord and Christ."[66] Undoubtedly the process leading to this conviction was dialectic in nature: the Jesus events push the readers to a new understanding of certain passages, while the passages themselves coerce the readers to understand the events of Jesus in a new way. The Road to Emmaus is a classic example of the mental mechanics of a revised "Christian" reading: the intellects of the heart "burn" as Jesus opens up the scriptures on the way, but it is also Jesus's gesture of the "breaking and distributing the bread" that breaks open the full illumination of this new understanding of "all that stands written about him" (Luke 24:13–35).

We have seen that this "plan" encapsulates "all that stands written" in "Moses, the prophets, and the psalms" about Jesus as the suffering Christ ("the Christ must suffer" and "Jesus is that Christ"[67]): ([ἡ] βουλὴ τοῦ θεοῦ ["the counsel/plan/will of God"]–Luke 7:30; Acts 2:23; 4:28; 5:38 [ironically]; 13:36; 20:27; compare

---

[66] Acts 2:36b, 23–24.
[67] See above nn. 13, 30.

27:42–43). Curiously Luke favors the impersonal verb δεῖ ("it is necessary") when showing Jesus as the suffering righteous anointed of the scriptures: Luke 9:22; 13:33; 17:25; 22:37; 24:7, 26, 44[68]; Acts 1:16, 22; 3:21; 4:12; 9:16; 14:22; 17:3; 19:21; 23:11; 27:24; compare Luke 2:49; 4:43; 13:16; 15:32; 19:5; 21:9; 22:7; Acts 9:6; 10:6; 25:10; 26:23; 27:21.

In sum, as distinct from the other authors of the NT, Luke looks globally over "written texts" that have, or are in the process of being read as authoritative scripture and pronounces them as pointing together severally, and as a whole, to the "Messiah who must suffer so that he might enter into his glory" (Luke 24:26). Read together these Jewish scriptures are becoming a proto-Christian 'Bible,' and it is in this sense, as we have already seen, that Luke can be called '*the first biblical theologian*' precisely as he is a composer of a two-volume Hellenistic *history*.

II. *Luke is a* Manager *(οἰκονόμος) of the Narrative 'Economy' (οἰκονομία). As rhetorical* elaborator, *Luke determines to a great extent how the parts combine to make a whole and, conversely, how the whole defines the parts. Through various protocols of 'arranging' Luke turns to tropes of conventional poetics to effect the grasp he wishes his audience to attain of the events he recounts. We may list some of these devices and 'methods of elaboration' that Luke the composer drafts for his poetic arsenal*:

While we have traced several 'types' of poetics schemes of 'arrangement' (οἰκονομία) through the Hellenistic era,[69] we have also discovered that these 'dispositions' are based upon operative conventions of narrative (*diegesis*) writing established well before this period. Aristotle's *Poetics* in fact articulates and expounds upon the prevailing 'state of the art' or default position for narrative rhetoric toward the beginning of the Hellenistic period: a triadic synergy of the poet's/author's art, consisting of authorial intention (διάνοια), the arrangement of the actions or events (μῦθος/πράξεις) through characters and their thought according to this intention, and the consequent impact upon the audience (for example, κάθαρσις [of fear and pity]). All three components are inter-dynamically intertwined such that no single component can operate without the concurrent engagement of the other two.[70]

All subsequent patterns of poetics, then, become variations spun around this linchpin of communicative exchange between writer and audience. Already by the time of Polybius, an intricate dynamic of poetics for multi-volume history writing is intact: a 'continuity of the narrative' (τὸ συνεχὲς τῆς διηγήσεως) ren-

---

[68] The "thus" (οὕτως) of Luke 24:46 is the epexegetical link with the δεῖ of 24:44.
[69] See esp. Chapters Five, Six, and Seven, above.
[70] See esp. Chapter Five § 1.

dered by an overall 'telos' (τέλος) of the author complete with a 'final' or 'closing event' (τελευτή), and a defining 'beginning' (ἀρχή), together with 'synchronistic' links and synchronic overlapping to illustrate the 'universal' interweavings of that curious coalition between human exigency and fate. This 'continuity of the narrative' establishes a targeted audience's ability to 'follow' (παρακολουθέω) the author's epistemological forays intended to capture their intellectual comprehension and affective consent.[71]

By the 1st century BCE, Diodorus, followed in the next generation by Dionysius, develops a more nuanced scheme. Diodorus is particularly intent to stake his reputation on "complete(d) narratives" (αὐτοτελεῖς) that entangle linear chrono-logical trajectories with lateral syn-chrono-logical networks of the known regions of the world to "ensemble forth" the finely meshed workings of the "one global village."[72] In Dionysius, Hellenistic literary criticism reaches a zenith through his application to 'narrative' of what he calls "the more technically-skilled" (τὸ τεχνικώτερον)[73] side of 'subject-matter' (τὸ πραγματικός), that which is called 'arrangement' (τὸ οἰκονομικόν), which is required in every kind of writing, whether one chooses philosophical or rhetorical subjects. It consists of 'division'/'partitioning' (διαίρεσις), 'sequence' (τάξις), and 'method of elaboration'" (ἐξεργασία) (*On Thucydides* 9). We have observed that the first element, 'division,' entails both a proper 'beginning point' and a known 'telos' and '*teleutē*' such that requisite 'sequencing' and 'effective elaboration' of the 'continuity' may be executed through the author's 'thought' (διάνοια).[74]

In his prologues, Luke taps into this conventional narrative hermeneutics to make his case that he is a skilled as well as a credentialed narrative composer. Already in his Gospel preface, Luke divulges his familiarity with the standards of Hellenistic narrative rhetoric by references to his 'scope' (διήγησιν περὶ τῶν πεπληροφορημένων ἐν ἡμῖν πραγμάτων ... πᾶσιν ... γράψαι), 'arrangement' (πᾶσιν ἀκριβῶς καθεξῆς σοι γράψαι)–including a 'beginning' (οἱ ἀπ' ἀρχῆς αὐτόπται καὶ ὑπηρέται γενόμενοι τοῦ λόγου), credentials–including in part his point of vantage or 'thought' (παρηκολουθηκότι ἄνωθεν πᾶσιν), and his 'purpose' or *telos* (ἵνα ἐπιγνῷς περὶ ὧν κατηχήθης λόγων τὴν ἀσφάλειαν) for the whole. And when his secondary *prooimion* is dovetailed into the entire narrative, Luke discloses his distinctive 'partitioning' (τὸν μὲν πρῶτον λόγον ἐποιησάμην περὶ πάντων ... ὧν ἤρξατο ὁ Ἰησοῦς ποιεῖν τε καὶ διδάσκειν, ἄχρι ἧς ἡμέρας ... ἀνελήμφθη, Acts

---

71 See Chapter Five §§ 1.1; 2.1–3.
72 See Chapter Six §II.
73 Cf. "technical" [Pritchett, *On Thucydides*], "artistic" [Usher, LCL].
74 See esp. Chapter Seven §§ 1–2.

1:1–2) of an "account" (διήγησις) of "all" the "traditions" that derive "from the beginning eyewitnesses and attendants of the message" (Luke 1:1–2, 4) but that also continue in the ongoing traditions of "witness" to that "message from the beginning" (Acts 1:6–8).[75]

Luke also reveals much about his 'ordering' (τάξις) or 'narrative sequence' (καθεξῆς) as he 'partitions' two 'beginnings,' one for the whole narrative work (e.g., Luke 1:2→Acts 1:22), the other for the scope and purpose of his second volume (Acts 1:1–2→11:15–16→15:7). How do these two 'beginnings' (ἀρχαί) collaborate and signify *vis-à-vis* each other?[76]

1. Luke's 'beginning' (ἡ ἀρχή) for his two-volume work forecasts the plot and sets the tone for the whole: Jesus's anointing by the Spirit through John the Baptist is linked inextricably to John's fate of a violent end, on one side (Luke 3:19–21), and to the fulfillment of the "beloved Son" in whom God "delights," on the other (3:22). Along with this "beloved Son" immediately hailed as a "son" of "Adam, son of God" (Luke 3:23–38), Luke announces the story of universal salvation through the "Christ" of Israel as one of suffering, and that Jesus as that suffering Christ will bring to fruition ancient words resonating through Israel's scriptures of an "anointed servant" and "beloved son" of Abraham.[77]

Luke's secondary 'beginning' (ἀρχή) ushers his audiences back inexorably to this rudimentary starting point. When Peter recalls the importance of his "witness" before Cornelius, he summons a second "beginning," when "the Holy Spirit fell upon them just as also upon *us at the beginning* (ἐν ἀρχῇ) and I remembered the word of the Lord [Jesus], how he had said, 'John baptized with water, but you shall be baptized by the Holy Spirit'" (Acts 11:15–16). But these are the words of Jesus in the linking prologue to Acts, when Jesus *at table* takes over the voice of the narrator and collapses his words and actions in the Gospel into the continuing plot of Acts (Acts 1:4b–5). Moreover, as he shares a meal with his apostles (1:4a), Jesus's words actually echo John the Baptist's distinction between his own baptism and that of "the mightier one who is coming," right at the point when Jesus is baptized (through John) by the Holy Spirit at the seminal "beginning" (Luke 3:15–22). Peter in fact had already reminisced with Cornelius how God had, "beginning (ἀρξάμενος) from Galilee after the baptism which John announced (Luke 3:16!), anointed Jesus from Nazareth with the Holy Spirit and power" who had "eaten and drunk" with them *at table* when God "had appointed

---

75 See esp. Chapters Three and Four above.
76 See esp. Chapter Nine §§ 2–3.3.
77 Gen 22:2, 12, 16; Isa 42:1–4.

them witnesses" to Jesus's anointed ministries of the Holy Spirit "after he had risen from the dead" (Acts 10:37–41).[78]

This secondary ἀρχή also enfolds Paul into the logical 'narrative sequence' (καθεξῆς) of the partitioned volumes, making Paul not only vital but also indispensable for the readers' comprehension of the primary beginning of Jesus the Christ's anointed calling. At the apostolic gathering in Acts 15, Peter, on the heels of Paul's and Barnabas's report of how the "turning" of the Gentiles had brought great joy to the "brothers and sisters" of Phoenicia and Samaria (15:3–5), reminded the "apostles and elders" that it was God who had first "from those beginning days" (ἀφ' ἡμερῶν ἀρχαίων) chosen him to announce the "word of the good news" to Gentiles. Cornelius's household response now confirms Paul's and Barnabas's "gospel," a "word" which does not require "circumcision" in the "turning" of the nations as they receive the "power of the Holy Spirit." Peter's words are his last in Acts and, in effect, pass *over to Paul* the mantle of the risen Christ's calling of the Twelve to "witness to the end of the earth" (Acts 1:8→15:7–11).[79] With that pronouncement, "the whole assembly became silent and they began to listen to Barnabas and Paul as they described in detail all the signs and wonders that God had done through them among the Gentiles" (15:12).[80]

Luke's 'division' thus imparts a coherence to the entire story. Israel's "Christ" of the anointing by the Spirit forms the 'continuity of the narrative' as Luke's 'sequencing' steers his audiences along that "way." Whether the Baptist or Paul at the beginning and ending, the calling of God's beloved Son and servant, along with the calling of Christ's witnesses to that calling in the power of the Spirit, expresses Luke's '*dianoia*' with a '*telos*' and the '*teleutē*' to the far reaches of the earth culminating in the "full flowering of those events in our midst" (Luke 1:1).

Luke engages a number of 'methods of elaboration' (ἡ ἐξεργασίαι) in his *poiesis*. We can list a few: 'contrasting through comparing' (ἡ σύγκρισις), especially between John the Baptist and Jesus throughout both volumes, where uneven parallels break the molds of previous understanding and expectations for

---

[78] See esp. Chapters Six §III and Seven § 3.1

[79] Acts 15:11 is one of the loudest echoes by Peter of Paul's emphasis on the role of "grace" and of "having trust/faith in" and uses the Gentile, not Jewish, believers as the models of the working of grace to receive the Holy Spirit (cf. Gal 3:2!).

[80] James, of course, provides the clinching argument: Not only does God's more recent working among Gentiles prove the legitimacy of a circumcision-free turning to the good news, but so does Moses who "from the generations of ancient times has been read every Sabbath in the synagogues" (Acts 15:13–21)! For "signs and wonders" as a function of the power of the Spirit in Acts, see esp. Stephen in 6:8–10.

the future.⁸¹ 'Synchronisms' (οἱ συγχρονισμοί) bind both the intra-textual material of the two volumes to each other as well as to external events and circumstances in the *metadiegetic* level or world of the author, thus opening up a wide 'cultural encyclopedia' for Luke's audiences.⁸² The 'genealogy' (ἡ γενεαλογία) of Luke 3:23–38 nudges the reader to assess Jesus's anointing in light of the 'beginnings' and the 'ends' of God's creation of humankind. And 'doublets' or 'repetitions' force the reader to re-combine previous understandings into more complex developments as the plot is 'raveled' or 'bound' more tightly. The twofold 'reiterations' or *relectures* of Saul's calling on the Damascus Road as well as the double repetition of the Cornelius event are prime illustrations of the author's enforcing his intended significance for his audiences *through these emplotted elaborations*.⁸³

2. As another trope of 'elaboration,' the *metalepsis* of Luke's secondary *prooimion* not only pulls Paul into the 'continuity of the narrative' as central to the larger story but, even more, structures the narrative poetics so that Paul will emerge as *chief* "witness" or '*the* witness of witnesses' of the Christ's anointed sending to Israel and the nations–to the "end of the earth."⁸⁴

We have seen that the metaleptic transfer of two narrative worlds or levels into the one realized Kingdom of God through the crucified-risen one makes Jesus the 'proclaimed proclaimer' and the 'enacted actor' through the rest of Acts.⁸⁵ Yet this metaleptic collapse comes to its most powerful expression in the words and actions of Paul. Though Peter's voice predominates in presenting the "word" and "name" of the Lord in the first five chapters of Acts,⁸⁶ it is Jesus's voice that takes over the narrator's and Paul's own voice in a fashion similar to the metaleptic transumption of Acts 1:4b:

---

81 See esp. the parallel panels comparing and contrasting John and Jesus in the first two chapters of Luke, each diptych followed by a scene combining each parallel into one new 'continuity' of the plot: 1:5–25 ‖ 1:26–38 → 1:39–56; 1:57–80 ‖ 2:1–40 → 2:41–52; something very similar occurs in 3:1–4:30! By the end of Jesus's preaching in Nazareth, both his continuity and discontinuity with John has through σύγκρισις been clearly 'elaborated.'
82 See Chapter Five above.
83 See esp. Chapter One § 3; Chapter Seven §§ 1–2.
84 See Chapter Seven §§ 2–3.
85 See esp. Chapter Seven § 3.
86 Peter must first undergo a major "change of thinking" about the relation of Jesus's active presence to the salvation of the rest of the non-Jewish world as he and the rest of the Twelve ignore and thus disregard Jesus's immediate command to take his salvation "to the ends of the earth" (Acts 1:8 → 10:1–11:18).

1) The first time Luke's auditors will hear again the voice of the Risen Jesus who breaks into the voice of the narrator in Acts 1:4b–5 is his abrupt breaking into Paul's journey to Damascus: "Saul, Saul, why are you persecuting *me*?" (Acts 9:4b).

2) In fact, unlike any of the apostles or disciples, "Jesus," "the Lord," after the initial *prooemial* interruption, speaks *directly only* to Paul, some seven times.[87] Thus Luke's auditors hear the voice of Jesus again–for the first time in the plotted story–only when Paul enters into the action. The upshot is that Jesus speaks, teaches, acts, and appears more directly to and through Paul than any other character in Acts.[88] Acts 26:23 sums up Paul's entire sending as Jesus's *witness* to be virtually the proclamation of the suffering risen Christ himself.[89]

3) It is Paul, and not the Twelve, nor Stephen and the Seven, who fulfills the mandate of Jesus's voice *to the Twelve* in Acts 1:8[90] to be his witness "to the end of the earth." Paul's calling in 9:1–19a with its two *relectures* stresses that, like the Twelve, Paul is sent both to the people of Israel *and* to non-Jewish peoples at "the end of the earth."[91] Though the apostles will suffer much for the sake of Jesus's name (see Acts 5:41), Paul's call is freighted with the *necessity* of much suffering in special solidarity with Jesus the Christ: "I myself [Jesus] will show him [Saul] how much he must suffer for the sake of my name" (Acts 9:16) → "Hurry up, get out of Jerusalem at once, because they will not accept your witness about me" (22:18) → "I will rescue you from your people and from the Gentiles to whom I am sending you" (26:17). *From* Jerusalem, Paul is sent to Israel and the nations far away by the *direct* voice of the Lord Jesus himself (22:18). Already in the conclusion to Paul's first major address, "I [the Lord] have appointed you [Paul and Barnabas and entourage] to be the light of the Gentiles, in order that you might extend salvation to the end of the earth'" (τέθεικά σε ... σε εἰς σωτηρίαν ἕως ἐσχάτου τῆς γῆς, Isa 49:6b in Acts 13:47b → Acts 1:8b).

---

[87] Acts 9:4b–6 (cf. 9:15–16 = direct speech of the Lord about Paul reported by Ananias); 13:47; 18:9–10; 22:10; 22:18, 21; 23:11; 26:14–18 (cf. 27:23–24, direct speech of an "angel of the God to whom I belong").
[88] Only for Paul does the narrator state explicitly that when Paul preaches or teaches, one should understand that it is actually Jesus who is speaking through him: Acts 13:38–39, 47 (corporate character of the servant mission); 14:3; 26:23!
[89] Cf. Acts 14:3.
[90] Actually eleven apostles; Matthias replaces Judas Iscariot later in plotted time in Acts 1. For a comprehensive treatment of Paul in Acts and the relation of this portrait to the Pauline epistles, see now Daniel Marguerat, *Paul in Acts and Paul in His Letters*, WUNT 310. (Tübingen: Mohr Siebeck, 2013), esp. 1–21.
[91] Acts 9:15–16; 22:14–15, 17–21.

In sum, through the metalepsis that engrafts Acts into the heart of the anointed Christ's "going in and out among us,"[92] Paul is ensconced at the center of the apostolic faith founded, interpreted, and energized by Jesus himself. Ironically, it is the non-apostle, non-witness–the one who did not "bear witness" to the deeds and words of Jesus during his public activity but rather had become prime "witness" to the stoning of Stephen–Paul–who becomes the chief "witness" and *hermeneutēs* of the words and works of Jesus of Nazareth in the two volume Luke and Acts. Through Paul, the "things concerning the Lord Jesus Messiah" and "the Kingdom of God" are proclaimed openly at the center of the 'kingdom' that controls "the ends of the earth" (Acts 28:30–31; Isa 45:4–6; compare *Pss. Sol.* 8:15). Consequently Luke's peculiar 'partitioning' and coordinating of the two 'beginnings' blends Paul's voice with the voice of the crucified-risen Christ. Paul thus becomes the premier definer and defender of the apostolic traditions that go back to the "beginning from the baptism of John" (compare Acts 13:24–25).[93] But that also means that Luke's 'school' pedigree for his entire storytelling projects its narrative voice as *conjoining with the living voice of Jesus himself.*

---

[92] Acts 1:21–22.
[93] Paul is entangled into two-thirds of the plot of Acts. Portraying Paul's solidarity with the apostolic traditions authored by Jesus himself must give evidence of one of the main reasons Luke has extended the "narrative" of "the many" into an elongated story "of those events which have come to fruition in our midst" (Luke 1:1)!

Finale:
Luke the Historian, Biblical Theologian of Israel's 'Christ'

Ancient Hellenistic historians reflect self-consciously on the purpose and means by which they convey information and persuade their audiences to specific ways of thinking about reality. *Luke the Historian of Israel's Heritage, Theologian of Israel's 'Christ.'* <u>A New Reading</u> *of Luke's 'Gospel Acts'* demonstrates that a full communicative model of authorial intent to impact an audience through a deliberately designed plot was a common poetic currency, and that Luke was fully versed in this culture. Indeed, the author of Luke and Acts exhibits a self-reflective, energetic engagement with this narrative hermeneutics through his desire to impart a greater, more reliable comprehension of the ongoing events of Jesus and his followers. Accordingly, if he proves persuasive, Luke's audience will perforce experience transformation in understanding, belief, and action.

As the first 'biblical' theologian, Luke construes authoritative scriptural texts as disclosing an overarching principle of divine activity or "plan." As a Hellenistic historian, Luke's "plan/counsel/will of God" epitomizes the divine rationale and 'steering' of history's entangled events to an intended 'goal.' As biblical theologian *and* Hellenistic historian, Luke perceives in both the whole and the parts of "the scriptures" a divine intent and action for Israel through Israel's Christ that comprehends all of human history for the salvation of the world. Luke's divine 'plan' is thus 'arranged' into a narrative plan or 'economy' of two volumes that re-presents the divine fulfillment in the life, death, and exaltation of Israel's Christ (Gospel of Luke) and the continuing events of Israel's risen, crucified Messiah speaking and acting through his followers in their movement to the "ends of the earth" (Acts of the Apostles). More than that, through all of Luke's narrative figuring and re-figuring, Luke the historian and theologian defends God's ways and actions through the suffering servants and prophets and kings of Israel that lead to "the Christ of God," as Jesus and the "church" through the apostles, Paul, and Luke himself "declare God to be right" and "the way of the Lord" as "just" in this grand performance of God's saving history.

Bibliography

Aland, Kurt. *Synopsis Quattuor Evangeliorum*. Stuttgart: Württembergische Bibelanstalt, 1964.
Aland, Kurt, and Barbara Aland. *The Text of the New Testament: An Introduction to the Critical Editions and to the Theory and Practice of Modern Textual Criticism*. Translated by E. F. Rhodes. 2nd ed. Grand Rapids, MI/Leiden: Eerdmans/Brill, 1989.
Alexander, Loveday. *Acts in its Ancient Literary Context: A Classicist Looks at the Acts of the Apostles*. LNTS 298. London: T&T Clark, 2005.
Alexander, Loveday. "'In Journeyings Often': Voyaging in Acts of the Apostles and in Greek Romance." In *Luke's Literary Achievement*, edited by Christopher M. Tuckett, 17–49. JSNTSup116. Sheffield: Sheffield Academic Press, 1995.
Alexander, Loveday. "Luke's Preface in the Context of Greek Preface-Writing." *NovT* 28 (1986): 48–74.
Alexander, Loveday. "The Preface to Acts and the Historians." In *History, Literature and Society in the Book of Acts*, edited by Ben Witherington III, 73–103. Cambridge: Cambridge University Press, 1995.
Alexander, Loveday. *The Preface to Luke's Gospel*. SNTSMS 78. Cambridge: Cambridge University Press, 1993.
Allen, O. Wesley. *The Death of Herod: The Narrative and Theological Function of Retribution in Luke-Acts*. SBLDS 158. Atlanta, GA: Scholars Press, 1997.
Allison, Dale C. Jr. *The Intertextual Jesus. Scripture in Q*. Harrisburg, PA: Trinity Press International, 2000.
Alter, Robert. *The Art of Biblical Narrative*. New York: Basic Books, 1981.
Aristotle. *Historia animalium*. In *Histoire des animaux*, vol. 1, edited by Pierre Louis. Paris: Les Belles Lettres, 1964.
Aristotle. *Poetics*. Translated by Stephen Halliwell. 1 vol. LCL. Cambridge, MA: Harvard University Press, 1995.
Augustine. *Sermons on Various Subjects*. Translated by Edmund Hill. Vol. 10, *The Works of Saint Augustine: A Translation for the Twenty-first Century*. Hyde Park, NY: New City Press, 1995.
Aune, David. *The New Testament in Its Literary Environment*. Philadelphia, PA: Westminster, 1987.
Aune, David. *Prophecy in Early Christianity and the Ancient Mediterranean World*. Grand Rapids, MI: Eerdmans, 1983.
Aune, David, ed. *Westminster Dictionary of the New Testament and Early Christian Literature and Rhetoric*. Louisville, KY: Westminster John Knox, 2010.
Avenarius, Gert. *Lukians Schrift zur Geschichtsschreibung*. Mesisenheim/Glan: Hain, 1956.
Bailey, Kenneth E. *Poet and Peasant*. Grand Rapids, MI: Eerdmans, 1976.
Balch, David L. "Two Apologetic Encomia: Dionysius on Rome and Josephus on the Jews," *Journal for the Study of Judaism* 13 (1982): 102–22.
Bann, Stephen, and John E. Bowlt, eds. *Russian Formalism*. Edinburgh: Scottish Academic, 1973.
Barr, David L., and Judith L. Wentling. "The Conventions of Classical Biography and the Genre of Luke-Acts: A Preliminary Study." In *Luke-Acts: New Perspectives from the Society of Biblical Literature Seminar*, edited by Charles H. Talbert, 63–88. New York: Crossroad, 1984.
Barrett, Charles K. "*Shaliah* and Apostle." In *Donum Gentilicium: New Testament Studies in Honour of David Danube*, edited by Ernst Bammel, Charles K. Barrett, and William D. Davies, 88–102. Oxford: Clarendon, 1978.

Barton, Stephen C. "Early Christianity and the Sociology of the Sect." In *The Open Text: New Directions for Biblical Studies?*, edited by Francis Watson, 140–62. London: SCM Press, 1993.
Barzel, Hillel. "Moses: Tragedy and Sublimity." In *Literary Interpretations of Biblical Narratives*, edited by Kenneth R. R. Gros Louis, James Stokes Ackerman, and Thayer S. Warshaw, 120–40. Nashville, TN: Abingdon, 1974.
Bauer, Bruno. *Die Apostelgeschichte: Eine Ausgleichung des Paulinismus und des Judenthums innerhalb der christlichen Kirche*. Berlin: Gustav Hempel, 1850.
Baur, Ferdinand Christian. *Paulus: Der Apostel Jesu Christi, sein Leben und Wirken, seine Briefe und seine Lehre*. 2nd ed. Leipzig: Fues, 1866–67; repr. Osnabrück: Zeller, 1968.
Baur, Ferdinand Christian. "Ueber den Ursprung des Episcopats in der christlichen Kirche." In *Ausgewählte Werke in Einzelausgaben*, edited by Klaus Scholder and Ulrich Wickert, 321–505. Stuttgart-Bad Cannstatt: Frommann, 1963.
Bellinger, William H., Jr. "The Psalms and Acts: Reading and Rereading." In *With Steadfast Purpose: Essays on Acts in Honor of Henry Jackson Flanders, Jr.*, edited by Naymond H. Keathley, 127–43. Waco, TX: Baylor University Press, 1990.
Berlin, Adele. *Poetics and Interpretation of Biblical Narrative*. Bible and Literature Series 9. Sheffield: Almond, 1983.
Bilde, Per. *Flavius Josephus between Jerusalem and Rome*. JSPSup. Sheffield: JSOT, 1988.
Blass, Friedrich, Albert Debrunner, and Robert W. Funk. *A Greek Grammar of the New Testament and Other Early Christian Literature*. Chicago, IL: University of Chicago Press, 1961.
Blinzler, J. "Die literarische Eigenart des sogenannten Reiseberichts im Lukasevangelium." In *Synoptische Studien: Alfred Wikenhauser zum siebzigsten Geburtstag [...] dargebracht*, edited by J. Schmid and A. Vögtle, 20–52. Munich: K. Zink, 1953.
Bock, Darrell L. *Luke*. BECNT. Grand Rapids, MI: Baker, 1994.
Boers, H. W. "Psalm 16 and the Historical Origin of the Christian Faith." *ZNW* 60 (1969): 105–10.
Bonner, Stanley Fredrick. *The Literary Treatises of Dionysius of Halicarnassus: A Study in the Development of Critical Method*. Cambridge Classical Studies 5. Cambridge: Cambridge University Press, 1939.
Boring, M. Eugene. *The Continuing Voice of Jesus. Christian Prophecy and the Gospel Tradition*. Louisville, KY: Westminster/John Knox, 1991.
Bouwman, Gilbert. *Das dritte Evangelium*. Düsseldorf: Patmos, 1968.
Bovon, François. "Tracing the Trajectory of Luke 13,22–30 back to Q: A Study in Lukan Redaction." In *From Quest to Q: Festschrift James M. Robinson*, edited by J. M. Asgeirsson, K. de Troyer, M. W. Meyer, 285–94. BETL 146. Leuven: Leuven University Press/Peeters, 2000.
Braumann, Georg. "Die lukanische Interpretation der Zerstörung Jerusalems." *NovT* 6 (1963): 120–27.
Brett, Mark. "The Future of Reader Criticisms?" In *The Open Text: New Directions for Biblical Studies?*, edited by Francis Watson, 13–31. London: SCM Press, 1993.
Brown, Schuyler. "The Role of the Prologues in Determining the Purpose of Luke-Acts." In *Perspectives on Luke-Acts*, edited by Charles H. Talbert, 99–111. Danville, VA: Association of Baptist Professors of Religion, 1978.
Bruce, F. F. *Commentary on the Book of Acts*. NICNT. Grand Rapids, MI: Eerdmans, 1954.
Buckwalter, H. Douglas. *The Character and Purpose of Luke's Christology*. SNTSMS 89. Cambridge: Cambridge University Press, 1996.
Burridge, Richard A. "About People, by People, for People: Gospel Genre and Audiences." In *The Gospels for All Christians: Rethinking the Gospel Audiences*, edited by Richard Bauckham, 113–45. Grand Rapids, MI: Eerdmans, 1998.

Burridge, Richard A. *What are the Gospels? A Comparison with Graeco-Roman Biography*. Cambridge: Cambridge University Press, 1992.
Burton, Anne. *Diodorus Siculus Book I: A Commentary*. Leiden: Brill, 1972.
Butcher, S. H. *Aristotle's Theory of Poetry and Fine Art*. New York: Dover Publications, 1951.
Byrskog, Samuel. *Story as History, History as Story: The Gospel Tradition in the Context of Ancient Oral History*. WUNT 123. Tübingen: Mohr Siebeck, 2000.
Cadbury, Henry J. *The Book of Acts in History*. New York: Harper and Bros., 1955.
Cadbury, Henry J. "Commentary on the Preface of Luke." Appendix C of *The Beginnings of Christianity: Part I, The Acts of the Apostles*, edited by F. J. Foakes-Jackson and Kirsopp Lake, 489–510. Vol. 2. New York: MacMillan, 1920–1933.
Cadbury, Henry J. "The Knowledge Claimed in Luke's Preface." *The Expositor* 8 (1922): 401–20.
Cadbury, Henry J. *The Making of Luke–Acts*. London: SPCK, 1968.
Cadbury, Henry J. "The Purpose Expressed in Luke's Preface." *The Expositor* 8 (1922): 431–41.
Cadbury, Henry J. "'We' and 'I' Passages in Luke-Acts." *NTS* 3 (1956–57): 128–32.
Caird, G. B. *Saint Luke*. Pelican New Testament Commentaries. Harmondsworth: Penguin, 1963.
Callan, Terrance. "The Preface of Luke-Acts and Historiography." *NTS* 31 (1985): 576–81.
Carroll, John T. *Luke. A Commentary*. NTL. Louisville, KY: WJK, 2012.
Carroll, John T. *Response to the End of History: Eschatology and Situation in Luke-Acts*. SBLDS 92. Atlanta, GA: Scholars Press, 1988.
Cicero. *On Invention*. Translated by H. M. Hubbell. LCL 386. Cambridge, MA: Harvard University Press, 1949.
Clark, Andrew C. *Parallel Lives: The Relation of Paul to the Apostles in the Lucan Perspective*. Paternoster Biblical and Theological Monographs. Carlisle: Paternoster Press, 2001.
Cohen, Shaye J. D. *Josephus in Galilee and Rome*. Leiden: Brill, 1979.
Cohen, Shaye J. D. "Josephus, Jeremiah, and Polybius." *History and Theory* 21 (1982): 366–81.
Colson, F. H. "Notes on St. Luke's Preface." *JTS* 24 (1923): 300–309.
Colson, F. H. "Τάξει in Papias: The Gospels and the Rhetorical Schools." *JTS* 14 (1913): 62–69.
Conzelmann, Hans. *Die Mitte der Zeit: Studien zur Theologie des Lukas*. BHT 17. 3rd ed. Tübingen: Mohr Siebeck, 1960.
Conzelmann, Hans. *The Theology of St. Luke*. New York: Harper and Row, 1960.
Cooper, Lane. *The Poetics of Aristotle: Its Meaning and Influence*. New York: Longman, Green and Co., 1927.
Cosgrove, Charles H. "The Divine *Dei* in Luke-Acts." *NovT* 26 (1984): 168–90.
Cross, Frank Moore. *Canaanite Myth and Hebrew Epic*. Cambridge: Harvard University Press, 1973.
Dahl, Nils A. "The Story of Abraham in Luke-Acts." In *Studies in Luke-Acts: Essays Presented in Honor of Paul Schubert*, edited by Leander E. Keck and J. Louis Martyn, 142–48. Nashville, TN: Abingdon, 1966.
Danker, Frederick W., ed. *A Greek-English Lexicon of the New Testament and Other Early Christian Literature*. 3rd ed. Chicago, IL: University of Chicago Press, 2000.
Danker, Frederick W. *Jesus and the New Age*. Philadelphia, PA: Fortress Press, 1988.
Daube, David. *The Exodus Pattern in the Bible*. All Souls Studies 2. London: Faber and Faber, 1963.
Davies, J. H. "The Purpose of the Central Section of Luke's Gospel." *SE II* (=TU 87). Berlin: Akademie, 1964: 164–69.

Degenhardt, Hans-Joachim. *Lukas, Evangelist der Armen: Besitz und Besitzverzicht in den lukanischen Schriften: Eine traditions- und redaktionsgeschichtliche Untersuchung*. Stuttgart: Katholisches Bibelwerk, 1965.
Devoldère, M. "Le prologue du troisième évangile." *NRTh* 56 (1929): 714–19.
Dibelius, Martin. *Die Formgeschichte der Evangelien*. Tübingen: Mohr Siebeck, 1971.
Dibelius, Martin. "Die Reden der Apostelgeschichte und die antike Geschichtsschreibung." In *Aufsätze zur Apostelgeschichte*, edited by Heinrich Greeven, 120–25. FRLANT 42. Göttingen: Vandenhoeck & Ruprecht, 1951.
Dihle, Albrecht. *Die Entstehung der historischen Biographie*. Heidelberg: Universitätsverlag, 1987.
Dihle, Albrecht. "Die Evangelien und die biographische Tradition der Antike." *ZTK* 80 (1983): 33–49.
Dihle, Albrecht. *Studien zur griechischen Biographie*. Göttingen: Vandenhoeck & Ruprecht, 1956.
Dillon, Richard J. *From Eyewitnesses to Ministers of the Word*. AnBib 82. Rome: Biblical Institute, 1978.
Dillon, Richard J. "Previewing Luke's Project from His Prologue (Luke 1:1–4)." *CBQ* 43 (1981): 205–27.
Diodorus Siculus. *The Library of History*. Translated by Charles Henry Oldfather. 12 vols. LCL. Cambridge, MA: Harvard University Press, 1933–1967.
Dionysius of Halicarnassus: The Critical Essays. Translated by Stephan Usher. 2 vols. LCL. Cambridge, MA: Harvard University Press, 1974–1985.
Doble, Peter. *The Paradox of Salvation: Luke's Theology of the Cross*. SNTSMS 87. Cambridge: Cambridge University Press, 1996.
Dodd, C. H. "The Fall of Jerusalem and the 'Abomination of Desolation.'" *JRS* 37 (1947): 47–54.
Donelson, Lewis R. "Cult Histories and the Sources of Acts." *Biblica* 68 (1987): 1–21.
Driver, S. R. *Deuteronomy*. ICC. 3rd ed. Edinburgh: T&T Clark, 1902.
Drury, John. *Tradition and Design in Luke's Gospel: A Study in Early Christian Historiography*. Atlanta, GA: John Knox, 1976.
Dungan, David L., and David R. Cartlidge. *Sourcebook of Texts for the Comparative Study of the Gospels*. SBLSBS 1. 4th ed. Missoula, MT: Scholars, 1974.
Dunn, James D. G. *The Acts of the Apostles*. Peterborough: Epworth Press, 1996.
Du Plessis, I. I. "Once More: The Purpose of Luke's Prologue (Luke I 1–4)." *NovT* 16 (1974): 259–71.
Dupont, Jacques. *The Salvation of the Gentiles: Essays on the Acts of the Apostles*. Translated by John R. Keating. New York: Paulist Press, 1979.
Eckstein, A. M. "Josephus and Polybius: A Reconsideration." *Classical Antiquity* 9 (1990): 175–208.
Eden, Kathy. *Poetic and Legal Fiction in the Aristotelian Tradition*. Princeton, NJ: Princeton University Press, 1986.
Edmonds, J. M. *The Fragments of Attic Comedy*. IIIA. Leiden: Brill, 1961.
Èjxenbaum, Boris Mixajlovic. "The Theory of the Formal Method." In *Readings in Russian Poetics: Formalist and Structuralist Views*, edited by Ladislav Matejka and Krystyna Pomorska, 3–37. Cambridge, MA: MIT University Press, 1971.
Elliott, John H. Review of *Israel und das gewaltsame Geschick der Propheten*, by Odil Hannes Steck. *JBL* 87 (1968): 226–27.
Ellis, E. Earle. *The Gospel of Luke*. NCB. Rev. ed. London: Oliphants, 1974.

Else, Gerald Frank. *Plato and Aristotle on Poetry*. Edited by Peter Burian. Chapel Hill, NC: University of North Carolina Press, 1986.
Enos, Richard L. *Greek Rhetoric before Artistotle*. Prospect Heights, IL: Waveland Press, 1993.
Enslin, Morton S. "Luke and the Samaritans." *HTR* 36 (1943): 277–97.
Esler, Peter. *Community and Gospel in Luke-Acts*. Cambridge: Cambridge University Press, 1987.
Eusebius. *The Ecclesiastical History*. LCL 153. Cambridge, MA: Harvard University Press, 1975.
Evans, Christopher F. "The Central Section of St. Luke's Gospel." In *Studies in the Gospels: Essays in Memory of R. H. Lightfoot*, edited by D. E. Nineham, 37–53. Oxford: Blackwell, 1955.
Evans, Craig A. with James A. Sanders. *Luke and Scripture: The Function of Sacred Tradition in Luke-Acts*. Minneapolis: Fortress, 1993.
Evans, Craig A. with James H. Charlesworth. *The Pseudepigrapha and Early Biblical Interpretation*. Sheffield: JSOT Press, 1993.
Fascher, Erich. "Theologische Beobachtungen zu δεῖ." In *Neutestamentliche Studien für Rudolf Bultmann*, edited by Walther Eltester, 228–54. BZNW 21. Berlin: Töpelmann, 1954.
Feldman, Louis H. *Josephus and Modern Scholarship (1937–1980)*. Berlin: de Gruyter, 1984.
Filson, Floyd V. "The Journey Motif in Luke-Acts." In *Apostolic History and the Gospel*, edited by W. Ward Gasque and Ralph P. Martin, 68–77. Grand Rapids, MI: Eerdmans, 1970.
Fitzmyer, Joseph A. *The Acts of the Apostles*. New York: Doubleday, 1998.
Fitzmyer, Joseph A. "The Composition of Luke, Chapter 9." In *Perspectives on Luke-Acts*, edited by Charles H. Talbert, 139–52. Danville, VA: Association of Baptist Professors of Religion, 1978.
Fitzmyer, Joseph A. *The Gospel according to Luke I–IX*. AB 28. Vol. 1. New York: Doubleday, 1981.
Flender, Helmut. *Heil und Geschichte in der Theologie des Lukas*. BEvT 41. Munich: Kaiser, 1965.
Freedman, David Noel, ed. *Anchor Bible Dictionary*. 6 vols. New York: Doubleday, 1992.
Frei, Hans. *Theology and Narrative: Selected Essays*. Oxford: Oxford University Press, 1993.
Fuhrmann, Manfred. *Aristoteles Poetik*. München: Heimeran Verlag, 1976.
Gasse, W. "Zum Reisebericht des Lukas." *ZNW* 34 (1935): 293–99.
Gaventa, Beverly R. *The Acts of the Apostles*. Nashville, TN: Abingdon, 2003.
Gaventa, Beverly R. "Theology and Ecclesiology in the Miletus Speech: Reflections on Content and Context." *NTS* 50 (2004): 36–52.
Geldenhuys, Norval. *Commentary on the Gospel of Luke*. NICNT. London: Marshall, Morgan & Scott, 1951.
Genette, Gerard. *Narrative Discourse: An Essay in Method*. Translated by Jane E. Lewin. Ithaca, NY: Cornell University Press, 1980.
Gill, David. "Observations on the Lukan Travel Narrative and Some Related Passages." *HTR* 63 (1970): 199–221.
Gingrich, F. Wilbur, and Frederick W. Danker, eds. *A Greek-English Lexicon of the New Testament and Other Early Christian Literature*. 2nd ed. Chicago, IL: University of Chicago Press, 1979.
Ginzberg, Louis. *The Legends of the Jews*. 7 vols. Philadelphia, PA: Jewish Publication Society of America, 1910.
Girard, Louis. *L'Evangile des voyages de Jésus ou La Section 9,51–18,14 de Saint Luc*. Paris: Gabalda, 1951.
Golden, Leon. *Aristotle on Tragic and Comic Mimesis*. American Classical Studies 29. Atlanta, GA: Scholars Press, 1992.
Goodman, Martin. "Josephus as Roman Citizen." In *Josephus and the History of the Greco-Roman Period*, edited by Fausto Parente and Joseph Sievers, 329–38. Leiden: Brill, 1994.

Goulder, M. D. "The Chiastic Structure of the Lucan Journey." *SE* II (= TU 87). Berlin: Akademie, 1964: 195–202.
Goulder, M. D. *Midrash and Lection in Matthew*. London: SPCK, 1974.
Goulder, M. D. *Type and History in Acts*. London: SPCK, 1964.
Green, Joel B. "Internal Repetition in Luke–Acts: Contemporary Narratology and Lucan Historiography." In *History, Literature and Society in the Book of Acts*, edited by Ben Witherington III, 283–99. Cambridge: Cambridge University Press, 1995.
Green, Joel B. *The Gospel of Luke*. NICNT. Grand Rapids, MI: Eerdmans, 1997.
Green, Joel B. *The Theology of the Gospel of Luke*. Cambridge: Cambridge University Press, 1995.
Gregory, Andrew. *The Reception of Luke and Acts in the Period before Irenaeus: Looking for Luke in the Second Century*. WUNT 2/169. Tübingen: Mohr Siebeck, 2003.
Gregory, Andrew F., and Christopher M. Tuckett, "Reflections on Method: What Constitutes the Use of the Writings that Later Formed the New Testament in the Apostolic Fathers?" In *The Reception of the New Testament in the Apostolic Fathers*, edited by Andrew F. Gregory and Christopher M. Tuckett, 61–82. Oxford: Oxford University Press, 2005.
Grube, G. M. A. "Dionysius of Halicarnassus on Thucydides." *The Phoenix* 4 (1950): 95–110.
Grube, G. M. A. *The Greek and Roman Critics*. London: Methuen, 1965.
Grundmann, Walter. *Das Evangelium nach Lukas*. THKNT. Berlin: Evangelische Verlagsanstalt, 1961.
Grundmann, Walter. *Das Evangelium nach Lukas*. THKNT 3. 8th ed. Berlin: Evangelische Verlagsanstalt, 1978.
Grundmann, Walter. "Fragen der Komposition des lukanischen Reiseberichts." *ZNW* 50 (1959): 252–70.
Guilding, Aieleen. *The Fourth Gospel and Jewish Worship*. Oxford: Clarendon, 1960.
Hadas-Lebel, Mireille. *Flavius Josephus: Eyewitness to Rome's First-Century Conquest of Judea*. Translated by Richard Miller. New York: Macmillan, 1993.
Haenchen, Ernst. *The Acts of the Apostles*. 14th ed. Oxford: Oxford University Press, 1971.
Haenchen, Ernst. "Das 'Wir' in der Apostelgeschichte und das Itinerar." *ZTK* 58 (1961): 329–66.
Halliwell, Stephen. *Aristotle's Poetics*. Chapel Hill, NC: University of North Carolina Press, 1986.
Halliwell, Stephen. *The Poetics of Aristotle: Translation and Commentary*. London: Duckworth, 1987.
Hallward, B. L. "The Roman Defensive." In *The Cambridge Ancient History*. Vol. 8. Cambridge: The University Press, 1930.
Harmless, William. *Augustine and the Catechumenate*. Collegeville, MN: Liturgical Press, 1995.
Hartl, Vinzenz. "Zur synoptischen Frage: Schließt Lukas durch 1,1–3 die Benutzung des Matthäus aus?" *BZ* 13 (1925): 334–37.
Hays, Richard B. "The Paulinism of Acts, Intertextually Reconsidered." In *Paul and the Heritage of Israel. Paul's Claim upon Israel's Legacy in Luke and Acts in the Light of the Pauline Letters*, edited by David P. Moessner, Daniel Marguerat, Mikeal C. Parsons, Michael Wolter, 35–48. Vol. 2, *Luke the Interpreter of Israel*. London/New York, NY: T & T Clark International, 2012.
Hays, Richard B. Preface to to the paperback edition of *Lord of the Banquet: A Literary and Theological Investigation of the Lukan Travel Narrative*, David P. Moessner. Harrisburg, PA: Trinity Press International, 1998.

Heath, Malcolm. *Unity in Greek Poetics*. Oxford: Clarendon Press, 1989.
Hengel, Martin. *The Four Gospels and the One Gospel of Jesus Christ: An Investigation of the Collection and Origin of the Canonical Gospels*. Harrisburg, PA: Trinity Press International, 2000.
Higgins, A. J. B. "The Preface to Luke and the Kerygma in Acts." In *Apostolic History and the Gospel*, edited by W. Ward Gasque and Ralph P. Martin, 78–91. Grand Rapids, MI: Eerdmans, 1970.
Holladay, Carl R. "Acts and the Fragments of Hellenistic Jewish Historians." In *Jesus and the Heritage of Israel*, edited by David P. Moessner, 171–98. Vol. 1, *Luke the Interpreter of Israel*. Harrisburg, PA: Trinity Press International, 1999.
Holladay, Carl R. *A Critical Introduction to the New Testament: Interpreting the Message and Meaning of Jesus Christ*. 2 vols. Nashville, TN: Abingdon Press, 2005.
Holladay, Carl R. *Fragments from Hellenistic Jewish Authors*. 3 vols. Chico, CA/Atlanta, GA: Scholars Press, 1983.
Homeyer, Helene. *Lukian: Wie man Geschichte schreiben soll. Griechisch und Deutsch*. München: W. Fink, 1965.
Jeremias, Joachim. "*paradeisos*." *Theological Dictionary of the New Testament*, vol. 5. Edited by Gerhard Kittel, 715. Grand Rapids, MI: Eerdmans, 1967.
Jervell, Jacob. *Luke and the People of God*. Minneapolis, MN: Augsburg, 1972.
Jervell, Jacob. *The Unknown Paul*. Minneapolis, MN: Augsburg, 1984.
Johnson, Luke Timothy. *The Acts of the Apostles*. SP 5. Collegeville, MN: Liturgical Press, 1992.
Johnson, Luke Timothy. "A Cautious Cautionary Essay." In *SBL Seminar Papers 1979*, edited by Paul J. Achtemeier, 1:87–94. Missoula, MT: Scholars, 1979.
Johnson, Luke Timothy. *The Gospel of Luke*. SP 3. Collegeville, MN: Liturgical Press, 1991.
Johnson, Luke Timothy. *The Literary Function of Possessions in Luke-Acts*. SBLDS 39. Missoula, MT: Scholars, 1977.
Jossa, Giorgio. "Josephus' Action in Galilee during the Jewish War." In *Josephus and the History of the Greco-Roman Period*, edited by Fausto Parente and Joseph Sievers, 265–78. Leiden: Brill, 1994.
Juel, Donald. "Social Dimensions of Exegesis: The Use of Psalm 16 in Acts 2." *CBQ* 43 (1981): 543–86.
Just Jr., Arthur A. *Luke*. Ancient Christian Commentary on Scripture. Downers Grove, IL: InterVarsity Press, 2003.
Karris, Robert J. *Luke: Artist and Theologian: Luke's Passion Account as Literature*. New York: Paulist Press, 1985.
Karris, Robert J. "Windows and Mirrors: Literary Criticism and Luke's *Sitz im Leben*." In *Society of Biblical Literature 1979 Seminar Papers*, edited by Paul J. Achtemeier, 47–58. Missoula, MT: Scholars, 1979.
Käsemann, Ernst. *Essays on New Testament Themes*. SBT 41. London: SCM, 1964.
Kennedy, George A. "The Evolution of a Theory of Artistic Prose." In *The Cambridge History of Literary Criticism*, vol. 1, edited by George A. Kennedy, 184–99. Cambridge: Cambridge University Press, 1989.
Kittel, Gerhard, and Gerhard Friedrich, eds. *Theological Dictionary of the New Testament*. Translated by Geoffrey W. Bromiley. 10 vols. Grand Rapids, MI: Eerdmans, 1964–1976.
Klauck, Hans-Josef. *The Religious Context of Early Christianity: A Guide to Graeco-Roman Religions*. Minneapolis, MN: Fortress Press, 2003.

Kodell, Jerome. "Luke's Use of '*Laos*,' 'People,' Especially in the Jerusalem Narrative (Lk 19,28–24,53)." *CBQ* 31 (1969): 327–43.

Korn, Manfred. *Die Geschichte Jesu in veränderter Zeit: Studien zur bleibenden Bedeutung Jesu im lukanischen Doppelwerk*. WUNT 2/51. Tübingen: Mohr Siebeck, 1993.

Kreissig, Heinz. "A Marxist View of Josephus' Account of the Jewish War." In *Josephus, the Bible, and History*, edited by Louis H. Feldman and Gohei Hata, 265–77. Detroit, MI: Wayne State University Press, 1988.

Krodel, Gerhard. *Acts*. Minneapolis, MN: Augsburg, 1986.

Kümmel, Werner Georg. "Current Theological Accusations against Luke." *Andover Newton Quarterly* 16 (1975): 131–45.

Kuhn, Karl Allen. *The Kingdom according to Luke and Acts. A Social, Literary, and Theological Introduction*. Grand Rapids, MI: Baker Academic, 2015.

Kurz, William S. "Luke 3:23–38 and Greco-Roman and Biblical Genealogies." In *Luke-Acts: New Perspectives from the Society of Biblical Literature Seminar*, edited by Charles H. Talbert, 169–87. New York: Crossroad, 1984.

Kurz, William S. "Luke 22:14–38 and Greco-Roman and Biblical Farewell Addresses." *JBL* 104 (1985): 251–68.

Kurz, William S. "Promise and Fulfillment in Hellenistic Jewish Narratives and in Luke and Acts." In *Jesus and the Heritage of Israel*, edited by David P. Moessner, 147–70. Vol. 1, *Luke the Interpreter of Israel*. Harrisburg, PA: Trinity Press International, 1999.

Kürzinger, J. "Lk 1,3: ... ἀκριβῶς καθεξῆς σοι γράψαι." *BZ* 18 (1974): 249–55.

Lampe, G. W. H. "The Lucan Portrait of Christ." *NTS* 2 (1955–56): 160–75.

Lamsa, George M., trans. *Peshitta*. San Francisco, CA: Harper & Row, 1933.

Lausberg, Heinrich. *Handbook of Literary Rhetoric*. Edited by David E. Orton and Dean Anderson. Leiden: Brill, 1998.

Leaney, A. R. C. *The Gospel according to Luke*. 2nd ed. London: A. C. Black, 1966.

Leiman, Sid Z. "Josephus and the Canon of the Bible." In *Josephus, the Bible, and History*, edited by Louis H. Feldman and Gohei Hata, 50–58. Detroit, MI: Wayne State University Press, 1988.

Lentz, Tony M. *Orality and Literacy in Hellenic Greece*. Carbondale, IL: Southern Illinois University Press, 1989.

Liddell, Henry George, and Robert Scott, eds. *A Greek-English Lexicon*. Rev. Henry Stuart Jones, Roderick McKenzie, and Eric A. Barber. Oxford: Clarendon, 1925/1968.

Lightfoot, R. H. *Locality and Doctrine in the Gospels*. London: Hodder & Stoughton, 1938.

Lindner, Helgo. "Eine offene Frage zur Auslegung des Bellum-Proömiums." In *Josephus-Studien*, edited by Otto Betz, Klaus Haacker, and Martin Hengel, 254–59. Göttingen: Vandenhoeck & Ruprecht, 1974.

Litwak, Kenneth. *Echoes of Scripture in Luke-Acts: Telling the History of God's People Intertextually*. New York: T&T Clark, 2005.

Lohfink, Norbert. "Darstellungskunst und Theologie in Dtn 1,6–3,29." *Bib* 41 (1960): 105–34.

Lohmeyer, Ernst. *Das Markus-Evangelium*. Kritisch-exegetischer Kommentar über das Neue Testament. 10th ed. Göttingen: Vandenhoeck & Ruprecht, 1937.

Lohse, Eduard. "Missionarisches Handeln Jesu nach dem Evangelium des Lukas." *TZ* 10 (1954): 1–13.

Lord, Albert B. *Epic Singers and Oral Tradition*. Ithaca, NY: Cornell University Press, 1991.

Lord, Albert B. "Words Heard and Words Seen." In *Epic Singers and Oral Tradition*, 15–37. Ithaca, NY: Cornell University Press, 1991.

Lucian. "How to Write History." Translated by K. Kilburn. 8 vols. LCL. Cambridge, MA: Harvard University Press, 1913–1967.
Lucian. "True Story." *Lucian*. Translated by A. M. Harmon. LCL. Cambridge: Harvard University Press, 1913.
Lührmann, Dieter. *Die apokryph gewordenen Evangelien: Studien zu neuen Texten und zu neuen Fragen*. NovTSup 112. Leiden: Brill, 2004.
Mallen, Peter. *The Reading and Transformation of Isaiah in Luke-Acts*. LNTS 367. London: T&T Clark, 2008.
Mann, Thomas W. "Theological Reflections on the Denial of Moses." *JBL* 98 (1979): 481–94.
Marguerat, Daniel. *The First Christian Historian: Writing the 'Acts of the Apostles.'* Translated by Ken McKinney, Gregory J. Laughery, and Richard Bauckham. SNTSMS 121. Cambridge: Cambridge University Press, 2002.
Marguerat, Daniel. *Paul in Acts and Paul in His Letters*, WUNT 310. Tübingen: Mohr Siebeck, 2013.
Marguerat, Daniel. "Voyages et voyageurs dans le livre des Actes et dans la culture gréco-romaine." *RHPR* 78 (1998): 33–59.
Marincola, John. *Greek Historians*. New Surveys in the Classics 31. Oxford: Oxford University Press, 2001.
Marshall, I. Howard. *Acts*. Grand Rapids, MI: Eerdmans, 1980.
Marshall, I. Howard. *The Gospel of Luke*. NIGTC. Exeter: Paternoster, 1978.
Marshall, I. Howard. *Luke: Historian and Theologian*. Exeter: Paternoster, 1970.
Mason, Steve. "Josephus, *Jewish Antiquities*." In *The Eerdmans Dictionary of Early Judaism*, edited by John J. Collins and Daniel C. Harlow, 834–38. Grand Rapids, MI: Eerdmans, 2010.
Mattill, A. J., Jr. "The Jesus-Paul Parallels and the Purpose of Luke-Acts: H. H. Evans Reconsidered." *NovT* 17 (1975): 15–46.
Mattill, A. J., Jr. "The Purpose of Acts: Schneckenburger Reconsidered." In *Apostolic History and the Gospel: Biblical and Historical Essays Presented to F. F. Bruce on His 60th Birthday*, edited by W. Ward Gasque and Ralph P. Martin, 108–22. Exeter: Paternoster, 1970.
Mauser, Ulrich. *The Gospel of Peace: A Scriptural Message for Today's World*. Louisville, KY: Westminster John Knox, 1992.
McCown, C. C. "The Geography of Luke's Central Section." *JBL* 57 (1938): 51–66.
Minear, Paul S. "Jesus' Audiences according to Luke." *NovT* 16 (1974): 81–109.
Minear, Paul S. "A Note on Luke xxii 36." *NovT* 7 (1964–1965): 128–34.
Minear, Paul S. *To Heal and to Reveal: The Prophetic Vocation according to Luke*. New York: Seabury, 1976.
Mitchell, Margaret M. "Rhetorical Shorthand in Pauline Argumentation: The Functions of 'the Gospel' in the Corinthian Correspondence." In *Gospel in Paul: Studies on Corinthians, Galatians and Romans for Richard N. Longenecker*, edited by L. A. Jervis and P. Richardson, 63–88. JSNTSS 108. Sheffield: Sheffield Academic Press, 1994.
Mittmann, Siegfried. *Deuteronomium 1,1–6,3: Literarkritisch und traditionsgeschichtlich untersucht*. BZAW 139. New York: de Gruyter, 1975.
Miyoshi, Michi. *Der Anfang des Reiseberichts: Lk 9,51–10,24*. AnBib 60. Rome: Biblical Institute, 1974.
Moessner, David P. "And Once Again, What Sort of 'Essence?' A Response to Charles Talbert." *Semeia* 43 (1988): 75–84.
Moessner, David P. "The Appeal and Power of Poetics (Luke 1:1–4): Luke's Superior Credentials (παρηκολουθηκότι), Narrative Sequence (καθεξῆς), and Firmness of Understanding

(ἡ ἀσφάλεια) for the Reader." In *Jesus and the Heritage of Israel, Luke's Narrative Claim upon Israel's Legacy,* edited by David P. Moessner, 84–126. Vol. 1, *Luke the Interpreter of Israel.* Harrisburg, PA: Trinity Press International, 1999.

Moessner, David P. "'The Christ Must Suffer': New Light on the Jesus-Peter, Stephen, Paul Parallels in Luke-Acts." *NovT* 28 (1986): 220–56.
Reprinted. In *The Composition of Luke's Gospel: Selected Studies from Novum Testamentum,* edited by David E. Orton, 117–53. Leiden: Brill, 1999.

Moessner, David P. "'The Christ Must Suffer,' the Church Must Suffer: Rethinking the Theology of the Cross in Luke-Acts." In *Society of Biblical Literature 1990 Seminar Papers,* edited by David John Lull, 165–95. Atlanta, GA: Scholars Press, 1990.

Moessner, David P. "'Completed End(s)ings' of Historiographical Narrative: Diodorus Siculus and the 'End(ing)' of Acts." In *Die Apostelgeschichte und hellenistische Geschichtsschreibung: Festschrift für Eckhard Plümacher,* edited by Cilliers Breytenbach and Jens Schröter, 193–221. AGAJU 57. Leiden: Brill, 2004.

Moessner, David P. "Diegetic Breach or Metaleptic Interruption? Acts 1:4b–5 as the Collapse between the Worlds of 'All that Jesus Began to Enact and to Teach' (Acts 1:1) and the 'Acts of the Apostles.'" *Biblical Research* 56 (2011): 23–34.

Moessner, David P. "Dionysius' Narrative 'Arrangement,'" in *Paul, Luke and the Graeco-Roman World: Essays in Honour of Alexander J. M. Wedderburn,* edited by Alf Christopherson, Carsten Claussen, Jörg Frey, and Bruce Longenecker, 149–64. JSNTSup 217. London: Sheffield Academic Press, 2002.

Moessner, David P. "How Luke Writes." In *The Written Gospel,* edited by Markus Bockmuehl and Donald A. Hagner, 149–70. Cambridge: Cambridge University Press, 2005.

Moessner, David P. "The Ironic Fulfillment of Israel's Glory." In *Luke-Acts and the Jewish People,* edited by Joseph B. Tyson, 35–50. Minneapolis, MN: Augsburg, 1988.

Moessner, David P. "Jesus and the 'Wilderness Generation': The Death of the Prophet like Moses according to Luke." In *Society of Biblical Literature 1982 Seminar Papers,* edited by Kent H. Richards, 319–40. Chico, CA: Scholars, 1982.

Moessner, David P. "The 'Leaven of the Pharisees' and 'This Generation': Israel's Rejection of Jesus according to Luke." *JSNT* 34 (1988): 21–46.

Moessner, David P. "'Listening Posts' along the Way: 'Synchronisms' as Metaleptic Prompts to the 'Continuity of the Narrative' in Polybius' *Histories* and in Luke's Gospel–Acts: A Tribute to David Aune." In *The New Testament and Early Christian Literature in Greco-Roman Context: Studies in Honor of David E. Aune,* edited by John Fotopoulos, 129–50. NovTSup 122. Leiden: Brill, 2006.

Moessner, David P. *Lord of the Banquet: A Literary and Theological Investigation of the Lukan Travel Narrative.* Minneapolis, MN/Harrisburg, PA: Fortress/Trinity Press International, 1989/1998.

Moessner, David P. "The Lukan Prologues in the Light of Ancient Narrative Hermeneutics: ΠΑΡΗΚΟΛΟΥΘΗΚΌΤΙ and the Credentialed Author." In *The Unity of Luke-Acts,* edited by Joseph Verheyden, 399–417. BETL 133. Leuven: Peeters Press, 1999.

Moessner, David P. "Luke 9:1–50: Luke's Preview of the Journey of the Prophet like Moses of Deuteronomy." *JBL* 102 (1983): 575–605.

Moessner, David P. "Luke's 'Plan of God' from the Greek Psalter: The Rhetorical Thrust of 'The Prophets and the Psalms' in Peter's Speech at Pentecost." In *Scripture and Traditions: Essays on Early Judaism and Christianity in Honor of Carl R. Holladay,* edited by Patrick Gray and Gail O'Day, 223–38. NovTSup 129. Leiden: Brill, 2008.

Moessner, David P. "Luke's 'Witness of Witnesses': Paul as Definer and Defender of the Tradition of the Apostles–'from the Beginning.'" In *Paul and the Heritage of Israel: Paul's Claim upon Israel's Legacy in Luke and Acts in the Light of the Pauline Letters*, edited by David P. Moessner, Daniel Marguerat, Mikeal Parsons, and Michael Wolter, 117–47. Vol. 2, *Luke the Interpreter of Israel*. London: T&T Clark, 2012.

Moessner, David P. "'Managing' the Audience: Diodorus Siculus and Luke the Evangelist on Designing Authorial Intent." In *Luke and His Readers: Festschrift A. Denaux*, edited by Reimund Bieringer, Gilbert Van Belle, and Joseph Verheyden, 61–80. BETL 182. Leuven: Peeters/University of Leuven Press, 2005.

Moessner, David P. "The Meaning of καθεξῆς in the Lukan Prologue as a Key to the Distinctive Contribution of Luke's Narrative among the 'Many.'" In *The Four Gospels, 1992: Festschrift Frans Neirynck*, edited by Frans van Segbroeck, C. M. Tuckett, G. Van Belle, and J. Verheyden, 2:1513–28. Leuven: Peeters/University Press, 1992.

Moessner, David P. "Ministers of Divine Providence: Diodorus Siculus and Luke the Evangelist on the Rhetorical Significance of the Audience in Narrative 'Arrangement.'" In *Literary Encounters with the Reign of God: Studies in Honor of R. C. Tannehill*, edited by Sharon H. Ringe and H. C. Paul Kim, 304–23. New York: T&T Clark International, 2004.

Moessner, David P. "Paul and the Pattern of the Prophet like Moses in Acts." In *Society of Biblical Literature 1983 Seminar Papers*, edited by Kent H. Richards, 203–12. Chico, CA: Scholars, 1983.

Moessner, David P. "Paul in Acts: Preacher of Eschatological Repentance to Israel." *NTS* 34 (1988): 96–104.

Moessner, David P. Preface to the paperback edition of *Lord of the Banquet: A Literary and Theological Investigation of the Lukan Travel Narrative*, David P. Moessner. Harrisburg, PA: Trinity Press International, 1998.

Moessner, David P. "Quirinius." In *NIDB*, edited by K. D. Sakenfeld, 4:704–5. 5 vols. Nashville: Abingdon Press, 2001–2009.

Moessner, David P. "Re-reading Talbert's Luke: The *Bios* of 'Balance' or the 'Bias' of History?" In *Cadbury, Knox, and Talbert: American Contributions to the Study of Acts*, edited by Joseph B. Tyson and Mikeal Parsons, 203–28. Atlanta, GA: Scholars Press, 1991.

Moessner, David P. "The 'Script' of the Scriptures in Acts: Suffering as God's 'Plan' (βουλή) for the World for the 'Release of Sins.'" In *History, Literature and Society in the Book of Acts*, edited by Ben Witherington III, 218–50. Cambridge: Cambridge University Press, 1995.

Moessner, David P. "Suffering, Intercession, and Eschatological Atonement: An Uncommon View in the Testament of Moses and in Luke-Acts." In *The Pseudepigrapha and Early Biblical Interpretation*, edited by James H. Charlesworth and Craig A. Evans, 202–27. Sheffield: JSOT Press, 1993.

Moessner, David P. "The Triadic Synergy of Hellenistic Poetics in the Narrative Epistemology of Dionysisus of Halicarnassus and the Authorial Intent of the Evangelist Luke (Luke 1:1–4; Acts 1:1–8)." *Neotestamentica* 42 (2008): 289–303.

Moessner, David P. "'*Two* Lords 'at the Right Hand'? The Psalms and an Intertextual Reading of Peter's Pentecost Speech (Acts 2:14–36)." In *Literary Studies in Luke-Acts: Essays in Honor of Joseph B. Tyson*, edited by Richard P. Thompson and Thomas E. Phillips, 215–32. Macon, GA: Mercer University Press, 1998.

Moessner, David P., and David L. Tiede. "Two Books but One Story?" In *Jesus and the Heritage of Israel. Luke's Narrative Claim upon Israel's Legacy* edited by David P. Moessner, 1–4. Vol. 1, *Luke the Interpreter of Israel*. Harrisburg, PA: Trinity Press International, 1999.

Momigliano, Arnaldo. *The Development of Greek Biography*. Cambridge, MA: Harvard University Press, 1993.
Mondésert, Claude, Chantal Matray, and Henri-Irénée Marrou, eds. *Clément D'Alexandrie: Le Pédagogue*. Livre III Texte Grec. Paris: Cerf, 1970.
Moore, Stephen D. *Mark and Luke in Poststructuralist Perspectives*. New Haven, CT: Yale University Press, 1992.
Morgenthaler, Robert. *Die lukanische Geschichtsschreibung als Zeugnis*. ATANT 14. 2 vols. Zurich: Zwingli, 1949.
Moulton, James Hope, and George Milligan. *The Vocabulary of the Greek Testament*. Grand Rapids, MI: Eerdmans, 1930.
Moxnes, Halvor. "Patron-Client Relations and the New Community in Luke-Acts." In *The Social World of Luke-Acts: Models for Interpretation*, edited by Jerome H. Neyrey, 241–68. Peabody, MA: Hendrickson, 1991.
Muhlack, Gudrun. *Die Parallelen von Lukas-Evangelium und Apostelgeschichte*. Theologie und Wirklichkeit 8. Bern: Lang, 1979.
Navone, John. "The Way of the Lord." *Scr* 20 (1968): 24–30.
Neyrey, Jerome H. "The Symbolic Universe of Luke-Acts: They Turn the World Upside Down." In *The Social World of Luke-Acts: Models for Interpretation*, edited by Jerome H. Neyrey, 271–304. Peabody, MA: Hendrickson, 1991.
Nicholson, Ernest W. *Deuteronomy and Tradition*. Oxford: Blackwell, 1967.
Nickelsburg, George W. E. *Jewish Literature between the Bible and the Mishnah*. Philadelphia, PA: Fortress, 1981.
Nicklas, Tobias with Michael Tilly. *Die Apostelgeschichte als Kirchengeschichte: Text, Texttraditionen und antike Auslegungen*. BZNW 120. Berlin: de Gruyter, 2003.
Noth, Martin. *Überlieferungsgeschichte des Pentateuch*. Stuttgart: Kohlhammer, 1948.
Noth, Martin. *Überlieferungsgeschichtliche Studien* I. Schriften der Königsberger Gelehrten Gesellschaft, Geisteswissenschaftliche Klasse 18/2. Halle: Niemeyer, 1943.
Ogg, George. "The Central Section of the Gospel according to St Luke." *NTS* 18 (1971): 39–53.
Old, Hughes Oliphant. *The Patristic Age*. Vol. 2, *The Reading and Preaching of the Scriptures in the Worship of the Christian Church*. Grand Rapids, MI: Eerdmans, 1998.
O'Neill, J. C. *The Theology of Acts in its Historical Setting*. 2nd ed. London: SPCK, 1970.
Ong, Walter J. "Writing is a Technology that Restructures Thought." In *The Written Word: Literacy in Transition*, edited by Gerd Baumann, 23–50. Oxford: Clarendon: 1986.
Origen. *Homilies on Luke, Fragments on Luke*. Translated by Joseph T. Lienhard. FC 94. Washington, DC: Catholic University of America Press, 1996.
Osswald, Eva. *Das Bild des Mose in der kritischen alttestamentlichen Wissenschaft seit Julius Wellhausen*. Theologische Arbeiten 18. Berlin: Evangelische Verlagsanstalt, 1962.
Osten-Sacken, Peter von der. "Zur Christologie des lukanischen Reiseberichts." *EvT* 33 (1973): 476–96.
Pao, David W. *Acts and the Isaianic New Exodus*. WUNT 2/130. Tübingen: Mohr Siebeck, 2000.
Papyrus 168 (2nd century BCE) of the Società italiana per la ricerca dei papiri greci e latini in Egitto. Pubblicazioni 45/52, *Papiri greci e latini*. Vol. 3. Rome: Firenze F. Le Monnier, 1914.
Papyrus grecs et démotiques. Recueillis en Égypte et publiés (Pap.18.15 [2nd bce]). Edited by Théodore Reinach, MM. W. Spiegelberg, S. de Ricci. Paris: 1905; reprinted. Milan: Cisalpino-Goliardica, 1972.

Parker, Pierson. "Herod Antipas and the Death of Jesus." In *Jesus, the Gospels, and the Church: Essays in Honor of William R. Farmer*, edited by E. P. Sanders, 197–208. Macon, GA: Mercer University Press, 1987.
Parsons, Mikeal C. *Acts*. Paideia: Commentaries on the New Testament. Grand Rapids, MI: Baker, 2008.
Parsons, Mikeal C. *Luke. Storyteller, Interpreter, Evangelist*. Peabody, MA: Hendrickson, 2007.
Parsons, Mikeal C. "Reading Talbert: New Perspectives on Luke and Acts." In *Cadbury, Knox, and Talbert: American Contributions to the Study of Acts*, edited by Joseph B. Tyson and Mikeal Parsons, 133–71. Atlanta, GA: Scholars Press, 1991.
Parsons, Mikeal C., and Richard I. Pervo. *Rethinking the Unity of Luke and Acts*. Minneapolis, MN: Fortress/Augsburg, 1993.
Patillon, M. *Aelius Théon. Progymnasmata … avec l'assistance, pour l'Arménien de G. Bolognesi*. Paris: Les Belles Lettres, 1997.
Penner, Todd. "Reading Acts in the Second Century: Reflections on Method, History, and Desire." In *Engaging Early Christian History. Reading Acts in the Second Century*, edited by Rubén R. Dupertuis and Todd Penner, 1–15. Durham: Acumen, 2013.
Pervo, Richard I. *Acts. A Commentary*. Hermeneia. Minneapolis, MN: Fortress, 2009.
Pervo, Richard I. "Israel's Heritage and Claims upon the Genre(s) of Luke and Acts: The Problems of a History." In *Jesus and the Heritage of Israel*, edited by David P. Moessner, 127–43. Vol. 1, *Luke the Interpreter of Israel*. Harrisburg, PA: Trinity Press International, 1999.
Pervo, Richard I. *Rethinking the Unity of Luke and Acts*. Minneapolis, MN: Fortress Press, 1993.
Petersen, Norman R. *Literary Criticism for New Testament Critics*. Philadelphia, PA: Fortress, 1978.
Philostratus. *The Life of Apollonius of Tyana*. Translated by Christopher P. Jones. LCL. Cambridge, MA: Harvard University Press, 1960.
Plato. *Theaetetus*. Translated by Harold North Fowler. LCL. Cambridge, MA: Harvard University Press, 1921.
Plümacher, Eckhard. "Die Apostelgeschichte als historische Monographie." In *Les Actes des Apôtres: Traditions, redaction, théologie*, edited by Jacob Kremer, 457–66. BETL 48. Gembloux: Leuven University Press, 1979.
Plümacher, Eckhard. *Lukas als hellenistischer Schriftsteller*. SUNT 9. Göttingen: Vandenhoeck & Ruprecht, 1972.
Plümacher, Eckhard. "The Mission Speeches in Acts and Dionysius of Halicarnassus." In *Jesus and the Heritage of Israel*, edited by David P. Moessner, 251–66. Vol. 1, *Luke the Interpreter of Israel*. Harrisburg, PA: Trinity Press International, 1999.
Plutarch. *Alexander*. Volume 7, *Lives*. Translated by Bernadotte Perrin. 11 vols. LCL. London: Heinemann, 1914–1926.
Polybius. *The Histories*. Translated by W. R. Paton, 6 vols. LCL. Cambridge, MA: Harvard University Press, 1922–1927.
Press, Gerald A. *The Development of the Idea of History in Antiquity*. Kingston: McGill-Queen's University Press, 1982.
Pritchett, W. Kendrick. *Dionysius of Halicarnassus: On Thucydides*. Berkeley, CA: University of California Press, 1975.
Quintilian III. *The Institutes*. Translated by Harold Edgeworth Butler. LCL. Cambridge, MA: Harvard University Press, 1921.

Rackham, R. B. *The Acts of the Apostles*. Westminster Commentaries. 8th ed. London: Meuthen, 1919.
Rad, Gerhard von. *Deuteronomium-Studien*. FRLANT N. F. 40. 2nd ed. Göttingen: Vandenhoeck & Ruprecht, 1948.
Rad, Gerhard von. *Deuteronomy: A Commentary*. OTL. Philadelphia, PA: Westminster, 1966.
Rad, Gerhard von. *Old Testament Theology*. 2 vols. New York: Harper & Row, 1962–1965.
Rad, Gerhard von. "Theologische Geschichtsschreibung im Alten Testament." *TZ* 4 (1948): 161–74.
Radl, Walter. *Paulus und Jesus im lukanischen Doppelwerk. Untersuchungen zu Parallelmotiven im Lukasevangelium und in der Apostelgeschichte*. EHST 49. Bern: Theologischer Verlag, 1975.
Reicke, Bo. *The Gospel of Luke*. Richmond, VA: John Knox, 1964.
Reicke, Bo. "Instruction and Discussion in the Travel Narrative." *SE* I (= TU 73 [1959]): 206–16.
Reicke, Bo. *The Roots of the Synoptic Gospels*. Philadelphia, PA: Fortress Press, 1986.
Reicke, Bo. "Synoptic Prophecies on the Destruction of Jerusalem." In *Studies in New Testament and Early Christian Literature: Essays in Honour of A. P. Wikgren*, edited by David E. Aune, 121–34. Leiden: Brill, 1972.
Reid, Robert S. "Dionysius of Halicarnassus' Theory of Compositional Style and the Theory of Literate Consciousness." *Rhetoric Review* 15 (1996): 46–64.
Reid, Robert S. "'Neither Oratory nor Dialogue': Dionysius of Halicarnassus and the Genre of Plato's Apology." *Rhetoric Society Quarterly* 27 (1997): 63–90.
Reid, Robert S. "When Words Were a Power Loosed: Audience Expectation and Finished Narrative Technique in the Gospel of Mark." *Quarterly Journal of Speech* 80 (1994): 427–47.
Renan, Ernst. *Les Evangiles et la seconde generation chrétienne*. Paris: Calmann Lévy, 1877.
Rengstorf, Karl Heinrich. *Das Evangelium nach Lukas*. NTD 3. 5th ed. Göttingen: Vandenhoeck & Ruprecht, 1963.
Resseguie, James L. "Interpretation of Luke's Central Section (Luke 9:51–19:44) Since 1856." *Studia Biblica et Theologica* 5 (1975): 3–36.
Richard, Earl. *Acts 6:1–8:4: The Author's Method of Composition*. SBLDS 41. Missoula, MT: Scholars, 1978.
Ricoeur, Paul. *Time and Narrative*. Chicago, IL: University of Chicago Press, 1984.
Robbins, Vernon K. "Prefaces in Greco-Roman Biography and Luke-Acts." *Perspectives in Religious Studies* 6 (1979): 94–108.
Roberts, W. Rhys. *Dionysius of Halicarnassus: On Literary Composition*. London: Macmillan, 1910.
Robinson, William C., Jr. *Der Weg des Herrn: Studien zur Geschichte und Eschatologie im Lukas-Evangelium*. TF 36. Hamburg: Evangelischer Verlag, 1964.
Robinson, William C., Jr. "The Theological Context for Interpreting Luke's Travel Narrative (9:51ff.)." *JBL* 79 (1960): 20–31.
Roloff, Jürgen. "Die Paulus-Darstellung des Lukas." *EvT* 39 (1979): 510–31.
Rowe, C. Kavin. *World Upside Down: Reading Acts in the Graeco-Roman Age*. Oxford: Oxford University Press, 2009.
Russell, Donald A. *Criticism in Antiquity*. Berkeley, CA: University of California Press, 1981.
Sacks, Kenneth S. *Diodorus Siculus and the First Century*. Princeton, NJ: Princeton University Press, 1990.

Sacks, Kenneth S. *Polybius on the Writing of History*. Berkeley, CA: University of California Press, 1981.
Sacks, Kenneth S. "Rhetorical Approaches to Greek History Writing in the Hellenistic Period." In *SBL 1984 Seminar Papers*. Atlanta, GA: Scholars Press, 1984.
Sanders, James A. "From Isaiah 61 to Luke 4." In *Luke and Scripture: The Function of Sacred Tradition in Luke-Acts*, edited by Craig A. Evans and James A. Sanders, 46–69. Minneapolis, MN: Fortress, 1993.
Sandnes, Karl Olav. "*Imitatio Homeri*? An Appraisal of Dennis R. MacDonald's 'Mimesis Criticism.'" *JBL* 124 (2005): 715–32.
Scafuro, Adele C. "Universal History and the Genres of Greek Historiography." Ph.D. diss., Yale University, 1984.
Schlatter, Adolf. *Das Evangelium des Lukas: Aus seinen Quellen erklärt*. Stuttgart: Calwer, 1931.
Schmidt, Daryl. "Rhetorical Influences and Genre: Luke's Preface and the Rhetoric of Hellenistic Historiography." In *Jesus and the Heritage of Israel*, edited by David P. Moessner, 27–60. Vol. 1, *Luke the Interpreter of Israel*. Harrisburg, PA: Trinity Press International, 1999.
Schmidt, Karl Ludwig. *Der Rahmen der Geschichte Jesu: Literarkritische Untersuchungen zur ältesten Jesusüberlieferung*. Berlin: Trowitzsch & Sohn, 1919.
Schmidt, Karl Ludwig. "Die Stellung der Evangelien in der allgemeinen Literaturgeschichte." In *Eucharisterion: Studien rur Religion und Literatur des Alten und Neuen Testaments: Hermann Gunkel zum 60.*, edited by Hans Schmidt. Göttingen: Vandenhoeck & Ruprecht, 1923.
Schmidt, Karl Ludwig. "Jesus Christus". In *Religion in Geschichte und Gegenwart*, vol. 3, 2nd ed. Edited by Hermann Gunkel and Leopold Zscharnack, 110–151. Tübingen: Mohr Siebeck, 1929.
Schmitt, Armin. "Ps 16,8–11 als Zeugnis der Auferstehung in der Apg." *BZ* 17 (1973): 229–48.
Schneckenburger, Matthias. *Ueber den Zweck der Apostelgeschichte*. Bern: Fischer, 1841.
Schneider, Johannes. "Zur Analyse des lukanischen Reiseberichtes." In *Synoptische Studien: Alfred Wikenhauser zum siebzigsten Geburtstag [...] dargebracht*, edited by J. Schmid and A. Vögtle, 207–29. Munich: K. Zink, 1953.
Schniewind, Julius. *Das Evangelium nach Markus*. NTD 1. Göttingen: Vandenhoeck & Ruprecht, 1963.
Schniewind, Julius. *Das Evangelium nach Matthäus*. NTD 2. Göttingen: Vandenhoeck & Ruprecht, 1950.
Schubert, Paul. "The Structure and Significance of Luke 24." In *Neutestamentliche Studien für Rudolf Bultmann*, edited by Walther Eltester, 165–86. BZNW 21. Berlin: Töpelmann, 1954.
Schuetz, Frieder. *Der leidende Christus*. BWANT 89. Stuttgart: Kohlhammer, 1969.
Schweizer, Eduard. *The Good News according to Luke*. Atlanta, GA: John Knox, 1984.
Sloan, Robert B. "'Signs and Wonders': A Rhetorical Clue to the Pentecost Discourse." In *With Steadfast Purpose: Essays on Acts in Honor of Henry Jackson Flanders, Jr.*, edited by Naymond H. Keathley, 145–62. Waco, TX: Baylor University Press, 1990.
Smend, Rudolf. *Das Mosebild von Heinrich Ewald bis Martin Noth*. BGBE 3. Tübingen: Mohr Siebeck, 1959.
Smith, David E. *The Canonical Function of Acts: A Comparative Analysis*. Collegeville, MN: The Liturgical Press, 2002.
Squires, John T. *The Plan of God in Luke-Acts*. SNTSMS 76. Cambridge: Cambridge University Press, 1993.

Stagg, Frank. "The Journey Toward Jerusalem in Luke's Gospel." *RevExp* 64 (1967): 499–512.
Stählin, Gustav. *Die Apostelgeschichte*. NTD 5. 13th ed. Göttingen: Vandenhoeck & Ruprecht, 1970.
Stanton, Graham N. *Jesus of Nazareth in New Testament Preaching*. SNTSMS 27. Cambridge: Cambridge University Press, 1974.
Steck, Odil H. *Israel und das gewaltsame Geschick der Propheten*. WMANT 23. Neukirchen-Vluyn: Neukirchener, 1967.
Sterling, Gregory C. *Historiography and Self-Definition: Josephos, Luke-Acts and Apologetic Historiography*. NovTSup 64. Leiden: Brill, 1992.
Stern, Menahem. "Josephus and the Roman Empire as Reflected in *The Jewish War*." In *Josephus, Judaism, and Christianity*, edited by Louis H. Feldman and Gohei Hata, 71–80. Detroit, MI: Wayne State University Press, 1987.
Sternberg, Meir. *The Poetics of Biblical Narrative*. Bloomington, IN: Indiana University Press, 1985.
Stonehouse, Ned B. *The Witness of Luke to Christ*. London: Tyndale, 1951.
Strait, A. J. "Gods, Kings and Benefactors: Resisting the Ruling Power in Early Judaism and Paul's Polemic against Iconic Spectacle in Acts 17:16–32." Ph.D. diss., University of Pretoria, 2015.
Stylianou, P. J. *A Historical Commentary on Diodorus Siculus Book 15*. Oxford: Oxford University Press, 1998.
Talbert, Charles H. "The Contribution of the View of Martyrdom in Luke-Acts to an Understanding of the Lukan Social Ethic." In *Political Issues in Luke Acts*, edited by Richard J. Cassidy and Philip J. Scharper, 99–110. Maryknoll, NY: Orbis, 1983.
Talbert, Charles H. "The Gospel and the Gospels." *Interpretation* 33 (1979): 351–62.
Talbert, Charles H. *Literary Patterns, Theological Themes and the Genre of Luke-Acts*. SBLMS 20. Missoula, MT: Scholars, 1974.
Talbert, Charles H. "Once Again: Gospel Genre." *Semeia* 43 (1988): 53–74.
Talbert, Charles H. *Reading Luke: A Literary and Theological Commentary on the Third Gospel*. New York: Crossroad, 1982.
Talbert, Charles H. "Shifting Sands: The Recent Study of the Gospel of Luke." *Int* 30 (1976): 381–95.
Talbert, Charles H. "Succession in Luke-Acts and in the Lukan Milieu." In *Reading Luke-Acts in Its Mediterranean Milieu*. NovTSup 107. Leiden: Brill, 2003.
Talbert, Charles H. *What Is a Gospel? The Genre of the Canonical Gospels*. Philadelphia, PA: Fortress, 1977.
Talbert, Charles H., and J. H. Hayes. "A Theology of Sea Storms in Luke-Acts." In *Jesus and the Heritage of Israel*, edited by David P. Moessner, 267–83. Vol. 1, *Luke the Interpreter of Israel*. Harrisburg, PA: Trinity Press International, 1999.
Tannehill, Robert C. *The Acts of the Apostles*. Vol. 2, *The Narrative Unity of Luke-Acts: A Literary Interpretation*. Minneapolis, MN: Fortress, 1990.
Tannehill, Robert C. "Rejection by Jews and Turning to Gentiles: The Pattern of Paul's Mission in Acts." In *Luke-Acts and the Jewish People*, edited by Joseph B. Tyson, 83–101. Minneapolis, MN: Augsburg, 1988.
Tannehill, Robert C. *The Sword of His Mouth: Forceful and Imaginative Language in Synoptic Sayings*. SemeiaSup 1. Philadelphia, PA/Missoula, MT: Fortress/Scholars Press, 1975.
Taylor, Vincent. *Behind the Third Gospel*. Oxford: Clarendon, 1926.
Thackeray, Henry St. John. *Josephus: The Man and the Historian*. New York: Ktav, 1967.

Thiselton, Anthony. *The Two Horizons: New Testament Hermeneutics and Philosophical Description*. Grand Rapids, MI: Eerdmans, 1980.
Thomas, Carol G., and Edward Kent Webb. "From Orality to Rhetoric: An Intellectual Transformation." In *Persuasion: Greek Rhetoric in Action*, edited by Ian Worthington, 3–25. London: Routledge, 1994.
Tiede, David L. "Glory to Thy People Israel." In *Luke-Acts and the Jewish People*, edited by Joseph B. Tyson, 21–34. Minneapolis, MN: Augsburg, 1988.
Tiede, David L. *Luke*. Minneapolis, MN: Augsburg, 1988.
Tiede, David L. *Prophecy and History in Luke-Acts*. Philadelphia, PA: Fortress, 1980.
Tompkins, Jane P. "The Reader in History: The Changing Shape of Literary Response." In *Reader-Response Criticism: From Formalism to Post-Structuralism*, edited by Jane P. Tompkins, 201–32. Baltimore, MD: Johns Hopkins University Press, 1980.
Toohey, Peter. "Epic and Rhetoric." In *Persuasion: Greek Rhetoric in Action*, edited by Ian Worthington, 153–75. London: Routledge, 1994.
Toye, David L. "Dionysius of Halicarnassus on the First Greek Historians." *AJP* 116 (1995): 279–302.
Treier, Daniel J. "The Fulfillment of Joel 2:28–32: A Multiple-Lens Approach." *JETS* 40 (1997): 13–26.
Trimpi, Wesley. *Muses of One Mind: The Literary Analysis of Experience and Its Continuity*. Princeton, NJ: Princeton University Press, 1983.
Trompf, G. W. *The Idea of Historical Recurrence in Western Thought: From Antiquity to the Reformation*. Berkeley, CA: University of California Press, 1979.
Trompf, G. W. "La section médiane de l'évangile de Luc: l'organisation des documents." *RHPR* 53 (1973): 141–54.
Trompf, G. W. "Polybius and the Elementary Models of Historical Recurrence in the Classical Tradition." In *The Idea of Historical Recurrence in Western Thought: From Antiquity to the Reformation*, 60–115. Berkeley, CA: University of California Press, 1979.
Tuckett, Christopher M. *Luke: New Testament Guides*. Sheffield: Sheffield Academic Press, 1996.
Tuckett, Christopher M., ed. *Luke's Literary Achievement: Collected Essays*. JSNTSup 116. Sheffield: Sheffield Academic Press, 1995.
Tuckett, Christopher M. and Andrew F. Gregory. "Reflections on Method: What Constitutes the Use of the Writings that Later Formed the New Testament in the Apostolic Fathers?" In *The Reception of the New Testament in the Apostolic Fathers*, edited by Andrew F. Gregory and Christopher M. Tuckett, 61–82. Oxford: Oxford University Press, 2005.
Tyson, Joseph B. *Images of Judaism in Luke-Acts*. Columbia, SC: University of South Carolina Press, 1992.
Tyson, Joseph B. "The Problem of Jewish Rejection in Acts." In *Luke-Acts and the Jewish People*, edited by Joseph B. Tyson, 124–37. Minneapolis, MN: Augsburg, 1988.
Tyson, Joseph B., ed. *Luke-Acts and the Jewish People: Eight Critical Perspectives*. Minneapolis, MN: Augsburg, 1988.
Unnik, Willem C. van. "The Book of Acts: The Confirmation of the Gospel." *NovT* 4 (1960): 26–59.
Unnik, Willem C. van. "Luke's Second Book and the Rules of Hellenistic Historiography." In *Les Actes des Apôtres: Traditions, redaction, théologie*, edited by Jacob Kremer, 37–60. BETL 48. Gembloux: Leuven University Press, 1979.
Unnik, Willem C. van. "Once More St. Luke's Prologue." *Neotestamentica* 7 (1973): 7–26.
Unnik, Willem C. van. "The Purpose of Luke's Historical Writing." In *Sparsa Collecta*. NovTSup 29. Leiden: Brill, 1973.

Vaughn, Stephen. "History as Rhetoric: Style, Narrative, and Persuasion." *The Journal of American History* 82 (1996): 1595
Verheyden, Joseph, ed. *The Unity of Luke–Acts*. BETL 142. Leuven: University/Peeters Press, 1999.
Vermes, Geza. "Die Gestalt des Moses an der Wende der beiden Testamente." In *Moses in Schrift und Überlieferung*, edited by Henri Cazelles and Fridolin Stier, 78–86. Düsseldorf: Patmos, 1963.
Virgil. *The Eclogues*. Translated by Guy Lee. London: Penguin Books, 1984.
Votaw, Clyde Weber. *The Gospels and Contemporary Biographies in the Greco-Roman World*. FBBS 27. Philadelphia, PA: Fortress, 1970.
Walaskay, Paul W. *'And so we came to Rome': The Political Perspective of St. Luke*. SNTSMS 49. Cambridge: Cambridge University Press, 1983.
Walbank, Frank W. *A Historical Commentary on Polybius*. 3 vols. Oxford: Clarendon Press, 1957, 1967, 1974.
Walbank, Frank W. "History and Tragedy." *Historia* 9 (1960): 216–34.
Walbank, Frank W. "The Idea of Decline in Polybius." In *Polybius, Rome and the Hellenistic World: Essays and Reflections*, 193–211. Cambridge: Cambridge University Press, 2002.
Walbank, Frank W. "Polybius and the Past." In *Polybius, Rome and the Hellenistic World: Essays and Reflections*, 178–92. Cambridge: Cambridge University Press, 2002.
Wall, Robert W. and Eugene E. Lemcio. The New Testament as Canon. A Reader in Canonical Criticism. JSNTSup 76. Sheffield: Sheffield Academic, 1992.
Walton, Steve. *Leadership and Lifestyle : The Portrait of Paul in the Miletus Speech and 1 Thessalonians*. SNTSMS 108. Cambridge: Cambridge University Press, 2000.
Wehnert, Jürgen. *Die Wir-Passagen der Apostelgeschichte: Ein lukanisches Stilmittel aus jüdischer Tradition*. Göttingen: Vandenhoeck & Ruprecht, 1989.
Weiner, Aharon. *The Prophet Elijah in the Development of Judaism: A Depth-Psychological Study*. London: Routledge and Kegan Paul, 1978.
Weinfeld, Moshe. *Deuteronomy and the Deuteronomic School*. Oxford: Clarendon, 1972.
Wenham, J. W. "Synoptic Independence and the Origin of Luke's Travel Narrative." *NTS* 27 (1981): 507–15.
Wilckens, Ulrich. *Die Missionsreden der Apostelgeschichte*. WMANT 5. Neukirchen-Vluyn: Neukirchener Verlag, 1974.
Witherington, Ben, III. *The Acts of the Apostles: A Socio-Rhetorical Commentary*. Grand Rapids, MI: Eerdmans, 1998.
Wolter, Michael. *Das Lukasevangelium*. HNT 5. Tübingen: Mohr Siebeck, 2008.
Wolter, Michael. "Israel's Future and the Delay of the Parousia, according to Luke." In *Jesus and the Heritage of Israel. Luke's Narrative Claim upon Israel's Legacy*, edited by David P. Moessner, 307–24. Vol. 1, *Luke the Interpreter of Israel*. Harrisburg, PA: Trinity Press International, 1999.
Worthington, Ian. *A Historical Commentary on Dinarchus: Rhetoric and Conspiracy in Later Fourth-Century Athens*. Ann Arbor, MI: University of Michigan Press, 1992.
Wright, G. Ernest. "Exegesis of Deuteronomy." In *IB*, edited by George A. Buttrick, 2:339–40. 12 vols. New York: Abingdon, 1951–1957.
Zeller, Eduard. *The Contents and Origin of the Acts of the Apostles, Critically Investigated*. 2 vols. London: Williams & Norgate, 1875–76.
Ziesler, J. A. "Luke and the Pharisees." *NTS* 25 (1979): 146–57.
Zimmerli, Walther. *Ezekiel 1*. Hermeneia. Philadelphia, PA: Fortress, 1979.

Subject Terms for *Luke the Historian* . . .

Abraham 16, 18, 22, 23 n.51, 36, 46, 59, 146, 149, 229, 237n.114, 241, 246–50, 260, 262, 310, 321, 326 n.114, 334
Ambrose 13, 16 n.21, 22 n.44
Aristotle 5, 29, 43, 78, 86, 109, 125, 128–134, 138, 140, 141, 146, 154–56, 163, 165, 173–74, 332
    role of the *Poetics* 128–133, 156, 163, 173–74, 184, 332–33
'arrangement' of narrative (*diegesis*) 4, 7, 13, 20, 28, 55, 64, 67, 72, 104, 105, 121, 125–126, 129, 131–32, 134, 136–38, 141–42, 156–57, 160–64, 166, 170–84, 198–99, 203, 306–07, 332–33, 338 n.93
    'continuity of the narrative' 126, 134–36, 138, 141–42, 143, 147, 153, 168 n.27, 179–80,
    'division'/'partitioning' 179–80, 306–07, 334–35, 338
    'order/sequence' 129–136–37, 149, 153, 161–62,164, 166–71
    'elaboration'/'tropes of development' 125–26, 335–38
    'ring composition' 28–33
ἀρχή/*archē* 52n.42, 69, 81, 82 n.19, 83, 95, 100, 101, 103, 104, 106, 114, 118, 139, 141, 144 n.53, 147–49, 169, 173, 182–84, 308, 333–35
    the 'beginning' 16–21, 52 n.42, 68–69, 81–82, 84–85, 95, 100–01, 104–06, 114–17, 139–42, 143–49, 152, 173, 182–84, 308, 333–35
    relation to 'narrative plot' 16–21, 52 n.42, 139–42, 143–49, 166–71, 184–85, 334–35, 338
Baur, F.C. and "Tübingen school" 238 n.3, 239, 303,
'biblical theology' 306–14
    Luke as 'biblical' theologian 21–38, 318–32, 339
βίος/*bios* as genre 2, 12, 39–65
    biography 33, 34 n.107, 39–65, 108 n.2, 174

Bultmann, Rudolf 40, 212 n.27, 252 n.47, 264 n.73, 290, 303–5
    Bultmann 'school' 290, 303–04
Burridge, Richard 34 n.107, 64–65
    Gospels as '*bioi*' 64–65
canon 2, 4, 11, 14, 15, 21, 34 n.109, 38, 40–43, 52–53, 320–21
    proto-Christian Bible 7–8, 318–24
    Luke as first 'biblical' theologian 7–8, 22–33, 36–38, 58–63, 318–24, 330–32, 339
Cassius Dio 43n.15, 44n.17, 315
'character' and 'characterization' in narrative 129–30, 145–47, 318, 320–323, 325, 330, 332, 337
Chrysostom 1 n.2, 2, 4 n.9
Cicero 1, 47, 113, 125, 315 n.2, 342
Conzelmann, Hans 25 n.67, 143 n.50, 205 n.3, 206 n.7, 209 n.16, 218 n.55, 231 n.96, 239–40, 290, 304–05
    Luke-Acts as *Heilsgeschichte* 206 n.7, 207, 239–40, 290, 304–05
    the de-eschatologized period of the church 304, 305
Cornelius 30, 52, 69 n.4, 110–17, 119–22, 169–70, 184, 190–96, 308, 310, 334–36
    role in overall 'arrangement' of Luke and Acts 111–15, 117, 122–23, 166–71, 184, 334
covenant 18, 22, 26, 41 n.6, 59, 60, 146, 202, 213, 226 n.76, 228 n.89, 229–30, 235, 237 n.110, 241, 243, 293 n.8, 321
    "old" and "new" testaments 2, 17 n.25, 320–21
    "new covenant" as fulfilled Passover of Exodus 22, 26
cross, crucifixion 23, 26, 58–60, 63, 143, 144, 152, 202, 210, 226, 228, 230, 236n.108, 244 n.27, 251, 273, 276, 277, 286, 290, 295, 297
    Jesus as the 'resurrected-crucified' one 20, 168, 279, 287
        relation to:
        'plan of God' 61–63

'atonement' 56–64, 143–45
'redemption' 56–64, 143–45
Cullmann, Oscar 290, 291, 302–14
    relation to Bultmannian 'existential exegesis' 304–05
    relation to Conzelmann's threefold scheme 304–05
    relation of Luke to Paul 304–05, 306–13, 314
Daniel 16–17, 21, 319 n.15
David 17–20, 23 n.48, 30, 36, 46, 48, 59, 14–46, 167, 201, 202, 204, 248, 272–87
    reign, throne of David 17, 19, 273, 284, 285,
    "my Lord" 204, 274, 277, 278, 279, 280, 282, 283, 284,
    suffering servant 272–87, 322, 339
    pioneer/trailblazer of the 'Christ' 202, 285, 322,
Deuteronomy 25–26, 34, 48, 203, 205, 208, 210–11, 212, 213–18, 219, 221, 225–26, 227, 230–32, 235, 236–37, 271
    Deuteronomistic history 34, 203, 218, 233–35, 236–37, 242–44, 245–51, 253–62, 263–72
    Deuteronomistic view of history (4-fold scheme) 233–34, 243, 247, 249–71, 293–99
διάνοια/*dianoia* 64–65, 84, 129–31, 146 n.59, 309, 316, 332–33, 335
    thought/perspective of a character 128–33,
    authorial intent or overall perspective 130–31,
diegesis (narrative) 6, 64, 84, 128, 134, 155–56, 172–74, 181, 189–90, 192, 201, 329, 332
see also 'arrangement' of narrative/*diegesis*
the *Poetics* as defining 'state of the art' 125–26, 128–31, 174
Demetrius Phalereus 95–96
Diodorus Siculus 19 n.34, 20 n.36, 21 n.41, 34 n.108, 35, 36, 44 n.17, 52 n.41, 104 n.47, 126, 133, 138 n.39, 143 n.48, 151 n.61, 154–66, 174 n.6, 330
    'half-completed'/'completed narrative' 160–63

'history writing' as 'minister of providence' 20 n.36,120, 157
'continuity of the narrative' 160–62, 168 n.27
syn-chronistic narration 159–60
    secondary 'linking' prologues 19 n.34, 143 n.48, 160, 165
'universal' history 157–66
Dionysius of Halicarnassus 1, 34 n.108, 35, 44 n.17, 104, 105 n.52, 126, 128, 133, 136 n.33, 161–62 n.13, 168 n.27, 169 n.31, 172–85, 323, 330, 333
    as literary critic 161–62 n.13, 174–80, 182–84
    his tripartite 'arrangement' 174–80
    as historian 174–77
    critique of Thucydides 177–80
Dodd, C.H. 258 n.63, 295, 297 n.22, 326 n.45
Elijah 24, 25, 60, 61, 203, 219–21, 226–27, 252, 253, 255, 261, 319, 321
Emmaus 13, 62, 201, 285, 331
Eupolemus 96
Eusebius, of Caesarea 13, 51 n.37, 87–89, 98, 105 n.53, 321 n.21
E(e)xodus 19, 23–28, 30, 34, 49, 60, 202, 203, 212, 216–20, 225–30, 234–37, 246–62, 269–70, 284, 319
    exodus pattern in Bible/Luke and Acts 202–03, 236–37
    New Exodus 212, 219, 229, 230, 237n.113
eyewitness 18 n.33, 44, 55, 56, 67, 68–73, 82, 89, 94–96, 100–1, 106–109, 122, 142, 172, 187, 192, 198, 215, 317, 329, 334
    importance for historian 55–56, 93–97, 328–29
fulfillment 17, 18, 22, 30, 35, 37, 45–50, 52n.41, 54, 59–63, 72, 104, 108, 110, 113, 116–17, 121–22, 137, 145, 147, 149, 166–67, 181, 185, 198–99, 209, 216, 230, 237, 240–42, 244, 246, 248–50, 261, 264, 269–70, 276, 277–78, 293, 296–98, 301, 318, 324, 334, 339
genre 5, 11–65, 131, 133–34, 155–66, 172, 176, 316

Gentiles/nations 17–18, 30–31, 51, 113, 115–17, 152, 169, 171, 196, 241, 245, 259, 261, 267–70, 273, 289–90, 292, 298, 300–1, 335, 337
Gennette, Gérard 187, 189–91, 199
good news 24, 57, 60, 115, 147–48, 150–51, 170, 194, 201, 204, 240, 241, 326, 328, 335
Hannah 16, 17, 22, 145, 147, 321, 323
Haenchen, Ernst 16, 17, 22, 145, 147, 321, 323
Heilsgeschichte 207, 213 n.31, 215, 237 n.112, 290–91, 302–14
    salvation history 57 n.61, 61, 206 n.7, 242–71, 290–91, 296–301, 302–14
Hellenistic historian, Luke as 3–8, 35–38, 47–56, 143–53, 166–71, 180–82, 184–91, 315–38
historia/historein 157, 315 n.2, 316
    historiography 12, 29 n.81, 39–65, 135, 156, 157, 174, 176, 274
    'history' as concept 315–16
    history as 'narrative' 47–56, 84–85, 157–66
    patterns of recurrence:
    from the Jewish scriptures 317–24
    synchronisms and world events 324–28
    author/narrator and "we" 54, 56, 101n.39, 106–7, 328–29
    providence/fate/divine necessity 330–32
    'universal history' 84–85, 134–35, 140, 139–40 n.46, 333
Isaiah 22, 26, 37 n.121, 54, 59, 62, 121, 147–49, 152 n.62, 185, 241 n.19, 261 n.66, 268 n.80, 289, 290, 295, 300, 321, 322, 326
    servant as Israel, smaller group, individual 62, 148–49, 290, 300–01
    as framework of the plotting of Luke and Acts 148–49, 184–85, 268n.80, 290, 300–01
Israel 3, 7–8, 11–14, 16–38, 41–42, 45–52, 54, 58–64, 94, 96, 103, 113, 115, 116, 118–21, 136, 137, 143–153, 155, 166–69, 172, 180–81, 185–87, 191–92, 195–98, 202–4, 213–16, 218, 220–21, 224, 229, 233–34, 236, 241–78, 284–87, 289–301, 302, 306–27, 331, 334–39
Jacob 17, 23, 33, 50, 51, 246, 248, 292,
Jerusalem 16–18, 21–25, 28, 30–32, 49, 50, 60, 61, 94, 113–21, 145, 147, 150–51, 167–70, 186, 188, 190, 194, 195, 198, 203–211, 226–37, 260–70, 276, 290, 293–301, 303, 309–312, 319, 320, 326, 337
Jervell, Jacob 292
Josephus 35–36, 93–106, 136, 138, 175, 247, 326–28, 330
journeys 19, 22–33, 49, 50, 60–62, 110–13, 116, 135, 198, 203, 205–30, 235–37, 245–70, 290, 293–300, 315, 319–20, 337
    journey framework of Luke and Acts 22–33, 245–51, 264–69, 270–71
    great journey/travel narrative 205–37, 24, 255–58, 264–69, 293–99
judgment 17, 24, 25, 27, 31, 32, 46–47, 50, 60, 87, 103, 109, 131, 147, 149, 170, 214, 233–35, 243–44, 247–48, 256, 258, 261, 267, 281, 289, 290, 292–301, 322, 326
καθεξῆς/*kathexēs* 44, 56, 67, 70 n.10, 84 n.22, 104, 108–23, 137, 166, 169 n.30, 173, 180, 184, 199, 210 n.21, 333–35
    narrato-logical sense' 109–14
King, David see David
Kingdom of God 7 n.14, 13, 20, 21, 23, 26, 29, 30 n.94, 32, 45 n.20, 50, 52–53, 57–58, 61, 152, 168, 181, 185–88, 191–92, 194, 196–99, 221–22, 232, 240, 247, 257, 259, 265, 289, 297, 320, 325, 336, 338
    'suffering' as necessary to enter 31–32, 59–63, 121, 220–28, 249–54, 264–69
law 7n.15, 22, 27, 49, 62, 103, 116, 145–147, 150, 152, 211nn.23 and 24, 213, 218, 233, 235, 236, 242, 243, 248, 250, 251, 255, 259, 261, 268, 269, 289, 318
    Law of Moses 7 n.15, 22, 27, 116, 145, 147, 152, 289, 318
    law and the preaching of the prophets – see Deuteronomistic view of history
Lucian 34 n.108, 35 n.112, 44–45, 52 n.41, 53, 55, 96, 128, 174, 316 n.6, 330 n.65, *How to Write History* 34 n.108, 44 n.17, 45 n.19, 128, 174

'omniscient' point of view 53–56, 146
Mariam 16–18, 30 n.87, 146,
Messiah 7, 12, 17–19, 29–32, 34–37, 41, 46 n.23, 48, 53, 61–63, 69, 114–17, 119–21, 127, 136, 143–44, 147, 150–52, 168, 171, 185, 187, 191, 194, 197–98, 202, 207, 223, 227, 242, 244, 260–61, 265, 272, 274–75, 277, 285–86, 299, 320, 322, 322–23 n.31, 326–27, 332, 338, 339
 Christ 61, 68–69 n.4, 91, 114, 127, 132, 137, 144, 146–52, 166–70, 180, 186–87, 191–94, 198–99, 201–4, 238, 240–41 n.15, 26061, 265–71, 272–76, 284–87, 289–91, 315, 318–19, 322–23 n.31, 324, 326, 327, 328 n.54, 330–31, 334–39
metalepsis 172, 187–91, 199, 336–38
 metaleptic shift 187–91, 197–99
 Gospel of Luke as collapsed into Acts 185–99,
mimesis 122 n.11, 125, 129, 134, 156–57, 173 n.4, 174, 321
Minear, Paul S. 241, 245n.30
Moses 145, 147, 151–52, 167, 197, 201–37, 245–71
 in Deuteronomy 213–18
 prophet like Moses 110, 203, 205–37, 245–71, 294 n.10,
 "(law of) Moses and the prophets and the psalms" 116, 167, 318
narrative as genre—see 'arrangement' of narrative/*diegesis*
 relation to the "many" attempts to write 44, 108–09, 125, 136–37, 155, 172–73, 180–82
narrative hermeneutics 3–8, 25n.67, 64–65, 67, 84–85, 333
narrative rhetorical criticism 5–6, 7–8, 84–85, 174–198, 202
nations, end of the earth 14 n.10, 18, 20–21, 30–32, 43, 46, 48–49, 51, 59, 62–63, 67, 114, 116–17, 136, 138, 140, 143–44, 147–53, 155, 158, 160 , 167–70, 181, 185, 188, 195–98, 201–3, 207, 243 n.25, 245, 248, 250, 263, 269–70, 274–79, 281, 284, 286 n.17, 289, 290, 296–98, 301 n.29, 320–21, 324–25, 327–28, 335–37

οἰκονομία/*oikonomia*, see 'arrangement' of narrative/*diegesis*
Origen 13
Papias 13, 87–89, 98, 105
παρακολουθέω/*parakoloutheō* 13 n.7, 55, 67, 68–107, 122, 140–145, 159, 169 n.30, 172 n.2, 178, 180, 183, 328–29, 333
Passover 22, 26, 28, 31, 50, 145–46, 259, 264, 319
 Jesus redefines the Passover lamb 22, 26, 31, 145–47, 319
Paul 3, 11, 13 n.8, 15 n.17, 30–32, 34 n.111, 37, 50–51, 53, 57 n.61, 69 n.4, 91, 98, 100–105, 110–11, 118–23, 137 n.35, 150–52, 167, 170, 172 n.1, 189, 193–203, 236 n.108, 238–44, 251, 262–71, 289–91, 292–301, 302–314, 320, 322, 324, 327 n.53, 329, 330 n.64, 335–38, 339
 quintessential representative of a hardened Israel 251, 263
 non-apostle, non-witness of Jesus' public actions and speech 199, 338
 becomes chief witness of Acts 197–98, 336–38
 aligned most closely with Jesus 195–99, 264–69, 299–301, 336–38
 voice of Jesus in Acts heard only directly to and through Paul 199, 336–337
 'Calling' of Paul in Acts 30–33, 195–97, 241n.19, 263–64, 290, 300–01
  two *relectures* of calling 195–96
 as corporate servant fulfilling Acts 1:8 290, 337
Pentecost 1 n.2, 20, 30–31, 52, 114–115, 143 n.48, 151, 169 n.29, 170, 184, 197, 201, 203, 230, 266, 272, 275–76, 278, 281–82, 285–86, 301, 320
people (of God) 31, 50, 51, 119, 219, 226, 228, 237, 259, 278, 289, 292, 301, 313
Peter 20, 30, 32 n.102, 34 n.111, 58 n.66, 63 n.78, 69 n.4, 88–89, 98, 100, 105, 110–117, 119, 121, 122, 137, 143 n.48, 166–71, 180, 184, 190, 193–94, 196–97, 203, 219–20, 222, 228 n.82, 238–91, 293 n.6, 321 n.23, 334–36
Philo, of Alexandria 90

Philo, the elder 96
"plan of God" 4, 7, 32, 35, 37, 148, 152, 274–87, 308–09, 330–32, 339
  will of God 7, 152–53, 289, 330–32, 339
  divine plan 37, 152–53, 289, 330–32, 339
Plato 74, 75, 130 n.13, 132, 156, 175–76, 190, 344, 352, 353
plot (see also the 'continuity of the narrative') 7, 8, 12, 19–21, 25, 28, 31, 34, 36, 42, 46, 49–50, 57, 59, 62, 64, 85, 97, 109, 113, 117, 126, 129–33, 135, 138 n.39, 143–44, 146, 148–49, 151, 159–61, 163, 165, 168–69, 174, 177, 179–84, 187–88, 191–92, 194, 198–99, 202–3, 209–10, 217, 222, 227, 231, 235, 237, 241–42, 245–46, 259, 266, 272 n.1, 276, 278–79, 283, 285–86, 290–91, 294 n.10, 296, 301, 318, 321–24, 334, 336–39
Plutarch 42, 43–44, 45, 47, 109 n.5
Polybius 34 n.108, 35, 37, 44 n.17, 50, 82, 84–85, 125–26, 127- 53, 173, 174 n.7, 318, 323, 325, 327, 330, 332,
  'continuity of the narrative history' 134–36, 138, 141–42, 143, 147, 153
  'universal' history 84–85, 134–35, 140, 139–40 n.46,
  "the beginning" of the plotted narrative 139–42, 149,
  symplokē/overlapping theatres/periods of inter-national events 137–139
prologue 4, 15, 28, 67, 69, 70, 82, 84–85, 97, 109, 117, 118, 141, 178, 186, (189), 198–99, 211, 317, 329, 333–34
prooemium, prooimion 16, 38, 71, 160, 168, 181, 182, 183, 317, 333, 336
  secondary prologue 19 n.34, 143 n.48, 160, 165,166–68, 185–88, 317, 333–34
prophecy 16, 22, 110 n.7, 143 n.48, 145, 181, 236, 241, 256–57, 261–62, 272
  prophet 16–18, 24–26, 29, 34, 48–50, 54, 59, 110, 148–49, 203–4, 205, 211, 212, 218–220, 222, 224, 229–37, 239, 241–62, 267–271, 289, 294–95, 319 n.15,
  the prophets 32, 37, 46 n.23, 47, 52 n.42, 59–63, 110, 116, 119, 127, 137 n.37, 151, 153, 167, 221 169, 181 n.25, 196–97, 201–4, 233, 236, 241–62, 266–271, 272–87, 289–90, 293–95, 298–301, 308–9, 312, 318, 320–25, 326 n.46, 331, 339
  prophetic view of history – see Deuteronomy, Deuteronomistic history
  prophet like Moses – see Moses
Psalms 18, 27, 63 n.7, 116, 167, 203, 204, 272–87, 318, 322, 331
  David and the suffering righteous 272–87 – see also David, suffering servant
  "opened" by the resurrected Christ 7 n.24, 18, 20, 62–63, 167, 171, 202, 275, 278, 286
Quintilian 125, 188
  Greek 'metalepsis' 187–91
reception – see 'arrangement' of narrative, esp. 'elaboration'/'tropes of development'
  reception of Luke and Acts 1–6
Redaktionsgeschichte 239
  redaction (criticism) 4, 25 n.67, 41 n.6, 58, 132, 207, 213 nn.28 and 31, 240, 293 n.7
redemption 16–17, 22, 25, 145–47, 149, 152, 202, 216, 227, 229 n.94, 231, 235, 244, 249, 250, 257, 318, 319, 321, 326 n.46
reign of God 12, 46, 48–49, 61, 195, 197, 290, 328
  – see also Kingdom of God
Renan, Ernst 1, 13
repentance 56, 60–61, 63, 115–16, 119, 148, 234, 238, 241, 243, 244, 260–62, 267–69, 276, 287, 290, 292–301, 322
resurrection 2, 6, 14, 19, 21 n.42, 41 n.6, 57–59, 61–63, 98, 110, 115, 120, 151, 185, 187, 193, 197, 201, 204, 229 n.94, 244, 260, 268, 272–74, 276, 279, 287, 325
revelation 17, 46, 56, 58, 61, 69, 113, 195, 204, 217, 220–21, 225, 228, 230–32, 246, 257, 263, 319, 321
rhetoric 1–7, 28 n.78, 29, 50, 64–65, 67, 71, 85, 88 n.28, 98, 100, 125–26, 128, 131, 133–135, 138, 153, 155–56, 160–65,

172–177, 187–89, 198, 202–203, 272–77, 286, 315–20, 329, 332–33
salvation 4 n.10, 14 n.10, 18, 29, 34, 41–42, 46, 48–50, 57, 60–63, 112–13, 115, 136, 147, 155, 166, 170, 185, 195–99, 204, 207, 212, 216, 218, 226, 229, 240, 242–45, 250, 260, 264, 269–70, 273–78, 289–91, 293, 297, 299–300, 302, 320–22, 324, 326 n.46, 331, 334, 336–37, 339
salvation history see *Heilsgeschichte*
scripture 2, 7, 11, 17–18, 20–21, 30–32, 34–37, 39, 47, 49, 51–53, 61–63, 95–98, 103, 116, 120–21, 148, 149, 151–53, 166–71, 181, 185, 198, 202, 241, 272–76, 279, 286, 297–98, 318, 320–24, 330–34, 339
   the Jewish scriptures 36–37, 98, 318–24
   Israel's scriptures 17, 34, 318, 323–24, 331–32
   Christian "old" and "new" testaments 2, 17n.25, 320–321
Septuagint/LXX 1, 16, 54, 55, 143n.49, 153, 272, 279, 320–21, 324,
Intertextuality of the scriptures 7–8, 33, 34, 36–37, 318–24
sequence/order, see 'arrangement' of narrative (*diegesis*)
servant 16, 22, 24, 26, 32, 37, 48, 59, 62, 69, 91, 146–52, 185, 193, 195–96, 201–4, 261, 276, 278, 285, 290, 318, 322, 325, 334, 335, 337, 339
   pattern of servant/suffering righteous 202–04, 233–37, 241n.19, 322
   Jesus as: 26, 49n.31, 62, 146–47, 149, 290, 322, 324
   the servant of Isaiah in Isa 40—55 62, 146–47, 149, 152n.62, 241n.19, 290, 318
Simeon 17, 22, 59, 145–47
speeches (*logoi*) 51n.39, 163–66, 167–70, 240n.15
Spirit 15 n.16, 19–20, 22–23, 29–31, 38, 47, 49 n.31, 52 n.42, 57–58, 112–17, 121–22, 143–44, 146, 149–50, 153, 168–70, 184, 186, 191–92, 196, 201–4, 242, 248, 250, 260, 264, 267, 272, 274, 276–79, 286, 289, 318, 320, 334–35
Steck, Odil H. 233, 243, 247–48, 255 n.56, 293 n.8, 294 n.11, 298 n.25
Stephen 30, 32 n.102, 34 n.111, 63 n.78, 194, 203, 210, 237–271, 285, 289, 293 n.6, 300, 321, 326 n.46, 337, 338
suffering righteous 23, 201–4, 264, 272 n.1, 279, 285, 289, 322, 332
   – see also David, suffering servant
Synchronisms 16, 37, 48, 51, 57, 126, 127, 135–43, 147, 152–53, 181, 326, 336
Talbert, Charles H. 12, 39–65
τέλος/*telos* (goal) 11, 19, 26, 35, 65, 127, 131, 134–35, 138, 141–43, 151, 159, 167, 182–84, 283, 296, 319 n.13, 331, 333, 335
Temple/Jerusalem Temple 16, 19, 22, 27–31, 49–50, 54, 59, 145–47, 188, 192, 194–95, 203, 205, 236, 248–49, 251, 253–56, 258, 260, 262–63, 265–70, 295–99, 318–19, 326
tradent, Luke as 72–73, 99–107, 198, 314, 317, 329
transfiguration 218–31, 252–54, 261, 263, 266 n.77, 270
travel narrative – see journeys
"way" of the Lord 113, 118–22, 148, 206–7, 339
Weyden, Rogier van der 1
"we" passages 54, 56, 101n.39, 106–7, 328–29
'will of God' see "plan of God"
witnesses 7, 18, 21, 27, 29, 30, 33, 45 n.20, 52, 55, 58 n.66, 69, 94, 106, 114, 116–18, 147, 152 n.62, 153, 167–70, 181, 184–85, 191–92, 194–95, 198, 201–2, 219, 225, 240, 255, 260, 262, 275–76, 289, 322, 335–36
Za(e)chariah 16–17, 22, 59, 144–48, 319
Zecharia ben-Jehoida 255, 293, 300, 325
Zeller, Eduard 239

Scripture (other than Luke and Acts)

Genesis
4:10 293
16:7–16; 17:1–22; 18:1–15   16
22:1–2 149
50:24–25 257

Exodus
3 36
3:16 257
4:31 145
6:6 145
6:14–27 36
7–12 36
13:1–6, 12–15 145
15:13 145
20:11 324
24:10, 17 219
29:38–42 319
40:35 219

Leviticus
12:2–4 145
19:20; 25:25; 27:31, 33   146
23:29 261

Numbers 18:15–19 146, 212

Deuteronomy 213–18, 220, 224, 227–31, 235, 247, 260
5:23–24 219, 225
9:24 226
10:11 226
18:15–19 219, 247, 252, 255, 261
27:15–26 293
31:14–29 298
32:1–43 298
34:10–12 34

Joshua 2:18; 4:6 322

Judges 13:2–25 16

Ruth 1:6 145

1 Samuel / 1 Kingdoms
1:24–2:10, 20 145
2:1–10 16, 17
2:26 48

2 Samuel / 2 Kingdoms 4:11 255

1 Kings / 3 Kingdoms
18:1–39 253
19:4–21 252, 255

2 Kings / 4 Kingdoms
2:9, 10, 11 61
9:7 255
17:18, 20 247
18:14 248
19:15 324

2 Chronicles 247, 255, 293

Ezra 247

Nehemiah 247–49, 261

Psalms 247
2:1–2 143
9:12 255
15[16] 20, 204
15:8 166
15:8–11 272–87
48:7, 8, 9 146
79:14 145
90[91] 23, 219
105:4 145
109[110] 20, 166–67, 204, 272–87
118:22 298
129:8 146
145[146]:6 324

Proverbs 18:11 219

Isaiah
3:12, 25–26 294, 295, 326
5 293

5:26 301
6:9–10 289, 292
7:11, 14 322
8:14–15 298
29:1–4, 6, 12 257, 293, 295, 326
37:16, 33 295, 324, 326
40–55 146–47, 152, 290
40:5 147
42:1, 6 147, 149, 253
45:22 151–52
46:13 147
48:20 301
49:6, 9 147, 152
52:10 147
52:15–53:2 152
53:1–12 62, 149, 318
63:4 146
66:1 248

Jeremiah 247–48
6:6–22 257, 301
7:8–15 295–96
12:7–13; 14:6a 256, 295
16:11–13 294
22:13–14 293
27:29 295

Ezekiel
4:2 295, 326
21:22 295, 326
31:12 326
33:6, 8 255, 294
34:2, 4–5 293, 300

Daniel 247
7:9–18 319
8:1–27 17
8:15–26; 9:20–27 16
9:3–19 256, 295, 319
9:20–27 21, 319

Joel
2:31–32 166
3 20
3:1–5 272–87

Amos
3:2 294
4:1–2 294
5:1,2, 18–20 293, 295
8:4–8 294

Micah
2:1–4 293
3:9–12 294

Habakkuk 2:11 257

Zechariah 247–49

Malachi 4:5–6 253

Matthew
17:17 223
22:7; 23:29–31 247
24:15 295
26:28 59
28:16–20 19

Mark
9:19 223
10:45 59
12:9 247
16:1–8 19

John 21:20–25 19

Romans 9–11; 15 290, 302–14

Galatians 3:2 335

1 Thessalonians 2:16 247

1 Timothy
1:1–2, 3, 18 91
4:6 91, 98, 102
6:12b, 20 91

2 Timothy
1:3–7, 13–14 103
3:10–11 90–91, 98, 102, 103
4:6–8 103

Deutero-Canonical, Pseudepigrapha, Rabbinic, and Qumran Texts

2 Maccabees
8:11 90
9:27 90

3 Maccabees 4:21; 5:30 35, 330

4 Maccabees 9:24 35, 330

Wisdom 6:7; 14:3 35, 330

Sirach 48:7–8 252

Tobit 247

Baruch 247–48, 255, 295

Prayer of Azariah 247

Testament of Levi 247, 255, 295

Testament of Judah 247

Testament of Issachar 247

Testament of Zebulun 247

Testament of Dan 247

Testament of Naphtali 247

Testament of Asher 247

1 Enoch 247, 252, 255, 293, 295

Jubilees 247–50

Psalms of Solomon 247, 301

Ascension of Moses 247

Biblical Antiquities 247

4 Ezra 247

2 Baruch 247, 255

Pesiq. Rab. 138a; 146a 247, 255, 295

4QDibHam 247

1QS 247–48

CD 247

Christian Writings

Ambrose
Exposition on the Gospel of Luke 1.4.7 13

Barnabas 2:4b, 13, 29; 3:8 247

Chrysostom
Homiliae in Principium Actorum [iii, p. 54] 2

Clement of Alexandria
Paedagogus 3.11.73 (Philemon 124) 76

Eusebius
Ecclesiastical History (Hist. eccle.)
III.39.4 87, 98
III.39.14–16 13
III.39.15 87, 98, 105

Irenaeus
Against Heresies III.1, 12, 18   3

Justin
Dialogues 16:4   247

Melito of Sardis
Extracts in Eusebius, *Hist. eccle.*
   IV.26.12–14   321

Other Ancient Sources

Aratus
Phaenomena   325

Archimedes
Arenarius   84

Aristophanes
Ecclesiazusae [The Women's Collectives]
   719–27   74

Aristotle
The History of Animals 496a29   78
Topica 125b.28–34   86
Poetics   125, 146, 156, 173,   184
   9.3   174
   6.15–40   129, 156
   14.1–13   130
   23.22–23   134
   25.23–24   131

Arrian
Anabasis V.1.2   35, 330

Artemidorus
Oneirocritica   84

Cicero
On Invention 2.40.117   113, 125
On Oratory   125

Cornelius Nepos
Pelopidas 16.1.1   52

Demetrius
On Style   324

Demosthenes
Against Meidias Oration 21 (14.69)   75
Against Phaenippus 42.21   89
Against Aristocrates 187.2   82, 106
Concerning the Crown Oration 18 (162, 172)   77, 81–82, 92, 101,   106
Against Olympiodorus 40.1–7   82, 106
On the Dishonest Embassy Oration 19 (257)   92
Orations: De falsa legatione 257.9   82
Polyclem 13.3   82

Dio Cassius
Roman History
   1.2   44
   45–56   41, 43

Diodorus Siculus   173
Library of History   165, 168
   I.1.3   35, 330
   I.2.1–3   36, 157
   I.3   157–60
   I.4   44
   I.6.1   160
   III.15.7, 19.2   35
   IV.1.1   36
   V.1,1–4   34, 161–62
   X.21.3   35
   XIII.21.4–5   35
   XV.63.2   35
   XVI.1.1–3   34, 52, 162–63
   XVIII.21–59   35, 330
   XX.1.1–2   164
   XXVI.1.1   166
   XXVI.15.3   35, 330
   XXXIV/XXXV.27.1   35, 330

Dionysius of Halicarnassus 173, 175
Letter to Gnaeus Pompeius 175–76, 179, 183
Literary Treatises 128, 175
On Demosthenes 175–76
On Thucydides
    9   104–105, 177–78, 333
    10   182–83
    10–11   34
    12   183
Roman Antiquities
    I.4.2, 5.2   35, 330
    III.5.2, 19.6   35, 330
    V.8.6   35
    VIII.32.3   35, 330
    IX.8.1   35
    X.45.4   35
    XI.1, 12.3   35, 330

Homer
Odyssey 189

Horace
Art of Poetry 125

Josephus
Antiquities
    I.4–5   97, 330
    I.14, 46   35, 330
    I.213–18   95
    II.174, 209, 332   35, 330
    IV.47, 114, 128, 185   35, 330
    V.277   35, 330
    IX.13–14   247
    X.177   35, 330
    XI.327   35, 330
    XVI.397–98   35
    XVIII.26, 29   327
Against Apion
    I.53–54, 213, 218   93, 101, 103, 106
    I.44–56   93–94
War
    I.49–50   96
    II.162–64   35
    III.387.91   35, 330
    IV.238   35, 330
    V.78, 120–22, 258–74   35, 326, 330
    VI.14, 44   35, 330

Lucian
How to Write History 128
    47   44
    47–51   55–56
    49   53, 55
    55   34, 44, 45, 52
"True Story" 1.247–357 316
Zeus Catechized 35 n.112

Papyrus 168 (PSI 3.168.24) 78

Papyrus grecs et démotiques. (PRein. 18.15) 79

Philemon 124 76

Philo, the Elder 95–97

Philo
The Sacrifices of Abel and Cain 70 90

Plato
Republic 10,607d 156
The Sophist 266c 75
Theaetetus 143 190

Plutarch
Alexander 1 42, 43, 52
Demosthenes 11.7 42
Pompey 8.6 43

Polybius 173
The Histories
    I.3.3–4   36, 127, 134
    I.3.9   44
    I.4–5   34, 35, 135, 330
    I.5.5   135, 138
    I.6.1   139, 140
    I.7.4   330
    I.12.6–7, 13.6, 10–11   140
    I.12.7   82
    I.74   35
    III.4–5   142
    III.6.7   34
    III.32   84, 142
    IV.1–2   135
    IV.28.1–4, 6   34, 139
    V.31.1–5   141

Quintilian
Institutes 125
    8.6.37–38 188

Rhetorica ad Herennium 125

Strabo 84

Tacitus
Agricola 44

Théon
Progymnasmata
    8 45

78–96 5
84.2 5
96.15 5

Theophrastus 84
Enquiry into Plants 6.4.8 80

Thucydides
War 2.2.-6 5
    104–105

Xenophon
"On the Art of Horsemanship" 8.14 86

Modern Authors

Aland, Barbara 38, 340
Aland, Kurt 38, 233, 340
Alexander, Loveday 28, 33, 69, 70, 108, 172, 340
Allen, O. Wesley 34, 340
Alter, Robert 53, 340
Aune, David 5, 33, 42, 44, 46, 50, 51, 52, 55, 127, 258, 293, 294, 297, 299, 326, 340, 349, 353
Avenarius, Gert 128, 340
Bailey, Kenneth E. 205, 208, 210, 340
Balch, David L. 175, 340
Bann, Stephen 210, 294, 340
Barrett, Charles K. 221, 340
Barton, Stephen C. 122, 341
Barzel, Hillel. 217, 341
Bauer, Bruno 73, 109, 167, 184, 238, 341
Bauer, Walter 87, 100
Baur, Ferdinand Christian 238, 239, 303
Bellinger, William H., Jr. 273, 341
Berlin, Adele 301, 341
Blass, Friedrich 341
Blinzler, J. 205, 206, 208, 341
Bock, Darrell L. 99, 341
Boers, H. W. 273, 341
Bonner, Stanley Fredrick 175, 341
Boring, M. Eugene 341
Bouwman, Gilbert 205, 341
Bovon, François 132, 341
Bowlt, John E. 210, 294, 340
Braumann, Georg 297, 341
Brett, Mark 118, 341
Brown, Schuyler 211, 341
Bruce, F. F. 237, 239, 266, 341, 348
Buckwalter, H. Douglas 143, 341
Burridge, Richard A. 34, 64, 341, 342
Burton, Anne 165, 342
Butcher, S. H. 129, 342
Byrskog, Samuel 18, 342
Cadbury, Henry J. 2, 15, 32, 33, 38, 39, 70, 71, 82, 94, 107, 342, 350, 352
Caird, G. B. 212, 229, 342
Callan, Terrance 45, 342
Carroll, John T. 100, 295, 342

Cartlidge, David R. 207, 343
Charlesworth, James H. 344
Clark, Andrew C. 240, 342
Cohen, Shaye J. D. 94, 138, 342
Colson, F. H. 70, 88, 342
Conzelmann, Hans 25, 143, 205, 206, 207, 209, 218, 231, 239, 240, 290, 304, 305, 342
Cooper, Lane 109, 129, 342
Cosgrove, Charles H. 62, 342
Cross, Frank Moore 249, 342
Cullmann, Oscar 290, 291, 302, 303, 304, 305, 306, 307, 309, 313, 314
Dahl, Nils A. 237, 248, 342
Danker, Frederick W. 87, 99, 100, 109, 342, 344
Daube, David 221, 236, 342
Davies, J. H. 205, 207, 218, 226, 252, 342
Debrunner, Albert 341
Degenhardt, Hans-Joachim 18, 343
Devoldère, M. 70, 343
Dibelius, Martin. 55, 226, 343
Dihle, Albrecht 33, 42, 43, 44, 46, 47, 48, 50, 343
Dillon, Richard J. 18, 70, 343
Doble, Peter 143, 343
Dodd, C. H. 258, 295, 297, 326, 343
Donelson, Lewis R. 317, 343
Driver, S. R. 217, 343
Drury, John 36, 205, 208, 211, 343
Dungan, David L. 207, 343
Dunn, James D. G. 273, 343
Du Plessis, I. I. 70, 343
Dupont, Jacques 273, 343
Eckstein, A. M. 136, 343
Eden, Kathy 129, 343
Edmonds, J. M. 76, 343
Èjxenbaum, Boris Mixajlovic 343
Elliott, John H. 243, 343
Ellis, E. Earle 208, 209, 211, 343
Else, Gerald Frank 130, 344
Enos, Richard L. 29, 133, 155, 344
Enslin, Morton S. 205, 344
Esler, Peter 17, 344

Evans, Christopher F. 205, 207, 208, 211, 344
Evans, Craig A. 34, 37, 344, 350, 354
Evans, H. H. 264, 292, 348
Fascher, Erich 264, 344
Feldman, Louis H. 94, 344, 347, 355
Filson, Floyd V. 237, 264, 344
Fitzmyer, Joseph A. 13, 15, 16, 68, 69, 71, 145, 205, 207, 211, 218, 227, 252, 253, 273, 344
Flender, Helmut 205, 207, 344
Freedman, David Noel 344
Frei, Hans 6, 344
Friedrich, Gerhard 346
Froehlich, Karlfried 302
Fuhrmann, Manfred 129, 344
Funk, Robert W. 341
Gasse, W 205, 344
Gaventa, Beverly R. 266, 273, 344
Geldenhuys, Norval 208, 344
Genette, Gerard 187, 189, 190, 191, 199, 344
Gill, David 24, 205, 207, 218, 344
Gingrich, F. Wilbur 87, 100, 344
Ginzberg, Louis 218, 344
Girard, Louis 205, 344
Golden, Leon 130, 344
Goodman, Martin 94, 344
Goulder, M. D. 205, 208, 210, 264, 345
Green, Joel B. 17, 32, 129, 143, 145, 342, 345
Gregory, Andrew 2, 3, 345, 348, 356
Grube, G. M. A. 129, 174, 175, 345
Grundmann, Walter 70, 205, 207, 218, 222, 240, 345
Guilding, Aieleen 205, 208, 210, 345
Hadas-Lebel, Mireille 94, 345
Haenchen, Ernst 70, 99, 105, 143, 273, 292, 345
Halliwell, Stephen 129, 130, 156, 173, 174, 340, 345
Hallward, B. L. 139, 345
Harmless, William 14, 345
Hartl, Vinzenz 70, 345
Hayes, J. H. 9, 32, 355
Hays, Richard B. 26, 251, 278, 294, 345
Heath, Malcolm 129, 133, 346
Hengel, Martin 14, 94, 346, 347
Higgins, A. J. B. 70, 346

Holladay, Carl R. 38, 272, 274, 275, 346, 349
Homeyer, Helene 128, 346
Jeremias, Joachim 227, 253, 346
Jervell, Jacob 292, 346
Johnson, Luke Timothy 15, 16, 99, 122, 145, 205, 207, 208, 235, 236, 237, 242, 245, 273, 346
Jossa, Giorgio 94, 346
Juel, Donald 273, 346
Just Jr., Arthur A. 1, 13, 14, 346
Karris, Robert J. 1, 236, 346
Käsemann, Ernst 143, 346
Kennedy, George A. 5, 128, 346
Kittel, Gerhard 346
Klauck, Hans-Josef 144, 327, 346
Kodell, Jerome 229, 347
Korn, Manfred 296, 347
Kreissig, Heinz 94, 347
Krodel, Gerhard 273, 347
Kuhn, Karl Allen 7, 347
Kümmel, Werner Georg 143, 236, 347
Kürzinger, J. 70, 347
Kurz, William S. 32, 36, 37, 47, 137, 181, 347
Lampe, G. W. H. 240, 347
Lamsa, George M. 99, 347
Lausberg, Heinrich 29, 347
Leaney, A. R. C. 99, 347
Leiman, Sid Z. 96, 347
Lentz, Tony M. 29, 347
Liddell, Henry George 73, 109, 347
Lightfoot, R. H. 205, 218, 344, 347
Lindner, Helgo 94, 347
Litwak, Kenneth 323, 347
Lohfink, Norbert 213, 214, 347
Lohmeyer, Ernst 225, 347
Lohse, Eduard 205, 207, 347
Lord, Albert B. 29, 133, 145, 347
Lührmann, Dieter 14, 348
Mallen, Peter 268, 348
Mann, Thomas W. 214, 215, 216, 217, 348
Marguerat, Daniel 28, 34, 147, 278, 337, 345, 348, 350
Marincola, John 316, 348
Marrou, Henri-Irénée 76, 351
Marshall, I. Howard 70, 99, 143, 205, 206, 208, 210, 219, 220, 222, 253, 273, 344, 348

Mason, Steve 96, 348
Matray, Chantal 76, 351
Mattill, A. J., Jr. 239, 264, 292, 348
Mauser, Ulrich 18, 348
McCown, C. C. 206, 218, 348
Milligan, George 99, 351
Minear, Paul S. 228, 229, 236, 241, 245, 348
Mitchell, Margaret M. 348
Mittmann, Siegfried 213, 348
Miyoshi, Michi 206, 348
Moessner, David P. 3, 13, 14, 18, 20, 23, 24, 25, 26, 31, 32, 33, 34, 37, 38, 39, 40, 59, 60, 63, 84, 108, 127, 137, 138, 147, 151, 154, 161, 169, 172, 181, 205, 233, 244, 250, 251, 252, 254, 260, 261, 264, 274, 278, 292, 293, 294, 296, 327, 345, 346, 347, 348, 349, 350, 352, 354, 355, 357
Momigliano, Arnaldo 33, 42, 43, 351
Mondésert, Claude 76, 351
Moore, Stephen D. 7, 249, 342, 351
Morgenthaler, Robert 206, 208, 351
Moulton, James Hope 99, 351
Moxnes, Halvor 17, 351
Muhlack, Gudrun 240, 351
Navone, John 206, 351
Neyrey, Jerome H. 17, 351
Nicholson, Ernest W. 213, 237, 249, 351
Nickelsburg, George W. E. 298, 351
Noth, Martin 213, 237, 351, 354
Ogg, George 206, 208, 351
Old, Hughes Oliphant 14, 351
O'Neill, J. C. 206, 207, 351
Ong, Walter J. 29, 133, 351
Osswald, Eva 213, 351
Osten-Sacken, Peter von der 206, 207, 218, 351
Pao, David W. 237, 351
Parker, Pierson 27, 352
Parsons, Mikeal C. 2, 5, 34, 39, 52, 53, 58, 59, 147, 278, 345, 350, 352
Patillon, M. 5, 352
Penner, Todd 3, 352
Pervo, Richard I. 2, 3, 33, 53, 172, 352
Petersen, Norman R. 57, 210, 294, 352
Plümacher, Eckhard 33, 51, 55, 151, 169, 349, 352
Press, Gerald A. 316, 352

Pritchett, W. Kendrick 175, 333, 352
Rackham, R. B. 239, 264, 353
Rad, Gerhard von 213, 214, 217, 218, 219, 227, 235, 237, 298, 306, 353
Reicke, Bo 13, 14, 23, 206, 207, 258, 297, 326, 353
Reid, Robert S. 155, 161, 175, 176, 177, 353
Renan, Ernst 1, 13, 353
Rengstorf, Karl Heinrich 208, 353
Resseguie, James L. 205, 206, 209, 353
Richard, Earl 245, 353
Ricoeur, Paul 129, 353
Robbins, Vernon K. 108, 353
Roberts, W. Rhys 175, 353
Robinson, William C., Jr. 132, 206, 207, 209, 353
Roloff, Jürgen 240, 353
Rowe, C. Kavin 7, 353
Russell, Donald A. 29, 129, 131, 133, 353
Sacks, Kenneth S. 29, 138, 165, 174, 353, 354
Sanders, James A. 37, 344, 354
Sandnes, Karl Olav 321, 354
Scafuro, Adele C. 37, 134, 138, 140, 159, 354
Schlatter, Adolf 257, 354
Schmidt, Daryl 33, 172, 354
Schmidt, Karl Ludwig 41, 206, 212, 354
Schmitt, Armin 279, 354
Schneckenburger, Matthias 239, 264, 348, 354
Schneider, Johannes 205, 206, 207, 354
Schniewind, Julius 225, 354
Schröter, Jens 151, 302, 349
Schubert, Paul 212, 226, 229, 237, 248, 252, 342, 354
Schuetz, Frieder 206, 207, 229, 354
Schweizer, Eduard 70, 99, 354
Scott, Robert 73, 109, 208, 344, 347
Sloan, Robert B. 278, 354
Smend, Rudolf 213, 354
Smith, David E. 2, 354
Squires, John T. 35, 62, 136, 330, 354
Stagg, Frank 206, 207, 355
Stählin, Gustav 240, 355
Stanton, Graham N. 13, 40, 355

Steck, Odil H. 233, 243, 247, 248, 255, 293, 294, 298, 343, 355
Sterling, Gregory C 355
Sternberg, Meir 53, 55, 355
Stern, Menahem 94, 355
Stonehouse, Ned B. 206, 208, 355
Strait, A. J. 324, 355
Stylianou, P. J. 165, 355
Talbert, Charles H. 12, 32, 33, 34, 36, 39, 40, 41, 42, 43, 44, 46, 47, 48, 52, 53, 56, 57, 58, 59, 63, 64, 99, 205, 206, 207, 211, 236, 340, 341, 344, 347, 348, 350, 352, 355
Tannehill, Robert C. 18, 20, 138, 273, 350, 355
Taylor, Vincent 206, 208, 355
Thackeray, Henry St. John 94, 96, 355
Thiselton, Anthony 132, 356
Thomas, Carol G. 29, 132, 356
Tiede, David L. 14, 18, 36, 59, 99, 241, 242, 350, 356
Tompkins, Jane P. 154, 155, 156, 158, 162, 163, 166, 171, 356
Toohey, Peter 29, 356
Toye, David L. 175, 356
Treier, Daniel J. 278, 356
Trimpi, Wesley 3, 129, 356
Trompf, G. W. 32, 128, 206, 323, 324, 356
Tuckett, Christopher M. 3, 15, 26, 28, 108, 340, 345, 350, 356

Tyson, Joseph B. 18, 34, 39, 59, 272, 349, 350, 352, 355, 356
Unnik, Willem C. van 33, 48, 50, 51, 55, 108, 356
Vaughn, Stephen 1, 357
Verheyden, Joseph 15, 84, 108, 154, 349, 350, 357
Vermes, Geza 218, 236, 357
Votaw, Clyde Weber 207, 357
Walaskay, Paul W. 292, 357
Walbank, Frank W. 83, 128, 135, 136, 138, 140, 174, 315, 318, 330, 357
Walton, Steve 266, 357
Webb, Edward Kent 29, 132, 356
Wehnert, Jürgen 54, 357
Weiner, Aharon 357
Weinfeld, Moshe 213, 357
Wenham, J. W. 206, 211, 357
Wentling, Judith L. 42, 340
Wilckens, Ulrich 143, 357
Witherington, Ben, III 20, 32, 33, 145, 172, 273, 340, 345, 350, 357
Wolter, Michael 99, 100, 147, 278, 296, 345, 350, 357
Worthington, Ian 29, 132, 356, 357
Wright, G. Ernest 217, 357
Zeller, Eduard 238, 239, 341, 357
Ziesler, J. A. 236, 357
Zimmerli, Walther 300, 357

Lightning Source UK Ltd.
Milton Keynes UK
UKHW011834080519
342334UK00002B/135/P